Adapted Physical Education and Sport

Fourth Edition

Joseph P. Winnick, EdD

State University of New York, College at Brockport

Editor

Human Kinetics

Library of Congress Cataloging-in-Publication Data

Adapted physical education and sport / Joseph P. Winnick, editor.-- 4th ed.
    p. cm.
  Includes bibliographical references and index.
  ISBN 0-7360-5216-X (hardcover)
  1. Physical education for people with disabilities. 2. Sports for people with
disabilities. I. Winnick, Joseph P.
  GV445.A3 2005
  371.9'04486--dc22

2004024997

ISBN-10: 0-7360-5216-X
ISBN-13: 978-0-7360-5216-0

The Web addresses cited in this text were current as of August 2004, unless otherwise noted.

Acquisitions Editor: Bonnie Pettifor; **Developmental Editor:** Melissa Feld; **Assistant Editors:** Kathleen D. Bernard and Michelle M. Rivera; **Copyeditor:** John Wentworth; **Proofreader:** Sarah Wiseman; **Indexer:** Betty Frizzéll; **Permission Manager:** Dalene Reeder; **Graphic Designer:** Fred Starbird; **Graphic Artist:** Denise Lowry; **Photo Manager:** Kelly Huff; **Cover Designer:** Robert Reuther; **Photographer (cover):** Empics; **Art Manager:** Kelly Hendren; **Illustrators:** Beth Young (medical and line drawings), except figure 13.1 by Tim Offenstein; **Printer:** Edwards Brothers

Printed in the United States of America   10   9   8   7   6   5   4

Human Kinetics
Web site: www.HumanKinetics.com

United States: Human Kinetics, P.O. Box 5076, Champaign, IL 61825-5076
800-747-4457
e-mail: humank@hkusa.com

Canada: Human Kinetics, 475 Devonshire Road Unit 100, Windsor, ON N8Y 2L5
800-465-7301 (in Canada only)
e-mail: orders@hkcanada.com

Europe: Human Kinetics, 107 Bradford Road, Stanningley, Leeds LS28 6AT, United Kingdom
+44 (0) 113 255 5665
e-mail: hk@hkeurope.com

Australia: Human Kinetics, 57A Price Avenue, Lower Mitcham, South Australia 5062
08 8277 1555
e-mail: liaw@hkaustralia.com

New Zealand: Human Kinetics, Division of Sports Distributors NZ Ltd., P.O. Box 300 226 Albany, North Shore City, Auckland
0064 9 448 1207
e-mail: info@humankinetics.co.nz

Contents

Chapter 18 Students With Temporary Disabilities and Other Special Conditions   323

Christine B. Stopka

PART III Developmental Considerations   341

Chapter 19 Motor Development   343

John C. Ozmun and David L. Gallahue

Chapter 20 Perceptual–Motor Development   359

Joseph P. Winnick and Barry W. Lavay

Chapter 21 Infants and Toddlers   373

Cathy Houston-Wilson

Chapter 22 Early Childhood Adapted Physical Education 385

Lauriece L. Zittel

PART IV Activities for Individuals With Unique Needs 399

Chapter 23 Health-Related Physical Fitness and Physical Activity 401

Francis X. Short

Chapter 24 Rhythmic Movement and Dance 415

Boni B. Boswell

Chapter **28** Winter Sport Activities   **503**

Luke E. Kelly

Chapter **29** Enhancing Wheelchair Sport Performance   **517**

Abu B. Yilla

Preface

It is with a great deal of satisfaction and motivation that I write this preface for the fourth edition of *Adapted Physical Education and Sport*. When I wrote the preface for the first, second, and third editions, I was confident that these books would benefit children with unique physical education needs by providing clear and concise information for teachers and others who provide quality services. In this fourth edition, the book is further developed and, in several places, reorganized to meet today's trends in adapted physical education and sport. This preface identifies and explains major influences on the content and organization of the book, briefly summarizes new and continuing features, provides an overview of the parts of the book, and closes with some comments about the value of adapted physical education and sport in the lives of youngsters today. As the editor, I strongly welcome comments on the strengths of the book and suggestions for improvement.

LEGISLATION: A MAJOR INFLUENCE ON THIS BOOK

There are many factors that shape the emphasis, approach, content, and organization of any book. This book is influenced by original and current versions of two landmark laws: the Individuals with Disabilities Education Act (IDEA) (originally signed in 1975 as PL 94-142, the Education for All Handicapped Children Act) and section 504 of the Rehabilitation Act (originally passed in 1973 as PL 93-112).

One of the major purposes of IDEA is to ensure that all children with disabilities have a free public education available to them that emphasizes special education and related services to meet their unique needs. IDEA makes clear that the special education to be made available includes physical education, which in turn may be specified as adapted physical education. As will be clearly communicated in this book, regulations associated with IDEA define physical education as the development of physical and motor fitness; fundamental motor skills and patterns; and skills in aquatics, dance, individual and group games, and sports

including intramural and lifetime sports. In this book, adapted physical education is defined in a manner consistent with key provisions of the IDEA definition, including the scope of physical education presented in the definition. This book helps schools and agencies in each state to develop and implement adapted physical education programs consistent with federal legislation.

The identification of unique needs, which is specified in the IDEA definition of special education, is also emphasized in this book. This book includes many ways of adapting physical education to meet individual needs. One of the most important concepts associated with federal legislation is the requirement of individualized education programs (IEPs) to meet the unique needs of children. In chapters 4 and 21 detailed information is presented about components and strategies for developing IEPs, 504 plans, and Individualized Family Service Plans (IFSPs).

In IDEA, the disabilities of children ages 3 to 21 are identified and defined. Information related to physical education is presented in this book in regard to each of the specific disabilities identified in IDEA. IDEA also defines infants and toddlers ages 0 to 2 with disabilities. One entire chapter (chapter 21) on physical education services related to infants and toddlers is presented in the book.

Both IDEA and section 504 require that education be provided in the most normal and integrated setting appropriate. In regard to physical education, this book encourages education in regular environments to the extent appropriate. The book prepares readers for working in inclusive environments, with extensive discussions about inclusion in several chapters. However, it recognizes that education in the *least restrictive environment* is the "law of the land" and also prepares readers to provide services in any setting. In regard to sport, this book recommends an orientation to sport and a sport continuum that enables and encourages participation in a variety of settings.

Thus, this book responds to legislative requirements in many ways, including compatibility with the definition of special education, the requirement of identifying unique educational needs of the individual within the context of a broad program of physical education, the requirement for IEPs, and the importance of education in the most normal, integrated setting possible. Because of the orientation used in this book, educators can be confident that they are implementing programs that respond to societal needs expressed through legislation.

NEW FEATURES IN THIS EDITION

Many changes influencing adapted physical education and sport have occurred since the third edition (2000) of this book. All chapters have been updated or revised to incorporate these changes. The inclusion movement continues to expand, and its coverage in this book has increased. The inclusion movement is introduced in chapter 1, and basic information regarding inclusion is expanded in chapter 2. Chapters dealing with children with disabilities include sections on inclusion, and several of the chapters focusing on activities also discuss and make applications relevant to inclusion.

Because individuals with disabilities are increasingly involved in sport, this book includes a separate chapter on adapted sport (chapter 3). Advances regarding classification, sport organizations, national governing bodies, the United States Olympic Committee, and the Paralympic Games are dramatic, and this chapter has been revised to communicate these changes. The chapter continues to be guided by a sport integration continuum, which serves to stimulate thinking about sport opportunities in integrated as well as segregated sport settings.

Although all chapters have been updated, major revisions are provided in several chapters. The chapter on measurement and assessment (chapter 4) has been significantly changed to reflect advances, particularly in regard to alternate assessment. The newly created Brockport Physical Fitness Test, a criterion-referenced health-related physical fitness test appropriate for youngsters with disabilities, is introduced in the chapter, and a DVD of an audiovisual presentation of the test is included in the sleeve of the book.

The increased attention on behavioral disabilities and ways to provide for youngsters with behavioral disabilities consistent with IDEA has resulted in more attention on this topic in chapters 6 and 9. In the last few years more and more attention has been given to pervasive developmental disabilities. In response, Dr. Cathy Houston-Wilson has developed a practical user-friendly chapter focusing on the implications of these conditions for the teaching of physical education. Also in this fourth edition, separate chapters have been written on visual disabilities and deafness by one of America's foremost authorities, Dr. Lauren J. Lieberman.

Six authors are contributing to this book for the first time. They are Dr. Douglas H. Collier, writing the chapter on instructional strategies for adapted physical education; Dr. Francis M. Kozub, writing the chapter on other health-impaired students; Dr. Christine B. Stopka, writing the chapter on students with temporary disabilities; Dr. Barry W. Lavay, writing the chapter on specific learning disabilities and cowriting the chapter on perceptual–motor development; Dr. Boni B. Boswell, writing the chapter on rhythmic movement and dance; and Dr. John C. Ozmun, coauthoring the motor development chapter. These six people were involved in writing six chapters, and their new perspectives result in significant changes and advances in these chapters.

CONTINUING FEATURES

In this and previous editions of this book, a good portion of the chapters have focused on physical education and sport rather than merely structuring the book by the names of the disabilities. The latter approach traditionally has been associated with a medical model for the structuring of know-ledge rather than a more educationally oriented model. On the other hand, relevant information regarding disabilities is presented in the text so that relationship between disabilities and their implications for physical education and sport are discussed.

This edition retains focus on physical education for youngsters from ages 0 to 21. No attempt is made to address the entire age span of individuals with disabilities, although much information in the book is relevant to the entire age span. This book is also delimited to the areas of physical education and sport and makes no claims to cover important allied areas such as recreation or therapeutic recreation. This clear focus in regard to the scope of the text makes the book focused, manageable, and easy to read.

A feature continued in this edition is the presentation of resources with each chapter. The presentation of written, audiovisual, and electronic resources in the text and instructor guide will be of much interest and help to both students and instructors.

In this fourth edition, we continue to use application examples and a vignette that begins each chapter to enhance to reader's understanding. The opening vignettes present real-life scenarios that introduce one or more concepts to be discussed in the chapter. Application examples provide readers with the opportunity to explore real-life situations and see how the concepts in the text can be applied to these situations to "solve" the problems at hand.

An electronic instructor guide has again been developed to accompany this book. For each chapter, the instructor guide provides objectives, suggestions for learning, and enrichment activities, resources, and PowerPoint® presentations. Because it is so important for college students to be aware of individuals with disabilities, to teach, and interact with them in a positive manner; the electronic instructor guide includes additional ideas to provide these opportunities. The guide also includes some ideas for an introductory course related to adapted physical education and sport as well as a sample course syllabus. Finally, an electronic bank of test questions has also been developed, which can be used to develop quizzes, exams, or study questions.

PARTS OF THE BOOK

The book is presented in four parts. Part I, Foundational Topics in Adapted Physical Education and Sport, encompasses chapters 1 though 7, which are designed to introduce the reader to adapted physical education and sport and cover general topics in the adapted physical education and sport subdiscipline. This part includes chapters on adapted sport, individualized education programs, measurement and assessment, and behavior management. Part I ends with chapter 7, which identifies major strategies for teaching adapted physical education.

Part II, Individuals With Unique Needs, includes 11 chapters. This part covers all the disabilities specifically defined in IDEA, a chapter on pervasive developmental disabilities, and a chapter related to students without disabilities who nonetheless have unique physical education needs. These chapters provide an understanding of disabilities—how they relate to physical education and sport—and educational implications associated with each disability covered. As appropriate, particular attention is given in each chapter to inclusion and sport programs.

The third part of the book, Developmental Considerations, includes four chapters. Chapters 19 though 22 in this part cover motor development, perceptual–motor development, adapted physical education for infants and toddlers, and children in early childhood programs.

Part IV, Activities for Individuals With Unique Needs, includes chapters 23 through 29. These chapters present physical education and sport activities for both school and out-of-school settings. A key aspect of this part is the presentation of activity modifications and variations for the various populations involved in adapted physical education and sport. This part concludes with a chapter on wheelchair sport performance. Part IV, in particular, serves as an excellent resource for teachers, coaches, and other service providers long after they have left colleges and universities and are involved in providing quality programs for youngsters.

The appendices consist of the latest definitions pertaining to infants, toddlers, and children with disabilities in IDEA; a list of addresses associated with adapted physical education and sport; information related to the Brockport Physical Fitness test; and a scale to rate or evaluate adapted physical education programs. Each of these complement information presented in the main body of the book. Also, as mentioned earlier, a DVD accompanies the text and presents an audiovisual presentation of the Brockport Physical Fitness Test.

CLOSING

As opportunities in adapted physical education and sport have increased, there has been a realization that individuals with disabilities are really individuals with abilities and individual differences capable of much more than society has ever believed. With greater participation, the value of physical activity has been more clearly recognized and accepted. More youngsters with disabilities, parents, medical professionals, educators, and others recognize the tremendous value of physical education and sport today than ever before. This recognition and acceptance extend throughout the world, as clearly demonstrated at international symposia related to adapted physical activity and international competition in sport.

As the field of adapted physical education and sport has advanced, many recognizable subspecialties have emerged. Thus, I continue to assemble top people in their areas of expertise to serve as a team of authorities who draw on many years of experience in adapted physical education and sport to contribute to the book.

This book has been designed to be comprehensive, relevant, and user-friendly. It has been designed as both a resource and text for adapted physical education and sport. As a resource, this book aids teachers, administrators, and other professionals as they plan and provide services. As a text it can be used to prepare students majoring in physical education, recreation sport management, special education, and related disciplines. Use of this book and the study questions presented in the electronic test bank accompanying the book will help prepare professionals to pass the Adapted Physical Education National Standards (APENS) exam established by the National Consortium for Physical Education and Recreation for Individuals with Disabilities (NCPERID). Passing this exam leads to nationally recognized qualifications in adapted physical education. Although the book can serve different purposes, its primary thrust is its emphasis on providing quality services to individuals with unique physical education needs, differences, and abilities.

Joseph P. Winnick

Acknowledgments

Boni B. Boswell—I wish to extend a warm thanks to Joe Winnick for the opportunity to contribute to this book and for his ongoing support of dance in the schools. I am sincerely grateful to the many students who have served as reviewers of this work and shared their creativity and humor. Also, thanks to my son, Glen, for his support of my work and his growing independence.

Douglas H. Collier—I would like to thank Joe Winnick for bringing me on board and for his thoughtful and positive contributions to the chapter I wrote and to our profession. Thanks also to my wonderful wife, Chris, for her constant support and friendship.

Cathy Houston-Wilson—I would like to thank Joe Winnick for giving me the opportunity to contribute to this text. Developing the PDD chapter was truly a "labor" of love.

Luke E. Kelly—I would like to thank the graduate students at the University of Virginia who serve as a sounding board for my ideas and as reviewers of my drafts. I would also like to thank Andrew, Zachary, and Melissa for their continuing support and for being the source of inspiration for my work.

Francis M. Kozub—I would like to acknowledge Joe Winnick and David Porretta. Both were instrumental in my professional development.

Patricia L. Krebs—Appreciation is extended to Joe Winnick for allowing me to continue as part of this incredible writing team, and for writing the section on cognitive development and part of the section on planned programs in chapter 8. Very special appreciation is extended to the 10,000 athletes of Special Olympics Maryland who make me smile every day and inspire me by their greatness.

Barry W. Lavay—I would like to thank Joseph Winnick for providing me with the opportunity to contribute to this book and for his major contributions, over the years, to the adapted physical activity profession. I would like to acknowledge my students and colleagues who continue to challenge me to learn and grow as a professional. I want to thank my family, my wife, Penny, and children, Nicole and Danielle, who have always been supportive of my work and who make life special.

Monica Lepore—I would like to acknowledge the supervisors, participants, families, and codirector Ray Zetts, of the WCU special physical education programs for their support. In addition, thanks and love to Ed Nutter, Pat, Frank, Anne, and Maria Lepore for their encouragement in my pursuit of making the world a better place for people with disabilities.

Lauren J. Lieberman—I would like to acknowledge the students from the Perkins School for the Blind and the many campers from Camp Abilities for their assistance in teaching me what I know about teaching individuals with sensory impairments. Special thanks to Dr. Jim Mastro, an associate professor of adapted physical education at Bemidji State University and a Paralympic athlete who is blind, and to Janet MacVicar, a vision teacher and adapted physical educator from Fredericton, New Brunswick, Canada, for their assistance with chapter 12. Special thanks to Dr. Kathleen Ellis, a Deaf associate professor of adapted physical education from the University of Rhode Island, Louise Britton, a Deaf Education teacher from Fredericton, New Brunswick, Canada, and Dr. Katrina Arndt from St. John Fisher College in Rochester, New York, a specialist on transition and higher education for students who are deaf-blind, for their feedback on chapter 13.

E. Michael Loovis—I would like to thank Don Krebs, president of Access to Recreation, Inc., for his assistance in acquiring a photograph used in chapter 27. I also extend thanks to Joe Winnick for his assistance with reconceptualization of chapter 9.

John C. Ozmun and David L. Gallahue—Our chapter is dedicated to Dr. Harold "Hal" Morris, whose commitment and devotion to the roles of mentor, colleague, professional, and friend were unsurpassed.

Michael J. Paciorek—I would like to express my sincerest thanks to one of my best friends and colleagues in helping me with this chapter. Jeff Jones, director of the Wirtz Sports Program at the Rehabilitation Institute of Chicago's Center for Health and Fitness and president of the United States Sled Hockey Association, provided great support and feedback in reviewing the rough drafts while riding the train to and from work. I deeply appreciate his efforts and friendship. I would like to thank Joe Winnick for his leadership in the field and his confidence in me. I would also like to acknowledge the efforts of Dr. Ron Davis at Ball State University for assisting me in the writing of the section on classification, and Sarah Nash, director of communication for the American Association of Adapted-Sports Programs, Inc., for her efforts. Most of all I would like to acknowledge the great contribution by my wife, Karen. Her comments, suggestions, and encouragement helped me significantly.

David L. Porretta—Recognition and appreciation go to Jerry McCole and the National Disabled Sports Alliance (NDSA) as well as USA Volleyball and ÖSSUR North America for providing selected chapter photos. Also, a special thanks goes to Joseph Winnick for inviting me to participate in this and previous editions of the book.

Francis X. Short—Appreciation is extended to Joe Winnick for helping to keep me "current"; to J.J. Brewer, Kevin Head, Jim Dusen, and Sommer Tiller for helping out with the photographs; and to all the folks at Human Kinetics for their hard work on the text.

Christine B. Stopka—I sincerely thank Dr. Joe Winnick for his invaluable and immeasurable contributions to our profession. I am honored to join his outstanding team of authors. Finally, I'd like to thank my students for their assistance, the readers who make this field a success, and my family for their amazing support.

Joseph P. Winnick—I wish to acknowledge the wonderful support and cooperation I have received from the outstanding authors involved in this edition. I very much appreciate the help and support I have received from many persons at the State University College at Brockport.

Abu B. Yilla—This work extends the work of Dr. Colin Higgs from the second edition of this book. Dr. Higgs' permission and contributions to this chapter are greatly appreciated. The support of the Dallas Wheelchair Mavericks basketball team and the department of kinesiology at the University of Texas at Arlington are also appreciated.

Lauriece L. Zittel—I would like to thank Joe Winnick for the opportunity to contribute to this edition of the text. A special thanks to my precious Claire Anne—you have shared your life, love, and development. I am learning so much as I watch you grow as a preschooler.

PART 1

Foundational Topics in Adapted Physical Education and Sport

Part I of this book, consisting of seven chapters, introduces adapted physical education and sport and presents topics that serve as a foundation for the book. Chapter 1 defines adapted physical education and sport and offers a brief orientation concerning its history, legal basis, and professional resources. Programmatic planning, inclusion, and qualities of service providers are topics also introduced. In chapter 2, the focus shifts to the organization and management of programs. Topics include programmatic and curricular planning and guidelines for the organization and implementation of adapted physical education programs. Human resources and program evaluation associated with adapted physical education and sport programs are also covered. Chapter 3 emphasizes information pertaining to adapted sport. Following a brief introduction, the chapter covers the status and issues associated with adapted sport from local school and community programs to Paralympic Games. Preparing physical educators to enhance involvement of individuals with disabilities in adapted sport is stressed in the chapter. Vital to the development of adapted physical education programs are several concepts related to measurement and evaluation. Chapter 4 presents basic information regarding measurement and assessment and recommends strategies and tests for use in adapted physical education. Chapter 5 contains a detailed discussion of individualized education programs developed for students with unique needs, including section 504 accommodation plans. Chapter 6 covers basic concepts and approaches related to methods of behavior management. Chapter 7 discusses instructional strategies related to adapted physical education.

The information in part I pertains to planning, assessing, prescribing, teaching, and evaluating relative to adapted physical education. Basic information related to overall program planning (chapters 1 and 2), student assessment and evaluation (chapter 4), individualized education programs, (chapter 5), instructional strategies, (chapter 7), and program evaluation, (chapter 2) is introduced and discussed. A chapter on behavior management is included in the foundational area before chapter 7 because of its importance in shaping appropriate social behavior and its influence in promoting skill acquisition.

CHAPTER 1

An Introduction to Adapted Physical Education and Sport

Joseph P. Winnick

Adapted physical education and sport programs relate to the unique needs and abilities of individuals, which vary quite widely. What is not often known is that individuals with disabilities involved in physical activity and sport achieve many goals that many would think impossible. For example, Heinz Frei (Switzerland) and Jean Driscoll (USA) attained record times in the Boston Marathon of 1 hour, 21 minutes, and 23 seconds, and 1 hour, 34 minutes, and 22 seconds, respectively, using wheelchairs. Jim Abbott, a pitcher for the New York Yankees born without a right hand, pitched a no-hitter against the Cleveland Indians in 1993. Wilma Rudolph—despite birth defects and polio—was a triple gold medalist in the 100-meter, 200-meter, and 400-meter relays in the 1960 Olympics in Rome. Tom Dempsey, born with only half a right foot, set a National Football League record in 1970 for the longest field goal kicked (63 yards). Casey Martin, with a serious impairment of his leg associated with the Klippel-Trenaunay-Weber syndrome, gained fame as a gifted golfer. These examples demonstrate what can be attained if opportunities are provided.

Individuals who pursue a career of teaching physical education and coaching sports typically enjoy physical activity and are active participants in physical education and athletics. Often, however, they do not become knowledgeable about adapted physical education and sport until they prepare for their careers. With increased awareness, they realize that people with unique needs might exhibit abilities ranging from very low to extremely high, as the opening examples illustrate. As they gain experience, students begin to appreciate that there are individuals with a variety of unique needs involved in adapted physical education and sport. They learn that those with unique needs include people with and without disabilities.

If physical education and sport opportunities are offered in educational institutions and other societal entities, they must be made available to all students, including those with disabilities. It is neither desirable nor permissible to discriminate on the basis of disability in regard to these opportunities. Adapted physical education and sport has evolved as a field to meet the unique physical education and sport needs of individuals. This chapter introduces the reader to adapted physical education and sport.

THE MEANING OF ADAPTED PHYSICAL EDUCATION

Because different people use different terms (and different definitions of the same term), we first should clarify the definition of adapted physical education. Adapted physical education is an individualized program involving physical and motor fitness, fundamental motor skills and patterns, skills in aquatics and dance, and individual and group games and sports designed to meet the unique needs of individuals. Typically, the word "adapt" means "to adjust" or "to fit." In this book, the word "adapt" is consistent with these definitions and includes the modification to meet unique needs of students. It encompasses traditional components associated with adapted physical education, including those designed to correct, habilitate, or remediate. Adapted physical education is viewed as a subdiscipline of physical education that provides for safe, personally satisfying, and successful experiences for students of differing abilities.

Adapted physical education is generally designed to meet long-term (more than 30 days) unique needs. Those with long-term unique needs include individuals with disabilities as specified in the Individuals with Disabilities Education Act (IDEA). According to IDEA, a child with a disability means a child having mental retardation, deafness or other hearing impairment, speech or language impairment, blindness or other visual impairment, serious emotional disturbance, orthopedic impairment, autism, traumatic brain injury, a learning disability, deafblindness, or multiple disabilities or other health impairments that require special education and related services (Office of Special Education and Rehabilitative Services (OSE/RS, 2002). The term "child with a disability" for a child aged three to nine years may, at the discretion of the state and the local educational agency, include a child experiencing developmental delays as defined by the state and as measured by appropriate diagnostic instruments and procedures in one or more of the following areas: physical development, cognitive development, communication development, social or emotional development, or adaptive development; and who, by reason thereof, needs special education and related services (OSE/RS, 2002). Adapted physical education might also include infants and toddlers (individuals under three years of age) who need early intervention services because (1) they are experiencing developmental delays in cognitive development, physical development, communication development, social or emotional development, or adaptive development or (2) they have a diagnosed physical or mental condition that has a high probability of resulting in developmental delay. At a state's discretion, adapted physical education might also include at-risk infants and toddlers (IDEA, 1997). The term "at-risk infant or toddler" means an individual under three years of age who would be at risk of experiencing a substantial developmental delay if early intervention services were not provided (OSE/RS, 2002).

Adapted physical education may include individuals with disabilities as encompassed within section 504 of the Rehabilitation Act of 1973 and its amendments. Section 504 defines a person with a disability as anyone who has a physical or mental impairment that substantially limits one or more major life activities, has a record of such an impairment, or is regarded as having such an impairment. Although every child who is a student with a disability under IDEA is also protected under section 504, all children covered under 504 are not necessarily students with a disability under IDEA. Individuals with disabilities who do not need or require services under IDEA are, nonetheless, entitled to accommodations and services that are necessary to enable them to benefit from all programs and activities available to students without disabilities.

Adapted physical education may include students who are not identified by a school district as having a disability under federal legislation but who might have unique needs that call for a specially designed program. This group might include students restricted because of injuries or other medical conditions; those of low fitness (including exceptional leanness or obesity), inadequate motor development, or low skill; or those individuals with poor functional posture. These individuals might require individually designed programming to meet unique goals and objectives.

According to IDEA, students aged 3 to 21 with disabilities must have an individualized education program (IEP) developed by a planning committee. In developing an IEP, physical education needs must be considered, and the IEP developed might include specially designed instruction in physical education. IDEA also requires the development of an individualized family service plan (IFSP) for infants and toddlers with disabilities (OSE/RS, 2002). Although physical education services are not mandated for this age group, they may be offered as part of an IFSP. In accordance with section 504 of the Rehabilitation Act of 1973 and its amendments, it is recommended that an accommodation plan be developed by a school-based assessment team to provide services and needed accommodations for individuals with disabilities. Although not covered or required by federal law, an individualized physical education program (IPEP) should also be developed by a planning committee for those who have a unique need but who have not been identified by the school as having a disability. Each school should have policies and procedures to guide the development of all individualized programs. More specific information on the development of programs and plans is presented in chapters 4 and 5 (ages 3 to 21) and chapter 21 (ages 0 to 2).

Consistent with the least restrictive environment concept associated with IDEA, adapted physical education may take place in classes that range from integrated (i.e., regular education environments) to segregated (i.e., including only individuals receiving adapted physical education). Although adapted physical education is a *program* rather than a *placement,* it should be understood that a program received is directly influenced by placement (the setting in which it is implemented). Whenever appropriate, students receiving an adapted physical education program should be included in regular physical education environments. Although an adapted physical education program is individualized, it can be implemented in a group setting and should be geared to each student's needs, limitations, and abilities.

Adapted physical education should emphasize an active program of physical activity (figure 1.1, a and b, p.6) rather than a sedentary alternative program. The program should be planned to attain the benefits of physical activity through meeting the needs of students who might otherwise be relegated to passive experiences associated with physical education. In establishing adapted physical education programs, educators work with parents, students, teachers, administrators, and professionals in various disciplines. Adapted physical education may employ developmental (bottom-up), community-based, functional (top-down), or other orientations and might employ a variety of teaching styles. Adapted physical education takes place in schools and other agencies responsible for educating individuals. Although adapted physical education is educational, it draws on related services (more on related services in chapter 2 and later in this chapter), especially medically related services, to help meet instructional objectives and goals.

In this text, adapted physical education and sport are viewed as part of the emerging area of study known as adapted physical activity, a term that encompasses the comprehensive and interdisciplinary study of physical activity for the education, wellness, sport participation, and leisure of individuals with unique needs. Adapted physical activity encompasses the total lifespan, whereas adapted physical education focuses only on the ages of 0 to 21. Although adapted physical education may exceed the minimal time required by policies or law, it should not be supplanted by related services, intramurals, sport days, athletics, or other experiences that are not primarily instructional.

ADAPTED SPORT

Adapted sport refers to sport modified or created to meet the unique needs of individuals with disabilities. Adapted sport may be conducted in integrated settings in which individuals with disabilities interact with participants without disabilities or in segregated environments that include only individuals with disabilities (see the sport continuum presented in chapter 3 on page

Figure 1.1 *(a)* Student with a lower-limb impairment moves briskly around a track, and *(b)* a student with a visual impairment confidently conquers a climbing wall.

40). Based on this definition, for example, basketball is a regular sport and wheelchair basketball is an adapted sport. Goal ball (a game created for individuals with visual impairments in which players attempt to roll a ball that emits a sound across their opponents' goal) is an adapted sport because it was created to meet unique needs.

Adapted sport encompasses "disability sport" (e.g., Deaf sport), which typically focuses on segregated participation in regular or adapted sport. Although disability sport terminology has been used as a term encompassing sport related to individuals with disability, adapted sport terminology is preferred for the following reasons: It is consistent with terminology in adapted physical education and adapted physical activity; it focuses on the modification of sport rather than on disability; it encourages participation in the most normal and integrated environment; it is consistent with normalization theory; it promotes the creation of sport opportunities; and it provides an opportunity for the pursuit of excellence in sport throughout a full spectrum of settings for participation. This orientation to adapted sport is consistent with the sport integration continuum presented in figure 3.1 (page 40). Many of us believe that this model will lead to more participation in sports by individuals with disabilities as well as to more

creative offerings and grouping patterns related to sport at every level of participation. Adapted sport terminology supports the development of excellence in sport while promoting growth in sport participation within many settings.

Adapted sport programs are conducted in diverse environments and organizational patterns for a variety of purposes. Educational programs are generally conducted in schools and include intramural, extramural, and interschool activities. Intramural activities are conducted within schools, involve only pupils enrolled in that school, and are organized to serve the entire school population. Extramural sport activities involve participation of pupils from two or more schools, and are sometimes conducted as play days or sport days at the end of instructional or intramural sessions. Interschool sports involve competition between representatives from two or more schools and offer enriched opportunities for selected and more highly skilled individuals. Adapted sport activity might also be conducted for leisure or recreational purposes within formal, open, or unstructured programs or as a part of the lifestyle of individuals or groups, or for wellness, medical, or therapeutic reasons. For example, sport or adapted sport might be used as part of recreational therapy, corrective therapy, sport therapy, or wellness programs. In general, involvement in sport or adapted sport has several purposes. In this book we focus on adapted sport in educational settings and in regional, national, and international competition under the governance of formalized organizations promoting sport for individuals with disabilities.

PLANNING: PURPOSES, AIMS, GOALS, AND OBJECTIVES

An important step in providing a good adapted physical education program is planning. A plan provides the direction of the program and includes identifying its purpose, aims, goals, and objectives. The purpose of a program should be consistent with the mission of its organization and with the regular or general physical education or sport program available for individuals without disabilities. In this book, it will be assumed that the purpose of adapted physical education is to promote self-actualization, which in turn promotes optimal personal development and contributes to the whole of society. This purpose is consistent with the humanistic philosophy interpreted by Sherrill, who says that humanism is a philosophy that pertains to helping people become fully human, thereby actualizing their potential for making the world the best possible place for all forms of life (2004).

There is no universal model or paradigm related to purposes, aims, or goal areas in adapted physical education. The framework presented in figure 1.2 is offered as a skeletal reference for physical education programs, which is consistent with federal legislation and the orientation used in this book. Figure 1.2 encompasses the statement of purpose presented as well as a program's aims, program goals, and content areas. This framework assumes that the adapted physical education program is part of the total school physical education program. In essence, the program strives to develop individuals to their maximum.

In this orientation, the physical education and sport program aims to produce physically educated individuals who live active and healthy lifestyles that enhance their progress toward self-actualization. The National Association for Sport and Physical Education (NASPE) has developed six content standards to reflect what the physically educated individual should know and do (see sidebar on page 8).

The development of a physically educated individual is accomplished through experiences associated with goals and objectives related to psychomotor, cognitive, and affective domains of learning. In this paradigm, program goals are accomplished by development of and through the psychomotor domain. In figure 1.2, education *of* the psychomotor domain is represented by solid lines connecting content and program goals. Development *through* the psychomotor domain is represented by dotted lines among cognitive, affective, and psychomotor development areas.

Program goals are developed through content areas in the physical education program. Content areas related to psychomotor development may

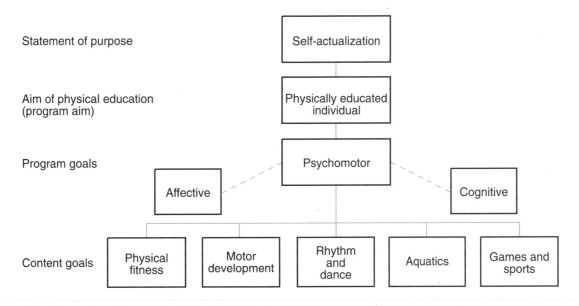

Figure 1.2 Aims and goals for an adapted physical education program.

NASPE Content Standards

The physically educated person . . .

Standard 1—demonstrates competency in motor skills and movement patterns needed to perform a variety of physical activities.

Standard 2—demonstrates an understanding of movement concepts, principles, strategies, and tactics as they apply to the learning and performance of physical activities.

Standard 3—participates regularly in physical activity.

Standard 4—achieves and maintains a health-enhancing level of physical fitness.

Standard 5—exhibits responsible personal and social behavior that respects self and others in physical activity settings.

Standard 6—values physical activity for health, enjoyment, challenge, self-expression, and social interaction.

Reprinted from *Moving Into the Future: National Standards for Physical Education: A Guide to Content and Assessment* (2004) with permission from the National Association for Sport and Physical Education, an association of the American Alliance for Health, Physical Education, Recreation and Dance, 1900 Association Drive, Reston, VA 20191.

be grouped in many ways. Figure 1.2 shows five content goal areas: physical fitness, motor development, rhythm and dance, aquatics, and games and sports. These content areas are consistent with the definition of adapted physical education used in this book and the definition of physical education associated with IDEA. Each of these content areas includes developmental areas or sport skills. For example, aerobic capacity might be a developmental area under physical fitness, and basketball is a sport within the content area of group games and sports.

The content goals shown in figure 1.2, as well as goals in affective and cognitive domains, may serve as annual goals for individualized programs. Specific skills and developmental areas associated with these goals may be used to represent short-term objectives. For example, an annual goal for a student might be to improve physical fitness. A corresponding short-term objective might be to improve health-related flexibility by obtaining a score of 25 centimeters on a sit-and-reach test. Objectives can be expressed on several levels to reflect the specificity desired. The emphasis given to the three developmental areas in a student's

program should be based on his or her needs. An adapted physical education program is established to meet objectives unique for each student.

In general, the purpose, aims, and program goals are the same for regular and adapted physical education. Differences between these programs exist mainly in the area of content goals, specific objectives, and performance standards and benchmarks. For example, goal ball may be a content goal for individuals who are blind, and an objective for them might relate to throwing and blocking. Teachers may select test items and standards that assess functional as well as physiological health, which relate to health-related physical fitness. Other differences might include the time spent on instructional units or objectives and the scope of the curriculum mastered.

SERVICE PROVIDERS

Individuals providing direct service are the key to ensuring quality experiences related to adapted physical education and sport. These individuals include teachers, coaches, therapists, and volunteers. In regard to teachers, it must be emphasized that adapted physical education and sport must be provided not only by individuals who specialize in this field but by regular physical educators as well. If services were provided only by specialists in adapted physical education, relatively few individuals needing services would be getting services because there are too few specialists in adapted physical education.

To meet the needs of children in adapted physical education and sport, teachers of physical education must assume responsibility for all children they teach. Each of these teachers must be willing to contribute to the development of each individual. This requires a philosophy that looks toward human service and beyond "won and lost" records as the ultimate contribution in one's professional life. Success for *all* students in physical education requires an instructor who has appropriate professional knowledge, skills, and values as well as a caring and helping attitude. A good teacher or coach of children recognizes the development of positive self-esteem as important and displays an attitude of acceptance, empathy, friendship, and warmth, while ensuring a secure and controlled learning environment. The good teacher or coach of adapted physical education and sport selects and uses teaching approaches and styles beneficial to students, provides individualized and personalized instruction and opportunities, and creates a positive environment in which students can succeed. The good teacher uses a praising and encouraging approach and creates a positive educational environment in which all students are accepted and supported.

Individuals studying to become teachers often have little or no experience working with individuals with disabilities or those with unique physical education needs. It is important to take advantage of every opportunity to interact with individuals with disabilities, to describe the value of physical activity to them, and to listen to their stories about their experiences in adapted physical education and sport. Being involved in disability awareness activities and having an opportunity to assume and function as if one has a disability provides important insights and values to prospective teachers.

BRIEF HISTORY OF ADAPTED PHYSICAL EDUCATION

Although significant progress concerning educational services for individuals with disabilities has been relatively recent, the use of physical activity or exercise for medical treatment and therapy is not new. Therapeutic exercise can be traced to 3000 B.C. in China. It is known that the ancient Greeks and Romans also recognized the medical and therapeutic value of exercise. However, the idea of physical education or physical activity to meet the unique needs of individuals with disabilities is a recent phenomenon. Efforts to serve these populations through physical education and sport has been given significant attention only during the 20th century, although efforts began in the United States in the 19th century.

Beginning Period

In 1838, physical activity began receiving special attention at the Perkins School for pupils with visual disabilities in Boston. According to Charles E. Buell (1983), a noted physical educator with a visual impairment, this special attention resulted from the fact that Samuel Gridley Howe, the school's director, advocated the health benefits of physical activity. For the first eight years, physical education consisted of compulsory recreation in the open air. In 1840, when the school was moved to South Boston, boys participated in gymnastic exercises and swimming. This was the first physical education program in the United States for students who were blind, and, by Buell's account, it was far ahead of most of the physical education in public schools.

Medical Orientation

Although physical education was provided to blind people, as well as individuals with other disabilities, in the early 1800s, most students of the history of adapted physical education recognized that medically oriented gymnastics and drills began in the latter part of the century as the forerunner of modern adapted physical education in the United States. Sherrill (2004) states that physical education prior to 1900 was medically oriented and preventive, developmental, or corrective in nature. Its purpose was to prevent illness and promote the health and vigor of the mind and body. Strongly influencing this orientation was a system of medical gymnastics developed in Sweden by Per Henrick Ling and introduced to the United States in 1884.

Shift to Sports and the Whole Person

From the end of the 19th century into the 1930s, programs began to shift from medically oriented physical training to sports-centered physical education, and concern for the whole child emerged. Compulsory physical education in public schools increased dramatically, and physical education teacher training (rather than medical training) developed for the promotion of physical education (Sherrill, 2004). This transition resulted in broad mandatory programs consisting of games, sports, rhythmic activities, and calisthenics designed to meet the needs of the whole person. Individuals unable to participate in regular activities were provided corrective or remedial physical education. According to Sherrill, physical education programs between the 1930s and the 1950s consisted of regular or corrective classes for students who today would be considered "normal." Sherrill (2004) has succinctly described adapted physical education during this period in the United States.

> Assignment to physical education was based upon a thorough medical examination by a physician who determined whether a student should participate in the regular or corrective program. Corrective classes were comprised primarily of limited, restricted, or modified activities related to health, posture, or fitness problems. In many schools students were excused from physical

education. In others, the physical educator typically taught several sections of regular physical education and one section of corrective physical education each day. Leaders in corrective physical education continued to have strong backgrounds in medicine and/or physical therapy. Persons preparing to be physical education teachers generally completed one university course in corrective physical education. (page 18)

The Emerging Comprehensive Subdiscipline

During the 1950s, more and more pupils described as handicapped were being served in public schools, and the outlook toward them was becoming increasingly humanistic. With a greater diversity in pupils came a greater diversity in programs to meet their needs. In 1952, the American Association for Health, Physical Education and Recreation (AAHPER) formed a committee to define the subdiscipline and give direction and guidance to professionals. This committee defined adapted physical education as "a diversified program of developmental activities, games, sports, and rhythms suited to the interests, capacities, and limitations of students with disabilities who may not safely or successfully engage in unrestricted participation in the rigorous activities of the regular physical education program" (Committee on Adapted Physical Education, 1952). The definition retained the evolving diversity of physical education and specifically included students with disabilities. Adapted physical education serves today as the comprehensive term for this subdiscipline.

Recent and Current Status

With the impetus provided by a more humanistic, more informed, and less discriminatory society, major advances continued in the 1960s. Many of these advances were associated with the Joseph P. Kennedy family. In 1965, the Joseph P. Kennedy, Jr., Foundation awarded a grant to the American Alliance for Health, Physical Education, Recreation and Dance (AAHPERD) to launch the Project on Recreation and Fitness for the Mentally Retarded. The project grew to encompass all special populations, and its name was changed in 1968 to the Unit on Programs for the Handicapped. As director of the unit, Dr. Julian Stein dramatically influenced

adapted physical education at every level throughout the United States.

In 1968, the Kennedy Foundation exhibited further concern for individuals with mental retardation by establishing the Special Olympics. This program grew rapidly, with competition held at local, state, national, and international levels in an ever-increasing range of sports. During the mid-1960s, concern for people with emotional or learning disabilities had a significant effect on adapted physical education in the United States. The importance of physical activity for the well-being of those with emotional problems was explicitly recognized by the National Institute of Mental Health, U.S. Public Health Service, when it funded the Buttonwood Farms Project. The project, conducted at Buttonwood Farms, Pennsylvania, included a physical recreation component. This project was valuable for recognizing the importance of physical activity in the lives of individuals with disabilities, bringing the problems of seriously disturbed youngsters to the attention of educators, and developing curricular materials to prepare professionals in physical education and recreation for work with this population.

During the same era, adapted physical education gained much attention with the use of perceptual–motor activities as a basis or modality for academic and intellectual development, particularly for students with learning disabilities. Newell C. Kephart, Gerald N. Getman, Raymond H. Barsch, Marianne Frostig, Phyllis Maslow, Bryant J. Cratty, and Jean A. Ayres were major proponents of motoric (movement or motor experiences) experiences as a basis or modality for perceptual, academic, and motor development. The contention that movement experiences serve as a basis for intellectual abilities has lost support in recent years. However, the use of movement experiences including active games for the development and reinforcement of academic abilities appears to be regaining popularity and research-based support.

Contemporary direction and emphasis in adapted physical education are heavily associated with the individual's right to a free and appropriate education. Because of litigation and the passage of various federal laws and regulations, change and progress have occurred in both adapted physical education and sport. This legal impetus has improved programs in many schools and agencies, extended mandated physical education for individuals ages 3 to 21, stimulated activity programs for infants and toddlers, and resulted in dramatic increases in participation in sport programs for individuals with disabilities. Legislation has also resulted in funds for professional preparation, research, and other special projects relevant to the provision of full educational opportunity for individuals with unique needs. Finally, the impact of federal legislation and a strong belief in the right and value of an education in the regular educational environment have resulted in a significant movement toward inclusion regarding the education of children with disabilities in the United States. The elements of contemporary direction and emphasis mentioned here are covered in great detail in several parts of this book.

Recent and Current Leaders

As fields of study emerge, evolve, and mature, individuals always appear who have provided leadership and achieved excellence in the field. These individuals serve as role models for contributions to philosophy, theoretical foundations, research, programs, teaching and other services to the field. In regard to adapted physical education, the periodical *Palaestra* has identified 10 individuals who have made significant contributions to adapted physical education in the late 20th century throughout distinguished careers. Their class of 1991 leaders included David M. Auxter, Slippery Rock University in Pennsylvania; Lawrence Rarick, University of California at Berkeley; Julian U. Stein, American Alliance for Heath, Physical Education, Recreation and Dance and George Mason University; Thomas M. Vodola, Township of Ocean School District in New Jersey; and Janet Wessel, Michigan State University. In the next decade *Palaestra* (2000), selected the following nationally and internationally

Figure 1.3 Recent and current leaders of adapted physical education: *(a)* David Beaver, *(b)* Gudrun Doll-Tepper, *(c)* John Dunn, *(d)* Claudine Sherrill, and *(e)* Joseph Winnick.

recognized individuals as leaders in the field of adapted physical education: David Beaver, Western Illinois University; Gudrun Doll-Tepper, Free University of Berlin; John Dunn, Oregon State University; Claudine Sherrill, Texas Women's University; and Joseph P. Winnick, State University of New York, College at Brockport (figure 1.3, p. 11). Detailed accomplishments of these individuals are presented in the Summer 2000 issue of *Palaestra.* Although these individuals have been recognized, it is important to realize that they constitute a tiny percentage of the individuals making significant contributions at many different levels every day in the field of adapted physical education.

THE INCLUSION MOVEMENT

Inclusion means educating students with disabilities in a regular educational setting. The movement toward inclusion was encouraged by and is compatible with the least restrictive environment (LRE) provisions associated with IDEA. Education in the LRE requires, to the maximum extent appropriate, that children with disabilities be educated with children without disabilities. However, according to LRE provisions in IDEA, a continuum of alternative environments (including segregated environments) may be used for the education of an individual if that is the most appropriate environment. A recommended continuum is presented in figure 2.1 (p. 24). The inclusion movement has also been given impetus by many who believe that separate education is not an equal education and that the setting in which a program is implemented significantly influences that program provided for a child. In the 24th annual report to Congress, it was reported that over 97 percent of students with disabilities, ages 6 to 21, attended schools with their peers without disabilities in the 1999–2000 school year (U. S. Department of Education, 2002). This is the reality of inclusion and why appropriately prepared educators are required. Although this book prepares teachers to serve children in all settings, it gives special emphasis to the skills and knowledge needed to optimally educate children with disabilities in regular educational environments.

LITIGATION

Much has been and can be written about the impact of litigation on the guarantee of full edu-cational opportunity in the United States. The most prominent of cases, which has served as an important precedent for civil litigation, was *Brown v. Board of Education of Topeka, Kansas* (1954). This case established that the doctrine of "separate but equal" in public education resulted in segregation that violated the constitutional rights of black individuals. Two landmark cases also had a heavy impact on the provision of free, appropriate public education for all children with disabilities. The first was the class action suit of the *Pennsylvania Association for Retarded Children v. Commonwealth of Pennsylvania* (1972). Equal protection and due process clauses associated with the Fifth and Fourteenth Amendments served as the constitutional basis for the court's rulings and agreements. The following were among the rulings or agreements in the case:

- Labeling a child as mentally retarded or denying public education or placement in a regular setting without due process or hearing violates the rights of the individual.
- All mentally retarded individuals are capable of benefiting from a program of education and training.
- Mental age may not be used to postpone or in any way deny access to a free public program of education and training.
- Having undertaken to provide a free, appropriate education to all its children, a state may not deny mentally retarded children the same.

A second important case was *Mills v. Board of Education of the District of Columbia* (1972). This action, brought on behalf of seven children, sought to restrain the District of Columbia from excluding children from public schools or denying them publicly supported education. The district court held that, by failing to provide the seven children with handicapping conditions and the class they represented with publicly supported specialized education, the district violated controlling statutes, its own regulations, and due process. The District of Columbia was required to provide a publicly supported education, appropriate equitable funding, and procedural due process rights to the seven children.

From 1972 to 1975, 46 right-to-education cases related to individuals with disabilities were tried in 28 states. They provided the foundation for much of the legislation to be discussed in the next section.

LAWS IMPORTANT TO ADAPTED PHYSICAL EDUCATION AND SPORT

Laws have had a tremendous influence on education programs for individuals with disabilities. Since 1969, colleges and universities in many states have received federal funds for professional preparation, research, and other projects to promote programs for individuals with disabilities. Although the amount of money has been relatively small, physical educators have gained a great deal from that support. The government agency most responsible for administering federally funded programs related to adapted physical education is the Office of Special Education and Rehabilitative Services within the Department of Education.

Four laws or parts of laws and their amendments have had significant impact on adapted physical education or adapted sport: IDEA, section 504 of the Rehabilitation Act of 1973, the Olympic and Amateur Sports Act, and the Americans with Disabilities Act (ADA). In January of 2002, PL 107-110, the No Child Left Behind (NCLB) Act of 2001 was signed into law to ensure that all children have a fair, equal, and significant opportunity to obtain a high-quality education. The provisions of the NCLB Act emphasize the attainment of academic achievement standards and academic assessment that affect students in special education. Although the central thrust of NCLB has less impact on adapted physical education and sport than the other four laws have, it is clear that the NCLB Act must be coordinated with the other laws. Table 1.1 (on page 14) shows a time line marking important milestones along with brief statements describing the importance of these laws.

Individuals With Disabilities Education Act (IDEA)

A continuing major impetus related to the provision of educational services for students with disabilities is the IDEA (Public Law 105-17). Definitions associated with this law can be found in appendix A. This act expanded on the previous Education for the Handicapped Act and amendments. However, IDEA reflects the composite and the most recent version and amendments of these laws (table 1.1). This act was designed to ensure that all children with disabilities have available to them a free appropriate public education that emphasizes special education and related services designed to meet their unique needs and that prepares them for employment and independent living (see sidebar). In this legislation, the term "special education" is defined to mean specially designed instruction at no cost to parents or guardians to meet the unique needs of a child with a disability, including instruction conducted in the classroom, in the home, in hospitals and institutions, in other settings, and in physical education (OSE/RS, 2002). IDEA specifies that the term "related services" means transportation and any developmental, corrective, or other supportive services required to assist a child with a disability to benefit from special education. These services include speech–language pathology and audiology services, psychological services, physical and occupational therapy, recreation (including therapeutic recreation), early identification and assessment of disabilities in children, counseling services (including rehabilitation counseling), orientation and mobility services, and medical services for diagnostic and evaluation purposes. Related services also include school health services, social work services in schools, and parent counseling and training (OSE/RS, 2002). The act also ensures that the rights of children with disabilities and their parents or guardians are protected and helps states and localities provide education for all individuals with disabilities. In addition, IDEA has established a policy to develop and implement a program of early intervention services for infants and toddlers and their families.

Highlights of the Individuals With Disabilities Education Act

IDEA and its rules and regulations require the following:

- A right to a free and appropriate education
- That physical education be made available to children with disabilities
- Equal opportunity for nonacademic and extracurricular activities
- An individualized program designed to meet unique needs for children with disabilities
- That programs are conducted within a least restrictive environment
- Nondiscriminatory testing and objective criteria for placement
- Due process
- Related services to assist in special education

Table 1.1 **Legislative Time Line: 1973-2003**

Law	Date	Importance
PL 93-112. The Rehabilitation Act of 1973	1973	Section 504 of this act was designed to prevent discrimination against and provide equal opportunity for individuals with disabilities in programs or activities receiving federal financial assistance.
PL 94-142. The Education for all Handicapped Children Act of 1975	1975	This act was designed to ensure that all children with handicapping conditions have available to them a free appropriate public education that emphasizes special education (including physical education) and related services designed to meet their unique needs.
PL 95-606. The Amateur Sports Act of 1978	1978	This act was passed to coordinate national efforts concerning amateur activity, including activity associated with the Olympic Games. This legislation led to the establishment of the Committee on Sports for the Disabled (COSD) as a standing committee of the United States Olympic Committee. The COSD coordinates American efforts for the Paralympics.
PL 98-199. Amendments to the Education for All Handicapped Children Act	1983	This act provided incentives to states to provide services to infants, toddlers, and preschoolers with handicapping conditions.
PL 99-457. Education for All Handicapped Children Amendments of 1986	1986	This act expanded educational services to preschool children ages three to five and established a discretionary program to assist states to plan, develop, and implement a comprehensive, coordinated, interdisciplinary program of early intervention services for infants and toddlers with handicapping conditions, birth to age 3 (or 0 to 2).
PL 101-476. Individuals with Disabilities Education Act (IDEA)	1990	This act replaced the term "handicapped" with "disabilities," expanded on types of services offered and disabilities covered.
PL 101-336. Americans with Disabilities Act	1990	This act extended civil rights protection for individuals with disabilities to all areas of American life.
PL 105-17. Individuals with Disabilities Education Act Amendments of 1997	1997	This act provided several changes in the law, including provisions for free appropriate education to all children with disabilities (ages 3 to 21); extension of a "developmental delay" provision for children ages 3 to 9; emphasis on educational results; required progress reports for children with disabilities that are the same as those for children without disabilities; and changes in individualized education program (IEP) requirements.
PL 105-277. Olympic and Amateur Sports Act	1998	This act continues services associated with the Amateur Sports Act of 1978. As a result of this legislation, the United States Olympic Committee assumed the role and responsibilities of the United States Paralympic Committee.

Definition and Requirements of Physical Education in IDEA

Regulations associated with IDEA (OSE/RS, 2002) define physical education as the "development of (a) physical and motor fitness, (b) fundamental motor skills and patterns, and (c) skills in aquatics, dance, and individual and group games and sports (including intramural and lifetime sports)." This term includes special physical education, adapted physical education, movement education, and motor development. IDEA requires that special education, including physical education, be made available to children with disabilities and that it include physical education specially designed, if necessary, to meet their unique needs. This federal legislation, together with state requirements for physical education, significantly affects adapted physical education in schools. Readers should notice that the definition of adapted physical education used in this book closely parallels the definition of physical education in IDEA.

Free Appropriate Public Education Under IDEA

The term "free appropriate public education" means special education and related services: (1) are provided at public expense, under public supervision and direction and without charge; (2) meet the standards of the state's educational agency; (3) include an appropriate preschool, elementary, or secondary school education in the state involved; and (4) are provided in conformity with an IEP (OSE/RS, 2002).

Least Restrictive Environment

IDEA requires that education be conducted in the least restrictive environment. See the student placement application example explaining the best possible setting for a child with behavioral problems. Education in the least restrictive environment means that individuals with disabilities are educated with individuals without disabilities and that special classes, separate schooling, or other removal of children with disabilities from the regular physical education environment occurs only when the nature or severity of disability of a child is such that education in regular classes with the use of supplementary aids and services cannot be achieved in a satisfactory way (OSE/RS, 2002).

Relevant to education in the most appropriate setting is a continuum of instructional placements (see figure 2.1 on page 24), which range from a situation in which children with disabilities are integrated into a regular class to a very restrictive setting (out-of-school segregated placement).

Focus on Student Needs and Opportunities

IDEA implicitly, if not explicitly, encourages educators to focus on the educational needs of the student instead of on clinical or diagnostic labels. For example, as the IEP is developed, concern focuses on present functioning level, objectives, annual goals, and so on. The associated rules and regulations also indicate that children with disabilities must be provided with an equal opportunity for participation in nonacademic and extracurricular services and activities, including athletics and recreational activities.

Section 504 of the Rehabilitation Act

The right of equal opportunity also emerges from another legislative milestone that has affected adapted physical education and sport. Section 504 of the Rehabilitation Act provides that no otherwise qualified individual with a disability, solely by reason of that disability, be excluded from participation in, be denied the benefits of, or be subjected to discrimination under any program or activity receiving federal financial assistance (Workforce Investment Act of 1998).

APPLICATION EXAMPLE

Student Placement

Setting: Individualized program planning committee meeting

Student: 10-year-old with behavior problems, inadequate physical fitness (as evidenced by failing to meet specific or general standards on the Brockport Physical Fitness Test), and below-average motor development (at or below one standard deviation below the mean on a standardized motor development test)

Issue: What is the appropriate setting(s) for instruction?

Application: On the basis of the information available and after meeting with the parents and other members of the program planning committee, the following plan was determined:

- The student will receive an adapted physical education program.

- The program will be conducted in an integrated setting with support services whenever the student's peer group receives physical education.

- The student will receive an additional class of physical education each week with two other students who also require adapted physical education.

An important intent of section 504 is to ensure that individuals with a disability receive intended benefits of all educational programs and extracurricular activities. Two conditions are prerequisite to the delivery of services that guarantee benefits to those individuals: Programs must be *equally effective* as those provided to students without disabilities, and they must be conducted in the *most normal and integrated settings* possible. To be equally effective, a program must offer individuals with disabilities **equal opportunity** to attain the same results, gain the same benefits, or reach the same levels of achievement as peers without disabilities.

To illustrate the basic intent associated with section 504, let us consider a student who is totally blind and enrolled in a course in which all other students in the class are sighted. A written test given at the end of the semester would not provide the student who is blind equal opportunity to demonstrate knowledge of the material; thus, this approach would not be equally effective. By contrast, on a test administered orally or in Braille, the blind student would have an equal opportunity to attain the same results or benefits as the other students. In giving an oral exam, the instructor would be giving equivalent, as opposed to identical, services. (Merely identical services, in fact, would be considered discriminatory and not in accord with section 504.) It is neither necessary nor possible to guarantee equal results; what is important is the equal opportunity to attain those results. For example, a recipient of federal funds offering basketball to the general student population must provide wheelchair basketball for students confined to wheelchairs, if a need exists.

A program is not equally effective if it results in indiscriminate isolation or separation of individuals with disabilities. To the maximum degree possible, individuals with disabilities should participate in the least restrictive environment, as represented by a continuum of alternative instructional placements (see chapter 2).

Compliance with section 504 requires program accessibility. Its rules and regulations prohibit exclusion of individuals with disabilities from federally assisted programs because of architectural or other environmental barriers. Common barriers to accessibility include facilities, finances, and transportation. Money available for athletics within a school district cannot be spent in a way that discriminates on the basis of disability. If a school district lacks sufficient funds, then it need not offer programs; however, it cannot fund programs in a discriminatory manner.

In accordance with section 504, children with disabilities who do not require special education or related services (not classified under IDEA), are still entitled to accommodations and services in the regular school setting that are necessary to enable them to benefit from all programs and activities available to students without disabilities. Every child who is a student with a disability under IDEA is also protected under section 504, but all children covered under section 504 are not necessarily students with a disability under IDEA.

Section 504 obligates school districts to identify, evaluate, and extend to every qualified student with a disability (as defined by this act) residing in the district a free and appropriate public education, including modifications, accommodations, and specialized instructions or related aids as deemed necessary to meet their educational needs as adequately as the needs of students without disabilities are being met. School districts across the United States are now developing section 504 accommodation plans to provide programmatic assistance to students so that they have full access to all activities. For example, a 504 plan related to physical education might seek specialized instruction or equipment, auxiliary aids or services, or program modifications. A sample 504 plan is presented in chapter 4.

The Rehabilitation Act is known as complaint oriented legislation. Violations of section 504 may be filed with the United States Office for Civil Rights (OCR) and, in addition, parents may request under section 504 an impartial hearing to challenge a school district's decision regarding their children.

The Olympic and Amateur Sports Act

The Amateur Sports Act (ASA) of 1978 (PL95-606), amended by PL 105-277, (Ted Stephens Olympic and Amateur Sports Act of 1998), has contributed significantly to the provision of amateur athletic activity in the United States, including competition for athletes with disabilities. This legislation has led to the establishment of the United States Olympic Committee (USOC) and gives it exclusive jurisdiction over matters pertaining to U.S. participation and organization of the Olympic Games, the Paralympic Games, and the Pan-American Games, including representation of the United States in the games. The USOC will encourage and provide assistance to amateur athletic programs and competition for amateur athletes with disabilities;

including, where feasible, the expansion of opportunities for meaningful participation in programs of athletic competition for able-bodied athletes. Additional information about the Paralympics is presented in chapter 3.

Americans With Disabilities Act

In 1990, PL 101-336, the Americans with Disabilities Act, was passed. Whereas section 504 focused on educational rights, this legislation extended civil rights protection for individuals with disabilities to all areas of American life. Provisions include employment, public accommodation and services, public transportation, and telecommunications. Related to adapted physical education and sport, this legislation has required that community recreational facilities including health and fitness facilities be accessible and, where appropriate, that reasonable accommodations be made for individuals with disabilities. Physical educators must develop and offer programs for individuals with disabilities that give them the ability to participate in physical activity and sport experiences within the community.

HISTORY OF ADAPTED SPORT

Athletes who are deaf were among the first Americans with disabilities to become involved in organized sports at special schools. As reported by Gannon (1981), in the 1870s the Ohio School for the Deaf became the first school for the deaf to offer baseball, and the state school in Illinois introduced football in 1885. Football became a major sport in many schools for the deaf around the turn of the century, and basketball was introduced at the Wisconsin School for the Deaf in 1906. Teams from schools for the deaf have continued to compete against each other and against athletes in regular schools.

Beyond interschool programs, formal international competition was established in 1924, when competitors from nine nations gathered in Paris for the first international silent games. In 1945, the American Athletic Association for the Deaf (AAAD) was established to provide, sanction, and promote competitive sport opportunities for Americans with hearing impairments.

The earliest formal, recorded athletic competition in the United States for individuals with visual disabilities was a telegraphic track meet between the Overbrook and Baltimore schools for the blind in 1907. In a telegraphic meet, local results are mailed to a central committee, which makes comparisons to determine winners. From this beginning, athletes with visual disabilities continue to compete against each other and against their sighted peers.

Since the 1900s, wars have provided impetus for competitive sport opportunities. Sir Ludwig Guttman of Stoke Mandeville, England, is credited with introducing competitive sports as an integral part of the rehabilitation of veterans with disabilities. In the late 1940s, Stoke Mandeville Hospital sponsored the first recognized games for wheelchair athletes. In 1949, the University of Illinois organized the first national wheelchair basketball tournament, which resulted in the formation of the National Wheelchair Basketball Association (NWBA). To expand sport opportunities, Ben Lipton founded the National Wheelchair Athletic Association (NWAA) in the mid-1950s. This organization has sponsored competitive sports on state, regional, and national levels for individuals with spinal cord conditions and other conditions requiring wheelchair use. Another recent advancement was the creation of the National Handicapped Sports and Recreation Association (NHSRA). This organization—known today as Disabled Sports, USA (DS/USA)—was formed by a small group of Vietnam veterans in the late 1960s. It has been dedicated to providing year-round sport and recreational opportunities for individuals with orthopedic, spinal cord, neuromuscular, and visual disabilities.

Special Olympics—created by the Joseph P. Kennedy, Jr., Foundation to provide and promote athletic competition for individuals with mental retardation—held its first international games at Soldier Field in Chicago in 1968. (A symbol for Special Olympics is shown in figure 1.4, p. 18) Special Olympics has served as the model sport organization for individuals with disabilities through its leadership in direct service, research, training, advocacy, education, and organizational leadership.

During the last quarter of the 20th century, other national multisport and unisport programs have been formed. These have expanded available sport offerings to an increasing number of individuals with disabilities. The latest opportunities have been organized for athletes with visual impairments, cerebral palsy, closed head injury, stroke, dwarfism, and les autres (i.e., other conditions).

The evolution of sport organizations within the United States has led to greater involvement in international competition. In fact, many American sport organizations have international

Figure 1.4 This symbol of the Special Olympics was a gift of the former Union of Soviet Socialist Republics on the occasion of the 1979 International Special Olympic Games, hosted by the State University of New York, College at Brockport. The artist is Zurab Tsereteli.

counterparts (see chapter 3). Especially notable in this regard is the International Paralympics, discussed in chapter 3. American organizations that participate in international games are also listed in chapter 3. These organizations are multisport programs—that is, several sports are included as a part of these programs. In addition to multisport organizations, several organizations are centered on single sports, such as the National Wheelchair Basketball Association. An important movement is underway today in which sport programs traditionally offering programs for athletes without disabilities are organizing opportunities and competition for athletes with disabilities. This approach reduces the need for sport organizations organized primarily for types of disability. Some of these programs are associated with international competition. Unisport organizations provide excellent opportunities for athletes with disabilities; several of these organizations are identified in other chapters of this book.

In the past few years, much of the impetus for sports for athletes with disabilities has been provided by out-of-school sport organizations. Although developing at a slower rate, other opportunities have begun to surface throughout the United States in connection with public school programs. An important milestone came in 1992 when Minnesota became the first state to welcome athletes with disabilities into its state school asso-

ciation. This made Minnesota the first state in the nation to sanction interschool sports for junior and senior high school students with disabilities. More recently, a Georgia-based nonprofit organization entitled the American Association of Adapted Sports Programs (AAASP) has been developed to build interscholastic sports leagues for students with physical disabilities or visual impairments. This group has developed a model for other programs throughout the country to imitate. This organization has joined forces with Project ASPIRE (Adapted Sports Programs in Recreation and Education) to promote programs. AAASP has been endorsed by the American Association for Adapted Lifestyles and Fitness (AAALF).

A few states now organize statewide competition for athletes with disabilities. Some of these are combined with community-based organized sport programs, and others are provided independently of other organized sport programs. Finally, sport programs in rehabilitation settings for individuals in communities are emerging in major cities in the United States. More detailed information on these programs is presented in chapter 3.

PERIODICALS

The increased knowledge base and greater attention to adapted physical education and sport in recent years has been accompanied by the founding and development of several periodicals devoted to the subject. Among the most relevant of these are the *Adapted Physical Activity Quarterly, Palaestra,* and *Sports 'N Spokes*. Other periodicals that publish directly relevant information from time to time include the *Journal of Physical Education, Recreation, and Dance; Strategies; Research Quarterly for Exercise and Sport; Journal of Visual Impairment and Blindness; Journal of Learning Disabilities; American Annals of the Deaf; Teaching Exceptional Children; American Journal of Mental Deficiency; Journal of Special Education; Therapeutic Recreation Journal; Journal of the Association for Persons with Severe Handicaps; Clinical Kinesiology;* and *The Physical Educator.*

ORGANIZATIONS

The American Alliance for Health, Physical Education, Recreation and Dance (AAHPERD) is an important national organization that makes significant contributions to programs for special populations. AAHPERD (called AAHPER before the dance discipline was added) has many members whose primary professional concern lies in adapted physical education and sport. AAHPER established a definition of adapted physical education in 1952. Over the years, its many publications, conferences, and conventions have given much attention to adapted physical education—not only on the national level but also within the organization's state, district, and local affiliates. Its professional conferences and conventions are among the best sources of information on adapted physical education and sport. At the national level, AAHPERD continues to advocate physical education and fitness for individuals with disabilities. Over the past few years, AAHPERD has continually developed its organization to help professionals in adapted physical education and sport, recreation, and dance, serve individuals with disabilities. It is expected that it will continue to provide key professional services and leadership in the future.

The National Consortium for Physical Education and Recreation for Individuals with Disabilities (NCPERID, or the Consortium) was established to promote, stimulate, and encourage professional preparation and research. The organization was started informally in the late 1960s by a small group of college and university directors of federally funded professional preparation or research projects seeking to share information. Its members have extensive backgrounds and interest in adapted physical education and therapeutic recreation. They have provided leadership and input on national issues and concerns, including the development of IDEA and its rules and regulations; federal funding for professional preparation, research, demonstration projects, and other special projects; and the monitoring of legislation. The Consortium holds an annual meeting and publishes a newsletter.

The International Federation for Adapted Physical Activity (IFAPA), which originated in Quebec, has expanded to a worldwide organization with an international charter. Its primary service has been to sponsor a biennial international adapted physical activity symposium. In alternating years symposia organized by IFAPA are also held in other regions throughout the world. The organization primarily solicits memberships from allied health therapists, therapeutic recreators, and adapted physical educators. With its international dimensions, IFAPA can disseminate valuable knowledge throughout the world.

The Office of Special Education and Rehabilitation Service, within the Department of Education, is responsible for monitoring educational services for individuals with disabilities and for providing grants to colleges and universities to fund professional preparation, research, and other special projects.

A private organization that has made a monumental contribution to both adapted physical education and sport is Special Olympics, Inc., founded by Eunice Kennedy Shriver. Although its leadership in providing sport opportunities for individuals with mental disabilities is well known, this organization has provided much more to adapted physical education and sport. Specifically, Special Olympics has played a key role in the attention to physical education in federal legislation and the provision of federal funding for professional preparation, research, and other projects in federal legislation through its advocacy activities. The organization has provided a worldwide model for the provision of sport opportunities; its work is acknowledged in several sections of this book.

SUMMARY

Over the past few years increased attention was given to adapted physical education and sport. This chapter described and presented a brief history of this field. Information regarding program direction was presented, and the importance and characteristics of those providing services in this field were recognized. The chapter stressed the importance of litigation, legislation, and the inclusion movement on programs affecting individuals with disabilities. Finally, periodicals and organizations significant to adapted physical education were identified and described to serve as part of this introductory chapter.

REFERENCES

Brown v. Board of Education of Topeka, Kansas 347 U.S. 483 (1954).

Buell, C.E. (1983). *Physical education for blind children.* Springfield, IL: Charles C. Thomas.

Committee on Adapted Physical Education (1952). Guiding principles for adapted physical education. *Journal of Health, Education and Recreation, 23*(15), 15-28.

Gannon, J.R. (1981*). Deaf heritage: A narrative history of deaf America.* Silver Spring, MD: National Association for the Deaf.

Individuals with Disabilities Education Act Amendments of 1997 (PL 105-17), 20 U.S.C. 1400 (1997).

Mills v. Board of Education of the District of Columbia, 348 F. Supp. 966 (1972).

No Child Left Behind Act (NCLB Act). Pub. L, 107-110, 115 Stat 1425 (2001).

Office of Special Education and Rehabilitative Services (OSE/RS), 34 CFR 300 (2002).

Palaestra (2000). Leadership in Disability Sport, Adapted Physical Education, & Therapeutic Recreation. *Palaestra* 16(3): 48-52.

Pennsylvania Association for Retarded Children v. Commonwealth of Pennsylvania, U.S. District Court, 343 F. Supp. 279 (1972).

Sherrill, C. (2004*). Adapted physical activity, recreation and sport: Crossdisciplinary and lifespan.* (6th ed.) Boston: McGraw Higher Education.

Ted Stephens Olympic and Amateur Sports Acts of 1998, U.S.C.A. 220501 et seq. (West 2001)

U.S. Department of Education. Office of Special Education Programs. (2002). The Twenty-Fourth Annual Report to Congress on the Implementation of the Individuals with Disabilities Education Act. Washington, D.C.: Author.

Workforce Investment Act of 1998 (PL 105-220), Sec 401 et seq. (1998).

WRITTEN RESOURCES

American Association of Adapted Sports Programs (AAASP).

This is a nonprofit organization that builds interscholastic sports leagues for students with physical disabilities or visual disabilities. Sports include beep baseball, indoor wheelchair soccer, wheelchair basketball, power wheelchair hockey, and track and field. Contact: Post Office Box 538, Pine Lake, Georgia, 30072, Phone: (404) 294-0070, AAASP@bellsouth.net, www.AAASP.org.

Metro Association for Adapted Athletics.

This organization provides leadership for and organizes interscholastic athletic opportunities for students with disabilities in the state of Minnesota. Detailed information can be obtained from Rich Matter, Minnesota State High School League, 763-560-2262 x497, rmatter@mshsl.org.

Block, M. E. (1995). American with disabilities act: Its impact on youth sports. *Journal of Education, Recreation and Game,* 66(1), 28-32.

This article summarizes major parts of the act and answers questions on how the act affects youth sports.

Winnick, J.P., Auxter, D., Jansma, P., Sculli, J., Stein, J., & Weiss, R.A. (1980). Implications of Section 504 of the Rehabilitation Act as related to physical education instructional, personnel preparation, intramural, and interscholastic/intercollegiate sport programs. In J.P. Winnick & F.X. Short (Eds.), *Special athletic opportunities for individuals with handicapping conditions.* Brockport, NY: SUNY College at Brockport (ERIC Ed210897) or *Practical Pointers,* 3(11) 1-20.

This chapter provides a full position paper related to section 504 of the Rehabilitation Act of 1973.

AUDIOVISUAL RESOURCES

Physical activity for all: Professional enhancement program (PAFA). (1999).

This is a digital video disc, read-only memory (DVD-ROM) with modules on 12 adapted physical education topics, including movement science foundations; legal and professional aspects; physical education: inclusive settings; physical education: special settings; family, community, and school; uniqueness (unique attributes of learners); collaboration; assessment; curriculum and instruction; principles and practices of physical fitness; play; leisure and sports. Source: Program Development Associates, P O Box 2038, Syracuse, NY 13220. Phone: 1-800-543-2119, Fax: 315-452-0710; Web site: www.disability training.com. Running time is approximately six hours.

ELECTRONIC RESOURCES

Challenge Publications. Web site: www.palaestra.com.

This is the home of *Palaestra,* published by Challenge Publications, PO Box 508, Macomb, IL 61455.

Human Kinetics. Web site: www.humankinetics.com.

This is the home of the *Adapted Physical Activity Quarterly,* published by Human Kinetics Publishers, Inc., 1607 N. Market Street, Box 5076, Champaign, IL 61825-5076.

Paralyzed Veterans of America. Web site: www.pva.org/.

This is the Web site of *Sports 'N Spokes,* published by the Paralyzed Veterans of America, 2111 East Highland Avenue, Suite 180, Phoenix, AZ 85016-4702.

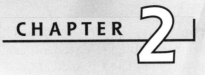

CHAPTER 2

Program Organization and Management

Joseph P. Winnick

Jimmy, an elementary student with cerebral palsy, could definitely benefit from an individu-alized program to meet his physical education needs. Unfortunately for Jimmy, there is a great deal of confusion at his school. Is he eligible for adapted physical education? In what setting should his program be implemented? What should he be taught? How much time should he receive in physical education? Should he receive physical therapy? In Jimmy's school, such confusion is not unusual—the same questions arise every time a student with a unique need enrolls. Should Jimmy's school have written guidelines to improve the educa-tional process for Jimmy and other students? The answer is yes, and in this chapter we will provide information to help develop these guidelines.

This chapter includes information that is helpful in developing and implementing adapted physical education and services in a school. The information presented will help schools organize and manage programs and write guidelines reflecting policies and procedures on how to implement adapted physical education programs. The guidelines can be a part of the overall plan for physical education or part of a separate document. In either case, guidelines should reflect current laws, rules and regulations, policies, procedures, and best practices.

PROGRAM AND CURRICULUM PLANNING

An important early step for organizing and managing programs and developing guidelines is to identify the purpose(s), aims, goals, standards, and objectives for physical education. As a part of this step, the similarities and differences between regular and adapted physical education should be addressed. This provides a good beginning framework for a program. There is no universal model for this framework, so educational entities must establish or adopt their own. A sample framework for adapted physical education is presented in the first chapter of this book and is outlined in figure 1.2 (on page 7). This framework can be adapted or modified for use for a school plan. It also serves as the framework or structure for this book.

ADMINISTRATIVE AREAS RELATED TO PROGRAM ORGANIZATION AND MANAGEMENT

Personnel who administer school programs must develop procedures for organizing and implementing an adapted physical education program. These administrators must ensure that the resources at their disposal adequately meet the needs of the pupils they serve. They should have procedures in place to identify pupils who should receive adapted physical education programs, and they should have a plan to select settings most appropriate for instruction. Because of the emphasis on inclusion today, understanding and promoting inclusion is an important consideration in implementing programs. Administrators must ensure that appropriate class sizes and groupings

are provided, schedules are developed to meet student needs, mandated time requirements are met, sport opportunities are provided, and programs are appropriately funded and conducted in accessible facilities. In the next few pages we will address these areas in more detail.

Identifying Pupils for Adapted Physical Education

In identifying students for an adapted physical education program, it is important at the outset to determine who is eligible or qualified. In some instances, the decision is obvious, and an elaborate system of identification is not necessary. In other instances, determination of a unique need can be made only after detailed assessment data are analyzed and compared to the criteria established to determine a unique need.

Essentially, an adapted physical education program is for students with unique needs who require a specially designed program exceeding 30 consecutive calendar days. In selecting candidates for such a program, procedures, criteria, and standards for determining unique needs are important (they are discussed in chapters 4 and 5). The inability to attain health-related criterion-referenced physical fitness standards appropriate for the individual is an example of a criterion for establishing a unique need. A unique need is exhibited because individuals are expected to meet standards appropriate for them.

Many procedures are used to identify students who require adapted physical education in a school. These procedures are associated with child find, a program that tries to determine which children in a school have unique needs, as referred to in IDEA. The procedures might include screening:

- all new school entrants,
- students with disabilities,
- *all* students annually,
- referrals, or
- students requesting exemption from physical education.

An important child-find activity is the screening of all new entrants to the school. For transfer students, records should be checked to determine if unique needs in physical education have been previously identified. In the absence of such information, the school, as part of its procedures, might decide to administer a screening test, particularly if a unique physical education need is suspected.

A second child-find source is a list of enrolled students identified as having a disability in accordance with IDEA. Every student who has been so identified and whose disability is frequently associated with unique physical education needs should be routinely screened. Many children with disabilities have participated in preschool programs, and records from these programs might indicate children with unique physical education needs.

A third activity is the annual screening of all students enrolled in school. Such a screening might involve informal observation as well as formal testing. Conditions that might be detected through informal screening and possibly warrant in-depth evaluation include (but are not limited to) disabling conditions, obesity, clumsiness, aversion to physical activity, and postural deviations.

Many students are referred to adapted physical education. School guidelines should permit referrals from:

- parents or guardians;
- professional staff members in the school district;
- physicians;
- judicial officers;
- representatives of agencies with responsibility for student welfare, health, or education; or
- students themselves (if they are at least 18 years of age or are emancipated minors).

Referrals for adapted physical education should be received by a specifically designated person in each school.

Medical excuses or requests for exemption from physical education should lead to referrals for adapted physical education. When an excuse or request is made, immediate discussion with the family physician might be necessary to determine how long adaptation might be required. For a period shorter than 30 consecutive days, required adjustments can be determined by the regular physical education teacher, following established local policies and procedures. If the period is longer than 30 consecutive days, the procedure for identifying pupils for adapted physical education for a school district should be followed. Typically, these procedures involve a planning committee.

Instructional Placements for Physical Education

Individuals who are referred or are otherwise identified as possibly requiring a specially designed program should undergo a thorough assessment to determine if a unique need exists. We discuss procedures for assessment in chapters 4 and 5. Once it is established that students have unique physical education needs and require an adapted physical education program, they must be placed in appropriate instructional settings. In this regard, it must be emphasized that adapted physical education may be implemented in a variety of settings. In accordance with IDEA, to the maximum extent appropriate, children with disabilities must be educated with students who are not disabled and in the least restrictive environment (LRE). To comply with the LRE requirement, various authors have proposed options on a continuum of instructional arrangements. Typical options on a continuum of instructional arrangements appear in figure 2.1 (on page 24). The number of options available is less important than the idea that students will be educated in the regular setting (to the extent appropriate and possible) and in the environment most conducive to their advancement. The continuum presented in figure 2.1 clearly depicts more possibilities than integrated or segregated placement and thus is consistent with IDEA.

The three levels at the base of the continuum provide placement in a regular educational environment, and it is within these levels that the continuum is consistent with education in regular or inclusive environments. Level 1 placement is for students without unique needs or those whose short-term needs are met in the regular physical education program. This placement is also appropriate for individuals with unique needs requiring an adapted education program that can be appropriately implemented in the regular physical education setting.

Level 2 is for students whose adapted physical education programs can be met in a regular class environment with support service assistance. For example, some students might function well in a regular class if consultation is available to teachers and parents. In another instance, regular class placement might be warranted if a paraprofessional or an adapted physical education teacher can work with the individual with unique needs.

Level 3 is a regular class placement with supplementary or resource room assistance, as appropriate. Supplementary services can be

contribute to successful inclusion. These functions include identifying unique needs; determining appropriate instructional settings and supplementary or support services; selecting strategies for individualizing instruction; adapting activities; preparing regular education students for inclusion, and preparing support personnel.

Identify Unique Needs

The first step toward promoting inclusion is to identify the unique needs of the individual student. Once this is accomplished, the program content and objectives can be selected. The identification of unique needs is basic to adapted physical education. In the absence of unique needs, the physical education that is appropriate is regular physical education. Chapter 4 includes information to help identify unique needs.

Determine Appropriate Instructional Settings and Support Services

Once unique needs are recognized, inclusive settings for instruction and supplementary or support services are identified. Possible settings are associated with levels 1 through 4 of the continuum of alternative instructional placements, as presented in figure 2.1. Settings for instruction depend on the support or supplementary services required. Support services might include ways to promote individualized attention through team teaching, peer tutoring, teaching assistants, paraprofessionals, or volunteers. In addition to (or as a part of) support services there might be a need to identify and provide 504 accommodations for

students with disabilities to promote inclusion. Examples include interpreters; facilities, equipment, or supply modifications; and even rule modifications. Examples of supplementary services include physical, occupational, or recreation therapy; orientation and mobility training, or extended services in physical education.

Individualize Instruction

The ability to individualize instruction is an important skill for teachers implementing inclusive programs. Individualization occurs when teachers make modifications in their objectives, methods of assessment, content, instructional materials, teaching styles, and instructional strategies and methods. Chapter 7 includes a detailed discussion of instructional strategies to meet individual differences. Strategies for individualization in inclusive environments will vary and build on the curricular content and objectives appropriate for each student. Inclusionary curricular options modified from the suggestions of Craft (1996) include: (1) the *same curriculum content* with objectives the same or different from other students in the class; (2) a *multilevel curriculum* in which specific skills or activity levels are varied to meet specific objectives but in which the content areas are the same for all students; (3) a *modified curriculum* in which activities are adapted to meet the same or different goals or objectives; and (4) a *different curriculum* in which the activities pursued are different in order to meet the same or different goals or objectives. Figure 2.2 shows how cycling equipment can be adapted to permit cycling to

© Joseph P. Winnick

© Joseph P. Winnick

Figure 2.2 Inclusive cycling activities.

© Sarah M. Rich

Figure 2.3 Inclusive settings allow students to perform modified or different activities while participating in class.

take place and contribute to aerobic objectives. Figure 2.3 presents a modified or different activity that enables the participant to pursue aerobic objectives in an inclusive setting.

Adapt Activities

Another critical function to promote integration is to adapt activities. Adapting activities increases the likelihood that individuals with different abilities will have the same opportunity to participate and gain equal benefits from participation (see the application example). Of course, not all adaptations are "equal," lead to the same results, or are "good." For example, permitting a player using a wheelchair to play in a traditional basketball game involving nine players without disabilities might jeopardize the education and safety of several of the remaining players and is probably not a good modification strategy. Permitting a double dribble in a basketball game by a student with low cognitive functioning might be considered a good strategy by some teachers and students but be viewed as unfair by others. With this in mind, it is useful to evaluate adaptations using established criteria for such a purpose. For the purpose of this book, the following five criteria are suggested in determining good adaptations.

- Promotes interaction and interplay—good adaptations enhance co-action, cooperation, competition, and reciprocity to the extent appropriate.
- Meets the needs of all students in the class—good adaptations meet the needs of

all students and do not jeopardize the education of any student in class.

- Improves or maintains self-esteem—good adaptations improve or maintain the self-esteem of all students. Adaptations should not embarrass or inappropriately draw attention to students.
- Provides physical activity—good adaptations promote physical activity for all classmates as much as possible (e.g., elimination-type activities would be contraindicated).
- Provides a safe experience for all—good adaptations sustain a safe environment for all participants.

Modifications to guide the adaptation of physical activities have been directly or indirectly categorized by different people in different ways. Lieberman and Houston-Wilson (2002) suggest four modification areas for adapting activities: equipment, rules, environment, and instruction. Each modification area involves a change or variation so that individuals with unique needs might be better able to participate in skills or games. As an example, table 2.1 (on page 28) provides some ways that the activities associated with softball can be modified using the four categories. The modifications may be applied to most or all physical activities and to one or more individuals participating in the activity. In this book, you will find many adaptations for physical education and sport based on these modification areas and others.

APPLICATION EXAMPLE

Inclusion

Setting: Seventh-grade physical education class

Student: 13-year-old student with intellectual disabilities and limitations in motor coordination

Unit: Basketball

Task: Dribbling and weaving around cones, alternating hands with each dribble

"Dribble the ball around five cones in a weaving manner, return, give the ball to the next person in line, then sit at the end of the line."

Application: The physical educator might include the following modifications of the task:

- Permit the use of either the same or alternating hands
- Permit the skipping of alternate cones
- Use a different ball size
- Dribble for a shorter distance around fewer cones

Table 2.1   Some Modifications of Softball Activities

Category	Modifications
Equipment	Beep ball, auditory ball, bright balls, Nerf balls, Wiffle balls, large balls, buzzers on bases, large bases, tee, large plastic bats, light bats
Rules	Hit off a tee, five-strike rule, no strike out, three swings and no strikes, running with a partner
Environment	Shorter distance between bases, increase in number of players in a game, reduction in the number of bases, batting cages, smaller field, partner activities
Instruction	Physical assistance, peer tutors, teaching in Braille, task analysis, sign language, hand signals, verbal cues, demonstration, auditory cues, one-on-one instruction

Modified from Lieberman, L.L. and C. Houston-Wilson. (2002) *Strategies for Inclusion.* Champaign, IL: Human Kinetics, p.137.

Although adapting physical activities via the four modification areas is a useful approach, adaptations can be enhanced in other ways as well. The sidebar presents seven helpful techniques to promote the integration of pupils with and without disabilities into physical education activities. The first suggested technique is to permit the sharing, substitution, or interchange of duties in an activity. This technique is patterned after the idea of a pinch hitter or a "courtesy" runner in softball. In an inclusive setting, for example, an able-bodied runner might run to first base after a nonambulatory student strikes a softball from a tee, or a blind runner might run bases with a sighted partner.

A second helpful technique is to select activities in which contact can be made and maintained with an opponent, partner, small group, or object. Youngsters who are deaf or those who have vision impairments might engage successfully in such activities as tug of war, chain tag, square dancing, and wrestling because continual contact is made with partners, team members, or opponents. Youngsters with vision impairments might use a rail to guide their approach while bowling.

A third helpful technique is to modify activities in such a way that all participants assume an impairment or disability. If not overused, this strategy can be useful in educating all children. Youngsters without disabilities might simulate lower-limb impairments during an activity by hopping on one foot; youngsters can close their eyes or be blindfolded while playing Marco Polo in a pool.

The next technique is a procedure generally recommended in regular physical education—that is, to modify or avoid elimination-type games or activities. In dodge ball, for example, rather than being eliminated from play when hit by a thrown ball, children might become throwers standing behind their opponents' end-line or simply have a point charged against them. In a game of "Jump the Shot," the winner could be the one who makes contact

Techniques for Integrating Pupils With and Without Disabilities Into Physical Education Activities

- Permit the sharing, substitution or interchange of duties in activity.
- Select activities in which contact is made and maintained with an opponent, partner, small group, or object.
- Modify some activities in a way that allows students without disabilities to assume disability.

- Modify or avoid elimination-type games and activities.
- Reduce play areas if movement capabilities are limited.
- Modify activities to use abilities rather than disabilities.
- Modify activities by "giving handicaps."

with the "shot" the least number of times rather than the last person remaining in the activity.

Inclusion is sometimes promoted when play areas are reduced for individuals with limited movement capabilities. For example, an individual with a below-the-knee amputation and a prosthesis might successfully play tennis, badminton, or volleyball in a narrower than normal court. Years ago, football players with vision impairments played on fields 10 yards wide. Reducing the size of play areas might be advisable to decrease activity intensity for children exhibiting cardiopathic disorders, severe forms of diabetes, or other conditions affected by exercise intensity.

The next technique is to emphasize abilities rather than disabilities. For example, youngsters who are deaf or those who have vision impairments might be more successfully included in activities if auditory or visual cues or goals are used. Instead of running to a line, children with impaired vision might be asked to run toward a bell, horn, whistle, drum, or clapping sound by another youngster. Youngsters with impaired vision might shoot baskets, perform archery, or play shuffleboard if an auditory goal locator is placed near the target. Youngsters with severe movement restrictions using wheelchairs might play a game in which the winner is the one who most closely predicts his or her time in negotiating 100 yards (thus practicing their cognitive abilities).

A final recommended technique, and perhaps the most helpful, involves modifying activities by "giving handicaps." The basis for this strategy stems from competition in games such as bowling or golf where "handicaps" are given. In a running relay, for example, a youngster with a lower-limb impairment is given a "distance handicap" and runs a shorter distance and returns to a starting point or is given a head start. In a basketball shooting

contest, an individual with less ability might compete or participate by standing closer to the basket, using a smaller ball, or shooting at a larger rim. When playing Wiffle ball, youngsters with eye–hand coordination deficits might be permitted to use a much larger plastic bat. In tennis, a player using a wheelchair might be permitted to strike the ball after it has bounced twice. In these instances, the idea is to determine who can participate or win under the conditions set at the outset.

Prepare Regular Education Students for Inclusion

A fifth key function for successful inclusion is preparing regular physical education students for an inclusionary physical education experience. Regarding regular education students, it is commonly accepted that prior positive experiences and disability awareness contribute to overall peer acceptance and healthy attitudes toward youngsters with disabilities and their involvement in physical education and sport activities. Block (2000), who used the term general physical education rather than regular physical education, has suggested several disability awareness activities for students without disabilities:

- Invite guest speakers with disabilities with successful experiences in physical education and sport to appear in your class.
- Role-play activities.
- Discuss current attitudes held by students in the class regarding individuals with disabilities.
- Discuss role models who are successful in physical education and sport.
- Teach general information about specific disabilities and how they are acquired.

In planning facilities in which to conduct adapted physical education and sport programs, attention must be given to indoor and outdoor areas, including teaching stations, lockers, and restrooms. Indoor facilities should have adequate activity space clear of hazards or impediments. The environment must have proper lighting, acoustics, and ventilation. Ceiling clearance should permit appropriate play. Floors should have a finish that enables all kinds of ambulation. When necessary, protective padding should be placed on walls. There should be plenty of space for wheelchairs to pass and turn.

As is true of indoor areas, outdoor areas should be accessible and properly surfaced. Facilities should be available and marked for activities, including special sports. Walkways leading to and from outdoor facilities should be smooth, firm, free of cracks, and at least 48 inches wide. Doorways leading to the facilities should have at least a 36-inch clearance and be lightweight enough to be opened without undue effort; when possible, doorways should be automatically activated. Water fountains with both hand and foot controls should be located conveniently for use by individuals with disabilities. Colorful signs and tactual orientation maps of facilities should be posted to assist individuals with visual disabilities.

Both participants in adapted physical education and athletes need adequate space for dressing, showering, and drying. Space must be sufficient for peak periods. The design of locker rooms should facilitate ambulation and the maintenance of safe and clean conditions. Adequate ventilation, lighting, and heating are necessary. The shower room should be readily accessible and provide enough showerheads to accommodate everyone. The facilities should be equipped with grab rails. Locker rooms should include adequate benches, mirrors, and toilets. Individuals with disabilities frequently prefer horizontal lockers and locks that are easy to manipulate. Planning must ensure that lockers are not obstructed by benches and other obstacles. All facilities must be in operable condition. Well-designed restrooms should have adequate space for manipulation of wheelchairs, easily activated foot or hand flush mechanisms, grab rails, and toilets and urinals at heights that meet the needs of the entire school population.

Swimming pools are among the most important facilities. Pool design must provide for safe and quick entry and exit (refer to chapter 25 for additional information). Water depth and temperature should be adjustable to meet learning, recreational, therapeutic, and competitive needs. Careful coordination of pool use is usually necessary to accommodate varying needs. Dressing, showering, and toilet facilities must be close by, with easy access to the pool.

Students in adapted physical education and sport programs must have equal opportunity to use integrated facilities. Too often, segregated classes in physical education for individuals with disabilities are conducted in boiler rooms or hallways. Administrators need to offer classes so that individuals with disabilities have the opportunity to attain the same benefits from school facilities as students without disabilities. Failure to do so is discriminating and demeaning to both pupils and school personnel.

Budget

An equitable education for a student with unique needs is more costly than that of a student without unique needs. To supplement local and state funds, the federal government has several programs that provide money for the education of people with unique needs. Funds associated with IDEA are specifically earmarked. To facilitate the receipt of federal funds for physical education, physical educators must be sure that they are involved in IEP development.

Funds associated with IDEA are available to help provide for the excess costs of special education (i.e., costs that exceed student expenditure in regular education). These funds "flow" through state education departments (which are permitted to keep a certain percentage) and on to local education agencies. This flow-through money can be used to help cover some excess costs already assumed by states. Because adapted physical education involves students who are not disabled as well as with those who are, it is less discriminatory for schools to fund teachers in physical education, whether regular or adapted, from the same local funding source rather than to rely on federal money. This is justifiable because states are responsible for the education of all their students.

In addition to meeting needs identified in IEPs, funding must support the preparation of teachers to provide quality services in adapted physical education and sport. For example, funds are needed for in-service education, workshops, clinics, local meetings, professional conferences and conventions, program visitations, and so on. Schools also need funds to maintain up-to-date libraries and other reference materials.

Interscholastic teams made up of students with disabilities must receive equitable equipment, supplies, travel expenses, officials, and so on. Although the funding level for curricular and extracurricular activities in a local community is not externally dictated, available funds cannot be used in a discriminatory fashion (e.g., available to males but not females, or available to students without disabilities but not to students with disabilities).

HUMAN RESOURCES

A quality program in adapted physical education and sport depends to a great extent on the availability of quality human resources and the ability of involved personnel to perform effectively within a group. People are needed to coordinate and administer services, fulfill technical and advocacy functions, and provide instruction. Many of these functions are carried out in important committees. To provide high-quality services for adapted physical education and sport, the teacher must work with various school and IEP committees. In doing so, it is helpful to understand roles and responsibilities and to realize that the concern for students with unique needs is shared by many. This section identifies key personnel and discusses their primary roles and responsibilities. Many perform their responsibilities by serving on committees identified in chapter 5.

Director of Physical Education and Athletics

Although not a universal practice, it is desirable for all aspects of physical education and sport programs to be under the direction of an administrator certified in physical education. Such centralization enhances coordination and efficiency in regard to personnel, facilities, equipment, budgeting, professional development, and curriculum. The director of physical education and athletics should oversee all aspects of the program, including the work of the coordinator of adapted physical education, if that position exists.

Because adapted physical education and sport is often in the developmental stage and not a well-advocated part of the total program, the physical education director needs to demonstrate genuine concern and commitment to this part of the program. A positive attitude serves as a model for others. With the assistance of other administrative personnel, the director can help the program in adapted physical education and sport by ensuring adequate funding, employing qualified teachers, and providing support services. The director must also be knowledgeable about adapted physical education and sport to work effectively with individuals and groups outside the department. The director must work with other directors, coordinators, building principals, superintendents, and school boards and must have positive professional relationships with medical personnel. Other important relationships are those with parents, teachers, students with disabilities, and advocacy groups. For this reason, the director of physical education and sport must be kept informed about all students who are identified as having unique needs.

Adapted Physical Educator or Coordinator

To provide a quality comprehensive school program in adapted physical education and sport, schools are advised to employ a qualified teacher of adapted physical education to provide direct teaching responsibilities and program coordination. In a small school, this might be a part-time position; in larger schools, a full-time adapted physical education teacher or coordinator might be needed. Although most states do not require a special endorsement, credential, or certification to teach adapted physical education, it is best to select an individual who has considerable professional experience. If possible, the teacher or coordinator should have completed a recognized specialization or concentration in adapted physical education and, where applicable, should meet the state competency requirements for certification. If a school cannot employ a person who has preparation in adapted physical education, the teacher or coordinator's duties should be entrusted to someone who demonstrates genuine interest in the field.

The role and functions of the teacher or coordinator depend on the size of the school, the number and types of students with disabilities within the school population, and the number and types of students involved in adapted physical education and sport. Generally, however, the teacher or coordinator needs to assume a leadership role in various functions associated with adapted physical education and sport. The specific functions often differ more in degree than in kind from those performed by regular physical educators. Table 2.2 identifies typical functions associated with adapted education and sport and indicates who is responsible for those functions. Functions may overlap or be shared; specific lines of demarcation should be drawn to suit local conditions.

A function adapted physical educators are being increasingly called on to do is to serve as a consultant or resource person for a school or school district. It would be ideal if every school district employed one of more individuals with a background and interest to serve not only as a teacher but also as a resource person. Colleges and universities preparing adapted physical education specialists are increasingly putting more attention on preparing individuals for the consulting role. Consultants are expected to serve as resource individuals or helpers to regular physical educators and anyone else who affects the quality of services in physical education and sport. They should be able to assess needs, plan and implement programs, and evaluate educational experiences for consultees. Consultants might provide information on many different topics, including information on disabilities and implications for teaching physical education; ways of adapting methods, activities, and assessment practices and procedures for students with unique needs; strategies for controlling

student behavior; information regarding recent legislation affecting students receiving special education; and information on developing individualized education and 504 plans for students with disabilities. Some characteristics of a good consultant are presented in the sidebar.

Regular Physical Educator

Although adapted physical educators are sometimes employed by a school, the regular physical educator plays an extremely important role in implementing quality programs in adapted physical education and sport. Table 2.2 presents several functions that are shared by or are the primary responsibility of regular physical educators. For example, they play an important role in screening. They might also implement instructional programs in integrated environments and help implement sport programs. One of the most important tasks is referral of pupils to appropriate committees. In the area of management or leadership, regular physical educators generally play a secondary role. With the present-day trend of including more and more students with disabilities in regular classes, it is often the responsibility of regular physical educators to implement and oversee such programs.

Nurse

The school nurse is an allied health professional with an important part in the successful development and implementation of adapted physical education and sport programs. The nurse must be knowledgeable about the adapted physical education and sport program and, ideally, should serve on its committee on adapted physical education. By helping convey information required for individual education planning, the nurse can be a valuable resource. If time permits, the school nurse can assist the physical education staff in testing students, particularly in the case of postural screening. The nurse can also keep medical records, communicate with physicians, and help parents and students understand the importance of exercise and physical activity.

Physicians

Physicians have an important relationship with the school's adapted physical education and sport program. The physician's role is so important that it is often addressed in federal, state, or local laws, rules, and regulations. In some instances, states

Some Characteristics of a Good Consultant

- Establishes a positive rapport in the consulting environment
- Is prepared in the field of consultation
- Has a passion for the consulting role
- Encourages others to provide information and share ownership of results
- Works as an equal rather than as an authority
- Asks for feedback during the consultancy (helping) process
- Establishes trust
- Employs empathetic listening
- Plans programs jointly
- Accepts constructive criticism

Table 2.2   **Primary Responsibility for Functions Relevant to Adapted Physical Education and Sport**

Function	Responsibility	
	Regular physical educator	Adapted physical educator or coordinator
Measurement, assessment, evaluation		
• Student screening	X	X
• In-depth testing		X
• Student assessment and evaluation		X
• APE or sport program evaluation		X
Teaching or coaching		
• Implement instructional programs for students with short-term unique needs	X	
• Implement instructional program to meet long-term unique needs in integrated environments	X	X
• Implement instructional and sport programs with guidance of adapted physical educator	X	
• Implement adapted sport program		X
Management and leadership		
• Consultation		X
• In-service education		X
• Advocacy and interpretation		X
• Recruitment of aides and volunteers		X
• Chair-adapted physical education committee		X
• Liaison with health professionals	X	X
• Referral and placement	X	X
• Organization of adapted sport program		X

look to a designated school physician for the final decision on participation in athletic opportunities. School physicians also provide and interpret medical information on which school programs are based. Using this information, the IEP planning groups plan appropriate programs. The responsibility for interpreting the adapted physical education and sport program to family physicians and other medical personnel also lies with the school physician.

In states where physical education is required of all students, physicians must know and support laws and regulations. They must be confident that if a student is unable to participate without restriction in a regular class, adaptations will be made. Physicians should be aware of how physical education and adapted physical education have

changed over recent years and should understand their role and responsibility within the existing programs.

One of a physician's important functions is to administer periodic physical examinations. Examination results are used as a basis for individualized student evaluation, program planning, placement, and determination of eligibility and qualification for athletic participation. It is desirable for students with unique physical education needs to receive an exam every three years, beginning in the first grade. Exams should be annual for those assigned to adapted physical education because of medical referrals. School districts that do not provide physical exams should require adequate examination by the family physician. For students covered by IDEA, medical examinations must be given in accordance with state and local policies and procedures. For athletic participation, exams should be administered at least annually.

Coaches

Adapted sport programs should be operated under the direction of qualified school personnel. When an adapted program includes interschool athletic teams, standards for coaches must be consistent with those for the regular interschool athletic program. Teachers certified in physical education may be permitted to coach any sport, including those whose participants have disabilities. Ideally, coaches of teams composed primarily of individuals with unique needs should have expertise in adapted physical education.

Coaches must follow acceptable professional practices, including maintaining a positive attitude and insisting on good sportsmanship, respect, personal control, and willingness to improve professionally through in-service programs, workshops, and clinics.

Related Service Personnel

Under IDEA, "related services" refer to transportation and other developmental, corrective, and supportive services required to assist children with disabilities to benefit from special education. Related services include speech-language pathology and audiology services; psychological services; physical and occupational therapy; recreation, including therapeutic recreation; social work services; counseling services, including rehabilitation counseling; orientation and mobility services; and medical services for diagnostic or evaluation purposes only. Related service providers who influence physical education include occupational and physical therapists. According to the rules and regulations for the implementation of IDEA, occupational therapy includes improving, developing, or restoring functions impaired or lost through illness, injury, or deprivation; improving ability to perform tasks for independent functioning when functions are impaired or lost; and preventing, through early intervention, initial or further impairment or loss of functioning. The same rules and regulations define physical therapy as services provided by a qualified physical therapist. These services have traditionally included physical activities and other physical means for rehabilitation prescribed by a physician. The rules and regulations specify that recreation includes

assessment of leisure function, therapeutic recreation services, recreation programs in schools and community agencies, and leisure education.

Much has been written about the relation of adapted physical education and the related services of physical and occupational therapy. The lines of responsibility among these areas are often blurred. One thing that is clear is the fact that related services must be provided if a student requires them to benefit from direct services. For example, both physical and occupational therapy must be provided to the extent a student needs them to benefit from physical education or other direct services in the school program. IDEA specifies that physical education must be made available to children with disabilities. Also, states have their own requirements concerning the provision of physical education. Clearly, physical therapy and adapted physical education are not identical, and related services should not supplant physical education or adapted physical education (which are direct services under IDEA).

Several assumptions about the role of physical education might underlie the decision of who will design programs to improve the physical fitness of students with disabilities. First, it is clearly the physical educator's responsibility to design these programs. Thus, the physical educator is involved with the development of strength, endurance, cardiorespiratory endurance, and flexibility (range of motion). His or her responsibility concerns *both* affected and unaffected parts of the body. For example, individuals with cerebral palsy should be helped to maintain and develop their physical fitness. When dealing with the affected parts of the body, the physical educator should consult and coordinate with medical or related service personnel in program planning and implementation.

Sometimes improvements in physical development cannot be attained by a physical educator using the usual time allotments, methods, or activities associated with physical education. In such cases, physical or occupational therapy can enhance physical fitness development. Activities included in the physical education programs of youngsters with disabilities should be those that are typically within the scope of physical education. These are the kinds of activities subsumed under the definition of physical education in the rules and regulations of IDEA and included in the scope of physical education, as described in chapter 1. Although the physical educator involves children in exercise, it is important *not* to limit physical education to an exercise prescription program. Instead, the physical educator must offer a broad spectrum of fun and well-liked physical education activities. Youngsters who require exercise to the extent that they would encompass an entire physical education period should meet this need in class time added to the regularly scheduled physical education period, or it should be a provided service. This approach would permit involvement in a broad spectrum of activities within the regularly scheduled physical education class. Physical educators should help students appropriately use wheelchairs and supportive devices in physical education activities. Thus, they must be knowledgeable about wheelchairs and other assistive devices. However, it is not their responsibility to provide functional training in the use of those aids for basic movement or ambulation.

Physical educators must consult physicians and other medical personnel as they plan and implement programs. Such consultations should be consistent with each school's adapted physical education program.

Although much can be written and discussed concerning roles and responsibilities, very often the quality of services provided depends on the interpersonal relationships of service providers. Successful situations are those in which professionals have discussed their roles and responsibilities and work hard to deliver supportive services to benefit individuals with unique needs.

GENERAL PROGRAM EVALUATION

At the beginning of this chapter, we stressed the importance of guidelines for program organization and management. This chapter has presented background information that can be used to develop such guidelines. Once in place, the guidelines can serve as a basis for program direction, implementation, and general program evaluation. Program evaluation might encompass the total physical education program or just the adapted physical education portion. Ideally, the guidelines (as a part of or separate from a comprehensive school plan) should be evaluated at five-year intervals and draw on data collected from a variety of relevant sources. Appendix D presents a sample rating scale to assess six essential areas related to program organization and management: curriculum, required instruction, attendance, personnel, facilities, and administrative procedures. This

appendix contains a series of criteria statements that reflect guidelines suggested in this chapter relative to these areas. The entire scale or parts may be used to collect data for program evaluation. Remember that an instrument for evaluation is least threatening if used for self-appraisal and as a point of departure for identifying and discussing strengths and weaknesses and developing a schedule to remedy weaknesses and reinforce strengths. The areas of evaluation in appendix D supplement the instructional outcomes associated with the Program Evaluation section presented in chapter 4.

SUMMARY

Well-organized and managed programs for adapted physical education are built on solid policies and procedures, which are enhanced and characterized by written guidelines on how to implement programs. This chapter has provided information that may be used for the development of programs and program guidelines. Information has been presented in four categories: program and curriculum planning, administrative procedures and program implementation, human resources, and general program evaluation.

REFERENCES

Block, M.E. (2000). *A teacher's guide to including students with disabilities in regular physical education.* Baltimore, MD: Paul H. Brookes.

Craft, D.H. (1996). *A focus on inclusion in physical education.* In Hennessy, B. (Ed.) Physical education source book. Champaign, IL: Human Kinetics.

Lieberman, L., and Houston-Wilson, C. (2002). *Strategies for inclusion.* Champaign, IL: Human Kinetics.

WRITTEN RESOURCES

Active Living Alliance for Canadians with a Disability. (1994). *Moving to inclusion.* Gloucester, Ontario, Canada: Author.

A curriculum consisting of nine books in English and French. Each book provides ideas for individualization for individuals with a specific disability. Available from Canadian Association for Health, Physical Education, and Recreation, 1600 James Naismith Drive, Gloucester, Ontario K1B 5N4, Canada; phone 613-748-5639.

Block, M.E. (2000). *Including students with disabilities in general physical education.* (2nd ed.). Baltimore, MD: Paul H. Brooks.

This source helps teachers include students with disabilities in regular physical education settings. Included are topics on planning, assessment, instructions, adaptation, and safety.

Craft, D.H. (Ed.) (1994). Inclusion: Physical education for all. *Journal of Physical Education, Recreation and Dance,* 65(1), 22-56.

This periodical provides a special issue on inclusion, including information on making curricular modifications, promoting equal status relationships among peers, teaching collaboratively with others, research on inclusion, ideas on infusion, and experiences implementing inclusion in two schools.

Lieberman, L., and Houston-Wilson, C. (2002). *Strategies for inclusion.* Champaign, IL: Human Kinetics.

This source provides background information and strategies for successful integration of a child with disabilities into a traditional physical education setting and contains teachable units that include assessment tools for curriculum planning.

Sherrill, C. (1998). *Adapted physical activity, recreation, and sport: Cross disciplinary and lifespan.* Madison, WI: WCB McGraw-Hill.

Includes a checklist for evaluating school district needs related to adapted physical education.

Winnick, J.P. (2004). Rating scale for adapted physical education.

This rating scale can be used as one self-assessment instrument on which to base evaluation of a school's adapted physical education program. The scale presents criteria statements reflecting guidelines implicitly suggested in this chapter. The rating scale can be found in appendix D.

CHAPTER

Adapted Sport

Michael J. Paciorek

During the ninth grade Jeffrey Kling was required to complete a one-mile run for his physical education class. It took him an entire grading period to accomplish this requirement. Jeffrey is of average intelligence but has a hearing impairment, cerebral palsy, and poor motor skills; he receives physical therapy. He is a student with a disability and is eligible for services as outlined in IDEA. Jeffrey's physical education teacher encouraged him to try out for the cross country team the next year. He and his father trained very hard during the summer, and as a 10th grader Jeffrey earned a letter as a member of his high school cross country and track teams despite coming in last in every race. Before the start of the 11th grade, Jeffrey's parents met with Mentor, Ohio, school officials and submitted proposed IEP goals and objectives addressing Jeffrey's need to run cross country. The school district officials refused to discuss the appropriateness of these goals and objectives as a part of the IEP. Additionally, the request to run cross country was denied because of the Ohio High School Athletic Association's (OHSAA) age limit for participation in athletic events (similar to most states). If a student enrolled in high school attains the age of 19 before August 1, that student shall be ineligible to participate in high school interscholastic athletics in the calendar year. Jeffrey missed the date by 16 days. His parents requested a due process hearing to decide whether the school district, by failing to consider the parents' request to make an individualized determination about the need for interscholastic cross country and track, denied Jeffrey free and appropriate public education (FAPE), and whether a school district, subject to federal law (IDEA), can summarily reject a special education program that contains an interscholastic athletic component in reliance on the rules of a private voluntary athletic association (OHSAA) (Siegel, 2000; Stewart, 2001).

In this chapter we will discuss the implications of Jeffrey's case and will provide information on the responsibility of the physical educator in providing meaningful sport participation and training opportunities for students with disabilities. We will present a continuum of sport participation and identify many multi- and unisport organizations available for individuals with disabilities. Although participation in sport programs should not be used as a substitute for adapted physical education, after reading this chapter teachers should be able to provide parents and students with information on the many sport resources available. Throughout this chapter, the physical educator should realize that the concept of least restrictive environment and free and appropriate public education (FAPE) also applies to sports and athletic opportunities and that athletic participation for students with disabilities is a logical extension of any good physical education program.

Although medical personnel and educators have seen for many years the potential that sport participation has for students with disabilities, opportunities for such participation have been slow to develop. Limited sport opportunities have been available for older individuals for some time, but sport opportunities for children with disabilities have been minimal. As noted in chapter 1, federal legislation affirms the rights of students with disabilities to have equal access and opportunities to physical education, intramural, and school sport programs.

As defined in chapter 1, adapted sport refers to sport modified or created to meet the unique needs of individuals. For many people, the definition of adapted sport refers only to competitive athletic opportunities. Although this chapter focuses on those opportunities to a great degree, the physical educator should refer to adapted sport in the broadest sense possible and use it to encompass not only competitive athletic experiences but those that include leisure-time recreational pursuits that enable a student with a disability to practice healthy living outside of the school setting. Adapted sport should be viewed as legitimate sport and competition of a high quality; it should not be seen as only a social experience.

INTEGRATION CONTINUUM

Over the past few years, increased attention has been given to providing sports opportunities for people with disabilities. In response to the intent of section 504 of the Rehabilitation Act of 1973, educational and extracurricular opportunities must be provided in the least restrictive (most normal and integrated) setting possible, on the basis of a continuum of setting ranging from the most restrictive (segregated) to the least restrictive (integrated). Figure 3.1 presents a framework for a sport continuum to promote integration to the maximum extent possible, help guide decisions on

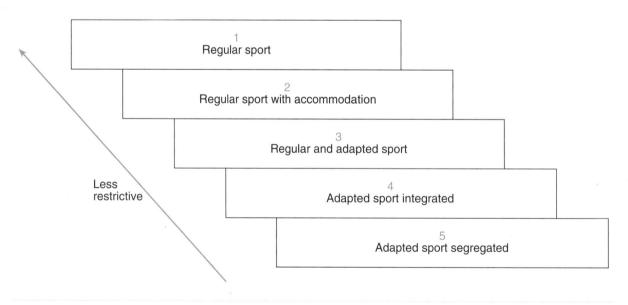

Figure 3.1 An integration continuum for sport participation.

Reprinted, by permission, from J.P. Winnick, 1987, "An integration continuum for sport participation," *Adapted Physical Activity Quarterly* 4: 158.

sport participation, and help stimulate the provision of innovative opportunities. Winnick (1987) published the continuum and related material in this section originally.

The continuum, which relates to the provision of programs in the least restrictive environment, encompasses opportunities in intramural and interschool programs and out-of-school sport and leisure programs. (For purposes of this book, all are encompassed under the designation of sport.) The athlete has many options available to participate in regular sport or adapted sport through a five-level continuum. Regular sport implies that the athlete with a disability can participate in a sport without modifications. Adapted sport implies that the athlete with a disability competes in a regular sport with the aid of an assistive device (e.g., sled hockey) or rule modification (e.g., smaller field, smaller goal, and fewer players for athletes with cerebral palsy who play soccer) *or* that the athlete participates in a sport designed for a particular disability, such as quad rugby (a sport for quadriplegics who use wheelchairs), or goal ball (a game for individuals with visual impairments). You can find information on these activities in chapters 24 through 29.

Levels 1 and 2 of the continuum are essentially regular sport settings distinguished only by a need for accommodation. In regular sport, the setting is integrated. Individuals with disabilities should be given equal opportunities to qualify for participation at these levels. An example of level 1 participation would be an athlete with mental retardation running the 800-meter dash for his or her high school track team or an athlete with an amputation playing on the local youth baseball team (or see figure 3.2).

In accordance with section 504, schools and agencies should provide modified or special activities only if the following four criteria are met (Department of Health, Education, and Welfare, 1977a; Winnick et al., 1980):

- Programs and activities are operated within the most normal and appropriate setting.
- Qualified students with disabilities are not denied opportunity to participate in programs and activities that are not separate and different.
- Qualified students with disabilities are able to participate in one or more regular programs and activities.
- Students with disabilities are appropriately placed in full-time special facilities.

© Bruce Coleman, Inc.

Figure 3.2 An amputee skier can compete on an equal basis in regular competition with his high school ski team.

A bowler who is blind competing against sighted athletes with only the accommodation of a guide rail falls under level 2. Other examples might include an athlete with a physical disability participating on a high school track team while using a field or throwing chair, or a blind swimmer competing with sighted swimmers while using tap sticks to know when to begin flip turns (see figure 3.3). In making accommodations at level 2, section 504 rules and regulations require that any accommodation provided be reasonable and allow individuals with disabilities an equal opportunity to gain the same benefits or results as other participants in an activity. At the same time, accommodations should not give an unfair advantage to an individual with a disability. In the case of the bowler who is blind, the guide rail serves as a substitute for vision for the purpose of orientation to the target; for the field athlete, the throwing chair provides the stability needed during competition. Because the activity remains essentially unchanged for all participants and no undue advantage is given, this accommodation constitutes regular sport participation.

Perhaps the most well-publicized and controversial level 2 situation occurred when professional golfer Casey Martin was denied participation on

Figure 3.3 Wheelchair racers competing against able-bodied runners is an example of a level 2 accommodation.

the Professional Golf Association (PGA) tour in the spring of 1998. Martin, who has a rare circulatory disorder in his leg that makes it painful to walk moderate distances without severe pain, uses a cart when golfing. The PGA alleged that the use of a cart constituted an unfair advantage and fundamentally altered the nature of the game. The U.S. Supreme Court ruled 7-2 that the Americans with Disabilities Act required the PGA to allow Martin to ride in a golf cart between shots at PGA tour events. In delivering the majority opinion, Justice John Paul Stevens said that allowing Martin to use a golf cart is not a modification that fundamentally alters the nature of the sport. Title III of the Americans with Disabilities Act, modeled on the Civil Rights Act's Title II, prohibits discrimination on the basis of disability in places of public accommodation. By its "plain terms, it prohibits the PGA Tour from denying Martin equal access to its tours on the basis of his disability" *(PGA Tour v. Martin,* 532 U.S. 661, 2001).

Level 3 includes both regular and adapted sport conducted in settings that are partly or fully integrated. Those with a disability compete against or co-act with all participants in a contest, including competitors with and without disabilities. For instance, an athlete participating in a wheelchair (adapted sport) might compete against all runners in a marathon, including athletes with and without

disabilities; athletes without disabilities run on foot (regular sport). In another level 3 example, an athlete without a disability and an athlete with a disability might play together as doubles partners in tennis. The ambulatory partner is permitted one bounce before returning the volley (regular sport); the wheelchair tennis player is permitted two bounces (adapted sport).

The Special Olympics Unified Sports program is another example of inclusion of athletes with and without disabilities participating together. Unified Sports, begun in 1989, is a program that places athletes with mental retardation and their peers without metal retardation on the same team for training and competition. Athletes benefit from physical and mental challenges by participating in competitions organized by Special Olympics or by community sport organizations. The use of Unified Sports rules and guidelines on age and ability grouping help ensure that all athletes play a meaningful and valued role on the team. Special Olympics now offer Unified Sports in all its summer and winter sports.

Level 3 also includes situations in which an athlete participates part time in regular sport and part time in adapted sport. For example, a person who is blind might participate in regular competition for power lifting, but in adapted sport competition for goal ball. Level 3 activities show either athletes with and without disabilities integrated and participating in regular sport and adapted sport, respectively, *or* athletes with disabilities participating part time in adapted sport and part time in regular sport.

At level 4 athletes with and without disabilities participate in a modified version of the sport. At this level, competition or co-action must include both an individual with a disability and a participant without a disability. One example is a game of tennis in which athletes with and without disabilities use wheelchairs in their competition against opponents who are likewise in wheelchairs.

At level 5, athletes with disabilities participate in adapted or regular sport in a totally segregated setting; as examples, athletes with mental retardation compete against each other in a Special Olympics program; athletes with physical disabilities compete in wheelchair fencing; or two teams of youngsters who are blind compete in a local goal ball tournament. The Challenger Division created by Little League Baseball for athletes with physical disabilities is another level 5 example. The Challenger Division provides boys and girls with disabilities the opportunity to experience the emotional development and the fun of playing Little League Baseball. This program enables every child, regardless of ability level, the opportunity to participate in a structured athletic program.

The conceptual framework for the sport continuum is primarily based on degree of integration (with co-actor or competitor) and sport type (traditional or adapted). The continuum stresses association or interaction among athletes with and without disabilities—the key ingredient in integration. To some extent, the continuum reflects severity of disability and ability to compete, but at other times it is less responsive to this concern. This is because *nature* of disability and *ability* to perform, as related to a specific sport, are greater factors than *severity* of condition.

SPORT ORGANIZATIONS

As legislation on behalf of individuals with disabilities has led to more inclusion in all aspects of daily living, an explosion has occurred in the number of organizations that provide sports programming for individuals with disabilities. These can be categorized into multisport and unisport organizations.

Community-Based Multisport Organizations

Multisport organizations provide training and athletic competition in sports for individuals with a particular disability. For instance, the National Disability Sports Alliance (NDSA), formerly the United States Cerebral Palsy Athletic Association (USCPAA), provides competition in 10 sports for individuals who have cerebral palsy, stroke, or traumatic brain injury. These organizations serve in much the same capacity as a sport national governing body for athletes without disabilities: to oversee the development and conduct of their sports and promote athletic involvement for their members. In addition to the athletic competition involved, athletes have used these organizations as support groups and discussion forums. There are seven multisport disabled sports organizations affiliated with the United States Olympic Committee (USOC), including the Dwarf Athletic Association of America (DAAA), Disabled Sports USA (DS/USA), Special Olympics, Inc. (SOI), United States Association of Blind Athletes (USABA), National Disability Sports Alliance (NDSA), USA Deaf Sports Federation (USADSF) and Wheelchair Sports USA (WSUSA). Each organization provides sports opportunities in different ways. Some organizations, such as the NDSA, rely on sport technical officers to oversee programs; others, such as WSUSA and USADSF, are divided into sport federations. The USADSF operates outside the Paralympic Sports Organization. Their athletes compete internationally in the Deaflympics, (formerly the Deaf World Games) and do not compete in the Paralympic Games. More information on the multisport organizations can be found in the later chapters on specific disabilities.

Unisport Organizations

Unisport organizations promote sport participation in a single sport, either for a single disability or for multiple disabilities. For instance, the North American Riding for the Handicapped Association (NARHA), through its affiliated programs, offers therapeutic and competitive horseback riding for individuals regardless of disability. The Handicapped Scuba Association International (HSAI) offers individual and instructor training programs in a similar manner, whereas the Achilles Track Club affiliates offer road-racing opportunities for athletes with disabilities. Examples of unisport

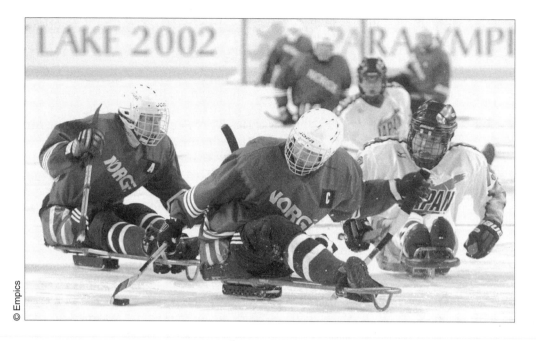

Figure 3.4 The United States Sled Hockey Association is an example of a unisport organization that competes against teams nationally and internationally.

organizations that promote one sport for individuals with disabilities include the United States Quad Rugby Association (USQRA), the United States Sled Hockey Association (USSHA) (see figure 3.4), the American Amputee Soccer Association (AASA), and the National Beep Baseball Association (NBBA), to name a few.

THE OLYMPIC AND AMATEUR SPORTS ACT AND THE ROLE OF THE USOC

A history of the adapted sport movement was presented in chapter 1, but the Amateur Sports Act (ASA) of 1978, amended in 1998 as the Olympic and Amateur Sports Act P.L. 105-277 (within the Omnibus Appropriations Bill), is perhaps the one piece of legislation that provided the catalyst for the explosion in adapted sport. Sponsored by Senator Ted Stevens of Alaska, this legislation reorganized the United States Olympic Committee (USOC) and administration of amateur sports in the United States. The amended act strengthened the linkage between the USOC and athletes with disabilities by including the Paralympic Games and amateur athletes with disabilities within the scope of the act and within the USOC. With the available resources and prestige attached to the

USOC, sport organizations for individuals with disabilities have a new sense of hope in building their programs. The USOC Constitution was rewritten to reflect the new commitment to adapted sport and intent of the law:

> To encourage and provide assistance to amateur athletic programs and competition for amateur athletes with disabilities, including, where feasible, the expansion of opportunities for meaningful participation by such amateur athletes in programs of athletic competition for able-bodied amateur athletes (USOC Constitution, 1998).

U.S. PARALYMPICS

Through the establishment of U.S. Paralympics in 2001 (a division of the USOC), the USOC mission now includes duties and responsibilities for development and training of elite athletes with disabilities (table 3.1). Because opportunities for elite athletes are becoming available, children with disabilities now have role models to emulate as they begin their training programs in local communities. Since 2001, funding for elite Paralympic athletes has increased from $632,000 to over $2.5 million (Huebner, 2003)—which is still, of course, a tiny fraction of the overall USOC budget of $491.5 million.

Table 3.1 **Relationship Among U.S. Olympic Committee Disabled Sport Organizations and International Sport Federations**

American sport organization	International counterparts	Disability areas
*Disabled Sports USA (DS/USA)	International Sports Organization for the Disabled (ISOD)	Amputations (winter sports for several disability areas)
*Dwarf Athletic Association of America (DAAA)	International Sports Organization for the Disabled (ISOD)	People with dwarfism ("little people")
*National Disability Sports Alliance (NDSA)	Cerebral Palsy–International Sports and Recreation Association (CP-ISRA)	Cerebral palsy, head injury, stroke
*Special Olympics	Special Olympics, Inc. (SOI)	Intellectual disabilities
**USA Deaf Sports Federation (USADSF)	International Committee on Silent Sports (CISS)	Deafness
*United States Association for Blind Athletes (USABA)	International Blind Sports Association (IBSA)	Blindness
*Wheelchair Sports USA (WSUSA)	Stoke Mandeville Wheelchair Sports Federation (SMWSF)	Spinal cord–injured amputee, other wheelchair users

* Paralympic affiliated organization

** Non-Paralympic organization (participates in the Deaflympics)

Note: Special Olympics, Inc., in conjunction with the USOC, has assumed the responsibility for athletes with intellectual disabilities participating in the Paralympic Games in the United States.

Additionally. U.S. Paralympics promotes the following efforts:

- Developing interest and participation throughout the United States in sports for individuals with disabilities
- Working with USOC national governing bodies to carry out the mandate of involving amateur athletes with disabilities in sports programs for athletes without disabilities
- Disseminating information on physical training, equipment design, coaching, and performance analysis for athletes with disabilities
- Encouraging and supporting more research in areas of sport medicine and sports safety pertaining to athletes with disabilities
- Helping to guarantee that Olympic training facilities are fully accessible to athletes with disabilities
- Seeking appropriate allocation of funds available to the USOC for sports for athletes with disabilities

The USOC and U.S. Paralympics works with both the sport national governing bodies and the disabled sports organizations to provide support services to elite athletes with disabilities in training and competing in the Paralympic and other quadrennial games for athletes with disabilities. The USOC Disabled Sports Services department manages the internal activities necessary to promote this process and addresses all issues related to national Paralympic concerns.

THE ROLE OF NATIONAL GOVERNING BODIES

National governing bodies (NGBs) and international federations (IFs) are organizations dedicated to the development and promotion of specific sports. These organizations generally sanction competitions and certify officials. By law, each of the NGBs affiliated with the USOC must allow participation by people with disabilities and assume a greater responsibility for elite athletes with disabilities. NGBs and IFs now routinely include information on adapted sport participation through the use of subcommittees, information on specific programming options, or the inclusion of adapted sports rules. For example, the United States Racquetball Association includes wheelchair racquetball rules in their official rule book. Some NGBs, such as United States Swimming (USS) and the United

States Tennis Association (USTA), offer extensive information on adapted sport programming in their literature. Some disabled sport organizations have merged with other organizations, such as the National Foundation of Wheelchair Tennis merging with the USTA, to offer expanded programming for athletes with disabilities. Similar mergers have occurred at international levels as well.

PARALYMPIC GAMES

The Paralympic Games (*para* meaning equal to) are the equivalent of the Olympic Games for athletes with physical disabilities or visual impairments. Individuals with hearing impairments compete in the Deaflympics. The history behind the Paralympics began in 1948, when the Stoke Mandeville Games were held in Aylesbury, England. This was the same year as the games of the XIV (14th) Olympiad were being held in London. The idea of holding these games is attributed to a doctor, Sir Ludwig Guttman, who included sport in his rehabilitation for injured World War II veterans.

The first Paralympic Summer Games as we now know were held in Rome in 1960 (the first winter Paralympic Games were held in Sweden in 1976), the same year that the Italians hosted the games of the XVII (17th) Olympiad. These first summer Paralympic Games drew 400 athletes representing 23 countries. Since then, the Olympic and Paralympic Games have led a parallel existence, whenever possible being held in the same city or same country. The 1988 Seoul games marked the beginning of the modern Paralympic Games, the first time the term Paralympics was used.

The 1992 Barcelona Paralympics marked the first time that a joint Olympic and Paralympic Committee was used. Then International Olympic Committee President Juan Antonio Samaranch was so deeply moved and impressed by the caliber of the Barcelona Paralympic Games, he decreed that after 1996 all bids for the Olympic Games must be submitted by joint Olympic and Paralympic Committees. "The Paralympic Games have been as successful as the Olympic Games," said Samaranch, "that it is an indication that we must take another look at, and think seriously about the subject of disabled people. It was the same organizing committee and the same volunteers that worked out very well." Since the 1984 games in Los Angeles, all Olympics have included two demonstration events for athletes with physical disabilities; the 1,500-meter wheelchair race for men, and 800-meter wheelchair race for women. Although full inclusion and merger with the Paralympic Games might not be possible or feasible, the recognition of events for athletes with disabilities in the Olympic Games demonstrates the strides made on behalf of athletes with disabilities in being recognized as true athletes.

The Paralympic Games, which began life as an event with strong social implications and therapeutic ends, has become the most important sporting event for people with disabilities. Every four years the participation of elite athletes at the Paralympic Games provides proof of the progress being made in terms of competitiveness and athleticism. The countless records broken and the marks achieved, as well as the increase in international attention, further demonstrates the great success of these games and the overall development of disability sport.

The Paralympic Games are recognized by the International Olympic Committee (IOC) and sanctioned by the International Paralympic Committee (IPC), a member organization of the IOC. Five disability group IFS, under IPC jurisdiction, provide technical guidelines for classification criteria to the Paralympics. Every country that participates in the Paralympic Games has identified a national counterpart to these federations (see table 3.1).

CLASSIFICATION

Classification systems are used widely in sports to allow for a fair and equitable starting point for competition (Richter, Adams-Mushett, Ferrara, & McCann, 1992). Youth football requires a minimum and maximum weight of players, whereas youth soccer and baseball might have age and gender restrictions, all with the express purpose of providing maximum enjoyment and fairness and to aid in the prevention of injuries. Within a specific type of disability is perhaps a wide continuum of ability or physical characteristics. For instance, the levels of acuity among people with visual impairments vary significantly, as do the levels of functional ability among individuals with cerebral palsy. This kind of continuum of functional ability is common to all disabilities.

It is accepted that some form of classification or groupings must be used for athletes with disabilities, but which is the most equitable type of classification to use remains a topic of debate and complexity. Classification systems are generally of two types: medical and functional.

Medical classification verifies minimum disability and is not concerned with the functional ability of the athlete (Davis & Ferrara, 1996). Examples include the level of visual acuity for a blind athlete, the level of spinal cord injury, or the location of an amputation (see figure 3.5). These kinds of evaluation provide a medically related equal starting point for competition. Success or failure in competition now depends on the physical skill and the level of training of athletes.

Figure 3.5 This Class A2 (single leg above the knee amputee) athlete competes against other runners of similar physical abilities.

The functional classification systems identify how an athlete performs specific sport skills (Davis & Ferrara, 1996). Functional systems combine medical information with performance information to evaluate an athlete's sport-specific skills and medical condition required in an athletic event. For instance, athletes with cerebral palsy might be observed by classifiers performing their sport to determine range of motion and physical capabilities prior to classification. This classification system can be used for both single disability and cross-disability competitions. In other words, function is primary and medical is secondary.

Special Olympics use a classification system based on age, gender, and past performances. Although Special Olympics place a premium on training of athletes, this type of system does not necessarily reward the athlete for training effects.

Whichever classification system is used, the system should ensure that the training and skill level of the athlete becomes the deciding factor in success, not the type or level of disability (Paciorek & Jones, 2001). Sport or health care professionals who have completed a certification course perform classification for national and international competition. Classifiers usually consist of physicians, physical therapists, occupational therapists, and others knowledgeable in kinesiology and disability. You can find classifications related to specific disabilities in the chapters in part II.

SCHOOL AND LOCAL COMMUNITY-BASED ADAPTED SPORTS PROGRAMMING

Although international competitions such as the Paralympic Games, Special Olympics World Games, and Deaflympics tend to receive much of the media's attention, very few athletes with disabilities have the necessary skills or opportunity to participate in these elite athlete events. The majority of athletes with disabilities participate in grass roots and youth sport programming in their local communities. These typically include recreation and park district programs, parent-sponsored sports programs, cross-disability sports programs affiliated with rehabilitation centers, and sports available through public school athletic programs.

Section 504 of the Rehabilitation Act of 1973 and the ADA have had great implications for participation of youth with disability in sports. Together, these complementary antidiscrimination pieces of legislation require agencies that provide sport programs, whether they receive federal funds or not, to provide comparable opportunities to individuals with disabilities. No sports program may discriminate against players or coaches with disabilities, including school-based programs. All players have the right to play on recreational sports teams and must be afforded the opportunity to try out for select or premier teams, even if segregated programs such as Challenger baseball leagues are available (Block, 1995). Schools, recreation programs, and communities must make reasonable accommodations to ensure that individuals with disabilities have equal access to programs. Reasonable accommodations might require the purchasing of an adapted piece of equipment, such as a wider bench for a power lifter with a spinal cord injury, or the use of facilities that are readily accessible to individuals with disabilities, such as the community fitness center.

REGULAR SPORT PARTICIPATION

Jeffrey Kling (whom you met at the beginning of the chapter) and other athletes with disabilities will continue to experience barriers in their attempts to participate in regular sport opportunities. No numerical data is available on participation of youth with disabilities in regular sport, though anecdotal records suggest that participation continues to increase despite these barriers. Reports of high school athletes with disabilities participating in cross country, swimming, track and field, and even football are highlighted in newspapers across the country. Many sport organizers are making reasonable accommodations for athletes with disabilities. Runners who are blind are being allowed to run track and cross country with sighted guides. Wrestlers who are blind are allowed to use a touch start. Athletes with amputations and mental retardation participate on football teams. And various accommodations are being made in recreation programs without fundamentally altering the competition. League officials must continue to consider and implement common-sense changes or modifications that would enable a student with a disability to meet the same eligibility requirements that other team members must meet.

Although not specifically addressed in ADA, the implications of this law prevent discrimination against coaches and athletes in youth sport programs (Block, 1995). Various court cases have upheld the right of baseball coaches who use wheelchairs to coach on the field *(Anderson v. Little League, 1992; Barrios v. California Interscholastic Association, 2002)*, and the case of *Kling v. Mentor School District* is another indication of the confusion that still exists regarding individuals with disabilities participating in regular sport. According to the National Federation of High

Schools (NFHS), high school athletes with disabilities must meet the same eligibility standards for participation as required of all athletes, including grade point average and submission of a medical clearance form from a physician. According to Block (1995), the law does exclude individuals whose participation poses a direct threat to the health and safety of others when modifications cannot be made. Three factors must be satisfied to use this part of the law to exclude individuals from participation: (1) the threat must be real and not perceived or speculative; (2) the threat must be based on objective information; and (3) if a real risk is found, attempts must be made to reduce or eliminate the risk (e.g., padding of a prosthesis or cast). Increased numbers of athletes with disabilities participating in regular sport will continue at a slow pace as more students are included in regular education environments, sport organizers become educated to disability rights issues, and court decisions clarify the confusion that still exists.

Over the past few years, much of the impetus for sports for athletes with disabilities has been provided by out-of-school sport organizations. Although developing at a slower rate, other opportunities have begun to surface throughout the United States in connection with public school programs (Matter, Nash, & Frogley, 2002). An important milestone was reached on November 11, 1992, when Minnesota became the first state to welcome athletes with disabilities into its state high school association. The Metro Association for Adapted Athletics (MAAA) is a member of the Minnesota State High School League, which each school year operates the adapted athletics program statewide for high school students with disabilities. This move made Minnesota the first in the nation to sanction interschool sports for middle and high school students with disabilities.

In a 2001–2002 high school athletics survey conducted by the NFHS, only one state (Minnesota) officially reported offering any type of adapted sports programming, although other states (Georgia, Illinois, Iowa, and Connecticut) do have sanctioned events for athletes with disabilities. Minnesota continues to lead the nation in programming for students with disabilities with over 280 middle and high schools offering coed adapted sports competition in bowling, soccer, floor hockey, and softball to over 1,500 students with physical and mental impairments. With advancements in technology, teleconference competition might soon be used. Sports such as bowling or power lifting, for instance, might have a televised link provided at sites many miles apart. Each athlete can bowl or lift during his or her turn and then watch the monitor for the performance of their competitor. Teleconferencing has tremendous potential for individual sports. We hope that in the not-too-distant future technology will allow increased participation for athletes in rural locations and areas where numbers of athletes with disabilities are low.

Another innovative adapted sports program is the American Association of Adapted Sports Programs, Inc., formed in 1980 in DeKalb County, Georgia, as an after-school program for students with physical disabilities in grades 1 through 12 (AAASP, 2003; see figure 3.6). In 2001, AAASP and the Georgia High School Association (GHSA) formed an alliance to promote the AAASP adapted sports model as a viable component of the state's overall athletic structure (along with its sister program, project ASPIRE). In this parallel relationship, GHSA looks to AAASP for guidance in adapting sports for students with physical disabilities or visual impairments within high schools. The GHSA has designated the AAASP as the official sanctioning and governing body for Georgia's interscholastic adapted athletics (AAASP, 2003).

Since 1992, the Connecticut Interscholastic Athletic Conference (CIAC) has had a partnership with Special Olympics to offer Unified Sports programming. Participation is open to all public and parochial schools in Connecticut. At the elementary level, students engage in noncompetitive athletic activities designed to develop skills in a variety of sports; middle and high school students compete in statewide Unified Sports tournaments. The CIAC currently holds tournaments in basketball, soccer, softball, and volleyball. The program boasts a participation of 1,300 athletes and 120 schools throughout the state.

A few other states now provide statewide competition for athletes with disabilities. According to Frogley and Beaver (2002), "these attempts have centered more on accepting certain events within already staged state championships, rather than the adoption of a state-wide program of interscholastic competition for student-athletes with disabilities, and have thus failed to provide comprehensive state-wide opportunities for competition." For example, Iowa offers limited track and field competition at their state high school championships, and New York offers regional and statewide competition for individuals with physical and sensory disabilities, ages 5 through 21, in connection with its Empire State Games for the Physically Challenged. These games, conducted with government financing, serve as an alternative to New York's Empire State Games designed for athletes without disabilities. The Illinois High School Association has become the first state to add wheelchair basketball as part of their programming (Matter, Nash, & Frogley, 2002). Currently 150 student-athletes are registered, with full-season

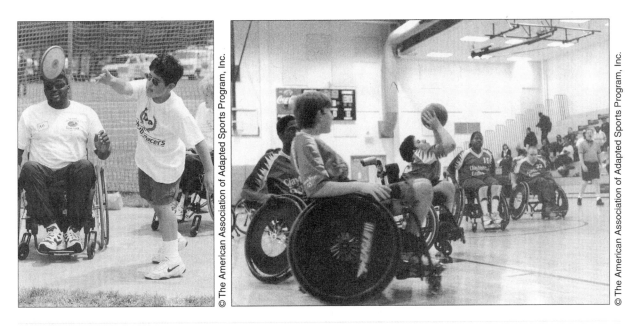

© The American Association of Adapted Sports Program, Inc.

Figure 3.6 Since 1996, AAASP has made competitive after-school athletics a possibility for hundreds of Georgia kids with physical disabilities or visual impairments in grades 1 through 12.

play to begin in 2005; the sport is sponsored and administered by the IHSA (Frogley, 2003).

Since 2001, Wheelchair Sports, U.S.A. (WSUSA) and the Glenn D. Loucks Games have run an integrated elite high school track meet in White Plains, New York. For 35 years, the Loucks Games have attracted the top high school athletes from the northeastern United States. With the inclusion of a wheelchair division, this meet is the country's only integrated nonstate high school track meet (Scorecard, Sports 'N Spokes, 2002).

Because of the tremendous health benefits, sport programs in rehabilitation settings are also increasing (Paciorek & Jones, 2001). Most of the larger programs are centered in major cities. Examples include the Wirtz Sports Program at the Rehabilitation Institute of Chicago's Center for Health and Fitness (see figure 3.7), Roosevelt Warm Springs Institute for Rehabilitation in Warm Springs, Georgia, Shepard Center in Atlanta, Georgia, and the Craig Rehabilitation Hospital in Denver, Colorado. These centers generally offer wide-based multisport, cross-disability programming for individuals in the community.

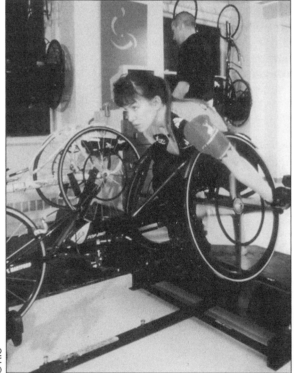

Figure 3.7 The Rehabilitation Institute of Chicago Center for Health and Fitness offers multisport programming for individuals with disabilities. World-class racer Linda Mastandrea works out on a wheelchair racer.

TRANSITION SERVICES

Important goals of physical education and adapted physical education programs are to provide students with functional motor skills, knowledge, and opportunities necessary for lifelong, healthy, independent living. Adapted sport programs can play a vital role in assisting with independent living and should be seen and used as a logical extension of the school-based program. These programs should provide for a clear transition between the school and community living. The Individuals with Disabilities Education Act (IDEA) is very clear on the transition issue and mandates that a statement be provided of the transition service needs for students beginning no later than age 16 and beginning at age 14, and when determined appropriate, a statement of needed transition services for the child including interagency responsibilities or any needed linkages. Please see the application example.

Although IDEA specifies that a transition plan must be provided at least by age 16, transition services in physical education and sport should begin at a much earlier age to foster independence and inclusion in community living. Taking into account the needs and desires of each student, the physical educator should use the individual education program (IEP) to identify and recommend extracurricular programs, including intramurals and sports. These activities promote the goals of adapted physical education as well as those of occupational and physical therapy. Physical therapists can play a large role by assisting with the athletes' exercise and conditioning program. Linking these interdisciplinary services makes for a greater chance that the recommendations will be implemented. Often, once parents are aware of programs available for their child, they can have more influence than teachers with school officials in encouraging the development of such opportunities. Adapted physical education and adapted sport can provide a vital link in the transition plan to assist the person with a disability in becoming fully integrated into community life (Megginson & Lavay, 2001).

ROLE OF THE PHYSICAL EDUCATOR IN ADAPTED SPORT

Opportunities for students without disabilities to participate in sport and leisure programs within and outside of school are well documented. Most

APPLICATION EXAMPLE

Transition Service

Setting: Individualized Education Planning Committee Meeting

Child: A 17-year-old student with spina bifida who is a wheelchair user.

Issue: At the beginning of the meeting, the student's parents ask about an educational program to teach their child about community recreation opportunities.

Application: Because federal law requires that transition services be included in a student's IEP at age 16, the physical educator has already considered the available options. The IEP contains the following information:

- Each week the student will be exposed to various community recreation opportunities. Every Thursday the student and other members of his class will leave the school for community recreation programs. The students will attend swimming and fitness classes at the local fitness facility, where they will receive instruction on the use of the equipment.

- Other facilities will be visited on alternate weeks, such as the local bowling alley and the town's recreation department.

- The physical educator has also planned trips to the disability sports program at the local rehabilitation hospital. The student will participate in the center's competitive sport program of sitting volleyball and sailing.

- The physical educator has also collaborated with the special education resource teacher to include instruction on using public transportation to get to recreational programs.

middle and high schools provide a full range of sports for the interested student. Opportunities for students with disabilities, however, are not always apparent or available. Although federal legislation supporting these programs has been available since 1973, many schools have been slow to respond to the needs and desires of their students with disabilities. Many court cases have documented the rights of students with disabilities to have access to the same quality of programs available to students without disabilities.

As long as physical educators do not understand the important role they play in promoting sports participation for students with disabilities, students such as Jeffrey Kling will sit idly by the sidelines, watching others participate and wondering what it feels like to experience the thrill of participation and competition.

The unqualified success of national and international sports events for people with disabilities, such as the Paralympics, Deaflympics, and Special Olympics, have documented the ability of people with disabilities to become elite athletes who train and compete just as hard as their counterparts without disabilities (see figure 3.8, p. 52). Television and media exposure of adapted sport continues to improve. The highly publicized Supreme Court case involving disabled golfer Casey Martin's successful attempt to compete in the PGA while using a golf cart, as well as other lower court cases, emphasize that people with disabilities can compete in regular competitions if reasonable accommodations are provided that do not change the nature of the sport or alter the skill required. No longer should one equate *disability* with *lack of ability.* Elite athletes with disabilities complete the wheelchair marathon in less than 90 minutes; athletes who are blind complete bicycle races of 80 miles or more; athletes with cerebral palsy play soccer at a high level; and athletes with amputations run the 100-meter dash in times less than two seconds off the Olympic record. Competitions such as goal ball, wheelchair soccer, and Special Olympic gymnastics now draw large numbers of spectators. People with disabilities are more visible in our communities, such as wheelchair users playing tennis, or children with cerebral palsy playing soccer or baseball, or people who are blind riding tandem bikes or in-line skating with sighted friends. It is clear that people with disabilities have the same desires and needs to participate in adapted sport as people without disabilities do. The physical educator plays a vital role in helping to make this happen.

Figure 3.8 This elite-level Nordic Sit-skier demonstrates the skills and accomplishments that can be attained through hard training.

WHAT ABOUT JEFFREY KLING'S CASE?

Legislation supporting athletic participation of individuals with disabilities is continuing to evolve, but it has had a dramatic impact on participation levels over the past 30 years. The ruling in the *Kling v. Mentor School District* case might have far-reaching implications and precedence. According to the ruling, under applicable federal statutes and regulations, the IEP team—and *not* the Ohio High School Athletic Association (OHSAA)—is charged with the responsibility to determine the need for a student with a disability to participate in interscholastic athletics. Where OHSAA rules conflict with, or are more restrictive than IDEA, and thereby operate to prevent compliance with IDEA, such conflicts shall be resolved in favor of IDEA (Siegel, 2000; Stewart, 2001).

With regard to the age rule limitation imposed by the OHSAA, the OHSAA's position is that the age 19 rule establishes a threshold standard through which to achieve desired goals of safety and fair-ness and is cast in concrete, without exception, regardless of season. Petitioners define this as "administratively convenient." The court's position was that the lack of a waiver provision seems to be justified by the ease of administration for the athletic association. In other words, the association and its members do not wish to be burdened by a case-by-case analysis of an individual student-athlete's particular situation. "The court wonders what either institution's (i.e., the school district or the OHSAA) mission may be if it is not the welfare and education of individual students."

Insofar as the OHSAA rules are more restrictive than IDEA and thereby operate to prevent compliance with IDEA, Jeffrey is not obligated follow them. Notwithstanding the fact that the Mentor and Mayfield school districts are members of the OHSAA, the age 19 rule cannot be blindly accepted and obeyed. Private agreements containing items inconsistent with federal law do not take precedence and to the extent the terms of the agreement cause an actor to violate the law, they are not enforceable *(Shelley v. Kramer,* 68 S Ct. 836, 1948).

School administrators, physical educators, and athletic directors should review policies for athlete participation and ensure that the rules are reasonable and sensible. School personnel should review individual cases to meet the needs of all students and not be blinded by past practice and inflexible rules. Administrators should be governed by best practice, not past practice. As the numbers of students with disabilities who are included in neighborhood schools increase, so does the likelihood that these students will want opportunities to participate in interscholastic activities.

SUMMARY

In the past 30 years many advances have occurred in adapted sport. Federal legislation, success of some disabled sport organizations, increased awareness of health benefits by physical educators and medical personnel, and involvement with the USOC are some reasons for the growth of adapted sport. Many opportunities exist today for people with disabilities to participate in sport and leisure activities throughout communities. Opportunities exist at regional, national, and international levels for the individual interested in high levels of competition through multi- and unisport organizations. A continuum of involvement exists within the least restrictive environment for participation in regular or adapted sport. Physical educators of today must be resource people. They need to be aware of the programs in their communities for their students with disabilities to take the skills and knowledge they have acquired in adapted physical education and use them. Adapted sport should be an important part of the transition plan specified in the IEP for students who have disabilities.

REFERENCES

American Association of Adapted Sports Programs (2003). www.aaasp.org/

Anderson v. Little League Baseball, Inc., 794 F.Supp. 342 (Dist. Ariz. 1992).

Barrios v. California Interscholastic Association, 277 F.3d 1128 (9th Cir. 2002).

Block, M.E. (1995). Impact of the Americans with Disabilities Act (ADA) on Youth Sports. Journal of Physical Education, Recreation and Dance, 66(1), 28-32.

Davis, R.W. (2002). Inclusion Through Sports: A Guide to Enhancing Sport Experiences. Champaign, IL: Human Kinetics.

Davis, R., & Ferrara, M. (1996). Athlete classification: An exploration of the process. Palaestra, 12(2), 38-44.

Department of Health, Education & Welfare (1977). Education of handicapped children. Federal Register, 42(163), 42434-42516.

Federal Register, 42(86), 22676-22702.

Federal Register, May 4, 1977, PL 93-112, the Rehabilitation Act of 1973, Section 504.

Federal Register, June 4, 1997, PL 105-17, Individual with Disabilities Education Act Amendments of 1997.

Federal Register, October 21, 1998, PL 105-277, Olympic and Amateur Sports Act in Omnibus Appropriations Bill.

Frogley, M., & Beaver, D.P. (2002). Editor's Corner: Is the time right—Interscholastic athletics for student-athletes with disabilities? Palaestra, 18(2), 4-5.

Frogley, M. (2003). Personal correspondence, July 23, 2003.

Huebner, C. (2003). U.S. Paralympics Forum. Palaestra, 19(2), 9.

Matter, R., Nash, S., & Frogley, M. (2002). Interscholastic athletics for student-athletes with disabilities. Palaestra, 18(3), 32-38.

Megginson, N.L., & Lavay, B.W. (2001). Providing disability sport opportunities in adapted physical education. Palaestra, 17(2), 20-23, 24-26.

Metro Association for Adapted Athletics (MAAA) (2003). www.mnadaptedathletics.com/

National Federation of State High School Associations (2003). 2002 High School Participation Survey. www.nfhs.org

Olympic and Amateur Sports Act (1998), Omnibus Appropriations Bill.

Paciorek, M.J., & Jones, J.A. (2001). Disability sports and recreation resources, (3rd ed). Traverse City, MI: Cooper Publishing Group.

PGA Tour v. Martin, 532 U.S. 661, (2001). United States Supreme Court Decision. Rehabilitation Act of 1973. Revisions of 1998, 29 U.S.C. Chapter 16.

Richter, K.J., Adams-Mushett, C., Ferrara, M.S., & McCann, B.C. (1992). Integrated swimming classification: A faulted system. Adapted Physical Activity Quarterly, 9, 5-13.

Scorecard (2002). Elite Wheelchair Track Meet. Sports 'N Spokes, 28(5).

Shelley V. Kramer, 334 U.S. 1, 68 S.Ct. 836, 92 L. Ed. 1161 [1948].

Siegel, N.G. (2000). Kling vs. Mentor School Board. www.nessasiegel.com/kling_vs_mentor.htm

Stewart, D.A. (2001). The Power of IDEA: Kling vs. Mentor School District. Palaestra, 17(4), 28-30, 32.

United States Olympic Committee Constitution (1998). Colorado Springs, CO.

Winnick, J.P., (1987). An integration continuum for sport participation. Adapted Physical Activity Quarterly, 4, 157-161.

Winnick, J.P., Auxter, D., Jansma, P., Sculli, J., Stein, J., & Weiss, R.A. (1980). Implications of Section 504 of the Rehabilitation Act as related to physical education instructional, personnel preparation, intramural, and interscholastic/intercollegiate sport programs. Practical Pointers, 3(11): 1-20.

WRITTEN RESOURCES

Block, M.E. (1995). Americans with disabilities act: Its impact on youth sports. Journal of Physical Education, Recreation and Dance, 66(1), 28-32.

This article provides information on the legal rights for participation in youth sports for children with disabilities.

Coaching Athletes with Disabilities. Australian Sports Commission.

This series of extensive manuals and videos can be purchased by contacting the Australian Sports Commission Disabilities Program, P.O. Box 176, Belconnen ACT 2616, Australia (02) 6214 1792, Web site: www.activeaustralia.org/dep/countmein/index.htm; E-mail: DEP@ausport.gov.au. The Australian Sports Commission offers education packages on sport and physical activity for people with disabilities through the Count Me In program and Coaching Athletes with a Disability (CAD) scheme. The Count Me In program has been designed to assist anyone and everyone involved or interested in providing sporting opportunities for people with disabilities.

Davis, R. (2002). Inclusion through sports: A guide to enhancing sport experiences. Champaign, IL: Human Kinetics.

This is an excellent resource for physical education teachers or recreation specialists to help establish a comprehensive physical education program for students with and without disabilities using the medium of sport. The book describes many disability sports and how activities can be modified and taught in physical education settings.

DePauw, K.P. & Gavron, S.J. (2005). Disability and sport, (2nd ed). Champaign, IL: Human Kinetics.

This source gives readers an understanding of the historical context for sport today and trends for the future, an awareness of sport modifications, and a multitude of sport opportunities available for individuals with disabilities.

Paciorek, M.J., & Jones, J.A. (2001). Disability sports and recreation resources. Traverse City, MI: Cooper Publishing Group.

A complete resource guide that provides information on 47 sports and recreation activities for people with disabilities. Information is provided on adapted equipment and manufacturers, disabled sport organizations, and national governing bodies.

Measurement, Assessment, and Program Evaluation

Francis X. Short

At a recent physical education staff meeting, teachers were discussing some of their frustrations about how students are assigned to physical education classes. "Something's definitely wrong," said Mr. Webb. "I seem to have three or four kids in every regular class who can't keep up with their classmates and should probably be learning more elementary skills than the others. Then my special education class comes into the gym, and two or three of those kids could handle the regular class, no sweat."

"That's because kids are assigned to physical education without any prior consideration of their ability," said Ms. Nelson. "What we need is a testing program to help get these students into the most appropriate program."

"Sure, but what should we test?" asked Ms. Mestre. "And which tests should we use?"

"Right," said Mr. Ferruggia. "And what cutoff scores would we use to decide on the best program for each student?"

M easurement and assessment serve several purposes in physical education. One of the more critical purposes in adapted physical education, to assess program eligibility, is characterized in the previous scenario. The goal of this chapter is to familiarize you with many of the important concepts of measurement and assessment as they relate to adapted physical education. Among the major topics covered include measurement and assessment strategies, measurement and assessment in adapted physical education, tests and measures for use in adapted physical education, and program evaluation.

MEASUREMENT AND ASSESSMENT STRATEGIES

In this section we will provide a brief overview of terminology and approaches generally used in physical education. In the first subsection we attempt to distinguish between norm-referenced and criterion-referenced standards as they are commonly used in physical education. In the second subsection we briefly discuss what we refer to as standardized approaches to measurement and assessment. The third subsection deals with what will be called alternative (or authentic) types of measurement and assessment. Alternative approaches include the use of rubrics, task analyses, functional assessments, checklists, and portfolios. In the final subsection we cover the relation between standardized and alternative approaches.

Standards for Assessment

In the title of this chapter, "measurement" refers to the process of administering tests to students and obtaining scores that represent students' abilities (or traits). The term "assessment" (sometimes called "evaluation") pertains to a subsequent step in which some kind of judgment is made about those test scores. These judgments are generally based on some standard of performance. The types of standards most commonly used to assess test scores in physical education are norm referenced and criterion referenced.

Norm-Referenced Standards

Norm-referenced standards allow teachers to compare one student's performance against the performance of others from a particular peer group (e.g., 10-year-old girls). Norm-referenced standards provide evaluations relative to other students and lead to statements such as, "Tucker's setting ability is above average for boys his age," "Tamiko is two years behind her age group on motor-based developmental milestones," and "Tim's body mass index scores are high for his age." Examples of norm-referenced standards include percentiles, age norms, T scores, z scores, and other kinds of "standard scores." Norm-referenced standards are generally established by testing large numbers of subjects from defined groups (usually gender and age groups and sometimes disability groups) and analyzing and summarizing the scores (often in one or more tables). Norm-referenced standards are usually associated with the standardized strategies discussed later in this chapter.

Criterion-Referenced Standards

Whereas norm-referenced standards typically provide scores for a theoretical "average" student of a particular age, criterion-referenced standards provide levels of "mastery" for the skill or ability being evaluated. This mastery score represents an acceptable level of performance for the test in question as determined by expert opinion, research data, logic, experience, or other means. The American Red Cross, for instance, uses criterion-referenced tests to certify lifeguards. Candidates for certification must demonstrate a level of aquatic performance deemed necessary to save lives.

Whereas norm-referenced assessment involves comparing scores of students, criterion-referenced assessment does not. If the Red Cross standards for lifeguard certification were norm-referenced, perhaps the top 25 percent of the class would qualify for certification, but that top 25 percent might or might not have the "mastery" necessary to save lives. With the criterion-referenced approach, theoretically all of the students in the class could qualify or, on the other hand, none might qualify. Certification depends on meeting mastery standards and has nothing to do with how one student compares to others. Thus, criterion-referenced assessment makes judgments about competency and leads to such statements as, "Grace's skinfold measures are in the healthy fitness zone," "Joe demonstrates a mature catching pattern," and "Louise is unable to push her wheelchair up a standard ramp."

Recently, greater attention has been placed on the development of tests with criterion-referenced standards in physical education. The Fitnessgram (Cooper Institute for Aerobics Research, 1999a) is a good example. The standards associated with Fitnessgram represent a level of performance thought to be necessary to attain objectives related to good health and improved function. For each test item (table 4.1), standards for a "healthy fitness zone" are provided by gender and age (5 to 17+). The healthy fitness zone is defined by a lower-end score and an upper-end score. All students are encouraged to achieve at least the lower-end criterion. Little emphasis is placed on going beyond the upper-end criterion, however, because health-related objectives can be attained simply by staying within the healthy fitness zone. As Fitnessgram demonstrates, criterion-referenced standards can be associated with standardized tests, but they can also be found with some of the alternative strategies discussed later in this chapter.

Standardized Strategies

Standardized strategies generally involve testing students by following established procedures in controlled environments. Students with like characteristics are tested in exactly the same way under exactly the same conditions. By controlling, or standardizing, the environment, teachers hope to improve the validity and reliability (including the objectivity) of the test. Standardized testing frequently is used to determine if a student is making reasonable progress on skill and fitness development compared to similarly defined students or to levels of achievement thought to be appropriate for students with certain characteristics (e.g., age, gender, disability). A few of the many existing standardized tests of physical fitness, motor development, and sports skills are described later in the chapter.

Alternative Strategies

In recent years standardized testing strategies have come under increasing criticism. Critics argue that many of the skills tested on standardized batteries have little "functional relevance" for the student (e.g., a test might require a student to touch her nose with her index finger as an indication of kinesthetic awareness, but this is not a skill that youngsters use a great deal either at home or at school); standardized tests are less likely to provide information important for instruction (e.g., when a standardized assessment reveals that a student is "below average" on a test, it might not directly identify *why* the performance was "below average"); and, because the controlled testing environment is often artificial, it is unknown if the results will generalize to other situations (e.g., if a student does a good job of passing a volleyball

Table 4.1 Fitnessgram and Brockport Physical Fitness Test (BPFT) Test Items Arranged by Components of Health-Related Physical Fitness

Fitnessgram		BPFT	
Aerobic capacity		Aerobic functioning	
PACER		PACER (20 m and 16 m)	
Mile run		Mile run	
Walk test		Target aerobic movement test	
Muscular strength, endurance, and flexibility		**Musculoskeletal functioning**	
Curl-ups		Reverse curl	Flexed arm hang
Trunk lift		Seated push-up	Extended arm hang
Push-up		40-m push/walk	Trunk lift
Modified push-up		Wheelchair ramp test	Curl-up
Pull-up		Push-up	Modified curl-up
Flexed arm hang		Modified pull-up	Target stretch test
Back-saver sit-and-reach		Dumbell press	Shoulder stretch
Shoulder stretch		Bench press	Modified Apley
		Dominant grip strength	Modified Thomas test
			Back-saver sit-and-reach
Body composition		**Body composition**	
Percent fat (triceps and calf skinfolds)		Skinfolds (triceps and calf; triceps and subscapular; triceps only)	
Body mass index		Body mass index	

against a wall, will that skill transfer to a game situation?) (Block, Lieberman, & Connor-Kuntz, 1998).

Proponents for alternative strategies suggest that authentic assessment is an approach that closely links assessment to instruction (so that it has day-to-day applicability for the teacher) and takes place in "natural" settings. It is designed to directly measure the skills that students need for successful participation in physical activity and emphasizes subjective evaluation through observation. Four techniques associated with authentic assessment—rubrics, task analysis, functional assessment, and portfolios—are briefly discussed.

Rubrics

Rubrics, or scoring rubrics, are gaining in popularity as a way of measuring student performance. A rubric provides a mechanism for a teacher to match a student's performance to one of multiple levels of achievement through a set of criteria (a form of criterion-referenced standards). A sample rubric for the volleyball serve is provided in figure 4.1.

One of the distinct advantages of testing and evaluating through rubrics is that students know exactly what they have to do to get the best possible score. For instance, in the volleyball serve example, an overhand serve is clearly valued in the scoring scheme. Because even a poor overhand serve scores better than a good underhand serve, students know what they need to practice and can analyze their own performances (as well as that of their classmates) accordingly. The volleyball serve can be evaluated with a scoring rubric as students play an actual game; thus, evaluating is "unobtrusive" and done in a "natural" environment. Rubrics also are easily modifiable via "rubric extensions" and "rubric analysis" (Block, Lieberman, & Connor-Kuntz, 1998). For higher-performing students, for instance, the volleyball rubric could be extended to include location and ball movement variables or could include a level for jump serving. For lower-performing students, the rubric might include the use of a lighter ball, a lower net, or a closer serving line, or it might place a higher value on the underhand serve (see the rubric extension, 1a-1d, in the example). When it is unclear why a student cannot attain a particular level of a rubric, analyzing some aspect of that level might be helpful (see the rubric analysis, 4a-4d, in the example.) For instance, if a student cannot get

5 Serves overhand. Toss brings ball consistently above the attacking shoulder. Wrist is firm at contact. Ball is rarely served out of bounds and can be served deep into the opponent's court with a low trajectory (ball velocity is good).

4 Serves overhand. Toss brings ball consistently over the attacking shoulder. Wrist is firm at contact. Ball is usually inbounds, although depth is inconsistent and trajectory tends to be high (ball velocity is moderate).

    a. Stands facing the net with opposite foot slightly forward.

    b. Stands with hips and shoulders at an angle of about 45 degrees to the net.

    c. Holds ball at chest level with either opposite hand or with both hands.

    d. Tosses ball two to three feet in the air above, and slightly in front of, the attacking shoulder

3 Serves overhand. Toss is inconsistent so that the ball is not always above the attacking shoulder. Wrist tends to collapse on contact. Ball is frequently served out of bounds (often in, or short of, the net; ball velocity is slow).

2 Serves underhand. Ball is usually inbounds, but the depth of the serve is often short and the trajectory tends to be high (ball velocity is moderate).

1 Serves underhand. Ball is usually out of bounds. Serves that are inbounds tend to be short or weak (ball velocity is slow).

    a. Serves a volleyball underhand from a line drawn six meters from the net. Most serves are inbounds.

    b. Serves a volleyball underhand from a line drawn six meters from the net. Most serves are out of bounds (or in the net).

    c. Serves a volleyball underhand from the attack line (three meters from the net). Most serves are inbounds.

    d. Serves a large foam ball underhand from the attack line (three meters from the net). Most serves are inbounds.

Figure 4.1 Sample rubric for the volleyball serve.

to level 4 because of an inconsistent ball toss, that aspect might be targeted for improvement.

In adapted physical education settings, assessment through rubrics translates nicely to individualized education program (IEP) development (see chapter 5) and personalized instruction. For example, if a student's present level of performance on the volleyball serve is level 3, a reasonable objective (or objectives) would be provided by the criteria associated with level 4 (i.e., a majority of serves inbounds, a more consistent ball toss above the attacking shoulder, a firm wrist at contact). One of the keys to incorporating rubrics into the measurement and assessment strategy is to clearly define the criteria associated with each level of performance. Explicit definitions help to reduce the subjectivity associated with alternative assessment.

Task Analysis

The process of task analysis involves breaking a skill or movement down into its component parts and sequencing those parts into a progression (either simple to complex or chronological). Many ways to conduct a task analysis have been described in the professional literature, and many names have been used with those descriptions. Regardless of the type (or name) of the task analytic approach employed, however, the value of the technique is that once a more difficult skill or movement has been reduced to a number of smaller, less difficult parts, the teacher is provided with both an assessment tool *and* an instructional strategy. Through task analysis the teacher can identify the components of the skill or movement the student can do (i.e., the assessment piece that describes the student's present level of performance), as well as those the student cannot do (i.e., the instructional strategy piece that targets components for future learning).

In this text the terms "traditional task analysis," "ecological task analysis," and "biomechanical task analysis" are used to describe different approaches to this technique. Traditional task analysis involves the identification of a progression of lead-up activities, ordered from simple to complex, in which the skill or movement being taught is the most complex step in the progression. Ecological task analysis not only looks at the skill or movement itself but also attempts to account for student characteristics and preferences, as well as possible environmental factors that might influence the execution of the skill or movement. Traditional and developmental task analyses are discussed in chapter 7 (with examples); the reader is reminded, however, that these techniques (as well as other task-analytic approaches) have implications for both assessment and instruction (by noting the tasks and subtasks the student can and cannot do).

As used here, the term biomechanical task analysis involves listing the biomechanical components or "focal points" of the task (usually in chronological sequence) so that an "idealized" performance is described. A basic biomechanical task analysis for the forehand stroke in tennis, for instance, might include the following components or focal points:

- Keeps eyes on ball throughout the skill
- Moves quickly to the ball, using proper footwork
- Positions body with hips and shoulders perpendicular to the net, knees bent
- Racket is brought back to waist level and parallel to the ground
- Leg drives off rear foot; weight transfers at contact with rotation of hips and shoulders
- Ball is ahead of hips at contact
- Wrist is firm at contact
- Opposite arm is away from body for balance
- Follow-through is high (hand finishes at or above opposite shoulder)

Using this analysis, a student's forehand tennis ability could be evaluated in a natural environment (i.e., while playing a game of tennis). Students who do not receive checkmarks for each of the focal points know which aspects of the forehand they need to learn. (Each of these focal points can be seen in checklist form as part of figure 4.2, p. 61)

Biomechanical (and other) task-analytic approaches, however, have been criticized for two main reasons (Davis & Burton, 1991): (1) they might do a good job describing the components of the task, but they fail to account for the capabilities (or limitations) of the student and (2) they might ignore important environmental factors in executing the skill. (The idea that the task, the individual, and the environment must all be considered in understanding, describing, or assessing human movement is consistent with current theory; see chapter 19.) One student with a disability, for instance, might be able to perform each of the components of the tennis skill; another might be able to perform them only if some of the environmental factors associated with the task are modified (e.g., bigger ball, smaller racquet, and the like); and a third student might be able to perform them only if some of the task components themselves are modified (including the elimination of some or the addition of others). Some of the environmental factors that a teacher could manipulate in the tennis example might include the size of the court, the type of racquet used, the type of ball, and the way the ball is "presented" to the student—whether it is hit, tossed, or placed on a tee. (Other environmental factors include wind and weather and the type of court surface, but these are not usually under the teacher's control.) Task components could be adjusted in ways that give the student the greatest chance for success in executing the skill—that is, the "idealized" performance for *that* student.

Figure 4.2 presents an example of how a biomechanical task analysis for the forehand stroke in tennis might be expanded to include individual (student) and environmental factors. The assessment form is printed with the standard components of the forehand with space to modify components as might be necessary for a particular student. Some of the key environmental factors are also listed and can become part of the analysis. In this example, some of the task components have been modified for a student who uses a wheelchair and who has good upper body functioning. The modified components, along with the remaining original components, are meant to represent good wheelchair tennis technique. The assessment focuses on which of the task components the student can perform and under what set of environmental conditions. So, the teacher writes in any necessary modifications to the original set of focal points, describes (via checkmarks) the environmental conditions during the assessment, and assesses (again, via checkmarks) the student's ability to perform the focal points (modified as necessary). The ultimate goal for the student might be to demonstrate all task components while playing an actual tennis match on a regulation court with a standard (or junior-size, as appropriate) racket and a regulation ball and under standardized rules (which might include a two-bounce rule for players in wheelchairs). In earlier stages of learning, of course, the student might not be able to execute all the task components or might need environmental adjustments to be successful; in fact, giving the student some choice in the adjustments is a good place to start. Nevertheless, this type of task analysis

can be used to assess performance frequently and provide both the teacher and the student with information to promote future learning.

Figure 4.2 provides an example of how a biomechanical task analysis can be expanded to increase its utility (both as an assessment tool and a teaching strategy) by also considering student and environmental factors in analyzing the task. Some adapted physical educators, however, have had success with, and recommend, a different modification to the biomechanical approach. Houston-Wilson (1995) describes a modification that considers the level of assistance required by a student in executing the components of a biomechanical task analysis. An example of this technique is provided in figure 4.3 (on page 62). In this example, six focal points for an isometric push-up are identified. The scoring system, however, is expanded to consider the amount of assistance provided to the student in performing each of the components. The level of assistance ranges from total physical assistance to independent performance and a "percentage of independence score" can be calculated (in this case, 66 percent). This approach to task analysis is especially useful with students who have more severe disabilities and frequently require assistance during physical activity.

Ecological Assessment

Some authorities have argued for a more functional approach to physical education for students with disabilities, including assessment strategies. Functional skills are those with a high likelihood of occurring in a student's natural environment, either currently or in the future. Proponents of the functional approach would argue that physical educators should not spend valuable instruction time working on nonfunctional skills (e.g., throwing a javelin or putting a shot) for students with disabilities because they very rarely pursue these activities outside of class (unless a student is on the track and field team). If Frisbee throwing, however, is a popular activity in the student's neighborhood, it might be a functional skill for that student. In identifying functional skills for students, teachers must consider the student's interests and abilities as well as environmental factors that might influence activity selection (facility and programming availability, activity interests of the family, popular activities in the community, and so on).

Block (2000) has supported an approach he calls a "top-down" strategy for assessing and teaching functional skills. By "top-down," Block suggests

Student's name: ___John_____   Date of observation: _10/5/04_____

Observed: ☐ During game   ☐ During skills test   ☑ During practice

Skill: __Forehand stroke in tennis_____

Performer adjustments necessary?   ☐ No   ☑ Yes (as indicated below)

☑ Eyes are on ball throughout the skill.

_____

☑ Moves quickly to the ball using proper footwork.
    _Self-propels wheelchair; thumb of racket hand is on top of rim or wheel_____

☑ Positions body with hips and shoulders perpendicular to the net; knees are bent.
    _Positions wheelchair at 45-degree angle relative to the net_____

☐ Racket is brought back to waist level and parallel to the ground.
    _Backswing is low to the ground and straight back from rear axle_____

☐ Leg drives off rear foot; weight transfers at contact; rotation of hips and shoulders occurs.
    _Body leans into the shot (toward the net)_____

☑ Ball is ahead of hips at contact.
    _Ball is at, or slightly ahead of, front foot at contact_____

☐ Wrist is firm at contact.

_____

☑ Opposite arm is away from body for balance.
    _Opposite hand is placed on ipsilateral knee or rim for support or balance_____

☐ Follow-through is high (hand finishes at, or above, opposite shoulder).

_____

Environmental factors and modifications:

Court size:	☐ Full court	☑ Half-court	☐ _____
Racquet type:	☐ Standard	☑ Junior	☐ Racquetball
	☐ Badminton		
Ball type:	☑ Tennis	☐ Foam	☐ _____
Ball mode:	☐ Hit by opponent	☐ Hit by facilitator	
	☐ Tossed by facilitator	☑ Hit from tee	
_____:	☐ _____	☐ _____	

(Others)

Figure 4.2 Example of a biomechanical task analysis that considers the task, the individual, and the environment.

that teachers should start with the desired final product, or end result, and work backward from there as a way of identifying the components of a functional physical skill. (*Note:* the top-down approach is actually the opposite of what most physical education teachers are trained to take. Most physical education teachers have been schooled in "developmental physical education,"

BIOMECHANICAL TASK ANALYSIS

Objective: To execute an isometric push-up correctly for three seconds.

Directions: Circle the minimal level of assistance an individual requires when correctly performing a task. Total each column. Total the column scores, and enter the total score achieved in the summary section. Determine the percentage of independence score using the chart in the summary section. Record the amount of time the position is held for the product score.

Isometric push-up	IND	PPA	TPA
1. Lie facedown.	③	2	1
2. Place hands under shoulders.	③	②	1
3. Place legs straight, slightly apart, and parallel to the floor.	3	2	1
4. Tuck toes under feet.	3	②	①
5. Extend arms while body is in a straight line.	3	2	1
6. Hold position for three seconds.	3	2	①
Sum of column scores:	6	4	2

Key to levels of assistance:

IND = Independent; the individual is able to perform the task without assistance.

PPA = Partial physical assistance; the indvidual needs some assistance to perform the task.

TPA = Total physical assistance; the individual needs assistance to perform the entire task.

Summary		Percentage of independence		
Total score achieved	12	6/18 = 33%	11/18 = 61%	16/18 = 88%
Total score possible	18	7/18 = 38%	12/18 = 66%	17/18 = 94%
% of independence score	66%	8/18 = 44%	13/18 = 72%	18/18 = 100%
Product score	1 sec.	9/18 = 50%	14/18 = 77%	
		10/18 = 55%	15/18 = 83%	

Reprinted, by permission, from C. Houston-Wilson, 1995, Alternate assessment procedures. In *Physical best and individuals with disabilities,* edited by J. Seaman (Reston, VA: AAHERD).

Figure 4.3   Example of a biomechanical task analysis that considers the level of assistance required by the student.

which takes a "bottom-up" approach. In developmental physical education, teachers believe that rudimentary movements are prerequisite to fundamental movements, which, in turn, are prerequisite to specialized movements such as games and sports. Thus, games and sports are not taught until prerequisites have been mastered. In the top-down approach the importance of prerequisites is reduced, and only those absolutely necessary for the task are taught.) So, if the desired final product is to play miniature golf, the top-down approach seeks to identify all the components of miniature golf (e.g., stance, grip, stroke, scoring, and rules). Those components, in turn, could then be task analyzed to provide assessment tools and strategies for teaching miniature golf.

Block (2000) and others also have argued that functional skills should be taught using a top-down strategy in the settings in which they most likely will be used. Often, those settings will be community based. So, if the desired final product is to independently play miniature golf at a local facility, an ecological assessment should be conducted. With an ecological assessment, the top-down approach is expanded to include additional cognitive and affective skills necessary to accomplish the goal. An ecological analysis for playing miniature golf at a local facility might include getting to the course (knowing the route and safely crossing streets), checking in (paying for the round, verifying the correct change, and getting the necessary equipment—putter, ball, scorecard, pencil), playing the game (including grip, stance, stroke, scoring, and rules), etiquette (such as allowing the group ahead to finish the hole before "teeing up"), checking out (returning the putter, ball, and pencil), and going home (retracing the original route with appropriate safety precautions).

Each of the components of this analysis could then be task analyzed to provide an appropriate assessment device for determining present level of performance. Results of the assessment then serve as the basis for instruction; that is, whichever necessary tasks or subtasks are not checked become the targeted skills for meeting the functional goal (i.e., independently playing miniature golf at the local facility). The notion of teaching functional skills via a top-down approach in community-based settings is gaining support and seems to be particularly appropriate for addressing IEP transition plans for older students (see chapter 5).

Portfolios

An important aspect of alternative or authentic assessment is the collection of evaluation data on multiple occasions in multiple settings. Another important aspect is documenting student learning through exhibits and work samples (rather than simply through some kind of grade). Consequently, the use of a student portfolio system is often associated with the alternative approach. Teachers can identify any number of items that students can choose to include in their physical education portfolio. Examples include videotapes, test results (including standardized tests), teacher observations, peer evaluations, rating scales, checklists, journals, self-reflections, self-assessments, and logs.

Materials, however, are not just "dumped" into a portfolio. Teachers must establish criteria for what goes in the portfolio and how it will be evaluated. The contents of a portfolio will vary, depending on the student's age and cognitive ability and the purpose of the portfolio. Lieberman and Houston-Wilson (2002) suggest that portfolios in inclusive settings should reflect assessments and performances related to all three domains of behavior (cognitive, affective, psychomotor), adapted as necessary for students with disabilities.

Synthesis

In recent years, the push for alternative or authentic types of assessment has gained momentum in physical education. Often, authentic approaches

hold the most promise for directly linking testing and learning. When conducted properly, authentic approaches inform students of their progress (which, to a large extent, they monitor themselves) and what they need to work on next. Testing and learning, in a sense, become seamless because students learn, in part, from the testing program.

Alternative approaches, however, are not without weaknesses. As mentioned earlier, alternative approaches put a premium on subjective observation. As Hensley (1997) has noted, such assessment practices "have frequently been criticized on the basis of questionable validity and reliability, being susceptible to personal bias, generosity error (the tendency to overrate), lack of objective scoring, as well as the belief that they are conducted in a haphazard manner with little rigor." Furthermore, the Individuals with Disabilities Education Act (IDEA) requires that the unique needs of youngsters be determined using valid, reliable, objective, and nondiscriminatory instruments. Authentic assessment strategies often do not meet these criteria.

Consequently, we recommend that measurement and assessment strategies include both standardized and alternative elements. Instructors should recognize that two continua influence the selection of tests in adapted physical education. Tests vary among their psychometric properties (including validity and reliability) and their authentic properties, and there tends to be a relation between these variables. Because the establishment of appropriate levels of validity and reliability requires controlled circumstances, tests with stronger psychometric qualities tend to have lower authentic qualities. Conversely, those with stronger authentic qualities tend to have weaker psychometric properties. Of course, teachers should attempt to select tests that have at least acceptable levels of both types of properties. Test selection, however, will also be influenced by the purpose of the testing. When important educational decisions pertaining to a student (e.g., eligibility for adapted physical education services) are based on testing, the teacher should give preference to tests with stronger psychometric properties. When a student is learning a skill to be used in a particular context (e.g., dribbling a basketball for eventual use in a game situation), the teacher should give preference to tests with stronger authentic properties to monitor student progress. The application of both standardized and alternative assessment strategies in adapted physical education is explored further in the next section.

MEASUREMENT AND ASSESSMENT IN ADAPTED PHYSICAL EDUCATION

There are many reasons for measuring and assessing in physical education, including increasing motivation, determining strengths and weaknesses, classifying students, determining degree of achievement, evaluating instruction and programs, predicting future success, and conducting research designed to answer questions and solve problems (Miller, 2002). In adapted physical education, measurement and assessment strategies are often employed to assist in the determination of unique need (and, subsequently, placement) and in providing a basis for instruction. The relation of measurement and assessment to each of these functions is discussed in the following sections.

Determination of Unique Need

Students suspected of having unique physical and motor needs should be referred to appropriate committees within the school for further testing. Referrals must document the reasons that the student should be considered for an adapted physical education program. Measurement and assessment at the referral level, usually called screening, are to document the need for an in-depth evaluation to determine if the student has a unique need in physical education.

Determining unique need is critical for two reasons. First, a student must have a unique need to be eligible for adapted physical education services. This is true both for students considered to have disabilities under IDEA and for those without disabilities but who are low in physical education–related abilities. Second, once a unique need is determined, the need serves as the basis for developing IEP goals and, possibly, objectives for the student. These aspects of unique need—eligibility and goals and objectives—are discussed in the following paragraphs.

In dealing with the question of eligibility, a distinction must be made between an adapted physical education *program* and the instructional *placement* to which a student is assigned. A student might qualify for an adapted program but receive that program in a regular class placement. Thus, placement is established after the appropriate program has been determined. When a student is referred to a school committee on the basis of preliminary screening, the committee must first determine whether the student is eligible for the adapted physical education program. It will probably be necessary for the adapted physical educator to conduct more assessments to determine if the student has a unique need. A long-term unique need must be established for a student to qualify for adapted physical education. In the absence of a medical referral, the criteria for entry into the adapted program (in most cases) should be based primarily on psychomotor performance. Usually, measurement and assessment for the purpose of determining program eligibility should focus, to the extent possible, on standardized testing (i.e., tests with strong psychometric properties and standards for evaluation).

Several states have developed criteria for admission into adapted physical education. In states without such criteria, it is recommended that school districts adopt local criteria for admission into adapted physical education. It is also recommended that districts consider one or more of the following (or similar) standards for admission based on test results that measure developmental aspects of physical education:

- The student scores below the 15th percentile.
- The student scores more than one standard deviation below the mean (e.g., a T score less than 40).
- The student exhibits a developmental delay of at least two years when age norms are used (although the use of age norms is not recommended for students older than seven).
- The student fails to meet criterion-referenced standards on one or more areas evaluated.
- The student fails to meet 70 percent or more of the competencies in the physical education curriculum.

Because formal testing often takes place under "artificial" conditions, districts might also consider additional criteria. For example, corroboration of standardized test results through observational techniques, authentic test results, or a temporary trial placement might also be required.

Once eligibility has been established, based on a documented unique need, appropriate goals and objectives are written. Typically, annual goals and short-term objectives are selected to improve the area(s) of unique need. Students in adapted physical education often have the same goals as the regular program (e.g., to improve physical fitness or ball-handling skills), but the objectives will usually be different because other activities might need to be substituted for those in the regular program or different performance criteria might need to be adopted. Although teachers must rely on their professional judgment in setting appropriate performance criteria, they should always consider the student's current level of performance. In some cases the teacher might choose to use standardized data to help establish reasonable objectives. For instance, if a student has an intellectual disability, the teacher might consult the criterion-referenced standards in the Brockport Physical Fitness Test (Winnick & Short, 1999a) to determine an appropriate grip strength score for an 11-year-old girl. The teacher would see that the specific standard (one adjusted for the influence of intellectual disability) is 12 kilograms and that the minimal general standard (one unadjusted for disability) is 19 kilograms. Armed with this information and knowledge of the student's present level of performance, the teacher is in a good position to establish a performance criterion that constitutes a reasonable expectation. In other cases, a teacher might choose to use authentic forms of assessment (e.g., rubrics and task analyses) to provide the criteria for an instructional objective.

After the goals and objectives have been determined, the most appropriate placement for obtaining them is selected. Every effort should be made to keep the student in a regular class placement. Teachers should attempt to modify activities and methodologies so that the student's objectives can be met in the regular class. Although there was one primary criterion for admission into the program (i.e., performance), there are several considerations in the selection of the appropriate placement. Placement, for instance, might depend in part on what is being taught in the regular class. A student who uses a wheelchair, for instance, could probably meet appropriate goals and objectives for individual sports (e.g., swimming, weight lifting, track and field) in a regular placement. But the same student might be assigned to a more restrictive setting when team sports (e.g., volleyball, soccer, football) are played in the regular class (although alternative activities also could be offered within the same placement). Another important consideration during placement is the input of the student and his or her parents. Whatever placement is selected, the student should be comfortable with it. In some cases, when students are unable to understand concepts or safety considerations being taught in the regular class place-

ment or if there are behavioral or other affective concerns, students might need to be assigned to a more restrictive placement (see the continuum of alternative instructional placements in chapter 2, p. 24).

Measurement in the Affective Domain

Students with disabilities, with or without unique needs in the psychomotor domain, might be placed in more restrictive physical education settings if they have unique needs in the affective domain. The affective (or social–emotional) domain is broad and encompasses elements such as attitudes, interests, values, beliefs, and personality, among others, but social behavior is the element of the affective domain that often gets the greatest attention in schools. The ability (and willingness) to follow directions, take turns, respect others, play fair, and demonstrate sportsmanship, for instance, is important in physical education.

Although physical educators can certainly make observations relative to a student's behavior in physical activity settings, it is unlikely they will administer any standardized tests to help determine a unique need in the affective domain. Such an assessment is most likely conducted by a school psychologist and might include the administration of tests such as the Vineland Social Maturity Scale or the Behavior Assessment System for Children. Physical educators would more likely assess behavior in an authentic context and, as such, would develop their own rubrics, checklists, task analyses, or rating scales to measure behavior. As an example, Gallo (2003) has recommended a rating scale (developed by a collaborative team of physical educators) to evaluate the affective domain (figure 4.4, p. 66).

Providing a Basis for Instruction

The role of measurement and assessment does not stop after the student has been assigned to a physical education program. Progress on the goals and objectives established for the student should be monitored closely. As suggested earlier, alternative tests can be designed and used for this purpose. Students, for instance, can work (individually, in pairs, or with the teacher) from task sheets or cards that include rubrics or task analyses for a particular activity. Teachers help students to devise practice regimens that promote learning, as evidenced by scoring at a higher level

Affective domain criteria

Etiquette

- Respects others' personal space and boundaries
- Honors activity dynamics
- Conforms to standards of conduct of the sport

Fairness

- Plays fair
- Accepts defeat and does not complain
- Accepts victory and does not gloat

Communication with peers

- Encourages others
- Accepts different individual skill levels
- Assists others in reaching personal success
- Uses active listening, positive words, and body language respectfully

Communication with instructor

- Uses active listening, positive words, and body language respectfully
- Accepts coaching cues in a positive manner
- Responds to instruction and seeks clarification
- Remains on task

Each of the four categories is rated on multiple occasions as follows:

A = appropriate = always meets behavioral criteria

NI = needs improvement = sometimes meets behavioral criteria

I = inappropriate = never meets behavioral criteria

Figure 4.4 Example of a rating scale for the affective domain.

Reprinted with permission from the April issue of the *Journal of Physical Education, Recreation & Dance*, a publication of the American Alliance for Health, Physical Education, Recreation and Dance, 1900 Association Dr., Reston, VA 20191 (www.aahperd.org)

on the rubric or by demonstrating previously missing techniques on the task analysis. Skills learned in practice situations also need to be transferred to natural environments, such as daily activities, games, and sports.

At the conclusion of the instructional program or unit, the teacher should conduct final testing to determine the student's "exit abilities." In some cases, grades are awarded based on this final assessment. Whether the program is graded or not, progress should be evaluated in terms of the written goals and objectives. For nongraded situations, Melograno (1996) suggests a progress report form that lists the student's goals as a checklist on which teachers can check "achieved," "needs improvement," or "working to achieve" for each goal listed. Summary sheets from portfolios can also be used for evaluating exit abilities. Some teachers might choose to give awards to students on the basis of their final test performances.

TESTS AND MEASURES FOR USE IN ADAPTED PHYSICAL EDUCATION

Many published tests are available to physical educators. Most of these tests are considered more "standardized" than "alternative" (as these terms have been used in this chapter). That is, most published tests tend to have established levels of validity and reliability, provide norm-referenced or criterion-referenced standards, and require controlled testing environments. Some of these tests, however, do contain alternative elements such as rubric-like scoring systems (e.g., Test of Gross Motor Development) or task-analytic sequences (e.g., Special Olympics Sports Skills Program Guides).

Available tests in physical education measure a range of traits and abilities. Most, however, fall within five traditional areas of physical and motor development and ability: reflexes and reactions, rudimentary movements, fundamental movements, specialized movements (including sports skills, aquatics, dance, and activities of daily living), and physical fitness. (Readers should note that these categories are somewhat arbitrary and do not encompass all possibilities. In some situations, for instance, teachers might routinely test and assess the posture or the perceptual–motor abilities of their students.) More recently, a sixth area, physical activity, has gained attention. The rest of this section of the chapter is devoted to a discussion of tests or measures from each of these six areas. One instrument from each area is highlighted. The highlighted instruments are meant to be representative of a particular content area and are recommended or used by many adapted physical educators. As you read the following material, remember that other tests are available within each area and that teachers always have the option of designing alternative measures to augment or replace "store bought" instruments, as appropriate. In adapted physical education, there are always circumstances when published instruments prove to be inappropriate for a particular student, and teachers must modify or design instruments in accordance with the student's abilities. (Additional tests are listed in this chapter's "resources" section.)

Measuring Reflexes and Reactions

The measurement and assessment of primitive reflexes and postural reactions is becoming increasingly common in adapted physical education. (See chapter 19 for information on reflexes and reactions.) As educational services are extended to infants and toddlers—as well as to those with more severe disabilities (especially those that are neurologically based, such as cerebral palsy)—physical educators need to understand the role of reflexes and reactions on movement.

Because primitive reflexes normally follow a regular sequence for appearing, maturing, and eventually disappearing, they are particularly helpful in providing information on the level of central nervous system maturation. If a primitive reflex persists beyond schedule, presents an unequal bilateral response (e.g., present on one side, but absent or not as strong on the other), is too strong or too weak, or is completely absent, neurological problems might be suspected. When primitive reflexes are not inhibited, they will undoubtedly interfere with voluntary movement because muscle tone involuntarily changes when reflexes are elicited. The Milani-Comparetti Motor Development Screening Test is a good example of an instrument that assesses reflexes and reactions.

Milani-Comparetti Motor Development Screening Test for Infants and Young Children

- Purpose: The Milani-Comparetti Test (Meyer Rehabilitation Institute, 1992) is designed to assess motor development in young children, birth to 24 months. Although the instrument has obvious use for infant and toddler programs, the inclusion of several reflexes and reactions in the battery makes it appropriate for older developmentally delayed individuals as well, especially those with cerebral palsy.
- Description: In all there are 27 items associated with this test. Nine of the items are classified as "spontaneous behaviors," which test for head control in four postures (vertical, prone, supine, and pulled from supine); body control in three postures (sitting, all fours, and standing); and two "active movements" (standing from supine and locomotion). The remaining 18 items are called "evoked responses" and test 5 primitive reflexes

(hand grasp, asymmetrical tonic neck, moro, symmetrical tonic neck, and foot grasp) and 13 righting, parachute, or tilting reactions. In evaluating most of the spontaneous behaviors, testers are required to evaluate the progression of development. For instance, for "all fours" the child progresses from a prone position propped up by forearms and hands, to hands and knees, and finally to hands and feet (i.e., "plantigrade"). For evoked responses, the tester need only note whether the reflex or reaction is absent or present. Age norms are associated with each of the test items.

- Reliability and validity: Interobserver and test–retest data provide evidence of acceptable levels of reliability. Age norms were established based on the performance of 312 subjects. Content validity is claimed based on general acceptance of test items by physicians and therapists.
- Comment: The primary advantage of the Milani-Comparetti is its relative ease of administration, which is due, in part, to the limited number of test items. Physical and occupational therapists are likely to have experience with this test and might be resources for the adapted physical educator.
- Availability: Munroe-Meyer Institute, University of Nebraska Medical Center, 985450 Nebraska Medical Center, Omaha, NE 68198-5450. Web site: www.unmc.edu/mmi/consumer/index.htm

Measuring Rudimentary Movements

Rudimentary movements are the first voluntary movements (see chapter 19). Reaching, grasping, sitting, crawling, and creeping are examples of rudimentary movements. Most instruments that assess rudimentary movements do so in some kind of developmental milestone format—that is, a series of motor behaviors associated with specific ages are arranged chronologically and tested individually. By determining which behaviors the child can do, the teacher can estimate the child's developmental age (because each milestone has its own "age norm") and can provide future learning activities (i.e., the behaviors in the sequence that the child cannot currently do). The Peabody Developmental Motor Scales (PDMS-2) is an example of this approach, with some additional enhancements (other instruments are discussed in chapters 21 and 22).

Peabody Developmental Motor Scales

- Purpose: The Peabody Developmental Motor Scales (Folio & Fewell, 2000) assesses the motor development of children ages birth to five years in both fine and gross motor areas. Items are subcategorized into the following six areas: reflexes, stationary (balance), locomotion, object manipulation, grasping, and visual–motor integration.

- Description: The PDMS-2 includes 249 test items (mostly developmental milestones) arranged across six areas. The items are arranged chronologically within age levels (e.g., 0 to 1 month, 6 to 7 months, 18 to 23 months), and each is identified as belonging to one of the six categories being assessed (e.g., reflexes, locomotion). It is recommended that testers begin administering items one level below the child's expected motor age. Items are scored on a 0, 1, 2 basis according to specified criteria. Testing continues until the "ceiling age level" is reached (a level for which a score of 2 is obtained for no more than 1 of the 10 items in that level). Composite scores for gross motor quotient (reflexes, stationary [balance], locomotion, and object manipulation), fine motor quotient (grasping and visual-motor integration), and total motor quotient (combination of gross and fine motor subtests) are possible.

- Reliability and validity: Empirical research has established adequate levels of reliability and validity. Information is provided for subgroups as well as for the general population.

- Comment: The PDMS-2 appears to have certain advantages over other rudimentary movement tests. First, the large number of test items represents a larger sample of behaviors than exist in many other tests. Second, the six categories help teachers to pinpoint exactly which areas of gross motor development are problematic. Finally, the scoring system and availability of normative data provide the teacher with more information on student performance than many other tests do. Supplementary materials, including a software scoring and reporting system and a motor activity program, also are available in conjunction with PDMS-2.

- Availability: Pro-Ed, 8700 Shoal Creek Boulevard, Austin, TX 78757-6897. Web site: www.proedinc.com/store/index.php? mode=product_detail&id=9280

Measuring Fundamental Movements

Fundamental movements are those associated with early childhood, such as throwing, catching, skipping, and hopping. Some fundamental movement test instruments use the developmental milestone approach discussed under rudimentary movements, but most use a point system to evaluate either the process of the fundamental movement or its product. Process-oriented approaches generally attempt to break down (or task analyze) a movement into its component parts and then evaluate each component individually. This approach assesses the quality of the movement, not its result. Product-oriented approaches are concerned primarily with outcome. Product-oriented assessment is more concerned with the quantity of the movement (e.g., how far? how fast? how many?) than with its execution. The Test of Gross Motor Development (TGMD-2) emphasizes a process-oriented approach to the assessment of fundamental movements.

Test of Gross Motor Development

- Purpose: The Test of Gross Motor Development (Ulrich, 2000) has four purposes: to design a test representing gross motor content frequently taught in preschool and early elementary grades including special education; to develop a test that could be used by various professionals with a minimum amount of training; to design a test with both norm-referenced and criterion-referenced standards; and to place a priority on the gross motor skill sequence rather than the product of performance.

- Description: The test measures ability in 12 gross motor areas divided into two subtests. The locomotor subtest is composed of the run, gallop, hop (figure 4.5), leap, horizontal jump, and slide. The object control subtest consists of striking a stationary ball, stationary dribble, catch, kick, underhand roll, and overhand throw. For each skill, the tester is provided with an illustration, equipment and condition requirements, directions, and performance criteria. Children receive one point for meeting each of the performance criteria given for each of two trials. These criterion-based scores can be added and compared to norm-referenced standards. Age norms are provided in half-year increments for ages three to eight for both subtests.

- Reliability and validity: Reliability coefficients are quite high (generally .84 to .96). Evidence of content-related, criterion-related, and construct-related validity is provided.

- Comment: The sound process of test construction should provide the user with a good deal of confidence that scores obtained by children accurately reflect their fundamental movement abilities. The fact that both criterion-referenced and norm-referenced standards are provided increases the test's utility.

- Availability: Pro-Ed, 8700 Shoal Creek Boulevard, Austin, TX 78757. Web site: www.proedinc.com/store/index.php?mode =product_detail&id=9260

© Human Kinetics

Figure 4.5 A student attempts the hopping item from the locomotor subtest of the Test of Gross Motor Development.

Measuring Specialized Movements

Of the five content areas described in this section, specialized movements present the greatest challenge for making summary statements relative to assessment and for choosing one test instrument as an example. This is because of the wide variety of possible activities that could be tested under this heading. Safrit (1990), for instance, lists 185 skills tests across 25 sports. Sports skills tests can take many forms, but often they are criterion referenced and teacher constructed (in fact, many teachers prefer to use authentic techniques to assess game and sport skills). Teachers who work with students with disabilities who compete in special sport programs, such as those sponsored by Wheelchair Sports, USA, the United States Association of Blind Athletes, or the National Disability Sports Alliance are encouraged to develop their own tests specific to the event in which the athlete competes. One example of a sports skills test that can be used with athletes with disabilities comes from the Special Olympics Sports Skills Program Guides.

Sports Skills Program Guides

- Purpose: The Sports Skills Program Guides (also called Coaches Guides) (Special Olympics, n.d.) complement or supplement existing physical education and recreation programs for people with disabilities (age eight and older) in sports skills instruction.

- Description: The Sports Skills series is a curriculum that includes 26 sports divided into 3 categories: Special Olympic Summer Sports, Special Olympic Winter Sports, and Nationally Popular Sports. Although not a test instrument per se, authentic assessment is a critical aspect of the program. The assessment consists of task analyses, and testers check off those focal points that the student is able to perform. For instance, in Athletics there are 11 test items corresponding to track-and-field events. Within each test, testers check the focal points an athlete can demonstrate (e.g., "performs a single-leg take-off for a running long jump"). Each focal point is also accompanied by an assessment of the student's readiness to perform that skill (e.g., "athlete can locate her starting mark").

- Reliability and validity: No information has been reported, but content validity probably could be claimed because the tests reflect task analyses of sports skills developed by "experts" in the field.

- Comment: A primary advantage of the program guides is convenience—a teacher or coach can adopt the existing task analytic curricula for many sport activities. The program has been used with participants with intellectual disabilities for some time and has been shown to have good utility for that group. A disadvantage is that neither reliability nor validity of the various test instruments has been formally established.

- Availability: Special Olympics, Inc., 1325 G Street, Suite 500, Washington, DC 20005. Web site: www.specialolympics.org

Measuring Physical Fitness

Over the years many standardized tests of physical fitness have become available to teachers. Older tests of fitness did not always distinguish between health-related and skill-related components of fitness and often used norm-referenced standards in the assessment. More recently developed tests have emphasized the measurement of health-related aspects of fitness and have employed criterion-referenced standards.

Recently, AAHPERD has joined with the Cooper Institute for Aerobics Research and Human Kinetics to create the American Fitness Alliance (AFA), a national resource center for fitness- and physical activity–related products and services. The AFA's objective is to promote physical activity and fitness throughout a lifetime. The AFA recommends two tests of physical fitness, each of which is health related and criterion referenced. The first is Fitnessgram, which was introduced earlier in this chapter. The second is the Brockport Physical Fitness Test (BPFT) (Winnick & Short, 1999a), which extends the health-related, criterion-referenced approach to youngsters with disabilities (table 4.1). A DVD on the BPFT has been included with this text.

Brockport Physical Fitness Test

- Purpose: The Brockport Physical Fitness Test (Winnick & Short, 1999a) provides a health-related, criterion-referenced physical fitness test appropriate for youngsters (ages 10 to 17) with and without disabilities.

- Description: The test battery includes 27 test items from which teachers can choose. (A brief description of all test items can be found in appendix C, and many are demonstrated on the DVD.) Typically, students would be tested on four to six test items from three components of fitness: body composition, aerobic functioning, and musculoskeletal functioning (muscular strength, endurance, and flexibility; see figure 4.6). Although specific test items are recommended for youngsters with intellectual disabilities, cerebral palsy, visual impairments, spinal cord injuries, and congenital anomalies and amputations (as well as for those in the general population), teachers are encouraged to "personalize" testing. Personalization involves identifying health-related concerns pertaining to the student, establishing a desired fitness profile for the student, selecting components and subcomponents of fitness to be assessed, selecting test items to measure those components, and selecting health-related, criterion-referenced standards to evaluate fitness. Thus, teachers have the option to modify any of the elements of the testing program as outlined in the test manual. Both "general" and "specific" standards are available, as appropriate. A general standard is one appropriate for the general population and has not been adjusted in any way for the effects of a disability. A specific standard is one that has been adjusted for the effects of an impairment or disability. Specific standards are available only for selected test items for particular groups of youngsters.

- Reliability and validity. The test items in the BPFT are believed to be valid and reliable. Evidence for validity and reliability is provided in a lengthy technical report (Short & Winnick, 1999) that readers can access through the Fitness Challenge Software, the computer program developed to support the BPFT.

- Comment: The BPFT was patterned after the Fitnessgram, and many of the standards, especially for the general population, were adopted from that test. Thus, teachers in "inclusive" settings should find it relatively easy to go back and forth between the tests as necessary. In addition to the test manual, the BPFT kit includes a training guide (Winnick & Short, 1999b), the computer software, an instructional videotape, skinfold calipers, curl-up strips, and the PACER audio CD or cassette.

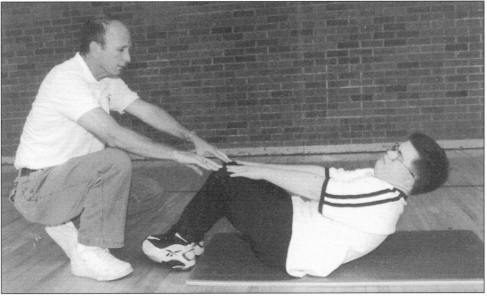

© Francis X. Short

Figure 4.6 A student performs a modified curl-up, a test of musculoskeletal functioning from the Brockport Physical Fitness Test.

- Availability: Human Kinetics, P.O. Box 5076, Champaign, IL 61820. Phone 800-747-4457. Web site: www.humankinetics.com

Measuring Physical Activity

Much research has established the positive relation between regular physical activity and health, and many physical education programs are promoting physically active lifestyles to their students as a primary goal of the program. Consequently, it is becoming increasingly important for physical educators to find ways of measuring physical activity that describe the status of a student's activity level and to document changes in that level. At present, four general types of activity measures are available to teachers: heart rate monitors, activity monitors (e.g., pedometers, accelerometers, motion sensors), direct observation, and self-report instruments (Welk & Wood, 2000). Heart rate monitors, despite their accuracy, have limited applicability in school situations because of the cost and limitations (only a few children can be measured at one time). Pedometers are relatively inexpensive and have good utility for measuring walking activity, but they do not have broad applicability in measuring physical activity in general. Coding student activity through direct observation is not expensive, but it can be time consuming because only a few youngsters can be monitored at one time by a trained observer. (These approaches—heart rate monitors, activity monitors, direct observation—might be more effective in adapted settings than regular settings because of smaller class sizes.)

Thus, almost by default, self-report instruments are probably the most appropriate means of measuring physical activity in most school settings. Self-report instruments require students to recall and record their participation in physical activity over a set amount of time (usually from one to seven days). Although many self-report instruments are available (see Welk & Wood, 2000, for examples), all seek to quantify the frequency, intensity, and duration of students' physical activity. If students with disabilities have difficulty with self-reports, teachers or parents might need to provide an estimate of the information instead. A computer software program called Activitygram provides teachers with an easy method for measuring student physical activity.

Activitygram

- Purpose: Activitygram (Cooper Institute for Aerobics Research, 1999b) records, analyzes, and saves student physical activity data and produces reports based on that data.
- Description: Activitygram is part of the Fitnessgram 6.0 software package. The program prompts youngsters to recall their physical activities over the previous day in 30-minute time blocks. Students select activities from within six categories: lifestyle activity, active aerobics, active sports, muscle fitness

activities, flexibility exercises, and rest and inactivity. Students are also asked to rate the intensity of the activity (light, moderate, vigorous). The printed Activitygram report summarizes the entered data in three ways. It reports the total number of minutes of at least moderate-level activity for up to three days; it provides a time profile for each day showing levels of activity (rest, light, moderate, hard) across the hours of the day; and it gives an activity profile that describes which of the six activity categories the student pursued.

• Reliability and validity: Because of the subjective nature of recall and reporting, measurement limitations are associated with all self-report instruments. Nevertheless, the Previous Day Physical Activity Recall instrument, on which Activitygram is based, has been shown to provide valid and reliable estimates of physical activity and also accurately identifies periods of moderate to vigorous activity (Weston, Petosa, & Pate, 1997).

• Comment: Although designed primarily with students without disabilities in mind, Activitygram can be useful in adapted physical education settings. Specific activities will vary (e.g., running vs. pushing a wheelchair), but the six categories of physical activity are appropriate for most students with or without disabilities. Younger children and those with intellectual disabilities, however, might have trouble recalling and entering activity data. Peer tutors, teacher aides, or parents could be trained to make direct observations and could enter the data on behalf of a student who has difficulty using the system.

• Contact: American Fitness Alliance, Human Kinetics, P.O. Box 5076, Champaign, IL 61820. Web site: www.americanfitness.net

Program Evaluation

One of the time-honored purposes of measurement in physical education is program evaluation. (As used in this section of the book, the term "program evaluation" relates to the evaluation of instructional programming. Other aspects of a program, including management and organizational aspects, can be evaluated in different ways; see chapter 2 and appendix D.) Program evaluation essentially seeks to answer the question, "Are we actually doing what we say we do?" This kind of information, of course, is important to teachers because if the answer to this question is, "No," something needs to change (and one hopes that "something" is under the teacher's control). Program evaluation, however, can also have a powerful public relations function in the schools. Physical education teachers are all too familiar with attacks on their programs by administrators or school boards when money (or instructional time) gets tight. Unfortunately, physical education has not always been able to successfully defend against these attacks. For instance, the Surgeon General reports that daily physical education among high school students declined from about 42 percent to about 25 percent between 1991 and 1995 (U.S. Department of Health and Human Services, 1996). To reverse this trend, and others like it, physical educators must overcome perceptions that their programs are merely "play time," "glorified recess," or "open recreation." Physical educators, certainly, must build good programs, but it is insufficient for them to simply *claim* the program is effective—they must *demonstrate* that it is effective.

To conduct program evaluation, program goals must be in place. These goals might be determined locally (in a specific school or school district), statewide, or even nationally. A school district, for instance, might choose to adopt the NASPE content standards (National Association for Sport and Physical Education, 2004) for its program goals. These six standards (reprinted here with permission) are as follows:

1. Demonstrates competency in motor skills and movement patterns needed to perform a variety of physical activities

2. Demonstrates understanding of movement concepts, principles, strategies, and tactics as they apply to the learning and performance of physical activities

3. Participates regularly in physical activity

4. Achieves and maintains a health-enhancing level of physical fitness

5. Exhibits responsible personal and social behavior that respects self and others in physical activity settings

6. Values physical activity for health, enjoyment, challenge, self-expression, or social interaction

Although helpful in articulating a direction for a program, these standards (and other more generally written program goals) in their current form are too broad to be used for program evaluation. It is up to the local physical education staff to "operationalize" the standards in ways that can be measured and evaluated. Examples of how a local staff might establish operational definitions for a few of the NASPE Standards are provided in the following list.

Standard 1. To evaluate standard 1 the terms "competency" and "variety" must be defined. A district, for instance, might choose to define beginning, intermediate, and advanced competencies for the motor skills and movement patterns taught in its curriculum and might simply define variety by the number of activities for which some level of competency is claimed. So, a physical education staff might rework standard 1 as follows:

> By the end of the year, at least 80 percent of all eighth-graders will master all beginning-level competencies in at least three sports and all intermediate-level competencies in at least one sport.

If the staff can specify beginning, intermediate, and advanced competencies for a variety of sports taught in the curriculum, it could adopt different program goals at different grades, so that perhaps by graduation the program goal might be for 80 percent of the students to have met beginning-level competencies in at least 10 activities, intermediate in at least 5, and advanced in at least 3. This, then, would be the district's operational definition for NASPE standard 1. Students and teachers could develop portfolios that "follow" students through their school years with different teachers helping students to acquire additional competencies in different sports as they move toward graduation.

Standard 3. A physical education staff might decide to adopt the Centers for Disease Control and Prevention and American College of Sports Medicine (CDC-ACSM) joint physical activity guidelines for its secondary students, as follows:

> For grades 7 to 12, 90 percent of all students will perform at least 30 minutes of moderate-intensity physical activity on at least four days per week during the school year.

The computer program Activitygram could be used to monitor progress on this program goal (although teachers might want to interact with students to encourage accurate self-reporting). Pedometers are relatively inexpensive and are becoming increasingly popular in the schools. Some models record "exercise time," which would be useful in evaluating this standard.

Standard 4. Computer software associated with Fitnessgram and the Brockport Physical Fitness Test (Fitness Challenge) could be used to evaluate a program goal based on standard 4. Fitness Challenge, for instance, provides a report that summarizes the performance of all members of a class for all items in the test battery. A physical education staff might operationalize standard 4 as such:

> At least 80 percent of all students aged 10 to 17 will meet either minimal general or specific health-related physical fitness standards for their age, gender, and, as appropriate, disability on at least one measure of aerobic functioning.

Other program goals could be written for other components of fitness and monitored with help from Fitness Challenge. Inasmuch as Fitness Challenge includes both general and specific standards, it has good utility in inclusive settings.

As a final note on program evaluation, it should be acknowledged that program goals that have been operationally defined for a general physical education program might not always be useful in evaluating an adapted physical education program. In the absence of general program goals that might apply to a very diverse student body in adapted physical education, teachers could choose to report program evaluation data as a function of success in meeting students' short-term objectives on their individualized education programs (IEPs; see chapter 5). Such a program goal might read:

> At least 80 percent of all short-term physical education objectives appearing on a student's IEP will be achieved for at least 90 percent of students enrolled in adapted physical education.

These short-term objectives would be based on the alternative or standardized measurement strategies discussed in this chapter.

SUMMARY

Measurement and assessment serve several important functions in adapted physical education. Most significantly, they are a means for determining if a student has a unique need in physical

APPLICATION EXAMPLE
Measurement and Assessment

Setting: A new student (age 10) with mild intellectual disabilities received special education services, including adapted physical education, at his previous school. The district, as a matter of policy, will reevaluate the student before deciding on proper programs and placements. A physical education teacher is invited to be a member of the IEP team.

Issue: How should the physical educator determine if the student should be assigned to the adapted program?

Application: The teacher might do the following:

- Administer the Brockport Physical Fitness Test (BPFT) to determine if the student's fitness is sufficiently developed (the expectation would be that the student would achieve at least specific standards for youngsters with intellectual disabilities).

- Administer the Test of Gross Motor Development (TGMD) to determine if fundamental movements are completely developed (maximum or near maximum scores would be expected for a 10-year-old).

- Compare standardized test results (i.e., BPFT and TGMD) to the district's guidelines or criteria for adapted physical education.

- Place the student in a trial placement (or placements) and collect authentic assessment data (determine, for instance, if the rubrics being used by other members of the class are reasonably appropriate, with or without modification, for the new student).

- Consider all assessment data when formulating a recommendation for the IEP team.

education, and they provide a foundation for structuring learning experiences and monitoring progress. This is illustrated in the Measurement and Assessment application example. Measurement and assessment strategies can range on a continuum from techniques with stronger psychometric properties conducted in less natural environments (often called standardized assessment) to those with weaker psychometric properties conducted in more natural environments (often called authentic assessment). Each of these approaches has strengths and weaknesses and should be selected in accordance with the purposes of the assessment. It is recommended that these approaches be combined to yield a more complete picture of the student. Ordinarily, assessment in adapted physical education should focus on physical fitness and motor development and ability (including reflexes, rudimentary movements, fundamental movements, activities of daily living, sports skills, aquatics, and dance, as appropriate). Standardized tests are commercially available for each of these areas and are especially useful for summative purposes, such as determining unique need. Standardized tests, however, might not be appropriate for every youngster with a disability.

Authentic techniques are useful when standardized tests are inappropriate and are especially useful for formative or instructional purposes, such as monitoring student progress on a daily basis. Test data generated from the assessment of individual students can be aggregated to yield information on the effectiveness of the physical education instructional program.

REFERENCES

Block, M. (2000). *A teacher's guide to including students with disabilities in general physical education.* Baltimore, MD: Brookes.

Block, M., Lieberman, L., & Connor-Kuntz, F. (1998). Authentic assessment in adapted physical education. *Journal of Physical Education, Recreation and Dance,* 69(3), 48-55.

Cooper Institute for Aerobics Research (1999a). *Fitnessgram.* Dallas, TX: Author.

Cooper Institute for Aerobics Research (1999b). Teacher Fitnessgram Software. Dallas, TX: Author.

Davis, W., & Burton, A. (1991). Ecological task analysis: Translating movement theory into practice. *Adapted Physical Activity Quarterly,* 8, 154-177.

Folio, M., & Fewell, R. (2000). *Peabody developmental motor scales* (2nd ed.). Austin, TX: Pro-Ed.

Gallo, A. (2003). Assessing the affective domain. *Journal of Physical Education, Recreation, and Dance,* 74(4), 44-48.

Hensley, L. (1997). Alternative assessment for physical education. *Journal of Physical Education, Recreation and Dance,* 68(7), 19-24.

Houston-Wilson, C. (1995). Alternate assessment procedures, In J. Seaman (Ed.), *Physical best and individuals with disabilities: A handbook for inclusion in fitness programs.* Reston, VA: AAHPERD.

Lieberman, L., & Houston-Wilson, C. (2002). *Strategies for inclusion.* Champaign, IL: Human Kinetics.

Melograno, V. (1996). *Designing the physical education curriculum.* Champaign, IL: Human Kinetics.

Meyer Rehabilitation Institute (1992). *Milani-Comparetti motor development screening test for infants and young children: A manual.* Omaha: Author.

Miller, D. (2002). *Measurement by the physical educator.* New York: McGraw-Hill.

National Association for Sport and Physical Education (2004). *Moving to the future: National standards for physical education.* Reston, VA: Author.

Safrit, M. (1990). *Introduction to measurement in physical education and exercise science.* St. Louis: Times Mirror/Mosby.

Short, F., & Winnick, J. (1999). *The Brockport physical fitness test technical manual. Fitness challenge software.* Champaign, IL: Human Kinetics.

Special Olympics (n.d.). *Coaches guides.* Retrieved December 8, 2003, from www.specialolympics.org.

Ulrich, D. (2000). *Test of gross motor development* (2nd ed.). Austin, TX: Pro-Ed.

U.S. Department of Health and Human Services (1996). *Physical activity and health: A report of the Surgeon General.* Atlanta, GA: U.S Department of Human Services, Center for Disease Control and Prevention, National Center for Chronic Disease Prevention and Health Promotion.

Welk, G., & Wood, K. (2000). Physical activity assessment: A practical review of instruments and their use in the curriculum. *Journal of Physical Education, Recreation and Dance, 71*(1), 30-40.

Weston, A., Petosa, R., & Pate, R. (1997). Validation of an instrument for measurement of physical activity in youth. *Medicine and Science in Sports and Exercise, 29*(1), 138-143.

Winnick, J., & Short, F. (1999a). *The Brockport physical fitness test manual.* Champaign, IL: Human Kinetics.

Winnick, J., & Short, F. (1999b). *The Brockport physical fitness training guide.* Champaign, IL: Human Kinetics.

WRITTEN RESOURCES

Brigance Inventory of Early Development—Revised (1999). Curriculum Associates, Inc., PO Box 2001, North Bellerica, MA 01862.

This is a criterion-referenced assessment of more than 200 skills in 11 major areas, including preambulatory motor, gross motor, and fine motor skills. Designed for ages birth to 7 years. Web site: www.curricassoc.com

Denver Developmental Screening Test (Denver II) (1989). Denver Developmental Materials, Inc., PO Box 371075, Denver, CO 80237.

Developmental milestones for normal gross motor development; age norms up to 6 years. Web site: www.denverii.com

President's Challenge (2003). President's Council on Physical Fitness and Sports, 200 Independence Avenue SW, Room 738H, Washington, DC 20001.

This is a physical activity and physical fitness awards program. Five awards are available—three related to physical fitness (including the Presidential Physical Fitness Award), one to health-related physical fitness, and one to maintaining a physically active lifestyle. Web site: http://fitness.gov

AUDIOVISUAL RESOURCES

Brockport Physical Fitness Test video. (1999). American Fitness Alliance, Youth Fitness Resource Center, PO Box 5076, Champaign, IL 61825-5076.

Discusses and demonstrates the proper techniques for administering the 27 items in the BPFT. Some background information is also provided. Running time is about 30 minutes. (A copy of the video is included with this book in a DVD format.)

ELECTRONIC RESOURCES

Fitness Challenge Software (1999). American Fitness Alliance, Youth Fitness Resource Center, P.O. Box 5076, Champaign, IL, 61825-5076.

This computer software program supports the Brockport Physical Fitness Test (BPFT). It prints goals, results, and fitness plans for individual students, and separate reports can be generated for instructors or parents. Also includes the technical manual for the BPFT, which provides validity and reliability information.

Fitnessgram 6.0 Software (1999). American Fitness Alliance, Youth Fitness Resource Center, P.O. Box 5076, Champaign, IL, 61825-5076.

Provides a sophisticated computerized system for administering Fitnessgram. Includes both teacher and student components. The student component allows students to enter their own test scores and track their progress. It also provides a system for monitoring their levels of physical activity through Activitygram, a subcomponent of the software.

Individualized Education Programs

Francis X. Short

Sandra Shockley, a physical education teacher at the local elementary school, was doing some paperwork at the dining room table when her husband looked over her shoulder.

"What's all this?" he asked.

"I'm working on a new IEP for Stevie, one of my students," she said. "I have a committee meeting tomorrow."

"All of this stuff is for one kid?"

"Yeah, but it's not that much—mostly test results, a copy of his current IEP, and some notes I've made."

"Is an IEP like a lesson plan?"

"No. I still have to write lesson plans, too. Mostly the IEP lists the student's goals and objectives and the resources that will be provided to reach them. Parents also have some input. We use the IEP to monitor progress during the year."

"Sounds like a lot of work for one student."

"Well, it does take a little time, but it really is helpful to develop an individualized program for a student with a disability. Besides, the IEP is required by law."

"Required by law? So, what happens if he doesn't make the goals and objectives as planned? Can you get in trouble?"

"You can relax," Sandra laughed. "They won't send me to the Big House if Stevie does only one curl-up!"

Federal legislation has mandated that students with disabilities receive individualized programs. Depending on age and other factors, a student's individualized program might be described in an individualized education program (IEP), an individualized family service program (IFSP), or a section 504 accommodation plan. Furthermore, students who are not disabled but who have unique needs in physical education might also have individualized programs developed for them. Such programs, though not required by federal legislation, are recommended in this text and are called individualized physical education programs (IPEPs). This chapter provides an overview of these programs and discusses in detail the requirements and procedures for developing IEPs, 504 plans, and IPEPs.

OVERVIEW OF INDIVIDUALIZED PROGRAMS

When President Ford signed PL 94-142, the Education for All Handicapped Children Act of 1975, the provision of special education in the United States was altered in several ways. One significant change was the provision that students classified as having a disability should have IEPs. More recent legislation, culminating with the amendments to the Individuals with Disabilities Education Act (IDEA) in 1997, has reaffirmed the importance of IEPs in developing appropriate educational plans for students with disabilities. An IEP is a written document that essentially describes the student's current level of educational achievement, identifies goals and objectives for the near future, and lists the educational services to be provided to meet those goals. IDEA requires that IEPs be developed for all students with disabilities between the ages of 3 and 21.

IDEA also has provisions for addressing the developmental needs of infants and toddlers with disabilities. Local agencies may provide early intervention services for infants and toddlers in accord with state discretion. These services are detailed in an IFSP, a document written for all eligible participants. (The IFSP is described in chapter 21.) Thus, IDEA addresses the needs of students (ages 0 to 21) who meet the criteria of infants, toddlers, and children with disabilities as defined by the act (see chapter 1 for an overview of IDEA).

Some students with disabilities, however, might not meet the criteria to qualify for special education services provided by IDEA. Youngsters who have (or who have the effects of) the following conditions might be in this group: HIV or AIDS, alcohol abuse, substance abuse, asthma, diabetes, ADHD, or mild learning disabilities not requiring special education. These students would not have IEPs, but they might be entitled to appropriate accommodations and services tailored to meet their individual needs as provided in a section 504 accommodation plan (see chapter 1 for a description of section 504).

In physical education there might be a third group of students (in addition to those covered by IDEA or by 504) who require individualized programs. These students are not considered disabled (by either piece of legislation) but have unique needs in physical education. Students recuperating from injuries or accidents or convalescing from noncommunicable diseases or those who are overweight or have low skill levels or low levels of physical fitness might fall into this category. Although this group of students is not covered by legislation, we recommend here that school districts develop IPEPs to document programs modified to meet students' unique physical education needs.

Whether or not a student is deemed to have a disability under the provisions of IDEA or section 504, physical education teachers should provide an individualized program for that student if the student has a unique need in physical education. A unique need is apparent when a student cannot safely or successfully participate in the regular physical education program. Figure 5.1 summarizes the individualized programs that are either required or recommended for students with unique needs in physical education.

THE STUDENT WITH A DISABILITY

The specially designed program for any child identified as having a disability by the school district in accordance with IDEA is detailed in the IEP. Local districts may determine and design their own IEP format; thus it is not unusual for neighboring school districts to use different IEP forms. Although formats might vary, each IEP must include certain components.

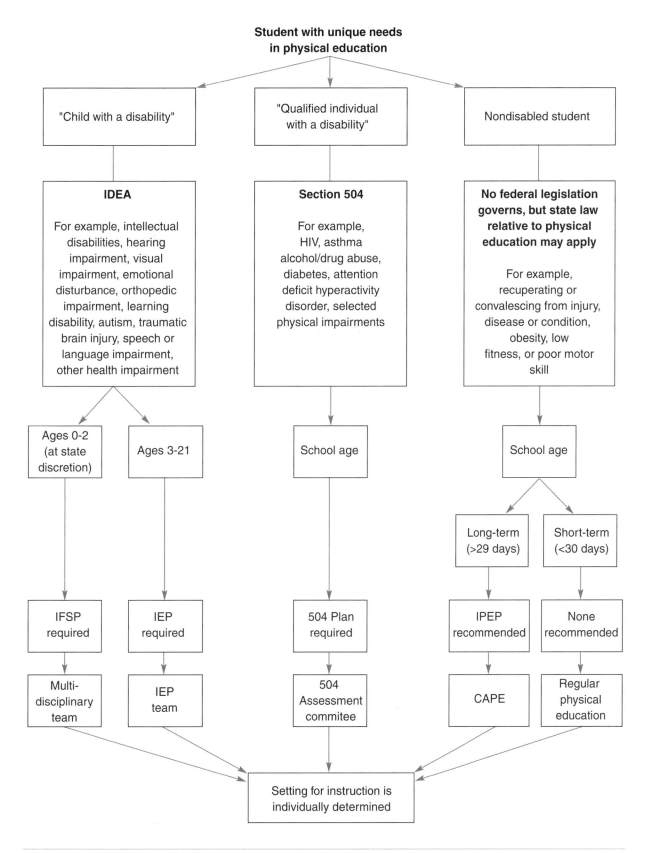

Figure 5.1 Individualized programs for students with unique needs in physical education.

COMPONENTS OF THE IEP

Although local IEP forms might include additional information, IDEA requires an IEP to contain eight components. Each of these required components is discussed in the following text, and sample physical education information that might be included in an IEP is shown in figure 5.2.

Present Level of Performance

Every IEP must include a statement of the child's present levels of educational performance, includ-ing how the child's disability affects the child's involvement and progress in the general curriculum or, for preschool children, how the disability affects the child's participation in certain activities (Department of Education, 2002). In essence, the present level of performance (PLP) component is used to establish the student's current "baseline" educational abilities and is where all relevant evaluation information is presented. This evaluation information has two general purposes: (1) to determine if a child has a disability (this is especially critical during the student's initial evaluation and any formal re-evaluations, which must

INDIVIDUALIZED EDUCATION PROGRAM

Student's name: Thomas Hernandez   Age: 16

Present Level of Performance

1. Completes 25 laps in the 20-m PACER (Brockport Physical Fitness Test [BPFT] specific standard is 38 laps).
2. Sum of triceps and subscapular skinfold measures is 35 mm (BPFT minimal general standard is 15 to 33 mm).
3. Performs 20 modified curl-ups (exceeds the BPFT specific standard but does not meet the minimal general standard of 24).
4. Dominant grip strength is 22 kg (BPFT specific standard is 28 kg).
5. Successfully performs the trunk lift at 12 in. (BPFT general standard is 9-12 in.).
6. Back-saver sit-and-reach score for both right and left sides is 8 in. (BPFT general standard is 8 in.).
7. Averages 4,700 steps per day on the pedometer.
8. Scores a 2 (out of a possible 3) on the throwing technique rubric (characteristics: ball is brought behind the head in preparation, high over the shoulder release, steps forward with the leg on the same side as the throwing arm, limited trunk rotation in preparation, trunk flexes slightly in follow-through).
9. Throws a baseball 42 feet.
10. Scores a 3 (out of a possible 10) on the throwing accuracy test (target is 4 ft by 4 ft with the bottom line 2 ft from the floor, student stands 30 ft away and attempts to throw an indoor baseball into the wall target 10 times, is given 1 point for each successful throw).
11. Averages 1.25 physical provocations (hitting, pushing others) per physical education class.

Effect of disability: Thomas has Down syndrome with mental retardation. His disability generally contributes to lower performance in physical fitness and sport activities. His muscle tone is poor, he is overweight, and he tends to tire easily. Thomas sometimes requires physical assistance or prompting when participating in physical activity and is occasionally physically aggressive toward others.

Annual Goals and Short-Term Objectives

1.0 Thomas will improve his aerobic functioning.

    1.1 Thomas will complete 40 laps on the 20 m PACER (meets BPFT specific standard).

2.0 Thomas will improve his muscular strength and endurance.

    2.1 Thomas will do 24 modified curl-ups (meets BPFT minimal general standard).

    2.2 Thomas will score 22 kg on dominant grip strength (meets BPFT specific standard).

3.0 Thomas will improve his throwing ability. *(continued)*

Figure 5.2 Sample physical education information for an IEP.

3.1 Thomas will score a 3 on the throwing technique rubric (characteristics: arm is swung backward, rather than upward, and ball will be above throwing elbow, throwing elbow moves horizontally during throw, thumb points down in follow-through, marked rotation of trunk in preparation, throwing shoulder drops slightly in preparation, steps forward with foot opposite the throwing arm with weight transfer from back foot to front).

3.2 Thomas will throw a baseball 60 feet.

3.3 Thomas will score 7 out of 10 on the throwing accuracy test.

4.0 Thomas will improve his behavior in physical education.

4.1 Thomas will average less than .5 physical provocations per 45-minute class period.

5.0 Thomas will increase his level of physical activity.

5.1 Thomas will average 7,000 steps per day on the pedometer.

Statement of Services and Supplementary Aids

Thomas will receive adapted physical education services with his intact special education class three times per week. In addition, Thomas will participate in the regular physical education class once per week during that class's weight training unit. No special equipment or aids are required, but a peer tutor will be used during the weight training unit in the general class.

Statement of Participation in Regular Settings

Most of Thomas's physical education program will be conducted with other students who have disabilities. During the weight training unit, however, Thomas will receive 25 percent of his physical education program in a placement with students with no disabilities.

Assessment Modifications

The BPFT includes appropriate modifications for health-related fitness assessment in accord with the FITNESSGRAM test that is administered district-wide (e.g., the curl-up is modified so that the hands slide along the thighs to the knee rather than sliding across a strip placed on the floor, and the grip strength test is substituted as a measure of musculo-skeletal functioning). The three throwing tests (technique, distance, accuracy) are tests that are ordinarily administered at the elementary level, but were deemed appropriate for Thomas given his interest in baseball. Thomas currently cannot score on the baseball skills test routinely given at the secondary level.

Schedule of Services

Thomas will have adapted physical education on Mondays, Tuesdays, and Thursdays from 9:30 to 10:15. During the weight training unit, he will attend the regular physical education class on Fridays from 1:15 to 2:00.

Transition Services

Thomas loves baseball and frequently attends games with his family or watches games on television. In the spring, Thomas will participate in the Challenger's Baseball program for the first time. Development of baseball skills, with an emphasis on throwing, will take place in the adapted physical education class. Rules of the game will be reinforced both in physical education and at home. Mr. Hernandez will spend additional time each weekend working on batting skills (off a tee and underhand pitch). During the winter Thomas will accompany his older brother to the Fitness Connection gym on Monday and Wednesday afternoons (for strength and aerobic-related activities). Mrs. Hernandez will take Thomas for walks around the community after dinner at least three times per week.

Procedures for Evaluation and Parental Report

Criteria for evaluation are contained in the short-term objectives. Progress on the objectives will be monitored weekly. A final assessment will be conducted during the week of June 1. The Brockport Physical Fitness Test pedometer readings, and the three throwing tests will be used for this evaluation, and the teacher will maintain a record of Thomas's physical provocations. A written report describing Thomas's progress on his goals and objectives will be sent to the parents at least quarterly.

Figure 5.2 *(continued)*

take place at least once every three years) and (2) to determine the educational needs of the child. PLP should also note how the disability affects the child's participation and success in the regular curriculum.

The present level of performance component is the cornerstone of the IEP. The information presented in all subsequent components is related to the information set forth in the PLP. If the PLP is not adequately and properly determined, chances are the student's specially designed instructional program will not be the most appropriate. PLP statements should be objective, observable, and measurable. Ordinarily, the PLP component consists primarily of test results, which can come from standardized tests with performance norms or criteria or from less formal teacher-constructed tests (including authentic assessments). Both standardized and authentic assessment results have roles to play in the IEP. When the purpose of the evaluation is to determine if the student qualifies as a "child with a disability" (especially during the initial evaluation and any triennial re-evaluations), it is important, whenever possible, that the assessment instruments be "technically sound" and have been validated for the purposes for which they are used. Standardized tests are more likely to address these considerations than less formal, teacher-constructed tests. On the other hand, teacher-constructed tests (i.e., authentic assessments) can be very helpful in clarifying the "educational needs of the child." In fact, IDEA requires "current classroom-based assessments and observations" as part of the evaluation of any student under consideration for special educational services. Authentic assessment techniques that are "curriculum embedded" are more likely to address this concern than commercially produced, standardized tests.

PLP information should be presented in a way that places the student on a continuum of achievement—that is, the test results shown should discriminate among levels of ability. For this reason, tests on which students attain either minimum (0 out of 10) or maximum (10 out of 10) scores are not very helpful in determining PLP (although some criterion-referenced tests might simply have pass–fail standards). Also, in situating a student on this continuum, the PLP component should note, to the extent possible, what the student *can* do, not just what he or she cannot do. Finally, PLP information should be presented in a way that is immediately interpretable; it should not require additional detailed explanation from the teacher. When standardized test results are included, it is helpful when percentiles, criterion-referenced standards, or other references are presented as well as the raw scores; teacher-constructed tests should be adequately described so the conditions can be replicated at a later date. (See chapter 4 for information on measurement and assessment in adapted physical education.)

Annual Goals and Short-Term Objectives

Also required on every IEP is a statement of measurable annual goals, including benchmarks or short-term objectives. These goals and objectives relate to: (1) meeting the child's needs that result from the disability so that the child can be involved in and progress in the general curriculum and (2) meeting each of the child's other educational needs that result from the child's disability (Department of Education, 2002).

An annual goal is a broad or generic statement designed to give direction to the instructional program. Once the PLP information has been obtained and studied, the teacher should identify one or more content areas to be emphasized in the student's program. An annual goal focuses on the student's unique needs as identified in the PLP. In fact, this link is a key element in writing an annual goal statement. The annual goal must clearly relate to information presented in the PLP component. For instance, if the PLP contains only information on ball-handling skills, it would be inappropriate to write an annual goal for swimming, physical fitness, or any content area unrelated to ball-handling skills. The need for emphasis on a particular content area must be demonstrated in the PLP.

Although the annual goal is broad or general, a short-term objective (STO) is narrow and specific. An STO is a statement that describes a skill in terms of action, condition, and criterion. Action refers to the type of skill to be performed, such as running. Condition indicates the way the skill is to be performed, such as running 50 yards (about 45 meters). Criterion refers to how well the skill is to be performed, such as running 50 yards in 8.5 seconds. Conditions and criteria used in physical education usually relate to such concepts as "how fast," "how long," "how far," or "how many," although it is also appropriate to describe "how mature." For instance, a 10-year-old student might throw a ball into a wall target 9 out of 10 times from a certain distance. The teacher might be pleased with the accuracy score ("how many"), but if the student does not step with the opposite foot when throwing, the teacher might not be pleased with the quality of the movement pattern ("how mature"). In this case, the teacher might write an STO that describes a movement pattern, rather than an accuracy score, to be attained.

Just as an annual goal must relate to PLP information, STOs must relate to an annual goal. If an annual goal stresses the content area of "eye–hand coordination," the STOs should include skills such as throwing, catching, and striking. The student's baseline (pretest) ability must also appear in the IEP, usually in the PLP component. For example, a short-term objective might specify that a student will be expected to do 15 curl-ups in 60 seconds at some future date; this statement has little meaning unless it is known how many curl-ups the student can do now. In fact, the easiest way to write an STO is to take a well-written PLP statement, copy the action and condition elements verbatim, and make a reasonable change in the criterion. (The teacher uses professional judgment based on experience to determine what constitutes a "reasonable" expectation for improvement.) It should be noted that although STOs are helpful in identifying activities to be conducted in class, they are not meant to supplant daily, weekly, or monthly lesson plans.

Statement of Special Education and Related Services and Supplementary Aids and Services

A third required component of the IEP is a statement of the special education and related services and supplementary aids and services to be provided to the student (or on behalf of the student) as well as a statement of the program modifications or supports for school personnel that will be provided for the student. These services, aids, and supports are provided to help the student progress toward the annual goals, to be involved and progress in the general curriculum as well as in extracurricular and nonacademic activities, and to participate with both students with disabilities and students without disabilities (Department of Education, 2002).

Once the present level of performance is determined and annual goals and short-term instructional objectives are written, decisions must be made regarding the student's educational placement, additional services (if any) to be provided, and the use of special instructional media and materials, as necessary. The placement agreed

on should be considered the least restrictive environment for the student.

In addition to appropriate placement, other special education and related services might be prescribed. A special education service means specially designed instruction that directly affects educational objectives, for example, physical education. Provisions for this service should be specified in this component of the IEP. A related service is designed to assist a student with a disability to benefit from special education. Examples include physical therapy, therapeutic recreation, occupational therapy, psychological services, and speech, language, or hearing therapy.

In some cases, modified pieces of equipment (e.g., a beep baseball, an audible goal locator, a snap-handle bowling ball, or a bowling ramp) and special support personnel (e.g., teacher assistants, paraprofessionals, peer tutors, or volunteers) are required for the education of students with disabilities. These should also be listed in this IEP component.

Statement of Participation in Regular Settings

The IEP must contain an explanation of the extent, if any, to which the child will not participate with children without disabilities in the regular class and in other extracurricular and nonacademic activities (Department of Education, 2002). If a child is removed from the regular physical education setting to participate in an adapted physical education program, for instance, this should be noted in this component of the IEP. Usually this explanation includes a percentage of time the student is excluded from (or included in) the regular educational setting and for what kinds of activities.

Assessment Modifications

Another required IEP component is a statement of individual modifications in the administration of state- or district-wide assessments of student achievement needed in order for the child to participate in such assessment. Further, if it is determined that the child will not participate in a particular assessment, the IEP must include a statement regarding why that assessment is not appropriate for the child and how the child will be assessed instead (Department of Education, 2002). Thus, if a school district routinely administers physical education tests (physical fitness, fundamental motor skills, sports skills, aquatics, and so on) to its students, the appropriateness of those tests for a student with a disability must be considered. In this case, test item modifications or test item substitutions must be provided as necessary and noted on the IEP.

Schedule of Services

A sixth required component is the projected date for the beginning of the services and modifications listed earlier in the IEP and the anticipated frequency, location, and duration of those services and modifications (Department of Education, 2002).

Transition Services

The IEP also requires that beginning at age 14 (or younger, if determined appropriate), a statement of needed transition services for the child must be added (Department of Education, 2002). This component includes goals and actions to help the student transition successfully from the school-based educational program to a community-

based option that will occur no later than age 22. Many students, for instance, might eventually be enrolled in vocational training programs, some will go on to college, and others might enter alternative adult service programs (e.g., group homes, sheltered workshops). School personnel attempt to prepare students for the most appropriate option once they "age out" of school.

For physical education teachers, transition includes extending opportunities for physical activity into the community. Examples include participation in community-based adapted sport, recreation, or leisure programs designed to enhance physical fitness, motor ability, sport skills, social skills, or community adjustment (Modell & Megginson, 2001). Adapted physical educators concerned with student transition should conduct student interviews or administer surveys to determine the sport, recreation, or leisure interests of their students (and their families); take field trips to expose students to community-based, physical activity–related facilities and programs; compile an inventory of community-based,

---

APPLICATION EXAMPLE

Transition Services

Issue: The physical education teacher of a 16-year-old female student must consider strategies for transitioning to community-based physical activity programs under IDEA. The teacher might consider the following steps:

Application:

- Interview the student to learn her physical activity preferences (including those related to sport, recreation, and leisure)

- Contact the family to determine their activity interests and their current and future expectations for their child relative to sport, recreation, and leisure

- Contact representatives from relevant community-based activity-related agencies to determine the feasibility of having the student participating in their programs, including the identification of necessary supports (e.g., equipment or procedural modifications, human assistance)

- Write a physical activity–based individualized transition plan (ITP) that includes goals

(e.g., participate appropriately in the free swim program at the local recreation center), activities to meet the goals (e.g., transportation; checking in; use of locker room, including using the locker, changing clothes, using the showers; swimming skills, pool rules and etiquette), and identification of the people responsible for supporting each activity, including evaluating the student's progress in the activity (e.g., physical education teacher, community service provider, family members, peer tutors, volunteers)

- Design a physical education curriculum that teaches the necessary skills to support transition goals (e.g., swimming skills, pool rules and etiquette)

- Teach those skills in the community-based setting whenever possible (e.g., at the local recreation center pool rather than at the school pool)

- Evaluate progress on the transition goal regularly

physical activity–related facilities and programs that can be used to match with student interests, abilities, and resources; and advocate with community-based, physical activity–related service providers to expand the possibilities for people with disabilities (Modell & Megginson, 2001).

Although IDEA requires only that transition services be included in the IEP (either as a separate component, as described here, or as imbedded in other components of the IEP), some authorities (e.g., Krebs & Block, 1992; Piletic, 1998) have suggested the development of an individualized transition plan (ITP) to address this important element of a student's education. An ITP might list transition goals and the necessary steps or activities for achieving the goals, and, because IDEA defines transition services as a "coordinated set of activities," identify those individuals responsible for each of the activities (see the application example).

Procedures for Evaluation and Parental Report

The final required component of the IEP is a statement of how the child's progress toward annual goals will be measured and how the child's parents will be regularly informed of that progress (IDEA, 2002). This component is used to specify how and when the student's progress will be evaluated. In most cases, progress is determined by testing the written objectives. The evaluation should indicate the extent to which the progress is sufficient to enable the child to achieve the goals by the end of the year. Evaluation can be scheduled to occur at any time within 12 months from the time the IEP takes effect; the IEP must be reviewed at least annually and re-evaluated at least triennially. Parental notification of the progress of a student with a disability must occur at least as often as parents are routinely informed of the progress of a student without disabilities (e.g., the frequency of regular report cards).

DEVELOPMENT OF THE IEP

Procedures for developing an IEP vary slightly from state to state, but essentially the process involves two steps: (1) to determine if the student is eligible for special education services and (2) to develop the most appropriate program, including establishing goals and objectives and determining appropriate placement. The process that results

in the development of an IEP usually begins with a referral. Any professional staff member at a school who suspects that a child might possess a disability can refer the child for an evaluation to determine eligibility for special education. A referral should outline the reasons a disability is suspected, including test results, records, or reports; attempts to remedy the student's performance; and the extent of parental contact before the referral (New York State Education Department, 2002). A sample referral form is shown in figure 5.3 (on page 86). Parents might refer their own children for evaluation when they suspect a problem. In fact, when parents enroll a youngster in a new school, the district will frequently ask them if they feel their child might have a disability. Physicians and judicial officers sometimes make referrals as well.

IDEA requires that an IEP team, consisting of one or both of the student's parents; at least one regular education teacher; at least one special education teacher; a representative of the school district qualified to provide or supervise the provision of special education; the student (when appropriate); and other appropriate individuals, at the discretion of either the parents or the school, be charged with the responsibility of determining special education eligibility (Department of Education, 2002). (The IEP team might go by a different name in different states; in New York, for instance, the team is called the "committee on special education.") In many cases the IEP team will determine unique needs by assessing the results of standardized tests. But before reaching a final decision, the team also considers other information, such as samples of current academic work; the role of behavior, language, and communication skills on academic performance; the amount of previous instruction; and anecdotal accounts, including parental input. On the basis of the information gathered and the ensuing discussion, the IEP team decides if the student is a "child with a disability" and thus qualified for special education; if so, the team recommends a program and a placement setting based on an IEP it has developed.

We should emphasize that the IEP is a negotiated document—both the school and the parents have input into its development and must agree on its contents before it is signed and implemented. In the event the two parties cannot agree on the content of the student's IEP, IDEA provides procedures for resolving the disagreement. These **due process** procedures are designed to protect the rights of the child, the parents, and the school district (figure 5.4, p. 87).

DEPARTMENT OF PHYSICAL EDUCATION REFERRAL FORM

This form should be used by teachers or administrators of physical education to refer students with unique needs to chairpersons of CSE, CPSE, CAPE, or the school building administrator. Referrals should be processed through the office of the APE coordinator to the director of physical education who shall forward the referral to appropriate individuals. Referrals may be made to change the program or placement of the student or for any other action within the jurisdiction of the CSE, CPSE, or CAPE.

Faculty member making referral: Date:

Student referred: Age: Gender:

Present physical education class (if any):

Student's primary or homeroom teacher:

A unique physical education need has been identified for the student:

      By the CSE?   Yes   No

      By the CPSE?   Yes   No

      By the CAPE?   Yes   No

If no, give reasons for believing a unique physical education need exists.

Give test results, records, or reports upon which a referral is based.

Describe prior attempts to remediate student's performance.

Has parental contact been made?   Yes   No   If yes, describe:

If a recommendation for placement or other action is included as a part of this referral, indicate the recommendation:

Referral processed by: Referral initiated by:

(Director of physical education):   (Staff member):

Legend: APE–Adapted Physical Education
         CSE–Committee on Special Education
         CPSE–Committee on Preschool Education
         CAPE–Committee on Adapted Physical Eduction

Figure 5.3   A sample referral form for adapted physical education.

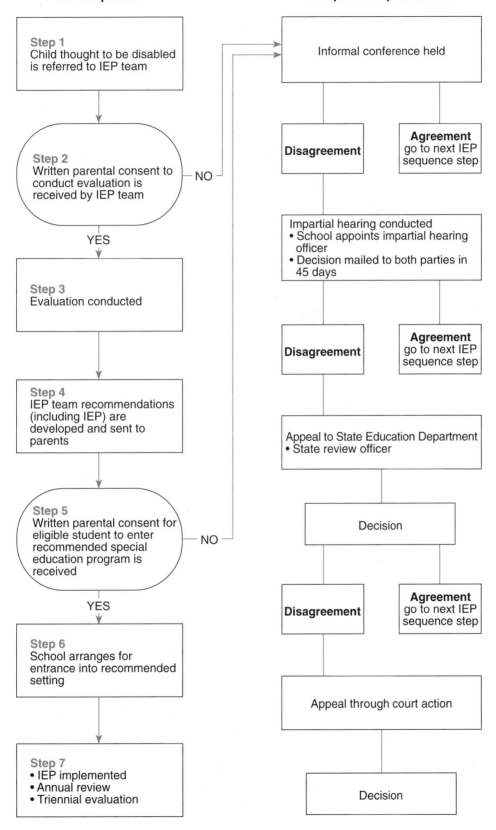

IEP sequence

Step 1
Child thought to be disabled is referred to IEP team

Step 2
Written parental consent to conduct evaluation is received by IEP team

— NO

YES

Step 3
Evaluation conducted

Step 4
IEP team recommendations (including IEP) are developed and sent to parents

Step 5
Written parental consent for eligible student to enter recommended special education program is received

— NO

YES

Step 6
School arranges for entrance into recommended setting

Step 7
• IEP implemented
• Annual review
• Triennial evaluation

Due process procedures

Informal conference held

Disagreement

Agreement go to next IEP sequence step

Impartial hearing conducted
• School appoints impartial hearing officer
• Decision mailed to both parties in 45 days

Disagreement

Agreement go to next IEP sequence step

Appeal to State Education Department
• State review officer

Decision

Disagreement

Agreement go to next IEP sequence step

Appeal through court action

Decision

Figure 5.4   Sample IEP sequence and due process procedures.

THE ROLE OF
THE PHYSICAL EDUCATOR

In the past, many physical educators have not been actively involved in the process of developing an IEP. It is clear, however, that if students with disabilities are to receive the free, appropriate education guaranteed by IDEA, physical education must be included in their IEPs. It is also clear that

An Important Question

When must physical education be described or referred to in the IEP? According to the *Federal Register* (Department of Education, 1998), the answer depends on the type of "PE program arrangement" the student is in.

- *Regular physical education with students without disabilities.* If a student with a disability can participate fully in the regular physical education program without any special modifications to compensate for the student's disability, it would not be necessary to describe or refer to physical education in the IEP. On the other hand, if some modifications to the regular physical education program are necessary for the student to be able to participate in that program, those modifications must be described in the IEP.

- *Specially designed physical education.* If a student with a disability needs a specially designed physical education program, that program must be addressed in all applicable areas of the IEP (e.g., present levels of educational performance, goals, objectives; services to be provided).

- *Physical education in separate facilities.* If a student with a disability is educated in a separate facility, the physical education program for that student must be described or referred to in the IEP. However, the kind and amount of information to be included in the IEP depends on the physical motor needs of the student and the type of physical education program to be provided. Thus, if a student at a residential school for students who are deaf is able to participate in that school's regular physical education program (as determined by the most recent evaluation), then the IEP need only note such participation. On the other hand, if special modifications are required for the student to participate, those modifications must be described in the IEP. Moreover, if the student needs an individually designed physical education program, that program must be addressed under all applicable parts of the IEP.

this is more likely accomplished when physical educators make sure they are involved in IEP development. Although physical education must be included in every IEP, the extent of IEP information required varies depending on the child's educational setting (see sidebar).

Unfortunately, many students are assigned to physical education settings more as a function of convenient scheduling than to meet their educational needs. It is not unusual for students to be evaluated by an IEP team without a physical education assessment being performed. Consequently, students are sometimes assigned to inappropriate physical education programs or placements, and physical education teachers might be assigned students for whom there are no assessment data, long-term goals, or short-term objectives. Thus, we highly recommend that school districts include the teacher of physical education on the IEP team. This educator would determine if the student qualifies for an adapted program and help write the eligible student's initial IEP.

To accurately determine eligibility for adapted physical education, a strong assessment program must be in place. Assessment should reflect as many content areas of physical education as possible. IDEA and this book define physical education as follows: "the development of (a) physical and motor fitness; (b) fundamental motor skills and patterns; and (c) skills in aquatics, dance, and individual and group games and sports (including intramural and lifetime sports)" (Department of Education, 2002, p. 18). The physical educator, therefore, should select assessment instruments that reflect these components. Test results help the physical educator to determine unique needs and justify a program adapted to meet unique needs.

Although documentation of subaverage test performance is important in determining the need for an adapted program, it is not the only criterion to use in making the decision. For instance, an emotionally disturbed student might be placed in a segregated, adapted physical education class even though his or her physical and motor skills are age appropriate. A unique need in the affective domain might prevent safe and successful participation in an integrated physical education class. In this case, a placement in a segregated setting might be justified on the basis of behavioral concerns; a large class size or an emphasis on competitive activities might make a regular physical education class inappropriate for such a student.

SECTION 504 AND THE ACCOMMODATION PLAN

Although section 504 of the Rehabilitation Act of 1973 is more than 30 years old, its implications have continued to be discussed in recent years (French, Henderson, Kinnison, & Sherrill, 1998). One such implication is that because the definition of a "qualified individual with a disability" covered under section 504 is broader than the definition of a "child with disability" covered under IDEA, some students with disabilities will not have IEPs but nevertheless might require (and be entitled to) appropriate accommodations and services. These accommodations and services must be documented in a section 504 accommodation plan, sometimes simply called a 504 plan.

Unlike the IEP, 504 plans do not have mandated components and, consequently, local districts usually develop their own. A sample 504 plan is presented in figure 5.5. The plan is developed by a committee consisting of at least two school professionals (e.g., teachers, nurses, counselors, administrators) familiar with the student and the school district's 504 officer (French, Henderson, Kinnison, & Sherrill, 1998). (School districts with more than 15 employees are required to have a 504 officer designated to monitor the implementation of section 504.) Technically, 504 does not require a full evaluation by a multidisciplinary diagnostic team as IDEA does, but clearly the assessment should focus on areas of student need that might necessitate evaluations by more than one professional.

The elements of the 504 plan found in figure 5.5 are self-explanatory, but the reader should note

SECTION 504 ACCOMMODATION PLAN

Name: Date of birth: Grade:

School: Date of meeting:

1. Describe the nature of the problem.

2. List evaluations completed, including dates of each evaluation.

3. List the basis for determining that the child has a disability (if any).

4. Describe the nature of the child's disability.

5. Does the disability affect a major life activity? If "yes," explain how.

6. List the accommodations (e.g., specialized instruction or equipment, auxiliary aids or services, program modifications, and so on) the team recommends as necessary to ensure the child's access to all district programs.

Review/reassessment date: (must be completed)

Participants (name and title):

cc: Student's cumulative file

Attachment: Information regarding Section 504 of the Rehabilitation Act of 1973 Due Process Notice

Date:

Figure 5.5   Sample 504 accommodation plan.

that item 5 ("Does the disability affect a major life activity?") is particularly important. To meet the definition of a "qualified person with a disability" under section 504, the student must have a physical or mental impairment that substantially limits one or more major life activities (Workforce Investment Act, 1998). Usually the accommodations listed in the plan (see item 6) are selected to help the student benefit from instruction in the regular classroom. More restrictive educational placements, although possible, would have to be justified.

THE STUDENT WITHOUT DISABILITIES WITH UNIQUE NEEDS

As mentioned at the beginning of this chapter, students without disabilities who have unique needs in physical education are not covered by IDEA or by section 504. School districts, however, still must provide an appropriate education for these students.

We recommend here that school districts establish a **Committee on Adapted Physical Education (CAPE)** to address unique needs of students without disabilities in physical education. This committee should consist of at least three members: the director of physical education or designee, the school nurse, and the teacher of adapted physical education. When possible, the student's regular physical education teacher should also be a member of the committee, and a school administrator should be available for consultation. The function of this committee is to determine the student's eligibility for an adapted program; define the nature of that program, including placement; and monitor the student's progress. A recommended procedure is outlined in figure 5.6 and discussed in the following seven steps. These may be modified as necessary to meet the needs of local school districts.

- Step 1. Referrals to CAPE ordinarily are made to the chairperson of the committee by a physical educator, family physician, parent, or even the student, when it is felt that the student has a unique need in physical education. CAPE should consider only those referrals in which the needs are believed to be long term (more than 30 days).

- Step 2. When CAPE receives a referral form (from a source other than the parents), the committee should notify the parents of the referral and indicate that an adapted program will be considered. The notification should point out

that physical education is a required subject area under state law (where applicable) and that "blanket" excuses, waivers, or substitutions are not appropriate options; that development of an "adapted" program would not mean that the district considers the student to have a disability under IDEA or section 504; and that any change in program will be reviewed periodically (at least annually). Parents should also be invited to submit their own concerns or aspirations for their child's physical education program.

- Step 3. In the case of a medical excuse or referral, CAPE should contact the family physician to determine the nature of the condition or disease and the impact on physical education. CAPE should also consult the student's regular physical education teacher to determine the student's performance level and any difficulties the student experiences in his or her current program. It might also be necessary to conduct additional testing to better understand the student's strengths and weaknesses.

- Step 4. After considering all the information collected in step 3, CAPE must decide if a specially designed (adapted) program is appropriate for this student. If the student does not have a unique need, the parents are informed, and the process is over. If, however, the student is eligible for an adapted program, CAPE must develop an individualized physical education program (IPEP) for the student. The IPEP is similar to the IEP and should include program goals, present level of performance (including any medical limitations), short-term objectives, placement and schedule of services, and a schedule for review.

- Step 5. Parents are notified of CAPE's decision. If the student is eligible, parents should receive an explanation of the adapted program and a copy of the IPEP. It is also recommended that the regular physical education teacher and, in the case of a medically initiated referral, the family physician receive copies of the IPEP as well. (The district should have due process procedures comparable to those depicted in figure 5.4 in place, if the parents do not agree with CAPE's decision or with the program outlined in the IPEP.)

- Step 6. The adapted program described in the IPEP is implemented. Most IPEPs can probably be implemented in an integrated placement. In cases in which a segregated placement is recommended, however, districts must obtain parental permission before changing the placement, unless the board of education has different and appropriate procedures.

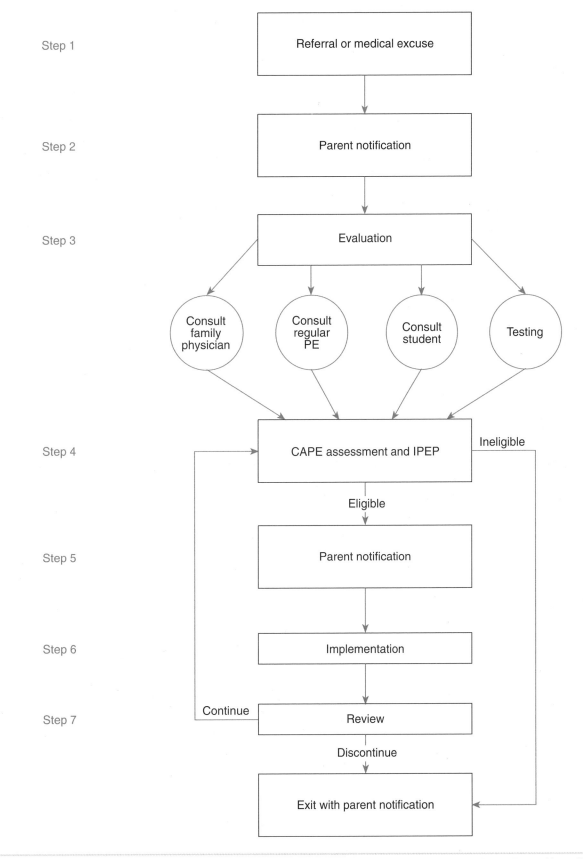

Step 1	Referral or medical excuse
Step 2	Parent notification
Step 3	Evaluation

Consult family physician   Consult regular PE   Consult student   Testing

| Step 4 | CAPE assessment and IPEP |

Ineligible

Eligible

| Step 5 | Parent notification |

| Step 6 | Implementation |

Continue

| Step 7 | Review |

Discontinue

Exit with parent notification

Figure 5.6 A recommended procedure for evaluating the need for adapted physical education services for students without disabilities.

- Step 7. The IPEP will be in effect for the time specified under "schedule for review." At the conclusion of this time, CAPE evaluates the student's progress and decides whether to continue or discontinue the program.

Formation of a CAPE (or equivalent) is solely at the discretion of the local school district. Districts must recognize, however, that a student need not be classified as having a disability to possess a unique need in physical education. Once that notion is acknowledged, it is incumbent on districts to develop procedures to ensure such students receive an appropriate education. Given the mounting prevalence of obesity in this country, for instance, the IPEP provides an option for schools looking to help all students defeat a serious fitness-related problem.

SUMMARY

Students might be eligible for adapted physical education, regardless of disability, if they exhibit a unique need. IDEA and section 504 of the Rehabilitation Act of 1973 provide procedures for the modification of educational programs for students with disabilities. These individualized programs are spelled out in documents required by the legislation. Infants and toddlers (ages zero to two) who meet the criteria established by IDEA may receive early intervention services under the act. These services must be documented in an IFSP. Similarly, individualized programs for qualified children (ages 3 to 21) also are governed by IDEA. In this case, however, the individualized program is documented in an IEP. Not all students with disabilities qualify for services under IDEA, but they might still be entitled to modified programs under section 504. These modified programs must be described in a section 504 accommodation plan. Finally, there might be students without disabilities in a school district who have unique needs in physical education. These youngsters would not qualify for services under either IDEA or 504 but might still require a modified physical education program. Although not required by law, it is suggested that districts develop written IPEPs to document the adapted physical education program.

REFERENCES

Department of Education (2002). *Code of Federal Regulations, 34 CFR, Parts 300 to 399, July 1, 2002.*

Department of Education (1998). *Federal Register,* 34 CFR Ch. III, July 1, 1998.

French, R., Henderson, H., Kinnison, L., & Sherrill, C. (1998). Revisiting Section 504, physical education and sport. *Journal of Physical Education, Recreation and Dance,* 69(7), 57-63.

Krebs, P., & Block, M. (1992). Transition of students with disabilities into community recreation: The role of the adapted physical educator. *Adapted Physical Activity Quarterly,* 9(4), 305-315.

Modell, S., & Megginson, N. (2001). Life after school: A transition model for adapted physical educators. *Journal of Physical Education, Recreation and Dance,* 72(2), 45-48, 53.

New York State Education Department (2002). *Part 200—Students with Disabilities.* Office of Vocational and Educational Services for Individuals with Disabilities, Albany, NY: Author.

Piletic, C. (1998). Transition: Are we doing it? *Journal of Physical Education, Recreation and Dance,* 69(9), 46-50.

Workforce Investment Act of 1998 (P.L. 105-220). Sec 401 *et seq.* (1998).

WRITTEN RESOURCES

Zirkel, P. (1993). *Section 504 and the schools.* Horsham, PA: LRP Publications.

This resource manual comes in a loose-leaf notebook format and addresses issues related to 504 and the education of students with disabilities. Bibliographic references and sample forms are included.

ELECTRONIC RESOURCES

A guide to the individualized education program. Web site: www.ed.gov/offices/OSERS/OSEP/Products/IEP_Guide/#IEPGuide

This site is designed to assist educators, parents, and state and local educational agencies in implementing IDEA with regard to IEPs. Links to regional resource centers.

Council for Exceptional Children. Web site: www.cec.sped.org/bk/catalog2/iep.html

This site provides a catalog of available books and resources related to IEP development.

IDEAPractices. Web site: www.ideapractices.org

Sponsored primarily by the CEC and U.S. Office of Special Education Programs, this site provides information on IDEA, including the opportunity to read or print the law and regulations, news, frequently asked questions, and professional development resources.

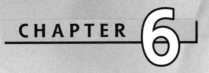

CHAPTER 6

Behavior Management

E. Michael Loovis

Mr. Smith, the physical education teacher at Middlefield Junior High School, has been assigned an eighth-grade class into which several students with behavioral disorders have been integrated. Although the class is reasonably well behaved, one student, Robert, has a difficult time staying on task, and he is constantly uncooperative, often getting into arguments with other students in class. Mr. Smith has instituted a token economy system in which time on task and reduced frequency of uncooperative behavior earn points that are displayed on a clipboard that he carries and that are available to Robert for him to assess his performance during class. During the first day that the token economy was in effect, Mr. Smith noticed that Robert was paying attention to his instructions and participating effectively in drills. Mr. Smith approached Robert and said, "Good work, Robert, you've earned one point." Then Mr. Smith placed one point on the chart. A little later, Robert told Sam, one of his teammates, that he had done a "good job." Mr. Smith told Robert, "That was a very nice thing to say to Sam; you've just earned another point." At this rate, Robert has a good chance to earn three points, which is the number required to exchange points earned for backup reinforcers. With help from Mr. Smith, Robert had previously determined what the reinforcers are. If Robert earns the prescribed number of points, he can redeem them for the opportunity to choose from a menu of reinforcers that include his choice for culminating activity of the day, free time in the gym on Friday, or serving as captain for his group during the next class period. Successful implementation of this behavior-modification strategy will result in Robert staying on task and significantly reducing, or even eliminating, the number of times he gets into arguments with classmates.

For years, educators confronting problems with inappropriate behavior have used a host of behavior-management practices, in worst cases including corporal punishment, suspension, and expulsion. In most cases, these practices are **reactive**—that is, a particular method is applied after a particular misbehavior has occurred. However, many of the problems that educators face on a daily basis could be prevented if they took a more **proactive** approach toward managing student behavior. Implicit in this statement is the discontinuation of ineffective practices (Mendler, 1992). For example, it is difficult for a physical educator to establish an appropriate instructional climate in a self-contained class for students with behavior disabilities when several students persist in being verbally and physically abusive toward the teacher and other class members.

From another perspective, behavior-management interventions include "all those actions (and conscious inactions) teachers . . . engage in to enhance the probability that children, individually and in groups, will develop effective behaviors that are personally fulfilling, productive, and socially acceptable" (Walker & Shea, 1999, p. 7). For example, a behavior-management approach can help a physical educator determine the appropriate level at which to begin instruction in golf for students with intellectual disabilities (mental retardation) and to maintain the students' enthusiasm for learning the activity over time. Behavior management has also been used to teach those appropriate social behaviors considered essential to performance in school, at home, and in other significant environments. In this chapter we offer several proactive approaches to help teachers and coaches achieve the goals and objectives of their programs in a positive learning environment. It should be noted that physical educators probably use an eclectic or pragmatic approach to behavior management, depending on what they perceive works best in a given situation. In this chapter, the following approaches are highlighted: behavior modification, psychoeducational, psychodynamic, ecological, biogenic, and humanistic. We will start by discussing behavior modification in some detail.

BEHAVIOR MODIFICATION

Behavior modification is a systematic process in which the environment is arranged to promote skill acquisition and shape social behavior. More specifically, behavior modification is the application of reinforcement learning theory derived from operant psychology. Behavior modification includes such procedures as **respondent conditioning** (the automatic control of behavior by antecedent stimuli), **operant conditioning** (the control of behavior by regulating the consequences that follow a behavior), **contingency management** (the relation between a behavior and the events that follow it), and **behavioral modeling**, also called **observational learning** (learning through observing another individual engaged in a behavior). All of these procedures have one thing in common: the planned systematic arrangement of consequences to alter an individual's response (or at least the frequency of that response). As it relates to an IEP designed to improve physical fitness, this arrangement could involve the use of rewards to encourage students with intellectual disabilities to engage in sustained exercise behavior when riding stationary bicycles. It could also mean establishing a contract with a student who has cerebral palsy to define a number of tasks to be completed in a unit on throwing and catching skills.

To understand behavior modification, you must understand some basic terminology. On the assumption that behavior is controlled by its effect on the environment, the first step toward understanding the management of human behavior is to define the stimuli that influence people's behavior. A measurable event that might have an influence on behavior is referred to as a **stimulus.**

Reinforcement is a stimulus event that increases or maintains the frequency of a response. In physical education, reinforcement may be thought of as feedback provided directly or indirectly by the teacher or coach. Reinforcers can be physical, verbal, visual, edible, or active in nature. Examples of reinforcers include a pat on the back (physical), an approving comment such as "Good job!" (verbal), a smile (visual), a piece of candy (edible), or a chance to bounce on a trampoline (active). All of these examples are usually considered positive reinforcers. Positive reinforcers, or rewards, are stimuli that individuals perceive as good, that is, as something they want. If a response occurs and it is positively reinforced, the likelihood of the response recurring under similar circumstances is maintained or increased. For example, a teacher might praise a student who demonstrates appropriate behavior during instruction in the gym. If praise is positively reinforcing to that student, the chances of the student's attending to instruction in the future are strengthened. **Positive reinforcement** is one of the basic principles of operant conditioning described in this section. Certainly positive reinforcement is the preferred strategy in adapted physical education; to the extent possible, the entire instructional experience should be positive. Figure 6.1 illustrates this principle as well as the others examined in this chapter. The presence of aversive or "bad" stimuli—something individuals want to avoid—is commonly called **negative reinforcement.** If a response occurs, and if it successfully averts a negative stimulus, the likelihood of the desired response recurring under similar circumstances is maintained or increased.

Because positive and negative reinforcement might produce similar results, the distinction between them is sometimes not readily apparent. An example might clarify the difference. Suppose that a student has been talking to a friend and distracting the teacher and the rest of the class while the teacher is explaining a lesson. If the teacher had warned that continual talking would result in after-school detention or a low grade for the day (possible aversive stimuli), and if the student perceived the stimuli as something to avoid, then the likelihood that the student would attend to instructions would increase. By listening in class the student would avoid staying after school or having his or her grade reduced. This is an example of negative reinforcement because the stimulus increased the likelihood of a desired behavior through the avoidance of an aversive consequence rather than the presentation of a positive one.

Just as teachers and coaches seek to maintain or increase the frequency of some behaviors, they might want to decrease the occurrence of others. When the consequence of a certain behavior has the effect of decreasing its frequency, the consequence is called **punishment.** Punishment can be either the presentation of an aversive stimulus or the removal of a positive stimulus. The intention of punishment is to weaken or eliminate a behavior. The following scenario illustrates the effect of punishment on the student in the example we just looked at. The student has been talking during instructional time. The teacher has warned the student that continual talking will result in detention or a grade reduction. The student ignores the warning and continues to talk. The consequence for talking when one is supposed to be listening, at least in this situation, will be the presentation of one of the two aversive stimuli.

A slightly different scenario illustrates the notion of punishment as the removal of a positive stimulus. Our student, still talking after the teacher's warning, is punished by being barred from a five-minute free-time activity at the end of class—an activity perceived as a positive stimulus. The removal of this highly desirable activity fits the definition of punishment and weakens or eliminates the disruptive behavior in future instructional episodes.

In contrast to punishment, withholding of reinforcement after a response that has previously been reinforced results in **extinction** or

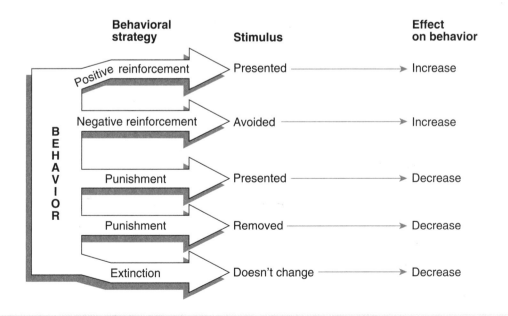

Figure 6.1 Principles of operant conditioning.

cessation of a behavior. Extinction differs from punishment in that no consequence follows the response; a stimulus (aversive or positive event) is neither presented nor taken away. For example, teachers or coaches who pay attention to students when they clown around might be reinforcing the very behavior they would like to see eliminated. If they ignore (i.e., stop reinforcing) the undesired behavior, the behavior will probably decrease in frequency.

Table 6.1 summarizes the basic principles of behavior modification. Each principle has a specific purpose; application of the principles requires that teachers or coaches analyze behaviors carefully before attempting to change them.

The examples provided in table 6.1 illustrate the range of learning principles available to teachers and coaches who want to change student behaviors. No one principle is the best choice all the time; which one to apply depends on the specifics of the situation. Later in this chapter (and again in chapter 9, p. 167), recommendations are provided that originate from the work of Dunn, Morehouse, and Fredericks (1986). After reading the section on their rules of thumb (chapter 9), you are encouraged to review table 6.1 to better understand the place of selected learning principles in behavior-modification strategies.

TYPES OF REINFORCERS

Several types of reinforcers can be used in behavior modification, including primary (unconditioned), secondary (conditioned), and vicarious reinforcers. The use of highly preferred activities to control the occurrence of less preferred responses, known as the **Premack Principle**, is another reinforcer.

- *Primary reinforcers.* **Primary (or unconditioned) reinforcers** are stimuli necessary for survival. Examples include food, water, and other phenomena that satisfy biological requirements such as the needs for sleep, warmth, and sexual stimulation.

- *Secondary reinforcers.* **Secondary (or conditioned) reinforcers** acquire their reinforcing properties through learning. A few examples are praise, grades, money, and completion of a task. Because secondary reinforcers must be learned, stimuli or events must often be paired repeatedly with other primary or secondary events before they will become reinforcers in their own right.

- *Vicarious reinforcers.* The essence of **vicarious reinforcement** is in observing the reinforcing or punishing consequences of another person's behavior. As a result of vicarious reinforcement, the observer will either engage in the behavior to receive the same positive reinforcement or avoid the behavior to avert punishment.

- *Premack Principle.* According to the Premack Principle (Premack, 1965), activities that have a high probability of occurrence can be used to elicit low-probability behaviors. To state it another way, Premack implies that activities in which an individual or group prefers to engage can be used as positive consequences or reinforcers for activities that are not especially favored.

Table 6.1 Behavior: Consequences, Classification, and Probable Effect

Behavior exhibited	Consequences	Classification	Effect
Susan engages effectively in drills.	Teacher praises Susan.	Positive reinforcement	Susan will continue to do well in drills.
Juan forgets to wear his gym uniform.	Teacher suggests that next time he will lose 5 points.	Negative reinforcement	Juan wears his gym uniform.
Tenora forgets her tennis shoes for the second day in a row.	Teacher deducts 5 points from her grade.	Punishment	Tenora will not forget her shoes next class.
Bill makes aggravating noises during class.	Teacher ignores Bill's noises.	Extinction	Bill will stop making noises during class.
Chris is overly aggressive during game play in class.	Teacher withdraws opportunity to participate in free time at end of class.	Punishment	Chris will tone down his aggressiveness during game play.

SCHEDULES OF REINFORCEMENT

When using the behavior-modification approach, the teacher or coach must understand when to deliver a reinforcer to attain an optimal response. During the early stages of skill acquisition or behavior change, it is best to provide reinforcement after every occurrence of an appropriate response. This is called **continuous reinforcement**. After a behavior has been acquired, continuous reinforcement is no longer desirable or necessary. In fact, behavior is best maintained not through a process of continuous reinforcement but through a schedule of intermittent or partial reinforcement. Several types of intermittent schedules exist, but the two most common ones are ratio and interval schedules.

In **ratio schedules**, reinforcement is applied after a specified number of "defined" responses have occurred. **Interval schedules**, on the other hand, provide reinforcement when a specified time has elapsed since the previous reinforcement. Thus, a ratio schedule is based on a preestablished number of responses, whereas an interval schedule is based on time between reinforcements. Associated with each of these major schedule types are two subtypes: **fixed** and **variable**. When these types and subtypes are combined, four alternatives for dispensing reinforcement are available. Both fixed and variable ratio schedules of reinforcement produce high response rates (e.g., providing praise every second successful throw or every third successful throw on average). In the case of interval reinforcement, a fixed schedule produces a high response rate just prior to the time for the next reinforcement. Conversely, there is a cessation of responding after reinforcement (e.g., praising the first successful throw at the end of each one-minute interval). Variable intervals of reinforcement, on the other hand, produce consistent response rates because the individual cannot predict when the reinforcer will be dispensed (e.g., praising the first successful throw at the end of an average three-minute interval).

PROCEDURES FOR INCREASING BEHAVIOR

Once it is determined that either a behavior not currently in a student's repertoire is desired or the frequency of a given behavior needs to be altered, the targeted response must be defined in measurable and observable terms. This response will be an observable instance of performance having an effect on the environment. After clear identification has been made, behavioral intervention can begin. The following discussion highlights several of the more popular strategies for increasing desirable behavior, including shaping, prompting, chaining, modeling, token economy, fading, and contingency management.

- *Shaping.* The strategy of **shaping** involves administering reinforcement contingent on the learning and performance of sequential steps leading to development of the desired behavior. Shaping is most often employed in the teaching of a new skill. Once the terminal or desired behavior has been learned, it is no longer necessary to perform all steps in the progression. For example, the use of shaping to teach a dive from a one-meter board might include the following progression: kneeling dive from a 12-inch elevation, squat dive from a 12-inch elevation, standing modified dive from a 12-inch elevation, squat dive from diving board, and standing modified forward dive from the diving board. Once the dive from the one-meter board has been learned, there is no longer any reason to perform the steps in the progression.

- *Chaining.* Unlike shaping, which consists of reinforcing approximations of a new terminal behavior, **chaining** develops a series of discrete portions or links that, when tied together, lead to enhanced performance of a behavior. Chaining is distinct from shaping in that the steps necessary to achieve the desired or terminal behavior are performed each time the response is emitted. In shaping, the steps in the progression are not considered essential once the terminal behavior has been mastered.

There are two types of chaining: forward and backward. In forward chaining, the initial step in the behavioral sequence occurs first, followed by the next step, and so forth until the entire sequence has been mastered (see the behavior management application example). A student learning to execute a lay-up from three steps away from the basket would take a step with the left foot, take a step with the left foot while dribbling once with the right hand, repeat the previous step and add a step with the right foot, and repeat the previous step with an additional step and jump off the left foot up to the basket for the lay-up attempt. In some cases a student's repertoire is limited, or the last step in the sequence is associated with a potent reinforcer. Under these circumstances, it might be necessary to teach the last step in a behavioral sequence first, followed by the next-to-last step, and so on until the entire sequence is learned. This is called backward chaining.

• *Prompting*. Events that help initiate a response are called **prompts**. These are cues, instructions, gestures, directions, examples, and models that act as antecedent events and trigger a desired response. In this way the frequency of responses and, subsequently, the chances of receiving reinforcement are increased. Prompting is very important in shaping and chaining procedures. Prompts can be thought of as a system of more or less intrusive or direct cues. Prompts are arranged in descending order of intrusiveness, from verbal to visual to physical assistance. The object of the system of least prompts is to encourage a response by using the least intrusive or direct cue; for example, a student who requires a visual prompt from a teacher is receiving a less intrusive prompt than one who requires physical assistance to perform the same behavior. Another form of prompting commonly used during instruction with individuals with mental retardation and autism is "redirection." The purpose of a "redirect" is to communicate an alternative means to engage the learner's attention on the task at hand. The redirect can be in the form of a physical or gestural cue, including pointing, touching materials, or touching the person's hand (if touching can, in fact, be tolerated) (Jones, 1998).

• *Fading*. The ultimate goal of any procedure to increase the frequency of a response is for the response to occur without the need for a prompt or reinforcer. The best way to reach this goal is with a procedure that removes or fades the prompts and reinforcers gradually over time. **Fading** reinforcers means stretching the schedule of reinforcement so that the individual must perform more trials or demonstrate significantly better response quality in order to receive reinforcement. For example, someone who has been receiving positive reinforcement for each successful basket must now make two baskets, then three baskets, and so on before reinforcement is provided.

• *Modeling*. The strategy of **modeling** is a visual demonstration of a behavior that students are expected to perform. From a behavioral perspective, modeling (compare it to vicarious reinforcement) is the process in which an individual watches someone else respond to a situation in a way that produces reinforcement or punishment. The observer thus learns vicariously.

• *Token economy*. Tokens are secondary reinforcers that are earned, collected, and subsequently redeemed for a backup reinforcer. Tokens, which might be poker chips or checkmarks on a response tally sheet, are earned and exchanged for consumables, privileges, or activities, which are the backup reinforcers. A reinforcement system based on tokens is called a **token economy**. Establishment of a token economy includes a concise description of the targeted behavior or behaviors along with a detailed accounting of the numbers of tokens administered for performance of targeted behaviors.

• *Contingency management*. When you change a behavior by providing a stimulus contingent on

APPLICATION EXAMPLE

Behavior Management

Setting: An elementary physical education class

Student: A 9-year-old student with high functioning autism with delays in throwing and catching

Unit: Fundamental motor skills and patterns

Task: Throwing with a mature, functional throw—at the very least stepping with the leg opposite the throwing arm

Application: The physical educator might do any of the following:

• Use forward chaining of the throwing mechanics

• Use a visual prompt, such as a footprint, to aid in the stepping action

• Use continuous reinforcement until correct throwing is well established

• Fade visual prompt (e.g., footprints) as student becomes more consistent in performance

the occurrence of a desired response, you are practicing **contingency management** (Walker & Shea, 1999). The most sophisticated form of contingency management is the behavioral contract. Basically, the contract (which is an extension of the token economy) specifies the relation between behaviors and their consequences. The well-developed contract contains five elements: a detailed statement of what each party expects to happen; a targeted behavior that is readily observable; a statement of sanctions for failure to meet the terms of the contract; a bonus clause, if desirable, to reinforce consistent compliance with the contract; and a monitoring system to keep track of the rate of positive reinforcement given (Kazdin, 2001). An example of a behavioral contract appears in chapter 9, page 163.

PROCEDURES FOR DECREASING BEHAVIOR

On occasion, the behavior of an individual or a group needs to be decreased. Traditionally, decreasing the frequency of behavior has been accomplished using extinction, punishment, reinforcement of alternative responses, and time out from reinforcement. In this section we will stress management techniques that are positive in nature because they have been successful in reducing or eliminating a wide range of undesirable behaviors. Moreover, these techniques model socially appropriate ways of dealing with troublesome behaviors and are free of the undesirable side effects of punishment. Reinforcement is ordinarily viewed as a process to increase, rather than decrease, behavior. Consequently, extinction and punishment are most often mentioned as methods for decreasing behaviors. In this section we highlight the use of reinforcement techniques to decrease behavior (Parrish, 1997).

• *Reinforcement of other behavior.* Reinforcing an individual for engaging in any behavior other than the targeted behavior is known as **differential reinforcement of other behavior.** The reinforcer is delivered as long as the targeted behavior (e.g., inappropriate running during the gym class) is not performed. Thus, the student receives reinforcement for sitting on the floor and listening to instructions, standing quietly and listening to instructions, sitting on the bleachers and listening to instructions—anything other than inappropri-

ate running during class. This reinforcement has the effect of decreasing the targeted response.

• *Reinforcement of incompatible behavior.* This technique reinforces behaviors that are directly incompatible with the targeted response. For example, a student has a difficult time engaging cooperatively in games during physical education class. The opposite behavior is playing cooperatively. The effect of reinforcing cooperation during game playing is the elimination of the uncooperative response. Unlike reinforcement of other behavior, this strategy defines diametrically opposed behaviors—playing uncooperatively versus playing cooperatively—and reinforces instances of positive behavior only.

• *Reinforcement of low response rates.* With a technique known as **differential reinforcement of low rates of responding,** a student is reinforced for gradually reducing the frequency of an undesirable behavior or for increasing the amount of time during which the behavior does not occur. For instance, a student who swears on the average of five times per day would be reinforced for swearing only four times. This schedule would be followed until swearing was eliminated completely.

The three techniques just discussed use positive reinforcement to decrease the frequency of undesirable behavior. Research does suggest, however, that acceptable levels of behavior might not be achieved without a punishment component (Lerman & Vorndran, 2002). For example, in cases in which the factors that maintain behavior cannot be identified or controlled or in which rapid behavior suppression is necessary to prevent physical harm, punishment might be part of the behavior-management strategy. (In recognition of the breadth and diversity of behavior-modification techniques, we will soon describe more traditional methods of decreasing inappropriate behaviors.)

• *Punishment.* Normally, punishment is thought of as the presentation of an aversive consequence contingent on the occurrence of an undesirable behavior. In the Skinnerian (or operant psychology) tradition, punishment also includes the removal of a positively reinforcing stimulus or event, which is referred to as **response cost.** In either case, the individual is presented with a consequence that is not pleasing or is deprived of something that is very pleasing. For instance, a student who is kept after school for being disobedient is most likely experiencing punishment.

Likewise, the student who has failed to fulfill a part of the contingency contract in the class and thus has lost some hard-earned tokens that "buy" free time in the gym is experiencing punishment. Response cost is most effective when used in combination with systematic reinforcement of appropriate behavior (Thibadeau, 1998). In each case the effect is to reduce the frequency of the undesirable behavior. Walker and Shea (1999) detail the advantages and disadvantages of using punishment. One advantage is the immediacy of its effect; usually, an immediate reduction occurs in the response rate. Punishment can also be effective: (1) when a disruptive behavior occurs with such frequency that reinforcement of an incompatible behavior is not possible and (2) for temporarily suppressing a behavior while another behavior is reinforced. The disadvantages of punishment are numerous, including undesirable emotional reactions, avoidance of the environment or person producing the punishment, aggression toward the punishing individual, modeling of punishing techniques by the individual who is punished, and reinforcement for the person who is delivering the punishment. Additionally, physical punishment might result in physical abuse to the person, although that may not have been the intent. For these reasons positive reinforcement is strongly encouraged in physical education for students with disabilities. Emphasis should always be on creating positive instructional environments that promote successful experiences.

- *Time out.* Time out is an extension of the punishment concept. We have mentioned that punishment often involves the removal of a positive event. The time-out procedure is based on the assumption that some positive reinforcer in the immediate environment is maintaining the undesirable behavior. In an effort to control the situation, the individual is physically removed from the environment and consequently deprived of all positive reinforcement for a specified time. The three basic types of time-out procedure are observational, exclusion, and seclusion (Lavay, French, & Henderson, 1997). In observational time out, the student is removed from an activity but is permitted to watch as classmates engage in the lesson. Exclusion time out, on the other hand, isolates the student within the physical education setting without opportunity to observe what is going on in the lesson. Finally, seclusion time out completely isolates the student, removing him or her from the physical education setting.

IMPLEMENTING A BEHAVIOR MODIFICATION PROGRAM

On a daily basis, behavior modification is used in some form by most people: parents, teachers, coworkers, and students. In ordinary situations, however, the use of behavior modification might not be thorough and regular. On the other hand, the deliberate application of reinforcement learning principles in an attempt to change behavior is a systematic, step-by-step procedure. Minimally there are four steps that, if implemented correctly, provide a strong basis for either increasing or decreasing the frequency of a particular behavior. These steps include identifying the behavior, establishing a baseline, choosing the reinforcer, and scheduling the reinforcer.

- *Identifying the behavior.* The first step is to identify the behavior in question. This is not as easy as it might sound because it entails fulfilling two criteria. The first is that the behavior must be observable; specifications that distinguish one behavior from another are clearly established. Measurability is the second criterion; it assumes that the frequency, intensity, and duration of a behavior can be quantified. Sportsmanship, for example, could be defined as the number of times students compliment their opponents for good performance during a game.

- *Establishing baseline.* Once the targeted behavior has been identified, the next step is to determine the frequency, intensity, and duration of its occurrence. This process, known as establishing baseline, consists of observing the individual or group in a natural setting with no behavioral intervention taking place. Baseline determination should occur across at least three sessions, days, periods, classes, or trials. Baseline is important as the comparison against which any programmatic gains are measured; it requires precise and accurate recording based on the criteria described in step 1. There are several recording systems; the choice depends on the nature of the behavior being observed. The most frequently used recording systems record event, duration, and interval. Event recording entails counting the exact number of times a clearly defined behavior occurs during a given period (e.g., the number of acts of good sportsmanship during a game or class period). Duration recording, on the other hand, measures the amount of time a student spends engaged in a particular behavior (e.g., cumulative time demonstrating good sportsmanship during a game). When reliable estimates of behavior are desired, and when these observations are made during specific time periods, interval recording may be used. An example of interval recording is counting the number of 10-second intervals during which students demonstrate good sportsmanship, as defined in the first (identification) step of the behavior-modification program.

- *Choosing the reinforcer.* Once it has been determined that a behavior requires modification and the baseline data confirms this suspicion, the success of the behavior-modification program depends on choosing the most effective reinforcer. Two important factors influence this choice. First, the type of reinforcer effective in a given situation depends on the individual. Not all reinforcers work with all people, you must ascertain which is best. A second factor is quantity. Within limits, more reinforcement is probably better. However, when teachers and coaches reinforce in excessive amounts, satiation results, and the reinforcer loses its value and effectiveness.

- *Scheduling the reinforcer.* With the reinforcer chosen, the next step is to schedule its use. The previous discussion of schedules is applicable here, with one very important reminder. When initiating a behavior-change strategy, try to reinforce continuously. Once the behavior has shown desired change, reinforcement should be reduced gradually. It is this shift that maintains the new behavior at a desirable rate. One last thing to say about scheduling: The longer reinforcement is delayed, the less effective it becomes.

USES OF BEHAVIOR MODIFICATION IN PHYSICAL EDUCATION AND SPORT

Dunn (1997) suggests that evidence supports the use of behavior modification in both segregated and inclusive programs for students with special needs. Dunn and colleagues (Dunn, Morehouse, & Fredericks, 1986) developed a Data-Based Gymnasium (DBG) for teaching students with severe and profound disabilities in physical education. Successful implementation of the DGB depends on systematic use of the behavioral principles discussed in this section. Additionally, Dunn and

colleagues have provided rules of thumb that guide the use of behavioral techniques in teaching skills and changing social behaviors. These include the use of naturally occurring reinforcers such as social praise or an extinction (i.e., ignoring a behavior). Tangible reinforcers such as food, toys, or desirable activities, which are earned as part of a token economy system, are not instituted until it has been demonstrated that the consistent use of social reinforcement or extinction is ineffective.

In skill-acquisition programs, task-analytic phases and steps are individually determined, and students move through the sequence at a rate commensurate with their ability. For example, a phase for kicking with the toe of the preferred foot consists of having students "perform a kick by swinging the preferred leg backward and then forward, striking the ball with the toes of the foot, causing the ball to roll in the direction of the target" (Dunn, Morehouse, & Fredericks, 1986, p. 81). Steps represent distances, times, or number of repetitions that might further subdivide a particular phase (e.g., kicking the ball with the toe of the preferred foot a distance of 10, 15, or 20 feet). Decisions about program modifications or changes in the use of behavioral strategies (rules of thumb) are made on an individual basis after each student's progress is reviewed. Further discussions of the DBG and the "rules of thumb" for managing inappropriate behavior in physical education with students with severe disabilities can be found in chapter 9.

Advantages of using behavior modification include the following:

- It considers only behaviors that are precisely defined and capable of being seen.

- It assumes that knowing the cause of a particular behavior is not a prerequisite for changing it.

- It encourages a thorough analysis of the environmental conditions and factors that might influence the behavior(s) in question.

- It facilitates functional independence by employing a system of least prompts—that is, a prompt hierarchy is used that is ordered from least to most intrusive.

- It requires precise measurement to demonstrate a cause-and-effect relation between the behavioral intervention and the behavior being changed.

Disadvantages of behavior management that should be considered before implementing such a program include the following:

- The actual use of behavioral principles in a consistent and systematic manner is not as simple as it might seem.
- Behavioral techniques might fail when what is thought to be the controlling stimulus is in fact not so in reality (e.g., a Premack falsely constructed on the assumption that an individual prefers a particular activity is destined to be unsuccessful).
- Behavioral techniques might not work initially, requiring more thorough analysis by the teacher to determine if additional techniques would be useful; this can entail implementing a new approach immediately, if necessary.

EXAMPLE OF BEHAVIOR ANALYSIS

The process for implementing a behavioral system requires reasonably strict adherence to several well-defined steps. This process is referred to as **applied behavior analysis.** The following example illustrates the teaching of a skill using a limited number of behavioral principles.

Skill: Standing long jump

Baseline: In a pretest condition, the student is observed on three occasions performing the long jump with faulty mechanics, most notably in the takeoff and landing portions of the jump.

Objective: When requested to perform a standing long jump, the student jumps a minimum of three feet, demonstrating appropriate form on takeoff, in the air, and on landing.

Choosing reinforcer: Teacher determines that social reinforcement (namely, verbal praise) is effective.

Scheduling reinforcer: Teacher decides to use continuous reinforcement initially and then switch to a variable ratio as learning and performance increase.

Prompt: Using the system of least prompts, the instructor employs prompts in the order presented from least to most intrusive depending on the ability of the student to perform the task: (a) "Please stand behind this line and do a standing long jump" (verbal prompt); (b) "Please stand behind this line, bend your knees, swing your arms backward and forward like this, and jump as far as possible" (verbal plus visual prompt); and (c) "Please stand behind this line, bend your knees, feel how I'm moving your arms so they swing back and forth like this, and jump as far as possible" (physical guidance prompt).

Behavior: Student acknowledges prompts, correctly assumes long-jump position, and executes long jump as intended.

Reinforcement: Teacher says, "Good job!" (verbal reinforcement).

Subsequent behavior: Student likely maintains or improves on the performance.

OTHER APPROACHES

The management of behavior has been the concern of individuals and groups with various theoretical and philosophical views. No fewer than five major approaches have been postulated to remediate problems associated with maladaptive behavior. Two models (either singly or in combination) guide most educational programs today (Hallahan & Kauffman, 2003): the behavioral and psychoeducational approaches. One of these approaches, behavior modification, we have already discussed. The second approach, psychoeducational, will be discussed in the next sections along with the psychodynamic, ecological, biogenic, and humanistic approaches. These interventions are discussed only briefly. Resources are suggested at the end of the chapter for those who wish to further explore a particular intervention and its primary proponents.

Psychoeducational

The psychoeducational approach views inappropriate behavior as students' maladaptive attempt to cope with their environment; it assumes that academic failure and misbehavior can be remediated directly if students are taught how to achieve and behave effectively. This approach emphasizes the education of the student's "self," balancing the educational and psychological perspectives. It focuses on the affective and cognitive factors associated with the development of appropriate social and academic readiness skills useful in home, school, and community. Its proponents recognize that some students do not understand "why" they behave as they do when their basic instincts, drives, and needs are not satisfied. Psychoeducation is concerned with the "here and now." Although it acknowledges the influence of past events on students' behavior and psyche, it is less concerned with explanations for this behavior. Identifying students' potentials for education and emphasizing their learning abilities are more important functions of this approach. Diagnostic procedures include observational data, measures of achievement, performance in situations requiring particular skills, case histories, and consideration of measures of general abilities.

The psychoeducational approach focuses on strengthening the student's ego and his or her relationships with teachers. This is accomplished through compensatory educational programs that encourage students to acknowledge that what they are doing is a problem, to understand their motivations for behaving in a certain way, to observe the consequences of their behavior, and to plan alternate responses or ways of behaving in similar circumstances.

When a behavioral crisis occurs (or shortly thereafter), a teacher trained in the psychoeducational approach conducts a **life-space interview (LSI)**, a term first used by Redl (1952). The purpose of LSI is to help the student either overcome momentary difficulties or work through long-range goals.

The psychoeducational approach assumes that making students aware of their feelings and having them talk about the nature of their responses will give them insight into their behavior and help them develop control. This approach emphasizes the realistic demands of everyday functioning in school and at home as they relate to improving inappropriate behaviors.

Among several strategies teachers can use to implement the psychoeducational approach are self-instruction, modeling and rehearsal, self-determination of goals and reinforcement standards, and self-reward.

Teachers are in an advantageous position to encourage students to use self-instructional strategies. This means helping students to reflect on the steps in good decision making when it is time to learn something new, solve a problem, or retain a concept. Fundamentally, the process involves teaching students to listen to their private speech, that is, those times when people talk either aloud or subvocally to themselves. For example, a person makes a faulty ceiling shot in racquetball and says, "Come on, reach out and hit the ball ahead of the body!" Self-instruction can be as simple as a checklist of questions for students to ask themselves when a decision is required. What is my problem? How can I do it? Am I using my plan? How did I do? Such questions are examples of the kind asked within the self-instructional process.

In the modeling-rehearsal strategy, students who have a difficult time controlling their behavior watch others who have learned to deal with problems similar to their own. Beyond merely observing the behavior, the students can see how the models respond in a constructive manner to a problematic situation. Modeling could include the use of relaxation techniques and self-instruction. Students can also learn appropriate ways of responding when time is provided to mentally rehearse or practice successful management techniques.

Another strategy that has proven effective in helping students control their behavior works by including them in the establishment of goals, reinforcement contingencies, or standards. An example of this process occurs when a group of adolescents with behavior disabilities determines which prosocial behaviors each member needs to concentrate on during an overnight camping trip. Likewise, the group establishes the limits of inappropriate behavior and decides what the consequences will be if anyone exceeds these limits.

A final strategy used in the psychoeducational approach is self-reward, which involves preparing students to reward themselves with some preestablished reinforcer. For example, a student who completes the prescribed tasks at a practice station might immediately place a check on a recording sheet posted at that station. When the checkmarks total a specified number, the student is thus instrumental not only in seeing that the goal of the lesson is achieved but also in efficiently implementing the reinforcement process.

Psychodynamic

Most closely associated with the work of Freud, the psychodynamic approach has evolved as a collection of many subtheories, each with its own discrete intervention. The focus of this approach, in any case, is the cause of psychological dysfunction. Specifically, the psychodynamic approach strives to improve emotional functioning by helping students understand *why* they are functioning inappropriately. This approach encourages teachers to accept students but not accept their undesirable behavior. The approach emphasizes helping students to develop self-knowledge through close and positive relationships with teachers. From the psychodynamic perspective, the development of a healthy self-concept, including the ability to trust others and have confidence in one's feelings, abilities, and emotions, is basic and integral to "normal" development. If the environment and significant others are not supportive, anxiety and depression might result. Self-perceptions and perceptions of others can become distorted; the result might be impaired personal relationships, conflicting social values, inadequate self-image, ability deficits, and maladaptive habits and attitudes.

In an attempt to identify the probable cause(s) of inappropriate behavior, the psychodynamic approach uses diagnostic procedures such as projective techniques, case histories, interviews, observational measures of achievement, and measures of general and specific abilities. Through interpretation of diagnostic results and an analysis of prevailing symptoms, the cause of the psychic conflict is, ideally, identified. Once the primary locus of the emotional disturbance is known, an appropriate treatment can be determined.

Conventional pyschodynamic treatment modalities include psychoanalysis, counseling interviews, and psychotherapeutic techniques (such as play therapy and group therapy). Treatment sessions involve the student alone, although some therapists see only the parents. Recently, family therapy has become popular, with students and parents attending sessions together. Regardless of how the session is configured, it is designed to help students develop self-knowledge.

The psychodynamic approach, including psychoanalysis and psychotherapy, is not regarded as an exemplary approach to intervention. Teachers might be employed at settings in which this approach is advocated, but such settings are usually directed by psychiatrists. Overall, it is not a common approach applied in traditional educational settings. An example of a psychodynamic approach was the Buttonwoods Farms project in Philadelphia. The psychodynamic approach has several inadequacies that include the following: diagnostic study is time consuming and expensive; the results of diagnostic study yield only possible causes for emotional conflict; and therapeutic outcomes are similar regardless of the nature of the intervention—whether students are seen alone or with parents, or are seen in play therapy or in group counseling.

But there are several prevalent misconceptions about the psychodynamic approach. Teachers should be aware that implementation of psychodynamic theory does not preclude working with groups. Its primary goal need not be increasing students' personal awareness. Teachers do not need to be permissively accepting, deal with the subconscious, or focus on problems other than those presenting real concerns in the present situation.

Ecological

The ecological approach assumes behavioral problems are caused by a disturbance in the student's environment or ecosystem. In effect, the student and the environment affect each other in a reciprocal and negative manner (i.e., some characteristic of the student disturbs the ecosystem, and the ecosystem responds in a way that causes the student to further agitate it). "The problem arises because the social interactions and transactions between the child and the social environment are inappropriate" (Hallahan & Kauffman, 2003, p. 222). Said another way, the problems that a student has are affected by the environment; the student is not the only one causing the problems. For example, a student who cannot get to class on time and is thus in conflict with teachers might be reflecting his culture's disdain for punctuality rather than disrespect for the teacher or the school schedule.

Evaluative procedures for assessing the cause(s) of disturbed behavior are difficult at best. Educators have purported to use a five-phase process for collecting ecological data: describing the environment, identifying expectations, organizing behavioral data, summarizing the data, and establishing goals.

Additionally, the Behavior Rating Profile (BRP-2) examines behaviors in several settings from several points of view. The profile consists of three student rating subscales, one teacher rating scale, one parent rating scale, and a sociogram (a diagram or chart that uses connecting lines to indicate choices made in groups). The purpose of the profile is to define deviant behavior specific to one setting or to one individual's expectations (Brown & Hammill, 1990).

The goal of the ecological approach is not simply to stop a disturbed or unwanted behavior but to change an environment, such as the home, in substantive ways so that it will continue to support desirable behavior once the intervention is withdrawn. Generally speaking, the focus of intervention within the ecological approach is on either one environment or, more likely, two or more environments. Interventions that focus on only one environment, however, are frequently unsuccessful, given that typically the behavior in question is prominent in more than just one location (Cullinan, Epstein, & Lloyd, 1991). For example, if a student is experiencing the same problems at home and in school, intervention must address how the behavior will be handled in both places.

Educational applications of the ecological approach are designed to make environments accommodate individuals rather than helping individuals to fit environments. In a classroom, this might require physical and psychological adaptations, such as individual or small-group work areas, time-out areas, or reinforcement centers. This approach entails having teachers create environments in which students succeed rather than anticipate failure. Changes in the home ecosystem might require parental involvement (e.g., talking with parents), respite care, or family therapy. At times, changes in several ecosystems are required (e.g., home, school, and community).

Present-day attempts to establish ecologically based programs include the creation and implementation of behavioral interventions as part of the IEP. Schools may no longer expel students with special needs regardless of whether the action was related to their disability; however, services may be provided in alternative settings. To develop an effective behavioral intervention, educators must engage in a three-step process: perform a functional assessment of the student's behavior, determine and implement intervention strategies, and evaluate the results. Assessing the student's behavior includes observation and recording of behavior patterns in several settings (e.g., classroom, playground, cafeteria, gym), with the intention of profiling the student's conduct. Establishing a baseline helps teachers understand either why a student is behaving in a certain way or who is controlling or reinforcing a student's behavior.

After completing the functional assessment, teachers develop and implement an intervention. The intervention should set realistic goals, including the acceptance of behaviors that would ordinarily not be deemed appropriate. For example, a student who fights with a teammate each time he misses a shot during a basketball drill will realistically be permitted to shout or curse at that same teammate, as long as he does not physically assault the student. After a while, shouting and cursing would be similarly faded. As many people as possible who work with the student should develop the intervention plan. Behavioral interventions must be team based so that the student experiences consistency. The student should also participate in developing the behavioral intervention.

Evaluation of the intervention plan is the final step. Teachers assess how effective the plan is and if modifications are necessary. Most experts agree that evaluation should occur monthly, if not weekly.

Biogenic

The central focus of the biogenic approach is neurophysiological dysfunction. Closely associated with the medical model, this approach relies on diagnostic techniques that explore signs and symptoms. Physicians attempt to localize problems using neurological soft signs (e.g., the results of gait and postural assessments); timed, repetitive movements; and visual motor sequencing tasks. Lack of definitive results might prompt the use of electroencephalography (EEG), computed tomography (CT), or magnetic resonance imaging (MRI) if lesser diagnostics prove uneventful. Identification of students with disabilities in this realm is made on the basis of general behavioral characteristics (e.g., hyperactivity, distractibility, impulsiveness, emotional lability) and specific functional deficits (e.g., disorders in perception, language, motor ability, and concept formation and reasoning). The manifestation of these characteristics and deficits is attributable to injury or damage to the central nervous system.

The biogenic approach places considerable importance on etiological factors. The integrity of the central nervous system is assessed on the basis of performance in selected activities or tests, such as walking a line with eyes closed, touching a finger to the nose, or reacting to various stimuli such as pain, cold, and light. Additionally, a neurological examination including an EEG is often a part of the diagnosis. Following diagnosis, treatment might include drug therapy, surgical procedures (e.g., removal of a tumor), physical therapy, sensory integrative therapy, or developmental training.

A major strategy associated with the biogenic approach is drug therapy (though the use of drugs as a means of controlling or modifying behavior cuts across several behavioral approaches).

Students are medicated for the management of such behaviors as short attention span, distractibility, impulsiveness, hyperactivity, visual motor impairments, and large motor coordination problems. Psychotropic drugs represent the major category of substances used to control emotional, behavioral, and cognitive changes of individuals with disabilities. These drugs include medications typically classified as antipsychotic, antianxiety, antidepressant, antimania, stimulant, or sedative–hypnotic. The most common categories of psychotropic drugs for the purpose of this discussion are stimulants, neuroleptics, and antidepressants.

• *Stimulants.* Stimulants are administered primarily for the management of attention deficit and hyperactive disorder (ADHD). In fact, ADHD is the only condition other than obesity and narcolepsy for which there is FDA approval for the use of stimulants. The most frequently prescribed family of stimulants is the methylphenidate hydrochlorides. These include Ritalin, (the most commonly prescribed), Concerta (a long-acting form prescribed for children under six years of age), Metadate CD, Metadate ER, and Methylin ER (Schatzberg, Cole, & DeBattista, 2003). All of these drugs are adjunctive therapy and are used with students who experience moderate to severe hyperactivity, short attention span, distractibility, emotional lability, and impulsiveness. Possible side effects include loss of appetite, weight loss, and insomnia. These effects are noted to be more profound in individuals with intellectual disabilities (Arnold, Gadow, Pearson, & Varley, 1998).

• *Neuroleptics.* These drugs, also called tranquilizers, remain the most widely prescribed class of psychotropic medications for individuals with intellectual disabilities. They are also used to control bizarre behavior in psychotic adults. In children they are used to control hyperactivity, aggression, self-injury, and stereotypic behavior. Tranquilizers are classified as either major or minor. Major tranquilizers, also called antipsychotics, include such drugs as Mellaril (thioridazine hydrochloride), Thorazine (chlorpromazine hydrochloride), and Haldol (haloperidol), all of which are prescribed for the management of psychotic disorders, including severe behavior disorders marked by aggressiveness and combativeness (Baumeister, Sevin, & King, 1998). Possible side effects of the major and minor tranquilizers include dizziness, drowsiness, vertigo, fatigue, diminished mental alertness (which could impair performance in physical activities), tardive dyskinesia (involuntary movements of the tongue and facial muscles), and movement disorders, referred to as the extrapyramidal effect.

• *Antidepressants.* Antidepressants are prescribed to adults to alleviate depression. In children they have a more diverse function, including not only the management of obsessive–compulsive disorder (OCD), affective disorders, and ADHD but also the treatment of nocturnal enuresis and, to a lesser extent, ritualistic behavior, self-injurious behavior, and aggression. Perhaps because of the documented side effects of the antidepressant drugs—ataxia, muscle weakness, drowsiness, anxiety, sleep disruption, decreased appetite, increased blood pressure, and mental dullness (Sovner et al., 1998)—physical educators and coaches should know when students are receiving such medication. Commonly prescribed antidepressants include Anafrani (clomipramine) and Tofranil (imipramine), which is used for ADHD where patients show excessive side effects or fail to respond favorably to stimulants.

Humanistic

Based on the work of Maslow (1970), the humanistic approach has as its basis the self-actualization theory. Five primary human needs are identified in ascending order, including physiological, safety, belongingness and love, esteem, and self-actualization. According to this theory of motivation, the human, who seeks to meet unsatisfied needs, will satisfy lower-level needs first and then satisfy needs at progressively higher levels as lower ones are met. For example, someone lacking food, safety, love, and esteem would probably hunger for food more strongly than for anything else. But when the need for food is satisfied, the other needs become stronger. In the need hierarchy, self-actualization is the fulfillment of one's highest potential. Maslow considered the following traits as among attributes of self-actualized people: accepting, spontaneous, realistic, autonomous, appreciating, ethical, sympathetic, affectionate, helpful, intimate, democratic, sure about right and wrong, and creative.

Self-actualization is the process of becoming all that one is fully and humanly capable of becoming. In large measure self-actualization is developed naturally by persons without disabilities. Persons with disabilities, on the other hand, might not achieve the same relative status of self-actualization as their peers without disabilities because they sometimes lack the intrinsic motivation and external assistance to become all they are capable of becoming. The desire to move people with disabilities toward self-actualization is supplied, at least initially, by those who care about these people as individuals first and foremost and as individuals with disabilities to a secondary degree.

In the sixth revision of her text on adapted physical education, Sherrill (2004) and colleagues have continued to draw extensively and build on self-actualization theory of Abraham Maslow—as well as the noted psychotherapist Carl Rogers' concept of the fully functioning self and the newer sources in attitude theory and disability studies—to guide a humanistic orientation to adapted physical education in general and to affective development in particular. She is not only the spokesperson for the humanistic philosophy but also its instrumentalist in that she applies its concepts in the gym and on the sports field. In an effort to demonstrate how the humanistic philosophy can be translated into action, Sherrill and her colleagues suggest that teachers and coaches of students with disabilities do the following:

- To the degree possible, use a teaching style that encourages learners to make some of the major decisions during the learning process. This implies that students should be taught with the least restrictive teaching style or one that most closely matches their learning styles.

- Use assessment and instruction that are success oriented. If learning tasks are sufficiently broken down (i.e., task analyzed), positive reinforcement and success will characterize the learning environment. No matter where students score in terms of the normal curve, they have worth as human beings and must be accepted as such.

- Listen to and communicate with students in an effort to encourage them to take control of their lives and make personal decisions affecting their physical well-being. Counseling students to become healthy, fit, and self-actualized requires the skills of active listening, acceptance, empathy, and cooperative goal setting. Such interaction helps individuals with disabilities reinforce their internal locus of control.

- Use teaching practices that enhance self-concept. The following practices are recommended: (a) show students that someone genuinely cares for them as human beings; (b) teach students to care about each other by modeling caring behavior in daily student and teacher interactions; (c) emphasize social interaction by using cooperative rather than competitive activities; and (d) build success into the instructional plan through the careful use of task and activity analysis.

SUMMARY

Behavior management approaches have been used successfully to facilitate skill acquisition, either directly, through systematic manipulation of content, or indirectly, through arrangement of the consequences of performance to produce more motivation. Additionally, lack of discipline has been identified as one of the most significant problems confronting public school teachers. An equally significant, albeit insidious problem, is how to replace old, worn-out thinking about how discipline should be delivered in favor of effective, proactive practices. A number of behavior-management systems are available that can significantly affect skill acquisition or reduce the need to discipline students. As students with behavior disabilities are integrated into a regular class and demonstrate persistent disruptive behavior, a behavior-management program designed to alleviate the problem might include any of the following: behavior modification using a token economy system; a psychoeducational approach using the life-space interview; a psychodynamic approach incorporating play therapy; a biogenic approach using medication; a humanistic approach using self-actualization, self-concept, and attitude theory; an ecological approach using a behavior intervention plan that includes the school as well as the student's home and community environment; or an eclectic use of these approaches, which in adapted physical education is the more common scenario. We should acknowledge that physical educators use mainly behavior modification, humanistic, and psychoeducational approaches, depending on the setting in which they are instructing.

REFERENCES

Arnold, L.E., Gadow, K., Pearson, D.A., Varley, C.K. (1998). Stimulants. In S. Reiss & M.G. Aman (Eds.), *Psychotropic medication and developmental disabilities: The international consensus handbook* (pp. 229-257). Washington, DC: American Association on Mental Retardation.

Baumeister, A.A., Sevin, J.A., & King, B.H. (1998). Neuroleptics. In S. Reiss & M.G. Aman (Eds.), *Psychotropic medication and developmental disabilities: The international consensus handbook* (pp. 133-150). Washington, DC: American Association on Mental Retardation.

Brown, L.L., & Hammill, D.D. (1990). *Behavior rating profile: An ecological approach to behavioral assessment* (2nd ed.). Austin, TX: Pro-Ed.

Cullinan, D., Epstein, M.H., & Lloyd, J.W. (1991). Evaluation of conceptual models of behavior disorders. *Behavioral Disorders, 16,* 148-157.

Dunn, J.M. (1997). *Special physical education: Adapted, individualized, developmental* (7th ed.). Madison, WI: Brown & Benchmark.

Dunn, J.M., Morehouse, J.W., & Fredericks, H.D.B. (1986). *Physical education for the severely handicapped: A systematic approach to a data based gymnasium.* Monmouth, OR: Teaching Research.

Hallahan, D.P., & Kauffman, J.M. (1997). *Exceptional children: Introduction to special education* (6th ed.). Englewood Cliffs, NJ: Prentice Hall.

Hallahan, D.P., & Kauffman, J.M. (2003). *Exceptional learners: Introduction to special education* (9th ed.). Needham Heights, MA: Allyn & Bacon.

Hellison, D.R. (2003). *Teaching responsibility through physical activity* (2nd ed.). Champaign, IL: Human Kinetics.

Jones, M.M. (1998). *Within our reach: Behavior prevention and intervention strategies for learners with mental retardation and autism.* Reston, VA: Division of Mental Retardation and Developmental Disabilities of the Council for Exceptional Children.

Kazdin, A.E. (2001). *Behavior modification in applied settings* (6th ed.). Belmont, CA: Wadsworth/Thomson Learning.

Lavay, B.W., French, R., & Henderson, H.L. (1997). *Positive behavior management strategies for physical educators.* Champaign, IL: Human Kinetics.

Lerman, D.C., & Vorndran, C.M. (2002). On the status of knowledge for using punishment: Implications for treating behavior disorders. *Journal of Applied Behavior Analysis, 35,* 431-464.

Maslow, A.H. (1970). *Motivation and personality* (2nd ed.). New York: Harper & Row.

Mendler, A.N. (1992). *How to achieve discipline with dignity in the classroom.* Bloomington, IN: National Educational Service.

Parrish, J.M. (1997). Behavior modification. In M.L. Batshaw (Ed.), *Children with disabilities* (4th ed.) (pp. 657-686). Baltimore, MD: Brookes.

Premack, D. (1965). Reinforcement theory. In D. Levine (Ed.), *Nebraska symposium on motivation.* Lincoln, NE: University of Nebraska Press.

Redl, F. (1952). *Controls from within.* New York: Free Press.

Safran, S.P., & Oswald, K. (2003). Positive behavior supports: Can schools reshape disciplinary practices? *Exceptional Children, 69,* 361-373.

Schatzberg, A.F., Cole, J.O., & DeBattista, C. (2003). *Manual of clinical psychopharmacology* (4th ed.). Washington, DC: American Psychiatric Publishing.

Sherrill, C. (2004). *Adapted physical education, recreation, and sport: Crossdisciplinary and lifespan* (6th ed.). St. Louis: McGraw-Hill.

Sovner, R., Pary, R.J., Dosen, A., Geyde, A., Barrera, F.J., Cantwell, D.P., & Huessy, H.R. (1998). Antidepressants. In S. Reiss & M.G. Aman (Eds.), *Psychotropic medication and developmental disabilities: The international consensus handbook* (pp. 179-200). Washington, DC: American Association on Mental Retardation.

Thibadeau, S.F. (1998). *How to use response cost.* Austin, TX: Pro-Ed.

Walker, J.E., & Shea, T.M. (1999). *Behavior management: A practical approach for education* (7th ed.). Upper Saddle River, NJ: Prentice-Hall.

WRITTEN RESOURCES

Hall, R.V., & Hall, M.L. (Eds.) (1999). *How to manage behavior series* (2nd ed.). Austin, TX: Pro-Ed.

This series consists of 15 self-instructional manuals that cover a broad range of behavioral topics including but not limited to selecting reinforcers; planning generalization; using group contingencies; using planned ignoring; using positive practice, self-correction, and overcorrection; and using prompts to initiate behavior. Each manual provides a clear definition of the procedure, examples of how the procedure is used, and opportunities for the reader to respond in a programmed text format.

AUDIOVISUAL RESOURCES

Almost everything you ever wanted to know about motivating people: Maslow's hierarchy of needs. (Videotape, 1987). Salenger Educational Media, 1635 12th Street, Santa Monica, CA 90404.

Basic needs such as food, shelter, security, recognition, and achievement are reviewed in light of Maslow's hierarchy of needs; their meaning for motivation in organizational settings is analyzed and illustrated using dramatized incidents. Running time is approximately 16 minutes.

Painting a positive picture: Proactive behavior management. (Videotape, 1994). Indiana Bureau of Child Development, 402 E. Washington Street, Indianapolis, IN 46204.

This video examines and illustrates how to manage children's behavior while maintaining a perspective between discipline and punishment. Includes scenarios portraying young children in childcare and daycare situations. Running time is approximately 28 minutes.

Teaching people with developmental disabilities. (Videotape, 1988). Research Press, Box 31775, Champaign, IL 60820).

This film is a hands-on training program illustrating how to use task analysis, prompting, reinforcement, and error correction to teach functional skills to individuals with mild to moderate developmental disabilities. Running time is approximately 88 minutes.

Three approaches to psychotherapy. III. Pt. 2. (Videotape, 1986). Psychological & Educational Films, PMB #252, E. Coast Highway, Corona Del Mar, CA 92625.

This video highlights Dr. Donald Meichenbaum illustrating his methods of cognitive behavior modification therapy. Running time is approximately 47 minutes.

ELECTRONIC RESOURCES

PsychoEd.Net, www.psychoed.net.

This site provides information about psychoeducation. It is primarily oriented toward educators of moderately and severely emotionally disturbed students. Childcare workers and mental health professionals might also find this information helpful. Psychoeducational approaches helpful for troubled children and youth are presented.

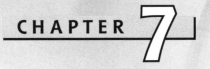

Instructional Strategies for Adapted Physical Education

Douglas H. Collier

"Whenever Peter and Jasmine come to physical education, I just get this tight feeling across my chest. Yes, I know I should be able to accommodate them, and I'd like to be able to, but I just don't feel qualified, so I get nervous. Peter has been diagnosed with Asperger's syndrome and Jasmine has Down syndrome. That's as much as I know. Oh, yes—I get an aide when they come to the gym with their 30 classmates. So, they have Asperger's syndrome and Down syndrome . . . what am I supposed to do with that information? On the one hand, I'm glad they're in the physical education class with their buddies. On the other hand, I wish I had better ideas of how to work with them. Do I change my approach? My curriculum? What if the other students get angry—or bored? What if I don't have time for all the others? Boy, with all the different skill levels and learning styles I see, I wish I'd been a little better prepared . . ."

Teaching physical education in an effective, efficient fashion so that students learn and retain meaningful content is a challenging undertaking, made more so by the increasing diversity of the student body (Siedentop & Tannehill, 2000). Although, as outlined in chapter 2, multiple physical education environments exist for students with identifiable disabilities, they are frequently being integrated into their neighborhood schools and are being taught in the same classes as their peers without disabilities (Block, 2000; Dunn, 1997). Thus, planning and presenting appropriate physical education content require—now more than ever—attention to individual differences. This does *not* mean coming up with a laundry list of instructional modifications based on perceived characteristics of a particular disability type. For example, it would be inappropriate to say, "If she has been diagnosed with autism, I'd better avoid physical prompts. Given he has Down syndrome, I'll expect oppositional behavior." Instructional decisions are not based only on a student's medical or behavioral diagnosis. Rather, instructional modifications, if needed, are also predicated on the individual learning style, strengths and shortcomings of the student, and the objectives of the class. For example, some students with autism will learn more effectively through a command style of teaching, whereas other students, with the same diagnosis, will learn more effectively when given options on how to perform a given skill. Langendorfer (1986) eloquently noted that physical educators have long known that all students come to physical education with different strengths, learning styles, and rates of learning and that the effective teacher takes these varying abilities or differences into account when planning, delivering, and assessing content. "The presence of persons in a group with more apparent differences does not alter the basic fact that differences were there all along. It simply forces the teacher and learner to better face those differences" (Langendorfer, 1985, p. 177).

Teaching quality physical education classes to typically developing students is a demanding and challenging undertaking that requires motivation, an extensive knowledge base, lots of practice, and appropriate feedback from skilled observers. When the classes include students with unique needs—whether the setting is integrated or segregated—the heterogeneity of our classes clearly is increased. Siedentop and Tannehill (2000) have noted that a committed and competent physical education teacher has extensive skills in the areas of conceiving and planning the curricula, managing behavior and teaching the content, optimizing the program through appropriate administration, and creatively linking the school-based program to community-based opportunities. These skills are required to an even greater degree when teaching students with unique needs. As well, the physical education teacher who works with students who have unique needs faces additional challenges that have not been traditionally emphasized in teacher preparation programs. These challenges include writing goals and objectives for individualized education plans (IEPs) or individualized family service plans (IFSPs), adapting activities, task analyzing activities (breaking skills into smaller parts), providing appropriate prompting, training and managing volunteers, working with parents and allied professionals as part of an interdisciplinary team, and effectively managing idiosyncratic or challenging behavior.

In this chapter we will provide information that directly relates to effectively instructing learners with unique needs. This information will assist the teacher in structuring an appropriate physical education environment that optimizes learning.

PHILOSOPHICAL APPROACHES TO ADAPTED PHYSICAL EDUCATION AND SPORT

Teachers of adapted physical education who implement individualized physical education programs of a high quality believe in each participant's inherent worth and are dedicated to the development of their full human potential. These general characteristics are present in two primary orientations that have influenced adapted physical education over the past quarter century—**humanism** and **applied behavior analysis.** Although humanism and applied behavior analysis (also referred to as behavior therapy, behaviorism, and behavior modification) have different traditions, emphases, and often employ different empirical tools, they share a commitment to providing the most advanced and highest quality instruction for people with and without disabilities. Both traditions emphasize nonaversive, affirming teaching strategies—in terms of both skill acquisition and the management of challenging behaviors. Teachers who embrace the humanistic approach as well as those who view themselves as applied behavior analysts recognize the inherent challenges of teaching learners with unique needs and believe that, despite these challenges, the learners are entitled to—and at all times deserve—respect. Instructional methodologies that best allow people to be self-reliant and productive while maintaining individual dignity are hallmarks of first-rate programs that embrace either of these philosophical perspectives. Although often cast as an "either-or" proposition, the thoughtful practitioner is able to embrace the best of each tradition without hypocrisy. Indeed, from an ethical and at times strategic perspective, proponents of each tradition have much in common. Both orientations, as noted, stress the importance of human dignity. There have been social policies and movements as well as economic priorities that have marginalized people with disabilities. Practitioners from both the humanistic and applied behavior analysis perspectives stand together in creating appropriate environments where people with unique needs can live full, positive, and valued lives.

Humanistic Philosophy

Humanism emphasizes the pursuit and teaching of such human qualities as creativity, choice, awareness, and personal and social responsibility. It is a hopeful and extremely positive view of human beings, holding that everyone—including, clearly, people with unique needs—has the capacity to develop a positive self-image, be self-determining, and be intrinsically motivated. Practitioners and researchers adhering to a humanistic philosophy view development in a holistic fashion. That is, mind, body, and spirit cannot be divided. Rather, educational experiences are designed to benefit the whole person. A catching activity would be constructed so that the student would be appropriately challenged physically, intellectually, and affectively. The activity, by its nature, would promote and preserve self-esteem (Sherrill, 2004). According to Carl Rogers, "An assumption unusual in psychology today is that the subjective human being has an important value which is basic; that no matter how he may be labeled and evaluated he is a human person first of all, and most deeply."

Humanistic philosophy began in the late 1950s with the work of Abraham Maslow (1908-1970) and Carl Rogers (1902-1987), considered two of the intellectual leaders of the movement. Their works in the area of human motivation, Maslow's self-actualization theory (Maslow, 1987), and Roger's fully functioning self theory gave humanistic psy-

chology its initial momentum. These researchers viewed human nature as essentially good, positing that all people have a substantial capacity to be self-determining.

Maslow's self-actualization theory informs practitioners embracing a humanistic approach to physical education. Evolving from his writings on the "hierarchy of human needs," self-actualization theory hypothesizes that basic physiological needs such as thirst and hunger must be taken care of—at least minimally—before the more creative or aesthetic needs can be satisfied (see figure 7.1). What Maslow refers to as "deficit needs" (physiological, safety, belonging, and esteem) must be taken care of hierarchically and generally require help from significant others in a student's environment (e.g., parents, teachers, peers). Once these "deficit needs" have been taken care of, self-actualization (an individual's fulfillment of his or her potential) can take place. Self-actualization, referred to as "being needs," are intrinsically motivated and are possible to attain once self-esteem has been achieved.

This hierarchy has implications for adapted physical educators. As students with unique needs take part in physical education, it must be established that physiological needs (food, water, appropriate medication, temperature) have been met. The teacher of adapted physical education, at times, meets this need. With regard to safety, adapted physical educators must go beyond

Figure 7.1 Maslow's theory of self-actualization.

physical considerations and address the psychological climate of the gymnasium. Are the students with unique needs learning in an environment free from anxiety and confusion? Have learning and assessment activities been selected that build trust and confidence and set the student up to succeed? In terms of Maslow's third tier—belonging—are students with unique needs accepted and appreciated by their peer group and teachers for who they are and not for what they can do? Students must feel safe and accepted before they can benefit from instruction that will improve competence and lead to enhanced self-esteem.

Often, people with unique educational needs demonstrate low fitness and movement skill levels and, at times, little motivation to improve. They might have done poorly in the past, possibly in a public forum, and see no reason for this state of affairs to change. It is up to the skilled teacher to design meaningful learning experiences that allow for success. Once basic self-esteem needs are met, the individual might be led to "feelings of self-confidence, worth, strength, capability, and adequacy, of being useful and necessary in the world" (Maslow, 1987, p. 21). This arrival at the "self-actualization" level (further subdivided into self-actualization, enlightenment, and aesthetic–creative levels) can be attained only to the degree that a student feels at home in the world.

Carl Rogers, Maslow's contemporary, has also made significant contributions in the areas of education, special education, and rehabilitation. Although known primarily for his client-centered approach to counseling, Rogers' **fully functioning self** theory presents a perspective that influences the education of people with disabilities. Rogers stresses the need for teachers to be warm, empathetic, and genuine as well as accepting of the learner—unconditionally. Within the fully functioning self theory, Rogers suggests that people have both an **ideal** self and an **actual** self. The closer the match between the ideal and the actual self, the more fully functioning an individual is. This ideal human condition results in a person who is open to experience, expresses feelings freely, acts independently, is creative, and lives a rich life. Movement toward this point of development requires **self-acceptance** as well as the unconditional acceptance of significant people in the student's life including family members and teachers. Although Rogers' fully functioning self theory has strong implica-

tions for adapted physical education and sport (see Sherrill, 2004, for a more in-depth treatment of the implications of fully functioning self theory), as a humanistic psychologist, his greatest contribution might be the strong emphasis he placed on the humane and ethical treatment of all individuals and a recognition of their inherent worth.

Applied Behavior Analysis

There is a rich tradition of employing the principles of applied behavior analysis to the teaching of physical education skills to students with unique needs (Alberto & Troutman, 1995; Dunn, 1997). Succinctly stated, applied behavior analysis involves the changing of behavior through the careful application of learning principles.

B.F. Skinner's work has been applied widely in the teaching of students with disabilities. Skinner stressed the importance of the consequences of an individual's actions—that is, what takes place after the behavior—on learning. His work demonstrated that **carefully selected consequences** could change the likelihood of the behavior that preceded it. Although consequences can be negative (punishing) to the individual, thus resulting in a decrease of the behavior, educators working with students who have unique needs should concentrate on positively reinforcing (that is, rewarding) behaviors that are helpful to the student, thus increasing the likelihood they will occur again.

The educational approach for students with unique needs that uses strategies derived from applied behavior analysis principles is commonly known as "behavior modification." Unfortunately, this term might conjure up images of punitive, controlling interventions. Although these powerful procedures have certainly been abused in the past, teachers educated in the use of behavioral interventions apply them ethically and positively with an eye on increasing and improving a learner's skills. By using this effective and ethical approach to teaching, many teachers have helped students significantly increase their repertoire of socially valued and individually meaningful abilities; as a result, the students live their lives with dignity and as self-reliant members of society.

Although teachers routinely employ behavioral principles, they are often unaware they are doing so. At times, without being aware of it, a teacher might reward (reinforce) a behavior, leading to an unexpected increase. For example, every time Peter called out, Mrs. Allen stopped the lesson and said, "Peter, we're all tired of your calling out. Please stop." Although Mrs. Allen felt she was firmly and effectively dealing with Peter's behavior, Peter thought all the individual public attention was great. As a result of Mrs. Allen's attention, Peter called out even more.

As noted, the applied behavior analysis approach to teaching physical education and sport to students with unique needs, although different in its approach, shares with the humanistic approach a positive and ethical approach to developing meaningful skills.

Clearly, the humanistic and applied behavior analysis traditions, along with other approaches in this text (discussed in chapter 6), are relevant to skill acquisition and behavior management. When teaching adapted physical education and sport, the practitioner must remain open-minded and, when appropriate, take the "best" elements of each tradition. It should also be recognized that, as noted earlier, the underlying goals of humanism and applied behavior analysis are not mutually exclusive. Within our individualized approach to teaching, the needs of our students must guide our choices. This text focuses on both approaches and subscribes to an eclectic perspective in implementing instruction. Chapters 6 and 9 include more information about the humanistic and applied behavior analysis perspective.

SYSTEMATIC TEACHING: HOW TO FACILITATE MOTOR LEARNING

Experts in the teaching of movement skills have stressed the importance of examining variables that relate to the learner, the task, and the environment when designing learning opportunities for students with unique needs (Reid, personal communication, October 7, 2003; Newell, 1986). It should be recognized that these three variables are not independent of one another; rather, they interact in sometimes complex ways, as shown in figure 7.2. Variables that relate to the learner include age, body build, gender, socioeconomic class, culture, attitudes, actual and perceived competence, creativity, motivations, and disability type. Some of these variables might change over the course of a unit or lesson, depending on the situation. For example, students with Down syndrome might be really excited about taking part in a jump rope activity, but after 10 minutes of doing the same thing with little success, their motivation level, as well as their perceived competence in jumping rope, might dwindle considerably. Conversely, students with cerebral palsy might come into the gym dreading the thought of taking part in line dancing, but given a really excellent breakdown of the skill, some thoughtful peer tutoring, and great tunes, their motivation to participate might increase dramatically.

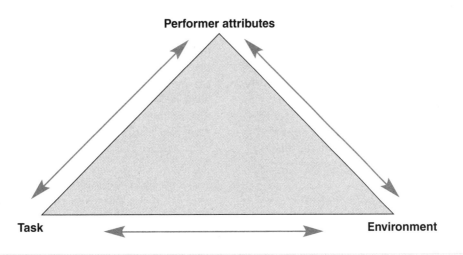

Figure 7.2 Interaction between performer, environment, and task.

Adapted from K.M. Newell, 1986, Constraints on the development of coordination. In *Motor development in children: Aspects of coordination and control,* edited by M.B. Wade & H.T. Whiting (Dordrecht, Netherlands: Nijhoff), 341-360. With kind permission of Springer Science and Business Media.

When examining environmental variables we must think beyond the physical. Although we must consider the nature of the indoor or outdoor setting, facilities, equipment, space, floor surfaces, lighting, temperature, and the like; it is also imperative that teachers of adapted physical education carefully consider the *emotional* environment. Do activities take place in a positive, affirming environment in which individual differences are embraced? Is there mutual respect? Are all students treated with dignity? Along with making sure the physical environment is safe and appropriate, effective teachers must also monitor the environment for emotional safety (Sherrill, 2004).

Our third variable—the task—gets at our curriculum. Are the movement skills that we've chosen to teach of interest and usefulness to our students? Do we teach skills because we enjoy them or because "it's always been done this way?" Or do we teach a skill because it is valued by the student, the family, or the community and will be useful now or in the next likely educational placement?

Research in the disciplines of motor learning, motor development, motor control, biomechanics, physiology, special education, and pedagogy have uncovered certain principles that—when applied appropriately—help significantly in the teaching and learning of movement skills. Keeping in mind the interaction of variables related to the learner, the environment, and the task to be accomplished, Dunn (1997) has compiled a list of motor skill tenets.

- *Growth and maturation influence the ability to learn a movement skill.* It is detrimental to the physical and emotional well-being of students to pressure them to take part in tasks that they are not ready to accomplish—motorically, cognitively, or socially. Although we encourage teachers to organize learning environments in which a child—with the appropriate supports—can explore his or her movement potential; cognitive, affective, and physical limitations must be carefully considered.

- *Mechanical and physiological principles of movement dictate the best way to perform a given skill.* The laws of stability and motion along with clearly established physiological principles of exercise apply to all people, regardless of functional level or disability. For example, the principle of stability posits that balance is enhanced when the center of gravity falls within the base of sup-

port. This principle should be considered when, for example, students with amputations are asked to perform movement skills in a gym or pool.

- *Reinforcement and repetition are needed when learning a new skill.* As discussed earlier in this chapter and in other chapters in this book, identifying consequences that will increase the likelihood that a response will take place is imperative. Although being intrinsically motivated by taking part in an activity is preferred, this is often not the case, especially with students that have intellectual disabilities. Thus, finding extrinsic reinforcers that are effective and applying them appropriately is imperative. In terms of repetition, students with unique needs must have multiple opportunities to perform a given movement skill. Too often, a student will not get the opportunity to practice enough, making it unlikely the skill will be established. The teaching situation must allow for plenty of perfect practice. Practice sessions must be structured so that students have the opportunity not only to repeat a given skill several times but to repeat it in a stimulating, exciting activity, in which their attention is focused on the relevant cues.

- *Emotion affects the process of learning motor skills.* During the learning of a given movement skill, extreme emotion (particularly anxiety, fear, embarrassment, or humiliation) negatively affects the learning process. As mentioned, the teacher of adapted physical education must be aware of the emotional atmosphere of the class, and work hard to establish a positive tone conducive to learning. Students might respond very differently to the same situation, so the teacher must be aware of each student's individual response. For example, although Miriam doesn't mind one bit when Alex and Stan good-naturedly joke with her about missing the target during a throwing activity, the same comments made to Nick result in a decreased desire to participate and occasionally in physical aggression toward Alex and Stan.

- *Success at a given task leads to improved learning.* As the old adage goes, "success breeds success." Activities should be chosen and taught in a way that students will perform them with a high degree of success. To increase the likelihood of success, prompts should be used effectively, and more complicated tasks should be broken down into smaller, more manageable parts. Teachers can also set up tasks that are "self-adjusting." That is, for example, students would choose a larger or smaller target depending on their previous success. Remember that reinforcers must be chosen carefully and provided effectively.

• *Learning takes place more quickly when practice sessions are separated by adequate rest periods.* Students learn more quickly when their interest is high and fatigue is not an issue. Even a well-designed activity loses its appeal if it goes on too long. Students with intellectual or physical disabilities are often in poor physical condition (Seidl, Reid, & Montgomery, 1987). Thus, keeping instructional periods short with brief rest periods and changing activities (even slightly) leads to increased learning. An associated benefit is a reduction in behavior problems because frustration, boredom, and fatigue are minimized.

• *Motor skills that are overlearned are retained longer.* Overlearning is the process of repeating a task until its performance is automatic, with no need for focused conscious effort. Although the point at which a skill becomes automatic varies from student to student, those with intellectual disabilities, in general, require more repetitions than their typically developing peers need. An example of an overlearned skill is cycling. Children who ride bikes frequently during their later elementary and middle school years as adults can pick up the skill—after many years of not riding—without any appreciable loss of skill.

When considering these tenets, a cautionary note should be considered because much of the research presented has been conducted with people who are developing typically, as opposed to those with identifiable disabilities. Although students with unique needs are more like their typically developing peers than not and thus it makes intuitive sense that these findings apply, additional research with a wider range of subjects (with identifiable disabilities) will significantly increase our knowledge base.

MEETING INDIVIDUAL DIFFERENCES

A major focus of this chapter (and the entire text) is to present information to help the reader address individual differences in a way that leads to significant and meaningful educational gains for students with unique needs. In the context of this chapter, the word "unique" applies not only to an individual's needs but to *all* of the attributes he or she has. As previously mentioned, teachers must focus on a learner's distinct learning style, strengths, and

limitations. Although a thorough understanding of the etiology and characteristics of a given disability (e.g., pervasive developmental delay or cerebral palsy) is important—and extensively covered in this text—an excellent understanding of that student standing in the gym is more important still. To borrow a phrase from research, our unit of analysis is one. That is, we look at students as individuals first and foremost.

Curricular Options: What to Teach?

Along with a thorough understanding of *how* to effectively teach students with disabilities come the equally important decisions regarding *what* should be taught—that is, decisions on the curriculum. One way to address individual differences is to individualize and formalize objectives and activities, as touched on in chapter 2.

Given that a significant number of students with disabilities are taught with their typically developing peers in integrated physical education settings, curricular modifications are often appropriate. In chapter 2, four categories have been suggested that allow for the meaningful integration of students with unique needs. These categories include the same curriculum, multilevel curriculum, modified curriculum, and different curriculum. Briefly presented, the *same* curriculum suggests that students with disabilities follow an *identical* curriculum to that of their typically developing peers, although their objectives might be different from those of the other students. Within the *multilevel curriculum* option, the student with a disability follows the regular physical education curriculum with modification(s) of the activities made if necessary (e.g., if a student with Down syndrome is playing a small-sided game of volleyball, she might serve from a distance eight feet closer to the net than "regulation." It should be noted that master teachers generally have activity modifications or options available for all students, thus appropriately challenging each at his or her own developmental level. In this way, everyone in the class is accommodated without anyone being singled out. A *modified curriculum,* appropriate for students with more severe disabilities, is used when the regular physical education curriculum is at least partly inappropriate for a student given his or her unique IEP objectives. However, these unique IEP objectives can be related to the curricular goals being followed by the rest of the class. For example, Peter, a sixth-grade student with cerebral palsy, is working on the grasp and release of a tennis ball (resulting in the knocking down of 3 bowling pins), whereas the other students are rolling eight-inch plastic bowling balls down a 15-foot alley to knock down 10 bowling pins. In this example, Peter's unique IEP objective (working on grasp and release) "overlaps" with bowling, part of the sixth-grade regular physical education curriculum. Although the activity Peter is doing is different from the one others are doing, it is clearly *related* to what the other students are doing—that is, all students are working on modified bowling tasks. When the unique physical education needs of a student with an identifiable disability cannot safely and meaningfully be overlapped with the regular physical education curriculum, work on unique IEP objectives might have to take place away from the main physical education activity; that is, the student might take part in an entirely *different curriculum.* In this case, the student with a disability works on skills unrelated to the curriculum pursued by other students in the class. For example, while classmates are playing small-sided games of ultimate Frisbee, the student with a disability is working on increasing upper-body strength through an individualized weight-training program. This is not necessarily an "all-or-nothing" proposition. That is, alternative activities might be necessary for a specific part of the curriculum, but not at other times. Block (2000) has suggested that peers without disabilities rotate away from their activities and take part in the alternative activity (in our example, weight training) for a set amount of time. In this way, all students receive the benefit of interacting with *all* class members while working on meaningful activities. As always, teachers must carefully examine task, environmental, and performer variables when deciding which curricular approach is the most appropriate for a given student at a given time.

A fundamental question related to curriculum concerns whether specific functional, age-appropriate movement skills should be the focus of instruction (referred to as a **top-down** approach to teaching) or whether it is more appropriate to follow a developmentally focused curriculum (referred to as a **bottom-up** approach to teaching).

Adapted physical education researchers and practitioners advocating the top-down approach target the movement and recreational skills a person needs to learn in order to independently recreate in their community. The curricular emphasis is on teaching age-appropriate leisure skills valued by the individual, his or her family, and the community at large. The learner's abilities

and shortcomings—with specific regard to the skill being taught—are carefully examined, and educational experiences are designed to achieve the end result. If a valued leisure skill in Shannon's family is playing two-on-two basketball on the driveway with her dad, mom, and sister, all the subskills needed to play (e.g., dribble, pass, shoot, rebound within a two-on-two "family" game) would be carefully examined in relation to Shannon's demonstrated abilities. If Shannon needs to work on passing the ball accurately with pace at the right time, this skill will be directly taught. Teaching age-appropriate and valued leisure skills in real world contexts is a hallmark of the top-down approach.

Those who advocate a bottom-up perspective (also called a **developmental** approach) believe that the ultimate goal of adapted physical education is to prepare students to engage in recreational and sports skills independently. Kelly (1989) and Graham, Holt-Hale, and Parker (2004) view the bottom-up approach as providing students with a broad foundation of fundamental movement skills during the elementary years. These foundational skills are then combined into games, dance, and athletics during the middle and high school years. Although the focus is on providing instruction in many different developmentally appropriate movement skills, if a student is considered at risk, a physical education teacher using the bottom-up approach will intervene early on in order to identify the "building blocks" (neurological, reflexive, or motor) that are lacking and to select activities to remedy the observed shortcomings, thus enabling participation in chronologically and developmentally appropriate movement activities. Moving back to our driveway basketball game, the teacher using a bottom-up approach would be sure that Shannon has mastered the locomotion and object control abilities important for success in basketball before she plays in the two-on-two game.

As is often the case in teaching adapted physical education, an open-minded and eclectic approach is recommended. If the student is very young and the disability (or delay) is minimal, the bottom-up approach might be best. Conversely, if a student has significant physical or intellectual deficits, extensive time spent working on the fundamental building blocks likely means the student will not be taking part in meaningful, socially valued activities with their typically developing peers. When making decisions about what to teach, always keep in mind individual characteristics and values as well as the unique ecology surrounding the learner.

Activity Modifications

As discussed, on deciding on the most appropriate curricular approach and activities to meet the individual's learning goals, it might become apparent that modifications of activities are necessary if the student is going to participate successfully. There are many strategies on which to base modifications. Lieberman and Houston-Wilson (2002) have suggested that activity modifications can be broken down into four categories: equipment, rules, environment, and instruction. The game of softball provides us with examples of activity modifications for students with different disabilities. If a student has below-average intellectual abilities, the rules might be simplified, whereas for those with visual impairments, the base paths could have a different texture than the field, and the ball and bases might include sound devices. If an individual struggles with muscular strength, the bat or ball could be lighter for students who have decreased coordination or cardiovascular fitness, reducing the distance between bases could help. Modified rules for making "outs" might help players with limited mobility compete at their highest level of ability.

Modifications do not have to affect every component of an activity; they should be limited to those necessary to meet individual needs. It must be stressed that modifications to equipment, rules, or the parameters of the activity must be done cautiously and carefully, keeping in mind the educational experiences of both the students for whom the modification(s) are being made and their classmates. When modifying an activity, the educator should try to maintain its inherent nature, keeping it as close to the traditional activity as possible. An example of an activity modification for a student with a visual impairment in an archery class is described in the activity modification application.

Teaching Style

"Teaching functions are usually performed within an instructional framework—a delivery system for getting content to the learner. . . . Many factors influence the choice of a teaching strategy, including the content itself, the characteristics of the learner, and the objectives and preferences of the teacher" (Rink, 2002, p. 177).

Regardless of the teaching style used and the format of the class, it is imperative that teachers consider the instructional and managerial tone of the physical education class. The tone is independent of both style and format and can

---

APPLICATION EXAMPLE

Activity Modification

Setting: High school physical education class

Student: 17-year-old student who is legally blind with a visual acuity of 2/200

Issue: Modifications for safe and successful inclusion of student with visual impairment into indoor archery unit

Application: After discussion among the physical education teacher, the student with the visual impairment, and class members, the following policies were instituted:

- Arrows of student with visual impairment will be identified with Braille tape by the arrow notch.
- A special target face will be used on which each scoring area will have a different texture.

- A raised rope will be used by all students as the shooting line.
- The archer with visual impairments will use an L-shaped wood template to align his feet and the target.
- A tape recorder will be attached to the back of the target to give auditory direction for the archer.
- A rope will be attached to the target, and foot templates will be placed on the ground to allow independent movement between the target and the shooting line.
- No one will go past the shooting line until an audible signal to retrieve arrows is given.
- Classmates will volunteer to assist with scoring, finding stray arrows, and so on when asked by the student with visual impairments.

range from clearly punitive to clearly positive and supportive. Some teachers of adapted physical education would be considered "upbeat" and excited, whereas others would be best described as relaxed. Some teachers interact frequently with students, and others do so much less. Teachers might be extremely demanding or, conversely, laid back. Their nature might, indeed, vary within and between classes, depending on the context. Students are exposed to this tone in large- and small-group settings as well as during individual interactions. When describing the tone of the class, terms such as "businesslike," "demanding," "aloof," "warm," and "caring" are often used. It is, of course, possible to be effective using a businesslike demeanor. It is also possible to be perceived as caring and nurturing, and be equally effective. Physical educators working with students with unique needs must ensure that the tone set in the classroom is accurately recognized. Furthermore, we should be aware of the tone's effect—both positive and negative—on the students. If for a given student a particular tone is ineffective, we should be prepared to modify the tone. For example, we might perceive ourselves, accurately, as being nurturing and caring. However, this laid-back approach might result in some students being off task because they perceive (mistakenly) that "it's okay" to goof around because Mr. C doesn't mind. Simply stated, does the tone we set lead to student achievement and their desire to spend time in physical education?

As used in this chapter, teaching style refers to how the teacher organizes and delivers instruction to learners. Figure 7.3 presents an overview of teaching styles.

There is no one best style; rather, effective instructors adapt their instruction to variables that include personal skills and preferences, the nature of the content being taught, characteristics of the learners, and the teaching context. In regard to personal skills and preferences, Siedentop and Tannehill (2000) have pointed out that teachers perform better when they are comfortable with and have a belief in the style being used. For example, if they feel pressured to use a more student-directed approach but are not convinced of its efficacy, teaching results will likely suffer. This is not to suggest that teachers should not attempt teaching styles they are less comfortable with (in some cases, they clearly should) but experimentation in this area should be the result of professional development and reflection, not an administrative directive.

Reproductive styles (also referred to as teacher-mediated instructional formats)

    Command

    Practice/task

    Reciprocal

    Self-check

    Inclusion/invitation

Productive styles (also referred to as student-mediated instructional formats)

    Guided discovery

    Convergent discovery

    Divergent discovery

Figure 7.3 Teaching styles.

Adapted from M. Mosston and S. Ashworth, 1994, *Teaching physical education,* 4th ed. (Upper Saddle River, NJ: Prentice-Hall), 248-249.

Certain content and objectives are more effectively taught via one teaching style than another. If, for example, a goal is to teach students how to throw a disk using a backhand motion and a forehand motion (the "flick"), a command style would probably be the most appropriate approach. If, later in the unit, the objective is to decide—given the defense being played—*which* motion is most appropriate, a convergent discovery style might be most effective. Clearly, teaching basic movement skills for a given activity is a different proposition than teaching higher-level strategies (Siedentop & Tannehill, 2000). Often, there is not one "correct" way to solve a movement task. Rather, one movement might be more appropriate than another, depending on the situation. Block (2000) has pointed out that although a teacher could point out to a learner which method would work the best in a given situation, students who learn through active experimentation are potentially more invested in their learning and retain the learning longer. Further, the domain (cognitive, affective, or psychomotor) that emphasizes the goal(s) of the class should be considered. If, for example, students are working together to solve a movement task, a student-directed style, such as cooperative learning, might be more appropriate.

The learner's characteristics are a third consideration, particularly when learners have identifiable disabilities. But teachers should take care not to jump to conclusions. Because a student has an intellectual disability or has ADHD, for example, this is not a sufficient reason to rule out a more student-centered teaching style. However, if behaving appropriately is an issue, where an individual struggles with attending to the task at hand, or a student's intellectual capacity is reduced, a teacher-mediated instructional format might be the best approach. Conversely, students who have a physical disability resulting in unique movement patterns might benefit more from a student-mediated instructional format—one that allows them to discover effective solutions themselves (with support).

Ultimately, when a teaching style is being considered, teacher attributes, comfort level, lesson goals, and learner attributes must be considered. Although it can be challenging to do so, using multiple styles within a given class is frequently the most effective approach. For example, while the majority of the class might be exploring (within a convergent discovery framework) how angling a disk alters how it flies through the air, a student with an intellectual disability might be receiving direct instruction (command style) on throwing a backhand. As a second example, while most of the class is learning how to serve a tennis ball (through the command style of instruction), a student in a wheelchair, a second with cerebral palsy, and a third whose injured back does not allow a turn of the shoulders might be encouraged to discover unique patterns that allow for fast and accurate serves. In general, the more severe the intellectual disability, the more direct the teaching style.

Siedentop and Tannehill (2000) have noted that the effectiveness of a teaching style ultimately depends on the learner and learning outcomes. Is there a considerable amount of academic learning time? Do students demonstrate a willingness to take part in the activities? Are goals of the unit being met? Ongoing program assessment regarding these questions aids in choosing the correct styles of teaching.

Class Format

Class format is an important instructional consideration related to teaching style (Block, 2000; Seaman and DePauw, 1989). In this section we will discuss nine formats that have been effectively used in the teaching of adapted physical education.

One-to-One Instruction

To promote acquisition, maintenance, and generalization of skills, students receiving adapted physical education sometimes require a 1:1 student-to-teacher ratio. This format allows for a highly individualized teaching session as well as multiple opportunities to respond on the part of the learner. An approach to 1:1 instruction that is extremely successful in teaching students with more severe disabilities is an instructional episode. Later in this chapter, this approach will be presented in considerable depth. In physical education settings, one-to-one instruction can be implemented by the physical education teacher, a trained teaching assistant, a parent, or a trained peer tutor.

Small-Group Instruction

Within a small-group instruction format, two to ten students generally work with one teacher or teaching assistant.

Large-Group Instruction

In this format, the entire class participates at the same time under the direction of one or more teachers or teaching assistants.

Mixed-Group Instruction

Within a mixed-group instruction approach, a variety of formats are used during the same class period. This format is particularly effective when students demonstrate different learning characteristics or are working toward different instructional objectives.

Peer Teaching or Tutoring

When peer teaching or tutoring takes place, lower-skilled students are taught by their more highly-skilled classmates or by highly-skilled students from other classes. A second approach—classwide peer tutoring or reciprocal teaching—utilizes all students in the class as both tutors and tutees.

Self-Paced Independent Work

As the name of this format suggests, self-paced independent work involves students working on their personal goals mostly by themselves. Often, "task cards" or input from the teacher or teaching assistant helps keep the students focused and on task.

Cooperative Learning

When students use a cooperative learning format, subsets of students within a given class work together to accomplish shared goals. This format can be particularly effective when the instructional objectives are affective in nature or target the development of social skills.

Reverse Mainstreaming

In this format, students without disabilities join their peers with unique needs in the self-contained class, taking part in movement activities along with them. Although not a substitute for meaningfully integrating students with unique needs into the regular education setting, reverse mainstreaming does provide opportunities for students with and without unique needs to work together. It is important that students with unique needs interact with their typically developing peers as these interactions provide benefits for all individuals.

Teaching Stations (Task Teaching)

Teaching stations allow for students to work on more than one task at the same time. Teaching stations are particularly effective when teaching a class of diverse learners at different stages of skill development, because stations can be designed to challenge students at their developmental level. Generally, three or more stations are set up throughout the gym, each focusing on a somewhat different skill or skill set. Students are placed into small groups and assigned, in the beginning, to a given station. On the teacher's command, or when a student has completed specified activities, students rotate to the next station. Siedentop and Tannehill (2000) have noted that under certain conditions, "task teaching" might occur without using multiple stations. For example, a single station, such as a climbing wall, could accommodate the class at one time. In this case, small groups might work on a set of related tasks, all occurring on the wall. Climbing "stations" might include a cargo net, climbing wall, and a horizontal bouldering wall.

Stations might involve skills related to each other, such as the tasks involved in playing hockey (namely, shooting, passing, stick-handling, and goaltending), or skills that are unrelated, such as having one station devoted to throwing and catching activities and another to jumping rope.

Stations can be organized in a hierarchical, progressive fashion. That is, as students progress in skill level they move to a station requiring more ability on the given task. Conversely, the "next" station might not require any prerequisite skill. Regardless of the progressive or nonprogressive nature of the task setup, or whether the tasks

are related to each other, each station should accommodate students of varying skill level by including multiple challenges. That is, opportunities for learning are individualized *within* stations. If juggling is the task being worked on at a station, then there should be an opportunity to, for example, juggle one ball, two balls, or scarves. If serving a tennis ball is the task, students should have the opportunity to serve from eight feet from the net, the service line, and the baseline. With multiple levels of performance, students have the opportunity to select their own "entry level." Well-designed stations provide options for students that relate to skill progressions and physical performance criteria. There are also choices of different implements (e.g., tennis racket versus badminton racket), sizes of targets (both service boxes or just one), and number of required repetitions. The students are given choices regarding *how* and *where* in the progression they will begin the task. Opportunities within the "task teaching" format to custom design individual stations—that is, offer multiple ways to accomplish a given task—make this approach particularly useful for learners with disabilities.

To let students know what is expected at a given station, effective teachers often supplement verbal descriptions with simply designed task cards or task posters. These cards or posters might use words, pictures, or a combination of the two. (Of course, the developmental level of students in the class must be considered when designing these cards or posters.) As noted, stations can be designed to challenge students with unique needs at their developmental level, offering progressively more difficult challenges within and between stations. Social skills can also be developed as students help each other at the stations. Figure 7.4 provides an example of a task poster.

An Instructional Episode

As noted, when working with students with unique needs, teaching must be structured carefully. Of particular importance are individual interactions with students. This instruction has been called "formal individual instruction" (Dunn, Morehouse, & Fredericks, 1986), "an instructional episode" (Reid & O'Neill, 1989), and "discrete trial training" (Koegel, Russo, Rincover, & Schreibman, 1982). In this chapter, we will use the Reid and O'Neill "instructional episode" terminology.

See table 7.1 for an outline of an instructional episode. The instructional episode is based on

How far can you jump?

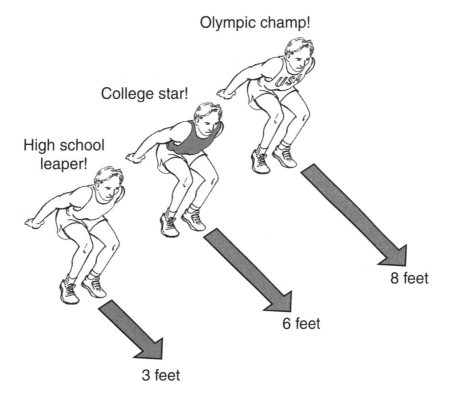

Figure 7.4 Task poster for jumping.

principles of learning derived from applied behavior analysis and, although used most extensively with children who have autism, is effectively used with a range of students. This approach has been used to teach skills including language skills, social skills, and fundamental movement skills. An **instructional episode** is a structured method that usually involves teaching in a one-on-one situation. Movement tasks are presented to the student in a series of separate, brief sessions. A particular trial can be repeated several times in a row, several times a day, or for several days—until the skill at hand is mastered. An important benefit of an instructional episode to the teacher of adapted physical education is the precision and care with which each trial is conducted, without sacrificing the important affective component. Specifically, the components of an instructional episode are, in this order: (1) an instruction or environmental cue, (2) an optional prompt, (3) a student's response, (4) consequences, and (5) an intertrial interval (see table 7.1 for an outline). We will look at each of the five components in some detail.

Table 7.1 Components of an Instructional Episode

Elements	To keep in mind
1. Instructional or Environmental	Salient, easy to discriminate Appropriate to the task Presented when the student is attending
2. Optional prompt	Presented subsequent to or concurrent with instruction Subsequent to or concurrent with the teacher's consequences Presented with an eye to fading
3. Student's response	Either correct, incorrect, or "no response" Must be in response to the instruction/request or environmental cue(s)
4. Consequences	Applied consistently Applied unambiguously Easy to discriminate
5. Intertrial interval	Three to five seconds

Instruction or Environmental Cue

The **instruction** or **environmental cue** is an event a learner responds to. Generally, these events are instructions or requests given by teachers, peers, or parents. However, the event could be an environmental cue, such as the blowing of a whistle or the ringing of a bell. For example, when the physical education teacher blows the whistle twice, what should the student do? Sit down on the carpet square? Return to home base? As can be seen, teaching responses to both instructions and environmental cues are important.

When giving instructions or setting up environmental cues, the teacher must ensure that the student is paying attention. If not, the odds of a correct response are extremely low. A simple and effective approach is to precede a request by using the learner's name: "Jim, please roll the ball down the alley."

Especially early on in the teaching–learning sequence, instructions should be simple and clearly stated. If the teacher does not present information in a manner that the learner can understand, confusion results. Thus, care must be taken to use language appropriate to the functional level of the learner, emphasizing clarity. Of course, as a student's skill level increases, the teacher should use more complex instructions. The key is to increase the complexity of the instruction systematically, always keeping in mind the skills of the student. Environmental cues may also be made more complex. Although distractions should be minimized initially, they might be systematically added to the learning environment as a student's abilities increase.

Optional Prompt

After the instruction (or environmental cue) is presented, the teacher might provide a prompt to the learner before the response is made. Although the terms "cue" and "prompt" have been used interchangeably in the special education and adapted physical education literature, for our purposes here cues refer to environmental information that lets the learner know what is expected of him or her. Prompts, on the other hand, refer to *extra* information—often verbal, visual, or physical in nature—added to the student's environment to ensure a proper response. Frequently used in special education and adapted physical education to teach students with unique needs a range of skills, prompts are an extremely important tool in the teaching of physical education. Prompts are presented at the same time as—or immediately following—instruction, or at the same time as—or immediately following—the teacher's consequences. Information on effective prompting was also discussed in chapter 6.

A prompting system proven effective with many learners is called a **system of least prompts** (Lieberman & Houston-Wilson, 2002). In this system, only as much verbal, visual, or physical assistance is given as is necessary for a task to be completed successfully. The objective is skilled **independent** performance. A system of least prompts is particularly effective in systematically reducing assistance when each of the major prompting levels (physical, visual, verbal, and "no prompts") is further subdivided. For example, at the physical prompt level are three degrees of physical assistance, each giving a different amount of assistance. This precision allows for the careful withdrawal (called **fading**) of assistance, leading to more autonomous performance on the part of the learner. Following is an example of a least prompts model (after Watkinson and Wall, 1982) in which prompts are broken down into four basic categories: physical, visual, verbal, and "no prompts." It is important to note that at any prompt level, the competent teacher will give more (or less) assistance to a learner, depending on the learner's skill level. Examples of the four levels of prompting are provided here.

- *Physical prompts.* When using physical prompts the teacher touches the student. This gives a high degree of physical assistance in which, for example, the teacher holds the student at the wrist as a pendulum swing is used to roll a bowling ball and moves the student's arm through the full range of motion. A reduced level of physical prompting might involve moving the student's arm only during the backswing. A further reduction might involve merely touching the student's wrist and applying slight backward pressure to indicate the direction of the backswing.

- *Visual prompts.* Visual prompts might involve a complete, sometimes exaggerated, demonstration of the skill in question. In our bowling example, if the skill was to roll the bowling ball from a stationary position, the teacher would demonstrate the complete skill—including the initial body position, backswing, follow-through, and release of the ball. As the learner's skill increased, less visual information would be given. For example, the teacher might demonstrate only the follow-through. Still less visual information might involve just pointing to the student's knees as a reminder to get into a deeper crouch.

• *Verbal prompts.* Verbal prompts include a sound, word, or instruction to focus the student's attention on the key features of the movements required to complete a skill. As with physical and visual prompts, the physical education teacher might give more or less verbal information, depending on the skill level of the learner. In our bowling example, a high degree of verbal prompting would involve a complete description of how to bowl. "Peter, I want you to bend your knees and then smoothly swing your arm backward and then forward." A reduced level of verbal prompt might involve merely a description of the skill to be performed: "Peter, it's your turn to bowl." A further reduction of verbal prompts would be a more general indication that it's Peter's turn to bowl or a motivating phrase: "Peter, what do you do now?" or "Peter, one, two, three, go!"

• *No prompts.* Although "no prompts" might not be an accurate description of this prompting level, the point is that the teacher doesn't use a physical, visual, or verbal prompt to help the student perform the skill; rather, the environment is set up for the student in such a way that the skill being worked on is elicited. One way of eliciting the skill is to place an object in the environment that—indirectly encourages—performance of the skill. The student enters the bowling alley from a direction that brings him or her alongside the bowling ball rack. This is enough of a prompt to pick up the ball and move to the correct lane. Another "no prompt" example would include the student performing the skill (bowling) after watching a peer perform the same skill.

These prompting categories are not mutually exclusive. Often, verbal prompts are paired with demonstrations or with physical prompts. Similarly, physical and visual prompts can be paired. In any case, the teacher must remember that skilled independent performance is the goal and that assistance should be systematically reduced.

To prompt a student effectively, the following guidelines should be kept in mind.

1. Use prompts that are meaningful to the student. Consider the learner's characteristics (skill level, preferred modality, specific disability). For example, if a student is more receptive to visual prompts than to physical prompts, focus on effectively using visual prompts during the instructional episodes. If a student is deaf, the emphasis might be on visual or physical prompts.

2. Be careful not to underprompt, because this might lead to frequent errors on the part of the learner.

3. Do not overprompt, because students might become reliant on prompts, thus hindering the development of an independently skilled performance. If assistance is not needed, do not give it.

4. Focus the learner's attention on the task. Some learners attend to the prompt being given instead of the task.

5. Make sure the prompt is effective. Adding an ineffective prompt to an instructional episode might delay or block learning.

6. Pretest and assess a student carefully before deciding on prompts—some students might need less assistance than first assumed.

7. Fade physical proximity. The distance between the student and teacher is an important variable involving the effectiveness of a prompt and the independence of the learner. As the student becomes more independent, move progressively further away.

8. Couple appropriate verbal prompting with other prompts. This way, when the physical or visual prompt is reduced (or eliminated), the student still responds to the verbal command.

9. Fade verbal prompts. Although learners should become able to respond to only verbal instructions, true independence means performing activities without even verbal help.

Although an "optional" component of an instructional episode, it should be stressed that the ability to effectively prompt, and fade prompts, is essential for effectively teaching students with unique needs.

Learner's Response

Following the instruction (or environmental cue) is the **learner's response.** The learner must be responding to the instructions or environmental cue. If the learner is responding to something other than the intended instruction or environmental cue, the instruction might have to be reconsidered.

Were the instructions too complicated? Was the learner attending to something other than the instructions? Was the environment too distracting? Frequently, more than one person is working with a given student. For this reason, criteria for correct responding should be described in detail and made known to all parties before the trials begin.

Consequences

The learner can respond in one of three ways during a given instructional episode: correctly, incorrectly, or not at all (that is, no response). In any case, after the student's response, the teacher delivers consequences, the type of which depend on the learner's characteristics and the nature of his or her response. Consequences should be based on the learner's behavior and be applied consistently and unambiguously. The learner should be able to easily pick out the consequence (i.e., it should be easily discriminable). If a response was correct (e.g., the ball was thrown accurately), this should be clear to the learner by the consequence that is elicited. Conversely, the learner should also clearly understand when a response is incorrect. Correct responses are reinforced when the learner receives a reward that he or she values. That is, the reinforcer should be something the student appreciates—not something the teacher appreciates or feels that the student *should* appreciate. For the reinforcement to be consistent and effective, the criteria for correct response—as previously noted—have to be well thought through, understood, and consistently used by all individuals working with the student. A lack of consistency severely undermines the teaching. If the learner responds incorrectly, either the response is ignored or corrective feedback is given. Any feedback should give the learner specific information about the performance. In general, punishing consequences should not be employed. Information on effectively applying consequences was presented in chapter 6.

Intertrial Interval

Following the consequences is an intertrial interval, a brief (three to five seconds) pause between consecutive instructional episodes. This pause lets the student know that an instructional episode has been completed. It also allows time for the reinforcement (e.g., a hug, a high five, a sticker placed in a book) to take place and for the teacher to write down data, if needed, about the instructional episode.

Task Analysis

It has been established that students who have good cognitive, affective, and movement skills benefit from daily interactions with the environment—especially when the environment is varied and thoughtfully arranged. This process has been called incidental learning. Because students with unique needs often find the learning of movement skills more difficult than their typically developing peers do, they require more systematic and planned learning experiences. When combined with effective reinforcement and prompting, task analysis is a powerful strategy to improve the learning of students with unique needs—in terms of both assessment and teaching. Although task analysis involves, broadly stated, the careful examination of all the factors or skills involved in the performance of a task, the term can be confusing because different authors, researchers, and theorists have used the term "task analysis" to describe somewhat different processes. A "traditional task analysis" (Dunn, 1997; Reid & O'Neil, 1989) involves the identification of components of an activity and then the ordering of the components according to their level of difficulty (from easiest to most difficult). Herkowitz (1978) has used the term "developmental task analysis" to examine the variety of task and environmental factors that influence motor performance. Short (chapter 5) uses "biomechanical task analysis" to refer to the breakdown of a continuous task, such as a long jump or overhand throw. In 1991, Davis and Burton coined the term "ecological task analysis" to describe an analysis that gave equal weighting to the attributes of the learner, the environment, and the task to be accomplished. Because biomechanical task analysis and ecological task analysis with reference to assessment has already been discussed in depth (chapter 5), we will discuss developmental task analysis and traditional task analysis in more detail in this chapter.

Developmental Task Analysis

Herkowitz (1978) has pointed out that several different task and environmental factors can influence motor performance and, by being aware of these factors, the teacher of adapted physical education can modify some (or all) of them to make the activity easier—or more challenging—for an individual student. Developmental task analysis has two components: general task analysis (GTA) and specific task analysis (STA).

Table 7.2   **An Example of a General Task Analysis (Throwing)**

Factors	Size of object being thrown	Distance object must be thrown	Weight of object being thrown	Accuracy required	Speed target is moving at	Acceleration or deceleration of the target	Direction in which target is moving at
Simple	Small	Short	Moderately light	None	Stationary	No movement	No move
							Left to right
to	Medium	Medium	Moderately heavy	Little	Slow	Steady speed	Right to left
				Moderate	Moderate	Decelerating	Toward thrower
Complex	Large	Large	Light or heavy	Much	Fast	Accelerating	Away from thrower

Adapted from Herkowitz, J. (1978). Developmental task analysis: The design of movement experiences and evaluation of motor development status. In M. Ridenour (Ed.), *Motor development: Issues and applications* (p. 141). Princeton, NJ: Princeton Book Co.

GTA (table 7.2) outlines all of the task and environmental factors that influence the performance of students in the general movement categories (e.g., throw, strike, jump). Under each of these factors, modifications are given, from simplest to most difficult.

Once teachers of adapted physical education have a good understanding of how task and environmental factors can influence movement proficiency through the GTA, they can develop a STA to look at how *select* factors influence movement skill. For example, in regard to throwing (table 7.2), if an instructor chooses to examine more precisely the effect of object size and weight on the learner's performance, the information presented with the STA will be much more precise. Instead of referring generally to ball size (small, medium, large), the instructor precisely manipulates the size (e.g., 6-inch, 8-inch, or 12-inch playground balls). Clearly, other variables (e.g., weight) may also be manipulated. Through the careful identification and manipulation of important variables, it is possible to break down and sequence tasks that are appropriate for given students, no matter their functional level. An example of a STA is shown in table 7.3.

Traditional Task Analysis

A traditional task analysis breaks a skill down into its tasks or related subtasks. These tasks are arranged into a sequence from easy to difficult with short-term outcomes being determined for each task and subtask. An effective approach to traditional task analysis involves separating the main task into several related subtasks (figure 7.5). As previously mentioned, each subtask has components arranged hierarchically from the most easy to the most difficult. Once all the components of a given subtask have been mastered, the learner then moves to the first component of the *next* subtask. Figure 7.5 provides a task–subtask traditional task analysis for jumping rope. In writing an appropriate traditional task analysis, the teacher must clearly identify the main skill

Table 7.3   **An Example of a Specific Task Analysis (Striking Behavior)**

Factors	Size of ball	Length of striking implement	Predictability of trajectory
Simple	S1: 12 in.	L1: hand	P1: rolled along ground
to	S2: 9 in.	L2: table tennis paddle	P2: bounced along ground
Complex	S3: 4 in.	L3: 18-in. dowel rod	P3: ball tossed in air
	S4: tennis ball	L4: plastic bat	

and terminal objective as well as any prerequisite skills. All potential steps (tasks and their associated subtasks) should be described in observable behavioral terms, thus aiding in the development of appropriate individualized education plans and in the assessment of learning.

There are many benefits to the traditional task analysis, particularly for students who struggle cognitively. First of all, there is clear recognition of progress by both student and teacher. With progress on meaningful tasks comes an avoidance of frustration, a reduction in off-task behavior, and a maintenance of interest in the task on the part of the teacher and the student. As discussed earlier in this chapter, the maintenance of self-esteem is of considerable importance. The mastery of components of a given task could have positive benefits with regard to empowering students. From a teaching perspective, traditional task analysis allows teachers to see that they have more options than they originally believed, leading to a "can do" perspective. Traditional task analysis allows the fading of prompts more quickly, thus increasing independence. Progress can be visually charted, thereby aiding communication with parents and other team members. The charting of progress (or lack of progress) allows clear observation of educational gains, allowing for sound educational decisions. For example, are more "steps" needed? Fewer steps? Increased level of prompting? Have inappropriate objectives (e.g., given the amount of time available) been pursued? Is the order of components appropriate?

Although an extremely effective educational tool, especially for students with more severe disabilities, the traditional approach to task analysis has been criticized (Dunn, 1997; Rich, 2000; Davis & Burton, 1991) because it might overemphasize the task while de-emphasizing characteristics of the performer and the environment. The teacher must attend carefully to both the environment and the learners. Although it helps to look at already available task analysis, it is important to come back to the idea of **individualizing** teaching. Students will likely differ from one another in terms of the type of breakdown needed, the number of components (and their order) that works best for them, and the preferred and most effective manner in which the material is presented. We must look at student strengths, shortcomings, and learning styles—and then be thoughtful and imaginative. The traditional approach to task analysis allows for the aforementioned individualization.

EXAMPLE OF A TASK ANALYSIS FOR ROPE JUMPING

Main task: For Mary to jump rope for a full (overhead) turn four times without verbal cue

Prerequisite skills: Ability to jump, ability to stand erect

I. Jump over painted line once over and back without verbal cue.
   a. Walk line down and back heel-to-toe with verbal cue.
   b. Face line with toes, jump over once with verbal cue.
   c. Stand parallel to line, jump over and back without verbal cue.

II. Jump over still rope over and back twice without verbal cue.
   a. Face rope with toes, jump over once with verbal cue.
   b. Stand parallel to rope, jump over and back with verbal cue.
   c. Stand parallel to rope, jump over and back twice without verbal cue.

III. Jump over wiggly (snake) rope 2 inches off ground without verbal cue.
   a. Jump wiggly rope on ground once with verbal cue.
   b. Jump wiggly rope 1 inch off ground over and back with verbal cue.
   c. Jump wiggly rope 2 inches off ground over and back without verbal cue.

IV. Jump over half-turned rope without verbal cue four times.
   a. Stand and jump on the back swing twice with verbal cue.
   b. Stand and jump on the forward and back swing twice with verbal cue.
   c. Stand and jump on the forward and back swing four times without verbal cue.

V. Jump rope a full turn overhead four times without verbal cue.
   a. Stand and jump once as the rope makes a full turn with verbal cue.
   b. Stand and jump twice as the rope makes a full turn with verbal cue.
   c. Stand and jump four times as the rope makes a full turn without verbal cue.

Figure 7.5 Example of a task analysis for rope jumping.

Activity Analysis

Activity analysis is a technique for determining the basic requirements of an activity needed for optimal student success in performing an activity. By breaking an activity into its components, the teacher can better understand the value of a certain activity and modify it to fit an individual learner's needs, as necessary. Thus, once a student's needs have been determined, the teacher can use activity analysis to assess whether a given activity can meet these needs.

Activity analysis facilitates the selection of program content based on the teacher's stated objectives. In making the analysis, the teacher must determine the physical, cognitive, social, and administrative requirements for performing the activity. When analyzing an activity from a physiological or biomechanical perspective, the teacher should examine such factors as basic body positions required, body parts used, body actions performed, fundamental movement patterns incorporated, required levels of coordination and fitness, and sensory systems used. Cognitive factors that should be examined include the number and complexity of rules and the need for memorization, concentration, strategies, and perceptual and academic skills. Social factors to consider in the activity analysis include the amount and type of interaction and communication required and whether the activity is cooperative or competitive. Such administrative demands as time, equipment, facility needs, and safety factors must also be determined. Table 7.4 shows an activity analysis for table tennis.

Table 7.4   An Activity Analysis for Table Tennis

Activity demands	Activity	Table tennis

Physical demands	1. Primary body position required?
	2. Movement skills required?
	3. Amount of fitness required?
	   a. Strength
	   b. Endurance
	   c. Speed
	   d. Flexibility
	   e. Agility
	4. Amount of coordination required?
	5. Amount of energy required?
		1. Standing
		2. Bending
		3. Minimal fitness level
		   a. Low ability to hold paddle
		   b. Low cardiovascular requirements
		   c. Quickness is an asset
		   d. Moderate
		   e. High level desirable
		4. Important, especially eye–hand coordination
		5. Little

Social demands	1. Number of participants required? 2. Types of interaction? 3. Type of communication? 4. Type of leadership? 5. Competitive or cooperative activity? 6. Amount of physical contact required? 7. Noise level?	1. Two for singles, four for doubles 2. Little; one-to-one 3. Little verbal, opportunity for nonverbal 4. None 5. Competitive mainly; cooperative if doubles 6. None in singles; much in doubles 7. Minimal
Cognitive demands	1. Complexity of rules? 2. Level of strategy? 3. Concentration level? 4. Academic skills needed? 5. Verbal skills needed? 6. Directional concepts needed? 7. Complexity of scoring system? 8. Memory required?	1. Moderate 2. Moderate 3. Moderate 4. Ability to count to 21 and to add 5. None 6. Yes 7. Simple 8. Little
Administrative demands	1. Time required? 2. Equipment needed? 3. Special facilities required? 4. Type of leadership required? 5. Safety factors to be considered?	1. Can be controlled by score or time 2. Paddles, balls, tables with nets 3. Area large enough to accommodate tables 4. Ability to instruct small group 5. Space between tables

Using Support Services

To teach physical education skills to students with identifiable disabilities, effective use of coteachers, support personnel, aides, volunteers, and peers is imperative. The following section outlines their effective use.

Team Teaching

If individuals with unique needs are in an inclusive physical education class, it is often best for two or more teachers to instruct the class together so that learner differences can be accommodated. This approach, called team teaching, is especially important in settings in which educators are not well prepared to work with students who have unique needs. This technique is often used in inclusive settings in which teachers of physical education, and perhaps an aide, work with children with special needs to allow them to participate with their peers.

Supportive Teaching

When students with disabilities are included in regular physical education classes it is often necessary for an aide or a volunteer assistant to help the student. This assistant supports the physical education teacher's efforts to include the child fully in the activity of the regular class and promotes successful participation by the student. The supportive teaching approach is particularly valuable for students just beginning the integration process.

Peer and Cross-Age Tutoring

Peer tutoring involves same-age students helping with instruction. Peer tutors can be used to reduce the student–teacher ratio. Cross-age tutoring programs enlist students of different ages (such as high school juniors or seniors) to work with young children receiving adapted physical education. Cross-age tutoring can provide satisfaction to tutors while increasing the level of learning for students with disabilities. The use of peer-age tutors has become common in inclusive physical education classes. Houston-Wilson, Dunn, Van der Mars, & McCubbin (1997) reported that the use of trained peer tutors assisting students with developmental disabilities resulted in improved motor performance when this technique was used in an integrated setting over a 36-day period.

PRESCRIPTIVE PLANNING AND INSTRUCTIONAL MODELS

Several curricular models developed since the 1970s have proven successful in providing a quality physical education experience for individuals with disabilities and have promoted the development of skills needed for inclusion. When used as guidelines, these models can help enhance the teaching process and ensure that students with unique needs are taught efficiently and effectively.

Project ACTIVE

The ACTIVE (All Children Totally InVolved Exercising) program was designed by Dr. Thomas Vodola (1976) to ensure that every child, regardless of disability, would have a chance to participate in a quality physical education program. Project ACTIVE incorporates a test-assess-prescribe-evaluate planning process and includes normative as well as criterion-referenced tests in the areas of motor ability, nutrition, physical fitness, and posture. (Materials are available from Joe Karp, Project ACTIVE, 103rd Place NE, Bothell, WA 98011-2455.)

The Data-Based Gymnasium

The Data-Based Gymnasium is a prescriptive instructional model that provides information on effectively managing the learning environment for individuals with severe disabilities. The Data-Based Gymnasium is unique in its delineation of applied behavior analysis techniques as a means of accomplishing meaningful learning objectives (see Dunn, Morehouse, & Fredericks, 1986). The Data-Based Gymnasium is discussed in detail in a subsequent chapter.

MOVE

The Mobility Opportunities Via Education (MOVE) model is a top-down activity-based curriculum developed to assist students with profound disabilities to learn the basic motor skills needed for everyday activities in the home and community. MOVE provides a sequence of age-appropriate motor activities valuable to the individual's quest for independence. (For additional information and training locations contact MOVE International, 1300 17th St., City Center, Bakersfield, CA 93301; phone 800-397-MOVE; e-mail: moveint@fc.kern.org; Web site: www.move-international.org.)

Moving to Inclusion

The Active Alliance for Canadians with Disability developed the Moving to Inclusion curriculum, which consists of nine books, available in English and French, that address a variety of disability groups. These resources are particularly valuable when planning to include students with disabilities in regular physical education classes. (The set is available from Canada Association for Health, Physical Education, and Recreation, 1600 James Naismith Drive, Gloucester, Ontario K1B 5N4, Canada; phone 613-748-5639.)

Special Olympics

This is a series of sport-specific instructional manuals, each including long-term goals, short-term objectives, skill assessment, task analysis, teaching suggestions, progression charts, and related information. (The manuals are available from Special Olympics, Inc., 1325 G St. NW #500, Washington DC 20005; 202-628-3630.)

I CAN

I CAN (Individualized instruction, Create social leisure competence, Associate all learnings, Narrow the gap between theory and practice) is a comprehensive physical education and leisure skills program for children with unique needs. The program is developmental in nature and provides a continuum of skills from preprimary motor and play skills to sport, leisure, and recreation skills. The Achievement Based Curriculum (ABC) model (Wessel & Kelly, 1986) is an enhancement of the I CAN curriculum and includes a systematic sequential process that enables teachers to plan, implement, and evaluate instructional programs for individuals based on selected goals and objectives (Wessel, 1979; Kelly, 1989).

I CAN Primary Skills K–3

The I CAN Primary Skills K–3 is a physical education curriculum based on a performance-based instructional model with feedback methods to improve and modify instruction based on stu-dent performance from kindergarten through third grade (see Wessel & Zittel, 1998).

SMART START Preschool Movement Curriculum

This curriculum provides teachers and caregivers a developmentally appropriate movement curriculum for preschool-aged children of all abilities (see Wessel & Zittel, 1995).

Both SMART START and the I CAN Primary Skills K-3 programs include skill checklists that can be used to collect information for individualizing movement programs.

SUMMARY

Many factors affect teaching for physical education and sport. Educators who can thoughtfully and imaginatively use many different approaches and teaching methods and match them to the needs of the learners in their classes are likely to have good success. Flexible educators teach the same content in different ways, thus allowing them to more fully adapt their teaching to meet individual needs. In this chapter the two major approaches to adapted physical education and sport—humanism and applied behavior analysis—were presented. The conclusion was reached that both approaches inform our teaching in a valuable, and often compatible, fashion. Important principles of motor learning that apply to students with unique needs were also discussed. The majority of the chapter examined how to effectively meet the very real challenge of individual differences in learners. Curricular options, activity modifications, teaching styles, and class formats were discussed along with several powerful educational tools, such as the instructional episode, task analysis, and activity analysis. Also discussed was the importance of using support services, especially with increased teacher–student ratios and an extremely diverse student body. Finally, selected prescriptive planning and instructional models were suggested. Familiarity with these excellent resources helps in optimizing the learning of students with unique needs.

REFERENCES

Active Living Alliance for Canadians with a Disability. (1994). *Moving to inclusion.* Gloucester, Ontario, Canada: Author.

Alberto, P.A., & Troutman, A.C. (1995). *Applied behavior analysis for teachers* (4th ed.). Englewood, NJ: Prentice-Hall.

Auxter, D., Pyfer, J., & Huettig, C. (2001). *Principles and methods of adapted physical education and recreation* (9th ed.). Boston, MA: McGraw-Hill.

Block, M. (2000). *A teacher's guide to including students with disabilities in general physical education* (2nd ed.). Baltimore, MD: Paul H. Brookes.

Burton, A., & Miller, D.E.(1998). *Movement skill assessment.* Champaign, IL: Human Kinetics.

Davis, W., & Burton, A.W. (1991). Ecological task analysis: Translating movement behavior theory into practice. *Adapted Physical Activity, 8*, 154-177.

Dunn, J.M. (1997). *Special physical education: Adapted, individualized, developmental.* Madison, WI: Brown & Benchmark.

Dunn, J.M., Morehouse, J.W., & Fredericks, H.D. (1986). *Physical education for the severely handicapped: A systematic approach to a data based gymnasium.* Austin, TX: Pro-ed.

Graham, G., Holt-Hale, S., & Parker, M. (2004). *Children moving: A reflective approach to teaching physical education* (6th ed.). Boston: McGraw-Hill.

Herkowitz, J. (1978). Developmental task analysis: The design of movement experiences and evaluation of motor development status. In M. Ridenour (Ed.), *Motor development: Issues and applications* (pp. 139-164). Princeton, NJ: Princeton Book Co.

Houston-Wilson, Dunn, J.M., van der Mars, H., & McCubbin, J.A. (1997). The effect of peer tutors on motor performance in integrated physical education classes. *Adapted Physical Education Quarterly, 14*(4), 298-313.

Kelly, L.E. (1989). Instructional time: The overlooked factor in PE curriculum development. *Journal of Physical Education, Recreation & Dance, 60*(6), 29-32.

Kelly, L.E. (1989). *Project I CAN-ABC.* Charlottesville, VA: University of Virginia.

Koegel, R.L., Russo, D.C., Rincover, A., & Schreibman, L. (1982). *Assessing and training teachers.* In R. L. Koegel, A. Rincover, & A.L. Egel (Eds.), Educating and understanding autistic children (pp. 178-202). San Diego, CA: College-Hill Press.

Langendorfer, S. (1985). Label motor patterns not kids: The developmental perspective for adapted physical education. *The Physical Educator, 42*(4), 175-179.

Lieberman, L.J., & Houston-Wilson, C. (2002). *Strategies for inclusion: A handbook for physical educators.* Champaign, IL: Human Kinetics.

Maslow, A. (1987). *Motivation and Personality.* NY: Harper Collins.

Newell, K.M. (1986). Constraints on the development of coordination. In M.G. Wade & H.T. Whiting (Eds.), *Motor development in children: Aspects of coordination and control* (pp. 341-360). Dordrecht, Netherlands: Nijhoff.

Reid, G., & O'Neill, K. (1989). *Adapted aquatics: Promoting aquatic opportunities for all.* The Canadian Red Cross Society.

Rich, S.M. (2000). *Instructional strategies for adapted physical education.* In J.P. Winnick (Ed.), Adapted physical education and sport (pp. 75-91). Champaign, IL: Human Kinetics.

Rink, J. (2002). *Teaching physical education for learning* (4th ed). NY: McGraw-Hill.

Rogers, C. R. (1980). *A way of being.* Boston: Houghton Mifflin.

Seaman, J.A., & DePauw, K.P. (1989). *The new physical education: A developmental approach.* Mountain View, CA: Mayfield.

Sherrill, C. (2004). *Adapted Physical Activity, recreation and sport: Crossdisciplinary and lifespan.* (5th ed.). Boston, MA: WCB/McGraw-Hill.

Seidl, C., Reid, G., & Montgomery, D.L. (1987). A critique of cardiovascular fitness testing with mentally retarded persons. *Adapted Physical Activity, 4*(2), 106-116.

Siedentop, D., & Tannehill, D. (2000). *Developing teaching skills in physical education* (4th ed.). Mountain View, CA: Mayfield Publishing.

Vodola, T. (1976). *Project ACTIVE maxi-model: Nine training manuals.* Oakhurst NJ: Project ACTIVE.

Watkinson, E.J., & Wall, A.E. (1982). PREP: Play skill manual. Ottawa: CAHPER.

Wessel, J.A. (1979). *I CAN—Sport, leisure and recreation skills.* Northbrook, IL: Hubbard.

Wessel, J.A., & Kelly, L.E. (1986). *Achievement-based curriculum development in physical education.* Philadelphia: Lea & Febiger.

Wessel, J.A., & Zittel, L.L. (1998). *I CAN primary skills K-3.* Austin TX: Pro-Ed.

Wessel, J.A., & Zittel, L.L. (1995). *SMART START: Preschool movement curriculum designed for children of all abilities.* Austin, TX: Pro-Ed.

WRITTEN RESOURCES

Please refer to the last section of this chapter (on page 128) for prescriptive planning and instructional models for developing curricula.

Gallahue, D.L. (1996). *Developmental physical education for today's children* (3d ed.). Madison, WI: Brown & Benchmark.

This source examines the developmental process from the prenatal period through age 12, including a discussion of psychomotor, cognitive, and affective factors influencing the motor development of children. Also described are teaching behaviors and styles that promote effective teaching of students with special needs. A helpful recourse in working with children that have developmental delays.

Graham, G., Holt/Hale, S., & Parker, M. (2001). *Children moving: A reflective approach to teaching physical education* (5th ed.). Mountain View, CA: Mayfield Publishing.

This comprehensive text on teaching elementary physical education outlines a reflective approach to teaching children. The developmental perspective presented applies to both typically developing children and those with unique needs.

ELECTRONIC RESOURCES

Adapt-talk, a subdivision of PE-Talk and sponsored by SportTime International.

Provides an e-mail opportunity to discuss adapted physical education challenges with peers and professionals worldwide. To subscribe to this service, send an e-mail (type "subscribe" in message) to adapt-talk-digestrequest@lists2. sportime.com.

PE Central Web site: http://pe.central.vt.edu.

PE Central is a frequently used online resource for regular physical educators and for teachers who work with students with unique needs. It includes curricular and lesson planning ideas and teaching suggestions.

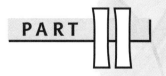
Individuals With Unique Needs

The first section of this part includes 10 chapters that relate to individuals with disabilities who are specially categorized in accordance with the Individuals with Disabilities Education Act (IDEA). A chapter discussing children with unique physical education needs who have not been classified as disabled by IDEA follows these chapters.

The disabilities discussed in the first 10 chapters include intellectual disorders (chapter 8); behavioral disabilities (chapter 9); pervasive developmental disorders (chapter 10); specific learning disabilities (chapter 11); visual impairments (chapter 12); deafness and deafblindness (chapter 13); cerebral palsy, traumatic brain injury, and stroke (chapter 14); amputations, dwarfism, and les autres (chapter 15); spinal cord disabilities (chapter 16); and other health-impaired students (chapter 17). These chapters examine the etiology of these conditions and the characteristics of affected groups. Particular attention is given in each chapter to implications for physical education. Sport programs associated with disabilities are presented. These chapters are critical for giving service providers the background and understanding they require about the individuals with unique needs they are preparing to serve.

CHAPTER 8

Intellectual Disabilities

Patricia L. Krebs

Loretta Claiborne was born with visual impairments, clubbed feet, and intellectual disabilities in the projects of York, Pennsylvania. After several surgeries to enable vision and correct her clubbed feet, she finally walked at the age of four and talked at the age of seven. Forbidden to participate in school sports because she was in special education, Loretta ran to get away from the bullies. At the age of 18, she became a Special Olympics athlete. Twenty-five years later, in 1996, Loretta Claiborne received the prestigious Arthur Ashe Award for Courage at ESPN's Espy Awards. In 1999, Disney aired a made-for-TV movie about her life, and Loretta appeared on The Oprah Winfrey Show. Along the way, Loretta completed three Boston Marathons, placing among the top 100 of all women finishers each time. In 1988 she finished in the top 25 women in the Pittsburgh Marathon and was named Special Olympics Female Athlete of the Year. In 1991, Loretta was named to Special Olympics Inc.'s board of directors and was selected by Runner's World magazine as the Special Olympics Athlete of the Quarter Century. The following year she was inducted into the York, Pennsylvania, Sports Hall of Fame and the William Penn High School Alumni Hall of Fame—the same high school that barred her from the track team because she had intellectual disabilities. Loretta introduced U.S. President Bill Clinton at the 1995 Special Olympics World Summer Games Opening Ceremonies in New Haven, Connecticut, and received an honorary doctorate degree of humane letters from Quinnipiac College in Hamden, Connecticut, the only known person with intellectual disabilities to receive an honorary doctorate. One of Loretta's most memorable races was a marathon in Harrisburg, Pennsylvania. Running strong, Loretta noticed another runner beginning to falter. Loretta slowed her pace and stayed with the man throughout the race, encouraging him on; they crossed the finish line together. The other runner? Former world heavyweight boxing champion Larry Holmes!

Intellectual disability is a condition currently in transition regarding terminology, definition, and treatment methods. In this chapter we will present current trends in definition, classification, and effective teaching techniques. As appropriate and to the extent possible, we will use the term *intellectual disabilities*. However, the term *mental retardation* will also be used, sometimes interchangeably with *intellectual disability,* because much of the previous literature and best practices have used this term. Also, the term *mental retardation* is used by the American Association on Mental Retardation (AAMR), the Individuals with Disabilities Education Act (IDEA), and other groups and individuals.

DEFINITION, CLASSIFICATION, AND INCIDENCE

Although there are several definitions and classification systems based on different criteria (e.g., medical condition, IQ score, needed supports), in this chapter we will use the 2002 definition and classification system proposed by the AAMR.

Definition

Individuals with intellectual disabilities present a diversity of abilities and potential, and educators must be prepared to accept this diversity. Intellectual disabilities present a substantial disadvantage to an individual attempting to function in society. They are characterized by cognitive limitations as well as functional limitations in such areas as daily living skills, social skills, and communication. Over the years, the AAMR's definition of and criteria for classification of mental retardation has changed dramatically, affecting the incidence of mental retardation.

To define the disability of mental retardation, public law 105-17, the Individuals with Disabilities Education Act (IDEA) amendments of 1997 uses the 1973 American Association on Mental Deficiency's (AAMD) definition of mental retardation (Grossman, 1973) and adds a phrase on how it affects educational performance: "Mental retardation means significantly subaverage general intellectual functioning, existing concurrently with deficits in adaptive behavior and manifested during the developmental period, that adversely affects a child's educational performance" (IDEA, 1997).

This definition doesn't differ much from the current AAMR definition of mental retardation, adopted in 2002, which states, "Mental retardation is a disability characterized by significant limitations in intellectual functioning and in adaptive behavior as expressed in conceptual, social, and practical adaptive skills. The disability originates before age 18" (Luckasson et al., 2002, p. 8).

Thus, three criteria must be met for someone to be diagnosed as having mental retardation. The first, "significant limitations in intellectual functioning," refers to a person scoring two or more standard deviations below the mean on a standardized intelligence test that is normed on the general population, including people with disabilities and without them. Two intelligence tests used extensively throughout the world are the Stanford-Binet IV and the Wechsler Intelligence Scale for Children III.

The second criterion, "significant limitations in adaptive behavior as expressed in conceptual, social, and practical adaptive skills" involves the collection of skills a person learns in order to function in everyday life. Limitations in adaptive behavior affect typical performance in both daily life and the ability to respond to changes in daily life and the environment. As with intellectual functioning, to determine significant limitations in adaptive behavior, an individual must score two or more standard deviations below the mean on a standardized assessment measuring one of the three adaptive skill areas or on an overall score measuring all three adaptive skill areas:

1. **Conceptual:** Language, reading and writing, money concepts, self-direction

2. **Social:** Interpersonal skills, responsibility, self-esteem, naiveté, obeys rules and laws, avoids victimization

3. **Practical:** Activities of daily living, occupational skills, maintains safe environments

The third criterion is that the disability originates before the age of 18. Conception through age 18 is considered the developmental period and is the period of the life cycle prior to adulthood. It is during this time that various developmental processes are being achieved. Adverse influences occurring during this time of brain growth and development may adversely impact these developmental processes. However, as long as the potential for continued growth exists (until about age 18), compensatory actions may occur to counteract these adverse influences and improve the ultimate structure and function of the brain. Thus an individual with normal intellectual functioning who sustains a brain injury or trauma after age 18 (adulthood), rendering deficiencies in both intellectual and adaptive behavior, is not considered to have mental retardation.

Classification and Description

Many systems exist for classifying intellectual disabilities: IQ level, intensity of needed supports, behavioral, and etiological. The World Health Organization's (WHO) International Classification of Diseases (ICD) (2001) and the American Psychiatric Association's Diagnostic and Statistical Manual of Mental Disorders DSM-IV (2000) use intelligence test scores to determine the level of severity of intellectual disabilities (table 8.1). AAMR used this classification system until 1992.

Table 8.1 Classification of Severity of Mental Retardation Based on IQ Scores

Mental retardation level	Intelligence test score
Mild mental retardation	IQ 50-55 to 70-75
Moderate mental retardation	IQ 35-40 to 50-55
Severe mental retardation	IQ 20-25 to 35-40
Profound mental retardation	IQ below 20-25

Although classification systems are necessary for service reimbursement, research parameters, service provision, and communication about selected characteristics, they also stigmatize people by assigning labels that tend to trigger absolute behavioral expectations and negative emotional reactions by society. Labels are also erroneously used as a global summary about people with mental retardation when in reality they reflect little information about the individual and thus have little application when developing support needs based on individual strengths and limitations.

Presently, however, AAMR's approach to classification has shifted from a deficit level within the individual to the relation between the individual's functioning and the environment and the supports needed to maximize his or her functioning (Luccasson et al., 2002). Thus, once the diagnosis of mental retardation has been made, a profile of individual strengths and limitations along five dimensions is determined. These five dimensions include:

- intellectual ability;
- adaptive behavior;
- participation (in everyday activities), interaction (with material and social worlds), and social roles (valued activities normal for an age group);
- health (physical, mental, and etiology); and
- context (involves the interrelated conditions within which people live their everyday lives—their families, communities, society, and culture).

Finally, a profile of needed supports is developed in each of nine areas. Supports are the resources and strategies that promote the development, education, interests, and personal well-being of a person and enhance individual functioning. The nine support areas profiled are the following:

- Human development
- Teaching and education
- Home living
- Community living
- Employment
- Health and safety
- Behavioral
- Social
- Protection and advocacy

The profile should address three aspects of supports in each of the nine support areas. The first aspect is the source of supports. The support source can be "natural," meaning supports are provided by people or equipment typically available and culturally appropriate within the individual's environment, or they can be "service based," which means supports are provided by people or equipment that are typically not part of the individual's natural environment. The second aspect is determining the support function. AAMR proposes eight support functions: teaching, befriending, financial planning, employee assistance, behavioral support, in-home living assistance, community access and use, and health assistance. AAMR also identifies many support activities corresponding to the eight support functions. The third aspect of supports which should be addressed in the profile is the intensity of needed supports. AAMR classifies supports into four intensity categories: *intermittent, limited, extensive, and pervasive.* This ILEP classification system emphasizes the interaction of supports to functioning, irrespective of an individual's IQ, and provides a way to classify and organize critical information about what he or she needs. These four intensity categories are determined by the type of support needed, how long and how often support is needed, the setting(s) in which the support is needed, the resources required to provide the support, and the degree of intrusiveness in one's life the support causes.

- **Intermittent supports** are episodic and short term in nature; most are provided on an as-needed basis. These are usually supports required during a job loss, medical emergency, or other life crisis.
- **Limited supports** are more consistent over time but are still time limited. They require few staff members and minimal cost, such as time-limited employment training or transition support from school to adulthood.
- **Extensive supports** are not time limited and are characterized by regular (daily) involvement in some (though usually not all) environments. Examples are long-term home living support, ongoing special education classes, or employment in special centers.
- **Pervasive supports** are constant, highly intense, and potentially life sustaining in nature; they are provided across all environments. Pervasive supports involve several people, significant costs, and significant intrusiveness in the individual's life.

A planning supports team develops an **individualized supports plan (ISP)** designed to improve the everyday life functioning of an individual with intellectual disabilities, enabling him or her to lead a more fulfilling and integrated life. For AAMR (Luckasson et al., 2002), the importance of supports is that they hold the promise of providing a more natural, efficient, and ongoing basis for enhancing personal outcomes related to independence, relationships, contributions, school and community participation, and personal well-being. In the remainder of this chapter we will generally use the intensity of support needs when describing students with intellectual disabilities, not levels of deficit identified by performance on an IQ test. This distinction is important in the education of students with intellectual disabilities in that the focus shifts from students with deficits to the types and intensities of supports these students need to succeed in physical education and the general curriculum. There are instances in this chapter, however, when classification by IQ level is used because it was the classification system used in the reported research.

Incidence

According to normal probability theory, it is estimated that 2.28 percent of the total population (with no known organic dysfunction) of any society has intellectual disabilities (2.15% + .13% = 2.28%). It is also estimated that .76 percent of

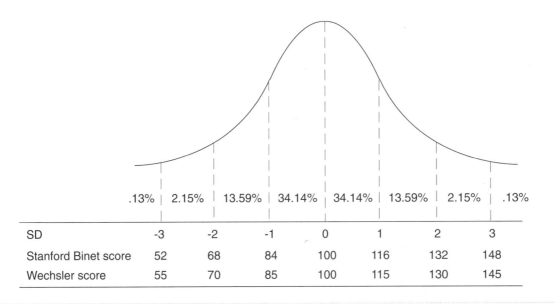

	.13%	2.15%	13.59%	34.14%	34.14%	13.59%	2.15%	.13%
SD	-3	-2	-1	0	1	2	3	
Stanford Binet score	52	68	84	100	116	132	148	
Wechsler score	55	70	85	100	115	130	145	

Figure 8.1 The normal curve and intelligence quotient scores.

the total population has known organic dysfunction that cause intellectual disabilities. These figures (2.28 percent plus .76 percent rounded to 3.0 percent) are used to estimate the incidence of individuals with intellectual disabilities in a particular geographic area (figure 8.1). The actual number of children and adults with intellectual disabilities receiving services through the educational system or governmental services systems is often much less than 3 percent of the population. This is because most people with intellectual disabilities do not need special services and thus are not on any lists identifying them.

CAUSES OF INTELLECTUAL DISABILITIES

There are nearly 500 disorders in which intellectual disabilities might occur as a specific manifestation of the disorder (Murphy, Boyle, Schendel, Decoufle, et al., 1998). These disorders are categorized according to when in the gestation period they occur—prenatally, perinatally, or postnatally. Depending on the population studied and the methods used, it has been reported that causes of mild and severe intellectual disabilities are as shown in table 8.2 (Hagberg & Kyllerman, 1983; McLaren & Bryson, 1987; Yeargin-Allsopp et al., 1997).

Table 8.2 Incidence of Mental Retardation Based on Gestation Period

Gestational stage	Mild ID	Severe ID
Prenatal	7-23%	25-55%
Perinatal	4-18%	10-15%
Postnatal	2-4%	7-10%

The most prevalent known cause of intellectual disabilities is fetal alcohol syndrome (as much as 1 in 333 births), in some studies accounting for up to half of all individuals with intellectual disabilities, but sophisticated genetic mapping research has recently determined that X-linked disorders are the most prevalent inherited disorders leading to intellectual disabilities (1 in 3,600 males and 1 in 4,000 to 6,000 females). X-linked disorders are caused by a recessive sex gene defect expressed in twice as many males as females. This is because

males inherit one X chromosome and one Y chromosome. Females inherit two X chromosomes. Thus, a male who receives the defective X gene will almost always display the disorder, whereas a female with a normal dominant X gene to oppose the abnormal recessive X gene will be clinically normal. However, a female risks transmitting the defective gene to half her offspring, including the sons, all of whom will be affected. An affected male with an X-linked disorder will transmit the defective gene to all his daughters, who will be carriers. His sons will be both clinically and genetically normal for the disorder. Fragile X syndrome is the leading inherited cause of intellectual disabilities. Other well-known X-linked disorders are Duchenne muscular dystrophy and hemophilia.

About half of the population with intellectual disabilities has more than one possible causal factor, and often the cause of the intellectual disability reflects the cumulative or interactive effects of many factors (McLaren & Bryson, 1987; Scott, 1988). For example, low birth weight is often considered to be an organic etiology, but other psychosocial factors such as maternal youth, poverty, lack of education, and inadequate prenatal care might also have contributed to the low birth weight. A multifactorial approach to etiology accounts for whether the causal factors affect the parents of the person with intellectual disabilities, the person with intellectual disabilities, or both; this approach extends the types of etiologic factors into four categories:

Biomedical—relates to biological processes, such as genetic disorders or nutrition

Social—relates to social and family interaction, such as stimulation and adult responsiveness

Behavioral—relates to potentially causal behaviors, such as dangerous (injurious) activities or maternal substance abuse

Educational—relates to the availability of educational supports that promote mental development and the development of adaptive skills (Luckasson et al., 2002)

Similarly, prevention efforts are directed toward the parents or the person at risk for developing intellectual disabilities. Primary prevention efforts are directed toward the parents of the individual with intellectual disabilities and aimed at preventing the problem from occurring (such as programs that prevent maternal alcohol abuse).

Secondary prevention efforts are directed toward the individual born with a condition that might result in intellectual disabilities and aimed at limiting or reversing the effects of existing problems (such as dietary programs to treat individuals born with phenylketonuria). **Tertiary prevention efforts** are directed toward the person who has intellectual disabilities and aimed at minimizing the severity of functional impairments or preventing secondary conditions (such as programs for physical, educational, or vocational habilitation).

COGNITIVE DEVELOPMENT

The 2002 AAMR definition of mental retardation is functionally and contextually oriented. Although this orientation is useful in determining individual strengths and limitations in present functioning, it is limited for understanding the dynamic nature of intellectual functioning and how it changes from age to age in the developmental process. Such a developmental orientation toward intelligence promotes effective instruction and programming.

To establish developmental orientation, it is necessary to draw on the extensive work of Piaget (1952). In his vast writing, Piaget proposed that children move through four stages of cognitive development: the **sensorimotor stage** (ages 0 to 2), the **preoperational stage** (ages 2 to 7), the stage of **concrete operations** (ages 7 to 11), and the stage of **formal operations** (age 11 or 12 to adulthood). These stages are depicted in table 8.3.

Sensorimotor Stage

During the sensorimotor stage, children develop, use, and modify their first schemata. For Piaget, schemata are forms of knowing that develop, change, expand, and adapt. A schema (singular) might be a simple response to a stimulus, an overt action, a means to an end, an end in itself, an internalized thought process, or a combination of overt actions and internalized thought processes.

Table 8.3 Stages of Cognitive and Play Development

Age (years)	Piagetian cognitive developmental stage	Type of play	Play group
0	Sensorimotor	Practice play and ritualization	Individual
1			
2	Preoperational	Symbolic	Egocentrism and parallel play
3			Reciprocal play (progressive reciprocity in dyads, triads, and the like)
4			
5			
6			
7	Concrete operations	Games with rules	Larger group play
8			
9			
10			
11	Formal operations		
12			
13			
14			
15			

Examples of schemata include grasping, sucking, and tossing a ball. During the sensorimotor stage, for example, a child develops the schema of grasping, which is internally controlled and can be used in grasping the mother's finger, picking up different objects, or picking up an object from various angles. A schema often functions in combination or in sequence with other schemata, such as when a child throws the ball, an action that combines the schemata of grasping and releasing.

To a great extent, the sensorimotor period is when a child learns about the self and the environment through the sense modalities. A great deal of attention is given to physically manipulating and acting on objects and on observing the effects of such actions. The child is stimulated by objects in the environment and observes how objects react to actions applied to them. Through exploration, manipulation, and problem solving, children gain information about the properties of objects, such as texture, size, weight, and resiliency, as they drop, thrust, pull, push, bend, twist, punch, squeeze, or lift objects that have various properties. At this stage, the functioning of the individual is largely sensorimotor in nature, with only rudimentary ability to manipulate reality through symbolic thinking.

Preoperational Stage

The preoperational stage includes the preconceptual substage, which lasts to about the age of four, and the substage of intuitive thought, which spans the ages of four to seven. Toward the end of the sensorimotor period, the child begins to develop the ability to symbolically represent actions before acting them out. However, the symbolic representation is primitive and limited to schemata associated with one's own actions. During the preoperational stage, progress occurs as the child is able to represent objects through language and use language in thinking. The child can now think about objects and activities and manipulate them verbally and symbolically.

Concrete Operations Stage

During the stage of concrete operations children achieve operational thought, which enables them to develop mental representations of the physical world and manipulate these representations in their minds (operations). The fact that operations are limited to those of action, to the "concrete," or to those that depend on perception distinguishes

this stage from the stage of formal operations. The fact that the child is able to develop and manipulate mental representations of the physical world distinguishes this stage from earlier stages. In the stage of concrete operations, the child is able to mentally carry through a logical idea. The physical actions that predominated in earlier stages can now be internalized and manipulated as mental actions.

During the period of concrete operations, increased sophistication is present in the use of language and other signs. In the preoperational phase the child developed word definitions without full understanding of what the words meant. In the stage of concrete operations, language becomes a vehicle for the thinking process as well as a tool for verbal exchange. In this stage, children can analyze situations from perspectives other than their own. This decentering permits thinking to become more logical and the conception of the environment to be more coherently organized. During the period of concrete operations, children's thinking becomes more consistent, stabilized, and organized. At the same time, although children are able to perform the more complex operations just described, they are generally incapable of sustaining them when they cease to manipulate objects or when the operations are not tied to physical actions.

Formal Operations Stage

Children functioning at the stage of formal operations are not confined to concrete objects and events in their operations. They are able to think in terms of the hypothetical and to use abstractions to solve problems. They enter the world of ideas and can rely on pure symbolism instead of operating solely from physical reality. They are able to consider all of the possible ways a problem can be solved and to understand the effects of a variable on a problem. Individuals at this stage can isolate the elements of a problem and systematically explore possible solutions. Whereas children at the stage of concrete operations tend to deal largely with the present, those functioning at the formal operations stage are concerned with the future, the remote, and the hypothetical. They can establish assumptions and hypotheses, test hypotheses, and formulate principles, theories, and laws. They not only can think but can also think about what they are thinking and why they are thinking it. During this stage, individuals are able to use systems of formal logic in their thinking.

Piaget and Play

Piaget called behaviors related to play **ludic** behaviors, which are engaged in to amuse or excite the individual. He held that behaviors become play when they are repeated for functional pleasure. Activities pursued for functional pleasure appear early in the sensorimotor period. According to Piaget, the most primitive type of play is practice play or exercise play. The child repeats clearly acquired skills (schemata) for the pleasure and joy of it. The infant repeats a movement, such as shaking a rattle over and over, and exhibits pleasure in doing so. This type of play does not include symbolism or make believe.

Later in the sensorimotor period, the play in which the child engages is called **ritualization.** More and more schemata are developed and used in new situations. Play becomes a happy display of mastered activities; gestures are repeated and combined as a ritual, and the child makes a motor game of them. As progress is made, the child forms still newer combinations from modified schemata. For example, a child might follow the ritual of sleeping after being exposed to the stimuli associated with sleeping (pillow, blanket, thumb sucking). Toward the end of the sensorimotor period, the child develops symbolic schemata and mental associations. These symbolic schemata enable him or her to begin to pretend or make believe in play. Some authors refer to symbolic play as make-believe play. Throughout the sensorimotor stage, play is individual or egocentric, and there are no rules involved.

The preconceptual period within the preoperational stage marks the transition from practice play to symbolic play. At the preconceptual stage the child's play extends beyond his or her own actions. Also, new ludic behaviors appear that enable children to pretend. At ages four through seven (the intuitive thought stage), an advance in symbolic play occurs. The child relates a story in correct order, is capable of a more exact and accurate imitation of reality, and uses collective symbolism (other people are considered during play). The child begins to play with one or more companions but also continues to display parallel play. In play, the child can think in terms of others, and social rules begin to replace individual ludic symbols. For example, games of tag and games related to the hiding of a moving object are now played. Although play is egocentric, opportunities for free, unstructured, and spontaneous play are important. Children at this level are not positively responsive to intuitive thought. Advancement occurs from egocentricity to reciprocity in play. Thus, opportunities for cooperative play become appropriate. It should be noted that the collective symbolism associated with cooperative play is at its beginning in this period. Guessing games, games based on looking for missing objects, games of make believe, and spontaneous games are stimulating for children during this stage. The fact that children are responsive to tag games, for example, indicates that they are beginning to play with others and to consider others during play.

At the stage of concrete operations there is an increase in games with rules. Rules might be "handed down," as in cultural games, or developed spontaneously. An expansion of socialization and a consolidation of social rules occur. Thus, the playing and construction of group games with rules becomes very attractive to children. As the child enters and moves through this period, play becomes less concerned with make believe and pretending and more concerned with "real" games. At this stage, play might be structured, social, and bound by rules. Although some children might be ready for such games by their seventh birthday, children with intellectual disabilities might not be ready for them until after adolescence, if then.

Application of Cognitive Development to Teaching

There are many teaching implications associated with cognitive theory. Because of space considerations, only a few examples are presented. First, because language is more abstract than concrete, teachers need to reduce verbalization of instructions and emphasize tactile, kinesthetic, visual, and other more concrete forms of instruction. Children who cannot readily transfer learning or apply past experiences to new situations need more gradual task progressions in smaller sequential steps and need to learn and practice skills in the environments in which they are used. It is also important to consider level of cognitive development in teaching rules and game strategies. As cognition develops, more complex rules and strategies can be introduced. Knowing the type of play and play groups associated with developmental stages can influence successful participation in games (table 8.3). Individuals at developmental age of six or earlier respond with greater enthusiasm for make-believe games played in small groups. Finally, language development should be considered in verbalization. For example, it is often helpful to emphasize action words and simple sentences when communicating instructions rather than multiple complex sentences. Demonstrations and physical assistance will facilitate the instructional process. Feedback on quality of performance should be short and specific. Cognitive theory also serves as a basis for some of the organizational and instructional methods suggested later in the chapter.

CHARACTERISTICS OF INDIVIDUALS WITH INTELLECTUAL DISABILITIES

Intellectual disabilities are multidimensional in that they affect all aspects of an individual's life. Following are characteristics typically manifested in individuals with intellectual disabilities.

Learning Characteristics

The area in which individuals with intellectual disabilities differ most from others is in cognitive behavior. The greater the degree of intellectual disabilities, the lower the cognitive level at which the individual functions. Most adults with intellectual disabilities needing **pervasive supports** function at the sensorimotor cognitive stage. Adults with intellectual disabilities needing **limited supports** might not be able to progress beyond the level of concrete operations. Others might be limited to simpler forms of formal operations or might be incapable of surpassing the preoperational substage.

Although the learning process and stages of learning are the same for both, children with intellectual disabilities learn at a slower rate than children without intellectual disabilities and thus achieve less academically. The learning rate of children with intellectual disabilities needing intermittent or limited supports is usually 40 to 70 percent of the rate of children without intellectual disabilities. Children needing extensive or pervasive supports often do not benefit from traditional schooling. Although self-contained classes and separate schools for children needing extensive or pervasive supports exist in most school systems, the primary educational objectives for them involve mastery of basic life skills

and communication skills needed for their care. Whereas adults needing extensive supports might learn to dress, feed, and care for their own hygiene properly and might even benefit from work activities, they will most likely need close supervision and care throughout their lives.

Social and Emotional Characteristics

Although children with intellectual disabilities exhibit the same ranges of social behavior and emotion as other children, they more frequently demonstrate inappropriate responses to social and emotional situations. Because they have difficulty generalizing information or learning from past experiences at the same rate or capacity as children without intellectual disabilities, they are likely to be unprepared to handle all the situations they encounter. Children with intellectual disabilities often do not fully understand what is expected of them, and they might respond inappropriately because they have misinterpreted the situation rather than because they lack appropriate responses.

Educational programs for children with intellectual disabilities should always include experiences to help them determine social behaviors and emotional responses for everyday situations. Personal acceptance and development of healthy social relationships are critical to independence. As is true for individuals without intellectual disabilities, the reason most individuals needing intermittent or limited supports lose jobs is inadequacy of social skills, such as poor work habits, and an inability to get along with fellow workers. On the other hand, when individuals develop basic social and emotional skills, they are happier and more accepting—and they are a joy to teach in physical activity settings.

Physical and Motor Characteristics

Children with intellectual disabilities differ least from children without intellectual disabilities in their physical and motor characteristics. Although most children with intellectual disabilities display developmental motor delays, they are often related more to limited attention and comprehension than to physiological or motor control deficits.

Generally, the greater the intellectual disability, the greater the lag in attaining major developmental milestones. As a group, children with intellectual disabilities walk and talk later, are slightly shorter, and usually are more susceptible to physical problems and illnesses than other children. In comparative studies, children with intellectual disabilities consistently score lower than children without intellectual disabilities on measures of strength, endurance, agility, balance, running speed, flexibility, and reaction time. Although many students with intellectual disabilities can successfully compete with their peers without intellectual disabilities, those students needing extensive or pervasive supports have a discrepancy equivalent to four or more years behind their peers without intellectual disabilities on tests of physical fitness and motor performance.

In general, the fitness and motor performance of children without intellectual disabilities exceeds that of children with intellectual disabilities needing intermittent or limited supports, who in turn perform better than children needing extensive or pervasive supports. The performance of boys generally exceeds that of girls, with the differences between the genders increasing as the intensity of needed supports increases (Eichstaedt, Wang, Polacek, & Dohrmann, 1991; Londeree & Johnson, 1974). Flexibility and balance seem to be the exceptions. Whereas girls without intellectual disabilities show greater flexibility and balance than boys without intellectual disabilities, boys with intellectual disabilities show greater flexibility and balance than girls with intellectual disabilities. Winnick and Short (1999a) recommend that children aged 10 to 17 with intellectual disabilities needing intermittent or limited supports should achieve levels of aerobic capacity, body composition, flexibility, abdominal strength, upper body strength, and endurance (necessary for positive health, independent living, and participation in physical activities) approaching the performance levels of their peers without disabilities. Winnick and Short (1999b) also offer activity guidelines for developing these functional and physiological fitness levels in children with intellectual and other disabilities. Also, children with Down syndrome exhibit more flexibility than other children with intellectual disabilities (Eichstaedt, Wang, Polacek, & Dohrmann, 1991; Rarick, Dobbins, & Broadhead, 1976; Rarick & McQuillan, 1977). Children with Down syndrome tend to have hypotonic musculature and hypermobility of the joints, which permits them greater than normal body flexibility and, because of weak ligaments and muscles, places them at greater risk of injury.

Many children with intellectual disabilities are hypotonic and overweight. Nutritional guidance and fitness activities might be necessary to enable a student to perform at a higher level of skill. Disproportionate bodies pose many problems with body mechanics and balance. Activities done on uneven surfaces or requiring rapid change of direction can cause anxiety and pose greater risk of injury and failure. Body alignment is in a total body slump. Club hands and feet, postural deviations, and cerebral palsy are all prevalent among children with intellectual disabilities; physical educators must consider this when planning each child's program (figure 8.2).

Figure 8.2 Many children with intellectual disabilities have other conditions as well.

Intellectual disabilities often coexist with other disabilities in children. The occurrence and number of coexisting conditions increase with increased severity of intellectual disabilities (Murphy et al., 1998), as shown in table 8.4.

Table 8.4 Coexistence of Intellectual Disabilities (ID) With Other Disabilities

Coexisting disability	With mild ID	With severe ID
Autism	9%	20%
Epilepsy	4-7%	20-32%
Cerebral palsy	6-8%	24-30%
Sensory deficits	2%	11%

DOWN SYNDROME

Down syndrome is the most recognizable genetic condition associated with intellectual disabilities. Because of its prevalence and unique sport and physical education implications, we will discuss it at length here. One in 700 children is born with Down syndrome. In the United States, about 5,000 such children are born each year. Although fathers are genetically responsible for the abnormality in about 25 percent of all cases, women over the age of 35 present the highest risk (1 in 290) of having a child with Down syndrome. At age 40 the risk increases to 1 in 150 births, and at age 45 the risk is 1 in 20 births (Cunningham, 1987).

Cause

Down syndrome results from one of three chromosomal abnormalities. The most common cause is trisomy 21, so named because of the presence of an extra number 21 chromosome. This results in a total of 47 chromosomes instead of the normal 46 (23 chromosomes received from each parent). A second cause of Down syndrome is nondisjunction, which occurs when one pair of chromosomes fails to divide during meiotic cell division, resulting in 24 chromosomes in one haploid cell and 22 in the other. A third and rare cause of Down syndrome is translocation, which occurs when two chromosomes grow together; they appear to be one chromosome but contain the genetic material of two chromosomes.

Characteristics

Although over 80 clinical characteristics are associated with Down syndrome, the most common physical characteristics are the following:

- Short stature
- Poor muscle tone
- Small nose with flat bridge
- Eyes slanted upward & outward
- Exaggerated folds of skin around eyes
- Mild to moderate obesity
- Underdeveloped respiratory and cardiovascular systems
- Short legs and arms in relation to torso
- Short neck
- Small low-set ears
- Small head and flat face
- Broad hands and feet
- Stubby fingers and toes
- Poor balance
- Perceptual difficulties
- Poor vision and audition

Many of these characteristics can be seen in the photo in figure 8.3.

Many people with Down syndrome also have medical problems. About 40 percent of these individuals develop congenital heart disease. They also have a greater risk of developing leukemia. Bowel defects requiring surgery and respiratory infections are common. People with Down syndrome age more rapidly, and almost all who live beyond age 40 develop Alzheimer's disease (Zigman, Silverman, & Wisniewski, 1996). In the United

© Special Olympics Maryland/Richard Lippenholz

Figure 8.3 Special Olympics athlete with Down syndrome.

States, a shocking racial disparity exists in the median lifespans of people with Down syndrome (Yang, Rasmussen, & Friedman, 2002). A 15-year study of 34,000 individuals with Down syndrome revealed that the median age at death for Caucasians with Down syndrome is 50 years, whereas it is 25 years for African-Americans and 11 years for people of other races. Individuals with Down syndrome are becoming increasingly integrated into our society and institutions, including schools, health care systems, community living, and the work force. Although there is always a degree of slow development and learning difficulties associated with Down syndrome, attainment and functional ability is much higher than previously thought possible (when people with Down syndrome attended only institutions and segregated schools).

Physical Education Programming

The many medical problems of individuals with Down syndrome require medical clearance for activity participation and careful planning of the physical education program. Aerobic activities and activities requiring maximal muscular contraction must be adapted and carefully monitored. Muscle hypotonia (low muscle tone) and hypermobility (above normal mobility) of the joints often cause postural and orthopedic impairments, such as lordosis, ptosis, dislocated hips, kyphosis, atlantoaxial instability, flat pronated feet, and forward head. Exercises and activities that cause hyperflexion are contraindicated because they put undue stress on the body that could result in hernias, dislocations, strains, or sprains. Rather, exercises and activities that strengthen muscles around the joints, thereby stabilizing them, should be encouraged. Poor eyesight and hearing in children with Down syndrome will require teachers to employ adapted equipment and teaching strategies typical for those with sensory impairments.

ASSESSMENT

Assessment is necessary to determine the status and needs of students with intellectual disabilities. Children with intellectual disabilities who need only intermittent or limited supports can often take the same tests as children without intellectual disabilities. In some instances standardized tests might require modification, or standardized tests designed specifically for students with intellectual disabilities might need to be selected. Children with intellectual disabilities needing intermittent or limited supports should also be able to complete methods of assessment used with the general student population. However, children needing extensive or pervasive supports often lack the levels of physical fitness, motor ability, motivation, and understanding required to perform standardized test items. Winnick and Short (1999a) recommend using task analysis or other measures of physical activity as an alternative to standardized tests designed to measure physical fitness of those with such support needs. Pedometers are being used more often to measure involvement in physical activity. Alternate assessments incorporating teacher-developed specially designed or adapted rubrics, analytic rating scales, and checklists are also appropriate to measure physical education abilities of this population.

We recommend three tests developed specifically for use with students with intellectual disabilities: the Brockport Physical Fitness Test (Winnick & Short, 1999a) designed to measure health-related physical fitness; The Ohio State University Scale of Intra-Gross Motor Assessment (Ohio State SIGMA) (Loovis & Ersing, 1979) designed to measure motor development; and the Special Olympics Sports Skills Guides (2000-2003) designed to measure gross motor development and motor skills and sports skills. Additional information regarding testing appears in chapter 4.

ORGANIZATIONAL AND INSTRUCTIONAL METHODS

Although many of the organizational and instructional methods used in teaching students without intellectual disabilities can be applicable to students with intellectual disabilities, certain methods are often stressed in the teaching of students with intellectual disabilities. When employed, these methods ensure successful positive experiences for students with intellectual disabilities in a physical education class where maximum participation takes place in a controlled environment.

Organizational Methods

Certain organizational methods have proven particularly successful in aiding the learning of students with intellectual disabilities and enabling them to be included in activities. They are using learning stations, peer tutoring, community-based instruction, and partial participation.

Learning Stations

Learning stations divide the gymnasium or play area into smaller units, each of which is designed for students to learn or practice a specific skill or sport. Students may be assigned to a single learning station for the entire activity period or might rotate from station to station after a set amount of time or after a learning goal has been achieved. Learning stations permit flexibility, allow students to progress at their own pace, and provide safe and successful learning experiences for both students with and without intellectual disabilities. Stations might focus on a theme (e.g., physical fitness, tennis, motor skills) and promote full integration while accommodating large numbers of students.

Peer Instruction and Cross-Age Tutoring

One of the most exciting developments in special education programs is the use of peers (other students with or without disabilities) to help children with unique needs. It is common for young children to rely on slightly older peers as role models. Cross-age tutoring is an excellent way of providing children with intellectual disabilities role models whom they can imitate. Peer instruction and cross-age tutoring increases personalized instruction time for students with intellectual disabilities.

Community-Based Instruction

Teaching skills in the "real" environment where the skills will ultimately be used is preferable to artificial environments such as the classroom or gym. Students with intellectual disabilities who need extensive or pervasive supports do not generalize well from one environment to another. In fact, teaching skills in artificial environments often entails reteaching the same skills in community environments. Thus, it is much more efficient to teach skills in environments where they will be used. One of the critical steps in the process of teaching skills in natural environments is identifying and prioritizing environments in which the skills will actually be used. For example, teaching students to access and use community health club facilities, bowling facilities, or community pools is preferred to teaching these activities in school gyms or pools.

Partial Participation

If a student with intellectual disabilities can acquire some of the skills needed to participate in an activity, the parts of the skills that cannot be performed can be compensated through physical assistance or adaptations of equipment. Often, peer tutors can provide the physical assistance, whereas modified equipment and rule changes can allow students to participate in an inclusive setting. For example, a student with cerebral palsy who uses a motorized wheelchair can be assigned a specially lined area of the soccer field. If the soccer ball enters this lined area, the peer tutor stops the ball. The student then has five seconds to maneuver his wheelchair to touch the ball. If the student is successful, the peer tutor then kicks the ball to a member of the student's team. If the student is unsuccessful, the peer tutor then kicks the ball to a member of the opposing team.

Instructional Methods

How you present information to your students with intellectual disabilities often makes the difference between success and failure. The following instructional strategies have proven successful for students with intellectual disabilities.

Concrete and Multisensory Experiences

Because children with intellectual disabilities are slower in cognitive development, their mental operations might be confined to concrete objects and events. Thus, concrete tasks and information are more easily learned and used than their abstract counterparts. Instruction should be concrete, emphasizing only the most important task cues. Because verbalization is more abstract, demonstration or modeling, physical prompting, or manipulation of body parts should accompany verbal instruction. Ensure that demonstrations and modeling are correct so that students do not copy incorrect ways of performing. Verbal instructions and cues should be short and simple and focus on action words; instead of saying, "go," say "run," "walk," or "hop."

Data-Based Teaching

Data-based instruction involves monitoring a student's progress and how such factors as environmental arrangement, equipment, task analysis, time of day, levels of reinforcement, and cueing techniques affect progress. By charting student progress, teacher and student can often determine when an objective will be accomplished (e.g., complete two laps around the track). Cooperative charting by teacher and student can provide motivation and direction to help a student estimate how long it will take to accomplish any new task, set personal objectives to accomplish a task within a reasonable margin of error, and identify practice techniques for reaching the objectives set.

Task Analysis

Because children with intellectual disabilities are generally unable to attend to as many task cues or pieces of information as children without intellectual disabilities, instructors should break skills down into sequential tasks when working with children with intellectual disabilities. Planned programs discussed later in the chapter employ task analysis.

Behavior Management

Applying behavior-management principles such as cueing, reinforcing, and correcting are critical to the success of task-analyzing skills and teaching all the smaller behaviors that enable a student to learn and perform the skill. Behavioral principles must be systematically employed and coordinated. Behaviors to be influenced must be pinpointed and systems designed to promote change in the identified behaviors. Substantial evidence indicates that the shorter the time lapse between student performance and feedback, the better learning is facilitated, especially for individuals with intellectual disabilities who need extensive or pervasive supports.

Move From Familiar to Unfamiliar

Because students with intellectual disabilities have difficulty applying past experience and previously learned information to new though similar tasks, they are more likely to view each new task as a novel one. Thus, the progression from familiar to unfamiliar must occur gradually and be strongly reinforced. Teachers should begin to teach well within the range of student skill and comprehension. Tasks to be learned should be divided into small, meaningful steps, presented and learned sequentially, and rehearsed in total, with as little change in order as possible. A word of caution, though: Children with intellectual disabilities often have short attention spans, and although progression to new tasks should be gradual, the teacher should plan many activities to sustain the student's attention. For example, if the lesson is practicing the fundamental motor skill of hopping, the teacher might need to plan several separate hopping activities in a 20-minute lesson. With younger children, using music and make believe often improve attention span and involvement.

Consistency and Predictability

Consistency of teacher behavior helps establish and maintain a sound working relationship between teacher and students. When students know what to expect, they can plan their behaviors knowing what the consequences will be. Children with intellectual disabilities are often less flexible in accepting or adapting to new routines. Thus, day-to-day consistency in class structure, teacher behavior, and expectations help promote learning.

Choice Making

Activities for individuals with intellectual disabilities are often provided without considering individual preferences. Choice making allows students with little control of their body and environment to have some control of their activity program. Choice making can consist of allowing students to choose which activity they want to play, which ball they prefer, how they would like to be positioned, who they would like to assist them, when they need to stop and rest, and so forth. Giving students choices sometimes makes the difference in whether they truly engage in an activity or just go through the motions.

Activity Modifications

When challenging skills are modified as necessary, students with intellectual disabilities can often participate successfully in physical education and sports alongside peers without disabilities. This is particularly true for children with intellectual disabilities who have associated health or physical impairments or who need extensive or pervasive supports. Among other ways, activities are often modified by:

- substituting fundamental motor skills and patterns for more highly developed sport skills,
- reducing the speed of skill execution or the force required to execute a skill, or
- reducing the distance required for skill execution.

ACTIVITIES

When selecting activities for students with intellectual disabilities, physical educators should be aware of the games, activities, and sports enjoyed by children within the neighborhood and available locally. These activities are good choices for the physical education class. Cooperative programming with local recreation agencies can promote successful inclusion of students with intellectual disabilities into structured community-based play groups. Activities should be fun yet challenging to the student with intellectual disabilities. Activities are not fun when they are beyond the understanding and skill of the participants. Music and make believe help stimulate interest and involvement in games when working with young children.

Selection of Activities According to Chronological Age

Instructors should base activities they select and skills they teach on a student's chronological age and on activities that the student's same-age peers enjoy. However, students' functional abilities and mental age must be considered when determining *how* to present skills and activities. Teaching chronologically age-appropriate skills and functional skills frequently used by all individuals in natural, domestic, vocational, community, and recreational environments minimizes the stigmatizing discrepancies between students with and without disabilities. Conversely, selecting activities based on mental age often involves keeping students needing extensive or pervasive supports at the lower end of the developmental continuum working on "prerequisite skills" that are often nonfunctional and extremely unlikely to be used in daily living or in community recreation and sport programs. A particular need of individuals with intellectual disabilities is to develop the motor skills and physical fitness levels required for optimal vocational training and use of leisure time.

Activities for Students Needing Intermittent or Limited Supports

Students with intellectual disabilities needing intermittent or limited supports often excel in sports; in fact, sports might be their primary avenue for success and self-esteem. They are more likely to be included in physical education classes than in any other subject. Their physical and motor needs are generally like those of students without intellectual disabilities, so their physical education activities can often be the same or quite similar.

Although students needing intermittent or limited supports often excel in physical education and sports, most of them generally do not achieve high skill levels. Still, basketball, soccer, hockey, baseball, and dancing are often popular among adolescents needing intermittent or limited supports, even though concepts of team play, strategy, and rules can be difficult for them to learn. Highly skilled students with intellectual disabilities can learn strategy and rules through concrete teaching experiences. Skill and sport activities such as those fostered by Special Olympics are successful and enjoyable for students with intellectual disabilities needing intermittent or limited supports.

Activities for Students Needing Extensive or Pervasive Supports

Individuals needing extensive or pervasive supports have not traditionally been placed into inclusive public school classes but rather into special classes, schools, or institutions. However, more and more of these students are functioning successfully in inclusive classroom settings when necessary and appropriate support systems are in place. Their level of intellectual and motor functioning is very basic. Their activity is generally characterized by little student interaction (i.e., parallel play), with most interactions occurring between teacher and student. School-age individuals needing extensive or pervasive supports generally need an educational program that uses sensorimotor skills, fundamental skills, movement patterns, and physical and motor fitness development (see the application example).

Sensorimotor programs involve the stimulation of a child's senses so that sensory channels are developed enough to receive information from the environment. Functional senses then permit the child to respond to the environment through movement and manipulation. In these programs, children are taught the normal infant motor progression of head control, crawling, grasping, releasing, sitting, creeping, and standing. Many students with these needs do not walk before the

APPLICATION EXAMPLE

Inclusion of Student With Intellectual Disabilities Needing Extensive Supports

Setting: Secondary physical education class

Student: 14-year-old student with intellectual disabilities who uses a motorized wheelchair and needs pervasive supports

Unit: Basketball

Issue: How to include the student in the basketball game in a meaningful way for both the student and the other basketball players

Application: The physical educator, after consultation with the adapted physical education specialist, uses partial participation with peer assistance as follows:

- A special area of the basketball court is marked off for use by the student and peer tutor.
- If the basketball enters this area, the peer tutor stops the ball. The student has five seconds to maneuver his wheelchair to touch the ball (any challenging task can be used).
- If the student is successful, the peer tutor

then throws the ball to a member of the student's team. If the student is unsuccessful, the peer tutor throws the ball to a member of the opposing team.

The following suggestions would also work:

- Within the special area, set up a target (smaller basket, box, trash can, or the like) and a throwing line a challenging distance from the target.
- If the basketball enters the special area, the peer tutor stops the ball. The student has 10 seconds to move his wheelchair to the spot where the ball entered the area and then to the throwing line, where he propels either the basketball or a more suitable smaller/lighter ball at the target.
- If the student hits the target, his team scores a basket. If the student misses the target, the peer tutor throws the ball to a member of the opposing team who is standing underneath the basket.

age of nine, and many never become ambulatory. Individuals needing pervasive supports might not readily respond to their environment and might exhibit little or none of the curiosity that would motivate them to investigate the environment and learn. Even the most rudimentary skills must be taught. Through partial participation and activity modification, many students needing extensive supports can participate in physical education classes alongside peers without disabilities. Many of these individuals enjoy and can benefit from participating in Special Olympics lower ability sports events or the Special Olympics Motor Activities Training Program.

Realistically, most students needing pervasive supports are unable to independently perform most age-appropriate functional skills. However, the addition of physical assistance and technologies in the form of adapted equipment, switches, and computers enable many such students to participate in chronologically age-appropriate functional activities in natural environments.

Planned Programs

Several established programs are good resources for instructional processes and methods, assessment procedures, and activities relating to physical education and sport for individuals with intellectual disabilities. Several of these, in fact, were originally designed for use with populations with intellectual disabilities. A program with particular relevance for individuals needing extensive or pervasive supports is the Data-Based Gymnasium (Dunn, 1997), which offers a behaviorally oriented instructional model for teaching students with extensive and pervasive support needs, as well as a system for analyzing behavioral principles for the socialization of behaviors. Finally, the Data-Based Gymnasium includes a game, exercise, and leisure sport curriculum. Skills within the curriculum are broken down into tasks and steps sequenced as phases representing shaping behaviors. Students are reinforced for successfully completing tasks that approximate the targeted behavior. The Data-Based Gymnasium includes a clipboard instructional and management system that helps to identify present status, objectives, and progress on skill development. Although the original text on Data-Based Gymnasium is no longer in print, many of the materials and ideas are incorporated in a text by Dunn (1997).

Mobility Opportunities via Education, or MOVE (Kern County Superintendent of School Office, 1995), is a top-down, activity-based curriculum for students with extensive and pervasive support needs that combines natural body mechanics with an instructional process that helps students acquire increased amounts of independence necessary to sit, stand, and walk. MOVE uses education as a means to acquire motor skills by having participants practice their motor skills while engaging in other educational or leisure activities. The motor skills sequence is age appropriate and based on a top-down model of needs rather than a developmental sequence of skill acquisition. The motor skills are usable for the participant into adulthood and range from levels of zero self-management to independent self-management.

The *Special Olympics Sports Skills Guides* created by Special Olympics, Inc., are also helpful in the development of sports skills. Initially designed for children and adults with intellectual disabilities, the guides are presented in a series of manuals that present long-term goals, short-term objectives, task-analyzed activities, sport-specific assessments, and teaching suggestions for many sports. Sports skills guides are available in all official summer and winter sports.

The many planned programs discussed in this section are particularly relevant for people with intellectual disabilities. However, because several have application for other populations in adapted physical education, they are discussed in more detail in other chapters.

STRATEGIES FOR INCLUSION

About 43 percent of all students with intellectual disabilities receive support services within an inclusive class, and 51 percent receive specially designed instruction in separate classes within a school (U.S. Department of Education, 2002). Physical education teachers face the task of providing successful, enjoyable, and challenging learning experiences for all students in inclusive classes. Their teaching strategies must ensure that students with intellectual disabilities will comprehend instructions and achieve success in the inclusive gymnasium. It must also ensure that students without intellectual disabilities accept and respect their peers with intellectual disabilities and understand how they can best support and communicate with them. Teachers can promote effective integration by using the teaching methods presented earlier.

Many students and adults with intellectual disabilities currently participate in general school and recreational sports programs. Another inclusive sports opportunity for individuals with intellectual disabilities is Special Olympics Unified Sports, in which teams are composed of about equal numbers of athletes with intellectual disabilities and their peers without intellectual disabilities. Whether participating in the general sports programs or in Special Olympics sports programs, all athletes with intellectual disabilities should be able to earn sport athletic letters and certificates, wear team uniforms, ride team buses to competitions, participate and be recognized in school and recreation award ceremonies, and represent their schools or agencies in Special Olympics local, regional, county, and state competitions.

SPECIAL OLYMPICS

Special Olympics—an international sports training and competition program open to individuals with intellectual disabilities of ages eight and older, regardless of ability level—was created in 1968 by Eunice Kennedy Shriver and the Joseph P. Kennedy, Jr., Foundation. Children with intellectual disabilities of ages 5 through 7 may participate in Special Olympics training programs but not in Special Olympics competitions. The mission of Special Olympics is to provide year-round sports training and athletic competition in Olympic-type sports for children and adults with intellectual disabilities.

Summer and Winter Special Olympics Games are held annually as national, program (state or province), sectional, area (or county), and local competitions. World Summer Special Olympics Games, which take place every four years, began in 1975. World Winter Special Olympics Games, also held every four years, began in 1977. Additional Special Olympics competitions that include two or more sports are defined as tournaments. To advance to higher levels of competition in a particular year (i.e., from local through area and sectional to program competition), an athlete must have trained in an organized training program in the sport(s) in which he or she is entered for higher-level competition. To advance, an athlete must have placed first, second, or third at the lower level of competition in the sport(s). Instruction for eight-week training programs is provided in the *Special Olympics Sports Skills Guides* (2000-2003).

The showcase for acquired sports skills of Special Olympics athletes in training is the many Special Olympics competitions held throughout the year. These competitions have the excitement and pageantry associated with Olympic Games, including a parade of athletes, lighting of the torch, declaring the Games open, and reciting the Special Olympics oath. In addition to showcasing their skills, Special Olympics athletes often get to meet entertainment and sport celebrities and community leaders, experience new sport and recreational activities through a variety of clinics, enjoy an overnight experience away from home with teammates, and develop the physical and social skills necessary to enter school and community sport programs.

Official Special Olympics summer sports are aquatics, athletics, badminton, basketball, bocce, bowling, cycling, equestrian, football (soccer), golf, gymnastics, powerlifting, roller skating, sailing, softball, table tennis, team handball, tennis, and volleyball. Official winter sports include alpine and cross country skiing, figure skating, speed skating, floor hockey, snowboarding, and snowshoeing.

To provide consistency in training, Special Olympics uses the sports rules of the International Sports Federation (given the responsibility by the International Olympic Committee for handling the technical aspects of Olympic Games) to regulate a sport, except when those rules conflict with the *Official Special Olympics Sports Rules* as outlined in the 2000-2003 revised edition.

Because of the wide range of athletic abilities among people with intellectual disabilities, Special Olympics training and competition programs offer motor activities training for athletes with the severest limitations, team and individual sports skills, modified competition, and regulation competition in most sports.

Special Olympics has developed three programs to help integrate Special Olympics athletes into existing community and after-school sports programs. In the first program, Sports Partnerships, students with intellectual disabilities train and compete alongside interscholastic or club ath-

letes. Varsity and junior varsity athletes serve as peer coaches, scrimmage teammates, and boosters during competition. Athletes with intellectual disabilities compete in existing interscholastic or club league competitions. For example, in a track and field meet, the varsity 100-meter race is followed by a Special Olympics 100-meter race. In distance races, all athletes start together. At the end of the meet, individual and school scores are tabulated for varsity and partnership teams. In team sports (soccer, softball, basketball, floor hockey, volleyball), partnership teams compete just prior to and at the same site as the varsity or junior varsity games.

The second program, Unified Sports, creates teams with approximately equal numbers of athletes with and without intellectual disabilities of similar age and ability. Unified Sports leagues can be part of a school's interscholastic, intramural, or community recreation sports program. Currently, these leagues are established in bowling, basketball, golf, softball, volleyball, and soccer (figure 8.4).

The third program, Partners Club, brings together high school and college students with Special Olympics athletes to perform regular sports skills training and competition and to spend

Figure 8.4 Special Olympics Unified Sports golf teams.

time enjoying other social and recreational activities in the school and community. The Partners Club should be a sanctioned school club with all the accompanying benefits.

Athlete Leadership Programs (ALPS) encourage athlete self-determination, include athletes in policy and program discussions, help athletes discover new roles in Special Olympics, create opportunities for athletes to maximize their potential, and encourage an attitude of service "with" as well as "for" athletes. ALPS include Global Messengers (public speakers), Athlete Congress, Athletes as Board Members, Coaches, Officials, Volunteers, Employees, and Media Reporters.

PARALYMPIC GAMES FOR INDIVIDUALS WITH AN INTELLECTUAL DISABILITY

The Paralympic Games are equivalent to the Olympic Games for the world's top athletes with disabilities. They include athletes with spinal cord injuries, amputations, blindness, deafness, cerebral palsy, intellectual disabilities, and "les autres." Unlike Special Olympics, which provides competition for all trained athletes with intellectual disabilities regardless of ability, the Paralympic Games provides international competition for elite athletes with intellectual disabilities, 15 years and older, who meet minimum qualifying sport standards. They are conducted every 4 years, just after the Olympic Games and at the same venues.

The Association Nacional Prestura de Servicio (ANDE) and the International Sports Federation for Individuals with Intellectual Disability (INAS-FID) held the first Paralympic Games for the Mentally Handicapped in September 1992 in Madrid, Spain. Fifty-six elite athletes with intellectual disabilities competed in swimming and athletics at the 1996 Paralympic Games in Atlanta. Two hundred forty-four elite athletes with intellectual disabilities competed in athletics, basketball, swimming, and table tennis at the 2000 Paralympic Games in Sydney, Australia. Athletes with intellectual disabilities will compete for the first time in Nordic skiing at the 2006 Winter Paralympic Games (Mulder, 2003).

SAFE PARTICIPATION

If the physical educator plans activities appropriate to the academic, physical, motor, social, and emotional levels of children with intellectual disabilities, there are few restrictions or contraindications for activity. Special Olympics has prohibited training and competition in certain sports that hold unnecessarily high risk of injury, especially injury that could have lifelong deleterious effects. Prohibited sports are the javelin, discus, and hammer throw, pole vaulting, boxing, platform diving, all martial arts, fencing, shooting, contact football, rugby, wrestling, judo, karate, nordic jumping, and trampolining.

Most individuals with Down syndrome have some increased flexibility of joints, called ligamentous laxity, which can affect any of their joints. Atlanto-axial instability describes an increased flexibility between the first and second cervical vertebrae of the neck. The instability of this joint could place the spinal cord at risk for injury if affected individuals participate in activities that hyperextend or radically flex the neck or upper spine. About 13 to 14 percent of individuals with Down syndrome show evidence of instability that is asymptomatic and discovered through X ray only. The condition can be detected through a physician's examination that includes X-ray views of full flexion and extension of the neck. Only 1 to 2 percent have symptoms that require treatment. Symptoms in these cases might include neck pain or persistent head tilt, intermittent or progressive weakness, changes in gait pattern or loss of motor skill, loss of bowel or bladder control, increased muscle tone in the legs, or changes in sensation in the hands and feet. Physical education teachers are encouraged to follow the lead of Special Olympics in restricting individuals who have atlantoaxial instability from participating in activities that, by their nature, result in hyperextension, radical flexion, or direct pressure on the neck and upper spine. Such activities include certain gymnastics activities, the butterfly stroke, diving, the high jump, heading a soccer ball, alpine skiing, and any warm-up exercises that place stress on the head and neck.

Because many children with intellectual disabilities, particularly those with Down syndrome, are cardiopathic, students should receive activity clearance from a physician. Appropriate activities within the limitations specified by the physician should then be individually planned.

Another common condition of individuals with intellectual disabilities is muscular hypotonia (flabbiness). Infants with this condition are often called "floppy babies." Although hypotonia decreases with age, it never disappears, and hernias, postural deviations, and poor body mechanics are prevalent because of insufficient musculature. Again, physical educators must take care not to plan exercises and activities that are beyond the capabilities of individuals with muscular hypotonia, because they can lead to severe injury. Abdominal and lower back exercises must be selected with care, and daily foot strengthening exercises are recommended.

SUMMARY

Intellectual disability is among the most prevalent of disabilities. It is a condition that can be viewed from both functional and developmental perspectives. Intellectual disabilities have many different causes, resulting in varied characteristics and affecting success and participation in physical education and sport. In this chapter we have suggested teaching methods, tests, and activities appropriate for this population and briefly reviewed selected sport and planned programs relevant to students with intellectual disabilities. Most people with intellectual disabilities have experienced and continue to experience success in physical education and sport experiences.

REFERENCES

Accardo, P.J., & Capute, A.J. (Eds.). (1998). Mental Retardations. *Mental Retardation and Developmental Disabilities Research Reviews*, 4 (1).

American Psychiatric Association. (2000). *Diagnostic and statistical manual of mental disorders* (4th ed., text rev.). Washington, DC: Author.

Burack, J.A., Hodapp, R.M., & Zigler, E. (Eds.). (1998). *Handbook of mental retardation and development*. Cambridge, United Kingdom: Cambridge University Press.

Cunningham, C. (1987). *Down syndrome: An introduction for parents* (rev. ed.). Cambridge, MA: Brookline.

Dunn, J.M. (1997). *Special physical education: Adapted, individualized, developmental* (7th Ed.). Madison, WI: Brown & Benchmark.

Eichstaedt, C.B., Wang, P.Y., Polacek, J.J., & Dohrmann, P.F. (1991). *Physical fitness and motor skill levels of individuals with mental retardation: Mild, moderate, and individuals with Down syndrome: ages 6 to 21*. Normal, IL: Illinois State University Printing Services.

Grossman, H.J. (Ed.). (1973). *A manual on terminology and classification in mental retardation* (rev. ed.). Washington, DC: American Association on Mental Deficiency.

Hagberg B., Kyllerman, M. (1983). Epidemiology of mental retardation—a Swedish survey. *Brain Development*, 5, 441-449.

Individuals with Disabilities Education Act Amendments of 1997, *Public Law No. 105-17,* 111 Stat. 37 (1997).

Kelly, L.E. (1989). *Project I CAN-ABC.* Charlottesville, VA: University of Virginia.

Kern County Superintendent of Schools Office. (1995). *M.O.V.E.: Mobility opportunities via education*. The Author: 1300 17th Street, City Centre, Bakersfield, CA 93301-4533.

Londeree, B.R., & Johnson, L.E. (1974). Motor fitness of TMR vs. EMR and normal children. *Medicine Science and Sport*, 6, 247-252.

Loovis, E.M., & Ersing, W.F. (1979). *Assessing and programming gross motor development for children*. Cleveland Heights, OH: Ohio Motor Assessment Associates.

Luckasson, R., Coulter, D.L., Polloway, E.A., Reiss, S., Schalock, R.L., Snell, M.E., Spitalnik, D.M., & Stark, J.A. (1992). *Mental retardation: Definition, classification, and systems of supports* (9th ed.). Washington, DC: American Association on Mental Retardation.

Luckasson, R., Borthwick-Duffy, S., Buntinx, W.H.E., Coulter, D.L., Craig, E.M., Reeve, A., Schalock, R.L., Snell, M.E., Spitalnik, D.M., Spreat, S., & Tassé, M.J. (2002). *Mental retardation: Definition, classification, and systems of supports* (10th ed.). Washington, DC: American Association on Mental Retardation.

McLaren, J., & Bryson, S.E. (1987). Review of recent epidemiological studies of mental retardation: Prevalence, associated disorders, and etiology. *American Journal of Mental Retardation*, 92, 243-254.

Mulder, Jos (jos.jopie.mulder@freeler.nl). 2003. *Answers to questions on INAS-FID*. July, 25. E-mail to P. Krebs (pkrebs@somd.org).

Murphy, C.C., Boyle, C., Schendel, D., Decoufle, P. et al. (1998). Epidemiology of Mental Retardation in Children. *Mental Retardation and Developmental Disabilities Research Reviews*, 4(1).

Official Special Olympics summer sports rules: 2000. Washington DC: Special Olympics.

Piaget, J. (1952). *The origins of intelligence in children*. New York: International Universities Press.

Rarick, G.L., Dobbins, D.A., & Broadhead, G.D. (1976). *The motor domain and its correlates in educationally handicapped children*. Englewood Cliffs, NJ: Prentice-Hall.

Rarick, G.L., & McQuillan, J.P. (1977). *The factor structure of motor abilities of trainable mentally retarded children: Implications for curriculum development*. (DHEW Project No H23-2544). Berkley, CA: Department of Physical Education, University of California.

Scott, K.G. (1988). Theoretical epidemiology: Environment and life-style. In J.F. Kavanagh (Ed.), *Understanding mental retardation* (pp. 23-33). Baltimore: Brookes

Special Olympics sports skills guides. (2000-2003). Washington, DC: Special Olympics.

U.S. Department of Education. (2002). *Twenty-fourth annual report to Congress on the implementation of the Individuals with Disabilities Education Act* (DOE Publication No. 2002-616-188/90444). Washington, DC: U.S. Government Printing Office.

Winnick, J.P., & Short, F.X. (1999a). *The Brockport physical fitness test manual*. Champaign, IL: Human Kinetics.

Winnick, J.P., & Short, F.X. (1999b). *The Brockport physical fitness training guide*. Champaign, IL: Human Kinetics.

World Health Organization. (2001). *International classification of functioning, disability and health (ICF)*. Geneva: Author.

Yang, Q., Rasmussen, S.A. & Friedman, J.M. (2002). Mortality associated with Down syndrome in the USA from 1983 to 1997: A population-based study. *The Lancet, 359*, 1019–1025.

Yeargin-Allsopp, M., Murphy, C.C., Cordero, J.F., et al. (1997). Reported biomedical causes and associated medical conditions for mental retardation among 10-year-old children, metropolitan Atlanta, 1985 to 1987. *Developmental and Medical Child Neurology, 39*, 142-149.

Zigman, W., Silverman, W., & Wisniewski, H.M. (1996). Aging and Alzheimer's disease in Down syndrome: Clinical and pathological changes. *Mental Retardation and Developmental Disabilities Research Reviews, 2*(2).

WRITTEN RESOURCES

Special Olympics. (2000-2003). *Sports skills program guides*. Washington, DC: Special Olympics, Inc., 1133 19th Street, NW Washington, DC 20036-3604; (202) 628-3630.

This is a series of sport-specific instructional manuals. Each manual includes long-term goals, short-term objectives, skill assessments, task analyses, teaching suggestions, progression charts, and related information.

Special Olympics, Inc. *Spirit: The Magazine of Special Olympics*. Washington, DC: Special Olympics, Inc., 1133 19th Street, NW Washington, DC 20036-3604; (202) 628-3630.

A published quarterly by Special Olympics to promote its aims and programs and provide information about Special Olympics to participants, volunteers, and others interested in Special Olympics.

AUDIOVISUAL RESOURCES

Let's get strong. (Videotape, 2001). Commack, NY: Healthy All Over, Ltd, P.O. Box 953, Commack, NY.

This exercise video is designed for people with developmental disabilities. All major muscle groups are targeted for a well-balanced body workout. Running time is 23 minutes. Cost is $24.95 plus S/H.

Let's have fun. (Videotape, 2001). Commack, NY: Healthy All Over, Ltd, P.O. Box 953, Commack, NY.

This exercise video is designed for people with developmental disabilities. The low-impact aerobics segment has visual aids to help stimulate imagination. The easy-to-follow routine helps develop a healthier and stronger body, increasing endurance for everyday activities. Running time is 23 minutes. Cost is $24.95 plus S/H.

The spirit of Special Olympics. (Videotape, 1997). Washington DC: Special Olympics, Inc., 1133 19th Street, NW Washington, DC 20036-3604; (202) 628-3630.

This is an orientation to the Special Olympics movement. It provides background and insight into Special Olympics as well as the myriad of volunteer opportunities. Running time is 20 minutes.

ELECTRONIC RESOURCES

Inas-Fid: www.inas-fid.org.

This is the Web site of the international sports federation for elite athletes with intellectual disabilities. The site provides information on eligibility for competition, member organizations, records and rankings of top competitors, upcoming competitions, and athlete registration.

Special Olympics, Inc.: www.specialolympics.org.

This Web site provides information on Special Olympics worldwide programs, upcoming games and competitions, individual profiles of Special Olympics athletes, and how to get involved.

Behavioral Disabilities

E. Michael Loovis

Several students from the seventh-period self-contained class for students with behavioral disorders are standing around before the start of physical education class. Ms. Thomas, the physical educator, enters the gym, blows her whistle, and says, "Line up and keep your mouths shut!" These students continue talking as they proceed to their predetermined spots on the gym floor where class attendance is taken. Ms. Thomas yells to the class, "Keep your mouths shut and pay attention!" Conversation among several students continues, and Ms. Thomas shouts, "Hey, you three, shut your mouths or you're going to the principal's office!" None of the students pays any attention to Ms. Thomas; they continue talking and mimicking her tone. At this point, Ms. Thomas sends them to the principal's office for the fifth time in two months. As the students leave the gym, all three turn toward Ms. Thomas and say, "Forget you! We'll be back!" They then slam the gym door so hard that the window shatters.

s. Thomas has just had one of what could turn out to be many experiences with students with behavioral disabilities. The keys to teaching these students effectively are: (1) understanding the types of behavioral conditions that exist and (2) understanding how to implement certain instructional strategies to teach them.

The fourth largest group of children and youth receiving special education pursuant to IDEA are those with emotional disturbances (National Center for Education Statistics, 2002). Although the number of students with emotional disturbance increased from 445,000 in 1995 to 1996 to 472,000 in 1999 to 2000, the relative percentage when compared with the number of all students with disabilities remained constant at 7.6 percent (figure 9.1). In the past, these students have been referred to as emotionally disturbed, socially maladjusted, behavior disordered, conduct disordered, and emotionally handicapped. Certain characteristics invariably associated with these students make them stand out. Not all of them exhibit the same characteristics; in fact, quite the opposite is true. Generally speaking, they tend to demonstrate behavior that is labeled hyperactive, distractive, or impulsive. Some of these students might exhibit aggression beyond what is considered normal or socially acceptable. Some lie, set fires, steal, and abuse alcohol or drugs. Some might behave in a manner that is considered withdrawn; they might act immature or behave in ways that

tend to highlight feelings of inadequacy. The terms emotional disturbance and behavioral disorder are used synonymously in this chapter.

Another segment of this population might demonstrate behavior directed in a very negative way against society; these individuals are known as juvenile delinquents. Increasingly, others fit the category called "at risk." These individuals are mired in an incompatibility between themselves and school, resulting in low academic achievement and high dropout rates (Davis & McCaul, 1990).

According to IDEA, emotional disturbance is defined as follows:

The term means a condition exhibiting one or more of the following characteristics over a long period of time and to a marked degree that adversely affects a child's educational performance:

- An inability to learn that cannot be explained by intellectual, sensory, or health factors
- An inability to build or maintain satisfactory interpersonal relationships with peers and teachers
- Inappropriate types of behavior or feelings under normal circumstances
- A general pervasive mood of unhappiness or depression
- A tendency to develop physical symptoms or fears associated with personal or school problems (Title 34 CFR, Section 300.7, 2002, p. 13)

Identification of individuals with emotional disturbance is perhaps the most perplexing problem facing school and mental health professionals. In addition, consideration is given to the ever-expanding number of children and youth who are at risk. Thus, it is beneficial to understand the three qualifiers that appear in the first paragraph of the federal definition—namely, duration, degree, and adverse effects on educational performance.

- Long period of time. This qualifier includes behavioral patterns that are chronic in nature, for example, a persistent pattern of physical or verbal attacks on a classmate. It excludes behaviors that conceivably could be construed as emotional disturbance but that are situational in nature and thus understandable or expected. For example, a death in the family, a divorce, or another crisis situation could alter a student's behavior in a way that makes it appear aberrant.

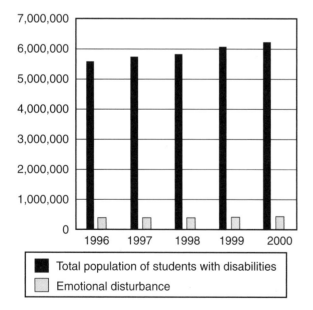

Figure 9.1 Relative frequency of students with emotional disturbance compared to all students with disabilities.

• **Marked degree.** Under consideration here are the magnitude and duration of a behavior. Intensity of behavioral displays, such as intensity of an altercation with a classmate, is considered. For example, a violent physical and verbal attack on a fellow student that requires extensive crisis intervention from teachers and counselors, in contrast to a "pushing and shoving" match, would qualify under this criterion. Also noted is the amount of time a student engages in a particular behavior—for example, if these attacks occur frequently.

• **Adversely affects educational performance.** There must be a demonstrable cause-and-effect relation between a student's behavior and decreased academic performance. This requires, at the very least, determining if students are performing at or near the level they would be expected to attain without behavioral disorder.

NATURE OF EMOTIONAL AND BEHAVIORAL DISORDERS

When endeavoring to understand students with a mild or moderate behavioral disorder, which is the group most likely to be found in an integrated classroom setting, a behavioral classification appears most serviceable. Quay (1986) conducted the seminal work in dimensional classification. Studies have shown that several dimensions (i.e., conduct disorder, anxiety-withdrawal, immaturity, and socialized aggression) are consistently found in special education classes for students who are emotionally disturbed. In 1987, Quay and Peterson, using the revised behavior problem checklist, expanded the dimensions identified previously. The six new dimensions (some of which are essentially the same as those listed previously) include the following:

• **Conduct disorder** involves attention-seeking behavior, temper tantrums, fighting, disruptiveness, and a tendency to annoy others.

• **Socialized aggression** typically involves cooperative stealing, truancy, loyalty to delinquent friends, associating with "bad" companions, and freely admitting disrespect for moral values and laws.

• **Attention problems–immaturity** characteristically involves short attention span, sluggishness, poor concentration, distractibility, lethargy, and a tendency to answer without thinking.

• **Anxiety–withdrawal** stands in considerable contrast to conduct disorders, involving, as it does, self-consciousness, hypersensitivity, general fearfulness, anxiety, depression, and perpetual sadness.

• **Psychotic behavior** insinuates saying things over and over and expressing strange, far-fetched ideas.

• **Motor excess** suggests restlessness and an inability to relax. (pp. 20-22)

An extension of Quay's work included the identification of two primary dimensions of disordered behavior, namely, externalizing and internalizing (Achenback, Howell, Quay, & Connors, 1991). Externalizing behavior involves attacks against others, which parallels Quay and Peterson's original conduct disorder and socialized aggression. Whereas, internalizing behavior involves internal, mental, or emotional conflict, such as depression and anxiety, which approximates Quay and Peterson's anxiety–withdrawal and immaturity dimensions.

Conduct disorders may be classified as either overt or covert (Kauffman, 2001) or undersocialized or socialized (Quay, 1986). Undersocialized (overt) behavior—especially behavior that is aggressive—is associated with violence. According to the American Academy of Experts in Traumatic Stress, students who are at risk for violent behavior typically demonstrate behaviors such as the following:

• Expressing self-destructive ideas
• Talking about specific plans to harm self or others
• Having difficulty controlling impulses
• Blaming other persons and events for their problems
• Engaging in substance abuse

The DSM-IV (APA, 1994) categorizes conduct disorders under four broad headings representing 15 characteristics. An individual is considered to have a mild conduct disorder if at least 3 symptoms from the list of 15 are present (table 9.1). Four or more symptoms indicate a moderate to severe conduct disorder. Of interest is the relation between oppositional defiant disorder (ODD) and conduct disorder. A significant percentage of children and adolescents who develop conduct disorders also show signs of ODD in early and middle childhood. According to the DSM-IV, ODD is "a recurrent pattern of negativistic, defiant, disobedient, and hostile behavior toward authority figures that persists for at least 6 months and is characterized by the frequent occurrence of at least four of the . . . behaviors" (p. 91) listed in table 9.1.

Psychiatric disorders are another area of concern for teachers in public schools. These disorders are likely to be more disabling and might require special therapeutic and medical treatments. Included in this category of disorders are anxiety disorders (e.g., obsessive–compulsive disorder and posttraumatic stress disorder), depression, and other mood disorders (e.g., bipolar or manic depressive disorder), as well as schizophrenic and other psychotic disorders (Forness, Walker, & Kavale, 2003). Combinations of psychopharmacology and behavioral intervention are usually employed in the treatment of these disorders (see chapter 6).

CAUSES OF BEHAVIORAL DISORDERS

Several factors conceivably having a causal relationship to behavioral disorders have been identified, including biological, family, school, and cultural factors. In addition, society is slowly becoming aware of children and students who are at risk. Although space here does not permit a detailed discussion of the forces or factors that place students at risk, we do recognize that broad societal factors have been shown to correlate with poor educational performance. These factors include poverty, minority racial or ethnic group identity, non-English or limited English language background, and specific family configuration (e.g., living in a single-parent household, limited education) (Rossi, 1994).

Biological Factors

According to Kauffman (2001), several biological aberrations might contribute to the etiology of behavioral disorders. These include genetic anomalies, difficult temperament, brain damage or dysfunction, nutritional deficiencies, physical illness or disability, and psychophysiological disorders. With these factors identified, we must reiterate Kauffman's (2001) contention, "When biological factors contribute to emotional or behavioral disorders, they do not operate in isolation from or independent of environmental (psychological) forces" (p. 220).

Table 9.1   **DSM-IV Diagnostic Criteria for Oppositional Defiant Disorder and Conduct Disorder**

Oppositional defiant disorder	Conduct disorder
Often loses temper	Often bullies, threatens, or intimidates others
Often argues with adults	Often initiates physical fights
Often actively defies or refuses to comply with adults' requests or rules	Has used a weapon
Often deliberately annoys people	Has been physically cruel to people
Often blames others for his or her mistakes or misbehavior	Has been physically cruel to animals
Is often touchy or easily annoyed by others	Has stolen while confronting a victim
Is often angry and resentful	Has forced someone into sexual activity
Is often spiteful and vindictive	Has deliberately engaged in fire setting
	Has deliberately destroyed other's property
	Has broken into someone else's house, building, or car
	Often lies to con others
	Has stolen items of nontrivial value without confronting the victim
	Often out late without permission, starting before age 13
	Has run away from home overnight at least twice
	Often truant, starting before age 13

Family Factors

Pathological family relationships are major contributory factors in the etiology of behavioral disorders. Family factors alone do not cause children's disordered behavior, except in complex interactions with other variables. Broken homes, divorce, chaotic or hostile family relationships, absence of mother or father, child abuse, and parental separation might produce situations in which youngsters are at risk to develop behavioral disorders. It is also clear that there is not a one-to-one relation between disruptive family relations and behavioral disorders. Many youngsters find parental discord more injurious than separation from one or both parents. Poverty is another factor statistically correlated with risk of disability (Fujiura & Yamati, 2000). Research also points to a multiplier effect: When two or more factors are present simultaneously, an increased probability exists that a behavior disorder will develop.

School Factors

It has become increasingly clear that, besides the family, school is the most significant socializing factor in the life of the child. For this reason, the school must shoulder some of the responsibility for causing behavioral disorders. According to Kauffman (2001) schools contribute to the development of behavior disorders in several ways:

- Insensitivity to students' individuality
- Inappropriate expectations for students
- Inconsistent management of behavior
- Instruction in nonfunctional and irrelevant skills
- Ineffective instruction in skills necessary for school success
- Destructive contingencies of reinforcement
- Undesirable models of school conduct

Cultural Factors

Frequently, there exists a discrepancy between the values and expectations that are embraced by the child, the family, and the school. Consequently, there is an increased probability that the student will violate dominant cultural norms and be labeled as deviant (Kauffman, 2001). Thus, educators should intervene only on behaviors inconsistent with achievement of core educational goals. Behaviors that have a cultural foundation should

be evaluated carefully in terms of whether the behaviors are inconsistent with educational goals or whether the behaviors do not conform to educators' cultural mores. In the latter case, disciplining a student would be considered inappropriate.

Part of the problem centers on conflicted cultural values and standards that society has engendered. For example, the popular media has elevated many high-status models whose behavior is every bit as violent as the villains they are apprehending; however, students who engage in similar behaviors are told that their choices are incompatible with society's expectations.

Another problem area involves the multicultural perspective, or rather a lack of it. Teachers find it extremely difficult to eliminate bias and discrimination when evaluating a student's behavior. Consequently, students are labeled as deviant when, in fact, it is only at school that their behavior is considered inappropriate.

Other cultural factors influencing behavior include the student's peer group, neighborhood, urbanization, ethnicity, and social class. These factors are not significant predictors of disordered behavior by themselves; however, in combination and within the context of economic deprivation and family conflict, they can have an adverse affect on behavior (Kauffman, 2001).

A significant sociocultural factor that portrays the relation between aberrant adult behavior and a spiraling incidence of behavioral disabilities is substance abuse. Children prenatally exposed to drugs and alcohol are affected in two ways. First, there is an increased incidence of neurological impairment because both drugs and alcohol can cross the placenta and reach the fetus, causing chemical dependency, congenital aberrations, neurobehavioral abnormalities, and intrauterine growth retardation. Second, these children are exposed to family situations that are, at best, chaotic. Typically, these children find themselves in the social service system bouncing from one substitute care situation to another (Bauer, 1991). Sinclair (1998) reported that prenatally drug-exposed children in Head Start programs were more likely to be classified as emotionally or behavioral disordered and placed in special education upon entrance into kindergarten. Van Dyke and Fox (1990) reported the long-range effects of fetal alcohol exposure. Their conclusions confirmed that a significant number of children diagnosed with fetal alcohol syndrome in the 1970s were having learning difficulties, behavioral problems, and attention deficits a decade later.

GENERAL IMPLICATIONS FOR PHYSICAL EDUCATION AND SPORT

Conceptual models that serve as the basis for understanding, treating, or educating students with behavioral disabilities are discussed comprehensively in chapter 6. These include the psychodynamic, psychoeducational, ecological, biogenic, humanistic, and behavioral approaches to teaching students with behavioral disorders. What follows is a discussion of instructional and managerial strategies that can be broadly applied in special education. These strategies can also be used effectively in adapted physical education with students who present mild and severe behavior disorders. See also the application example.

Instructional and Management Considerations

Research confirms that students with emotional disturbance and behavioral difficulties learn best in well-managed environments characterized by effective instruction. In this section emphasis is placed on those instructional and managerial strategies that work for physical educators in both inclusive and segregated settings when working with students considered to have mild to severe behavior problems. Additionally, two programmatic options are suggested as exemplars of effectiveness for adapted physical education.

Differentiated Instruction

Differentiated instruction is the hallmark of special education in the earliest years of the 21st century. Defined as the "planning of curriculum and instruction using strategies that address student strengths, interests, skills, and readiness in flexible learning environments" (Gartin, Murdick, Imbeau, & Perner, 2002, p. 8), differentiated instruction acknowledges that there is not one consistently correct way of instructing children, including those with behavioral disabilities. Effective teachers tailor their instructional techniques according to a student's type of behavioral disorder. In physical education, differentiated instruction could and probably should include consideration of the learning environment. Specifically, physical educators should attend to the organization of the gym (e.g., well-established routines, clearly posted rules, and the establishment of a positive instructional climate, including confirmed behavioral expectations). Additionally, arrangement of the environment includes designing flexible grouping. Students might benefit from large-group instruction, or they might be served better by employing small-group instruction, peer teaching, independent study, one-on-one instruction, or cooperative learning groups. Another way to differentiate is to use multilevel instruction that consists of engaging students in the same curriculum but with different goals and different levels of difficulty. For example, in a basketball unit related to learning and performance of the jump shot, the physical educator might employ peer teaching and conceivably alter the distance from the basket and reduce the criteria for achievement.

Praise

Praise has been documented to have a positive effect on both academic and behavioral outcomes with students with behavioral disorders. However, Sutherland (2000) found that although

APPLICATION EXAMPLE
Behavioral Disabilities

Setting: High school physical education class

Student: A 10th-grade student with oppositional defiant disorder who is frequently verbally and physically abusive to his peers and constantly challenges the authority of the physical educator.

Issue: What are some strategies for handling this situation?

Application: The physical educator could try . . .

- employing the conflict-resolution process;
- examining events or conditions that spark the episodes of abusive behavior; and
- praising instances of appropriate behavior (or implementing Hellison's responsibility model).

these students complied with teacher requests 80 percent of the time, teachers provided praise only 2 percent of the times that students complied. There is also a potential relation between how much praise is given and whether the praise is given effectively (i.e., conveyed in a tone that is earnest and reinforcing). Kamps, Kravits, Stolze, and Swaggart (1999) demonstrated that multicomponent prevention programs were successful in reducing inappropriate behavior in elementary school–age children with behavior difficulties. Multicomponent programs employ a combination of social skills training, peer tutoring, and behavior management.

Precision Requests

More specifically, special educators have devised programs such as precision requests, which have proven effective with students who have serious emotional disturbance and which could easily be used in physical education. Musser, Bray, Kehle, and Jenson (2001) described precision requests as having the following steps:

Step 1: An initial request for compliance is made by using the word "please." If the student complies, reinforcement is provided. If there is no compliance, step two is implemented.

Step 2: A second request is made with the phrase "you need to ____." If the student complies, reinforcement is provided. If there is no compliance, the final phase of the program is implemented.

Step 3: Noncompliance causes the use of reductive techniques such as a time-out.

At the very core of effective instruction with students with behavioral disorders is an examination of the ways people communicate. To communicate effectively, individuals must be able to give and receive information clearly and use the information to achieve a desired result. Giving and receiving information clearly is a goal of effective interpersonal communication that results from active listening.

Active Listening

Three basic skills are essential to the technique of active listening. The first is attending, a physical act that requires the listener to face the person speaking, maintain eye contact, and lean forward, if seated. These actions communicate to the speaker that the listener is, in fact, interested in what is being said. Listening, the second com-

ponent skill, means more than just hearing what is being said. It involves the process of "decoding," an attempt by the listener to interpret what has been said. Consider the following example:

Sender code: "Why do we have to do these exercises?"

Possible receiver decoding:

a. "He doesn't know how to perform them and is embarrassed to admit it."

b. "He's bored with the lesson and is anxious to get to the next class."

c. "He's unclear about why the exercises are necessary and is seeking some clarification."

Suppose that the most accurate decoding was *a* or *c,* but the listener decoded the message as *b.* A misunderstanding would result, and the communication process would start to break down. Such scenarios as this occur frequently, with neither the speaker nor the listener aware that a misunderstanding exists. The question then becomes, "What can be done to ensure that the correct message is being communicated?" The answer is contained in the third and final step of the active listening process. The third component of active listening is responding. The listener sends back the results of his or her decoding in an attempt to ascertain if there are any misunderstandings. In effect, the listener simply restates the interpretation of the sender's message. For example, in the previous illustration, the listener might say, "You're bored with the lesson and anxious to get to the next class?" If the sender responds, "No," then the receiver can reasonably rule out boredom as a cause for the original statement.

Active listening helps prevent misunderstandings, promotes problem solving, and demonstrates warmth and understanding. As with any new skill, active listening requires practice for maximum effectiveness.

Verbal Mediation

A second communication technique is verbal mediation, which involves individuals verbalizing the association between their behavior and the consequences of that behavior. Of particular importance in verbal mediation is having students take an active role in the process rather than passively hearing teachers make the association for them. The following exchange illustrates verbal mediation. A student has just earned 10 minutes of free time by successfully completing the assigned drill at a circuit-training station.

Teacher: "What did you do to earn free time?"

Student: "I followed directions and finished my work."

Teacher: "Do you like free time?"

Student: "Yes, it's fun."

Teacher: "So when you do your work, then you can have fun?"

Student: "Right."

Teacher: "Good for you! Keep up the good work."

In this example, the teacher has promoted the student's verbal mediation of the positive association between the appropriate behavior and the positive consequence.

Conflict Resolution

There is a greater than average risk of confrontation as a way of resolving conflict when teaching students with behavioral disorders. This does not imply that interpersonal confrontation need be punitive or destructive. On the contrary, a healthy use of confrontation provides the opportunity to examine a set of behaviors in relation to expectations and perceptions of others as well as to establish rules.

The goal of confrontation is resolution of conflicts through constructive behavior change. Several steps are necessary in reaching this desired goal through confrontation: making an assertive, confrontive statement (one that expresses honestly and directly how the speaker feels about another's behavior); being aware of common reactions to confrontation; and knowing how to deal effectively with these reactions.

Although assertive confrontation can be an effective means of resolving conflicts, it requires skillful use of each step in the process. Without question the most crucial component of the conflict-resolution process is the formulation of an effective confrontive statement. There are three main components, namely, a nonjudgmental description of the behavior causing the problem, a concrete effect that the behavior is having on the person sending the message, and an expression of the feelings produced from the concrete effect of the behavior. Together these components form what is referred to as an I-message. When combined with active listening, which further reduces defensiveness, the conflict resolution process can be an excellent means to avoid major conflicts, as exemplified in the following conversation:

Teacher: "Robert, your disruptive behavior during class is causing me a problem. When you argue and fight with the other students in class, I have to stop teaching. It's distracting to me, and I'm frustrated." (I-message)

Student: "I get that stuff at home. I don't need it here."

Teacher: "I see. Lately, you're having some problems at home with your parents." (active listening)

Student: "My dad and I have been fighting all week."

Teacher: "You're really upset about the problem you're having with your father." (active listening)

Student: "Yeah! I don't know how much longer I can put up with his bulls—t."

Teacher: "So you're angry because of the situation at home, and it's carrying over into school." (active listening)

Student: "Yeah! I know you're upset about me fighting and not getting along in class. You know I've tried to get along."

Teacher: "You're a little surprised that it's such a problem for me even though the incidents are not always all that extreme." (active listening)

Student: "Well, not really. I see what you're saying. You have to stop teaching and stuff. Mostly I'm taking my anger out on the guys in class. I'll just have to remember that it's not their fault that my dad and me aren't getting along. I'll try harder not to get angry and fight with the guys, okay?"

Teacher: "That would sure help me. Thanks, Robert."

In this example, the teacher has blended effectively the use of an I-message and the skill of active listening to diffuse a situation that could have erupted into a major confrontation between teacher and student.

Frank, Paget, Bowman, and Wilde (1998) suggest "Houdini" techniques to avoid destructive confrontational episodes with ODD students. These techniques involve curtailing teacher behaviors that can promote power struggles. For example, teachers should not threaten students, respond emotionally, confront students near their peers, respond quickly, remain in the interaction too long, use bribes, try "convincing" strategies, or use "put downs." According to the authors, teachers should defuse power struggles by doing the following:

- Use simple directions and choices.
- Make consequences for behavior public.
- Employ active listening and verbal mediation.
- Give brief and direct instructions in a calm tone.
- Discuss problems with the student in private.
- Walk away from the situation before it gets out of hand.

Behavioral Contracting

Contingency management is especially helpful with students who experience behavioral difficul-ties. As briefly discussed in chapter 6, behavioral contracting is a written document that specifies the relation between behaviors (in most cases behaviors that the teacher would like to see extin-guished) and their consequences. An example of a behavioral contract is illustrated in figure 9.2.

Physical Restraint

Passage of the Children's Health Act of 2000 (PL 106-310) awakened in education and health care providers an awareness of the legal ramifications of using physical restraint and seclusion (table 9.2) as a tool for managing the behavior of students with behavioral or mental health difficulties. State education agencies such as the Massachusetts Department of Education have codified the regu-latory requirements of PL 106-310 for use by school

BEHAVIOR CONTRACT IN PHYSICAL EDUCATION

The terms of this contract are detailed below:

The student will earn one point for every positive statement or action made to or about an opponent during par-ticipation in the class basketball unit. Student must earn 10 points to qualify for free time in the gym on Friday afternoons.

The teacher will record every demonstration of the student's positive interactions as evidenced by the chart pub-licly displayed in the gym. The teacher will award points during class and supervise free time in the gym on Friday afternoons if student earns the prescribed number of points.

This agreement is between [student's name] and [teacher's name]. The contract begins on [specify date] and ends on [specify date]. It will be reviewed on [specify date].

Student's signature _____ Date _____

Teacher's signature _____ Date _____

Figure 9.2 Behavioral contract in physical education.

Table 9.2 Physical Restraint: Types and Definitions

Types of restraint	Definition
Mechanical	The use of devices as a means of restricting a [student's] freedom of movement
Physical escort	The temporary touching or holding of the hand, arm, shoulder, or back for the purpose of inducing a [student] who is acting out to walk to a safe location
Physical restraint	A personal restriction that immobilizes or reduces the ability of an individual to move his or her arms, legs, or head freely; the term does not include a physical escort
Seclusion	A behavior-control technique involving locked isolation; such term does not include a time-out
Time out	A behavior-management technique that is part of an approved treatment program and might involve the separation of the [student] from the group, in a nonlocked setting, for the purpose of calming; time-out is not seclusion

districts. School personnel receive training on an annual basis. Training includes the development of knowledge and skill as it relates to the school restraint policy, methods of preventing the need to physically restrain, types of restraint employed and concomitant safety considerations, administration of restraint based on individual needs and limitations, and documentation and reporting of incidents.

Assessment and Activities

According to Steinberg and Knitzer (1992), effective physical education programs for students with emotional and behavioral disturbance are the exception rather than the rule. They suggest that this is especially perplexing in light of increased academic performance and decreased student absenteeism when students are involved in vigorous and systematic exercise programs. Poor motor performance in students with behavioral disorders is often attributed to indirect factors—attention deficits, poor work habits, impulsivity, hyperactivity, feelings of inadequacy, and demonstration of aggressive behavior—rather than to some innate inability to move well.

A local educational agency's approved policies and procedures should be followed when assessing students with behavioral disorders for the purpose of establishing IEP goals and objectives in physical education. Valid and reliable tests should be used to assess physical fitness and gross motor skills. Instruments such as the Test of Gross Motor Development–2 and the Brockport Physical Fitness Test should be used, when appropriate. Additionally, ecological or functional assessment techniques might be used when standardized testing protocols are inappropriate. Ecological and functional approaches were discussed in chapter 4.

Exercise programs have been shown to exert a positive influence on disruptive behavior. As little as 10 or 15 minutes of jogging daily has produced a significant reduction in the disruptive behavior of children (Yell, 1988). Elliot, Dobbin, Rose, and Soper (1994) reported a reduction in maladaptive and stereotypic behaviors in adults with autism and intellectual disabilities subsequent to vigorous aerobic exercise.

Depending on students' developmental abilities and behavioral characteristics, they should be placed in a class that can meet their needs. Regardless of placement, the type of programming chosen and the degree of peer interaction are two variables of considerable import. The first area of concern is the program itself. Because some students with behavioral disabilities might demonstrate a lag in physical and motor abilities, the physical educator must provide them with appropriate developmental activities. The emphasis should be on physical conditioning, balance, and basic movement. In this regard, Bar-Eli, Hartman, and Levy-Kolker (1994) determined that goal setting, more specifically the establishment of both short- and long-term goals, produced the greatest increase in performance of a fitness task with a group of adolescent male and female subjects with behavioral disorders. The development of fundamental locomotor and nonlocomotor movements will also require attention. In addition, it might be necessary to emphasize perceptual–motor activities because students with behavioral disabilities often demonstrate inadequacies in this area.

Relaxation is another program component that deserves a special place in the normal movement routine of many students with behavioral disorders. Making the transition from gym to classroom can be difficult for students with hyperactive behavior. This difficulty is not a reason to eliminate vigorous activity from these students' programs; rather, it is a reason to provide additional time, a buffer, during which the students can use relaxation techniques they have been taught. The ability to play effectively is crucial to success in physical education. Because games are a part of the physical education program for most students with behavioral disorders, it is essential for teachers to be aware of the direct relation between the type of activity chosen and the degree to which inappropriate behavior is likely to occur. The type of programming chosen directly relates to the amount of aggression demonstrated by students during activity. Reduced body contact, simplified rules, and fewer skill requirements are some of the variables that seem to control aggression. Not to be overlooked is the New Games approach, which has a cooperative rather than competitive orientation. In light of the problems surrounding self-concept and the antisocial behavior exhibited by some students with behavioral disorders, the least desirable situation is one that prescribes winners and losers or that rewards overly aggressive behavior.

Nontraditional activities such as initiatives and low-ropes challenges also have a place in the physical education curricula for students with behavioral disorders. Cluphf (2003) describes the use of these activities as a useful tool in developing physical skills as well as the value of teamwork and personal persistence in the face of failure.

SPECIFIC APPROACHES FOR PHYSICAL EDUCATION AND SPORT

This section provides two examples of specific approaches used in physical education and sport for students with behavioral disorders. The humanistic orientation is more common with students who have milder forms of behavioral disorders, whereas the behavioral approach is employed by individuals working with both mild and severe behavioral difficulties.

Humanistic

In physical education, students with behavior disabilities who function at higher levels can be taught through a humanistic approach. Generally speaking, some techniques suggested by Sherrill (2004) for improving self-concept are singularly applicable with this population; for example, teachers should strive to do the following (Sherrill, 2004, p. 234):

* Conceptualize individual and small group counseling as an integral part of physical education
* Teach students to care about each other and show that they care
* Emphasize cooperation and social interaction rather than individual performance
* Stress the importance of genuineness and honesty in praise
* Increase perceived competence in relation to motor skill and fitness
* Convey that they like and respect students as human beings, for themselves as whole persons, not just for their motor skills and fitness

More specifically, the approach outlined by Hellison (2003) has immediate relevance for practitioners confronted with students who lack self-control and consequently present management problems. Hellison has developed a set of alternative goals or levels for physical education that he believes focus on human needs and values rather than on fitness and sport skill development per se. The goals (levels) are developmental in nature and reflect a loosely constructed level-by-level progression of attitudes and behaviors. They include self-control and respect for the rights and feelings of others, participation and effort, self-direction, and caring and helping.

Level 0: Irresponsibility. This level defines students who fail to take responsibility either for their actions or inactions; they blame others for their behavior and typically make excuses.

Level I: Respecting the rights and feelings of others. This level deals with the need for control of one's own behavior. Self-control should be the first goal, according to Hellison, because learning cannot take place effectively if an individual cannot control impulses to harm other students physically and verbally.

Level II: Participation and effort. Level II focuses on the need for physical activity and offers students one medium for personal stability through experiences in which they can engage on a daily basis. Participation involves getting uninterested students to at least "go through the motions," experiencing different degrees of effort expenditure to determine if effort leads to improvement, and redefining success as a subjective accomplishment.

Level III: Self-direction. Level III emphasizes the need for students to take more responsibility for their choices and to link these choices with their own identities. Students at this level can work without direct supervision and can take responsibility for their intentions and actions. At this level, students begin to assume responsibility for the direction of their lives and to explore options in developing a strong and integrated personal identity. This level includes developing a knowledge base that will enhance achievement of their goals, developing a plan to accomplish their goals, especially more difficult ones, and evaluating their plan to determine their success.

Level IV: Caring and helping. Level IV is the most difficult for students; it is also not a requirement for successful engagement in the responsibility model. At this level students reach out beyond themselves to others to commit themselves genuinely to caring about other people. Students are motivated to give support, cooperate, show concern, and help. Generally speaking, the goal of level IV is the improvement of the entire group's welfare.

• *Self-stimulatory behavior.* This category includes behaviors that interfere with learning because students become engrossed in the preservative nature of the activities. Examples include head banging, hand flapping, body rocking, and eye gouging. As a rule of thumb, Dunn and associates recommend a formal behavioral program to deal with this type of behavior. An in-depth discussion of formal behavior modification principles and programs is presented in chapter 6.

POSITIVE BEHAVIORAL SUPPORT SYSTEMS

If students with a disability violate a school's conduct code, those students can be suspended for up to 10 days in a school year. Likewise, if students with disabilities are involved with drugs, bring weapons to school, or place themselves or other students in danger, those students can be assigned to an alternative placement for up to 45 days. In these cases the IEP team must determine the appropriate interim alternative education setting (IAES). As such, the IEP team must determine if the student's misbehavior is a function of a disability (i.e., was the student's ability to understand the consequences of the behavior or to control the behavior subject to disciplinary action impaired?). This process is called "manifestations determination." If the student's behavior is determined to be related to the disability, the student is subject to IDEA disciplinary procedures that consist of conducting a functional behavioral assessment and developing a behavior intervention plan.

Positive behavioral supports (PBS) are required in cases in which students' behaviors impede their ability to learn or interfere with others' learning. In consideration of these needs, school personnel are directed to address individual needs by altering environments and explicitly teaching new skills to students with challenging behaviors so they genuinely appreciate positive behavior. Implementing a two-stage process—namely, conducting a functional behavioral assessment (FBA) and designing a behavioral intervention plan (BIP)—accomplishes this task.

Functional Behavioral Assessment

Students with disabilities (particularly behavioral disorders) who exhibit dangerous or unruly behavior are not exonerated from responsibility for their behavior that is considered extreme. The 1997 reauthorization of IDEA created due process policies to ensure that students with disabilities who violate school conduct codes would continue to receive an appropriate education as specified in their IEP. Additionally, the IEP must also specify an appropriate intervention plan to ameliorate the student's inappropriate behavior.

IDEA requires that prior to expelling, ruling on an alternative school placement, or suspending for more than 10 days, a student with a disability must have a functional behavioral assessment. FBA is "a method of gathering information about the situational events that predict and maintain problem behavior" (Crone & Horner, 2003, p. xii). FBAs can be as simple as an interview with the student's teacher or as involved as direct observation for perhaps 20 or more hours and experimental manipulation of variables to promote behavioral control. For example, a member of the IEP team could observe a student during physical education class and record the frequency of an undesirable behavior, such as physical or verbal abuse during competitive team activities. Additionally, the observer would attempt to identify antecedent events such as occasions when the student is in a one-on-one situation with a particular student that might cause an increase in the physical or verbal abuse.

Behavior Intervention Plan

Once the behavior(s) in question are understood, intervention is designed and implemented. BIPs are designed to address students' motives for misbehaving, their likes and dislikes, and the effectiveness of various positive (and negative) reinforcers. BIPs are intended to emphasize positive interactions and behaviors. They should not be designed to punish the student or in any way to catch the student misbehaving. BIPs should also include or be developed by as many people as necessary who have interactions with the student. It is for this reason that physical educators must understand the purposes and design of the BIP and participate in its implementation.

Scott and Nelson (1999) proposed a process that links FBA and BIP. This process involves 10 steps:

• Determining the function of the undesirable behavior

• Determining an appropriate alternative behavior

- Determining how frequently the alternative behavior should occur
- Developing a teaching sequence
- Manipulating the environmental context to increase the probability of success
- Altering the environment to decrease the probability of failure
- Determining how positive responses will be reinforced
- Determining consequences for instances of problem behavior
- Developing a data-collection system
- Developing goals and objectives in behavioral and measurable terms

In many respects development and implementation of the 10-step FBA and BIP process parallel the applied behavior analysis approach outlined in chapter 6. Figure 9.3 is an example of the 10-step process linking functional behavioral assessment and the behavior intervention plan.

INCLUSION

Based on data collected through 1999 (National Center for Education Statistics, 2002), students with behavioral disorders are receiving their education in greater and greater numbers in the regular education classroom. Clearly, 25.3 percent of students with behavioral disorders spend more than 80 percent of the school day in regular classrooms; another 23 percent spend between 40 and 79 percent of the school day in the regular classroom. Students with behavioral disorders who spend less than 40 percent of the day in regular classrooms equal 33.2 percent. The remaining 18.3 percent are distributed across separate facilities,

---

1A. *Identification of problem behavior*—When engaged in team sports such as basketball in the physical education class and when the student makes continuous mistakes causing embarrassment, the student physically and verbally abuses opposing players. This has resulted in physical injury to several students and a general reluctance on the part of most students to want to compete against this student.

1B. *Function of undesirable behavior*—The student uses physical and verbal attacks against fellow students to deflect attention away from his fundamentally inadequate motor skills.

2. *Appropriate alternative behavior*—The student will use compliments and positive physical gestures that show respect for classmates.

3. *Frequency of alternative behavior*—The student will engage in alternative behaviors on a ratio of at least 5 to 1.

4. *Teaching sequence*—The student will learn personal responsibility by participating in and progressing through Hellison's model using appropriate levels and strategies (e.g., student initiates awareness talks with teacher and other students when an abusive episode seems imminent).

5. *Manipulating environment*—The student will be teamed with peers who understand his problem and who have volunteered to prompt appropriate behavior.

6. *Decreasing probability of failure*—The student is placed in instructional situations that require fewer skills, such as small-sided games or lead-up games, that reduce the likelihood of embarrassing mistakes that typically precipitate abusive episodes.

7. *Reinforcement of positive responses*—The student will receive social praise from the teacher and classmates for each occurrence of desirable behavior.

8. *Consequences for problem behavior*—The student's verbal abuse will be ignored; physical attacks will result in a time-out.

9. *Data collection system*—The teacher will record the frequency of physical and verbal abuse during scheduled class time. Results will be shared with the student in an effort to communicate the frequency and perhaps the severity of instances of abuse. The teacher will also attempt to ascertain if particular situations or combinations of students appear to precipitate these episodes of abusive behavior.

10. *Goals and objectives*—The IEP team will develop appropriate goals and objectives that serve as a measure of the BIP's effectiveness.

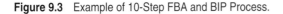

Figure 9.3 Example of 10-Step FBA and BIP Process.

residential facilities, and home or hospitals, which represent 13.3, 3.6, and 1.4 percent, respectively. These data would seem to indicate that physical educators are likely to have students with behavioral disorders in their regular physical education classes.

The inclusion of students with behavioral disorders into the "regular" class should be based primarily on the frequency and intensity of behavioral episodes. These students will demonstrate behavioral characteristics ranging from mild to severe. For those with mild behavioral profiles, the regular class is easily the placement of choice. The decision becomes more difficult if student behaviors are unmanageable, even with a management plan in effect.

In terms of students with behavioral disorders, inclusion is facilitated much of the time through development and implementation of a BIP. These plans describe in detail student expectations and consequences if behavioral expectations are not achieved (see chapter 6). Students who have severe behavior disorders such that they are either disruptive and interfere with the operation of the regular class or are harmful to themselves or other students in the class might require a segregated approach.

SUMMARY

Behavioral conditions correspond to the categories of behavior disorders and emotional disturbance, as defined in IDEA. In this chapter we provided ideas for teaching and managing students with identified behavioral disorders in integrated physical education classes. Effective interpersonal communication was discussed, specifically, active listening, verbal mediation, and conflict resolution. The work of Hellison and the contributions of Dunn and his colleagues were cited as effective approaches to physical education and sport for students with behavioral disorders and students considered at risk.

Physical educators are called on to promote positive behavioral supports (Safran & Oswald, 2003). They are asked to contribute as members of schoolwide behavior-management systems that not only provide sound and consistent discipline policies but also address the need for positive behavioral instruction. These models (ERIC/OSEP Special Project, 1997) share several features:

- Total staff commitment to managing behavior, whatever approach is taken

- Clearly defined and communicated expectations and rules
- Consequences and clearly stated procedures for correcting rule-breaking behaviors
- An instructional component for teaching students self-control and social skill strategies
- A support plan to address the needs of students with chronic, challenging behaviors

REFERENCES

Achenbach, T.M., Howell, C.T., Quay, H.C., & Conners, C.K. (1991). National survey of problems and competencies among four- to sixteen-year-olds: Parents' reports for normative and clinical samples. *Monographs of the Society for Research in Child Development,* 56(3), serial no. 225.

American Academy of Experts in Traumatic Stress. (2003). *A practical guide for crisis response in our schools.* Commack, NY: Author.

American Psychiatric Association. (1994). *Diagnostic and statistical manual of mental disorders* (4th ed.). Washington, DC: Author.

Bar-Eli, M., Hartman, I., & Levy-Kolker, N. (1994). Using goal setting to improve physical performance of adolescents with behavior disorders: The effect of goal proximity. *Adapted Physical Activity Quarterly,* 11, 86-97.

Bauer, A.M. (1991). Drug and alcohol exposed children: Implications for special education for students identified as behaviorally disordered. *Behavioral Disorders,* 17, 72-79.

Children's Health Act (PL 106-310), U.S. Department of Health and Human Services. (2000).

Cluphf, D. (2003). A low-ropes initiative unit for at-risk students. *Strategies,* 17, 13-16.

Code of Federal Regulations. (July 1, 2002). Title 34, Section 300.7, Assistance to States for the Education of Children with Disabilities. Washington, DC: Department of Education, Office of Special Education and Rehabilitative Services, p. 13.

Crone, D.A., & Horner, R.H. (2003). *Building positive behavior support systems in schools.* New York: Guilford Press.

Davis, W.E., & McCaul, E.J. (1990). *At-risk children and youth: A crisis in our schools.* Orono: University of Maine, Institute for the Study of At-Risk Students.

Dunn, J.M. (1997). *Special physical education: Adapted, individualized, developmental* (7th ed.). Madison, WI: Brown & Benchmark.

Dunn, J.M., Morehouse, J.W., & Fredericks, H.D.B. (1986). *Physical education for the severely handicapped: A systematic approach to a data based gymnasium.* Monmouth, OR: Teaching Research.

Elliot, R.O., Dobbin, A.R., Rose, G.D., & Soper, H.V. (1994). Vigorous, aerobic exercise versus general motor training activities: Effects on maladaptive and stereotypic behaviors of adults with both autism and mental retardation. *Journal of Autism and Developmental Disorders,* 24, 565-576.

ERIC/OSEP Special Project. (1997). *Research connections in special education.* Reston, VA: The ERIC Clearinghouse on Disabilities and Gifted Education/The Council for Exceptional Children.

Forness, S.R., Walker, H.M., & Kavale, K.A. (Nov/Dec, 2003). Psychiatric disorders and treatments: A primer for teachers. *Teaching Exceptional Children, 36*, 42-49.

Frank, K., Paget, M., Bowman, B., & Wilde, J. (1998). *Creative strategies for working with ODD children and adolescents.* Chapin, SC: Youthlight.

Fujiura, G.T., & Yamati, K. (2000). Trends in demography of childhood poverty and disability. *Exceptional Child, 66*, 187-199.

Gartin, B.C., Murdick, N.L., Imbeau, M., & Perner, D.E. (2002). *How to use differentiated instruction with students with developmental disabilities in the general education classroom.* Arlington, VA: Council for Exceptional Children.

Hellison, D.R. (2003). *Teaching responsibility through physical activity* (2nd ed.). Champaign, IL: Human Kinetics.

Hellison, D.R., & Georgiadis, N. (1992). Teaching values through basketball. *Strategies, 5*, 5-8.

Hellison, D.R., & Templin, T.J. (1991). *A reflective approach to teaching physical education.* Champaign, IL: Human Kinetics.

Kamps, D., Kravits, T., Stolze, J., & Swaggart, B. (1999). Prevention Strategies for students at risk and identified as serious emotionally disturbed in urban, elementary school settings. *Journal of Emotional and Behavioral Disorders, 7*, 178-188.

Kamps, D., Kravits, T., Rauch, J., Kamps, J.L., & Chung, N. (2000). A prevention program for students with or at risk for ED: Moderating effects of variation in treatment and classroom structure. *Journal of Emotional and Behavioral Disorders, 8*, 141-154.

Kauffman, J.M. (2001). *Characteristics of emotional and behavioral disorders of children and youth* (7th ed.). Upper Saddle, NJ: Prentice-Hall.

Musser, E.H., Bray, M.A., Kehle, T.J., & Jenson, W.R. (2001). Reducing disruptive behaviors in students with serious emotional disturbance. *School Psychology Review, 30*, 294-304.

National Center for Education Statistics. (2002). *The condition of education, 2002.* Washington, DC: Department of Education.

Quay, H.C. (1986). Classification. In H.C. Quay & J.S. Werry (Eds.), *Psychopathological disorders of childhood* (3rd ed., pp. 1-34). New York: Wiley.

Quay, H.C., & Peterson, D.R. (1987). *Manual for the revised behavior problem checklist.* Coral Gables, FL: Authors.

Rossi, R.J. (Ed.). (1994). *Schools and students at risk.* New York: Teachers College Press.

Safran, S.P., & Oswald, K. (2003). Positive behavior supports: Can schools reshape disciplinary practices? *Exceptional Child, 69*, 361-373.

Scott, T.M., & Nelson, C.M. (1999). Using functional behavioral assessment to develop effective behavioral intervention plans: A practical classroom application. *Journal of Positive Behavioral Support, 1*, 242-251.

Sherrill, C. (2004). *Adapted physical activity, recreation and sport: Crossdisciplinary and lifespan* (6th ed.), Madison, WI: Brown & Benchmark.

Sinclair, E. (1998). Head start children at risk: Relationship of prenatal drug exposure to identification of special needs and subsequent special education kindergarten placement. *Behavioral Disorders, 23*, 125-133.

Steinberg, Z., & Knitzer, J. (1992). Classrooms for emotionally and behaviorally disturbed students: Facing the challenge. *Behavioral Disorders, 17*, 145-156.

Sutherland, K.S. (2000). Promoting positive interactions between teachers and students with emotional/behavioral disorders. *Preventing School Failure, 44*, 110-115.

Van Dyke, D.O., & Fox, A.A. (1990). Fetal drug exposure and its possible implications for learning in the preschool and school-age population. *Journal of Learning Disabilities, 23*(3), 160-163.

Yell, M.L. (1988). The effects of jogging on the rates of selected target behaviors of behaviorally disordered students. *Behavioral Disorders, 13*, 273-279.

WRITTEN RESOURCES

Dunn, J.M., Morehouse, J.W., & Fredericks, H.D.B. (1986). *Physical education for the severely handicapped: A systematic approach to a data based gymnasium.* Austin, TX: Pro-Ed.

This text is a "nuts and bolts" approach to working with students who have severe disabilities in the physical education setting. It combines detailed information on learning theory with examples to illustrate the principles advocated for use in the gymnasium.

Goldstein, A.P., Sprafkin, R.P., Gershaw, N.J., & Klein, P. (1980). *Skillstreaming the adolescent: A structured learning approach to teaching prosocial skills.* Champaign, IL: Research Press.

This innovative program is designed to help adolescents develop competence in dealing with interpersonal conflicts, increasing self-esteem, and contributing to a positive classroom atmosphere.

Wood, M.M., & Long, N.J. (1991). *Life space intervention: Talking with children and youth in crisis.* Austin, TX: Pro-Ed.

This is an updated version of the pioneering work of Fritz Redl with emphasis on the "intervention" because crisis implies verbal intervention. "Talking strategies" are presented and applied to particular types of problems.

AUDIOVISUAL RESOURCES

Conflict resolution. (Interactive videodisc, 1993). University of South Florida, I'm Special Production Network, Tampa, FL 33620-8600.

This level III interactive application (external computer that uses a videodisc player as a peripheral device) teaches students how to send appropriate "I" messages, use active listening, and conduct the conflict–resolution process. The videodisc is aimed at undergraduate students and career teachers who will teach students with behavioral disabilities.

Understanding the defiant child. (Videotape, 1997). Guilford Publications, 72 Spring Street, New York, NY 10012.

Dr. Russell Barkley presents a clear and easily understood resource for clinicians, teachers, and parents who must deal with children who have Oppositional Defiant Disorder (ODD). Using real-life scenes of family interaction and parental commentary, Dr. Barkley helps viewers distinguish ODD from milder forms of misbehavior. The video likewise addresses long-term outcomes for defiant children and the correlation between ODD and ADHD.

Dylan and Marcia both have behaviors that deviate from typical childhood development. According to the *American Psychiatric Association's Diagnostic and Statistical Manual* (DSM IV) (1994) these two disorders fall under the category of "pervasive development disorders" (PDD) and include not only autism and Asperger syndrome but also Rett's disorder, childhood disintegrative disorder (CDD), and pervasive developmental disorder, not otherwise specified (PDD-NOS). The term "pervasive" means the condition affects total development. Table 10.1 provides an overview of these conditions.

HISTORY OF AUTISM AND ASPERGER SYNDROME

Although autism was evident in individuals for quite some time beforehand, it was not until 1943 when Dr. Leo Kanner, a child psychiatrist at John Hopkins University Medical School, described the common characteristics of 11 children he had studied between 1938 and 1943. These children were withdrawn and engaged in isolated activities. They did not relate well to people, including their own parents; they insisted on routines and displayed unusual body movements, such as flapping their hands. Many of the children could talk, for example, say the alphabet or recite whole books, but they rarely used speech to communicate with others (Ozonoff, Dawson, & McPartland, 2002). In addition, these behaviors were exhibited at an early age, before the age of three. Dr. Kanner borrowed the term "autism" from a Swiss psychiatrist who coined the term to describe adults with a certain form of schizophrenia. Dr. Kanner identified these children as having "early infantile autism." Choosing this terminology proved to be a grave mistake because it led parents to believe that their children were making a conscious effort to withdraw from a hostile and unnurturing environment. We now know conclusively that this is not the case: Autism is not caused by an unloving or unnurturing environment. Thus, the term "autism" has remained, but the descriptor "early infantile" is no longer used (Powers, 2000).

For many years, only those children who exhibited the same behavior patterns that Dr. Kanner noted were diagnosed with autism. However, today it is clear that autism ranges in severity, and individuals with autism can fall anywhere within

Table 10.1 Summary of the DSM-IV Diagnostic Criteria for Pervasive Developmental Disorders (1994)

Condition	Criteria
Autism	Impairment in social interaction with at least two of the following: • Impairment in the use of nonverbal behaviors (e.g., facial expressions, eye gaze, and body postures) • Failure to develop appropriate peer relationships • Lack of spontaneous seeking to share enjoyment, interests, or achievement with other people • Lack of social or emotional reciprocity Impairment in communication with at least one of the following: • Delay in or total lack of the development of spoken language • Marked impairments in the ability to initiate or sustain a conversation with others • Stereotyped and repetitive use of language or idiosyncratic language • Lack of spontaneous make-believe play Repetitive and stereotyped patterns of behavior with at least one of the following: • Preoccupation with one or more stereotyped and restricted patterns of interest that is abnormal in either intensity or focus • Inflexible adherence to specific, nonfunctional routines or rituals • Stereotyped and repetitive motor mannerisms Delays or abnormal functioning in at least one of the following: • Social interaction • Language as used in social communication • Symbolic or imaginative play The disturbance is not better accounted for by Rett's disorder or childhood disintegrative disorder.

Condition	Criteria
Asperger syndrome	Impairment in social interaction with at least two of the following: • Impairment in the use of nonverbal behaviors (e.g., facial expressions, eye gaze, body postures) • Failure to develop appropriate peer relationships • Lack of spontaneous seeking to share enjoyment, interests, or achievement with other people • Lack of social or emotional reciprocity Repetitive and stereotyped patterns of behavior with at least one of the following: • Preoccupation with one or more stereotyped and restricted patterns of interest that is abnormal in either intensity or focus. • Inflexible adherence to specific, nonfunctional routines or rituals • Stereotyped and repetitive motor mannerisms Condition causes clinically significant impairment in social, occupational, or other important areas of function. There is no clinically significant delay in language development. There is no clinically significant delay in cognitive development or self-help skills. Criteria are not met for other specific PDD or schizophrenia.
Rett's disorder	All of the following are used to diagnose the child with Rett's Disorder: • Apparently normal prenatal and perinatal development • Apparently normal psychomotor development through the first 5 months after birth • Normal head circumference at birth Onset of all of the following after the period of normal development: • Deceleration of head growth between ages 5 and 48 months • Loss of previously acquired purposeful hand skills between ages 5 and 30 months with the subsequent development of stereotyped hand movements • Loss of social engagement • Poor coordination and trunk movements • Severely impaired expressive and receptive language development with severe psychomotor delays
Childhood disintegrative disorder	Apparently normal development for at least the first 2 years after birth Clinically significant loss of previously acquired skills (before the age of 10) in at least two of the following areas: • Expressive or receptive language • Social skills or adaptive behaviors • Bowel or bladder control • Play • Motor skills Abnormal functioning in at least two of the following areas: • Impairment in social interaction • Impairment in communication • Stereotyped and repetitive motor mannerisms The condition is not better accounted for by another specific PDD or schizophrenia
PDD—not otherwise specified	This category is used when there is a severe and pervasive impairment in the development of reciprocal social interaction, verbal or nonverbal communication skills, or stereotyped behaviors, but the criteria are not met for a specific PDD, schizophrenia, or other personality disorder.

a spectrum of behaviors, from high functioning ability to low functioning ability.

At around the same time that Dr. Kanner first described autism, another researcher, Dr. Hans Asperger, an Austrian pediatrician wrote a paper published in 1944 that described a condition that became to be known as Asperger syndrome. The children described by Dr. Asperger were between the ages of 6 and 11 years; these children, despite typical communication and cognitive skills, had significant problems with social interactions. The paper was virtually unknown in the United States and other non–German speaking countries because the paper was written in German. It was not until 1981, when Dr. Lorna Wing, a prominent British researcher, discovered the paper, summarized it, and noted the similarities between Asperger syndrome and autism. Even today, some people question whether autism and Asperger syndrome are really one condition. Because Asperger syndrome is relatively new (to North America), research continues in this area. The greatest similarities between autism and Asperger syndrome can be found in those individuals diagnosed with high-functioning autism (Ozonoff, Dawson, & McPartland, 2002).

PERVASIVE DEVELOPMENTAL DISORDERS

In the following section we will describe each of the five conditions known as pervasive developmental disorders. As we progress, it will become evident that the characteristics associated with each condition are quite similar in nature. Although the *Diagnostic and Statistical Manual of Mental Disorders, Fourth Edition* (DSM IV) (APA, 1994), clearly distinguishes each condition, there are overlaps. For this reason, researchers have begun to adopt the term "autism spectrum disorders" to identify these related conditions.

Autism

Of the five PDD conditions, only autism is identified in federal legislation as a specific disability category. Federal legislation has defined autism as a severe and chronic developmental disability that affects communication and behavior. Autism is diagnosed on the basis of the behaviors a child exhibits during early development (usually before the age of three). A child with autism will usually experience difficulties with speech, language, and communication; relating to people, objects, and events; responses to sensory stimuli; and developmental discrepancies (OSE/RS, 2002). Each of these difficulties is discussed in the following sections.

Difficulty with Speech, Language, and Communication

According to Powers (2000), about 40 percent of children with autism do not speak at all, and others have what is known as echolalic speech (echolalic meaning "echo"). For example, if a physical education teacher says, "Ryan, throw the ball," Ryan might repeat word for word the phrase "Ryan throw the ball" without really comprehending what is being asked of him. In other cases, the echolalia might not occur immediately but might come at odd times. A child might recall a TV commercial he saw that morning and begin singing a jingle in the middle of class. In other individuals with autism who have language skills, the sound of their speech might be flat or monotonous, with no apparent control over pitch or volume. In addition to having speech pattern problems, some individuals with autism might not comprehend the social norms of communication and might continue to talk about a preferred topic long after the conversation should have ended. Similarly, a person might stand too close to another person when speaking or might say inappropriate things without realizing the statement will offend others.

Difficulty Relating to People, Objects, and Events

Powers (2000) notes that one of the most noticeable characteristics of individuals with autism is their inability to develop normal social relationships. Often these individuals prefer to be alone and engaged in isolated activities. They show few or unusual signs of attachment. When attachment is observed, it is typically one-sided and odd. For example, a child might sit on your lap and peck at your cheek. Eye contact is limited and often appears as if the child is looking "through you" rather than at you.

Relating to objects and events is also unusual in individuals with autism. Many individuals with autism have a "need for sameness" (Ozonoff, Dawson, & McPartland, 2002). Objects need to be placed in a pattern that only they understand. If the placement of the object is disrupted, the individual might become enraged. Objects might also be played with in a peculiar manner. For example, children might spin their toys over and over again or look at the toys for hours from various directions. Routines also must be followed, such as the way one travels from home to school and back again. Whereas these examples might strike some as troublesome, they demonstrate the nature of autism and the need that individuals with autism have for a predictable environment.

Abnormal Responses to Sensory Stimuli

Individuals with autism have difficulty screening out irrelevant information within the environment. Their senses allow them to overattend to some stimuli and underattend to others, so it is difficult for them to determine the most important part of a task (Ozonoff, Dawson, & McPartland, 2002). Some individuals with autism crave physical pressure. For instance, some have been known to lie under couch cushions so they could be sat on and squeezed (some believe the sensation of being in tight quarters provides security and relieves stress). Others do not want to be touched at all. The discrepancies among individuals with autism are quite wide. All have some form of difficulty with sensory stimuli, but the degree varies significantly among individuals.

Developmental Discrepancies

We know that most children develop in a certain sequence, at a certain rate, and within a certain time frame. For children with autism, however, the sequence and rate of development is not consistent with typical development except in the area of motor development (Ozonoff, Dawson, & McPartland, 2002). Cognitively, some children with autism are able to read with no understanding of vowels or consonants. Others can begin to talk normally, and then suddenly language ceases.

In addition to the behaviors just described, the sidebar provides an overview of the processing problems noted in individuals with autism. Armed with an understanding of how individuals with autism process information, physical educators can design their physical education program to meet the unique needs of the learner.

Asperger Syndrome

The defining characteristics of individuals with Asperger syndrome are impaired social interactions, impaired communication, and unusual interests and behaviors. These characteristics are discussed in the following sections. As noted in table 10.1 (pp. 174-175), individuals with Asperger syndrome typically have no delays in the onset of speech and language and have no significant delays in cognitive skills or self-help skills. The impairments become most apparent in social situations.

Information Processing Characteristics of Students With Autism

Difficulty processing sensory information. Often results in a state of overarousal.

Inability to focus consistently on the important elements of a task. Student is unable to screen out irrelevant information.

Chunks of information that occur simultaneously or very close together in time are quickly associated and remembered and are not organized in a relevant manner.

Information is not retrieved in the correct sequence.

Concept of time is impaired.

Possesses a literal understanding of language.

Processes auditory information more slowly than is typical.

Meaning is not automatically attached to visual information.

Difficulty solving problems or generating new responses.

Inability to control motor or verbal responses. Student might engage in repeated hand flapping or loud outbursts.

Adapted from Janzen, 1996.

Impaired Social Interaction

Individuals with Asperger syndrome typically do not follow the conventions of social interaction. They might wish to have friends and be part of a group, but because of their inability to adhere to social protocol, such as making eye contact or nodding during a conversation, their success is often limited. In addition, these individuals might be blatantly honest and say things that are inappropriate without realizing the comment was hurtful. They might not seem to understand other people's feelings or point of view. It is difficult for individuals with Asperger syndrome to put themselves in another person's shoes. They lack empathy and often do not understand why everyone is upset over something they did or said (Ozonoff, Dawson, & McPartland, 2002).

was given ("Good job"). At times, the feedback could be a treat or a sticker. The trials were repeated five or six times a minute for up to two hours. This frequent repetition increased the rate of learning and reduced the tendency of children with autism to withdraw. Over time, the physical prompting is faded, and the learning situation requires less structure (Lovaas, 1987).

The Lovaas study indicated that some of the children in the treatment group were able to enter kindergarten with minimal assistance and required only 10 hours of discrete trial training per week. In a follow-up study 6 years later, McEachin and colleagues were not able to distinguish among the most successful kindergarteners with autism and those in the control group (McEachin, Smith, & Lovaas, 1993). It appears, then, that in order for this method to be successful it must be continued over time. Although this form of intervention has its detractors because of the rigidity of the program, no published studies have successfully refuted the effectiveness of this approach.

TEACCH

Another popular program used around the nation to assist students with PDDs, particularly autism, is the North Carolina statewide program known as TEACCH, developed by Eric Schopler in the early 1970s. This program uses a combination of approaches and methods to meet the unique needs of the learner. It is more a behavior-management system than a teaching or learning system. The program is based on the students' skills, interests, and needs. Structured teaching is an important component. To promote independence, the focus of the program is on organizing the physical environment, developing daily work schedules, providing clear and explicit expectations, and using visual cues for presenting materials and prompting instructional sequences (Mesibov, 1996).

The TEACCH program also uses sensory integration therapy to determine the cause of inappropriate behaviors or lack of skill acquisition. It is theorized that pain is often the cause of inappropriate behaviors of individuals with PDDs. For example, if a child is overstimulated in an environment, he or she might be caused undue pain and stress. Rather than making the child tolerate the environment, the child is removed from the environment (Trehin, 1998). Proponents of this model espouse the use of the "culture of autism" as the basis for the intervention. That is, individuals with autism as a whole respond best to structure

and routines. The model builds on the learning strengths of the individual rather than forcing the learner to conform to socially accepted norms of behavior.

Floor Time

A new and exciting early intervention approach for children with autism and other PDDs is the DIR–Floor Time approach developed by Stanley Greenspan (1998). Floor time is based on Greenspan's theories of six functional milestones necessary for a child to succeed in further learning and development. According to Greenspan (1998, p. 3), these milestones are as follows:

1. The dual ability to take an interest in the sights, sounds, and sensations of the world and to calm oneself down
2. The ability to engage in relationships with other people
3. The ability to engage in two-way communication with gestures
4. The ability to create complex gestures, to string together a series of actions into an elaborate and deliberate problem-solving experience
5. The ability to create ideas
6. The ability to build bridges between ideas to make them reality-based and logical

The program requires interactive experiences that are child directed in a low stimulus environment. Using a child-directed versus adult-directed approach encourages the child to want to relate to the outside world. Time required varies from two to five hours a day. Greenspan advocates that the program begin as soon as possible. He contends that the longer the child is allowed to remain uncommunicative and the more parents lose their sense of their child's attachment, the more deeply the child will withdraw and become perseverative and self-stimulatory. The goal of the program is to transform "perserveration into interaction." Once this occurs, the children become more purposeful in their interactions and can imitate gestures, sounds, and play (Greenspan, 1998). Because Floor Time is a relatively new treatment approach, more empirical studies must be conducted to determine its overall effectiveness. However, preliminary reports suggest that Floor Time is quite promising in promoting and stimulating appropriate social behaviors of children with PDDs.

IMPLICATIONS FOR TEACHING PHYSICAL EDUCATION

In the following section we provide an overview of basic teaching strategies for working with children with PDDs, including activity selection, assessment, instruction, and inclusion.

Activity Selection

When selecting activities for children with PDDs, the most important consideration is the needs and interests of the learners and their families. In addition, the functional value of the activity should be considered. Activities that have a high probability of success for children with PDDs are generally more individual in nature. Individual activities such as swimming, running, and bowling tend to yield high success levels. However, no one should assume that children with PDDs cannot participate and enjoy team sports. Team sports might need modifications to enhance success, but all children should have the opportunity to explore a range of physical education activities. The learner's age must be taken into account. Both developmental appropriateness and age appropriateness should always be considered when selecting activities. Although elementary-aged children spend a great deal of time learning and improving their fundamental motor skills, it would be inappropriate to focus on such skills at the middle school or high school level. When selecting activities, instructors should also consider family and community interests. Does the child come from a family that enjoys hiking or skiing? Or is the family more involved in soccer or softball? Considering these factors helps shape the activity selection so that the child with PDD can more fully integrate within the family and community structure.

Assessment

Reid and O'Connor (2003) provide a model potentially useful for assessing the motor skills of children with PDDs. Within the model, the instructor examines the interaction of three factors: the individual being assessed, the environment, and the task. To derive a good understanding of the individual, the assessor should seek information about the child from several sources, including parents, teachers, therapists, and teacher aids. Reinforc-

ers and modes of communication should be fully understood before attempting to assess the child. The assessor should also spend time developing a rapport with the child prior to assessing. When beginning the assessment, start with activities the child understands and is able to perform and then move on to more difficult tasks. This approach allows for early success and, typically, better compliance throughout the assessment.

The second factor that needs to be examined is the environment. Keeping in mind that children with PDDs might be hypersensitive to environmental stimuli, the assessor should provide an environment with limited distractions and focus on one task at a time. Environmental cues should be naturally occurring, not forced. For example, if you want to assess a child on stair climbing, try using a slide; instead of using an artificial stair device, the child can climb stairs to the top of the slide and then slide down.

The final factor to consider in the model is the task—that is, what you are asking the child to do. To determine if the task selected is appropriate, consider the following questions: Is the task age-appropriate? Is it functional? Will the information gained assist in the development of IEP goals and objectives? How about in program development and instruction? If the answer to these questions is yes, the task being assessed can be considered appropriate. To assess the task, the assessor might use a task-analysis approach in which requisite skills are identified and either further broken down or assessed as a whole. For example, in assessing soccer skills, the assessor would determine the requisite skills for soccer (e.g., dribbling, passing, trapping, and shooting). Each of these skills could be broken down into components assessed separately, or the skill could be assessed as a whole.

Once the assessment is complete, the information is used to develop goals and objectives based on unique needs and to serve as a basis for instruction. The following section is an overview on strategies for instructing children with PDDs.

Instruction

Reid and colleagues have identified several factors to consider when instructing children with PDDs (Reid, O'Connor, & Lloyd, 2003). These include allowing time for familiarity with the instructor and the activity, promoting eye contact as much as possible, using clear and consistent cues and prompts, and providing effective reinforcement and feedback. In addition, Houston-Wilson and

Lieberman (2003) identify strategies that can be helpful in teaching children with PDDs. These techniques are consistent with the TEACCH approach. They focus on organizing and structuring the environment through routines and schedules so that daily tasks are more predictable and yield a higher success rate.

Routines with set beginning and end points allow for more predictability and thus reduced sensory overload. Routines are also useful in introducing new information or behaviors. By keeping some information familiar and gradually introducing new information, students can respond appropriately. Routines also help to reduce verbal directions and allow children to work independently.

The use of schedules and calendars are helpful in establishing routines. Children with PDDs often demonstrate inappropriate behavioral responses when new or incongruent information is presented to them in a random or haphazard manner. A calendar, with significant events highlighted, coupled with a schedule of daily activities helps to alleviate the stress associated with not knowing what to expect (Geckler et al., 2000).

The following scenario illustrates a typical routine that can be established for physical education. Before Justin goes to physical education class, a classroom teacher gives Justin a picture of the physical education teacher and says, "Justin, it is time for PE." The picture of the physical education teacher allows Justin to understand what is going to happen next. When the class enters the gym, Justin gives the picture card to the physical education teacher. The physical education teacher then shows Justin the daily schedule that lists the day's activities with either words or pictures. Figure 10.1 shows a sample schedule for physical education. When using words, each activity can be erased after it is completed. This way Justin understands that the activity has ended and the next activity will soon begin.

If pictures are used, use only one item because children with PDDs have a tendency toward overselectivity, meaning they are not able to screen out irrelevant information. Teachers should help students focus on the most relevant information. For example, if a child is working on basketball skills, do not use a picture of a basketball court with students playing on the court because there is too much information on the picture, making it difficult for the child to screen out irrelevant information. Figure 10.2 depicts a picture of a basketball isolated from the rest of the activity, making it clear that basketball is the next task. At

PHYSICAL EDUCATION SCHEDULE

Enter gym
Warm-up: jump rope for three minutes

Ball skills
Bouncing

Passing

Fitness activity
Jog for five minutes

Game
Parachute

Cool-down
Relaxation activity

PE ends

Figure 10.1 Physical education schedule.

the completion of each activity the picture can be turned over.

Children with PDDs also have difficulty with sensory overload. When they are entering a new environment, such as a gym, the atmosphere might create extreme sensory overload (Janzen, 1996). Teachers can structure the physical education space in many ways. First, the teacher needs to identify to the child where things are done (in the gym, on the field, on a mat), where things are located (balls in bin, ropes on hangers, rackets on hooks) and how to move from one place to another (rotating stations, rotating positions, moving from inside to outside). Second, the teacher needs to establish concrete boundaries. For example, if a child is to remain on one half of the field, cones indicating the halfway point should be in place. Labels can also help organize space. Equipment areas and boxes should be clearly labeled so that the child can easily retrieve and put away equipment.

At the conclusion of the physical education lesson, the physical education teacher should have a consistent cue to transition the child back to the classroom. This could be a picture of the classroom teacher or a desk. Forewarning is another effective way to transition a child back

Figure 10.2 A basketball with no other distractors.

© Cathy Houston-Wilson

to the classroom. For example, the teacher might say: "Justin, in three minutes PE will be over." This helps the child better understand time and prepare for the change in routine. A second warning might be given at two minutes and a third at one minute. Through proper preparation, anxiety levels are reduced because the child begins to understand that a change in the task will occur after the "one minute" signal from the instructor. Again, the child must understand what will be happening next. When he or she arrives back in the classroom, physical education can be crossed off his or her daily schedule.

The implementation of routines and schedules might at first seem time consuming for the teacher. However, once these systems are in place, dramatic improvements in behavior and participation usually occur, which makes the extra time feel worthwhile.

Teachers should also take advantage of support personnel to assist them in implementing programs. Teaching assistants, teacher aides, and peer tutors are all valuable resources that can provide some individualized instruction to students with PDDs.

In addition to the methods described previously, it might also be necessary for physical educators to implement selected behavior-management techniques to reduce the occurrence of inappropriate behaviors, such as verbal outburst or self-injury, or to promote appropriate behaviors, such as on-task behavior and language skills. Behavior-management strategies can also help children with PDDs learn new skills. In the following paragraphs key strategies are presented to help shape social behaviors and promote instruction of children with PDDs based on selected behavior-management techniques.

Focus on Antecedents

Antecedents are events that occur within the environment that yield a response or a behavior. After the behavior occurs, a consequence, good or bad, typically follows. For example, if a child enters the gym and is greeted warmly by the teacher (antecedent), the behavior that follows might be on-task behavior during the warm-up; if so, the consequence would be positive reinforcement by the teacher or the reward of a token. However, if a child enters the gym, and unbeknownst to the teacher, a peer intentionally trips the child (antecedent), the behavior that follows might be an outburst or an unwillingness to participate in the warm-up activity. As a result of noncompliance with the activity, the child might receive an undesirable consequence, such as loss of a privilege. In the past, it was common practice to correct inappropriate behavior by focusing on the consequence (what happens to the student after an inappropriate behavior occurs) rather than the antecedent (what led to the behavior). An example demonstrating an overfocus on the consequence rather than a proper focus on the antecedent is described here:

> Seth often banged his head against the wall when he became frustrated. The teacher, Ms. Walker, would take Seth's hands and hold them down on his lap and say, "No head banging." Ms. Walker repeated this process each time Seth banged his head against the wall. Soon Seth began holding his hands down on his lap while he banged his head against the wall.

As demonstrated, focusing on the consequence rather than the antecedent was ineffective in this situation because there is no connection between head banging and holding hands down and saying "no." A better approach would be to focus on the antecedent—that is, consider what is happening in the environment or with the child to elicit the undesired behavior. If the antecedent can be determined (e.g., overstimulation caused by the gym setup), then the intervention would be to remove the child from the environment or to redirect him or her away from the inappropriate behavior (e.g., jogging around the gym).

Use Natural Environment Cues

In teaching new skills to children with PDDs, instructors are urged to use natural cues within the environment and to minimize verbal cues. If the goal is for the child to kick a soccer ball into a goal, the natural cues would be a soccer ball and a goal. To achieve the desired objective, the instructor might need to break the task down to smaller steps, which might include lining the child up at the shooting line, placing the ball on the shooting line, and signaling for the child to take a shot. Demonstrations also prove helpful in fostering the acquisition of new skills. If the child performs the task correctly, continue with the lesson. For example, teach the child how to stop a ball being passed to the shooting line or add a defensive player. If, however, the child is unsuccessful in shooting the ball toward the goal, use physical assistance to help him or her gain a better understanding of what the task requires. Allow the child to repeat the task until no physical assistance is needed. Once he or she has performed the task correctly, teach the rest of the lesson.

Correction Procedure Rule

Another effective technique in instructing children with PDDs is the correction procedure rule, which is applied by taking the child back to the last component of the skill done correctly. Using a batting example, say a child maintains a proper batting stance and properly swings the bat at the ball, but then he or she runs to first base with the bat; in this case, following the correction procedure rule, the instructor would ask the child to repeat the swing and then physically assist him or her in placing the bat on the ground before running to first. The instructor returns the child to the last correct response prior to the incorrect response. The following application example is another scenario in which the correction procedure rule can be used (see also figure 10.3).

Parallel Talk

To promote language and skill acquisition, instructors are encouraged to embed language throughout the lesson. One way to accomplish this is using parallel talk, in which the teacher verbalizes the actions of the learner. For example, if Marci is rolling a red ball to the teacher, the teacher would say, "Marci is rolling the red ball." Parallel talk can also help children associate certain skills with their verbal meaning, such as spatial concepts (e.g., in,

out, under, over) and motor skills (e.g., dribbling, shooting, striking). Another way to foster language acquisition is to create print-rich physical education environments. Pictures, posters, and action words should be displayed prominently around the gym. Labeling the action as it is being performed helps students acquire both receptive and expressive language skills.

Other Techniques

These techniques are quite easy to implement and go a long way toward creating a positive learning environment for the child. In addition, more formalized behavioral techniques might be needed to eliminate inappropriate behaviors and to elicit desired behaviors of students with PDDs in physical education. Chapters 6 and 7 of this text provide additional information on behavioral and instructional strategies helpful in instructing children with PDDs in physical education. Two examples discussed in chapter 6 have yielded a degree of success in teaching students with PDDs: the token economy system and the Premack Principle. A token economy is a system in which the student is rewarded with a reinforcer that can be collected and later redeemed for a desirable object or privilege. For example, if Justin enjoyed roller skating, he would need to collect a certain amount of coins before earning an opportunity to roller skate. Similarly, the Premack Principle requires the student to participate in a less preferred activity prior to the preferred activity. Once again, using Justin's preferred activity of roller skating, he would be required to participate in other physical education–related activities before he could roller skate. Be careful when using the Premack Principle because if misused, a desirable object, privilege, or preferred activity could quickly become undesired or nonpreferred. If Justin is constantly forced to do things he does not enjoy in order to roller skate, roller skating might quickly become a nonpreferred activity.

Finally, instructors should be aware that students with PDDs might experience "meltdowns." Despite best efforts, structure, and routines, students with PDDs sometimes find it difficult to participate in any activity. In most cases, a behavioral plan has been created by a group of professionals (that may or may not include the physical education teacher) to deal with such instances, and the child might be permitted to sit it out or go to a quiet space and regain composure. Once the episode has subsided, the student is encouraged to participate in the planned activity.

APPLICATION EXAMPLE

The Importance of Visual Cues

Setting: Physical education field

Students: Elementary physical education class

Task: Participating in a tee-ball game

Application: Using visual cues to create a positive learning environment

Kiera is seven years old and has autism. Her physical education teacher, Mr. Greer, is teaching Kiera how to play tee-ball. They have practiced in a hand-over-hand manner to swing the bat at the ball, make contact with the ball, put the bat down, and run to first base. It appeared that Kiera really had the hang of the skill, so Mr. Greer allowed Kiera to bat independently. Kiera stood in the ready position; Mr. Greer placed the ball on the tee and took a step back. Just then a gust of wind came, and the ball fell off the tee. Kiera immediately placed the bat on the ground and began running to first base, although she did not make contact with the ball. This example illustrates that Kiera still did not understand the purpose of the game, which was to contact the ball with the bat before running. Mr. Greer then demonstrated to Kiera what to do if the ball falls off the tee. Mr. Greer put the ball on the tee loosely so that it would fall off. When the ball fell off, Mr. Greer picked the ball up again and replaced it on the tee; then he struck the ball with the bat. Mr. Greer then signaled to Kiera to try. Again he placed the ball loosely on the tee and gave the bat to Kiera. The ball fell off the tee and Kiera picked the ball up and replaced it on the tee. She then struck the ball and ran to first base. This example illustrates the need for students with

autism to visually see and understand a task. In no way was Kiera being uncooperative or off task. She simply did not understand the task. When she understood the task, Kiera was able to participate in the game independently.

Figure 10.3 Kiera practices her swing in tee-ball.

Inclusion

The techniques described in this chapter are useful in assisting physical educators to include children with PDDs in physical education. Keeping in mind that adapted physical education is a program, not a placement, these ideas are easy to incorporate in an inclusive setting. Using resources within the IEP, physical educators can request support personnel to help provide any one-on-one teaching that might be necessary throughout the lesson. In addition, supplemental aids and equipment that might be required to

more successfully include the child should be identified on the IEP. Goals and objectives developed for children with PDDs should parallel the physical education curriculum. In some instances, children with high-functioning autism or Asperger syndrome might not need any form of modification nor an IEP to be successfully included in the class. Determining whether to include students with PDDs in regular physical education must be based on the individual needs of the learner. In some instances, inclusion is most appropriate; in others, it is not. Responding to the unique needs of the learner is the best approach.

SUMMARY

This chapter provided an overview of pervasive developmental disabilities and implications for physical education. PDDs include autism, Asperger syndrome, Rett's disorder, Childhood Disintegrative Disorder (CDD), and Pervasive Developmental Disorder, Not Otherwise Specified (PDD-NOS). Each of these conditions has been explained in detail. The cause of PDDs is unknown, but research indicates they are probably attributed to a neurological or genetic link. The incidence of PDDs, especially autism, has increased significantly over the last several years. Many attribute this increase to better screening and detection; others believe it is caused by an increase in environmental toxins.

Research on the physical and motor characteristics of students with PDDs varies depending on the condition. Although it appears that some children with Asperger syndrome, Rett's disorder, CDD, and PDD-NOS have physical and motor delays, the physical and motor status of individuals with autism is less clear. Additional research is needed in this area.

Many treatment approaches have been used to assist students with PDDs live more productive lives. This chapter provided a review of three approaches: applied behavior analysis, the TEACCH program, and the DIR–Floor Time approach. These approaches all have merit, and each has led to significant gains in participants. Based on the treatment approaches presented, strategies for teaching students with PDDs in physical education were presented. Focus on teaching is based on using the strengths of the learner (structure, routines), maintaining a positive learning environment, and using behavior-modification techniques to help shape the lives of individuals with PDDs.

REFERENCES

American Psychiatric Association (1994). *Diagnostic and statistical manual of mental disorders* DSM-IV, Washington, DC.

Bryan, L.C., & Gast, D.L. (2000). Teaching on-task and on-schedule behaviors to high-functioning children with autism via picture schedules. *Journal of Autism and Developmental Disorders, 30*(6), 553-567.

Geckler, A.S., Libby, M.E., Graff, R.B., & Ahearn, W.H. (2000). Effects of reinforcer choice measured in single-operant and concurrent-schedule procedures. *Journal of Applied Behavior Analysis, 33*(3), 347-351.

Gillberg, C., & Wing, L. (1999). Autism: Not an extremely rare disorder. *Acta Psychiatricia Scandinavica, 99,* 399-406.

Grandin, T. (1988). Teaching tips from a recovered autistic. *Focus on Autistic Behavior, 3,* 1-8.

Greenspan, S.I. (1998). A developmental approach to problems in relating and communicating in autistic spectrum disorders and related syndromes. *SPOTLIGHT on Topics in Developmental Disabilities, 1*(4), 1-6.

Hanks, S. (1990). Motor disabilities in the Rett's syndrome and physical therapy strategies. *Brain and Development, 12,* 157-161.

Houston-Wilson, C., & Lieberman, L. (2003). Strategies for teaching students with autism in physical education. *Journal of Physical Education, Recreation and Dance, 74*(6), 40-44.

Janzen, J.E. (1996). *Understanding the nature of autism: A practical guide.* San Antonio: Therapy Skill Builders.

Levinson, L.J., & Reid, G. (1993). The effects of exercise intensity on the stereotyped behaviors of individuals with autism. *Adapted Physical Activity Quarterly, 10,* 255-268.

Lovaas, O.I. (1987). Behavioral treatment and normal educational and intellectual functioning in young autistic children. *Journal of Consulting and Clinical Psychology, 55,* 3-9.

McEachin, J.J., Smith, T., & Lovaas, O.I. (1993). Long term outcome for children with autism who received early intensive behavioral treatment, *American Journal of Mental Retardation, 4,* 359-372.

Mesibov, G.B. (1996). Division TEACCH: A collaborative model program for service delivery, training, and research for people with autism and related communication handicaps. In M.C. Roberts (Ed.), *Model programs in child and family mental health* (pp. 215-230. Mahwah, Nj: Lawrence Erlbaum.

Office of Special Education and Rehabilitative Services (OSE/RS). 34 CFR (2002).

Ozonoff, S., Dawson, G., & McPartland, J. (2002). *A parent's guide to Asperger syndrome and high-functioning autism.* New York: The Guilford Press.

Powers, M.D. (2000). *Children with autism: A parent's guide.* Bethesda, MD: Woodbine House.

Reid, G., & Collier, D. (2002). Motor behavior and the autism spectrum disorders—Introduction. *Palaestra, 18,* 20-27/44.

Reid, G., & O'Connor, J. (2003). The Autism Spectrum Disorders: Activity selection, assessment, and program organization—Part II. *Palaestra, 19,* 20-27/58.

Reid, G., O'Connor, J., & Lloyd, M. (2003). The Autism Spectrum Disorders: Physical activity instruction—Part III. *Palaestra, 20,* 20-26/47.

Rimland, B. (1964). *Infantile autism: The syndrome and its implications for neural theory of behavior.* New York, NY: Appleton-Century-Croft

Sigman, M., & Capps, L. (1997). *Children with autism: A developmental perspective.* Cambridge, MA: Harvard University Press.

Stodgell, C.J., Ingram, J.L., & Hyman, S.L. (2001). The role of candidate genes in unraveling the genetics of autism. In L.M. Glidden (Ed.) *International Review of Research in Mental Retardation* (Vol. 23, pp. 57-81). New York, New York: Academic Press.

Sulzer-Azaroff, B, & Mayer, R. (1991). *Behavior analysis for lasting change.* Fort Worth, TX: Holt, Reinhart & Winston, Inc.

Trehin, P. (1998). *Some basic information about TEACCH.* www.asatonline.org/about_autism/autism_info14.html.

WRITTEN RESOURCES

Cohen, D.J., & Volkmar, F.R. (Eds.). (1997). *Handbook of autism and pervasive developmental disorders,* (2nd ed.). New York: John Wiley & Sons.

A comprehensive and up-to-date professional textbook on autism and related conditions.

Grandin, T. (1996). *Thinking in pictures: And other reports from my life with autism.* New York: Vintage Press.

Written by Temple Grandin a recovered autistic, who has gained national fame for her insights and discoveries in the world of autism.

Harris, S.L., & Weiss, M.J. (1998). *Right from the start: Behavioral intervention for young children with autism.* Bethesda, MD: Woodbine House.

An introductory guide to applied behavior analysis and early intervention programs for young children.

Howlin, P. (1998). *Children with autism and Asperger syndrome: A guide for practitioners and carers.* New York: John Wiley & Sons.

Written for professionals but also beneficial for parents, this book provides a comprehensive look at autism and Asperger syndrome, covering major issues of treatment, education, and behavior.

Koegel, R., & Koegel, L.K. (1996). *Teaching children with autism: Strategies for initiating positive interactions and improving learning opportunities.* Baltimore, MD: Paul H. Brookes.

Describes the positive behavioral support strategies that can be applied to classroom and home settings.

AUDIOVISUAL RESOURCES

Asperger's syndrome: Crossing the bridge (Videotape). Michael Thompson Productions, PO Box 9334, Naperville, IL 60567.

A comprehensive look at Asperger syndrome through the eyes of Dr. Liane Holliday Willey, an adult diagnosed with the disorder. Running time is approximately 28 minutes.

Autism: A world apart (Videotape). Fanlight Productions, 4196 Washington Street, Boston, MA 02131.

Presents the day-to-day life of three families who have a child with autism. Running time is approximately 29 minutes.

Breakthrough: How to reach students with autism (Videotape). Child Development Media, Inc. 5632 Van Nuys Blvd., Suite 286, Van Nuys, CA 91401.

Includes video and curriculum manual. Follows a preschooler in a school setting and demonstrates how the use of high expectations, physical prompting, modeling, and attending to task increases the child's educational progress. Running time is approximately 26 minutes.

The spectrum of autism (Videotape). Fanlight Productions, 4196 Washington Street, Boston, MA 02131.

Presents the experiences of several families and professionals who care for children at different points on the spectrum of autism. Running time is approximately 34 minutes.

Understanding autism (Videotape). Fanlight Productions, 4196 Washington Street, Boston, MA 02131.

Discusses the nature and symptoms of autism and outlines a treatment program based on behavioral modification that can be used in schools or at home. Running time is approximately 19 minutes.

ELECTRONIC RESOURCES

Autism Research Review International: www.autism.com/ari.

This site is the home of the Autism Research Institute.

PDD network newsletter: www.PDDAspergerSupportCT.org.

This site is the home of the PDD/Asperger's Support Group.

The advocate: www.autism-society.org.

This site is the home of the Autism Society of America.

CHAPTER 11

Specific Learning Disabilities

Barry W. Lavay

Calvin is 13 years old, tall for his age with blond hair and bright blue eyes. Since first grade, Calvin has been receiving special education services after being diagnosed with a learning disability and attention deficit/hyperactivity disorder (ADHD). This year Calvin is attending seventh grade at Lexington Junior High and spends the first two periods of each school day in a special education resource room in math and reading. During the remaining five periods, Calvin is included in general classes with his peers without disabilities, including sixth period regular physical education class. Calvin struggles with physical education class, partly because the acoustics and the noise level make it difficult to concentrate and understand class instructions. Calvin also finds the large gym space with the different floor markings to be a distraction. Every three weeks after a sport unit is completed, Mr. Santos gives the class a 15-minute written test that Calvin has difficulty reading and completing in such a short time. Recently, two of the more skilled boys whose team he played on in a basketball unit began to make fun of him, taunting him and calling him names each time he dropped the ball. During these times, Mr. Santos comes over to help Calvin, but then Calvin gets really nervous and drops the ball even more. He doesn't want Mr. Santos to find out that he has a learning disability and is different from the other kids.

As you read this chapter, think about Calvin and other children like him with a learning disability, ADHD, or poor motor skills and consider the challenges each faces. Keep in mind that not all children with a learning disability have ADHD or poor motor skills, but some do. No two children with learning disabilities are alike; a wide range of characteristics exist. Children with learning disabilities, such as Calvin, will often be included in regular physical education classes. Consider how the information discussed in this chapter can be used to provide a more successful learning experience. The chapter's topics include definitions, causes, and incident rates of specific learning disabilities, a description of common characteristics, general educational approaches, and recommendations for teaching physical education and sport.

WHAT IS A SPECIFIC LEARNING DISABILITY?

No other disability has been more misunderstood and caused more confusion among professionals and parents than the condition identified as learning disability. In the past, such terms as "perceptually handicapped," "brain injured," "minimal brain dysfunction," "dyslexia," and "developmentally aphasic" were commonly used to identify this population.

In 1963, Sam Kirk of the University of Illinois, who is considered the father of the field of learning disabilities, coined the term "learning disability" in a meeting of parents and professionals in Chicago, Illinois. He shared with conference attendees that he had been using the term to refer to children who had learning problems but showed no signs of mental retardation or emotional disturbance. Parents quickly adopted the term as a more appropriate label than those used at the time (e.g., minimal brain dysfunction or neurologically impaired) (Dunn, 1997; Smith, 2001).

Learning Disability Defined

Professionals are unable to agree on one specific definition of learning disability (Kavale & Forness, 2000). What experts do agree on is that this group does not learn for a variety of reasons. Many believe that children with a learning disability have a neurological disorder that results in problems in storing, processing, and producing information in the central nervous system, thus causing a deficit in understanding spoken or written words.

This difficulty can manifest itself in an imperfect ability to listen, think, speak, read, write, spell, do mathematical calculations, or motor plan. Possible other indications that a learning problem exists are when individuals consistently have difficulty remembering newly learned information, expressing thoughts orally or in writing, understanding information presented, following directions and routines, or moving in space from one activity to the next. More specific difficulties include reversal of letters or words, difficulty with the steps necessary to complete an addition or division math problem, or spatial awareness difficulties, such as bumping into objects.

Since mid-1970, the Individuals with Disabilities Education Act (IDEA) definition has been used in public schools to determine if a child with a learning disability qualifies for special education services. Here is that definition:

> "Specific learning disability" means a disorder in one or more of the basic psychological processes involved in understanding or in using language, spoken or written, that may manifest itself in an imperfect ability to listen, think, speak, read, write, spell, or do mathematical calculations. The term includes such conditions as perceptual disabilities, brain injury, minimal brain dysfunction, dyslexia, and developmental aphasia. The term does not apply to children who have a learning problem that are primarily the result of visual, hearing, or motor disabilities; of mental retardation; or of environmental, cultural, or economic disadvantage. (IDEA amendment, 2001)

To some degree, most children have difficulty in some of these areas at one time or another. But only when these behaviors occur in more than one setting, persist over an extended time, and interfere with learning do they need special attention. The term "specific" was added to learning disabilities to underscore that these children have learning difficulties only in specific areas (e.g., reading, speaking, calculating), and that there are other areas of learning in which they are at least of average ability or even gifted in their learning.

The IDEA definition of a specific learning disability has undergone little change since being introduced in 1975. The definition still includes such terms as minimal brain dysfunction, dyslexia, and developmental aphasia. Many professionals believe this definition is difficult to put into practice and fails to provide significant insight into the true nature of a condition (Kavale & Forness,

2000). Despite this controversy, the IDEA definition continues to be used in the public schools to determine if a child qualifies for special education services.

Unexpected Underachievement

Experts agree that a key or defining feature of learning disability is that an educationally significant discrepancy exists between estimated intellectual potential and actual academic achievement. Discrepancy in this context means a difference between ability and actual achievement and is sometimes called "unexpected underachievement." Unexpected underachievement is a disorder related primarily to language and mastering academic areas (particularly reading) that is not attributed to other disabilities. A learning disability can't be caused by cultural differences, lack of educational opportunities, poverty, or other such conditions. Experts believe the problem is the result of an individual's inability to store, process, and produce information in the central nervous system. Specific learning disability does not occur as a result of other conditions but might coexist with other conditions, such as ADHD and developmental coordination disorder (DCD). Although the majority of students with a learning disability possess normal intelligence, their academic performance lags behind that of their peers, and they do not perform at grade level. This population has difficulty learning in traditional ways; we all must remember that a learning disability affects *how* the individual learns and not *how well* they learn (Kavale & Forness, 2000; Smith, 2001).

The Hidden Disability

Specific learning disability is not easily recognized or accepted. It is considered a hidden disability because no easily identifiable physical signs exist. When a person is missing a limb or using a wheelchair, for instance, his or her disability is easily visible. But when a person's disability involves dysfunction to the central nervous system and processing information, it is often not visible at all. Many individuals exhibit deficits in the perceptual motor process, such as when taking in, storing, and retrieving information. Chapter 20 includes an overview of information processing and the tactual, kinesthetic, visual, and auditory sensory systems.

Because they are often hidden, learning disabilities are frequently misunderstood; sometimes the main problem is in educating people who do not have the disability. Recognition is made even more difficult because many individuals with learning disabilities spend much of their time and energy hiding their disability. They might not read in public, for example, or they might shy away from activities on the playground. Parents might be in denial about their child's disability and feel that it will go away or can be quickly fixed. The truth of the matter is a learning disability will present lifelong challenges to those children and their families. Professionals and parents must realize that with modifications and the right type of intervention many individuals with learning disabilities will go on to be productive members of society. For example, Ben Franklin, Woodrow Wilson, Albert Einstein, and Winston Churchill did not perform well in school and are believed to have had a learning disability involving some type of attention deficit that was later adjusted.

Individuals With Learning Disabilities and Accompanying Disabilities of ADHD and DCD

Many individuals with learning disabilities exhibit additional characteristics of ADHD or DCD. The prevalence of children with learning disabilities who display accompanying characteristics of ADHD and DCD makes it important for us to discuss these two conditions in this chapter. However, children with ADHD and DCD are not recognized as a distinct disability category under IDEA and do not automatically qualify for special education services. Children with ADHD who do qualify for services must have, as their primary disability, one of the 13 disabilities identified in IDEA. The primary disability is usually a learning disability or a behavioral disability (see chapter 9). Some children with ADHD might qualify under the "other health impairment" category in IDEA if it can be shown that the child's deficit affects educational performance. Although IDEA does not recognize motor disabilities alone as a diagnosis for a learning disability, most authorities believe a higher than average percentage of children with learning disabilities have perceptual motor- and movement-related difficulties that require intensive intervention (Harvey & Reid, 2003; Sherrill, 2004).

Because the federal legislation does not clearly identify and recognize ADHD and DCD in the public schools as distinct conditions, programming for students with learning disabilities and such secondary conditions as ADHD and DCD becomes problematic (Beyer, 1999). For example, Henderson and Henderson (2002) believe the high degree of overlap between DCD and other childhood disorders appear to deemphasize its acceptance as a distinct syndrome. Other professionals feel it is not important what labels children wear as long as they receive services designed to meet their unique educational needs. In this chapter, the terms learning disability, ADHD, and DCD are used to denote that the information provided applies to students with one or more of these conditions.

What Is Attention Deficit or Hyperactivity Disorder?

Attention deficit or hyperactivity disorder (ADHD) is an official clinical label clearly defined and recognized by the American Psychiatric Association (APA) The diagnostic criteria to determine an individual with ADHD is shown in the sidebar (APA, 2000). It is important to note that no single test to determine ADHD exists; a comprehensive battery of assessment tests administered by a qualified professional, such as a school psychologist, is necessary for diagnosis.

ADHD is divided into three subtypes: combined type, predominantly inattentive type, and predominantly hyperactive–impulsive type. The defining features of an individual with ADHD are inattention and hyperactivity–impulsivity. Based on the criteria used to diagnose this condition, ADHD is defined as a persistent pattern of inattention or hyperactivity with impulse behaviors that are more inappropriate, excessive, frequent, and more severe than are observed in children of comparable development (criterion A). Six or more of these symptoms from category 1 or 2 must be excessive and pervasive or present over at least a six-month period. Some hyperactive–impulsive or inattention symptoms must be present before the age of seven years; exhibited in multiple (at least two or more) settings such as the home, school, and or social settings (criterion B); and not be explained by another disorder (see Diagnostic Criteria sidebar). The hyperactivity must be excessive, inappropriate, and occur in different settings. Children with ADHD are easily distracted by irrelevant stimuli and frequently shift from one incomplete activity to the next. Inattention occurs in academic, occupational, or social situations and is more difficult to observe than hyperactivity (APA, 2000). Children who exhibit inattention without hyperactivity may even be hypoactive.

What Is Developmental Coordination Disorder?

Since 1987, developmental coordination disorder (DCD) has been recognized officially by the APA, which identifies four diagnostic criteria for determining the presence of DCD:

1. An individual's performance in daily activities must be substantially below that expected for a person's age and IQ.
2. The deficiency must interfere with academic achievement activities of daily living.
3. The motor deficiency cannot be caused by a general medical condition, such as cerebral palsy, muscular dystrophy, or pervasive developmental disorder. For example, children with ADHD might fall and bump into things, but this is usually a result of distractibility or impulsiveness.
4. If mental retardation is present, the motor difficulties must be in excess of those associated alone with this disability (APA, 2000; Henderson & Henderson, 2002).

DCD is often operationalized as an individual entity two standard deviations below age norms on a standardized motor test. In general, children with DCD demonstrate a marked delay in meeting motor developmental milestones, such as walking, and the child appears clumsy, exhibits poor handwriting, and performs poorly in sports. Children with DCD often do not exhibit the classic neurological signs of clumsiness, but they lack the motor competence required to cope with the everyday demands of living (Henderson, 1994). Many children do not grow out of their motor difficulties; DCD can be a lifelong challenge.

Suspected Causes of Specific Learning Disability, ADHD, and DCD

A specific learning disability is complex, multidimensional, and possibly the culmination of many causes. Presently, the most common theory is a neurological condition, such as a dysfunction in the central nervous system in producing, processing, or storing information. Central nervous system dysfunction means that brain or neurological damage is present that impedes the individual's motor or learning abilities. Teachers must recognize the uncertainty about what

Diagnostic Criteria for Attention-Deficit/Hyperactivity Disorder

A. Either (1) or (2):

1. Six (or more) of the following symptoms of inattention have persisted for at least 6 months to a degree that is maladaptive and inconsistent with developmental level:

Inattention

a. Often fails to give close attention to details or makes careless mistakes in schoolwork, work, or other activities

b. Often has difficulty sustaining attention in tasks or play activities

c. Often does not seem to listen when spoken to directly

d. Often does not follow through on instructions and fails to finish schoolwork, chores, or duties in the workplace (not due to oppositional behavior or failure to understand instructions)

e. Often has difficulty organizing tasks and activities

f. Often avoids, dislikes, or is reluctant to engage in tasks that require sustained mental effort (such as schoolwork or homework)

g. Often loses things necessary for tasks or activities (e.g., toys, school assignments, pencils, books, or tools)

h. Is often easily distracted by extraneous stimuli

i. Is often forgetful in daily activities

2. Six (or more) of the following symptoms of hyperactivity-impulsivity have persisted for at least 6 months to a degree that is maladaptive and inconsistent with developmental level:

Hyperactivity

a. often fidgets with hands or feet or squirms in seat

b. often leaves seat in classroom or in other situations in which remaining seated was expected

c. often runs about or climbs excessively in situations in which it is inappropriate (in adolescents or adults, may be limited to subjective feelings of restlessness)

d. often has difficulty playing or engaging in leisure activities quietly

e. is often "on the go" or often as if "driven by a motor"

f. often talks excessively

Impulsivity

g. often blurts out answers before questions have been completed

h. often has difficulty awaiting turn

i. often interrupts or intrudes on others (e.g., butts into conversations or games)

B. Some hyperactive-impulsive or inattentive symptoms that caused impairment were present before age 7.

C. Some impairment for the symptoms is present in two or more settings (e.g., at school [or work] and at home).

D. There must be clear evidence of clinically significant impairment in social, academic, or occupational functioning.

E. The symptoms do not occur exclusively during the course of a pervasive developmental disorder, schizophrenia, or other psychotic disorder and are not better accounted for by another mental disorder (e.g., mood disorder, anxiety disorder, dissociative disorder, or a personality disorder).

Code Based on Type

Attention-deficit/hyperactivity disorder, combined type: if both criteria A1 and A2 are met for the past 6 months

Attention-deficit/hyperactivity disorder, predominantly inattentive type: if criterion A1 is met but criterion A2 is not met for the past 6 months

Attention-deficit/hyperactivity disorder, predominantly hyperactive-impulsive type: if criterion A2 is met but criterion A1 is not met for the past 6 months

Coding note: for individuals (especially adolescents and adults) who currently have symptoms that no longer meet full criteria, "in partial remission" should be specified.

Taken From American Psychiatric Association. (2000). *Diagnostic and statistical manual of mental disorders*. (4th ed.). Washington D.C.: Author.

causes learning disabilities and not make assumptions that brain damage exists when there is no physical evidence or an actual medical diagnosis. Labeling individuals with such terms as "brain injured" might lead educators and parents to presume that nothing can be done to remediate the educational difficulties, and consequently student expectations might be set too low with educational potential never met (Smith, 2001). Other possible causes of learning disabilities include brain damage from an accident; lack of oxygen before, during, or after birth; genetics or heredity (Kavale & Forness, 2000).

As is the case with learning disabilities, the cause of ADHD is unclear and controversial, though experts agree it is a multidimensional disability caused primarily by an interaction of neurological, genetic, and psychosocial factors. Several studies support the theory that the condition is biological, because certain regions of the brain are associated with ADHD. In addition, the condition is believed to be highly genetic because it is inherited, often running in families. For example, if one person in a family is diagnosed with ADHD, a 25 to 35 percent probability exists that another family member also has ADHD (compared to 4 to 6 percent probability in the general population). Physical educators must be aware of the probable biological basis for the lack of social control that individuals with ADHD might exhibit that can become more erratic in environments with decreasing amounts of social support (Harvey & Reid, 2003).

Incident Rates of Specific Learning Disability, ADHD, and DCD

Approximately 2.9 million students (5 percent) enrolled in the public schools in the United States are identified as having learning disabilities, which makes this group the largest category of special education (Smith, 2001). The category has grown considerably, from 25 percent of special education students in 1976 to 50 percent in 2004—the greatest percentage of the school-age special education population (Kavale & Forness, 2000). Although criteria are based on the federal IDEA definition, actual interpretation of the definition and identification of students can vary slightly from state to state and district to district, with statistics of students identified as having a learning disability ranging from 1.7 to 5.8 percent. This

category of disability is large because the definition of learning disability is so broad, and because children who are not succeeding in general education classes are often identified as having a learning disability (Smith, 2001). The learning disability label has become a "dumping ground" for unsuccessful students in general education as well as for students with different disabilities, such as ADHD.

A high percentage of children with learning disabilities (ranging from 25 to 50 percent) also display ADHD (Smith, 2001). About half of the children identified with ADHD also have oppositional defiant disorder or conduct disorder (APA, 2000). The symptoms of this condition are more likely to occur in a group setting, such as a playground or classroom, rather than in an individualized setting. This fact has important implications for physical education in which most activities occur in large group settings.

The prevalence of ADHD in school-age children is between 3 and 7 percent, but estimates have been reported as high as 20 percent, depending on the nature of the population sampled (APA, 2000). Within this group, 50 percent do not qualify for special education services (Smith, 2001). It has long been believed that boys with ADHD outnumber girls 3 to 1. However, many experts believe that females with ADHD are under recognized and that the actual number of females might be close to or equal to the number of males. The incident rate of children 6 to 11 years of age identified with DCD has been estimated to be as high as 6 percent (APA, 2000).

CHARACTERISTICS PRESENT UNIQUE CHALLENGES

The movement characteristics or behaviors of individuals with learning disabilities, ADHD, or DCD vary. Some individuals might be skilled movers and exceptional athletes, but the majority are at risk for developmental delays compared to peers without disabilities (Harvey & Reid, 2003). In general, this population exhibits a wide range of physical, cognitive, and social behaviors that affect their ability to move (Milne, Haubenstricker, & Seefelt, 1991). Some behaviors, such as a short attention span, are not specific motor problems but can make it difficult to attend to directions, and consequently affect movement outcomes (Horvat, Eichstaedt, Kalakian, & Croce, 2002). The sidebar provides a description of the most common physical, cognitive, and social–behavioral characteristics that teachers encounter that can affect movement and interfere with the ability of students with a specific learning disability, ADHD, or DCD to learn. When designing physical education programs, teachers must be aware of these behaviors and the unique challenges each can bring in order to provide students with a safe and positive experience. Other perceptual motor and sensory characteristics are discussed later in this chapter.

GENERAL EDUCATIONAL APPROACHES

Physical educators might be involved in some educational approaches for teaching students with learning disabilities, ADHD, and DCD, but others, such as the decision to prescribe medication, are beyond their responsibility (Craft, 2000). Yet these general educational approaches must be well understood so that physical educators can support

Common Physical, Cognitive, and Social Behavioral Characteristics That Affect Movement for Individuals With LD, ADHD, and DCD

These behavioral characteristics will vary among individuals.

Physical (developmental delay)

A marked developmental delay: lag behind their same age peers in fundamental gross motor skills such as running, throwing, and catching.

Movements are not performed in a smooth and efficient manner: require extra movements and the use of unnecessary body parts to perform skills. Movements appear clumsy or uncoordinated and there is difficulty moving one body part independently from others.

Skill sequencing: unable to initiate a movement that puts the correct parts into a proper sequence such as breaking down or analyzing the movements needed to successfully plan and perform the skill.

An inability to control movements: rush to complete the activity and do not perform at a pace or speed needed to successfully perform the task.

Inconsistency in skill performance: vacillates from practice session to practice session and even within the same session. Skill retention is difficult.

Cognitive (average or above average intellectual ability)

Process information: more time is required to take in, organize, or produce instructional information. The individual is taking in too much extraneous information or stimuli at one time and has difficulty remaining focused on the specific instruction or task. Difficult to take in more than one given direction at a time.

Difficulty completing tasks in allotted time: avoids or fails to stay on tasks that require a sustained mental effort. Overall, has difficulty organizing or planning tasks.

Fails to pay attention to details: Tasks are not completed or are finished quickly, makes careless mistakes in order to move on to the next task.

Perseveration: inability to shift easily from one activity to the next. This is the opposite of distractibility.

Language delays: in expressive, receptive, retention and or sequencing.

Perceptual and sensory delays: in tactile, proprioception, kinesthetic, visual, and auditory systems. May be hyper- or hyporesponsive to sensory stimuli.

Uneven academic achievement: there is uneven development among educational subject areas.

Social (lack of social expectations and low self-esteem)

Impulsive: acting before considering the consequences of actions and shows little inhibition before speaking or acting in front of others. Often interrupts others.

Hyperactive, easily distracted, and short attention span: demonstrates excess energy that is difficulty to control. This can lead to difficulty staying on task, taking turns, or remaining focused.

Poor self-concept: exhibits a low frustration and perceived competence level.

Bishop & Beyer, 1995; Milne, Haubenstricker, & Seefelt, 1991; Sherrill, 2004

and collaborate effectively with other professionals to meet student needs. More specific recommendations and methods for teaching physical education and sport are discussed at the end of the chapter.

Because students with learning disabilities, ADHD, and DCD are a very heterogeneous group, it follows that there are many ways of teaching to meet these students' needs. Currently, no one approach is universally supported; rather, several different approaches have been successful with students with learning disabilities, ADHD, and DCD. Three of these approaches—multisensory, behavior management, and multifaceted—are described briefly here. For consistency and when practical, the physical educator might want to determine which approach is used in the student's classroom or home and follow that same approach in the physical education setting (Craft, 2000).

Multisensory Approach

The ability to learn and function effectively is affected by the sensory systems. The characteristics of learning disabilities, ADHD, or DCD (see the Common Characteristics sidebar) are also affected by the sensory systems. Deficits related to the sensory systems are often identified as characteristics of individuals with learning disabilities, ADHD, or DCD. These deficits might include poor spatial orientation, poor body awareness, immature body image, poor visual motor coordination, clumsiness or awkwardness, coordination deficits, or poor balance. Considering these deficits, effective instruction needs to include a multisensory teaching approach with an understanding of the perceptual motor development process and the sensory systems (as described in chapter 20).

The multisensory approach emphasizes teaching through learning strengths and focuses on the use of three or more sensory channels in the teaching–learning process, the most typical being tactile, kinesthetic, visual, and auditory. A teaching method that integrates three of these modalities might have the student watch a demonstration of a movement (visual), listen to the teacher describe the movement (auditory), and be physically manipulated through the movement (kinesthetic). For example, a student might learn letters by looking at a printed letter, hearing the names of the letters, feeling their shape by tracing the letters, and moving the entire body to form the letter's shape. Many special educators have promoted the idea that teaching students with learning and attention deficits is best accomplished by matching the teaching method to the student's preferred learning style. Good teaching practice appeals to different learning styles simultaneously (Craft, 2000).

Behavior Management

The foundation of effective instruction is managing student behavior. Many behavior-management approaches (e.g., behavioral, psychoeducational, psychodynamic, psychoneurological) are used in the schools to maintain and increase appropriate behaviors and prevent or decrease inappropriate behaviors in children with learning disabilities, ADHD, or DCD (Lavay, French, & Henderson, 2006). In the behavioral approach, the teacher analyzes the behaviors of the student or class by focusing on the actions occurring before the behavior (called the antecedents) and the consequences occurring after the behavior. This sort of analysis helps the teacher evaluate the student or class situation and make appropriate changes (usually to the environment) to alter the behavior. A variety of effective behavior-management methods for individuals with learning disabilities, ADHD, or DCD are presented in chapter 6. Also see an upcoming section in this chapter: Recommendations for Teaching Physical Education and Sport.

Multifaceted Approach

Individuals with learning disabilities, ADHD, or DCD often have difficulty learning in traditional ways; no one method or cookbook approach works best. Rather, an eclectic or multifaceted approach is required, one that offers a combination of program services based on what is best for each individual. Taking a multifaceted approach means that a variety of approaches are used in conjunction and synthesized (Smith, 2001). Such an approach (more than any other) needs to be long term, consistent, and systematic. In many cases, a team approach among school personnel and other appropriate individuals (e.g., the special education classroom teacher and the child's family) works best. A multifaceted approach that develops both school and home interventions might include the following strategies and techniques:

- Applied behavior analysis
- Cognitive–behavioral therapy, such as "stop and think" techniques to counteract impulsivity
- Family education, with individual and family counseling that includes helping the child develop coping strategies

- Stress-reduction techniques
- Learning strategies to foster a positive self-concept
- Medication

A section later in the chapter, Learning Through Movement, provides good examples of a multifaceted approach to teaching.

RECOMMENDATIONS FOR TEACHING PHYSICAL EDUCATION AND SPORT

Unfortunately for many individuals with learning disabilities, ADHD, or DCD, physical education can be a series of miserable failures, such as being repeatedly picked last or dropping a fly ball in front of peers. For physical education class to be a positive and successful student experience, effective programming must be based on the teacher's understanding of many factors that affect student learning. In the next section we provide recommendations and best teaching practices that have proven effective in physical education and sport

for individuals with learning disabilities, ADHD, or DCD. Included are information, methods, and activities regarding safety, medication, behavior management, ecological task analysis, perceptual motor development, inclusion, interdisciplinary teaching, relaxation, and youth sport.

Safety

Always keeping student safety first and foremost in mind, physical educators must be aware of any potentially harmful activities and periodically check all facilities and equipment for potential hazards. Equipment needs to be developmentally appropriate to individuals' age, body type, and skill level. Unstructured physical activity designed to "blow off steam" needs to be avoided and is considered contraindicated because it might overstimulate students, especially students with ADHD. When this occurs the potential exists for individuals to get out of control and become confused and frustrated. Instead of using unstructured activities, provide students with opportunities to perform skills under control and at a slower rate, allowing time to motor plan before they perform the activity. Physical educators must remember that some

Medication

Ritalin (methylphenidate), *Dexedrine* (dextroamphetamine), and *Cylert* (permoline) are medications most often taken by children identified as hyperactive. Each is a stimulant to the central nervous system, has a paradoxical effect by calming the hyperactivity, increasing the student's attention and ability to focus on learning. During the past 40 years, Ritalin, the medication most often prescribed by physicians, has been safely and successfully used in the treatment of millions of children with ADHD (Huber & Duhuis, 2002). Research conducted on medication and its effect on learning is well documented; however, the majority of the work has been in the classroom and not on motor performance in physical education settings (Beyer, 1999).

Medication must never be viewed as an educational panacea or an easy fix and needs to be a part of the student's entire treatment package. Professionals caution against the quick prescription of medication and believe it should only be prescribed after other interventions have been explored. Medications like Ritalin are not to be taken by students six years and younger. These stimulant drugs are fast acting and can take effect from one to eight hours with Ritalin taking effect within one to four hours.

The physical educator needs to consider a number of factors regarding medication and students with LD, ADHD, and DCD (Howell, Evans, & Gardiner, 1997; Lavay, French, & Henderson, 2006). Identify those students who are on medication by receiving a list from the school nurse, asking the student's special education teacher, checking school files, or sending a note home to the student's parents to provide general information about their child. While physical educators will not dispense medication, it is still important to be aware of medication type, dosage, schedule, and side effects. Poor motor performance and an elevated heart rate may be due to potential adverse side effects. Students on medication may exhibit drowsiness, fatigue, headaches, loss of sleep, dizziness, blurred vision, irritability, and mood swings. There is also the possibility of the "rebound effect" that occurs when the medication wears off causing irritability and mood swings. The physical educator must insist on being informed of any "drug holidays" when the student is taken off the medication or transitional periods when the physician adjusts the dosage to determine optimal medication.

students might be taking medication to help manage behavior and learning (see sidebar).

Physical educators need to protect students from both physical and psychological harm. Students making fun of one another should never be tolerated, and discussions should be held in class about respecting individual differences. Instructors must design their programs to promote cooperation and positive interactions among students. When possible, a buddy or teammate may be assigned to socialize with an individual with a learning disability, ADHD, or DCD. Strategies for inclusion and activities that involve cooperation are described throughout this book.

Behavior Management

Organizing the environment and using instructional strategies that are responsive to students with learning disabilities, ADHD, or DCD is an effective way for the teacher to emphasize student success and provide a positive experience. A structured, consistent, and proactive behavior-management approach is important to student success. Being proactive means spending time before class designing a structured setting consisting of clear rules; consistent routines; smooth transitions, with signals for changing activities; and reinforcement methods that motivate students to participate. During instruction these methods are consistently implemented and practiced so that students clearly understand and follow class expectations. For example, during instruction, the physical educator can tell students to "attend, think, and act."

Class Structure

It is important to design clear and concise rules and routines that are posted and followed consistently during each class session. Students must know where to go when entering and exiting the gym. Starting class the same way each time allows students to feel comfortable with the program. For example, class can be started in the same location with an exercise warm-up, followed by certain activities each individual knows and feels comfortable with before introducing new activities. To help alleviate possible apprehension in certain students, the instructor should briefly explain the day's lesson.

Provide clear transitions, using signals for changing activities or moving from one activity area to the next to alert students that a change is about to occur. Consistent transitions and routines help students stay comfortable in class and learn what is expected of them. Examples of possible transition signals to use include hitting a tambourine, clapping hands, tossing a scarf into the air, or playing music. When it is time to transition, students "freeze" and listen for the next set of instructions. It might be helpful to establish an area, such as a big circle in the middle of the gym, where students know to go. Consider giving a two-minute verbal warning prior to each transition. Provide a one-on-one cue or a secret signal for a student having difficulty following transitions and signal the student a few minutes before the transition is to occur.

Class Organization

When teaching students with ADHD, instructors should eliminate irrelevant stimuli that might cause distraction. Keeping each individual active and on task cuts down on wait time and reduces behavior problems (and provides more opportunities to practice skills). Skill-learning opportunities can also be increased by shortening lines, providing each individual with a piece of equipment, and individualizing instruction. Consider using one-on-one instruction (self-paced), partner work, small groups, and learning stations.

Learning stations allow students to perform activities at their own pace and ability level while freeing instructors to work with individuals who need extra time for instruction. Remember to minimize distractions and reduce irrelevant stimuli at learning stations by using marked cones, chalking the area, or positioning folding gymnastic mats vertically (Bishop & Beyer, 1995). Another effective strategy to minimize distractions is to position students in learning stations away from the center of the gym with their back toward the extraneous stimuli or in a quiet area with reduced background noise.

Teaching Prompts or Cues

Some students with learning disabilities, ADHD, or DCD might have difficulty attending to the relevant aspects of the learning task. A prompt or a cue is a verbal, physical, or environmental reminder to the individual to perform the task. During instruction, it might be helpful to position the individual in front of and near the instructor. It is also helpful for the entire class to see the instructor and, if outside, have the class positioned away from looking into the sun. The teacher can help students focus on only the most relevant teaching prompts or cues by keeping directions simple and not providing too much information. This is especially important for students with limited attention spans. The application example provides the reader with a variety of verbal, physical, or environmental prompting or cueing strategies for a student with a short attention span who demonstrates difficulty staying on task.

Reinforcement

For students with short attention spans who do listen and stay on task, it is important for the teacher to provide positive feedback and reinforcement. Trocki-Ables, French, and O'Connor (2001) found that boys with ADHD stayed on task and performed better when verbal praise and tokens were used to reinforce their mile-run fitness performance. Nonverbal feedback can be a high-five or thumbs up. Provide positive specific verbal feedback. For example, say, "Nicole, that's great—you remembered to step with your opposite foot when throwing the ball!" Reinforce students who are accurate and move under control rather than those who demonstrate speed or how quickly they can complete an activity. Consider

---

APPLICATION EXAMPLE

Prompting and Cueing Strategies

Setting: Elementary to high school physical education class

Student: Students with LD, ADHD, and DCD who have a short attention span

Issue: What are some possible strategies for handling this situation?

Application: Prompting and cueing strategies for getting and keeping student attention during instruction

- Have the student make eye contact, listen, and do not let him or her begin the activity until the directions are completed.

- Give one set of age-appropriate directions at a time; provide time for the student to take in the information and respond to the directions. Have the student repeat the instructions before performing the task to determine if he or she is paying attention.

- Encourage *verbal mediation* in which the student plans and states aloud the task to be conducted; this strategy will help the student get organized (Mach, 2000).

- Provide *verbal reference points.* For example, to teach a soccer throw-in, the teacher can say, "Danielle, hold the ball with both arms above your head with your thumbs together."

- Determine the form of instruction or teaching cue that works best for each student, including verbal (auditory); demonstration, visual aids, or hand signals (visual); and physical guidance (kinesthetic or tactile).

- Use the least amount of prompts or cues possible. Start by providing verbal instructions, followed by a *demonstration or model,* followed by *physical guidance.* For example, the teacher might say, "Calvin, turn your body to the side before you throw the ball." Have Calvin then try to the throw the ball. Give Calvin time to respond to the directions. If he's unsuccessful, say, "Watch me" and then demonstrate or model the throw. Again provide time for Calvin to respond to the demonstration. If Calvin is still having difficulty, then physically assist: "Let me help you turn your body to the side." Be careful not to overassist. Many individuals with LD might feel more comfortable watching peers before starting the activity. See chapter 7 for more information.

- Provide *visual or environmental cues* by using a cone, footprints, poly spot, pictures, or a sign with an arrow that marks where and when to move. This will make the directions more concrete, gain student's attention, and help students who have difficulty listening and reading directions. In the previous example of Calvin throwing the ball, footprints or a hula hoop can also be placed on the floor to prompt or cue Calvin on where to step. In another example of cuing or prompting that is more complex, the instructor says, "Danielle, take five steps forward and then turn toward the cone, run in the direction of the arrow on the cone, and I'll throw you the Frisbee."

spending a shorter amount of time on an activity than you might with same-age peers. Frequently changing the activity adds variety and keeps students on task.

Task Analysis

Task analysis, described earlier in chapters 4 and 7 (pp. 59-63, 124-127), is another effective teaching approach to use with students with a learning disability. The teacher must carefully observe movement, be able to task analyze or break down skills, and, when necessary, make modifications to equipment and facilities. For example, there should be enough equipment available to accommodate task changes and different skill levels, such as providing various types (e.g., bats, rackets) and sizes (e.g., larger dimensions) of striking implements.

Perceptual Motor Development

As discussed earlier, individuals with a learning disability, ADHD, or DCD will exhibit a variety of perceptual and sensory challenges when engaged in physical education. However, perceptual difficulties can be managed and sometimes overcome by a physical educator who teaches fun and positive movement activities that help develop the tactual, kinesthetic, visual, and auditory sensory systems. See chapter 20, Perceptual Motor Development, for activities that contribute to an individual's development in these areas.

Inclusion Into Regular Physical Education

The majority of students with a learning disability, ADHD, or DCD will be taught in a general or regular physical education class with their peers without disabilities. Schools need to avoid placing a large group of students with learning disabilities, ADHD, and DCD into the same regular physical education class based on schedule convenience but instead distribute students across different classes. Neither is it an educationally sound practice to place a student with a disability into a regular physical education class setting without a plan that includes teacher support (Rizzo & Lavay, 2000).

The teacher will need to be more patient and perhaps provide students with a learning disability, ADHD, or DCD with more time to complete certain tasks. This includes providing the student with plenty of repetition and practice. Break skills down into simple parts, progressing from one step to the next in a well-planned sequential order. Teach from simple to complex. For example, kick a stationary ball before a moving ball.

Peer tutor programs, described earlier in the book (see page 128), is one of the most effective methods to promote inclusion. A major benefit is that the student with a learning disability, ADHD, or DCD receives increased instruction, practice, reinforcement, and feedback on a continuous and individual basis from the tutor (Lieberman & Houston-Wilson, 2002). However, peer tutors must never overassist or treat an individual with a disability in any way other than as a member of the class. An effective method to use with students with a mild learning disability, ADHD, or DCD is reciprocal peer tutoring in which the entire class is placed in pairs and take turns tutoring. For example, one student tutors and provides feedback while the other performs the activity, and then the partners switch roles. Mach (2000) believes that providing students with a learning disability, ADHD, or DCD the opportunity to be a peer tutor to classmates or younger students can improve self-esteem.

Learning Through Movement

Learning through movement or interdisciplinary teaching is an educational process with two or more subject areas integrated to promote learning in each subject area (Cone, Werner, Cone, & Woods, 1998). This approach lends itself well to the multisensory approach because many children with learning disabilities, ADHD, or DCD are concrete learners who learn best through actively moving. Conceptual information that is abstract is presented in a concrete manner that actively engages student learning. Movement or motor activities taught in physical education (i.e., perceptual motor) can be integrated into other subject areas throughout the school curriculum. Learning through movement in education has been used successfully in the past (Humphrey, 1965; Cratty, 1976).

Recently, there has been a resurgence of this approach (Morris & Stiehl, 1999). Advantages to using the movement medium include the following (Cone, Werner, Cone, & Woods, 1998):

- Helps in learning abstract concepts
- Promotes active rather than passive involvement in learning
- Provides a natural medium for learning
- Stimulates expression and communication
- Reinforces learning in a fun and meaningful way

- Helps promote collaboration among professionals, such as the physical educator working with the classroom teacher

This approach must never be viewed as a substitute for a sound, well-rounded physical education curriculum and is certainly not a panacea to overcome all the academic problems that students with learning disabilities, ADHD, or DCD might exhibit. Rather, it should be understood as a fun and educational strategy to enhance and motivate movement and learning.

Initially, the physical educator can start simple and integrate the motor, cognitive, and affective educational learning domains into a teaching lesson. For example, ask a young child with language delays who is striking a balloon (i.e., motor) to tell you the color of the balloon (i.e., academic). Young students with a learning disability, ADHD, or DCD can work with a peer tutor or in a small group (i.e., affective) to shape their body (i.e., motor) in various ways to form letters or words (i.e., academic) (figure 11.1).

The physical educator and classroom teacher can collaborate using a thematic approach and present to students such themes as the human body, animals at the zoo, transportation, holidays,

seasons, Olympics, and cultures from around the word. For example, students can form different letters of the alphabet with their body or move their body like different animals at the zoo or farm. Using transportation as a theme, the teacher can guide the child to move their body like a plane, car, boat, or train. Another approach is to link a subject area such as math to movement. For example, students can toss beanbags onto a number grid to solve addition and subtraction problems. To supplement spelling, the teacher can have the student hop on a letter grid and spell out words.

Relaxation

Relaxation in physical education is often overlooked as a way of assisting students in focusing their attention. Relaxing unneeded muscle groups conserves energy and makes for smoother, more coordinated movements, as well as teaching individuals how to problem solve and motor plan. Relaxation is a socially appropriate way to control emotions when upset and to handle stressful situations. When students lose focus, become too excited, or encounter stressful situations, the physical educator can immediately begin relaxation methods. These methods can be used at the end of class as a cool-down or closure activity. Ending with relaxation might help calm individual students or the group before returning to the next scheduled class. Relaxation methods used in physical education might include progressive relaxation, yoga, tai chi, static stretching, imagery, or impulse control games (Lavay, French, & Henderson, 2006).

Instruct individuals to take slow, deep breaths, inhaling through the nose and exhaling out through the mouth while maintaining a rhythm. Teachers use a smooth, calm voice in a setting that is as quiet as possible with the lights dimmed to reduce stimuli. Have students dress in loose clothing and lie in a comfortable position. Play soft background music to help students relax. Always set aside a few minutes of the class period to teach students to move under control and apply proper force to movements. For example, impulse control games can be introduced by instructing students to move their body parts as slowly as possible by walking on the moon, moving in a sea of jello, or being a slowly melting ice cream cone on a hot summer day. The student can use visual imagery and imagine a pleasant scene, such as walking in a forest along a stream, sitting by a campfire, or

© Human Kinetics

Figure 11.1 Having students shape their bodies to form letters is an example of learning language through movement.

watching a sunset. The teacher can also introduce a progressive relaxation activity, in which muscle groups are tightened for 5 to 10 seconds and then relaxed for 15 seconds. Edwards and Hofmeier (1991) believe it is important that the instructor use descriptive terms when teaching relaxation. For example, a relaxed muscle is loose and soft, like a sock, and a tense muscle is hard and tight, like a stick. Instructors can develop relaxation training scripts, asking students to make their arm loose like a dog's tongue or having them pretend to have a wet sponge or washcloth in their hand and squeeze all the water out as hard as possible (Ballinger & Heine, 1991).

Youth Sport

Individuals with a learning disability, ADHD, or DCD can enjoy the same benefits of youth sport participation as their peers without disabilities. However, inferior movement skills or the inability to socially interact with others often creates barriers that inhibit successful sport participation (Decker & Voege, 1992). Physical educators can help students overcome these barriers by teaching skills in their physical education program that students require in youth sport programs. Physical educators can also be resources for students and their parents by telling them about youth sport programs that exist in their community (Lavay & Seamark, 2001). Initially, an individual sport that a student enjoys, such as dance, karate, tennis, or swimming, might be a better choice than a team sport because the student will receive more individual attention, and the complexities of working with teammates are minimized. Many individual sports can become lifelong leisure activities.

Proper coach selection is also important for students with a learning disability, ADHD, or DCD. Parents can assist the coach by telling them all the necessary information about their son or daughter. For example, provide the coach with such information as the child's unique behaviors, strategies for overcoming these behaviors, reinforcements that motivate, and learning strategies that have worked well with the child.

SUMMARY

For many students with a learning disability, ADHD, or DCD, physical education might be the one area in which they can experience success during the school day because there is seldom the requirement to sit still, read, or write. Physical educators can showcase these students' movement skills. For others with a learning disability, ADHD, or DCD whose movement performances need maturing, physical education can still be an enjoyable experience when conducted in a manner that does not dwell on the student's movement deficits. This chapter has examined the importance of physical educators being sensitive to the characteristics and unique needs of students with a learning disability, ADHD, or DCD.

Craft (2000) suggests that in preparing to teach students with a learning disability, ADHD, or DCD, physical educators ask the following questions: What are the student's strengths and needs? How does this student best learn? How can I as the teacher change the environment and the task to help this student learn? What approaches and programs are already in place for this student at school and at home? What support systems will I need, and how will I work to get them? And, finally, how can I collaborate with others to ensure this student's success?

To help answer these questions, we have examined in this chapter the most effective general educational approaches used in the schools today, including the multisensory approach, behavior management, and a multifaceted approach. Also included are specific recommendations and activities based on the students' characteristics and needs for teaching physical education and sport, including safety; behavior management that includes class structure and organization, teaching prompts or cues, and reinforcement; ecological task analysis; perceptual motor development; inclusion practices; and learning through movement and relaxation. Teachers must remember that positive movement experiences can translate into a healthy lifestyle and a lifetime of quality physical activity for students with a learning disability, ADHD, and DCD.

REFERENCES

American Psychiatric Association. (2000). *Diagnostic and statistical manual of mental disorders* (4th ed.). Washington, DC: Author.

Ballinger, D.A., & Heine, P.L. (1991). Relaxation training for children—A script. *Journal of Physical Education, Recreation and Dance,* 62(2), 67-69.

Beyer, R. (1999). Motor proficiency of boys with attention deficit hyperactivity disorder and boys with learning disabilities. *Adapted Physical Activity Quarterly.* 16, 403-414.

Bishop, P., & Beyer, R. (1995). Attention deficit hyperactivity disorder (ADHD): Implications for physical educators. *Palaestra,* 11(4), 39-46.

Cone, T.P, Werner, P., Cone, S.L, & Woods, A.M. (1998). *Interdisciplinary teaching through physical education.* Champaign, IL: Human Kinetics.

Craft, D.H. (2000). Learning disabilities and attentional deficits. In Winnick, J.P. (Ed.) *Adapted physical education and sport* (3rd ed.). Champaign, IL: Human Kinetics.

Cratty, B. (1976). *Active learning: Games to enhance academic abilities.* Englewood Cliffs, NJ: Prentice Hall.

Decker, J., & Voege, D. (1992). Integrating children with attention deficit disorder with hyperactivity into youth sport. *Palaestra, 8,* 16-20.

Dunn, J.M. (1997). *Special physical education: Developmental, individualized and developmental* (7th ed.). Madison, WI: Brown Benchmark.

Edwards, V.D., & Hofmeier, J. (1991). A stress management program for elementary and special populations children. *Journal of Physical Education, Recreation and Dance, 62* (2), 61-64.

Harvey, W.J., & Reid, G. (2003). Attention-deficit/hyperactivity disorder: A review of research on movement skill performance and physical fitness. *Adapted Physical Activity Quarterly, 20,* 1-25.

Henderson, S.E., (1994). Developmental coordination disorder editorial. *Adapted Physical Activity Quarterly, 11,* 111-114.

Henderson, S.E. & Henderson, L. (2002). Toward an understanding of developmental coordination disorder. *Adapted Physical Activity Quarterly, 19,* 11-31.

Horvat, M., Eichstaedt, C., Kalakian, L., & Croce, R. (2002). *Developmental/adapted physical education: Making ability count* (4th ed.). San Francisco: Benjamin Cummings.

Howell, K.W., Evans, D., & Gardiner, J. (1997). Medication in the classroom: A hard pill to swallow. *Teaching Exceptional Children, 29,* 58-61.

Huber, J., & Duhuis, P. (2002). Ritalin and ADHD—Recent developments. *Palaestra, 18*(3), 12.

Humphrey, J. (1965). *Child learning.* Dubuque, IA: Brown.

Individuals with Disabilities Education Act (IDEA) *Amendments of 1997* (PL 105-17), U.S. Department of Education. (2001).

Kavale, K.A., & Forness, S.R. (2000). What definitions of learning disability say and don't say: A critical analysis. *Journal of Learning Disabilities, 33*(3), 239-256.

Lavay, B., French, R., & Henderson, H. (2006). *Positive behavior management in physical activity settings* (2nd ed.). Champaign, IL: Human Kinetics.

Lavay, B., & Seamark C. (2001). Everyone plays: Inclusion of special needs children into youth sport programs. *Palaestra, 14*(4), 40-43.

Lieberman, L.J., & Houston-Wilson, C. (2002). *Strategies for inclusion. A handbook for physical educators.* Champaign, IL: Human Kinetics.

Mach, M.M. (2000). Teaching and coaching students with learning disabilities and attentional deficits. *Strategies, 13* (4), 12; 29-31.

Milne, D.C., Haubenstricker, J.L., & Seefelt, V. (1991). Remedial motor education: Some practical suggestions. *Strategies, 4* (4), 15-18.

Morris G.S.D., & Stiehl, J. (1999). *Changing kids' games.* Champaign, IL: Human Kinetics.

Rizzo, T., & Lavay, B. (2000). Inclusion why the confusion? *Journal of Physical Education, Recreation and Dance.* 71 (4), 32-36.

Sherrill, C. (2004). *Adapted physical activity, recreation and sport: Crossdisciplinary and lifespan* (6th ed.). Boston: McGraw Hill.

Smith, D.D. (2001). *Introduction to special education: Teaching in an age of opportunity* (4th ed.). Boston: Allyn & Bacon.

Trocki-Ables, P., French, R., & O'Connor, J. (2001). Use of primary and secondary reinforcers after performance of a 1-mile walk/run by boys with attention deficit hyperactivity disorder. *Perceptual and Motor Skills, 93,* 461-464.

WRITTEN RESOURCES

Bishop, P., & Beyer, R. (1995). Attention deficit hyperactivity disorder (ADHD): Implications for physical educators. *Palaestra,* 11(4), 39-46.

Provides a variety of useful teaching suggestions for the physical education setting.

Harvey, W.J., & Reid, G. (2003). Attention-deficit/Hyperactivity disorder: A review of research on movement skill performance and physical fitness. *Adapted Physical Activity Quarterly, 20,* 1-25.

Provides the most comprehensive review to date of research on the movement performance and physical fitness of children with ADHD.

Smith, D.D. (2001). *Introduction to special education: Teaching in an age of opportunity* (4th ed.). Boston: Allyn & Bacon.

Provides a comprehensive chapter on learning disability in the classroom and includes definitions, identification types, history, incidence rates, causes and prevention, learning characteristics, and general educational interventions.

AUDIOVISUAL RESOURCES

Lavoie, Richard D. *Understanding learning disabilities: How difficult can this be? The FAT City Workshop.* (Videotape, 1989). PBS Home Video, Box 751089, Charlotte, NC, 28275. Phone 800-424-7963; fax 703-739-813; Web site: www.shopPBS.org.

This video looks at the world through the eyes of a child with a learning disability by taking the viewer to a unique workshop attended by parents, educators, psychologists, and social workers. There they join in a series of classroom activities that cause frustration, anxiety, tension, and emotions that are all too familiar to the student with a learning disability. This company offers a variety of videos regarding learning disability.

Sweeney, G., & Lynch, T. *A mind of your own.* (Videotape, 1999). Fanlight productions. PO Box 1084, Harriman, NY, 10926. Phone 800-937-4113; fax 201-652-1973; Web site: www.fanlight.com.

It's been estimated that every classroom has two or three kids with learning disabilities. This video profiles four courageous kids who don't let learning disability hold them back or get them down. This company offers a variety of videos on such social issues, including disability.

ELECTRONIC RESOURCES

Children with Attention Deficit Disorders (CHADD). 8181 Professional Place, Suite 201, Landover, MD, 20785. Phone 800-233-4050; fax 301-306-7090. Web site: www.chadd.org.

This site provides information on conferences, legislation, news releases, local chapters, and research studies.

Council for Learning Disabilities. (CLD) PO Box 40303, Overland Park, KS, 66204. Phone 913-492-8755; fax 913-492-2546. Web site: www.cldinternational.org.

This site is run by an international organization that promotes new research and effective ways to teach people with learning disabilities. Offers conference information, updates on scholarly initiatives, general information about learning disabilities, and research reports.

Division on Learning Disabilities (DLD) within the Council for Exceptional Children (CEC). 1920 Association Drive, Reston, VA 220191-5989; phone 703-620-3660; fax 703-264-9494. Web site: www.cec.sped.org.

This site includes the division on learning disability mission statement, events calendar, resources, and publications. Also included is TeachingLD.org: an electronic newsletter that provides trustworthy and up-to-date professional resources and information about learning disabilities and teaching students who learning disabilities.

Visual Impairments

Lauren J. Lieberman

Mr. Joseph has two students with visual impairments included in his regular middle school physical education classes. Peter has partial vision caused by **retinitis pigmentosa.** Sarah is totally blind. Both of her eyes were removed when she had **retinoblastoma.** She now wears prosthetic eyes. Throughout the year, Mr. Joseph teaches units in which Peter and Sarah can participate with minimal adaptations and includes the students in regular physical education on a flexible schedule. Mr. Joseph lets Peter and Sarah decide in which of the two physical education units offered they would like to participate. Mr. Joseph is beginning a basketball unit; the other physical educator is beginning a swimming unit.

Sarah opts for swimming. She has no sight, making it difficult for her to play basketball and other sports that involve seeing a ball. But Sarah can participate in swimming with few adaptations. Peter opts for basketball. His neighbors enjoy shooting hoops, and Peter hopes to improve his game enough to join them.

On this particular afternoon, Peter stood ready to receive the basketball from a sighted teammate but was not aggressively moving toward the ball in the scrimmage. Mr. Joseph required Peter's teammates to pass Peter the ball twice during all possessions when Pete was in the game. But each time the ball was passed to Peter, it was immediately stolen by the opposition. After the game, when Mr. Joseph saw how much Peter had been involved—15 seconds of contact with the ball over a 35-minute class period—he was disappointed. Such a low level of participation went against his philosophy of teaching.

Mr. Joseph reread the chapter on blindness in his college text in adapted physical education, browsed the Internet for additional appropriate adaptations, and made a call to his district's adapted physical education specialist. One week later, the scene in Peter's physical education class was quite different. Two thirds of the class time was now devoted to skill practice, with the final third allotted to game play. Plus, the rules were changed. To teach passing skills and cooperation, each team was now required to pass the ball to each team member before scoring. Peter's team always wore yellow jerseys to make it easier for Peter to see them. A five-second rule was in effect when Peter had the ball—the defense could not defend him for the first five seconds he had possession. His teammates could call out to indicate where they were, and the other team had to remain silent until he passed the ball. On that day Peter scored two baskets for his team and passed the ball 10 times.

Just like anyone else, individuals with visual impairments want to be accepted and respected; they want their visual impairment to be one of many personal characteristics, not their defining characteristic. Tim Willis, a track star with total blindness (see figure 12.1), once said, "Lack of sight does not mean lack of vision." Tim was absolutely right—all people, no matter their degree of disability, want to strive for success. A vigorous physical education program is beneficial and important for individuals who are blind or have low vision (Butcher, 2002; Williamson, 2002). The challenge for physical educators, as it is for Mr. Joseph, is planning and teaching so that individuals with visual impairments can actively participate in physical education, recreation, and sport in school and throughout their lifetime (Walker, 2003). But sometimes the adaptations to minimize visual impairments are the least of a teacher's concerns. Often, a higher priority is the emotional and social issues resulting from

how others treat individuals who are blind. It can be that learned helplessness—the countless acts of overprotection by family, teachers, and well-intended strangers and the eagerness of others to "do for" instead of expecting individuals with visual impairments to do for themselves—can teach individuals with visual impairments that they are helpless and limited in what they can do for themselves. In much of the discussion in this chapter we seek to provide ideas for overcoming learned helplessness. A primary task for the physical educator is to adapt activities as necessary, but they should also expect students with visual impairments to do much on their own and to be active, contributing members of the class and community.

DEFINITION OF VISUAL IMPAIRMENT

What is a visual impairment? Who is blind? The educational definition from the regulations of the Individuals with Disabilities Education Act (IDEA) is as follows:

> Visual impairment, including blindness, means an impairment in vision that, even when corrected, adversely affects a child's educational performance. The term includes both partial sight and blindness (Office of Special Education and Rehabilitation Services, 2002). These classifications of visual impairments are presented in table 12.1.

Most people who are visually impaired still have some usable sight. Perhaps one in four individuals with visual impairments is blind. Among students with total loss of vision, about half of them lost their vision before or at birth.

CAUSES OF VISION LOSS

People have vision loss for many reasons. In most cases, vision loss is associated with aging, but, in children, loss of vision occurs before or at birth (congenital) or in childhood or later (adventitious). Some of the causes of blindness are the following:

- **Macular degeneration:** Affects central vision, causing photophobia (sensitivity to light) and poor color vision, but peripheral vision is normal (see figure 12.2a, p. 208).

© Photo courtesy of USABA

Figure 12.1 When at age 10 Tim Willis lost his sight, he decided that was all he would lose—and nothing more. Years later, as a Class B1 total blind athlete, Tim has broken 13 national records and 2 world records, making him one of the top track athletes in the world.

Table 12.1   **Classifications of Visual Impairments**

Classification	Description
Visual impairment	Umbrella term encompassing total blindness and partial sight
Partial sight	Can read print through use of large print or magnification
Blind	Inability to read large print even with magnification
Legal blindness	Acuity of 20/200 or less in the better eye with best possible correction or a field of 20 degrees or less diameter in the better eye.
Travel vision	Ability to see at 5 to 10 feet what the normal eye can see at 200 feet (5/200 to 10/200) Motion perception: Ability to see at 3 to 5 feet what the normal eye can see at 200 feet; this ability is limited almost entirely to the perception of motion.
Light perception	Ability to distinguish a strong light at a distance of three feet from the eye but the inability to detect a hand movement at three feet from the eye (<3/200)
Total blindness	Inability to recognize a strong light directly into the eyes

- Retinoblastoma: A malignancy of the retina in early childhood, which usually requires enucheation (removal of the eye); vision loss can occur in one or both eyes.
- Rubella: During the third trimester of pregnancy, complications from rubella might cause limited vision.
- Albinism: Characterized by a total or partial lack of pigment, causing abnormal optic nerve development; might or might not affect skin color. Individuals with albinism might have one or more of the following conditions: decreased visual acuity, photophobia, high refraction error (the shape of the eye does not refract light properly, so images are blurred), astigmatism (blurred vision), nystagmus (uncontrollable eye movements that are involuntary, rapid, and repetitive), central scatomas (a blind or partially blind area in the visual field), and strabismus (the inability of one or both eyes to look directly at an object at the same time).
- Retinitis pigmentosa: A progressive disorder that causes loss of peripheral vision, night blindness, tunnel vision, decreased acuity and depth perception, spotty vision because of retinal scarring, and photophobia (see figure 12.2b, p. 208)
- Glaucoma: Blockage in the normal flow of fluid in the aqueous humor causes increased pressure in the eye. Vision loss might be gradual, sudden, or present at birth. Individuals with glaucoma might also have an increased sensitivity to light and glare.
- Cataracts: Usually bilateral; opacity of the lens restricts the passage of light, reducing acuity, blurring vision, causing poor color vision, photophobia, and sometimes nystagmus. Visual ability fluctuates according to light (see figure 12.2c, p. 208).
- Retinopathy of prematurity: Occurs in some infants born prematurely, resulting in reduced acuity or total blindness.

CHARACTERISTICS OF INDIVIDUALS WITH VISUAL IMPAIRMENTS

There is tremendous diversity among individuals with visual impairments, but some traits seem to occur with greater frequency than they do among individuals with sight. We discuss some of these in the following sections. Keep in mind that these traits are generalities and do not apply to all individuals with visual impairments.

Affective and Social Characteristics

Habits such as rocking, hand waving, finger flicking, or digging the fingers into the eyes are examples of repetitive movements some individuals with visual loss or multiple disabilities develop. These repetitive movements are also known as blindisms or self-stimulation. Although debate continues regarding the cause for these movements, adults

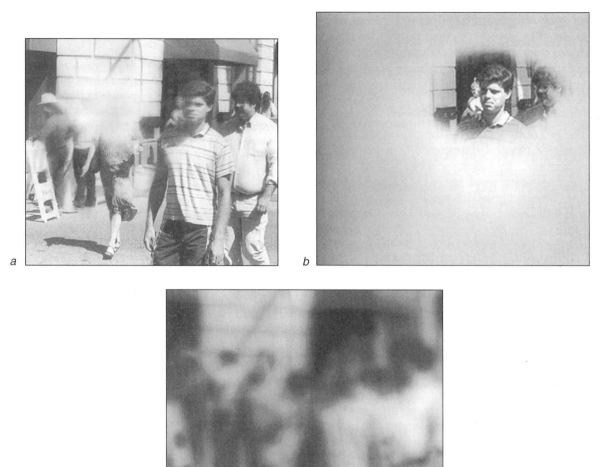

Figure 12.2   Three photos of what a person with a visual impairment might see. *(a)* In age-related macular degeneration, central vision is impaired, making it difficult to read or do close work. *(b)* In retinitis pigmentosa, night blindness develops; tunnel vision is another frequent result. *(c)* In cataracts, a clouding of the lens causes reduced ability to see detail.

Reprinted, by permission, from I. Bailey and A. Hall, 1990, *Visual Impairment: An Overview* (New York: American Foundation for the Blind). Courtesy AFB.

can simply accept these movements as variations of nervous habits most people show. Or, parents and teachers might together decide that it is in the child's best interest to stop these movements in certain situations. If these movements are not affecting the child's education or those individuals around the child, then some self-stimulating behaviors might be best overlooked (McHugh & Lieberman, 2003).

Fearfulness and dependence might characterize some individuals with vision loss, whether the loss is attributed to congenital or adventitious blindness. These characteristics might develop not as a result of the lack of vision but rather as a result of the overprotection experienced by many individuals who are blind. This overprotection usually leads to reduced opportunities for students to freely explore their environments, thus creating possible delays in perceptual, motor, and cognitive development.

Socialization Opportunities

Children with visual impairment tend to have less extensive social networks and fewer friendships than their sighted peers. Observations of children with visual impairments in inclusive settings indicate that children often are in the vicinity of their teacher and seldom socialize with sighted children. Children with visual impairments have described schools as unfriendly, lonely places or as places where they are teased and ignored by other children (Nikolaraizi & De Reybekiel, 2001). Robinson and Lieberman (2004) found that children with visual impairments had low levels of perceived control over their ability to make and retain friendships. Children who experience movement difficulty often experience lower self-perceptions, which likely lead to a reduction in movement confidence and often extend beyond the athletic domain, resulting in adverse psychosocial consequences (Bouchard & Tetrault, 2000).

Implications for Teaching Physical Education: Motor, Physical, and Fitness Characteristics

The lack of sight does not directly cause any unique motor or physical characteristics. But the reduced opportunity to move, which often accompanies blindness, might result in many distinct characteristics. The following are possible motor, physical, and fitness characteristics of visual impairments and corresponding implications.

- *Characteristic.* Motor delays in young children with visual impairments have multiple causes, including the reduced opportunity for "rough and tumble" play with parents, heightened protective instincts of parents and caregivers, the infant's own fear of being moved suddenly, the lack of vision that motivates movement, and the lack of opportunity to observe others moving.

- *Implication.* Students with visual losses must be provided with the opportunity and motivation to move in a safe environment to minimize the development of motor delays. Enthusiastically encourage and positively reinforce movements by physically demonstrating and verbally encouraging students that it is safe to move. Motor delays are not usually observed among individuals who are now blind but who were sighted for years. These individuals who were once sighted but now visually impaired need corrective feedback from observers, as a substitute for monitoring their own movements, so that skills once mastered are retained.

- *Characteristic.* Postural deviations might be prevalent among individuals with partial sight who may hold their heads in unique positions to maximize vision. Postural deviations are sometimes more pronounced among individuals who have been blind since birth and never have had the opportunity to see how others sit, stand, and move. Examples include a shuffling gait, forward tilt, or rounded shoulders.

- *Implication.* Corrective postural exercises might help improve posture and thereby reduce stress on the body. Verbal or physical prompts can remind the person to "sit up tall" with "head up."

- *Characteristic.* Body image and balance might also be delayed in students who are blind. One likely cause is decreased opportunities for regular physical activity through which balance and body image are refined. Also, sight enhances balance by "seeing" a reference point for aiding stability.

- *Implication.* Participation in activities such as dance, yoga, and movement education can be excellent means of developing body image and balance.

- *Characteristic.* A slow, shuffling gait characterizes many individuals who are blind. This can be demonstrated by asking sighted students to close their eyes and walk across the room. Likely, when unaided by sight, their gait will show shorter strides, a pronounced shuffle, slower pace, more time spent in the support phase, and a tendency, over a distance, to veer away from the stronger leg.

- *Implication.* Physical educators can increase stride length by generating greater hip extension during the drive phase and greater hip flexion during the recovery stage of the sprint run (Arnhold & McGrain, 1985; Wyatt & Ng, 1997). This can be facilitated through improving running techniques by using the guide-running techniques presented later in this chapter.

- *Characteristic.* Health-related fitness levels of individuals with visual impairments are generally below those of their sighted peers (Lieberman & McHugh, 2001; Winnick & Short, 1986). This might be of particular concern because Buell (1966) suggests that individuals with visual impairments need higher levels of physical fitness than their sighted counterparts. He notes many instances in which individuals without sight need to spend more energy to reach the same goals as those with sight. For example: using a cane utilizes energy from the arm, shoulder, and obvious mental energy to navigate the environment.

- *Implication.* Health-related fitness levels of individuals who are blind have the potential to match those of their sighted peers. Lack of opportunity to train and difficulty arranging for sighted guides for running can be obstacles to developing fitness (Tepfer, 2002). It is very important for physical educators to develop fitness programs for students with visual impairments and to work with families in finding fitness activities students can pursue at home. Samples of these are jumping rope, weight training, aerobics, bicycling (tandem, or single in a secluded area), and walking (Lieberman, 2002).

In summary, the missing component in the development of normal patterns of movement and fitness among students with visual impairments is not ability but the opportunity to experience physical activity. The physical educator must encourage students to feel safe and good about their movements. This can be accomplished through instruction in physical education and through collaboration with parents and caregivers and other influential individuals in the child's life (Lieberman, James, & Ludwa, 2004). In the following section we offer suggestions for helping students with visual impairments enjoy physical activity.

INCLUSION: TEACHING STUDENTS WITH VISUAL IMPAIRMENTS IN PHYSICAL EDUCATION

With the current emphasis on inclusive education, many students with disabilities are taught in regular physical education classes. This inclusive approach can work well if support systems are provided as needed. When teaching a student with a visual impairment in physical education, keep in mind that this student can do many of the same physical activities that sighted peers can do. Simple modifications, such as changing the ball color to one that contrasts sharply with the background, are sometimes all that are needed to enable the student with partial sight to participate fully in class. Other times, more extensive support systems are needed, such as team teaching with an adapted physical education specialist to help a student with visual impairments and severe behavioral disorders to remain focused and on task throughout class. All too often students with visual impairments are placed in regular physical education classes without the necessary support

systems. This "dumping" under the guise of inclusion is unfair to the student, the classmates, and the teacher. A result of this dumping might be a teenager who is blind and has never bicycled (tandem), roller bladed, or jogged with a friend; has never danced, bowled, or done a host of other physical activities that are well within his or her capabilities but beyond their experience.

Enlist the assistance of parents and other caregivers in advocating for appropriate support systems. Collaborate with others. Problem solve with a resource specialist in adapted physical education, vision teacher, or orientation and mobility specialist. Seek to have any needed support systems recorded on the student's individualized education program (IEP).

Fortunately, the teacher is not the only source of ideas for adaptations. The student with the visual impairment and all students in the class are also excellent sources. Teachers have had much success in developing accommodations by making it a class effort.

The curriculum and programming for students with visual impairments should include a mix of open and closed sports and activities. Open sports are those that have variables that change often, such as tennis, volleyball, football, soccer, and lacrosse. In other words, the game is unpredictable, and the speed, angle, and direction of the ball and defenders change often and without notice. Closed sports are those that are consistent and predictable, such as archery, bowling, shot put, horseshoes, discus, and bocce. The skill in and love of movement can be developed through active participation in physical education. Students with visual impairments should be introduced to all sports, games, and activities. Lifetime activities such as tandem biking, running, goal ball, swimming, wrestling, judo, and bowling should be included as well.

In the following three sections we will present ideas for adapting instruction for students with visual impairments based on learning about the student's abilities, fostering the student's independence, and exploring options for instructional modifications. Please refer to the inclusion of a student with impaired vision application example.

Learning About the Students' Abilities

Assess to determine each student's present level of performance. Generally, students with visual impairments are capable of taking the same formal

APPLICATION EXAMPLE

Inclusion of a Student With Impaired Vision

Setting: Middle school physical education class

Student: Andrea is a very active sixth-grade student who enjoys biking, swimming, in-line skating, and studying judo after school and on weekends. She has retinitis pigmentosa resulting in a progressive visual impairment. She has some residual vision and is adjusting to her current visual ability.

Issue: Andrea's IEP states that she must be fully included in her two 45-minute physical education classes each week, but her teacher believes that her blindness limits her abilities. He has her exercising on a stationary bike and walking the perimeter of the gym while her classmates are involved in physical activities and games. Andrea is becoming more and more frustrated, and this is affecting her performance in other subject areas.

Application: The following was determined as a result of a meeting with the school administrator, the teacher of the visually impaired, and Andrea's physical educator:

- Andrea will participate in all physical education activities with her peers.

- To assist him in adapting games, sports, and activities, the physical educator will purchase books such as *Games for People with Sensory Impairments, Adapted Physical Education and Sport,* and *Adapted Physical Activity, Recreation, and Sport.*
- The teacher will search the Internet for information and adaptations to assist him in supporting Andrea in an inclusive setting.
- The school will buy bright-colored balls, auditory balls, and set up a guide wire system in the gym and outside on the track.
- The curriculum will include a variety of games and activities conducive to full participation by Andrea, such as weight training, aerobics, goal ball, and cross-country skiing.
- Three of Andrea's friends will be trained as peer tutors to assist her in class.
- An additional class with supplemental physical education instruction will be offered should Andrea need more time to grasp a skill or activity.

assessments and attaining the same standards as students with sight. In case of mobility limitations caused by blindness, teachers can modify mobility test item standards, use assistive devices, or use sighted guides based on suggestions throughout this chapter. For example, auditory cues might be added so students know where to throw and how far to skip or run. However, caution should be used when interpreting test norms that do not include students with visual impairments or are based on test items that have been modified. The Brockport Physical Fitness Test (Winnick & Short, 1999) assesses the health-related fitness of youngsters who are blind. For more information on measurement and evaluation, refer to chapter 5. The teacher might seek to learn the answers to the following five critical questions in addition to assessing current performance:

- *What can the student see?* Ask the student, "What can you see?" rather than "How much can

you see?" Ask the same question of others familiar with the student's vision, including the student's previous teachers, parent or caregiver, and low-vision specialist. Read the student's educational file for further information regarding what the student can see.

- *When (at what age) was the loss of vision experienced, and over what period of time did it progress?* Is it still progressing? Ask the student when the vision loss was experienced. If the student gradually lost all vision because of a disease before the ages of 8 to 10, then he or she (as these skills are acquired before the age of 8 to 10 in sighted children) might require less time preparing for some activities, such as hitting a sound-emitting softball and running to a sound-emitting base, than a student who is congenitally blind and has never had the chance to see a game of baseball. A student with congenital blindness might need more detailed explanations that do not depend on analogies for which the student has no basis of understanding. For example, the teaching cue, "jump like a bunny" might not be useful to a child who does not have any visual memory of rabbits moving. The teacher might need to teach the child how to jump this way.

- *How can I maximize use of existent sight?* Learn from the students what helps them see best. For most visual impairments, bright lighting maximizes vision. For some conditions, such as glaucoma and albinism, however, glare is a problem. Teach these students in lighting free of glare to maximize vision. When outside, these students might need tinted glasses or a hat to reduce glare.

- *Are there any **contraindicated** physical activities?* To determine if there are any contraindicated (not recommended) physical activities, seek medical consultation. Note the cause of blindness. Consult reference texts on the etiology of visual impairments found in libraries and on the Internet, and read about the specific visual impairment the student has. There are few contraindications for individuals with total blindness, as there is no sight to seek to preserve. For individuals with partial sight there might be activity restrictions imposed in an effort to preserve remaining sight. Discuss the condition with the student's eye specialist to determine what, if any, restrictions are necessary, especially following recent eye surgery. For example, jarring movements are usually contraindicated for individuals with a detached retina. Contact sports, as well as diving and swimming underwater, might need to be avoided. Glaucoma occurs when the fluid within the eye is unable to drain and pressure increases within the eye, causing blindness. Inverted positions and swimming underwater are often contraindicated with glaucoma because of increased pressure on the eye.

- *What are the student's favorite scholastic, social, and physical activities?* Also ask what adaptations the student prefers. For example, How do you like to run? With a sighted guide? Using a guide wire? Independently on a clearly lined track? Learn about the opportunities that exist for the child to participate in physical activities with family, friends, and in the community. The opportunity to try all the options is important because a student might not know his or her preferences until he or she has had repeated opportunities to try each one. Seek to incorporate these activities and adaptations into the child's physical education program.

Fostering the Students' Independence

If they are not taught the skills to be independent, individuals with visual impairments might rely on others for mobility, instruction, socialization, and activities of daily living. To be independent, they must have the skills, socialization ability, stamina, and strength to complete everyday tasks. Through physical activity, individuals with visual impairments can acquire necessary stamina, socialization, strength, and skills to be independent.

Consider these five suggestions for teaching:

- *Develop and maintain a positive attitude about all students.* The attitude of the teacher is the determining factor in the classroom. If the teacher is truly interested in teaching all students, including a student with a visual impairment, and if this teacher provides accommodations and makes adaptations to teach to the diverse needs of all students without a fuss, then the students in the class will pick up on this attitude and be more likely to also accept students with visual impairments or other differences.

- *Encourage participation of all students in physical activities.* To encourage participation, discuss with students how they feel about various activities. Respect any fears they might express, and work with them to create an environment in which they feel safe and are more willing to participate in physical activity. The following scenario might help illustrate the importance of talking with students to understand their concerns and encouraging them to participate. A young girl who had been totally blind since birth performed very well in swimming. But she seemed unable to learn to swim underwater. When asked why she had such difficulty learning to swim underwater, she replied, "No one will see me if I go underwater. That scares me." After it was explained that water is clear and can be seen through, the girl was reassured and soon learned to swim underwater.

- *Help parents see their children's abilities.* Parents are most children's biggest advocates. Based on their fears for the child who does not have use of a major sense organ, some caregivers might dwell on what the child cannot do rather than on what he or she can do. In these cases the child will rarely have the opportunity at home to try new things, play games that sighted children play, or take risks. Physical educators can collaborate with parents about their children's capabilities by sending home data used in assessment, personal notes, or newsletters describing students' accomplishments, photographs of the student doing activities, and lists of the student's favorite physical activities. By learning about their children's current performance and abilities, parents might derive a better understanding of their children's potential and might allow or encourage more opportunity for physical activity at home and in the community.

• *Challenge students with visual impairments so they can be successful.* Reward and recognize all students' accomplishments to help improve self-esteem and motivate them to continue to work on their next goals. Using a realistic test that includes assessment of process and product and level of independence assists the student in observing improvement. An example of this type of assessment specifically for children with visual impairments is the Camp Abilities Activity Analysis Checklist (visit www.campabilities.org). Teachers help as they work with the student to set realistic goals and recognize achievements. Bulletin boards, student newspapers, and announcements are all ways to recognize student achievement.

• *Expect the student to move as independently as possible during physical education.* At the beginning of the school year, thoroughly orient the student with a visual impairment to playing fields, gyms, and equipment to increase independence and feelings of security. Together, identify landmarks that can help students orient themselves (e.g., a landmark might be the mats along the walls at either end of the gym). Allow individuals to walk around and touch everything as often as they need in order to create the visual map in their minds that will enable them to negotiate the area with confidence. Always keep equipment in the same position within the gym. Permit students extra time before class to orient themselves to the new configuration of equipment. If a change is necessary, forewarn and reorient students. In the locker room, be sure the locker is in an easily accessible location, and provide a lock that opens with a key rather than a combination. A trained peer tutor might be most helpful with mobility, skill acquisition, and feedback for children who are totally blind. Training the peer tutor is imperative to ensure safety, improved skill acquisition, and communication (Wiskochil, 2002). In addition to holding the initial training, meet with the student and peer tutor a few minutes before each class to introduce the student to the concepts and move-

ments to be taught that day. The sidebar offers more suggestions of things to keep in mind when teaching students with visual impairments. These suggestions must be shared with the peer tutor.

When Teaching Students Who Are Blind or Visually Impaired, Remember . . .

• What seems like ordinary, everyday happenings might need to be explained. Narrate during a game so students can understand what everyone is doing, or appoint a student narrator.

• Some experiences are not part of every student's direct experience. Tell the child about the martial art of judo and allow the child to experience judo.

• Students might need help in putting parts together to form a whole. Allow children to feel the entire playground set, the entire gym space, and the entire horse.

• Imitation is hard. Physically guide or tactile model a student through movements rather than show them.

• Feedback is needed because students cannot always tell how they are doing. Tell students where they threw the ball. Even better, use a beeping ball so they know where they threw the ball. (See resources for places to purchase auditory balls.)

Young children with visual impairments need additional incentives to move. Fundamental phylogenetic skills (skills that humans inherently develop, such as crawling, sitting, and walking) are more difficult to learn because of the deprivation of the most motivating sense—sight. Parents, specialists, teachers, and therapists must work together to give the child a reason to move and develop basic motor skills such as sitting, scooting, crawling, rolling, and walking. Here are suggestions to instill a yearning for movement in the young child with a visual impairment:

• Bell Balloon Bash: The child chases a balloon with a bell in it around the room while crawling, walking, or running. Guide the child, if necessary, and encourage him or her to kick the balloon when possible (Lieberman & Cowart, 1996).

- Parachute Swing: Two people swing a parachute while the child is inside.
- Incline Roll: Place the child on top of a low incline and allow him or her to roll or crawl to a motivating sound source at the bottom.
- Scooter Pull: The child sits on a scooter and holds one part of a hula hoop. The teacher holds the opposite part of the hula hoop and pulls the child around the gym. The teacher then decreases support until the child is doing the movements alone.
- Therapy Ball Push: In an assisted sitting position (an adult sits directly behind the child, supporting the child's back), the child pushes a large, heavy therapy ball to a sound source or a person. This builds upper-body strength to assist in crawling and creeping.
- Rebounder Heaven: The child jumps on a rebounder (minitrampoline) while holding the wall, the teacher, or a bar for support.
- Movement Exploration: Place the child on a mat and ask him or her to move forward, backward, high, low, fast, slow, and so on.

Exploring Options for Instructional Modification

So much of what a person learns is not directly taught but learned through watching and listening to what is happening around them. Incidental learning occurs when information that is observed from the surroundings. When a person's vision is impaired, the opportunity for incidental learning is dramatically reduced. Teachers need to directly teach much more information to a child with a visual impairment than other children. Every opportunity should be used to explain what is happening around the child and why.

Different students with visual impairments require different levels of instruction. Some might need a physical demonstration for certain skills, whereas others might learn the same skills through verbal instruction. In some cases, the complexity of the activity drives the level of instruction. This varied level of instruction is sometimes called "the system of least prompts" (Dunn, Morehouse, & Fredericks, 1986). The following system of least prompts provides examples specific to teaching children with visual impairments. Note that the instructor might use one or more of the following teaching strategies to help the student perform the skill. Instructors should know that physical guidance and tactile modeling have both shown to improve self-efficacy in novel tasks for children with visual impairments (O'Connell, 2000).

Verbal explanations by the instructor

- Explain what the child is to do in simple terms.
- Use the child's preferred mode of communication.
- If the child does not understand the first time, repeat in a different way.
- If the child has any usable vision, demonstrate to increase understanding.
- Give feedback using precise, unambiguous descriptions. A statement such as, "Hold the racket three to four inches above your left shoulder" provides more feedback than "Hold the racket like this." Use of precise language benefits all students, visually impaired or not.
- Include students with visual impairments during spectator events by assigning a student "announcer" to describe the action for spectators, much as a radio announcer describes a ball game. Select an announcer with a lively sense of humor to make the event more fun for everyone.

Demonstrations by the instructor or peer

- Show the child the desired skill or movement.
- Demonstrate within the child's field of vision.
- Ask someone close to the student's size and ability to model.
- Use whole-part-whole teaching when possible—demonstrate the whole skill, then the parts (based on task analysis), and then the whole task again.

Physical assistance or guidance from the instructor or peer

- Assist the student physically through the movement.
- Record which skills require physical assistance, including how much and where on the student's body assistance was needed. If asked, the teacher can explain when, where, and why the teacher touched a student.
- To avoid startling the student, forewarn him or her before giving physical assistance.
- Fade assistance to minimal physical prompts as soon as possible.

Tactile modeling of the instructor or a peer

- Allow the student to feel a peer or the instructor execute a skill or movement that was previously difficult to learn using the three previous approaches (Lieberman & Cowart, 1996).
- Tell the student where and when to feel you or a peer executing a skill.
- For legal purposes, document how much assistance was given, when and where the student felt you or a peer, and why.
- Repeat tactile modeling as many times as necessary to ensure understanding.
- Combine tactile modeling with other teaching methods to increase understanding.

(Dunn, Morehouse, & Fredericks, 1986)

Add sound devices

- For softball, use a large playground ball that is hit off a bounce, or use a beeper ball (a ball with an audible buzzer inside is available for purchase through the American Printing House for the Blind [www.APH.org]). The base coach calls continuously to direct the batter to the base.
- Make playground balls audible by cutting the ball, inserting bells, and then resealing the ball with a bicycle tire patch.
- Make scoring a goal audible by tying bells onto net goals. Everyone can hear the jingling sound when a goal is scored.
- Make a basket audible by tying a can with rocks to a string and to the rim and have a peer jiggle the string to emit an audible sound.

Enhance visual cues

- Most individuals with visual impairments have some residual vision. Evaluate each activity to decide what types of visual cues are needed and how to highlight these cues. Color, contrast, and lighting are important. Be sure to ask students what enhances their vision. For example, a student might not be able to distinguish a blue pinny from a red pinny but might see a yellow pinny clearly.
- Use colored tape to increase the contrast of equipment with the background, such as high jump standards and poles or the edges of a balance beam.
- Use brightly colored balls, mats, field markers, and goals that contrast with the background. (Some individuals with albinism and glaucoma require solid colored objects under nonglare lights.)
- Make the gym lighting brighter (or darker for students who have difficulty with glare or who tend to self-stimulate on the bright lights).

SPORTS FOR ATHLETES WITH VISUAL IMPAIRMENTS

There are two major organizations for athletes who have visual impairments. The goal of the United States Association for Blind Athletes (USABA) and the International Blind Sport Organization (IBSA) is to promote competitive sport opportunities for athletes with visual impairments. These organizations also seek to change attitudes toward individuals with visual impairments.

USABA

USABA is the major sport organization in the United States for athletes 14 years of age and older who have a visual impairment. Organized in 1976, USABA provides competitive sport opportunities at the local, state, regional, national, and international level. Individuals with visual impairments may choose to participate in integrated sports with their sighted peers or in sports exclusively for individuals with visual impairments, or both. Many individuals with visual impairments enjoy participation in sports for the blind because of the opportunity to meet and compete with others who are blind. Physical educators are encouraged to contact USABA for the location of the nearest local sport organization for athletes who are blind, and then share this information with students who are blind.

Although there is increased recognition and opportunities for elite athletes who are blind, there remain few programs designed to bring young people with visual impairments into sport. Physical educators can help by reviewing their physical education curriculum, noting those sports offered that are also USABA sports. While teaching these sports, physical educators are encouraged to make an extra effort to promote the sport among any students with visual impairments and assist them in learning how to pursue the sport through USABA.

USABA offers competition in nine sports:

Alpine and Nordic skiing

Athletics (track and field)

Goal ball

Judo

Powerlifting

Swimming

Tandem cycling

Wrestling

USABA athletes who reach an elite athletic level compete in the World Blind Championships and in the summer and winter Paralympics. USABA classification for competition is based on residual vision, as shown in table 12.2. Rules for each sport are modified slightly from those established by the national sport organizations. For example, track and field follows most NCAA rules, except that guide wires are used in sprints; sighted guides may be used on distance runs; hurdles are eliminated; and jumpers who are totally blind touch the high bar and then back off and use a one- or two-step approach. The use of guides depends entirely on the athlete's visual classification and the particular event. Guides facilitate the activity by running alongside the athlete, with both runners holding on to a tether. Alternatively, stationary guides are positioned around the track to call directional signals to the runner. The following list provides descriptions of guiding techniques for running:

- Sighted guide: The runner grasps the guide's elbow, shoulder, or hand depending on what is most comfortable for the runner and guide (see figure 12.3a).

- Tether: The runner and guide grasp a tether—a short string, towel, or shoelace. This allows the runner full range of motion of the arms while remaining in close proximity to the sighted runner (see figure 12.3b).

- Guide wire: The runner holds onto a guide wire and runs independently for time or distance. A guide wire is a rope or wire pulled tightly across a gym or track. A rope loop, metal ring, or metal handle ensures that the individual will not receive a rope burn and allows for optimal performance. Runners hold onto the sliding device and run for as long as they wish independently. Guide wires can be set up permanently or temporarily (see figure 12.3c).

- Sound source from a distance: The runner runs to a sound source, such as a clap or a bell. This can be done as a one-time sprint or continued for a distance run.

- Sound source: The guide rings bells or shakes a noisemaker for the runner to hear while they run side by side. This works best in areas with limited background noise.

- Circular running: In a large clear grassy area, a 20- to 25-foot rope is tied to a stake in the grass. The student takes the end of the rope, pulls it taut, and runs in circles independently. The circumference of the circle can be measured to determine distance, or the athlete can run for time. A beeper or radio can be placed at the starting point to determine number of laps completed.

- Sighted guides shirt: The runner with partial vision runs behind a guide with a bright shirt. Ask the runner what color he or she can see best to ensure maximum vision. This must be done in uncrowded areas.

- Independent running: A runner with travel vision runs independently on a track marked with thick white lines.

- Treadmill: Running on a treadmill provides a controlled and safe environment. Select a treadmill with the safety feature of an emergency stop.

- Wheelchair racing: An individual who is blind and in a wheelchair can use any of the adaptations listed previously, as needed. Aerobic conditioning results from pushing over long distances around a track, on neighborhood sidewalks, or along a paved path.

Table 12.2 USABA Classification for Sport Competition

Level	Classification
B1	From no light perception at all in either eye up to light perception and inability to recognize objects or contours in any direction and at any distance
B2	From ability to recognize objects or contours up to a visual acuity of 2/60 or limited visual field of 5 degrees
B3	2/60 to 6/60 (20/200) vision or field of vision between 5 and 20 degrees

Running is fundamental to many sports and activities. It is extremely important to allow the student opportunities to experience each technique and decide which he or she prefers. Students might even prefer one technique for speed and another for distance (Lieberman, Butcher, & Moak, 2001).

Figure 12.3   Running using *(a)* a sighted guide, *(b)* a tether, and *(c)* a guide wire.

Wrestling rules are modified slightly to require that opponents maintain physical contact throughout a match. Wrestlers with visual impairments have a long history of victories and state championships against sighted opponents (Buell, 1966).

Female gymnasts compete according to the rules of USA Gymnastics (the national governing body of the sport), except that vaulters who are blind may start with their hands on the horse and use a two-bounce takeoff; coaches on the balance beam may warn competitors when they near the end of the beam and no jumps are used; floor exercise competitors may count their steps to the edge of the mat; and music may be placed anywhere near the mat to aid directionality.

Swimming also follows NCAA rules. Athletes commonly count their strokes to anticipate the pool's edge. Coaches may also tap a swimmer, using a long pole with soft material at the end, such as a tennis ball, to signal the upcoming edge of the pool. On the backstroke, flags are hung low over the pool to brush the swimmers' arms to signal the pool's edge. Water can be sprayed on the surface of the pool to designate the end of a lane. This can be done for an individual or across the end of all lanes. When necessary, a spotter may use a kickboard to protect a swimmer's head from hitting the wall on one side of the lane.

Goal ball is a sport designed to be played by athletes with visual impairments. The object of the game is to roll a ball that contains bells past the opposing team's end-line (see figure 12.4).

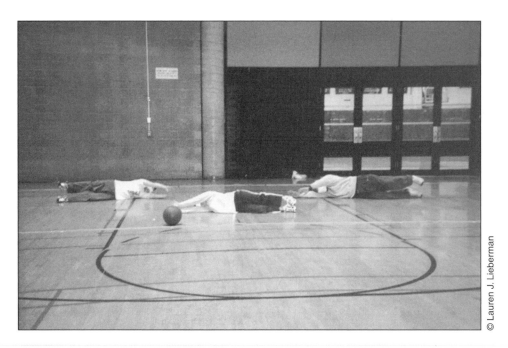

© Lauren J. Lieberman

Figure 12.4 Physical educators might introduce goal ball in an integrated class as a challenge to students who are sighted.

International Blind Sports Association

The international counterpart of USABA is IBSA. For international competition, USABA athletes participate in the Paralympic Games and the World Blind Championships.

National Beep Baseball Association

Beep baseball is a popular modification of baseball, governed by the National Beep Baseball Association (NBBA). Competition culminates with the NBBA World Series. Details on beep baseball are provided in chapter 26 (pp. 466-468).

SUMMARY

This chapter has focused on physical education for students with visual impairments. Whether the student is in inclusive physical education or in a segregated class, it is extremely important to know their abilities and focus on what they can do. It is up to the physical education teacher to make modifications necessary to ensure a high-quality physical education experience for students who are blind or have visual impairments.

REFERENCES

Arnhold, R.W., & McGrain, P. (1985). Selected kinematics patterns of visually impaired youth in sprint running. *Adapted Physical Activity Quarterly, 2,* 206-213.

Bouchard, D., & Tetrault, S. (2000). The motor development of sighted children and children with moderate low vision. *Journal of Visual Impairment and Blindness, 94,* 564-574.

Buell, C.E. (1966). Physical education for blind children. Springfield, IL: Charles C Thomas.

Butcher, J. (2002). Fit for life. *Future Reflections, 22*(1), 38-42.

Dunn, J., Morehouse, J., & Fredericks, H.D. (1986). *Physical education for the severely handicapped: A systematic approach to data based gymnasium.* Austin, TX: Pro-Ed.

Lieberman, L.J. (2002). Fitness for individuals who are visually impaired and deaf-blind. *Re:View, 1*(34), 13-23.

Lieberman, L.J., Butcher, M., & Moak, S. (2001). Preferred guide-running techniques for children who are blind. *Palaestra, 17*(3), 20-26, 55.

Lieberman, L., & Cowart, J. (1996). *Games for people with sensory impairments: Strategies for including individuals of all ages.* Champaign, IL: Human Kinetics.

Lieberman, L.J., & Houston-Wilson, C., (2002). *Strategies for inclusion: A handbook for physical educators.* Champaign, IL: Human Kinetics.

Lieberman, L.J., & McHugh, B.E. (2001). Health related fitness of children with visual impairments and blindness. *Journal of Visual Impairment and Blindness, 95*(5), 272-286.

Lieberman, L.J., James, A. R., & Ludwa, N. (2004). The impact of inclusion in general physical education for all students. *Journal of Physical Education, Recreation and Dance, 75*(5), 37-41,55.

McHugh, B.E., & Lieberman, L.J. (2003) The impact of developmental factors on incidence of stereotypic rocking among children with visual impairments. *Journal of Visual Impairment and Blindness, 97*(8), 453-474.

Nikolaraizi, M., & De Reybekiel, N. (2001). A comparative study of children's attitudes toward deaf children, children in wheelchairs, and blind children in Greece and in the UK. *European Journal of Special Needs Education,* 16, 167-182.

Office of Special Education and Rehabilitative Services (OSE/RS), 34 CFR 300 (2002).

O'Connell, M.E. (2000). *The effects of physical guidance on the self-efficacy of children who are blind.* Unpublished Masters Thesis: SUNY Brockport

Robinson, B., & Lieberman, L.J. (2004). Effects of level of visual impairment, gender and age on self-determination of children who are blind. *Journal of Visual Impairment and Blindness,* June, 352-366.

Tepfer, A. (2002). *Socialization into sport and barriers encountered by elite blind athletes.* Unpublished Masters Thesis, SUNY Brockport.

USABA. (1998). *Athletes' profile.* Colorado Springs, CO: Author.

Walker, S. (2003). PE in inclusive education. *Visibility,* 37, 19-20.

Williamson, M. (2002). Me and my PE teacher. *Future Reflections,* 22(1), 31-33.

Winnick, J., & Short, F. (1986). The influence on physical fitness test performance. *Journal of Visual Impairment and Blindness,* 80, 729-731.

Winnick, J., & Short, F. (1999). *The Brockport physical fitness test manual.* Champaign, IL: Human Kinetics.

Wiskochil, B. (2002). *The effects of peer tutors on the academic learning time of students who are visually impaired in physical education.* Unpublished Master's Thesis: SUNY Brockport.

Wyatt, L., & Ng, G.Y. (1997). The effect of visual impairment on the strength of children's hip and knee extensors. *Journal of Visual Impairment and Blindness,* 91(1), 40-46.

WRITTEN RESOURCES

Celese, M. (2002). A survey of motor development for infants and young children with visual impairments. *Journal of Visual Impairments and Blindness,* 96(3), 169-174.

Kuusisto, S. (1998). *Planet of the blind: A memoir.* New York: Dial Press.

This acclaimed writer has been legally blind since birth. Readers gain insights into his experiences with blindness through his excellent prose.

Lieberman, L., & Cowart, J. (1996). *Games for people with sensory impairments: Strategies for including individuals of all ages.* Champaign, IL: Human Kinetics.

This practical reference provides teachers and recreation specialists with 70 games that people with sensory impairments—both visual and hearing—can play.

Lieberman, L.J., Modell, S., Jackson, I. (in press). *Going PLACES: A transition guide to physical activity for youths with visual impairments and deafblindness.* Louisville, KY: American Printing House for the Blind.

Uriegas, O. (2001). Almost 100 motor activities for infants and toddlers. *See/Hear,* Summer 2001, 19-21.

Because early intervention is a necessity for young children with visual impairments, this resource is valuable in giving parents and teachers ideas on motor activities.

AUDIOVISUAL RESOURCES

Portraits of possibility. (Videotape, 1996). Insight Media, 2162 Broadway, P.O. Box 621, New York, NY, 10024-0621; fax 212-799-5309.

This 20-minute tape explores issues raised by participation in sports for individuals who are blind. Training methods are included.

Access sports model. (Videotape, 1996). Western Michigan University.

This 15-minute tape describes modifications and adaptations to boundaries, equipment, and rules in sport and physical activity to increase success for individuals who are visually impaired or blind.

ELECTRONIC RESOURCES

American Foundation for the Blind (AFB). Web site: www.afb.org.

This site provides information about advocacy, resources, programs, and publications by AFB, a major organization serving individuals who are blind. For more information, write AFB, 11 Penn Plaza, New York, NY 10001; 800-232-5463.

Camp Abilities: A developmental sports camp for children who are visually impaired, blind, or deafblind.

For more information, contact Lauren Lieberman PhD, Director, SUNY Brockport, Department of Physical Education, Brockport, NY, 14420; Phone 585-395-5361; llieberm@brockport.edu; Web site www.campabilities.org

International Blind Sport and Recreation Association (IBSA). Web site: www.ibsa.es/.

This site contains information about IBSA. For further information, contact Enrique Sanz, IBSA President, c/o Quevedo, 1-1 28014, Madrid, Spain; phone (3491) 589-45-33/34/36; fax (3491) 589-45-37; e-mail ibsa@ibsa.es.

National Beep Baseball Association (NBBA). Web site: www.nbba.org.

This site offers information about NBBA competitions and how to play Beep Baseball. For more information, contact NBBA, 9623 Spencer Highway, La Porte, TX, 77571; phone 713-476-1592.

CHAPTER 13

Deafness and Deafblindness

Lauren J. Lieberman

Ms. Goodwin, an elementary school physical education teacher, has been teaching for three years and loves what she is doing. At the beginning of her fourth year, she has a class of second graders, including a 10-year-old girl named Rachel, who is Deaf and uses sign language to communicate. Rachel has a full-time educational interpreter with her, Mr. Colgan. Ms. Goodwin has never taught a child with a disability and has been caught by surprise. She wants to make sure she does everything right, so she refers back to her old textbook on adapted physical education, where she reads of minor instructional modifications she can make in the class to ensure Rachel learns everything she needs to. At all the stations around the gym, Ms. Goodwin posts picture descriptions and clear explanations for fitness warm-ups. She learns that flashing the gym lights on and off is a good way to signal when she wants all of her students, including Rachel, to stop activity and look at her. When the class begins each day, Ms. Goodwin has students form a semicircle for class discussion so that Rachel can view everyone in the class at once. During instruction, she uses visual demonstrations, with checks for understanding along the way.

A few weeks into the class, although Ms. Goodwin is pleased with Rachel's progress and believes she is learning as she should, she does not feel she knows Rachel very well. Also, she has noticed a new trend lately—Rachel is always the last one in class selected when the children choose partners. Mr. Colgan and Ms. Goodwin decide that learning Rachel's language would solve some of these problems. Ms. Goodwin understands that she needs not only to learn the signs to communicate to Rachel (expressive language) but also to understand what Rachel is communicating back to her (receptive language). To achieve this, Ms. Goodwin takes a few minutes out of each day and learns the signs for the day's lesson. When she teaches kicking, for instance, she learns the signs for kick, hard, soft, far, short, stop, start, good job, more, and try again. Each class she learns a few new signs, and she and Rachel teach the signs to students in the class as well. Some of the kids pick up other signs that Mr. Colgan shares with them throughout the day and, before long, Rachel is communicating well with a few of her peers. Ms. Goodwin, quickly becoming skilled at the signs, notices that Rachel appreciates the effort and is trying harder than ever. Rachel eventually becomes one of the highest-skilled students in the class, and when Ms. Goodwin has students choose partners, they choose Rachel near the top every time.

eaching children who are Deaf, hard of hearing, or deafblind can be difficult if the instructor does not plan appropriately and become proactive about instruction. In this chapter we will discuss the definition of hearing loss, types of hearing loss, general characteristics of Deaf students, considerations for teaching, cochlear implants and physical education, inclusion strategies (including how to use interpreters), and sport opportunities within the Deaf community. We will also cover information on how to teach children who are deafblind, including types of deafblindness, general characteristics of children who are deafblind, and adaptations for teaching students who are deafblind.

DEFINITIONS OF HEARING LOSSES

Being Deaf in the United States today often means being a member of a subculture of American society that has its own language, its own customs, and its own way of perceiving the Deaf person's role within the hearing world. Understanding the perspective of the Deaf culture makes effective teaching of Deaf students in physical education more likely. Awareness of this perspective might begin with the knowledge that many Deaf people do not consider themselves "disabled" but rather members of a cultural and linguistic minority. Unlike members of most populations with disabilities, most who are Deaf do not want "person first" terminology used to describe them. Most Deaf individuals prefer to be called a "Deaf person" rather than a "person who is Deaf." The use of the uppercase "D" in the word "Deaf" is a succinct proclamation by the Deaf that they share more than a medical condition; they share a culture and a language—sign language. For many Deaf people, the term "hearing impairment" suggests that deafness is a condition in which something is damaged and in need of being fixed (or "cured," as some medical professionals promoting cochlear implants have been known to indicate). One of the reasons Deaf people do not like the term "hearing impaired" is that they think nothing is wrong with them and nothing needs to be fixed, thus nothing is impaired.

Deaf refers to a hearing loss in which hearing is insufficient for comprehension of auditory information, with or without the use of a hearing aid. The Individual with Disabilities Education Act (IDEA) defines "deaf" as having a hearing loss so severe that the individual is unable to process language through hearing, with or without the use of an amplification device. The loss must be severe enough to adversely affect the student's educational performance (Individuals With Disabilities Education Act, 1997).

Hard of hearing refers to a hearing loss that makes understanding speech through the ear alone difficult, but not impossible. Amplification with a hearing aid or remedial help in communication skills often benefits people who are hard of hearing. IDEA defines hard of hearing as having a hearing loss that might be permanent or fluctuating and adversely affects the student's educational achievement or performance (Individuals With Disabilities Education Act, 1997).

Most people with hearing losses are hard of hearing, not totally deaf. It is also important to note that two students might have the same degree of hearing loss but use their residual hearing differently because of age differences when their hearing loss occurred. Motivation, intelligence, presence of disabilities, environmental stimulation, and response to a training program might also affect the degree to which residual hearing is used.

Degree of hearing loss and residual hearing are described in terms of decibel (dB) levels. The ability to detect sounds in the 0 to 25 dB range is considered normal for children. Ordinary conver-

Table 13.1 **Degrees of Hearing Loss in Decibels (dB)**

Hearing threshold	Degrees of hearing loss	Levels of loudness
27-40 dB	Slight	Faint speech
41-55 dB	Mild	Normal speech
56-70 dB	Marked (moderate)	Loud speech
71-90 dB	Severe	Shouted speech
Greater than 90 dB	Profound	Any speech, even amplified

sation occurs in the 40 to 50 dB range, whereas noises in the 125 to 140 dB range are painfully loud. The 55 dB hearing loss level is a standard for the level at which communication difficulties begin to become apparent (Moores, 1996). Degrees of hearing loss are presented in table 13.1.

Deaf children use several communication modes depending on parental influence, educational background, speech therapy, and technological enhancements (such as cochlear implants). Communication ranges from speaking and hearing to using signed exact English (SEE) with speech (also known as "total communication") to using Pidgin sign language—a combination of SEE and American Sign Language (ASL)—to using strictly ASL. Some children use a combination of these methods depending on audience, experience, and comfort level.

TYPES AND CAUSES OF HEARING LOSS

The three major types of hearing loss are conductive, sensorineural, and mixed. With a conductive loss, sound is not transmitted well to the inner ear (analogous to a radio with the volume on low). There is no distortion, but words are faint. Some children with conductive loss might have intelligible speech. Because a conductive loss is a mechanical problem in which nerves remain undamaged, it can sometimes be corrected surgically or medically. Often, hearing aids work effectively to increase volume. A frequently observed condition is serous otitis media, or middle ear effusion, which often is treated by placing a plastic tube through the ear drum for several months to allow fluid to drain from sound-conducting inner ear bones.

A sensorineural hearing loss is caused by nerve damage. In comparison to a conductive loss, sensorineural loss is much more severe and likely to be permanent. Children with a sensorineural loss (analogous to a radio that is not well tuned) have more difficulties with speech than those with a conductive loss do. Sensorineural losses affect fidelity as well as loudness, so there is distortion of sounds. The words might be loud, but they are distorted and garbled. While raising one's voice or using a hearing aid might help the voice be heard, the words still might not be understood. Typically, low-pitched vowel sounds are heard, but the high pitch consonants such as "t," "p," and "k" are not heard clearly. This makes it difficult to distinguish

words such as "pop" from "top." Also note that only 20 to 30 percent of speech is visible on the lips. In some cases a child might be fitted with a cochlear implant to help make words clearer. A requirement for being a candidate for a cochlear implant is that you must be profoundly deaf and have a sensorineural hearing loss.

Students with a sensorineural loss will likely use sign language, are less likely to use speech, and might have balance difficulties as a consequence of damage of the semicircular canal. A mixed loss is a combination of conductive and sensorineural losses.

Among Deaf students, approximately two thirds have congenital deafness (present at birth) and one third have acquired deafness (developed some time after birth). Medical advances have enabled more severely premature babies and children with meningitis and encephalitis to survive. These survivors might have multiple disabilities, including deafness. Injuries, allergies to drugs, repeated exposure to loud music, infections such as herpes viruses, and toxoplasmosis can all cause hearing loss.

CHARACTERISTICS OF DEAF STUDENTS

Individuals who are classified as hard of hearing typically share the same characteristics as the general population. Their hearing impairments are mild and might not present major obstacles to speech. But most people who are postlingual profoundly deaf or prelingual severely or profoundly deaf might have unique characteristics caused by the need to communicate through a means other than spoken language. These characteristics are the focus of the following section.

Language and Cultural Characteristics

American Sign Language (ASL) is the preferred means of communication within the Deaf culture in the United States. This shared language is the basis of the shared identity in Deaf culture. Just like English, ASL is a language used to communicate, having its own grammar and structure to convey subtle nuances of abstractions, in addition to describing concrete objects. Most hearing people see only the signs that name objects and directions (figure 13.1, p. 224) and are unaware of the subtleties of ASL. Currently, many prelingually Deaf children do not develop intelligible speech despite speech training. So, communication between hearing and Deaf people remains a major problem until many more hearing persons learn ASL. Courtesies to aid communication among hearing and Deaf persons are presented in the sidebar.

Deaf students in the hearing community have fewer opportunities for incidental learning than hearing students because they cannot overhear conversations. Rarely do hearing parents, teachers, and friends sign when not addressing Deaf children. So there is little opportunity to "oversee" conversations, and continuity with life's events is often missing. This is where the use of sign language becomes universally important in the socialization and language development of Deaf children.

When Communicating With a Deaf Person, Remember to . . .

- maintain eye contact throughout the conversation,
- use paper and pencil to augment conversation,
- signal that you understand only when you really do (do not pretend to understand),
- use polite ways to gain a Deaf person's attention,
- learn to use a teletypewriter (TTY) to transmit typewritten words over the telephone lines to another TTY,
- discourage interruptions to the conversation, and
- correct a Deaf person's English only if asked.

Graybill & Cokley, 1993.

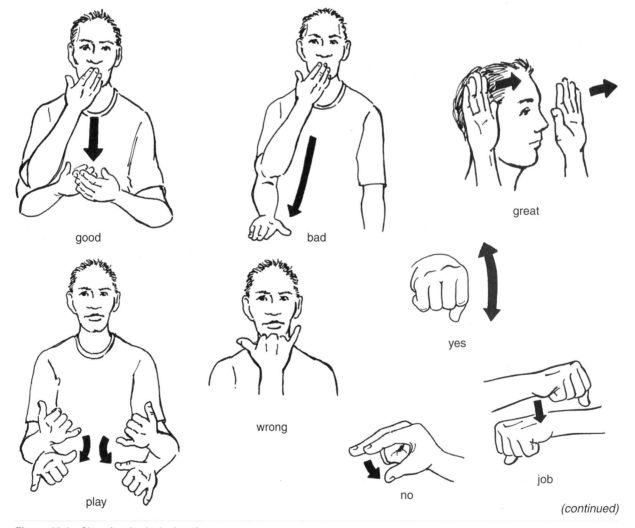

good

bad

great

play

wrong

yes

no

job

(continued)

Figure 13.1 Signs for physical education.

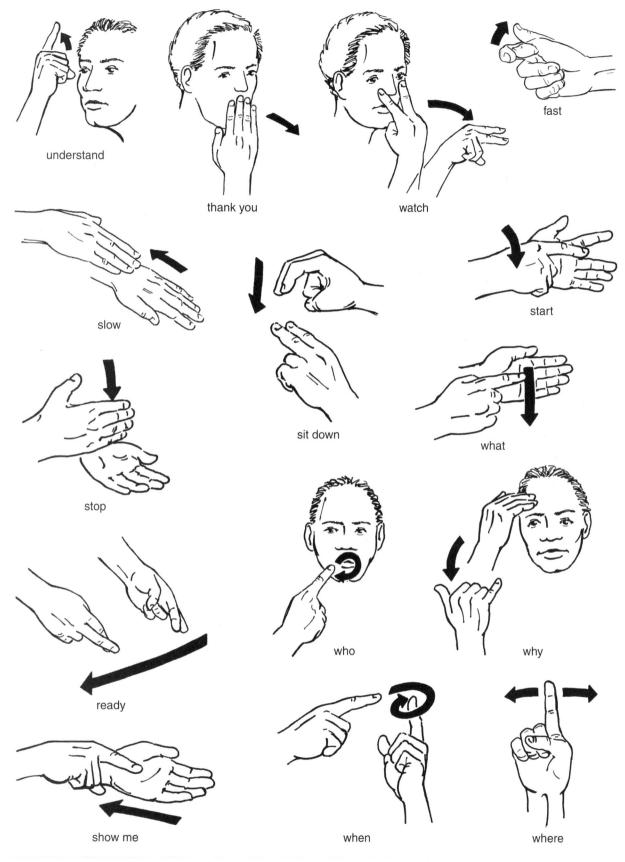

understand

thank you

watch

fast

slow

sit down

start

stop

what

ready

who

why

show me

when

where

Figure 13.1 *(continued)*

225

Behavioral and Affective Characteristics

Sometimes Deaf students are regarded as slow learners or behavior problems when their inappropriate behavior is actually a result of an undetected mild hearing loss. The incidence of perceived impulsivity seems to be greater among Deaf students than among hearing students. Perhaps this is because Deaf students learn visually and want to look around to check their surroundings more frequently. Some behavioral problems are a direct result of frustrations on the part of the Deaf child caused by a lack of understanding and communication.

Motor Characteristics

If the semicircular canals of the inner ear are damaged as a part of the hearing loss, as in sensorineural deafness, balance problems are likely. These balance problems—which occur as a result of vestibular damage, not deafness—can in turn cause developmental delays and motor ability delays. Research results that show poor motor performance for Deaf students as a group could reflect the very poor performance of those students with vestibular damage along with the average performance of the rest of the Deaf students. Given equal opportunity to learn movements and participate in physical activity, Deaf children should equal their same-age peers in motor skills (Lieberman, Volding, & Winnick, 2004). If these children are not afforded equal opportunity, they might lag behind in motor skills.

When comparing the results of fitness testing of children and youth with hearing losses to standardized norms, the outcome becomes drastically different, with Deaf children and youth showing more appropriate fitness levels (Ellis, 2001; Winnick & Short, 1986). Ellis (2001) reported that because hearing loss is a sensory rather than physical disability, there is no reason for Deaf children and youth to demonstrate lower fitness levels than their hearing peers. Thus, Ellis set out to determine what factors influenced the physical fitness of deaf children. In both studies it was found that two primary factors influenced the physical fitness of deaf children: physical activity participation (just as with hearing children) and parental influence. It was also discovered that Deaf children with Deaf parents had greater encouragement and activity participation than Deaf children with hearing parents (Ellis, 2001; Stewart, 1991).

GENERAL CONSIDERATIONS FOR TEACHING PHYSICAL EDUCATION TO DEAF OR HARD-OF-HEARING STUDENTS

Although movement is an area that does not heavily depend on auditory cues, receiving feedback about movement can be problematic. Usually, visual cues can be substituted for the auditory cues that are distorted or absent. According to Graziadei (1998), teaching conceptual aspects of physical education to Deaf students in a hearing class with a teacher who is not fluent in sign language can be problematic. It is recommended that Deaf students demonstrate learned skills in order to increase involvement and understanding.

Recall the scenario at the beginning of this section. Rachel now has a physical education teacher and friends who have basic means of communication with her. But she still faces some complex problems. It is unlikely that subtle sport strategy and rule concepts can be completely conveyed to her. Interpreters seldom have the sport-specific ASL vocabulary with which to explain the subtle movement or sports concepts.

Deaf students who are included in regular schools often experience isolation, social deprivation, and ridicule from teachers and peers because they lack a common language with their hearing classmates (Graziadei, 1998; Nowell & Innes, 1997). If a Deaf student is placed in an inclusive classroom, a peer tutor program should be created to alleviate these problems. Peer tutor programs have been shown to improve physical activity in inclusive physical education classes (Lieberman, Dunn, van der Mars, & McCubbin, 2000). As tutors learn many signs, new opportunities for appropriate socialization among peers emerge. Additional information on peer tutor programs can be found in Lieberman and Houston-Wilson (2002).

TEACHING CONSIDERATIONS FOR STUDENTS WITH COCHLEAR IMPLANTS

A cochlear implant is a surgical procedure that implants a device into an individual's inner ear. It takes the place of part or all the functions of the inner ear structures. The goal of the implant is to improve recognition of speech and acoustic information. The implanted device eliminates residual hearing in the implanted ear (Hilgenbrinck, Pyfer, & Castle, 2004; see figure 13.2). Students with cochlear implants have unique needs when it comes to physical education. The following are teaching considerations for students with cochlear implants according to Hilgenbrinck and colleagues (2004):

- Avoid sports that might result in serious blows to the head, such as football, hockey, lacrosse, soccer, wrestling, tumbling, and other contact sports. These activities might be modified to eliminate contact and can be enjoyed with adaptations.

- Avoid activities that increase the risk of falls or blows to the head, such as rollerblading, skateboarding, using a scooter, and climbing walls. With proper instruction, removal of the device, and use of helmets, these activities might be enjoyed.

- Use caution when participating in winter activities, such as skiing, snowboarding, sledding, and ice skating. These situations might create uncomfortable sensations around the head and neck regions.

- During water activities remove the device parts and place them in water-tight containers. This eliminates any hearing the student had with that ear, so follow the teaching techniques for Deaf students when the student does not have the device connected.

- Excessive sweating creates moisture inside the device. This might cause what is known as "motor boating," which is unwanted and unnecessary noise. Either take the device off before vigorous activity or wear a headband or hat to keep the device dry.

- At the time of implant, each device is individually calibrated by an audiologist to custom fit each recipient. This is called "mapping" the cochlear implant device. The interference of static electricity might "demap" the device, rendering it unusable. Avoidance of static electricity (balloons, rubber, dry mats) reduces the risk of demapping the device.

INCLUSION STRATEGIES FOR TEACHING DEAF AND HARD-OF-HEARING STUDENTS

When teaching Deaf students, physical educators might find it helpful to learn the answers to the following questions. When seeking answers to these questions, ask the student, if possible. Also look at the student's IEP and ask questions of the student, his or her parents or caregiver, and his or her educational interpreter (if there is one).

- To what extent can the student hear? How can the teacher maximize the use of remaining hearing?

- What is the student's preferred mode of communication? How can the teacher maximize communication with the student?

- Are there any contraindications or activities that should be avoided? How can these activities be modified?

Most Deaf individuals have no restrictions on participation in physical education. Children with frequent ear infections might have tubes placed in their ears, so they might need to wear ear plugs when swimming. Children susceptible to earaches should avoid exposing unprotected ears to cold weather. Evaluate balance prior to activity. Not all Deaf children have balance problems. If there are balance issues, work on tasks to improve balance. If balance problems and vertigo are found, only climb to heights, jump on a trampoline, or dive into a pool if adequate safeguards have been taken to ensure the student will not be hurt if he or she loses balance during the activity. Tumbling activities that require rotation, such as diving forward rolls, cartwheels, and handsprings, should be performed only with close spotting.

Students who are Deaf might benefit from the use of an interpreter. The role of an educational interpreter is to ease communication among Deaf or hard-of-hearing persons and others, such as teachers, service providers, and peers within the educational environment (RID, 2002). In inclusive physical education classes, the following suggestions from Graziadei (1998) and Best, Lieberman, and Arndt (2002) improve success, communication, and socialization:

- Encourage the interpreter to stand next to the teacher.

- Give lesson plans to the interpreter days in advance so both the interpreter and Deaf student can review and understand the lesson before it begins. Include a list of any specialized vocabulary.

- Face the Deaf student (not the interpreter) when addressing the student.

- Meet with the interpreter before beginning each unit to clarify sport terminology, instructional cues, and idioms that are likely to be used.

- Teach sport-specific signs at the beginning of each new unit.
- Pair each Deaf student with a hearing peer, *not* the interpreter.
- Use the interpreter to communicate with Deaf students. Do not ask them to speak if they do not feel comfortable using their voice; allow them to use their interpreter to communicate.
- Understand the interpreter's role does not include reprimanding a student.
- The interpreter is not a teacher assistant and should not be expected to take attendance or distribute and collect equipment.
- Include the Deaf student in information taught during "teachable moments."

For students with residual hearing, Graziadei (1998) has these suggestions:

- Minimize background noise—turn off any music and expect silence when others are speaking.
- Encourage the student to remove the hearing aid or adjust the volume if there is excessive unavoidable background noise.
- Consider use of an audible trainer or an FM loop system (microphone worn by the teacher to amplify the voice into the hearing aid worn by the Deaf student) if recommended by an audiologist.

The following are general considerations when teaching or coaching Deaf or hard-of-hearing students in either integrated or segregated settings:

- Use visual teaching cues when instructing activities that are easily understood.
- Give Deaf students copies of lessons modified to their reading levels.
- Use stations with cue cards providing written explanations and illustrations.
- Use clear signals for starting and stopping activities.
- Use demonstrations liberally.
- Use a scoreboard and a visual timer if playing a game.
- Develop highly recognizable and easily visible signals for communication at a distance.

- When possible, stand near the Deaf student and tap the student on the shoulder to gain attention.
- Face the student so that lips and facial expressions are fully visible.
- Avoid chewing gum or covering the mouth; consider shaving a beard or mustache.
- Position student directly in front of the teacher.
- Ensure the teacher is not standing directly in front of the sun or a bright light.
- When indoors, provide bright lighting (behind the student).
- When outdoors, take care that the student does not face into the sun.
- Check for understanding. Ask all students if they understand the activity before beginning. Help hearing students appreciate that if the Deaf students do not follow the rules it might be because they do not understand them and not because they intend to cheat or seek unfair advantage.
- Promote leadership skills among Deaf students.
- Give Deaf students choices (and honor the choices).
- Encourage Deaf students to be team captains, group leaders, and referees.
- Have Deaf students help hearing students as well as vice versa.
- Provide clear instructions so Deaf students do not need to wait and watch others before participating.
- If teaching students who sign, learn as much sign language as possible. A hearing person is encouraged to practice and learn ASL, which takes as much effort as learning any other language. With this practice, a hearing person can look forward to communicating with Deaf persons beyond a superficial level.
- Include Deaf students in information taught during "teachable moments." These moments often occur in the middle of a game, when an interpreter is on the sidelines and the Deaf student is down the field. Two options for including Deaf students are to review the teachable moments at the end of the lesson with either the entire class or only the Deaf students, or to gather all students along with the interpreter together on the field during a teachable moment (Graziadei, 1998).

- Dance and rhythms can be especially helpful for Deaf students. To help them better feel the vibrations of music, place speakers face down on a wooden floor, turn up the bass, and dance in bare feet. Butterfield (1988) suggests adding strobe lights that flash in rhythm with the music to provide visual cues. You can also use balloons so students can "feel the music" through their hands.

- Provide extra supervision when swimming underwater for students with vestibular damage. Pair Deaf students with hearing partners, and use signals developed for communication between the teacher and the class. Flashing lights might be a quick way to gain student attention (Butterfield, 1988).

- Allow Deaf students the option of taking written tests with an interpreter to clarify and sign test questions. In this way, physical education knowledge is tested, not the Deaf students' knowledge of English, a second language (Graziadei, 1998).

APPLICATION EXAMPLE

Inclusion of a Deaf Student

Setting: Elementary school physical education class

Student: Samuel is a boy in fourth grade who is hard of hearing and benefits from sign language and speech. Samuel has been going to his elementary school since kindergarten and has many friends. When he was in second grade, Samuel's parents asked for an interpreter to assist him in his academic areas. Ms. Wert has been his interpreter for two years, and he likes her a lot. Unfortunately, Ms. Wert takes her break during physical education class. The administrators made this decision because they viewed physical education as visual and felt there was no need for an interpreter. Many of Samuel's friends know some sign language and use it on the bus and in classes. They only know the signs he teaches them and a few they have picked up from the interpreter in passing.

Issue: The issue here was that Samuel loves physical activity but was reserved in physical education because he did not always understand the directions. He always waited a minute or two at the start of each activity to be sure he knew what the activity involved before starting. Mr. Wineberg noticed Samuel's reservations and became concerned. He missed at least six minutes of activity during each class as he watched his peers participate in fear of doing the wrong thing. Unfortunately, Mr. Wineberg did not know enough sign language to ask him what was wrong, so he asked to make an appointment.

Application: The following was determined as a result of a meeting with the school administrator, the Deaf education consultant, the interpreter, Samuel and his parents, and Mr. Wineberg:

- Samuel will continue to participate in physical education with his peers.

- The interpreter, Ms. Wert, will take short breaks at reading time, lunch, and recess instead of during physical education classes.

- Mr. Wineberg will meet with Ms. Wert before each unit and learn the necessary signs so he can start to communicate with Samuel himself during class. Ms. Wert will also teach Samuel's peers the signs commonly needed for each unit so they can communicate with him during class.

- Mr. Wineberg and Ms. Wert created an appropriate list of modifications to activities, such as using start and stop signals, sitting in a semicircle instead of rows, and facing Samuel when instructing.

- Mr. Wineberg will start a peer tutor program with trained peer tutors so that when Samuel is in class and he cannot see the interpreter, or if he is playing a game, the peer tutor can relay important information to him. This will also increase his self-confidence and increase the number of peers he can communicate with and increase his depth of conversation.

- An additional class with supplemental physical education instruction will be offered should Samuel need more time to grasp a skill or activity, such as dancing or rollerblading.

- When there is only one Deaf student in the class, teach signs to the entire class so there is clear communication no matter who is in the student's group.
- Schedule Deaf students into the same physical education class and encourage them to work together during class so they can help each other understand the lesson.
- Hold the same expectations for hearing and Deaf students regarding motor performance, fitness, and behavior. Clearly communicate these expectations in writing to Deaf students. Educators who are unusually understanding, or offer excessive assistance when students are not prepared for class, teach Deaf students that they can rely on others rather than accept responsibility for their own actions. It is suggested that teachers ask themselves, "Am I really helping? Is the assistance I am giving helping students to cope more effectively with the world that they will be living in after graduation? Or is it better to let them experience the real consequences of their behavior?"
- Encourage students to become involved in Deaf sport. The United States of America Deaf Sport Federation (USADSF) can be contacted through the Web site www. USADSF.org.

Refer also to the application example for an example of including a Deaf student in physical education class (p. 229).

Most physical fitness and motor tests can be administered to Deaf students, provided that visual cues are substituted for auditory cues. Examples of this are dropping the arm in addition to shouting "Go!" to signal the start of an event, or using strobe lights or cable lights as starting signals when doing a shuttle-run test. ASL is not semantically similar to English, so care must be taken when signing instructions. Be sure the person giving instructions is skilled in signing and able to give signed instructions that are semantically identical to spoken instructions (Stewart, Dummer, & Haubenstricker, 1990). Deaf children whose native language is ASL perform better on motor tests when the test is administered in ASL instead of English.

The strategies described previously apply to both the segregated and integrated setting for Deaf students. In addition to a quality physical education program, Deaf students need quality sport opportunities in hearing and Deaf sport.

SPORT OPPORTUNITIES

The greatest opportunity for most Deaf students is to participate in after-school sport programs. It is important for physical educators and coaches to encourage participation with hearing peers. Another opportunity for involvement in sport for Deaf students is Deaf Sport through the USADSF.

David Stewart's (1991) view of Deaf Sport follows:

> There is something about being "Deaf" that is quietly comforting to those who have this identity. . . Deaf sport can be thought of as a vehicle for understanding the dynamics of being deaf. It facilitates a social identification among Deaf people that is not easily obtained in other sociocultural contexts. . . . It relies on a Deaf perspective to define its social patterns of behaviors, and it presents an orientation to hearing loss that is distinctly different from that endorsed by hearing institutions. Essentially, Deaf sport emphasizes the honor of being Deaf, whereas society tends to focus on the adversity of hearing loss. (p. 1)

Physical educators have the important role of introducing Deaf students to both hearing and Deaf sport. For many Deaf students attending public schools, the majority of their exposure to Deaf culture is through Deaf sport. Many Deaf athletes choose to compete against other Deaf athletes under the auspices of the USADSF. The organization was established as the American Athletic Association for the Deaf (AAAD) in Ohio in 1945. Individuals with moderate or severe hearing loss (55 dB or greater in the better ear) are eligible for USADSF competition.

The USADSF has national sport organizations in the following sports for men and women:

Athletics (track and field),

Badminton

Baseball

Basketball

Bowling

Cycling

Flag football

Golf

Hockey

Orienteering

Skiing and snowboarding

Soccer

Team handball

The worldwide counterpart of USADSF is the International Comité des Sport des Sourds (CISS), which translates to the International Committee of Silent Sports. Currently, CISS is not a member of the International Paralympic Committee (IPC). Instead of participating in the Paralympic Games, Deaf sport continues to hold its own summer and winter Deaflympics every four years. Winter events include Alpine and Nordic skiing, speed skating, and ice hockey.

The rules followed by USADSF and CISS are nearly identical to those used in hearing national and international competitions. To equalize competition, athletes are not allowed to wear hearing aids. A few changes have been made to use visual rather than auditory cues. For example, in team sports a whistle is blown and a flag is waved to stop play. Strobe lights are used at the starting blocks for swimming events. In track, lighting systems placed 50 meters in front of the starting blocks and to the side of the track are used to signal the start of a race.

Involving youth in Deaf sport is an important objective of USADSF. The Annual Mini Deaf Sports Festival, held in Louisville, Kentucky, is specifically designed for the participation of 6- to 18-year-old Deaf students (Paciorek & Jones, 2001). This event is particularly important in fostering pride in Deaf sport and increasing involvement among Deaf youth who will form the future of Deaf sport. Physical educators are encouraged to refer to the Resource section of this chapter to learn more about student involvement in Deaf sport and to share this information with their Deaf students.

The sports skills of Deaf athletes span the range found in the hearing population, from unskilled to highly skilled. Deaf athletes are capable of competing as equals with hearing athletes, and some do so with significant success. As far back as 1883, Deaf athletes were competing in professional sports in this country. In that year Edward Dundon became the first recorded Deaf professional baseball player and is reported to be the reason for the development of umpire hand signals. Curtis Pride is Deaf and competed in the MLB, Terence Parkin is Deaf and won the silver medal in the 200-meter breaststroke at the 2000 Sydney Olympics, and Terry Clayton is Deaf and plays football for the University of Kentucky. Deaf athletes have also excelled in sports such as swimming, wrestling, bowling, and football. In fact, the huddle is said to have been first used by the Gallaudet University football team to prevent competing Deaf teams from eavesdropping on their plays.

DEAFBLINDNESS

Individuals who are deafblind do not have effective use of either of the distance senses—vision or hearing. Although the term "deafblind" suggests that these people can neither hear nor see, this is rarely the literal truth. Most individuals who are deafblind receive both visual and auditory input, but information received through these sensory channels is usually distorted. So, the term "deafblind" is often misleading—it is frequently more accurate to say that these people are both hard of hearing and partially sighted. Only in rare instances, such as with Helen Keller, is a person totally blind and profoundly deaf. See the sidebar for considerations when teaching students with deafblindness.

There are many causes of deafblindness. Understanding the cause might give an indication of the age of onset and whether remaining vision and hearing are likely. Usher syndrome is a congenital disability characterized by hearing loss present at birth or shortly thereafter and the progressive loss of peripheral vision. Usher type I is congenital deafness and progressive retinitis pigmentosa, whereas Usher type II is adventitious deafness and progressive retinitis pigmentosa. Usher syndrome is the major cause of deafblindness in the United States (Sauerbuger, 1993).

Another cause of deafblindness is CHARGE syndrome, so named because the following cluster of symptoms occur together:

C—coloboma of the eye (hole in the eye)

H—heart (congenital heart defect)

A—atresia of the choanae (nasal blockage that affects eating and swallowing)

R—retardation of growth

G—genital anomalies such as undescended testes or small genitalia

E—ear malformations such as low-set, rotated, or mis-shapen ears

Rubella can cause deafblindness when it is contracted by the mother during the first trimester of the pregnancy. Deafblindness can also be associated with meningitis, prematurity, parental use of drugs, sexually transmitted diseases (STDs), and unknown causes (McInnes, 1999).

When Teaching Students With Deafblindness, Remember . . .

- Offer activities that promote movement because children who are deafblind enjoy activities such as swimming, swinging, biking, walking, climbing, and sliding (Lieberman & MacVicar, 2003).
- Use multiple teaching modes (explanation, demonstration, tactile modeling, and physical assistance).
- Encourage choice making, such as choice of activity and equipment.
- Set up the environment to accommodate the students' strengths. For example, if you want a student to bat a ball, offer a variety of size, color, and textured bats, balls, and several ways to deliver the ball, such as on a string, on a tee, or via a thrown pitch. This way students can choose the size, weight, and color of the bat, ball, and preferred trajectory of the ball.

- Be flexible, patient, and creative.
- Facilitate socialization because individuals who are deafblind often experience isolation and loneliness (Lieberman & MacVicar, 2003). This can be done by implementing a peer tutor program, teaching the student's mode of communication to other students in the class, and encouraging the student who is deafblind to become involved in after-school programs and community activities.
- Provide all incidental information.
- Link movement to language. Teach the word for each skill learned and explain the purpose of each sport and activity.
- Learn the student's form of communication, including gestures and body language.

Characteristics of Children With Deafblindness

Although there is often a tendency for caregivers to focus on the medical aspects of deafblindness, physical educators can help parents begin to focus on the quality of life opportunities for their child with deafblindness. Physical educators can work to introduce the person who is deafblind to activities that they might come to enjoy. They can help him or her experience joy in living rather than focus only on survival. Teaching students who are deafblind is a unique experience that cannot be learned from a book. In fact, teaching students with visual impairments and deafblindness is a topic that is difficult to cover comprehensively in the limited time allotted to professional preparation courses (Lieberman, Houston-Wilson, Kozub, 2002). Camp Abilities, a developmental sports camp for youth and adolescents with visual impairments and deafblindness, is held for one week each summer at SUNY in Brockport, New York, and other locations throughout the country. This camp is an excellent opportunity for professional preparation students to learn how to teach the deafblind population. For more information on Camp Abilities, visit www.campabilities.org. See the resource list for more great resources for educating individuals who are deafblind.

A major consideration with students with deafblindness is isolation. Some people who are deafblind move to communities where there are several other people who are deafblind. Many attend camps for other people who are deafblind. Physical education and sport can provide opportunities to reduce this isolation and introduce the person who is deafblind to rollerblading, swimming, biking, gymnastics, and other sports to increase socialization.

Deafblindness presents very limited opportunities for incidental learning—that is, the student needs to be taught everything. It is becoming more common to use an intervenor, a person who works one on one with the individual who is deafblind, signing exactly what is happening in the person's environment (Morgan, 2001). For example, the intervenor signs such complex information as "a child is on the swings over there," "the instructor just entered the room," and "Kelly is telling classmates what she did in the game yesterday." The range of communication methods is similar to the range for children who are only deaf. The exception with a child who is deafblind is that signing might need to be done in the child's limited field of vision, which might be close up to the child's face, far away from the child, or in a limited space. If there is no vision, signing might be done tactually in the deafblind child's hand. See figure 13.2 for an example of tactile sign language.

© Lauren J. Lieberman

Figure 13.2 A sample of tactile sign language with a student with a cochlear implant.

Adaptations for Teaching

Many students who are deafblind will need modifications to successfully participate in regular activities. The teaching tips for children with visual impairments and for Deaf children also apply for students who are deafblind. Refer to the sidebar on page 232 for additional considerations when teaching students with deafblindness. Keep in mind that a multisensory approach is optimal when teaching these students. Modifications might include changing the rules, equipment, instruction, or environment, as described in chapter 2.

Students with deafblindness uncomplicated by additional disabilities can participate in most sports, both at a competitive and recreational level. Weight lifting, dance, roller skating, swimming, skiing, bowling, hiking, goal ball, track and field, cycling, and canoeing are some of the possibilities. As with students who are visually impaired, it is important to teach a combination of open and closed skills. Deafblind athletes wishing to compete in sports might choose to compete in sports for persons who are blind (USABA) or deaf (USADSF).

An experience with a student named Eddie might illustrate the importance of not placing ceilings on expectations for students who are deafblind. Eddie is 15 years old, Deaf, and blind.

He asked to learn to ride a unicycle. Using the same task analysis his physical education teacher had used to learn to ride, Eddie learned to ride the unicycle independently. Teaching students who are deafblind challenges physical educators to adapt appropriately to enable these students to learn.

SUMMARY

This chapter reviews types of deafness, characteristics, strategies for teaching, issues related to cochlear implants, Deaf sport, and deafblindness. Children with sensory impairments are born with the same potential as their hearing and sighted peers. Early intervention and exposure to a variety of sports and physical activities increases fitness and skill level and helps maintain a high quality of life. Physical educators are key in instilling confidence in movement among Deaf, hard-of-hearing, and deafblind individuals.

REFERENCES

Best, C., Lieberman, L.J., & Arndt, K. (2002). The use of interpreters in physical education. *Journal of Physical Education, Recreation and Dance, 73*(8), 45-50.

Butterfield, S.A. (1988). Deaf children in physical education. *Palaestra, 6*(4) 28-30, 52.

Ellis, K.M. (2001). Influences of parents and school on sports participation and fitness levels of deaf children. *Palaestra, 17*(1), 44-49.

Graybill, P., & Cokely, D. (1993). *Introduction to the Deaf community, videotape.* Burtonsville, MD: Sign Media.

Graziadei, A. (1998). *Learning outcomes of deaf and hard of hearing students in mainstreamed physical education classes.* Unpublished doctoral dissertation, University of Maryland, College Park.

Hilgenbrinck, L., Pyfer, J., & Castle, N. (2004). Students with cochlear implants: Teaching considerations for physical educators. *Journal of Physical Education, Recreation and Dance, 75*(4), 28-33.

Individuals With Disabilities Education Act Amendments of 1997. U.S. Public Laws 105-17. *Federal Register,* 4 June, 1997.

Lieberman, L.J., Dunn, J.M., van der Mars, H., & McCubbin, J.A. (2000). Peer tutors' effects on activity levels of deaf students in inclusive elementary physical education. *Adapted Physical Activity Quarterly, 17*(1), 20-39.

Lieberman, L.J., Houston-Wilson, C., (2002). *Strategies for inclusion: A handbook for physical educators.* Champaign, IL: Human Kinetics.

Lieberman, L.J., Houston-Wilson, C., & Kozub, F. (2002). Perceived barriers to including students with visual impairments and blindness into physical education. *Adapted Physical Activity Quarterly, 19*(3), 364-377.

Lieberman, L.J., & MacVicar, J. (2003). Play and recreation habits of youth who are deaf-blind. *Journal of Visual Impairment and Blindness, 97*(12), 755-768

Lieberman, L.J., Volding, L., & Winnick, J.P. (2004). A comparison of the motor development of Deaf children of Deaf parents and hearing parents. *American Annals for the Deaf, July.*

McInnes, J.M. (1999). *A guide to planning and support for individuals who are deafblind.* Toronto, Canada: University of Toronto Press.

Moores, D.F. (1996). *Educating the Deaf: Psychology, principles, and practices* (4th ed.). Boston: Houghton Mifflin.

Morgan, S. (2001). "What is my role?" A comparison of the responsibilities of interpreters, intervenors, and support service providers. *Deaf-Blind Perspectives,* 9(1), 1-3.

Nowell, R., & Innes, J. (1997). *Educating children who are deaf or hard of hearing: Inclusion.* Reston, VA: *ERIC Clearinghouse on Disabilities and Gifted Education.* ERIC Digest # E557.

Office of Special Education and Rehabilitative Services (OSE/RS), 34 CFR 300 (2002).

Paciorek, M.J., & Jones, J.A. (2001). *Disability sport and recreation resources* (3rd ed.). Carmel, IN: Cooper.

Registry of Interpreters for the Deaf. (2002). *RID's code of ethics.* Retrieved January, 13, 2002, from www.rid.org/coe.html.

Sauerburger, D. (1993). *Independence without sight and sound.* New York, NY: American Foundation for the Blind.

Stewart, D.A. (1991). *Deaf sport: The impact of sports within the deaf community.* Washington, DC: Gallaudet University.

Stewart, D., Dummer, G., & Haubenstricker, J. (1990). Review of administration procedures used to assess the motor skills of deaf children and youth. *Adapted Physical Activity Quarterly,* 7, 231-239.

Winnick, J. P., & Short, F. X. (1986). Physical fitness of adolescents with auditory impairments. *Adapted Physical Activity Quarterly,* 3, 58-66.

WRITTEN RESOURCES

Lieberman, L.J. (1996). *Adapting games, sports, and recreation for children and adults who are deaf-blind.* Deaf-Blind Perspectives, 3(3) 1-5. Available through Deaf Blind Link.

This fact sheet presents information on how to adapt games and sports for persons who are deafblind.

McInnes, J.M. (1999). *A guide to planning and support for individuals who are deaf-blind.* Toronto, ON: University of Toronto Press.

This book takes an international perspective on teaching students who are deafblind. Teaching strategies, modifications, communication techniques, and curriculum ideas are abundant in this excellent resource

Stewart, D., & Kluwin, T.N. (2002). Teaching deaf and hard-of-hearing students: Content, strategies and curriculum. Needham Heights, MA: Allyn & Bacon.

A book written by individuals who are Deaf themselves. Highlights teaching techniques and instructional strategies beneficial to Deaf children.

Smith, T. (2002). Guidelines: Practical tips for working and socializing with deafblind people. Burtonsville, MD: Sign Media.

This excellent resource offers a step-by-step guide to working and socializing with deafblind individuals.

AUDIOVISUAL RESOURCES

Graybill, P., & Cokely, D. *Introduction to the Deaf community.* (Videotape, 1993). Burtonsville, MD: Sign Media, 4020 Blackburn Lane, Burtonsville, MD 20866; 301-421-0268.

Basic information is provided to assist hearing persons interact comfortably with Deaf persons. The running time is about 30 minutes.

ELECTRONIC RESOURCES

American Association for the Deaf-blind: www.aadb.org e-mail aadb@rols.com.

This is the home Web site for the American Association for the Deaf-Blind (AADB). Information about annual activities, membership, and current issues are provided. For more information, contact AADB, 814 Thayer Avenue, Suite 302, Silver Springs, MD 20910-4500; TTY 301-588-6545; relay 800-735-2258; fax 301-588-8705.

The CHARGE Syndrome Foundation: www.chargesyndrome.org.

This is the web site for the CHARGE Syndrome Foundation where there is information on CHARGE syndrome.

Comité International des Sports des Sourds: www.ciss.org.

This site provides information on the CISS member organizations and committees, regional federations, calendar of sports events, CISS bulletin, and photo gallery. For more information, contact John M. Lovett, CISS President, 31 Clive Street, East Brighton, Victoria 3187, Australia.

USA Deaf Sport Federation: www.usadsf.org.

Provides information about USADSF competition, events calendar, history of the organization, and news. For more information, contact Dr. Bobbie Beth Scoggins, USADSF President, 911 Tierra Linda Drive, Frankfort, KY 40601-4633; TTY 801-393-7916; fax 801-393-2263.

Cerebral Palsy, Traumatic Brain Injury, and Stroke

David L. Porretta

He was once one of the most feared defensemen in the National Hockey League. But following a near fatal automobile accident, Vladimir Constantinov acquired a brain injury severe enough that he might never skate independently again. Within a short time he went from a highly skilled hockey player to an individual who needed to relearn many motor skills and sports skills he had once taken for granted. No doubt Vladimir Constantinov will play hockey again—but it might be in a wheelchair and in a game adapted to his needs. In this chapter we will discuss traumatic brain injury and other conditions that cause damage to the brain, including cerebral palsy and stroke. Physical education teachers and coaches must be aware of problems associated with damage to the brain and the possible ways in which brain conditions can affect the learning process. With the help of **adapted physical educators, allied health professionals,** and **physicians,** individuals such as Constantinov can enjoy physical education and sport in settings that are safe, enjoyable, and beneficial to health.

Although cerebral palsy (CP), stroke, and traumatic brain injury (TBI) have their own causes, each of these conditions results in damage to the brain. Thus, people with CP, stroke, and TBI might exhibit common motor, cognitive, and behavioral characteristics. Discussing them together in this chapter highlights their commonalties. Individuals with CP, stroke, and TBI at one time were restricted from physical activity for fear that it would aggravate their conditions. Now they are encouraged to participate in a wide range of physical education and sport activities.

CEREBRAL PALSY

Cerebral palsy (CP) is a group of permanent disabling symptoms resulting from damage to the motor control areas of the brain. It is a nonprogressive condition that might originate before, during, or shortly after birth; it manifests itself in a loss or impairment of control over voluntary musculature. The term *cerebral* refers to brain and *palsy* to disordered movement or posture. Depending on the location and the amount of damage to the brain, symptoms vary widely, ranging from severe (total inability to control bodily movements) to very mild (only a slight speech impairment). Damage to the brain contributes to abnormal reflex development in most individuals; this results in difficulty coordinating and integrating basic movement patterns. It is rare for damage to be isolated in a small portion of the brain. For this reason, the person with CP commonly exhibits many other impairments, possibly including seizures, speech and language disorders, sensory impairments (especially those involving visual–motor control), abnormal sensation and perception, and intellectual disability. CP can result from a myriad of prenatal, natal, or postnatal causes. Some of the more common causes are rubella, Rh incompatibility, prematurity, birth trauma, anoxia, meningitis, poisoning, brain hemorrhages or tumors, and other forms of brain injury caused by accidents or abuse. It is interesting to note that a premature infant is five times more likely than a full-term baby to have CP.

Incidence

According to the most recent figures published by the United Cerebral Palsy Associations, Inc. (2002), it is estimated that there are between 550,000 and 764,000 people in the United States with CP. Of this number about 10 percent of the cases are considered to be acquired—that is, they occur during the first two years of life. Most of the acquired cases are a consequence of some form of head trauma. The number of new cases of children with CP has increased 25 percent over the past decade. It is estimated that about 8,000 babies and infants are diagnosed with CP each year. In addition, about 1,200 to 1,500 preschool-age children are identified each year as having CP. However, enhanced technology and treatment in neonatal intensive care units have led to a decrease in the number of high-risk infants who might have otherwise acquired the condition. The most recent data from eight European countries suggest that their figures are quite similar to those of the United States (Johnson, 2002).

Classifications

Individuals with CP typically exhibit a variety of observable symptoms, depending on the degree and location of brain damage. Over the years, classification schemes have evolved that categorize CP according to topographical (anatomical site), neuromotor (medical), and functional perspectives (of which the functional classification is the most recent).

Topographical

The topographical classification is based on the body segments afflicted and is typically used by the medical community. Classes include the following:

- Monoplegia—any one body part involved
- Diplegia—major involvement of both lower limbs and minor involvement of both upper limbs
- Hemiplegia—involvement of one complete side of the body (arm and leg)
- Paraplegia—involvement of both lower limbs only
- Triplegia—any three limbs involved (a rare occurrence)
- Quadriplegia—also known as total body involvement (all four limbs, head, neck, and trunk).

Neuromotor

The American Academy for Cerebral Palsy currently uses a neuromotor classification system to describe cerebral palsy. This classification has undergone revisions over the years. Today, three main types are commonly described (United Cerebral Palsy Associations, 2003). It is important to understand that the characteristics described under each type might overlap each other; they are not as distinct as one would assume. The most common overlapping symptoms include spastic and athetoid movements.

Spasticity

Spasticity results from damage to motor areas of the cerebrum and is characterized by increased muscle tone (hypertonicity), primarily of the flexors and internal rotators, which might lead to permanent contractures and bone deformities. Strong, exaggerated muscle contractions are common, and in some cases muscles continue to contract repetitively. Spasticity is associated with a hyperactive stretch reflex. The hyperactive reflex can be elicited, for example, when muscles of the anterior forearm (flexors) are quickly stretched in order to extend the wrist. When this happens, receptors that control tone in the stretched muscles overreact, causing the stretched muscles to contract. This results in inaccurate and jerky movement, with the wrist assuming a flexed position as opposed to an extended or middle position. If muscles of the upper limb are prone to spasticity, the shoulder will be adducted, the arm will be carried toward the midline of the body, and the forearm will be flexed and pronated. The wrist will be hyperflexed, and the hand will be fisted.

Lower-limb involvement results in hip flexion, with the thigh pulling toward the midline, causing the leg to cross during ambulation. Lower-limb involvement causes flexion at the knee joint because of tight hamstring muscles. Increased tone in both the gastrocnemius and soleus muscles, along with a shortened Achilles tendon, contributes to excessive plantar flexion of the foot. A scissoring gait characterized by flexion of the hip, knee, and ankle along with rotation of the leg toward the midline is exhibited (figure 14.1). With their narrow base of support, people with a scissoring gait typically have problems with balance and locomotor activities. Because of increased muscle contraction and limited range of motion, they might have difficulty running, jumping, and throwing properly. Intellectual disability, seizures, and perceptual disorders are more common in spasticity than in any other type of CP.

Athetosis

Damage to the basal ganglia (masses of gray matter composed of neurons located deep within the cerebral hemispheres of the brain) results in

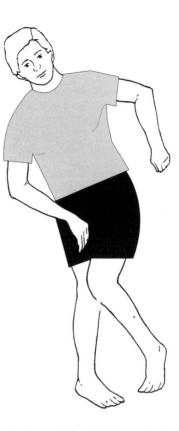

Figure 14.1   Person exhibiting spastic cerebral palsy.

an overflow of motor impulses to the muscles, a condition known as athetosis. In some cases basal ganglia damage can be caused by blood incompatibility problems during birth. However, most blood incompatibility problems can now be controlled. Slow, writhing movements that are uncoordinated and involuntary are characteristic of this type of CP. Muscle tone tends to fluctuate from hypertonicity to hypotonicity; the fluctuation typically affects muscles that control the head, neck, limbs, and trunk. Severe difficulty in head control is usually exhibited, with head drawn back and positioned to one side. Facial grimacing, a protruding tongue, and trouble controlling salivation are common. The individual has difficulty eating, drinking, and speaking. Because lack of head control affects visual pursuit, individuals might have difficulty tracking thrown balls or responding to quick movements made by others in motor activity situations. They will have difficulty performing movements that require accuracy, such as throwing a ball to a target or kicking a moving ball. A lordotic standing posture in which the lumbar spine assumes an abnormal anterior curve is common. In compensation, the arms and shoulders are placed in a forward position. Individuals with athetosis typically exhibit aphasia (impairment or loss of language) and articulation difficulties.

Ataxia

Damage to the cerebellum, which normally regulates balance and muscle coordination, results in a condition known as ataxia (figure 14.2). The cerebellum is located below and essentially behind the cerebral cortex. Muscles show abnormal degrees of hypotonicity. Ataxia is usually not diagnosed until the child attempts to walk. When trying to walk, the individual is extremely unsteady because of balance difficulties and lacks the coordination necessary for proper arm and leg movement. A wide-based gait is typically exhibited. Nystagmus, a constant involuntary movement of the eyeball, is commonly observed, and individuals able to ambulate frequently fall. People with mild forms of ataxia are often considered clumsy or awkward. They have difficulty with basic motor skills and patterns, especially locomotor activities such as running, jumping, and skipping.

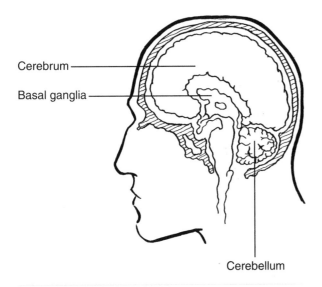

Figure 14.2 General areas of the brain involved in major neuromotor types of cerebral palsy.

Adapted, by permission, from P.D. Miller, 1995, *Fitness programming and physical disability* (Champaign, IL: Human Kinetics), 16.

Functional

A functional classification scheme is commonly used today in the field of education. According to this classification system, individuals are placed into one of eight ability classes according to the severity of the disability (table 14.1). Class I denotes severe impairment, whereas class VIII denotes minimal impairment. This scheme has

important implications for physical education and sport because individuals are categorized according to ability levels. For example, participants in classes VII and VIII might be good candidates for inclusion in several regular physical education activities. Teachers and coaches can also use this system, as does the National Disability Sports Alliance (NDSA), formerly known as the United States Cerebral Palsy Athletic Association (NDSA, 2002), and the Cerebral Palsy–International Sport and Recreation Association (CP–ISRA) to assist in equalizing competition among participants. In activities requiring competition between two individuals, players of the same classification can compete against each other. In team activities, players of the same class can be placed on separate teams so that each team is composed of players of similar functional levels. These suggestions for equalizing competition can be followed in either inclusive or noninclusive settings.

General Educational Considerations

Because CP is not a disease, most medical professionals agree that CP is not treated but rather managed. Management for CP is aimed at alleviating symptoms caused by damage to the brain and helping the child achieve maximum potential in growth and development. This consists of managing both motor and other associated disabilities. Managing motor dysfunction usually entails developing voluntary muscle control, emphasizing muscle relaxation, and increasing functional motor skills. In some instances, braces and orthotic devices are used to help prevent permanent contractures or to support affected muscle groups; this is especially true for those with spasticity. Surgery can be performed to lengthen contracted tendons (especially the Achilles tendon) or to reposition an unimpaired muscle to perform the movement of an impaired one. A repositioning operation known as the Eggar's procedure relieves flexion at the knee joint and helps to extend the hip by transferring the insertion of the hamstrings from the pelvis to the femur. In rare instances, brain surgery can be performed to alleviate extreme hypertonicity. A procedure known as chronic cerebellar stimulation (CCS), in which electrodes are surgically implanted on the cerebellum, has recently been developed. This procedure has demonstrated improvement; however, long-range effects on the central nervous system have not yet been documented, and it seems

Table 14.1   Functional Classification Profiles for Cerebral Palsy Used by NDSA and CPISRA

Class	Description	Locomotion	Object control
I	Severe spasticity or athetosis with poor functional range of motion and strength in all extremities; poor to nonexistent trunk control	Motorized wheelchair or assistance for mobility	Only thumb opposition and one finger possible; can grasp only beanbag
II	Severe to moderate spastic or athetoid quadriplegic; poor functional strength in all extremities, and poor trunk control; classified as II lower if one or both lower extremities are functional; otherwise classified as II upper	Propels wheelchair on level surfaces and slight inclines (lower class II with leg only); sometimes might be able to ambulate short distances with assistance	Can manipulate and throw a ball (II upper)
III	Moderate quadriplegic or triplegic; severe hemiplegia; fair to normal strength in one upper extremity	Can propel wheelchair independently but might walk a short distance with assistance or assistive devices	Normal grasp of round objects but release is slow; limited extension in follow-through with dominant arm
IV	Moderate to severe diplegic; good functional strength and minimal control problems in upper extremities and torso	Assistive devices used for distances; wheelchair is usually used for sport	Normal grasp is seen in all sports; normal follow-through is evident pushing a wheelchair or throwing
V	Moderate to severe diplegic or hemiplegic; moderate to severe involvement in one or both legs; good functional strength; good balance when assistive devices are used	No wheelchair; might or might not use assistive devices	Minimal control problems in upper limbs; normal opposition and grasp seen in all sports
VI	Moderate to severe quadriplegic (spastic–athetoid or ataxic); fluctuating muscle tone producing involuntary movements in trunk and both sets of extremities; greater upper-limb involvement when spasticity or athetosis present	Ambulates without aids; function can vary; running gait can show better mechanics than when walking	Spastic–athetoid grasp–release can be significantly affected when throwing
VII	Moderate to minimal spastic hemiplegic; good functional ability on nonaffected side	Walks and runs without assistive devices but has marked asymmetrical action; obvious Achilles tendon shortening when standing	Minimal control problems with grasp and release in dominant hand; minimal limitation seen in dominant throwing arm
VIII	Minimal hemiplegic, monoplegic, diplegic, or quadriplegic; might have minimal coordination problems; good balance	Runs and jumps freely with little to no limp; gait demonstrates minimal or no asymmetry when walking or running; perhaps slight loss of coordination in one leg or minimal Achilles tendon shortening	Minimal incoordination of hands

Adapted, by permission, from National Disability Sports Alliance, 2002, *NDSA sports rules manual*, 6th ed. (Kingston, RI: National Disability Sports Alliance), 6-13.

that this procedure results in little direct clinical application at this time. Some research questions now being addressed by the United Cerebral Palsy Research and Educational Foundation and other organizations include the following: What are the risk factors that predispose the developing brain to injury? Why are prematurity and low birth weight in full-term infants important risk factors for CP? Which available treatments are most effective for disabilities of individuals with CP?

Because of central nervous system damage, many individuals with CP exhibit abnormal reflex development that interferes with the acquisition of voluntary movement. If abnormal reflex patterns are present, young children with CP most likely receive some type of physical therapy designed to inhibit abnormal reflex activity in addition to enhancing flexibility and body alignment. However, recent scientific data show that passive activities and manipulations during the early years might not provide as much assistance in the remediation of abnormal reflex activity as once thought. Treatment emphasis should be directed toward having individuals perform and refine motor tasks through active self-control. Functional motor skills such as walking, running, and throwing should be developed and attained.

Attention must also be given to the psychological and social development of individuals with CP. The disabilities associated with CP increase the possibility of adjustment problems. Because of the negative reactions that other people might have to their condition, individuals with CP might not be totally accepted. As a result, guidance from psychologists or professional counselors should be sought for both parents and their children when emotional conflicts arise.

The primary concern should be for the *total* person. From an educational perspective, a team approach in which both medical and educational personnel work together with the parent and, when appropriate, with the student, is strongly recommended.

TRAUMATIC BRAIN INJURY

Traumatic brain injury (TBI) refers to an injury to the brain that might produce a diminished or altered state of consciousness and result in impairments of physical, cognitive, social, behavioral, and emotional functioning. Possible physical impairments include lack of coordination, difficulty planning and sequencing movements, muscle spasticity, headaches, speech disorders, paralysis, and seizures as well as a variety of sensory impairments (including vision and hearing problems). Physical impairments often cause varying degrees of orthopedic involvement that require the use of crutches or wheelchairs. Even when individuals exhibit no loss of coordination, motor function deficits, or sensation, apraxia might be evident. Cognitive impairments many times result in short- or long-term memory deficits, poor attention and concentration, altered perception, communication disorders in such skills as reading and writing, slowness in planning and sequencing, and poor judgment. Social, emotional, and behavioral impairments might include mood swings, lack of motivation, lowered self-esteem, self-centeredness, inability to self monitor, difficulty with impulse control, perseveration, depression, sexual dysfunction, excessive laughing or crying, and difficulty relating to others. Any or all of these impairments vary greatly depending on the extent and location of damage to the brain and the success of the rehabilitation process. Thus, impairments could range from mild to severe. However, with immediate and ongoing therapy these impairments sometimes decrease in severity. Because of the developmental nature of the central nervous system, children with TBI recover motor and verbal skills faster than adults. However, children's head injuries tend to be more diffuse than focal. A diffuse injury might affect the entire range of academic achievement and, thus, has significant educational implications for the child.

TBI is often referred to as the "silent epidemic" because impairments continue although no external visible signs are present on or around the face and head area. TBI can result from motor vehicle, sports and recreation accidents, child abuse, assaults and violence, and accidental falls. In addition, TBI can be caused from lack of oxygen (anoxia), cardiac arrest, or near drowning. Motor vehicle accidents, violence, and falls are the leading causes of TBI.

Brain injuries cause more deaths than any other sports injury. The Brain Injury Association of America (2001) has compiled information pertaining brain injuries related to various sports and recreational activities. For example, brain injury accounts for about 75 percent of all football deaths and 60 percent of all equestrian-related deaths. In soccer, about 5 percent of players sustain a brain injury. As a subgroup, children are especially at risk of brain injury. According to Appleton (1998), the majority of head injuries to children and adolescents are a result of one of the following:

- Road traffic accidents (pedestrian, passenger, cyclist)
- Falls from buildings, play equipment, or trees
- Injuries from objects (e.g., golf club, ball, stones, firearm)
- Child abuse
- Sports-related injuries (e.g., horseback riding, skateboarding, rollerblading, football)
- Seizures and other causes of lost consciousness

Because TBI is so common, it is now identified as a separate categorical condition in the Individuals with Disabilities Education Act (IDEA). In addition, in 1996 Congress passed the Traumatic Brain Injury Act (PL 104-166) authorizing states to obtain information on incidence, causes, and severity of brain injury.

Incidence

TBI is the leading killer and cause of disability in children and young adults under 45 years of age in the United States. It is estimated that 5.3 million people in the United States live with functional loss resulting from brain injuries. Every year in the United States about 1.5 million people sustain a new TBI (Palmer-McLean & Harbst, 2003). Of this number, hundreds of thousands die or sustain an injury severe enough to require hospitalization. Of those who survive, approximately 85,000 have a permanent long-term disability. Twice as many males are likely to sustain a TBI than females, and the highest rate of injury is among young males between the ages of 14 and 24.

Classification

Generally there are two classifications of head injury: open head injury and closed head injury. An open head injury might result from an accident, gunshot wound, or blow to the head by an object resulting in a visible injury. A closed head injury might be caused by severe shaking, anoxia, and cranial hemorrhages, among other causes. If the head injury is closed, damage to the brain is usually diffuse, but if the head injury is open (e.g., a bullet wound) damage is usually to a more limited area of the brain. In a closed head injury, the brain is actually shaken back and forth within the skull. This type of injury either bruises or tears nerve fibers in the brain that send messages to other parts of the central nervous system and all parts of the body. TBI can range from very mild to severe. Severe brain injury is characterized by a prolonged state in which the person is unconscious (comatose) and a number of functional limitations remain following rehabilitation. An injury to the brain can be considered minor when no formal rehabilitation program is prescribed and the person is sent directly home from the hospital. However, minor brain injury should never be treated as unimportant.

The Ranchos Los Amigos Hospital Scale describes eight levels of cognitive functioning and is typically used in the first few weeks or months following injury. These levels consist of the following:

Level 1—No response: deep sleep or coma

Level 2—Generalized response: inconsistent and nonspecific response to stimuli

Level 3—Localized response: might follow simple commands in an inconsistent and delayed manner; vague awareness of self

Level 4—Confused or agitated response: severely decreased ability to process information; poor discrimination and attention span

Level 5—Confused and inappropriate response: consistent reaction to simple commands; highly distractible; in need of frequent redirection

Level 6—Confused and appropriate response —responses might be incorrect because of memory loss but are appropriate to the situation; exhibits retention of tasks relearned; inconsistently oriented

Level 7—automatic and appropriate: oriented and appropriate behavior but lacks insight; poor judgment and problem solving; requires minimal supervision

Level 8—purposeful and appropriate: ability to integrate recent and past events; requires no supervision once new activities are learned

This scale should not be used in later years as a gauge for improved function.

General Educational Considerations

Many people with TBI, depending on the severity of the injury, need an individualized rehabilitative program. Individuals suffering from severe injury initially need to be provided intense rehabilitation in which therapy begins as soon as the patient is medically stable. An interdisciplinary team of medical professionals (e.g., physicians, nurses, speech and occupational therapists) provide such a therapy program, which usually lasts for three to four months, depending on the nature of the injury. For individuals of school age, the rehabilitative program takes precedence over educational considerations. According to Wehman, Keyser-Marcus, West, Target, & Bricout (2001), reentry planning needs to occur immediately following hospital admission. Hospital outreach personnel (e.g., social worker) should contact appropriate school personnel. Ongoing communication should include the child's status and prognosis, implications for school services, accessing school records, and providing education to family, school personnel, and peers.

Following the acute rehabilitation program, individuals are provided a long-term rehabilitation program, which provides a structured environment for those who make slow improvements. As long as progress is being made, school-age individuals remain at this level of rehabilitation and typically receive their educational program within the rehabilitative facility.

Some individuals, because of the severity of their injuries, require extended therapy programs following long-term care. These extended and structured therapy programs might last from 6 to 12 months following injury and usually emphasize cognitive skills, speech therapy, activities of daily living, the relearning of social skills, recreation therapy, and, when appropriate, prevocational and vocational training. Individualized educational programming continues in this environment. Only after individuals have attained the maximum benefit of rehabilitation programs will they re-enter their local educational environment.

Educators play a key role in the overall rehabilitation and educational process. Ylvisaker and Feeney (1998) stress that educational re-entry programs need to be flexible and creative. And because of the uniqueness of each person, no one re-entry program fits every student with TBI. Rather, educators should rely on basic principles to guide the implementation of their re-entry programs. These principles include the following: (1) each student should present unique cognitive, behavioral, and psychosocial challenges, (2) assessments need to be functional, collaborative, and contextualized, (3) supports (e.g., teacher's aide) need to be systematically reduced when appropriate, and (4) collaborative decision making (among educators, rehabilitation professionals, parents, student, and possibly others) should be fostered.

Educators need to work closely and cooperatively with the student's family to ensure the best re-entry educational program possible. Walker (1997) recommends that when building effective parent–professional partnerships teachers must do the following:

- Remember that collaboration means sharing control with parents in educational planning

- Acknowledge the value of parents as the primary decision makers in determining quality of life and intervention decisions on behalf of their child
- Strive to establish and maintain rapport and trust in relationships with parents in order to negotiate family-centered decisions
- Strive for educational programs that include equal proportions of parent and professional goals,
- Work to resolve disagreements and interpersonal tension between them and parents. Establishing positive relationships with parents of students with TBI is important. This can be a stressful time for parents, who up to this point in their child's education did not need to interact with special education teachers and therapists.

The development and implementation of transitional plans for high school–age students with TBI is of particular educational importance. Educators are encouraged to follow a functional skills transitional approach. Transitional skills related to physical education include learning recreation and leisure activities such as bowling, cycling, or swimming as well as learning to access community recreation facilities. Regardless of the transitional outcomes agreed on, educators must plan appropriate school experiences and establish links with community and postschool (e.g., vocational or technical schools) resources. See the application example for more information.

Several instructional strategies are recommended for teachers and coaches. Top-down instruction (Driver, Harmon, & Block, 2003) emphasizing functional activities is one such strategy. Functional physical activities are identified that the student enjoys and that can be performed within the student's community environment. The instructor then assesses the student to determine what elements of the activity need to be learned for the student to be successful. Some additional instructional strategies include using frequent reminders regarding tasks to be completed, providing additional time for review, rewriting or re-explaining complex directions into simple steps, using cooperative learning activities so that the student is not required to complete an entire task alone, having the student use a diary or datebook (or Palm Pilot) to help organize information, breaking up a task into smaller and distinct sequential parts

APPLICATION EXAMPLE

Transition

Setting: Hector is a 16-year-old male with traumatic brain injury. He uses a wheelchair and has lost many of the sport-related skills he learned previous to his injury.

Task: Teach functional recreation and leisure skills so that Hector can successfully maintain a healthy, active lifestyle during adulthood.

Application: Skills and activities once deemed important and necessary in regular secondary physical education might now need to be reevaluated relative to Hector's functional needs.

To determine the functional recreation and leisure skills and activities to be learned, the physical education teacher needs to

- be part of Hector's IEP team;
- consult with therapists and educators;
- talk with Hector's parents about their hopes and expectations for Hector after graduation;
- seek Hector's input about his interests and desires in leisure-time activities;
- identify, contact, and visit community resource centers (e.g., the local YMCA, recreation, and adult fitness centers) that can provide services to Hector after graduation; and
- implement Hector's physical education program in at least one site (when feasible) to aid him in the transitional process.

---

so that they can be put together meaningfully at the end, and color-coding materials for each class or activity.

STROKE

Stroke (**cerebral vascular accident** [CVA]) refers to damage to brain tissue resulting from problems caused by faulty blood circulation. Stroke can result in serious damage to areas of the brain that control vital functions. These functions might include motor ability and control, sensation and perception, communication, emotions, and consciousness, among others. In certain cases, stroke results in death. Individuals who survive a stroke have varying degrees of disability, ranging from minimal loss of function to total dependency. Because of the nature of the cerebral arterial system, stroke commonly causes partial or total paralysis on either the left or right side of the body. This might be one limb (monoplegia) or body segment or one entire side (hemiplegia). Individuals with right-sided hemiplegia are likely to have problems with speech and language; they tend to be slow, cautious, and disorganized when approaching new or unfamiliar problems. Individuals with left-sided hemiplegia are likely to have difficulty with spatial–perceptual tasks (e.g., ability to judge distance, size, position, rate of movement, form, and how parts relate to the whole) and tend to

overestimate their abilities. They often try to do things they cannot do and that might be unsafe. This trait has significant implications for those performing in physical education, leisure, and sport settings.

According to Yager (1999) stroke during the neonatal period might present itself as acute hemiparesis with or without seizures. However, there might be no detectable neurological signs at onset. Rather, neurological signs might appear during the first year after the stroke as motor skills develop. Children who exhibit seizures tend to have a worse prognosis for intellectual development and an increased incidence of recurrent seizures than those who do not.

Several factors contribute to the occurrence of stroke, including uncontrolled hypertension (high blood pressure), smoking, diabetes mellitus, diet, drug abuse (such as heroin and cocaine), obesity, and alcohol abuse, among others. Many of these risk factors can be controlled through lifestyle changes. The past few years have seen a substantial increase in the amount of knowledge regarding stroke and how it is treated, especially regarding the promotion of healthful behaviors. For example, in a controlled study, leisure-time physical activity has been shown to decrease the occurrence of stroke in elderly, multiethnic, urban U.S. participants (Sacco et al., 1998). In a longitudinal study outside of the United States it was found that physical activity is associated with a reduced risk of death from stroke in middle-aged and elderly women (Ellekjaer, Holmen, Ellekjaer, & Vatten, 2000). As a result of better education and treatment, more people are living who otherwise might have died because of stroke.

Depending on the location of the damage, symptoms mirror those of CP and TBI. Individuals might exhibit cognitive or perceptual deficits, motor deficits, seizure disorders, and communication problems, among others. That is why a collaborative approach to stroke rehabilitation is necessary. Whereas individuals with TBI and stroke can expect varying degrees of improvement following their injury, individuals with CP cannot. Research indicates that children show more improvement following brain trauma (TBI and stroke) than adults do.

Incidence

Stroke is a leading cause of long-term disability in the United States. About 4.7 million people in the United States are living today with neurological impairment because of stroke. About 750,000 people experience a stroke each year (Palmer-McLean & Harbst, 2003). In 2000, females accounted for 61 percent of all stroke fatalities. Stroke is the third largest cause of death in the United States following heart disease and cancer. Recent statistics also indicate that more than half of all individuals experiencing a stroke will survive their first stroke, although only about 10 percent of these individuals completely recover. Males have a higher incidence rate than females, and black individuals are more prone to strokes than white individuals. Typically, stroke affects older segments of the population and is a common form of adult disability. However, current data (American Stroke Association, 2002) indicate that 28 percent of annual stroke victims are younger than 65 years of age. Stroke occurring in infants, children, and adolescents is relatively rare but has significant implications for educators.

Classification

Although there are many types, stroke can generally be divided into two categories: **hemorrhagic** and **ischemic.** Hemorrhage within the brain is a result of an artery that loses its elasticity and ruptures, resulting in blood flowing into and around brain tissue. This type of hemorrhage is commonly called cerebral hemorrhage and is the most serious form of stroke. Ischemia, on the other hand, refers to the lack of an appropriate blood supply to brain tissue. The lack of blood results from a blocked artery leading to or within the brain itself. Typically, the blockage results from a progressive narrowing of the artery or from an embolism. An embolism is usually a blood clot or piece of fat deposit (plaque) that lodges in small arteries. An insufficient or absent blood supply means that oxygen, vital for proper brain functioning, is absent or diminished. This interruption might be permanent or for a brief period of time. If the attack is very brief, it is termed a transient ischemic attack (TIA). About 10 percent of all strokes are preceded by a TIA, which might occur days, weeks, or months before a major stroke. This type of ischemia results in full recovery but might indicate a future attack that is more severe. Aside from a TIA, when an individual experiences a hemorrhagic or ischemic stroke, brain tissue (cells) dies, which results in long-term reduced brain function or death.

General Educational Considerations

Although many strokes strike without warning, some people receive warning signs. Teachers and coaches should be aware of common warning signs of stroke, including sudden weakness or numbness of the face or an arm and leg on one side of the body, sudden dimness or loss of vision in only one eye, sudden loss of speech or trouble understanding speech, sudden severe headache with no apparent cause, and unexplained dizziness, unsteadiness, or sudden falls, especially with any of the previous symptoms. Teachers and coaches should have students with any of these symptoms seek medical attention immediately. If a student showing one or more symptoms has heart or circulatory problems or has experienced a previous stroke or brain injury, consider the situation an emergency.

Immediately following a stroke, individuals surviving will need to be placed on a planned, systematic, and individualized rehabilitation program. The intensity and duration of the rehabilitation program depends on the degree of disability. Someone who exhibits paresis (muscle weakness) or paralysis in one limb and retains normal voluntary movement for the remainder of the body will need little in the form of therapy. But someone who exhibits complete paralysis of all four limbs will need intense, long-term therapy. From an educational standpoint, individuals of school age will follow a school re-entry program similar to that followed by individuals with TBI, as described in the previous section.

PROGRAM IMPLICATIONS

All people with CP, TBI, or CVA (stroke) can benefit from physical education and sport activities. The type and degree of physical disability, motor educability, interest level, and overall educational goals determine the modifications and adaptations required. With these factors taken into account, an IEP can be planned and implemented.

General Guidelines

Several guidelines apply to programs for individuals with CP, TBI, or CVA. The guidelines that follow pertain to safety considerations, physical fitness, motor development, psychosocial development, and implications for sports.

Safety Considerations

All programs should be conducted in a safe, secure environment in which students are free to explore the capabilities of their own bodies and to interact with surroundings that nurture their physical and motor development. Teachers and coaches should closely monitor games and activities, especially for individuals prone to seizures or who lack good judgment (e.g., individuals with TBI). In fact, about 60 percent of individuals with CP exhibit seizures or have tendencies toward seizures (Laskin, 2003). Many of these individuals take antiseizure medication and, as a result, side effects (e.g., slowing physiologic responses to exercise, irritability, hyperactivity) might affect the person's performance in physical education and sport activities.

Students with severe impairments need special equipment, such as crutches, bolsters (to support the upper body while in the prone position), standing platforms (to assist them in maintaining a standing posture), orthotic devices, or seating systems to help them perform certain motor tasks (figure 14.3). Most students with mild impairments require no specialized equipment. Because many individuals with physical disabilities have difficulty maintaining an erect posture for extended periods of time, some activities are best done in a prone, supine, or seated position.

Figure 14.3 Athlete with CP using crutches to assist in running.

Individuals with physical limitations should be encouraged to experience as many different postures as possible not only in physical education classes but also throughout the school day. This is particularly important for individuals in wheelchairs.

Because of abnormal muscle tone and reduced range of motion, many individuals with neuromotor involvement have difficulty moving voluntarily. The teacher might need to assist by getting a student into and out of activity positions, physically supporting him or her during activity, or helping him or her perform a skill or exercise. The teacher might also need to position students by applying degrees of pressure with the hands to key points of the body, such as the head, neck, spine, shoulders, elbows, hips, pelvis, knees, or ankles. An example is applying both hands symmetrically to both of the individual's elbows in order to reduce flexion at the elbow joints. However, these techniques should be performed only after instruction by a therapist or physician. The ultimate aim of handling, positioning, and lifting individuals with CP is to continually encourage them to move as independently as possible. This is accomplished by gradually reducing the amount of support to key points of the body over time. When possible, teachers should consult with therapists in an effort to coordinate these procedures, especially for individuals possessing severe physical disabilities. Finnie (1997) provides excellent information on appropriate ways to handle children with characteristics associated with CP. In addition, teachers should closely monitor the physical assistance that a student with a disability receives from trained peers. Peer assistance should be discouraged if it poses a safety risk.

Because the conditions described in this chapter are of medical origin, it is important that physical educators and coaches consult medical professionals when establishing programs to meet unique needs. This is especially important for students with TBI or those receiving physical or occupational therapy, such as students with CP and stroke.

Physical Fitness

It is generally agreed that appropriate levels of health-related physical fitness assist individuals with disabilities in performing activities of daily living, recreation, and leisure activities, which, in turn, promote a healthy lifestyle. Although the health-related physical fitness needs of individuals with CP, TBI, or CVA are similar to the needs of individuals without disabilities, some aspects of fitness are particularly important to individuals with CP, TBI, or CVA. Reduced muscular strength, flexibility, and cardiovascular endurance levels are common in individuals with CP, TBI, or CVA and might lead to the inability to maintain balance, independently transfer or move one's body, perform activities of daily living, or participate in functional leisure activities. Because restricted movement is common for individuals with CP, TBI, or CVA, it is vitally important that strength and flexibility be developed to the maximum extent possible. Weak musculature and limited range of motion, if unattended, will lead to permanent joint contractures that result in significant loss of movement capability. For example, individuals with more severe forms of spastic CP might have significant range of motion and flexibility needs. Individuals with TBI or who have experienced a stroke might have a need to develop and sustain an adequate level of aerobic activity, especially if the trauma is recent. Whatever health-related profiles individuals with CP, TBI, or CVA exhibit, a personalized approach to the enhancement of health-related fitness is recommended.

The Brockport Physical Fitness Test (BPFT; Winnick & Short, 1999a) is the most recent fitness assessment instrument used for individuals with CP, TBI, or CVA based on a personalized approach to health-related fitness. This criterion-referenced test provides test items, modifications for disabilities, and criterion-referenced standards for achieving fitness. The test includes components of aerobic functioning, body composition, and musculoskeletal functioning (flexibility, muscular strength and endurance) vital for achieving health-related physical fitness. Various test items may be selected within each of the three components, depending on the student's individual desired profile (e.g., a target aerobic movement test; upper arm skinfold measures for body composition; a modified Apley test for flexibility; seated push-ups for muscular strength and endurance). The BPFT incorporates the eight level functional classification system used by CP–ISRA and NDSA (see table 14.1), which identifies the person's functional level. Based on the person's functional level, specific test items are selected. Detailed information regarding this test can be found in chapter 4.

As is true for anyone who has a low health-related fitness level, certain precautions might need to be taken as programs are established for students with CP, TBI, or CVA. It is especially important that the teacher be sensitive to the frequency, intensity, duration, and mode of exercises and activities. Fatigue might cause the person to become frustrated, which might adversely affect proper performance. The instructor should permit rest periods and player substitutions when endurance-related activities such as soccer and basketball are offered. It might be beneficial for those with reduced fitness levels to perform exercises and activities more frequently but with less intensity and duration. Exercises and activities should be selected that are found enjoyable by individuals with CP, TBI, or CVA. Performing enjoyable exercises and activities increases the likelihood that health-related fitness will be maintained over a lifetime.

Motor Development

CP, TBI, and CVA restrict individuals from experiencing normal functional movement patterns essential to normal motor development. As a result, delays in motor control and development are common. Individuals with CP typically exhibit motor delays because they often have fewer opportunities to move, lack movement ability, or have difficulty in controlling movements. Individuals with varying degrees of TBI or CVA might have difficulty planning and performing movements because of damage to the motor control and related areas of the cerebrum. Children with CP and TBI are frequently unable to execute fundamental movements in an appropriate manner.

Physical education programs should encourage the sequential development of fundamental motor patterns and skills essential for participation in games, sports, and leisure activities. Authentic assessment, which emphasizes the evaluation of functional skills, should be used in physical education programs. When attempting to enhance motor development, the physical educator should be concerned primarily with the manner in which a movement is performed rather than with its outcome. The goal of every physical education program should be to encourage individuals to achieve maximum motor control and development related to functional activities (e.g., recreation and daily living activities). Standardized motor development tests recommended for use with younger students include the Denver Developmental Screening Test II, the Milani–Comparetti Developmental Chart, and the Peabody Developmental Motor Scale.

Psychosocial Development

Many people with CP, TBI, or CVA lack self-confidence, have low motivational levels, and exhibit problems with body image. An appropriately designed physical education program can provide successful movement experiences that motivate students and help them gain the self-confidence they need to develop a positive self-image, which is vitally important for emotional well-being. A realistic body image can be developed when the physical education teacher does not expect students to perform skills and activities perfectly. It is far more important that the student perform the activity as independently as possible with a specified degree of competence. The teacher should promote the attitude that it is acceptable to fail at times when attempting activities because failing is a natural part of the learning process. Physical activities perceived as fun and not hard work can motivate students to perform to their maximum potential.

Implications for Sports

Physical education teachers are encouraged to integrate many of the sport activities described in the Adapted Sport section of this chapter into their programs. For example, the club throw, a NDSA field event, can be incorporated into a physical education program as a means of developing strength and also offers an opportunity for sport

competition. The club resembles a thin wooden bowling pin. The athlete grasps the top or thin portion of the club and throws the club in the air as far as possible. Other events such as bowling, archery, cycling, and bocce can be taught. Bowling, bocce, and cycling are excellent activities for individuals to engage in for lifelong leisure. Team games and sports might include volleyball, basketball, soccer, and floor hockey.

Individual and dual activities include tennis, table tennis, riflery, archery, badminton, horseback riding, billiards, and track and field. Winter activities including ice hockey, ice skating, downhill and cross-country skiing, tobogganing, and sledding are also popular in northern regions. All of these games and sports can be offered with a view toward future competition or leisure activity.

Disability Specific Guidelines

The previous section described general program guidelines applicable to CP, TBI, and CVA. However, there are also several guidelines specific to each condition. These guidelines focus chiefly on health-related physical fitness and motor ability components.

Cerebral Palsy

According to Winnick and Short (1999a), individuals with CP should possess the ability to sustain moderate physical activity (aerobic functioning), have body composition consistent with positive health, and musculoskeletal function (muscular strength and endurance, flexibility) so that participation in a variety of sport and leisure activities is possible. Sustaining moderate physical activity (70 percent of maximum predicted heart rate adjusted for mode of exercise) for 15 minutes represents the general aerobic standard for youngsters with CP (Winnick & Short, 1999a). The ability to perform this general standard has positive implications for sport and leisure activities. Minimum and preferred general standards are also presented for body composition and musculoskeletal functioning.

Inappropriate reflexive behavior in individuals with CP contributes to reduced aerobic activity and imbalances in muscle functioning and flexibility throughout regions of the body. Inappropriate reflexive behavior can also contribute to motor coordination and equilibrium difficulties, which can compromise the ability to attain acceptable health-related fitness and the ability to learn and perform certain motor skills, especially those needed to perform recreation and leisure-time activities. Because of either restricted or extraneous movements, an individual with CP might exert more energy than a person without impairment to accomplish the same task. Even with more energy output, individuals with CP can exhibit a 50 percent reduction in physical work capacity when compared to peers without disabilities (Laskin, 2003). In addition, the added energy output requires a greater degree of endurance. As a result, the duration of physical activities might need to be shortened.

When a child is receiving therapy for inappropriate reflexive behavior, it is important for the physical educator to work in conjunction with therapists to foster the suppression of certain abnormal reflexes and the facilitation of righting and equilibrium reactions. Although many physical education activities help in the development of righting and equilibrium reactions, others might elicit abnormal reflexes. Some of the more common reflexes affecting the performance of physical education and sport skills include the asymmetrical tonic neck reflex (ATNR), the symmetrical tonic neck reflex (STNR), the crossed extension reflex, and the positive supporting reflex. The ATNR can prevent the effective use of implements such as bats, rackets, and hockey sticks. When present, the STNR can affect the ability to perform scooterboard activities in the prone position or other activities requiring the chin to be tucked toward the chest (e.g., looking down to control a soccer ball or catch a ground ball in baseball). Difficulty in kicking from a standing position can be affected by the crossed extension and positive supporting reflexes.

As the young student progresses in age, even with therapy, inappropriate reflexes will not be inhibited. Thus, professionals responsible for the student's physical education program must pursue attainment of functional skills, including sport skills. The attainment of functional skills such as creeping, walking, running, and throwing are important to future skill development and should be incorporated into the student's program. Asking students with CP to repetitively perform activities that elicit unwanted reflexes will not aggravate the condition of CP (as once thought by professionals) once children have aged beyond seven or eight years. The following sections address components of strength, flexibility, speed, motor coordination, and perceptual–motor disorders as they pertain to physical education and sport.

Strength

In addressing the development of strength, it is important to note that muscle tone imbalances between flexor and extensor muscle groups are common in individuals with CP. For those with spastic tendencies, flexor muscles might be disproportionately stronger than the extensors. Thus, strength development should focus on strengthening the extensor muscles. For example, even though a student might have increased tone of the forearm flexors, he or she might perform poorly on pull-ups. This being the case, one should not continue to develop forearm flexors as opposed to forearm extensors. The goal is to develop and maintain a balance between flexor and extensor muscles throughout the regions of the body. When muscular strength imbalances are present among regions of the body, DiRocco (1999) suggests that individuals with CP can use handheld weights or flexible tubing so that the appropriate resistance is applied to a particular body segment or region.

When participating in a resistance training program some individuals might exhibit an increase in spasticity in the involved limb or segment of the body when a contralateral nonspastic limb is involved in a resistance exercise. It is suggested that strength-building exercises be performed at a moderate speed rather than a fast speed to reduce the spasticity. Baxter and Lockette (1995) suggest that increased spasticity is a temporary phenomenon and the increased spasticity should subside soon after the session. In any case, spastic muscles should not be subjected to work loads above 60 percent of maximum (DiRocco, 1999).

Individuals with CP can benefit from rigorous strength training programs. Isokinetic resistance exercises are particularly useful for developing strength, probably because they provide constant tension through the full range of motion and aid in inhibiting jerky movements that are extraneous and uncontrolled. Moving limbs in diagonal patterns (e.g., moving the entire arm across the body in a diagonal plane) encourage muscle groups to work in harmony. Involving individuals in a variety of gross motor activities such as throwing, striking, and kicking can elicit such movements.

Flexibility

Tight muscles in both the upper and lower limbs and the hip region contribute to reduced flexibility, especially for students with spastic CP. If left unattended, restricted range of motion leads to contractures and bone deformities. Thus, flexibility exercises and activities should be a regular part of physical education and sport programs. Individuals with spastic CP benefit from a prolonged warm-up period (15 to 20 minutes) of static flexibility exercises (DiRocco, 1999). The instructor might want to begin a flexibility program session by helping students relax target muscle groups. This can be accomplished by teaching students relaxation techniques, which they can then perform independently. When stretching exercises are used, they should be of static, as opposed to a ballistic nature, and they should be done both before and after strength and endurance activities (Surburg, 1999). If an individual is participating in a ballistic type of activity such as a club throw, ballistic stretching can be used, but static stretching should precede it. Surburg also recommends that stretching exercises for more severely affected body parts possessing spasticity should be done on a regular basis. When flexibility exercises are done, it is recommended that fewer repetitions and longer periods of stretching be performed.

When possible, students should perform stretching exercises on their own. This type of stretching (performed with no assistance) is called active range of motion. Should the teacher or coach need to assist an individual with spasticity in performing flexibility exercises (known as active–assistive range of motion), his or her hand should be placed on the extensor muscle, not the flexor (spastic) muscle (Mushett, Wyeth, & Richter, 1995). For individuals who because of severe spasticity or limited motor control cannot voluntarily move their body part(s), passive range of motion (movement performed entirely by the teacher or coach without assistance from the student) can be performed under general medical supervision.

Speed

Many students with CP have difficulty with games and sport skills that include a speed component because quickly performed movements tend to activate the stretch reflex. However, an appropriate program can permit students with CP to increase their movement speed. Speed-development activities for individuals with CP differ little from those for nonimpaired individuals except that such activities should be conducted more frequently than for students without impairments (daily activities are recommended). Students with CP should be encouraged to perform movements as quickly as possible but to do them in a controlled, accurate, and purposeful manner. Activities with a speed component include throwing and kicking for distance, running, and jumping. Initially, the

student should concentrate on the pattern of the movement while gradually increasing the speed of its execution. To develop arm and leg speed, the student can be asked to throw or kick a ball (or some other object) in a "soft" manner to a target; gradually, the throw or kick can increase in speed.

Motor Coordination

Varying degrees of incoordination (dyspraxia) are common in individuals with CP and contribute to delayed motor control and development. Those who are significantly uncoordinated might have problems ambulating independently or with appliances and might need to wear protective headgear. Because they frequently fall, they should be taught to fall in a protective manner. Because of abnormal movements and posture, individuals with CP have difficulty controlling balance and body coordination. Obstacle courses, horseback riding, bicycling and tricycling, balance beam, and teeter (stability) board activities can assist in controlling movements.

Motor control difficulties notwithstanding, individuals with CP (as well as those with TBI and CVA) can learn to become more accurate in their performance. Because individuals with CP can have difficulty planning movements involving accuracy, they should be allowed sufficient time to plan the movement before executing it. Many times, the use of a weighted ball, bat, or other implement assists in decreasing abnormal flailing or tremor movements. Adding weight to the implement helps in reducing exaggerated stretch reflexes, which, in turn, aids in controlling movements. Individuals with CP possessing motor control deficiencies resulting from athetoid, tremor, or ataxic tendencies can be expected to throw or kick for distance better and to exhibit freer running patterns than others who have limited range of motion because of spastic or rigid tendencies.

Loud noises and stressful situations increase the amount of electrical stimulation from the brain to the muscles; this tends to increase abnormal and extraneous movements, which, in turn, make motor activities difficult to perform. In an attempt to deal with this situation, students should be taught to concentrate on the activity they are performing. Individuals exhibiting spastic tendencies tend to relax more when encouraged to make slow, repetitive movements that have a purpose, whereas those with athetoid tendencies perform better when encouraged to relax before moving. Highly competitive situations that promote winning at all costs might increase abnormal movements. Thus, competitive situations might need to be introduced gradually. The teaching of relaxation techniques, which consciously reduce abnormal muscle tone and prepare the student for activity and competition, has been found to be beneficial. Another way to help individuals with CP improve general motor control and coordination is to have them construct a mental picture of the skill or activity prior to performance. This technique, called mental imagery, might help to integrate thoughts with actions.

In motor skill development for students with CP, the skills taught should be broken down into basic component parts and presented sequentially. This method is particularly useful for uncoordinated students seeking to learn more complex motor skills. However, because of the general lack of body coordination, activities should initially focus on simple repetitive movements rather than on complicated ones requiring many directional changes. Thus, activities that help to develop basic fundamental motor skills and patterns, such as walking, running, jumping, throwing, catching, and so forth, should be taught.

Perceptual–Motor Disorders

Perceptual–motor disorders also contribute to poor motor performance. Because of these disorders, many children with CP exhibit short attention spans and are easily distracted by objects and individuals in the immediate environment. Activities might need to be conducted in an environment as free from distractions as possible, especially during early skill development.

Visual perceptual disorders are common among students with CP and can adversely affect activities and events that involve spatial relations. These might include player positioning in team sports such as soccer, remaining in lanes during track events, and determining distances between objects such as bocce balls. Students might have difficulty with accuracy and aiming tasks such as throwing, tossing, or kicking an object to a specified target, as well as with activities involving fine motor coordination, such as rifle shooting, angling, or pocket billiards.

Traumatic Brain Injury and Stroke

Previous to their brain trauma, individuals with TBI were once involved in learning and performing a host of physical education and sport skills in a "normal" manner. It is commonly known that the learning of motor skills requires varying amounts of cognition, depending on the level of difficulty. Skills once thought to be quite simple to learn, following trauma require constant practice and planning by the person with TBI or CVA. Depending on the age of the individual at the time of trauma some skills might have already been learned for quite some time (e.g., running, throwing, catching), whereas other skills have been yet to be acquired (e.g., specific sport skills). Although some individuals with TBI or CVA might fully recover the motor skills lost, others with more significant and permanent injury might never regain them. For individuals with TBI and stroke to regain skills to their maximum potential, physical education and sport programs need to be individualized and offered on a frequent, regular basis.

Because of the nature of the disability, those with TBI or CVA might commonly exhibit weak muscles and balance difficulties. Thus, context-specific exercises, activities, and training programs are necessary to regain functional balance, walking, manipulation, and strength (Carr & Shepherd, 2003). Inadequate balance might hinder the performance of many physical education and sport activities. Readers interested in exercise testing and programming for individuals with stroke and head injury should consult the writing of Palmer-McLean and Harbst (2003). The following sections address physical fitness and motor coordination as they pertain to physical education and sport.

Physical Fitness

Acquiring and maintaining an adequate level of health-related physical fitness is important. This is especially true for individuals who have been severely injured through TBI and those who have been immobile for long periods of time after a stroke. The health-related fitness needs can be considered similar to individuals with CP. As such, individuals with CVA or TBI need to develop and sustain at least moderate levels of aerobic activity to maintain body composition consistent with good health and musculoskeletal functioning sufficient to participate in sport and leisure activities. Thus, depending on individual need, the physical education program should allow for activities to develop and maintain these health-related components. The BPFT (Winnick & Short, 1999a) highlights items and standards that can be used in the assessment of health-related fitness for individuals with disabilities. A personalized process might be used to design a test for youngsters with CVA and TBI.

Many students will fatigue easily, especially as they begin their re-entry into school. Thus, fitness exercises and activities should be introduced on a gradual basis, and sufficient rest periods should occur between activities, especially if physical education is near the end of the school day. For individuals immobilized for large periods of time, aerobic activities should be preceded by muscular strength and endurance activities performed in a progressive manner.

The neurological deficits associated with head injury many times affect the person's ability to ambulate efficiently. Thus, the individual with head trauma uses a significant amount of energy that would otherwise not be used. According to Palmer-McLean and Harbst (2003), appropriately planned fitness programs can improve cardiorespiratory endurance and muscle strength, thereby allowing individuals to raise energy levels to perform locomotor activities (e.g., sport, leisure, and activities of daily living) in a more efficient manner. Raising functional health-related fitness levels also increases a person's chance of living a more fulfilling and productive life.

Some individuals who exhibit spasticity (similar to CP) will need to focus on relaxation and flexibility exercises and activities. Other individuals exhibiting partial paralysis need to maintain residual functioning through muscular strength and endurance exercises and activities. Weight training and flexibility exercises and activities will not be new to the person recovering from TBI or CVA because physical and occupational therapy rehabilitation programs typically focus on these areas.

Universal gym equipment is convenient and safe to use to develop strength and endurance because individuals need not be concerned with placing free weights on barbells and dumbbells. Except for the bench press exercise, individuals can stay seated in their wheelchairs (although getting out of the wheelchair is important and should be encouraged). For individuals who can independently, or with assistance, remove themselves from their chairs, isokinetic equipment is also beneficial to use. However, according to DiRocco (1999) weight machines might not be the choice of equipment for individuals with TBI or CVA. Muscle weakness on one side of the body might prevent the successful use of weight machines because several exercises require the use of both arms or both legs at once. This considered, free weights, which allow limbs to be exercised individually, should be made available.

For individuals who do not have the availability of free weights, stretch bands are an economical way to conduct resistance training.

Because individuals with more severe brain injury are more likely to be sedentary, aerobic activities, which develop cardiorespiratory endurance levels, should be performed on a regular basis. These might take the form of low-impact aerobics for individuals who can ambulate or aerobics done from a sitting position for those using wheelchairs. Those who can perform activities from a standing position but who have limited endurance should have the availability of a stationary object for rest or support as needed. Aquatic activities are especially good for developing physical fitness. It is recommended that individuals with TBI and CVA participate in physical fitness programs that address all areas of fitness. *The Brockport Physical Fitness Training Guide* (Winnick & Short, 1999b) includes additional exercise and activity suggestions for promoting health-related fitness.

Motor Control

Depending on the location and severity of injury, individuals with TBI or CVA have difficulty planning, initiating, and controlling gross and fine motor movements. Individuals with TBI typically have difficulty performing movements sequentially. This has important implications for physical education and sport activities, especially when combinations of separate skills need to be linked together in succession. Individuals with TBI or CVA typically need to relearn movements and movement patterns they could easily perform before the injury. To assist in this process, more complex skills should be broken down into simpler subskills, which should be practiced sequentially. Because these individuals typically have problems processing information, allow enough time for movements to be planned before they are executed.

As is true for individuals with CP, visual perception might also be affected in individuals with TBI or CVA. As such, individuals might exhibit difficulty with activities requiring spatial relationships and those requiring object control like catching, kicking, and striking. Of course, activities incorporating object control will need to be individualized. Adolescents with TBI or CVA should be given choices about the type of sport and leisure activities to be learned in physical education classes. This gives the adolescent the needed sense of independence and self-control and contributes to smooth transition from school to community.

INCLUSION

Unless otherwise decided by IEP team members, students with CP, TBI, or CVA are to be included in regular physical education classes. Of course, such a decision must be made on an individual basis. Generally, those with mild to moderate degrees of impairment can be safely and effectively included in regular physical education settings. Most students with CP, TBI, or CVA unless severely intellectually impaired will understand verbal and written directions as well as rules and strategies for various games and sports. In certain cases, teachers might need to structure activities to suit participants' abilities. For example, students with CP affecting the lower limbs could play goalie in soccer or floor hockey and could pitch or play first base in softball. Providing appropriate inclusive environments gives these students opportunities for enhancing social and emotional development.

ADAPTED SPORTS

At almost all age levels, people with CP, TBI, or CVA now have the opportunity to become involved in competitive sports. In addition to individuals with CP, individuals with TBI and CVA are included in NDSA competition as well as a select group of sports for athletes with other physical disabilities, including muscular dystrophy, multiple sclerosis, and osteogenesis imperfecta. As the national governing body, the National Disability Sports Alliance (NDSA) is responsible for the conduct and administration of approved sports in the United States. The NDSA offers a variety of modified sporting events (figure 14.4). Athletes can participate in these events on the basis of their functional abilities. In addition to local and regional competitions, national championships are held by the NDSA on an annual basis.

NDSA is a member of the Committee on Sports for the Disabled (COSD) of the United States Olympic Committee and a member of the International Sports Organization for the Disabled (ISOD). NDSA athletes are eligible to participate in international competition governed by ISOD as long as they meet ISOD classification standards and qualify for events. The ISOD oversees the Paralympic Games, World Championships, World Games, and World Cup competition. The Paralympic Games are organized every fourth year, with competition in multidisabled games and sports.

The World Championships are organized relative to a specific sport; participants generally have single or multiple disabilities. World Games, on the other hand, are organized relative to competition in one or more sports for specific disability groups (e.g., CP) or games, which might deviate from existing rules. Finally, World Cup competition refers to international competition for national or club teams in team and individual sports. The international governing body for NDSA is CP–ISRA (Cerebral Palsy–International Sports and Recreation Association).

© Jerry McCole and USCPA. Printed by permission.

Figure 14.4 Athlete with CP performing the distance kick in NDSA competition.

Competition for athletes with CP, TBI, or CVA is based on the eight-level classification system described at the beginning of this chapter (see table 14.1). Athletes are placed in a specific class through two testing procedures. In the first, a functional profile is established through observation and questioning regarding the individual's daily living skills. The second testing procedure involves the measurement of speed, accuracy of movement, and range of motion for upper extremity and torso function and, for ambulant athletes, the assessment of lower extremity function and stability. Athletes generally compete within their designated classes in a variety of events. Table 14.2 identifies events and associated classification levels.

Table 14.2 Classes Eligible for NDSA Events

Events	Classes
Archery	1-8 (all classes)
Bocce (wheelchair—individual and team)	1 and 2 only
Bowling	1-8 (all classes)
Cross country (3,000 m)	5-8
Cycling	
• Bicycling	5-8
• Tricycling	2, 5, and 6
Equestrian	1-8 (all classes)
Power lifting (bench press)	1-8 (all classes)
Slalom	1-4
Soccer	
• Seven-a-side soccer	5-8
• Indoor wheelchair soccer	1-8 (all classes)
Swimming	1-8 (all classes)
Shooting	2-8
Table tennis	3-8
Track	
• 60 m weave (wheelchair)	1 only
• 100 m, 200 m, 400 m, 800 m	2-8
• 1,500 m	3-4 and 6-8
• 4 × 100 m relay, 4 × 400 m relay	2-8
Field Events	
• Soft shot, precision throw, height toss, soft discus	1 only
• Medicine ball thrust, distance kick	2 only
• Club throw	2-6
• Shot, discus	2-8
• Javelin throw	3-8
• Long jump	6-8

Adapted, by permission, from National Disability Sports Alliance, 2002, *NDSA sports rules manual*, 6th ed. (Kingston, RI: National Disability Sports Alliance), 6-13.

NDSA competition is divided into three age divisions: junior (up to 18 years of age); open (any age), and masters (over 40 years of age). The junior division is subdivided into five groups: Futures (age 6 and under); Division A (7 to 9 years of age); Division B (10 to 12 years of age); Division C (13 to 15 years of age); Division D (16 to 18 years of age). There are sports for both wheelchair and ambulatory classes in all three age divisions. The Futures subdivision stresses participation rather than competition. Depending on age and classification, junior athletes compete in events that are the same as those for adult athletes (e.g., ambulatory soccer, swimming). The NDSA hosts or sanctions several regional events across the United States each year. It also hosts the annual Youth Nationals Competition, which brings together junior athletes from across the country.

Each year, the NDSA holds clinics for professionals and volunteers that focus on coaching, training, and officiating techniques. The NDSA publishes an approved sports rules manual (NDSA, 2002) and a separate training guide. The association also publishes *Update,* a newsletter that provides readers with current information on competition, rules, classification, and training.

SUMMARY

In this chapter we have described the conditions of CP, TBI, and CVA as they relate to physical education and sport. Physical and motor needs were described and program and activity suggestions presented. Recognizing the medical nature of these conditions, teachers and coaches are encouraged to plan activities on the basis of input from physicians and allied health professionals.

REFERENCES

American Stroke Association (2002). *Impact of a stroke.* Retrieved from www.strokeassociation.org

Appleton, R.E. (1998). Epidemiology: Incidence, causes, and severity. In R.E. Appleton & T. Baldwin (Eds.), *Management of brain-injured children* (pp. 1-11). Oxford, England; New York, NY: Oxford University Press.

Baxter, K.F., & Lockette, K.F. (1995). Resistance training with stretch bands: Modifying for disability. In P.D. Miller (Ed.), *Fitness programming and physical disability* (pp. 91-100). Champaign, IL: Human Kinetics.

Brain Injury Association of America (2001). *Facts and stats —Sports and Recreation.* Retrieved from www.biausa.org/pages/facts_and_stats.html

Carr, J., & Shepherd, R. (2003). Stroke rehabilitation: Guidelines for exercise and training to optimize motor skill. London, England: Butterworth-Heinmann.

DiRocco, P.J. (1999). Muscular strength and endurance. In P. J. Winnick & F. X. Short (Eds.), *The Brockport physical fitness training guide* (pp. 39-73). Champaign, IL: Human Kinetics.

Driver, S., Harmon, M., & Block, M. (2003). Devising a safe and successful physical education program for children with a brain injury. *The Journal of Physical Education, Recreation, and Dance,* 74(7), 41-48, 55.

Ellekjaer, H., Holmen, J., Ellekjaer, E., & Vatten, L. (2000). Physical activity and stroke mortality in women. *Stroke: Journal of the American Heart Association,* 31, 14-18.

Finnie, N.R. (1997). *Handling the young child with cerebral palsy* (3rd ed.). Boston: Butterworth-Heinemann.

Johnson, A. (2002). Prevalence and characteristics of children with cerebral palsy in Europe. *Developmental Medicine and Child Neurology,* 45, 633-640.

Laskin, J. (2003). Cerebral palsy. In J.L. Durstine & G.E. Moore (Eds.), *ACSM's Exercise management for persons with chronic diseases and disabilities* (2nd ed.) (pp. 288-294). Champaign, IL: Human Kinetics.

Mushett, C.A., Wyeth, D.O., & Richter, K.J. (1995). Cerebral Palsy. In B. Goldberg (Ed.), *Sports and exercise for children with chronic health conditions* (pp.123-134). Champaign, IL: Human Kinetics.

National Disability Sports Alliance (2002). *Sports rules manual* (6th ed.). Newport, RI: Author.

Palmer-McLean, K., & Harbst, K.B. (2003). Stroke and brain injury. In J.L. Durstine & G.E. Moore (Eds.), *ACSM's Exercise management for persons with chronic diseases and disabilities.* (2nd ed.) (pp. 238-246). Champaign, IL: Human Kinetics.

Sacco, R.L., Gan, R., Boden-Albala, B., Lin, I., Kargman, D.E., Hauser, W.A., Shea, S., & Paik, M. (1998). Leisure-time physical activity and ischemic stroke risk: The Northern Manhattan stroke study. *Stroke: Journal of the American Heart Association,* 29, 380-387.

Surburg, P.R. (1999). Flexibility/range of motion. In J. P. Winnick & F. X. Short (Eds.), *The Brockport physical fitness training guide* (pp. 75-119). Champaign, IL: Human Kinetics.

United Cerebral Palsy Associations, Inc. (2003). *Research foundation and fact sheets— prevention, diagnosis and treatment.* Retrieved from www.ucp.org/ucp_generalsub.cfm/1/4/11654.

Walker, B.R. (1997). Creating effective educational programs through parent-professional partnerships. In A. Glang, G. H. Singer, & B. Todis (Eds.), *Students with acquired brain injury: The school's response.* (pp. 295-322). Baltimore, MD: Paul Brookes Publishing.

Wehman, P., Keyser-Marcus, L., West, D., Targett, P., & Bricout, J. (2001). Applications for youth with traumatic brain injury. In P. Wehman (Ed.), *Life beyond the classroom: Transition strategies for young people with disabilities* (3rd ed.). (pp. 449-490). Baltimore: Paul H. Brookes Publishing.

Winnick, J.P., & Short, F.X. (1999a). *Brockport physical fitness test manual.* Champaign, IL: Human Kinetics.

Winnick, J.P., & Short, F.X. (Eds.) (1999b). *Brockport physical fitness training guide.* Champaign, IL: Human Kinetics.

Yager, J.Y. (1999). Stroke in neonates, infants and children. In A. Shuaib & L. Goldstein (Eds.), *Management of acute stroke.* (pp. 141-171). New York, New York: Marcel Dekker, Inc.

Ylvisaker, M., & Feeney, T.J. (1998). School re-entry after traumatic brain injury. In M. Ylvisaker (Ed.), *Traumatic brain injury rehabilitation: Children and adolescents* (2nd ed.) (pp. 369-387). Oxford, England; Boston, MA: Butterworth-Heinemann.

WRITTEN RESOURCES

Fitness Canada. (1994). *Moving to Inclusion: Cerebral Palsy.* Glouster, Ontario: The Active Living Alliance for Canadians with a disability.

This is one in a series of nine manuals designed to provide physical education teachers with practical ways in which to integrate students with disabilities into regular physical education classes. This manual includes programming for inclusive physical education, manipulation skills, sport skills, fitness, outdoor education, intramural and interschool programs, and professional support services. The manual can be obtained by writing to The Active Living Alliance for Canadians with a Disability, 1600 James Naismith Dr., Glouster, Ontario, Canada, K1B 5N4.

Heartland Educational Agency II (1993). School Reentry of Students Experiencing Traumatic Brain Injury: Physical Education Considerations. Johnston, IA: Heartland AEA 11.

This paper provides current information regarding traumatic brain injury as it relates to physical education. An overview of TBI is provided along with information relative to assessment, teaching, programming strategies, and sport-related issues. This publication can be acquired from Heartland Educational Agency II, 6500 Corporate Drive, Johnston, IA 50131-1603.

AUDIOVISUAL RESOURCES

Physical activity. (Videotape, n.d.) American Heart Association, 7272 Greenville Avenue, Dallas, TX 75231.

The video illustrates how regular physical activity can help reduce heart attack and stroke risk as well as improve overall health.

Aerobics for Cerebral Palsy. (Videotape, n.d.) Disabled Sport, USA/Videotapes, 451 Hungerford Drive, Suite 100, Rockville, MD 20850.

This video illustrates vigorous exercise for ambulatory and nonambulatory individuals with muscular coordination difficulties. Program features prolonged warm-up followed by exercise using easy-to-follow upper body movements. Low-impact rhythmic full body actions are demonstrated.

A stroke survivor's workout. (Videotape, n.d.) American Heart Association, 7272 Greenville Avenue, Dallas, TX 75231.

This 28-minute video contains flexibility and strength exercises. Some exercises are done from a standing position and, if needed, using the support of a chair; other exercises are done seated in a chair or wheelchair.

ELECTRONIC RESOURCES

Brain Injury Association of America: www.biausa.org.

The Brain Injury Association of America is the national clearinghouse for information related to brain injury. The organization promotes awareness, understanding, and prevention of brain injury through education, advocacy, and research.

Amputations, Dwarfism, and Les Autres

David L. Porretta

The crowd cheers as Marlon finishes first in the 100-meter dash. His time is 10.97 seconds, just over one second off the Olympic record! No, Marlon is not a member of the U.S. Olympic team; he is a member of the U.S. Paralympic team and current Paralympic world-record holder in the 100-meter dash. Although Marlon Shirley has a lower-limb amputation, he has used state-of-the-art prosthetic technology to become one of the world's fastest humans. Marlon's accomplishment is one of the many achievements in sport today of people with disabilities, providing evidence that with the right equipment, training, and desire these athletes can attain elite levels of performance.

Individuals with amputations, dwarfism, and les autres (a French term meaning "the others") impairments were at one time restricted from physical activity for fear that it would aggravate their conditions. Today these individuals are encouraged to participate in many physical education and sport activities. In fact, as Marlon has shown, people with disabilities are approaching many of the national records set by athletes without disabilities. In this chapter we provide an overview of amputations, dwarfism, and les autres impairments within a physical education and sport context. Specific information is covered relative to program and activity perspectives.

AMPUTATIONS

Amputation refers to the loss of an entire limb or a limb segment. Amputations are categorized as either acquired or congenital. Acquired amputations can result from disease, tumor, or trauma; congenital amputations result from failure of the fetus to properly develop during the first three months of gestation. In most cases, the cause or causes of partial or total congenital limb absence are unknown. Generally, there are two types of congenital deformities. In one type, a middle segment of a limb is absent, but the proximal and distal portions are intact; this is known as phocomelia. Here, the hand or foot is attached directly to the shoulder or hip without the remaining anatomical structures present. The second type of deficiency is similar to surgical amputation, in which no normal structures, such as hands or fingers, are present below the missing segment. In many cases, however, immature fingerlike buds are present; this deficiency is usually below the elbow and unilateral in nature.

Incidence

Hundreds of thousands of people in the United States are amputees, and more than two thirds of these are missing a lower limb. Of this number, about 8 percent of those with missing limbs are under 24 years of age. Across all age groups, trauma is the leading cause of limb loss. However, congenital limb loss accounts for about 45 percent of all amputations in children 15 years of age or younger.

Classification

Amputations can be classified according to the site and level of limb absence or from a functional point of view. Nine classes, which are now in use

by Disabled Sports, USA (DS/USA), and the International Sports Organization for the Disabled (ISOD), are identified as follows:

- Class A1—Double above the knee (AK)
- Class A2—Single AK
- Class A3—Double below the knee (BK)
- Class A4—Single BK
- Class A5—Double above the elbow (AE)
- Class A6—Single AE
- Class A7—Double below the elbow (BE)
- Class A8—Single BE
- Class A9—Combined lower- plus upper-limb amputations

According to this system, class A8 represents functional ability greater than class A1. Information on sport competition can be found in the Adapted Sports Section of this chapter.

General Educational Considerations

In nearly all cases, a prosthetic device is prescribed and selected for the amputee by a team of medical specialists. The prosthetic device is designed to compensate, as much as possible, for the functional loss of the limb. Devices are chosen according to the size of the individual and the area and extent of limb absence. Most authorities favor the use of a prosthetic device as early as possible following the loss of the limb because the device tends to be more easily incorporated into the person's normal body actions the earlier it is introduced. Learning to use a device takes time and effort, and some individuals with more extensive lower-limb amputations need training with canes or crutches. Special consideration within the educational environment is needed for students with prosthetic devices. For example, classroom teachers can assist therapists in helping students acquire and maintain important fine motor skills, such as cutting, pasting, and drawing. Physical education teachers can assist therapists in helping students acquire and maintain important gross motor skills, such as catching, throwing and handling implements such as bats and rackets.

With recent technological advances, new types of both upper- and lower-limb prosthetic devices are now commonly seen in educational and sport settings. New types of lower-limb prosthetic devices are commonly used in sports to provide athletes with the most realistic sense of normal foot function. These devices provide an active push-off in which the device propels the body in a forward or vertical fashion. These prostheses, made of carbon graphite, contain a type of "dynamic response" in that they can store and release energy, simulating the function of a normal foot. They respond smoothly, gradually, and proportionally to pressure applied by the user. Individuals are fit individually with the assistance of computer-generated designs. As such, many athletes with both below-the-knee and above-the-knee amputations use these prostheses for competitive purposes in sports such as volleyball, basketball (both of which involve jumping), football, and sprint and distance running (figure 15.1). Many companies now offer these dynamic response devices commercially. Cosmetic foot covers are also now available to amputees, which simulate the form and look of the natural foot. These natural looking foot covers are shells, which accommodate prostheses. Unless closely examined, these cosmetic devices make it look as if nothing is missing. Of course, the use of these cosmetic devices is a personal choice.

Individuals with limb deficiencies often have additional educational needs in the psychosocial domain. Many feel shame, inferiority, and anxiety when in social and educational settings—feelings that might result from the stares or comments from their school-age peers. The new cosmetic covers might be of help, especially if students are self-conscious about their prosthetic devices within an educational setting. Finally, individual counseling by a psychologist or professional counselor might be necessary to promote healthy emotional functioning. To address the social stigma associated with limb loss in children, the Amputee Coalition

Figure 15.1   Kelly Bruno and Roderick Green, two elite athletes performing with state-of-the-art prosthetic devices.

of America has created a school-based curriculum entitled the Limb Loss Education and Awareness Program (LLEAP). Through multisensory activities, children are taught to recognize and appreciate differences in themselves and others.

DWARFISM

Dwarfism is a condition in which a person is of short stature (152.4 centimeters [5 feet] or less in height). When compared to the general population, individuals with dwarfism are shorter than 98 percent of all other people. Generally, dwarfism results from either the failure of cartilage to form into bone as the individual grows or from a pituitary irregularity. Aside from their short stature, people with dwarfism are no different from the majority of the population. Most people with dwarfism prefer to be called "little people."

Incidence

About 150,000 people in the United States possess a degree of dwarfism. At least 75 percent of all infants born with dwarfism are born to average-size parents. Achondroplasia is considered the most common type of disproportionate dwarfism. According to the Little People of America (2003) as many as 1 in 26,000 infants are born with achondroplasia.

Classification

Dwarfism can be classified into two categories: proportionate and disproportionate. Those individuals who possess proportionate dwarfism have all proportionate body parts but are very short. This type of dwarfism results from a deficiency in the pituitary gland, which regulates growth. Short arms and legs with a normal torso and a large head, on the other hand, characterize disproportionate dwarfism. This type of dwarfism might be caused by a faulty gene that results in failure of the bone to fully develop. Individuals with disproportionate dwarfism are the most prevalent. This type of achondroplasia is most common. Achondroplasia literally means the absence of normal cartilage formation and growth and begins in utero. This type of dwarfism can manifest itself in a waddling gait, lordosis, limited range of motion, and bowed legs. Additional anatomical features include a large head and flattened face. Many individuals with achondroplasia are overweight or obese. Because of abnormal stature, additional weight is carried in the buttocks, hips, and legs. The average adult height in achondroplasia is about four feet for men and women. In more severe cases, in which spinal involvement as well as additional bone deformities are present, the individual with achondroplasia might require ambulation devices such as crutches. Lumbrosacral spinal stenosis with compressed spinal cord or nerve roots is common. This condition is a structural abnormality of the spine in which the canal that houses the spinal cord is too small. As a result, muscle weakness, pain, and loss of sensation might occur. In severe cases, spinal surgery can alleviate the condition.

Some individuals with dwarfism who do not have achondroplasia might have cervical vertebrae abnormalities, similar to atlanto–axial instability in Down syndrome, which might lead to very serious neck injury. As such, the Dwarf Athletic Association of America (DAAA) requires a medical screening for all nonachondroplasia athletes before participation in running, jumping (basketball), or swimming (diving start) events.

General Educational Considerations

In general, a physical education program for individuals with dwarfism can and should follow the same guidelines as a program developed for individuals without disabilities. On an intellectual level, students with dwarfism do not function any different from average-size students. Thus, these individuals are to be treated the same as other students with regard to cognitive ability and academic achievement. Delayed motor milestones and otitis media are common in children with achondroplasia. Frey and Palmer (1999) identify several psychoeducational implications for children with dwarfism. As such, individuals with dwarfism should have the opportunity to develop a positive self-image in a psychologically safe educational environment. Many times students with obvious physical differences and limitations are subject to ridicule. It is the responsibility of the teacher to maintain an environment that encourages positive interactions and social contacts among all students.

Physical education teachers and coaches need to be aware of certain factors associated with physical education and sport activities for individuals with dwarfism. Because of delayed motor milestones in children with achondroplasia, elementary physical education programs should focus on the attainment of fundamental motor skills and patterns prior to the performance of more advanced activities. In addition, because of limited stature and disproportionate body segments, individuals with dwarfism might have a disadvantage in certain activities, such as track and field, tennis, baseball, softball, and basketball. From a safety perspective, because of joint defects, certain activities (e.g., gymnastics, acrobatics, contact sports) that place stress on joints should be modified.

LES AUTRES

Les autres is a categorization for several disabilities, including muscular dystrophy, juvenile rheumatoid arthritis, osteogenesis imperfecta, arthrogryposis, multiple sclerosis, Friedreich's ataxia, myasthenia gravis, and Guillain-Barré syndrome.

Muscular Dystrophy

Muscular dystrophy is actually considered a group of inherited diseases characterized by progressive, diffuse weakness of various muscle groups. Muscle cells within the belly of the muscles degenerate and are replaced by adipose and connective tissue. The dystrophy itself is not fatal, but secondary complications of muscle weakness predispose the person to respiratory disorders and heart problems. It is quite common for individuals with dystrophy in advanced stages of the disease to die from a simple respiratory infection or as a result of myocardial involvement. Disease symptoms might appear any time between birth and middle age, but most cases affect children and youth.

There are various types of muscular dystrophy, including the myotonic, facio-scapulo-humeral, limb-girdle, and Duchenne types. **Myotonic muscular dystrophy,** also known as Stienert's disease, manifests itself through muscle weakness and affects the central nervous system, heart, eyes, and endocrine glands. It is a slowly progressing disease generally occurring between the ages of 20 to 40 years. Congenital myotonic dystrophy is rare, occurring almost exclusively in infants of mothers with the adult form. With appropriate care, their conditions often improve; however, delayed motor development and intellectual disabilities in late infancy and early childhood are common. The **facio-scapulo-humeral** type of muscular dystrophy initially affects muscles of the shoulders and face and, in some instances, the hip and thigh.

Life expectancy is usually normal because this type of dystrophy might arrest itself at any time. In **limb-girdle muscular dystrophy,** degeneration might begin in either the shoulder or the hip girdle, with eventual involvement of both. Unlike the facio-scapulo-humeral type, degeneration continues at a slow rate. Facio-scapulo-humeral dystrophy manifests itself during adolescence or adulthood. The limb-girdle type might be exhibited at any time from late childhood on, though it usually occurs during the teenage years. With both facio-scapulo-humeral and limb-girdle dystrophy, males and females are equally affected.

Duchenne muscular dystrophy (DMD) is the most common and severe childhood form of the disease. It affects more boys than girls. Symptoms usually occur between the ages of 2 and 6 years. An almost identical form of DMD is called **Becker muscular dystrophy.** However, it is much less severe and onset is typically between 2 and 16 years of age. Many times Becker muscular dystrophy is not diagnosed until an adolescent or young adult cannot fully participate in physical education or recreational activities. The Duchenne type is commonly referred to as **pseudohypertrophic muscular dystrophy.** A pseudohypertrophic appearance, especially of the calf and forearm muscles, is the result of an excessive accumulation of adipose and connective tissues within the interstitial spaces between degenerated muscle cells. It is yet to be determined precisely how this happens; however, the gene responsible for causing Duchenne dystrophy has been identified. Linked to this gene is a protein called dystrophin (dis-tro-pin). This protein (one of many) allows muscle cells to function properly; without it, the muscle cells eventually die. In individuals with Duchenne dystrophy, this protein is absent. Research has shown that dystrophin is attached to other proteins at the edge of muscle fibers and that it most likely helps anchor the fibers to connective tissue surrounding them.

DMD manifests itself in atrophy and weakness of the thigh, hip, back, shoulder girdle, and respiratory muscles. The anterior tibialis muscle of the lower leg becomes extremely weak, resulting in a "drop" foot, in which the foot remains angled in a downward manner, making the individual prone to falling. Steady and rapid progression of the disease usually leads to the inability to walk within about 10 years after onset. The child exhibits characteristics that include:

- a waddling gait,
- difficulty in climbing stairs,

- a tendency for falling, and
- difficulty in rising from a recumbent position.

An additional characteristic is a high level of creatine phosophokinase (CPK), a protein commonly appearing in muscle. An abnormal CPK level found in blood serum is an important laboratory finding in the diagnosis of DMD.

Lordosis frequently develops from weakness of the trunk musculature (figure 15.2). As the disease progresses, the child eventually needs to use orthopedic devices (e.g., leg braces, walker) in order to continue walking. However, even with these devices and continued physical therapy, the child eventually becomes confined to a wheelchair and grows obese. Contractures might form at the ankle, knee, and hip joints, and muscle atrophy is extensive. Soon after the child begins using a wheelchair, scoliosis (a lateral curvature of the spine) also develops. Although weakness of the arms is present in the early stages of the disease, it does not cause real problems until the individual begins using a wheelchair. At that time, progressive loss of strength in these muscles continues until it becomes impossible to lift objects or even lift the hands to the mouth. Death often results in about the third decade of life. With continued research, such as muscle cell transplants, a cure for this type of dystrophy might be forthcoming. However, at present no treatment exists to stop muscle atrophy; any treatment given is basically symptomatic. A major treatment goal is to maintain ambulation as long as possible through exercise and activity.

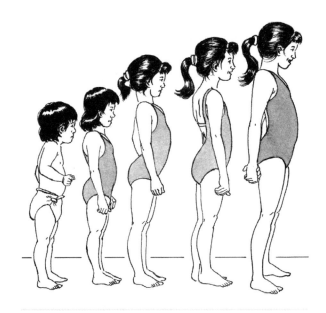

Figure 15.2 The developmental posture sequence of a child with Duchenne Muscular Dystrophy. Notice the increased lordosis as the child gets older.

Cognitive difficulties are present in some children with DMD, but many of these children exhibit above-average intelligence. Sometimes slowness of movement and limitations in physical abilities are misinterpreted as cognitive difficulties. It is important to recognize that should a child have cognitive difficulties, they are stable and do not worsen as the disease progresses.

Physical education can play an important role in managing muscular dystrophy, especially when exercises and activities are performed during the initial stage of the disease. Muscular strength

APPLICATION EXAMPLE

Breathing Activities

Setting: Parents of Jerrance, a child with muscular dystrophy, ask the adapted physical education teacher to suggest a couple of breathing activities that can be done at home so that Jerrance can maintain appropriate function of his respiratory muscles.

Student: Jerrance, an 8-year-old boy with muscular dystrophy beginning to exhibit weak respiratory muscles

Application: The adapted physical education teacher recommends that Jerrance perform the

following two activities with a friend, sibling, or parent on a daily basis:

- Jerrance and a partner face each other (about a yard apart) and try to keep a balloon in the air as long as possible by blowing it to each other without letting it touch the ground.

- While sitting and facing each other at opposite ends of a small table (about a yard long), Jerrance and his partner attempt to blow a Ping-Pong ball toward and across each other's goal (end of table).

and endurance activities programmed on a regular basis can have a positive effect on muscular development and can serve to counteract muscular atrophy. Particular attention should be given to the development of the lower leg, hip, abdomen, and thigh because muscles of these areas are used for locomotion. For people with weak respiratory muscles, especially those confined to wheelchairs, breathing exercises and activities should be given priority and performed on a daily basis (see the application example for more information). Strength and endurance can be developed through aquatic activities that use water as resistance. Performed on a regular basis, flexibility activities and exercises help to develop or maintain the person's range of motion so that permanent joint contractures do not develop; flexibility activities that keep the child's attention might be chosen. Low-intensity aerobic activities are also helpful in managing obesity, which is common in individuals with muscular dystrophy. Dance movements are particularly helpful for improving flexibility and cardiorespiratory efficiency. Arm and upper-body movements for those in wheelchairs can be performed to music. Postural exercises and activities help reduce postural deviations and give the individual an opportunity to perform out of the wheelchair.

Juvenile Rheumatoid Arthritis

Juvenile rheumatoid arthritis (JRA), or Still's disease, manifests itself in childhood and is one of several forms of juvenile arthritis. While the American College of Rheumatology uses the term JRA, the European League Against Rheumatism uses the term juvenile chronic arthritis (JCA). JRA is the most common type of arthritis in children and one if the more frequent chronic diseases in children today (Cassidy & Petty, 2001). As with adult rheumatoid arthritis, the cause of JRA is unknown. Depending on the degree of involvement, JRA affects joint movement. Joints become inflamed, which result in reduced range of motion. In some cases, permanent joint contractures develop, and muscle atrophy is pronounced. Some authorities suggest that inflammation of the joints results from abnormal antibodies of unknown origin that circulate in the blood and destroy the body's normal structures. The disease is not inherited, nor does it seem to be a result of climate, diet, or patterns of living. JRA is characterized by a series of remissions and exacerbations (attacks). One cannot predict how long affected children will

remain ill or how long they will be symptom free. Generally, the prognosis for JRA is quite encouraging—only about 15 percent of children with JRA will have moderate to severe functional disability in adulthood. The highest frequency of onset is between one to three years of age and before the age of 16. According to recent figures, about 285,000 infants, youngsters, and teenagers possess some form of arthritis, of which JRA is the most common (Arthritis Foundation, 2001). There are three main types of JRA: polyarticular, pauciarticular, or systemic. Polyarticular JRA affects five or more joints, which might include hand and finger joints as well as knees, hips, ankles, feet, neck, and jaw. It affects more girls than boys. The same joints on both sides of the body are typically affected. Malformation of the temporomandibular joint can result in slower jaw growth. Other symptoms could include a low-grade fever and anemia. Pauciarticular JRA affects four or fewer joints, which can include knees, ankles, and elbows. Children with pauciarticular have the highest probability for developing uveitis (chronic eye inflammation). Pauciarticular JRA typically affects one side of the body. The systemic type of JRA affects the entire body, including joints and internal organs. It is the least common form of JRA and affects boys and girls equally. In addition to joint inflammation, additional symptoms include a high spiking fever lasting for weeks or months and a body rash. In some instances there is inflammation of the heart and lungs along with enlarged liver or spleen. In a majority of cases, the high spiking fever and inflammation of the internal organs might disappear completely; however, joint inflammation will be chronic.

At present, there is no cure for juvenile arthritis. However, research is now being conducted in the areas of genetics and immunology. Treatment for severe periods of exacerbation consists of controlling joint inflammation, which is accomplished through medicine, rest, appropriately designed exercises, and, in some cases, surgery. During acute stages, complete bed rest is strongly recommended, and excessive weight bearing by inflamed joints should be avoided. In some instances, surgery might be performed to remove damaged tissue from the joint to prevent greater deterioration to bone and cartilage. Total hip replacements are now performed in some cases with great success.

Even during acute stages of JRA, joints should be exercised through the greatest possible range of motion at least once or twice a day so range of motion can be maintained. For individuals unable to exercise independently, teachers or therapists can provide partial or total assistance.

The physical education program should stress exercises and activities (e.g., swimming and bike riding) that help increase or maintain range of motion so that permanent contractures do not develop and normal bone density is maintained. Muscular strength and endurance activities should also be offered to decrease muscle atrophy. Isometric activities, such as hooking the fingers of both hands together and trying to pull them apart or placing the palms together and pushing, may be particularly helpful to encourage the development of hand muscles. Another hand exercise involves squeezing objects of various sizes and shapes. Hand exercises are most important in order to maintain appropriate manipulative skills. Most people with severe joint limitation or deterioration should refrain from activities that twist, jar, or place undue stress on the joints; activities such as basketball, volleyball, and tennis might need to be modified accordingly.

Osteogenesis Imperfecta

Osteogenesis imperfecta (OI), also known as brittle bone disease, is an inherited condition in which bones are imperfectly formed. An unknown cause produces a defect in the protein matrix of collagen fibers. The defect reduces the amount of calcium and phosphorus (bone salts), which in turn produces a weak bone structure. Bones are very easily broken. When healed, they take on a shortened, bowed appearance. According to the Osteogenesis Imperfecta Foundation (2003), up to 50,000 people in the United States might be affected with OI.

Essentially, there are four types of OI, which vary in characteristics and severity. The mildest and most common form of OI is type I in which bones are easily susceptible to fractures. Those with type I experience most fractures before puberty, but bone deformity is minimal or nonexistent. Collagen fibers are normal but about half the normal amount. Type I individuals attain normal stature, but they have a tendency toward spinal curvature and a triangular shaped face. Abnormal joint elasticity and low muscle tone is present. In addition, individuals with type I exhibit a thinning sclera (white portion of the eye) that takes on a blue, purple, or gray tint. About 50 percent of individuals with type I OI acquire a hearing loss in early adulthood. Many individuals with type I do not exhibit all the characteristics

described here. The most severe and least common form of OI is type II, which results in death at or shortly after birth. In type II the child is born with multiple severe deformities and fractures, is of small stature, and has underdeveloped lungs. In type II, collagen fibers are improperly formed. Children with type III OI have fractures present at birth, and bone deformity is often severe. Children have poor muscle development and abnormal joint elasticity. They are short of stature and exhibit a barrel-shaped chest, triangular shaped face, and spinal curvatures. As in type I OI, eye sclera is abnormal in color, and hearing loss is possible. However, in type III collagen fibers are improperly formed. Type IV is between types I and III in severity. Those with type III have easily fractured bones; most fractures occur before puberty. Children have a tendency to be shorter than average height, have moderate bone deformity, a barrel-shaped chest, a tendency for spinal curvature, and a triangular shaped face. Like types II and III, individuals with type IV have collagen fibers that are improperly formed. As with types I and III, hearing loss is possible, but unlike types I and III, eye sclera is normal in color.

Students with severe fractures and deformities might require the use of wheelchairs. Multiple fractures over a prolonged period have resulted in limb deformities and significant lower-limb limitations. Individuals with milder types of OI can ambulate independently, whereas those with more moderate degrees of impairment need to use canes or crutches. There is no cure for the disease. At the present time, surgery—which consists of reinforcing the bone by inserting a steel rod lengthwise through its shaft—is the most effective treatment.

Physical education activities such as swimming, bowling (with the use of a ball ramp), and the use of beach balls for striking and catching are safe to perform because they do not place undue stress on the joints or bones. Because of abnormal joint elasticity, strength-building exercises and activities, which can increase joint stability, should be encouraged. This might be accomplished in a swimming environment because water buoyancy promotes movement without risk of new fractures. Most people with the disorder should not play power volleyball, basketball, or football unless the games are modified appropriately.

Arthrogryposis

Arthrogryposis (ar-throw-gry-po-sis), also known as multiple congenital contractures, is a nonprogressive congenital disease of unknown origin.

About 500 infants in the United States are born with arthrogryposis each year. The condition affects some or all of the joints and is characterized by stiff joints (contractures) and weak muscles. Instead of normal muscle tissue surrounding the joints, fatty and connective tissue is present. The severity of the condition varies; an individual might be in a wheelchair or be only minimally affected. Limbs commonly exhibit deformities and can be fixed in almost any position. In addition, affected limbs are usually small in circumference, and joints appear large. Surgery, casting, and bracing are usually recommended for people with deformities. Most typically, upper-limb involvement includes turned-in shoulders, extended and straightened elbows, pronated forearms, and flexed wrists and fingers; trunk and lower-limb involvement includes flexion and outward rotation of the hip, bent or straightened knees, and feet turned in and down. Other conditions associated with arthrogryposis include congenital heart defects, respiratory problems, and facial abnormalities. Individuals with arthrogryposis almost always possess normal intelligence and speech.

Because people with arthrogryposis have restricted range of motion, their physical education program should focus on exercises and activities that increase flexibility. In addition, they should be taught games and sports that effectively make use of leisure time. In most cases, exercises and activities appropriate for individuals with arthritis are also acceptable for those with arthrogryposis and OI. Swimming, an excellent leisure activity, encourages the development of flexibility and strengthens weak muscles surrounding joints. Other activities, modified when needed, include cycling, miniature golf, bowling, shuffleboard, bocce, and track and field events.

Multiple Sclerosis

Multiple sclerosis (MS) is one of the most common central nervous system diseases among young adults. Worldwide it is estimated that MS affects between 1 to 1.25 million people (Waubant & Goodkin, 2000). It is a slowly progressive neurological disorder that might result in total incapacitation. About two thirds of all those afflicted with the disease experience onset between the ages of 20 and 40, and the disorder affects more women than men. The disease might manifest itself in young children or the elderly as well, but this is rare. MS is characterized by changes in the white matter covering (myelin sheath) of nerve fibers at various locations throughout the central nervous system (brain and spinal cord). The cause of MS is unknown, but some scientists believe that the disease might be a result of a virus attack, an immune reaction, or a combination of the two. Current research studies are focusing on myelin formation and its changes, drug therapy, immunotherapy, and diagnostic tests, among others. MS is diagnosed through a variety of tests, including neurological examination, blood tests, and magnetic resonance imaging (MRI), which can show lesions in the central nervous system.

In MS, the myelin sheath is destroyed and replaced by scar tissue; a lesion might vary from the size of a pinpoint to about 1 or 2 centimeters in diameter. Individuals with MS exhibit various symptoms, depending on the location of the damage. The most common symptoms are extreme fatigue, heat intolerance, hand tremors, loss of coordination, numbness, general weakness, double vision, slurred speech, staggering gait, and partial or complete paralysis. According to current estimates, about 75 percent of people with MS experience extreme fatigue. The early stage of the disease is characterized by periods of exacerbation followed by periods of remission. As scar tissue continues to replace healthy tissue, symptoms tend to continue uninterrupted.

Because most people with MS are stricken in the most productive and enjoyable years of life, many are unable to cope emotionally with the disease. Additional stress results from the fact that there is no established treatment to cure it. The main treatment objective is to maintain the person's functional ability as long as possible. Treatment should be directed toward preventing loss of range of motion (which would result in permanent contractures) and preserving strength and endurance. Many times, the disease progresses to a point at which the person needs braces or a wheelchair. Intensive therapy or physical conditioning during acute phases of MS might cause general body fatigue. Thus, physical activities should be judiciously programmed for the individual with MS.

Recent evidence suggests that moderate physical activity on a regular basis significantly reduces non–activity related fatigue, which a vast majority of people with MS experience. In addition to the physiological effects, regular physical activity provides psychological benefits as well. According to the National MS Society, although current fatigue medications are helpful, moderate, regular physical activity seems to be more effective. Mild forms of physical activity that emphasize strength and endurance should be performed for short periods of time. However, the duration and intensity of the activity should be programmed according to the individual's exercise tolerance level. Activities such as bowling, miniature golf, and table tennis are acceptable if regular rest periods are provided. Stretching exercises and activities are also recommended to maintain adequate range of motion. Activities incorporating balance and agility components might prove to be helpful for those exhibiting a staggering gait or varying degrees of paralysis. Many of these activities can be done in water. However, because of heat intolerance by many individuals with MS, water temperature must remain in the 80s.

Friedreich's Ataxia

An inherited neurological disease, Friedreich's ataxia usually manifests itself in childhood and early adolescence (boys and girls 8 to 15 years of age), but it can occur as late as the age of 20. The disease was first identified in the 1860s by German neurologist Nikolaus Friedreich, who described the disease as a gradual loss of motor coordination and progressive nerve degeneration. The sensory nerves of the limbs and trunk (peripheral nerves) are affected as well as the loss of tendon reflexes, and the disease might progress either slowly or rapidly. When the disease progresses quickly, many people become wheelchair bound by the late teens and early 20s. Early symptoms include poor balance and lack of limb and trunk coordination, resulting in a clumsy, awkward, wide-based gait almost indistinguishable from the gait of ataxic cerebral palsy. This is caused by the brain's inability to regulate the body's posture and the coordination of its muscle movements. Fine motor control of the upper limbs tends to be impaired because tremors might be present. Atrophy is common in muscles of the distal limbs. Individuals typically exhibit slurred speech and are prone to seizures. Most develop foot deformities such as clubfoot, high arches, and hammertoes, a condition in which the toes are curled because of tight flexor tendons of the second and third toes. As the disease progresses, spinal deformities, such as kyphosis and scoliosis, are common. Most individuals exhibit heart problems, such as heart murmur, enlarged heart, and constriction of the aorta and pulmonary arteries. Diabetes develops in 10 to 40 percent of people with Friedreich's ataxia. Visual abnormalities include nystagmus and poor visual tracking. There is no known cure at this time, but research is ongoing to find the gene responsible for the condition. Very recently, researchers have narrowed the gene responsible for the disease to 1 of 46 chromosomes. Therapy consists of managing foot and spinal deformities and cardiac conditions. Medication might be prescribed to control diabetes as well as cardiac, tremor, and seizure disorders. Some common diagnostic tests include electromyogram, which measures electrical activity of muscle cells; nerve conduction velocity, which measures how fast nerves are transmitting impulses; and electrocardiogram, which determines if heart abnormalities exist.

Physical education activities should be planned to promote muscle strength and endurance and body coordination. Activities that develop muscles of the distal limbs such as the wrist, forearm, foot, and lower leg are recommended. The development of grip strength is essential for activities that use implements, such as rackets and bats. Individuals exhibiting poor balance and lack of coordination are in need of balance training and activities that encourage development of fundamental locomotor movements. For those with fine motor control difficulties, activities might take the form of riflery, billiards, or archery. Remedial exercises are recommended for people with foot and spinal deviations. Games, exercises, and activities should be programmed according to individual tolerance levels for those with cardiac conditions; those prone to seizures should be closely monitored.

Myasthenia Gravis

Myasthenia gravis (MG) is a neuromuscular disease characterized by a reduction in muscular strength ranging from minimal to severe. Worldwide, MG affects about 2 of every 1 million people each year. In the United States, the disease affects about 25,000 people (Muscular Dystrophy Association, 2001). The disease was first identified and named in 1890 by a German medical professor, Wilhelm Erb. Even when strength is greatly reduced, the individual still has enough strength to perform activities, but often this demands maximum or near maximum effort. In some cases, MG is confused with muscular dystrophy because muscle weakness affects the back, lower extremities, and intercostal muscles. It affects more females than males. Women often develop MG in their late teens and early 20s whereas men usually acquire it after the age of 60. Although the exact cause is unknown, nerve impulses are prevented from reaching muscle fibers because of the production of destructive antibodies by the immune system.

The antibodies block the muscle receptors at the neuromuscular junction (points at which nerve endings meet muscle cells).

One of the main symptoms is abnormal fatigue. Muscles generally appear normal except for some disuse atrophy. Weakness of the extraocular and lid muscles of the eye occurs in about half of all cases; this results in drooping of the eyelid (ptosis) and double vision (strabismus). Because facial, jaw, and tongue muscles become easily fatigued, individuals might have problems chewing and speaking. Weakness of the neck muscles might prevent holding the head erect. Back musculature might also be weakened, which leads to misalignment of the spinal column, which can further restrict movement. Muscle weakness makes the execution of the activities of daily living difficult and contributes to low levels of cardiorespiratory efficiency. The disease is not progressive; it might appear gradually or might be sudden. It commonly goes into remission for weeks, months, or years. Thus, affected individuals live in fear of recurrent attacks. Among other treatments, MG is commonly treated with the use of drugs that help strengthen the neuromotor transmission or suppress the immune system. However, these drugs have serious side effects when taken over a prolonged period. Most recently, a blood flow exchange process is now being used that removes antibodies from the blood that might interfere with the transmission of nerve impulses.

Physical activities should focus on the development of physical fitness. Because people with MG fatigue easily, their activities should be programmed in a progressive manner and according to individual tolerance levels that take into account the duration, intensity, and frequency of the activity. When the muscles of respiration are weakened, breathing activities are strongly recommended. It is important to strengthen weak neck muscles, especially when the program includes such activities as heading a soccer ball or hitting a volleyball. Fitness levels can be maintained during acute stages through swimming activities incorporated into the program. Poor body mechanics resulting from weak musculature will ultimately affect locomotor skills. Thus, remedial posture exercises and activities should be offered.

Guillain-Barré Syndrome

Guillain-Barré (ghee-yan bah-ray) syndrome (GBS), also known as infectious polyneuritis, is a neurological disorder characterized by ascending paralysis of the peripheral nerves resulting in acute and progressive paralysis. Initially, the lower extremities become easily fatigued, and numbness, tingling, and symmetrical weakness are present. Paralysis, which usually originates in the feet and lower legs, progresses to the upper leg, continues on to the trunk and upper extremities, and finally affects the facial muscles. Symptoms usually reach their maximum within a few weeks. When initially affected, people involved in locomotor activities of an endurance nature, such as distance running, typically find themselves stumbling or falling during the activity session as muscles of the feet and lower legs fatigue prematurely. The condition is frequently preceded by a respiratory or gastrointestinal infection, which suggests that a viral or bacterial infection might be the cause. Some authorities believe that the syndrome is an autoimmune disease. Neurologists, immunologists, and virologists are cooperatively investigating the syndrome.

Although rare, Guillain-Barré syndrome occurs worldwide, affecting both genders equally and all ages and races. The National Institute of Neurological Diseases and Strokes (2001) reports the syndrome affects about 1 person per 100,000. It can affect both infants and the elderly but seems to cluster in childhood and middle age. About 90 percent of individuals recover either completely or with minimal paralysis, and most walk unassisted. However, about 10 percent can die as a result of pulmonary complications. Acute stage treatment includes passive range of motion, exercise, and rest.

For people who have made complete recovery, no restrictions in physical activities are needed. However, some individuals who do not completely recover exhibit weakness in limb and respiratory muscles. Their activities can focus on maintaining or improving cardiorespiratory endurance and strength and endurance of unaffected muscles. When a significant amount of weakness remains in the lower extremities, activities might need to be modified accordingly.

PROGRAM IMPLICATIONS

All people with amputations, dwarfism, or les autres conditions can benefit from physical education and sport activities. Should modifications or adaptations be needed, the type and degree of physical involvement, motor educability, interest level, and overall educational goals will determine them. Especially for individuals with unique physical and motor needs, physical education instruction needs to individualized and personalized.

General Guidelines

Several general guidelines can be applied to programs for people with amputations, dwarfism, and les autres conditions. The guidelines that follow pertain to safety considerations, physical fitness, motor development, and implications for sports.

Safety Considerations

The physical impairments presented in this chapter are of a medical origin and, as such, the physical education teacher or coach needs to be aware of key safety considerations. Individuals with physical limitations should be encouraged to experience as many postures as possible so that contractures do not develop, thus leading to decubitus ulcers that might require hospitalization. This is especially true for individuals in wheelchairs, such as students with advanced cases of Duchenne MD. Before getting a student into or out of a wheelchair, or positioning a person who has obvious physical limitations, it is important to consult the student's special education teacher and physical therapist or occupational therapist (should the student be receiving such services).

Individuals with disabilities described in this chapter might tire easily, especially when performing large muscle activities over an extended period of time. Fatigue exhibited for example in MS and Duchenne MD might cause someone to become frustrated, which in turn adversely affects proper performance. The instructor should permit rest periods and player substitutions when endurance-related activities such as soccer and basketball are being played. Should teachers fail to take this fatigue factor into account and program activities without regard to students' personal intensity and duration levels, the risk of medical problems is high, especially for individuals with cardiopathic conditions. For example, children with DMD typically have cardiopathic involvement as an accompanying condition to muscle degeneration.

Thus, it is important that physical educators consult medical professionals before establishing physical education and sport programs to meet unique needs. This is especially important for students currently under the care of a physician and those receiving physical or occupational therapy. Teachers should be in direct contact with the school nurse. Typically, the school nurse understands the student's medical condition and knows whether the student is taking any prescribed medication. Usually, the nurse has direct contact with the child's parents and personal physician should medical problems arise during the school day.

Physical Fitness

Today, a sufficient amount of evidence suggests that appropriate levels of health-related physical fitness contribute to the overall wellness of people with amputations, dwarfism, and les autres conditions. In fact, the Amputee Coalition of America has recently created a new youth fitness program called Bio-fit. The fitness program is designed for children with amputations as well as their parents and caregivers in which physical activities are led by Paralympians. Winnick and Short (1999) recommend that youngsters with amputations and congenital anomalies be evaluated and achieve physical fitness standards that promote functioning consistent with positive health. This level of functioning includes appropriate fitness levels to adequately perform activities of daily living, including physical education and sport activities. The Brockport Physical Fitness Test (BPFT; Winnick & Short, 1999) provides selected test items as well as projected standards for the evaluation of aerobic functioning, body composition, and musculoskeletal functioning (flexibility, muscular strength, and endurance). Because the conditions described in this chapter are of a medical nature, certain precautions might need to be taken as health-related fitness programs are established and implemented. It is especially important that the teacher be sensitive to the frequency, intensity, duration, and mode of exercises and activities. Because of low levels of fitness it is recommended that intermittent training be used, especially for students who fatigue easily. Activities performed with greater frequency and with less intensity and duration are recommended. Exercises and activities that are enjoyed will tend to be continued over time, which increases the chances of these individuals adopting lifelong active lifestyles.

Because restricted movement is common in individuals whose conditions are described in this chapter, it is important that strength and flexibility be developed to appropriate levels of physical fitness. Range of motion is basic to overall fitness. Maximizing range of motion allows individuals the opportunity to perform physical education and sport skills, as well as activities of daily living in the most efficient and effective manner possible. Weak musculature and limited range of motion, if unattended, lead to permanent joint contractures that result in significant loss of movement capability which, in turn, reduces the person's level of health-related fitness. Surburg (1999) provides flexibility and range-of-motion guidelines and exercise and activity examples that can be applied to individuals with different physical conditions, including amputations, MS, Duchenne MD, and JRA.

Motor Development

Many times, amputations and les autres impairments (and to a lesser extent dwarfism) restrict individuals from experiencing normal movement patterns essential to normal motor development. As a result, delays in the development of motor skills and patterns are common. Lack of ability to control movements contributes to the performance of inappropriate motor skills and patterns. Children with congenital amputations, for example, are frequently unable to execute fundamental movements in an appropriate manner. And children born with the absence of a lower limb might be delayed in acquiring locomotor patterns such as creeping, walking, and running. Muscle atrophy or weakness prevents individuals from developing the strength and endurance levels needed to perform fundamental movements vital to overall health.

Physical education programs should encourage the sequential development of fundamental motor patterns and skills essential for participation in games, sports, and leisure activities. When attempting to enhance motor development, the physical educator should be concerned primarily with the manner in which a movement is performed rather than with its outcome. For example, he or she should be concerned with the mechanics of the movement within the physical limitations of the student (e.g., dwarfism). The goal of every physical education and sport program should be to encourage individuals to achieve maximum motor control and development within their ability levels. The motor development of youngsters with disabilities covered in this chapter might be assessed using standardized tests as well as less formal procedures, including task analysis and rubrics. Interested readers are encouraged to consult chapter 4 for information on assessment of motor development and skills.

Implications for Teaching Sports in Physical Education

Physical education teachers are encouraged to integrate many of the sport activities described in the Adapted Sports section of this chapter

into their physical education programs. For example, sitting volleyball, a Disabled Sports/USA (DS/USA) event can be incorporated into a physical education program as a means of developing eye–hand coordination as well as offering an opportunity for sport competition. Other events included in organized competition such as DAAA (e.g., bowling, archery, cycling, bocce) can be taught.

Amputations

In general, a physical education program for individuals with amputations can follow the same guidelines as are developed for individuals without disabilities. Aside from missing limb(s), people with amputations are considered "able bodied." However, the location and extent of the amputation(s) might require modifications in some activities.

Most individuals with amputations typically use prosthetic devices in physical education activities. A person with unilateral lower-limb amputation usually continues to use the device for participation in football, basketball, volleyball, and most leisure activities. As previously stated, more mechanically efficient devices are now being worn by athletes with unilateral lower-limb amputations. In some situations, a unilateral BE, AE, or shoulder amputee might consider the device a hindrance to successful performance and discard it during participation; this is common in baseball or softball. Such is the case with Jim Abbott, a former Major League baseball pitcher who did not wear a prosthetic device for his BE congenital amputation. Of course, in some activities, such as swimming, the prosthetic device must be removed. Currently, the National Federation of State High School Associations allows participating athletes to wear prosthetic devices for interscholastic sports such as football, wrestling, gymnastics, soccer, baseball, and field and ice hockey. However, a device cannot be used if it is more dangerous to other players than a corresponding human limb or if it gives the user an advantage over an opponent (National Federation of State High School Associations, 2003).

Participation in physical education and sport activities requires some adaptations depending on the location and extent of the amputation and the type of activity. Table 15.1 (p. 268) provides some general participation guidelines for individuals with amputations.

Table 15.1   Participation Guide For Students With Amputations in Selected Physical Education and Sport Activities

Activity	Upper extremity	Lower extremity (BK)	Lower extremity (AK)
Archery	[R]A	R	R
Baseball or softball	R	R	[R]A
Basketball	R	R	[WC]A
Bicycling	R	R	R
Bowling	R	R	R
Field hockey	R	I	[WC]A
Football	R	R	I
Golf	[R]A	R	R
Rifle shooting	[R]A	R	R
Skiing (downhill)	R	R	[R]A
Cross-country skiing	R	R	[R]A
Soccer	R	R	I
Swimming	R	R	R
Table tennis	R	R	R
Tennis	R	R	I
Track	R	R	[WC]A
Volleyball	R	R	[WC]A

Note: A = adapted; R = recommended; I = individualized; WC = wheelchair.

Adapted, by permission, from R.C. Adams and J.A. McCubbin, 1991, *Games, sports, and exercises for physically disabled*, 4th ed. (Philadelphia, PA: Lippincott, Williams, and Wilkins), 181.

Physical Fitness

Like people with other physical conditions, individuals with amputations might need to increase their levels of health-related physical fitness. The Brockport Physical Fitness Test (BPFT) can be used to assess the health-related fitness of youngsters with amputations and congenital anomalies. Depending on the site of amputation, various test items might be chosen to assess aerobic functioning, body composition, and musculoskeletal functioning. For example, a person with a unilateral AK amputation would perform the Target Aerobic Movement Test (TAMT) to assess aerobic functioning. In this test, appropriate physical activities can be chosen to assess aerobic functioning. An activity would be deemed appropriate if it is of sufficient intensity to reach a minimal target heart rate and sustain that rate within a given target zone. Sustaining a level of moderate physical

activity for at least 15 minutes would be a minimal general standard for youngsters with amputations and congenital anomalies. Other BPFT items for a youngster with a unilateral AK amputation would be a triceps and subscapular skinfold measure (body composition) and a bench press (muscular strength and endurance). Individuals with bilateral BK or AK amputations often have lower levels of aerobic functioning level than upper-limb amputees because their locomotor activities might be severely restricted. For long-term aerobic training programs for individuals with lower-limb amputations, activities should be chosen that do not cause overuse injuries or skin breakdown (Pitetti & Pedrotty, 2003). Suggested aerobic activities include swimming, an arm-propelled tricycle, or arm, rowing, and cycle ergometers. To further encourage aerobic development, the physical educator could offer activities in which a wheelchair can be used, such as marathon racing or slalom events.

Muscular strength and endurance and flexibility should be developed for all parts of the body, even at the site of the amputation or anomaly. The remaining muscles surrounding the amputation or anomaly also need to develop so that they remain in balance with the nonaffected side. For a person with only a partial limb amputation, such as an ankle or wrist disarticulation, exercises and activities should be programmed to encourage the most normal possible use of the remaining limb segment. Absence of a limb can also affect balance and leverage when performing resistance activities. Some muscle strength activities are better and more safely performed without the use of a prosthetic device. DiRocco (1999) recommends that if a force of resistance runs through the shaft of the prosthetic device, then it would be acceptable to wear it for that particular exercise. For example, it would be acceptable if a person were wearing a prosthetic device when performing the bench press, because the weight would be distributed through the shaft of the prosthesis when the person attempted to lift the weight.

Both unilateral and bilateral AK amputees have a tendency to be obese and thus should be encouraged to follow a weight-reduction diet along with a program of regular, vigorous physical activity. Short, McCubbin, and Frey (1999) describe several desirable characteristics of a weight loss physical activity program for individuals with disabilities. Some of these characteristics include raising daily total energy expenditure, de-emphasizing activity intensity and emphasizing activity duration, exercising daily, participating with partners or small groups, and doing well-liked activities. Before an individual begins a physical activity program, Lockette and Keyes (1994) recommend that amputation type, functional range of motion, strength, balance and stability, and skin integrity be assessed.

Motor Skills

Limb deficiency of the upper or lower limb can affect an individual's level of motor skills. For example, acquired BE/AE or BK/AK amputations of the dominant limb can initially result in awkward or clumsy performance of motor skills. This might be more pronounced for adolescents and adults who have already mastered motor skills with their dominant limbs (e.g., overarm throw, kicking a ball). The absence of a limb most often affects the center of gravity, to a greater degree in lower-limb amputees than in upper-limb amputees. The result is difficulty with activities requiring balance. Developing static and dynamic balance is crucial to the performance of locomotor skills such as walking, running, hopping, or, for that matter, sitting in a wheelchair. Activities that foster the development of balance and proper body alignment should be encouraged; these might include traversing an obstacle course, performing on a mini-trampoline, or walking a balance beam. Speed and agility might also be adversely affected, especially in those with lower-limb deficiencies. People with unilateral AK and bilateral BK or AK amputations are most affected and might have difficulty in locomotor activities that require quick change of direction, such as basketball, football, soccer, and tennis.

Although unilateral BK or BE amputees can participate most effectively in physical education and competitive sports, those with bilateral upper or lower amputations will have activity restrictions. Bilateral upper-limb amputees can successfully engage in activities that involve the lower extremities to a significant degree—for example, skating, soccer, and jogging.

Unilateral AK amputees can effectively participate in activities such as swimming, water skiing, snow skiing, weightlifting, and certain field events like the shot put and javelin, which do not emphasize locomotion and agility. Those with bilateral BK amputations will be more limited in activities such as track events, football, or basketball, which involve jumping, hopping, or body contact. Bilateral AK amputees are much more restricted in their activities, usually relying part time on a wheelchair and using crutches at other times. Activities such as archery, badminton, and riflery, which can be performed from a sitting or prone position, are appropriate.

Dwarfism

Individuals with dwarfism should be encouraged to perform in regular physical education and sport activities. The development of health-related physical fitness and motor skills are important aspects of any physical education program. As such, individuals with dwarfism should have the same opportunities to develop as other individuals. This is especially true because many individuals with achondroplasia are overweight or obese. However, there are some considerations that need to be addressed in programs when developing physical fitness and motor skills.

Physical Fitness

Restricted range of motion, obesity, and joint defects might predispose an individual to dislocations and joint trauma. This is especially true for individuals with achondroplasia. Thus, maintaining flexibility, especially at the elbow joint, is important. Exercises and activities that place undue stress on weight-bearing joints should be avoided or modified to accommodate this limitation. For example, jogging can be replaced with walking or riding a bicycle, and volleyball can be performed with a lighter ball. Swimming, which promotes flexibility and cardiovascular endurance, is an excellent activity for individuals with achondroplasia because it does not place undue stress on the joints.

Motor Skills

Because of shorter limbs, the quality of movement might be affected in some activities, including ball throwing and catching, striking, and locomotor skills such as running, jumping, and hopping. Implements such as golf clubs, rackets, and hockey sticks will need to be adjusted according to the size of the individual. Failure to use appropriate sized implements results in the execution of inappropriate or inefficient motor skills.

Les Autres

Atrophied or weak muscles (e.g., Duchenne MD), reduced range of motion (e.g., JRA), and balance and coordination problems (e.g., Friedreich's ataxia) many times hinder (or prevent) individuals with les autres conditions in performing physical activities. Many of the conditions presented in this chapter are progressive (e.g., Duchenne MD, Friedreich's ataxia, MS, Myasthenia Gravis)—that is, muscles become weaker regardless of the amount of exercise or activity. As a result, it is important to maintain current levels of muscular strength and endurance as long as possible. DiRocco (1999) suggests that individuals with progressive muscular disorders not go beyond 50 percent of their maximum resistance weight when performing muscular strength activities. According to DiRocco, the exercise intensity level is too great if functional strength does not return within 12 hours of the exercise. This should be monitored closely by the teacher or coach. When affected muscles are weaker than antigravity strength (e.g., DMD), added weight resistance (like formal weights) is of no use in developing strength (Tarnopolsky, 2003). Rather, the goal is to maintain full range of motion against gravity. Once this is accomplished, gradual resistance exercises can be employed.

Exercises and activities that are fun increase the likelihood that they are performed on a regular basis. For young children, activities should be of short duration and might include rhythmic activities, active lead-up games, and obstacle courses. For adolescents, emphasis should be placed on activities with a focus on lifetime participation such as racket sports, skating, cycling, hiking, and swimming. Individuals in wheelchairs can participate in activities such as sledge hockey, rugby, seated aerobics, and wheelchair tennis.

Because limitations presented in this chapter prevent extended periods of activity, low aerobic fitness levels are common. For example, individuals with MS typically exhibit general body fatigue (not related to exercise), which reduces their capacity to perform physical activity over an extended period of time. This inactivity makes individuals with les autres conditions prone to obesity (e.g., Duchenne MD, amputations) and ultimately places them at greater risk for coronary heart disease and other associated conditions (osteoporosis). For individuals with moderate degrees of orthopedic impairments, low-impact aerobics, cycling, swimming, and brisk walking for extended periods of time can achieve aerobic gains. Maintaining a satisfactory level of health-related fitness reduces the risk of other associated debilitating conditions, such as osteoporosis.

Severe limitations in strength and flexibility, for whatever reason, can also hinder people with les autres conditions from acquiring the motor skills they need to become successful in sport and leisure activities. The inability to perform these skills reduces the person's chances of being physically active and, in turn, places these individuals at greater risk of reduced health.

Whether physical activity is performed for purposes of fitness or enhanced motor skills, a proper period of warm-up and cool-down, which places emphasis on enhanced flexibility, is needed. This is especially true for those with conditions that limit joint flexibility, such as JRA, OI, and other les autres conditions that might elicit spasticity. Daily range-of-motion exercises are recommended for those who have joint-limiting conditions such as JRA, arthrogryposis, and Guillain-Barré syndrome. Surburg (1999) offers several excellent recommendations in the development of flexibility and range of motion for individuals with disabilities.

INCLUSION

As is true for other disabilities, students with amputations, dwarfism, and les autres conditions must be encouraged to participate in regular physical education classes unless the IEP team decides otherwise. Most, if not all, people with these conditions can be safely and effectively included in regular physical education settings. And, unless those with les autres conditions are severely physically impaired, most can also be safely and effectively included in regular physical education settings as well. Even students with severe physical impairments can succeed in regular physical education settings as long as appropriate activities are performed and support services (e.g., teacher aides) are provided. In all cases, however, decisions about inclusion must be made on an individual basis in consultation with the student's IEP team. The impairments described in this chapter affect physical functioning, not intellectual functioning, so students will clearly understand verbal and written directions as well as rules and strategies for games and sports. In certain cases, teachers might need to structure activities to suit the participants' abilities.

Students with amputations or other lower-limb deficiencies could play goalie in soccer or floor hockey and could pitch or play first base in softball. These students with lower-limb amputations can be provided the option of riding a stationary bike when other students without disabilities are required to run over a long distance. Students with dwarfism can be safely and effectively included in regular physical education classes as long as the proper size equipment is used to accommodate short limbs. This would include shorter and lighter weight implements such as bats, rackets, and hockey sticks. Students with reduced muscular strength and aerobic capacity (e.g., muscular dystrophy, MS, Friedreich's ataxia) can also be safely and effectively included in regular physical education classes as long as activities are modified or activity options are provided. For example, when programming activities for the development of arm and shoulder strength, students with reduced strength can perform modified push-ups (performed with knees touching the floor) or chin-ups with a horizontal bar (performed from a supine position on the floor), whereas students without disabilities perform push-ups and chin-ups in a traditional manner. Students with joint limitations or deficiencies, such as those with JRA, arthrogryposis, and osteogenesis imperfecta,

can also benefit from regular physical education classes. For example, when programming activities to enhance aerobic capacity, these students can swim or participate in low-impact aerobics while students without disabilities participate in more traditional forms of rope skipping, jogging or running over distance, and bench stepping.

ADAPTED SPORTS

At almost all age levels, people with amputations, dwarfism, and les autres conditions now have the opportunity to become involved in competitive sports. Organizations such as Disabled Sports, USA (DS/USA), and the Dwarf Athletic Association of America (DAAA) assist individuals in reaching their maximum potential in sport. DS/USA and DAAA offer a variety of sporting events that in many cases have been modified for specific disabilities. Athletes are able to participate in these events on the basis of their functional abilities. These organizations are members of the Committee on Sports for the Disabled (COSD) of the United States Olympic Committee and members of the International Sports Organization for the Disabled (ISOD).

Amputations

DS/USA sponsors organized competition for athletes with amputations (as well as competition for individuals with birth defects, visual impairments, and neurological conditions). Founded in 1967 by disabled Vietnam veterans, DS/USA is the nation's largest multisport and multidisability organization. National and international competition for athletes with amputations is based on the nine-level classification system described earlier in this chapter. People with combinations of amputations not specified in the classification system are assigned to the class closest to the actual disability. For example, a combined AK and BK amputee would be placed in class A1, whereas a combined AE and BE amputee would be in class A5. People with single-arm paralysis are tested for muscle strength of the arms and hands. The following movements are tested and scored on a scale from 0 to 5 (5 being the greatest function):

- Shoulder flexion, extension, abduction, and adduction
- Elbow flexion and extension
- Wrist dorsal and volar flexion

- Finger flexion and extension at the metacarpophalangeal joints
- Thumb opposition and extension

Classification for participants with single-arm paralysis is limited to A6 (AE) or A8 (BE).

Amputee competition at both the national and international level takes place in track events such as 100-, 200-, and 400-meter dashes and 800- and 1,500-meter runs, and in field events such as shot put, discus, javelin, long jump, and high jump. National and international competition might also be offered in basketball, volleyball, lawn bowling, pistol shooting, table tennis, cycling, archery, weightlifting, and swimming (100-meter backstroke, 400-meter breaststroke, 100- and 400-meter freestyle, and 4 × 50-meter individual medley). Volleyball and basketball are offered in both sitting and ambulatory categories. In each sport, athletes of similar classifications compete with prostheses, except for those with double AK or combined upper and lower amputations.

In addition to national and regional competitions sponsored by DS/USA, amputees are eligible to compete in events sponsored by Wheelchair Sports, USA (WS/USA), the National Wheelchair Basketball Association (NWBA), and the National Federation of Wheelchair Tennis (NFWT), as long as they have an amputation of the lower extremity and require the use of a wheelchair.

Dwarfism

The DAAA was established in 1985 for the purpose of providing organized sport competition to individuals with dwarfism. Although independent of the Little People of America, DAAA maintains ties with that organization. Sports include track (15-, 20-, 40-, 60-, 100-meter runs and 4 × 100-meter relay), field (shot put, tennis and softball throw, discus, soft discus, and javelin), swimming (freestyle, backstroke, and breaststroke at 25, 50, and 100 meters), basketball, bocce (individual and team), equestrian, soccer, volleyball, table tennis, and power lifting. Separate competition is offered for men and women except for basketball, volleyball, and team bocce in which both men and women play on the same team. Skiing is offered in the winter.

Individuals are classified for open division (ages 16 to 39) track, field, and swimming events. There are three classes for track alone, which are based on a ratio of standing height to sitting height, and three classes for field and swimming, which

are based on the ratio of arm span to biacromial breadth. This system, which is now being refined, is used only for National DAAA events. For International events, the ISOD functional classification system is used.

To be eligible for competition, individuals with disproportionate dwarfism must be equal to or less than 152.4 centimeters (5 feet) in height, whereas individuals with proportionate dwarfism must be equal to or less than 147.3 centimeters (4 feet, 10 inches) in height. Individuals participate in one of five divisions (open, youth, master, wheelchair, or futures). Youth events (7 to 15 years) emphasize achieving one's personal best, whereas the futures division is for children younger than seven years of age. In this division a limited number of events are offered on a noncompetitive basis. DAAA also offers clinics and developmental events.

Les Autres

Historically, the les autres movement was associated with cerebral palsy sports. Les autres athletes performed at the National Cerebral Palsy Games in 1981 and 1983 along with CP athletes. At the National Cerebral Palsy/Les Autres games in Michigan in 1985, they participated in their own separate competition. In 1988 the United States Les Autres Sports Association (USLASA) held a national competition in Nashville. Currently, the National Disability Sports Alliance (NDSA) serves les autres athletes. These athletes compete among themselves in events such as track and field, swimming, volleyball, archery, bocce, cycling, shooting, table tennis, wheelchair team handball, and power lifting. Currently, the classification system for les autres athletes coincides with ISOD. Classes are divided into wheelchair and ambulatory sections. The number of eligible classes might vary with each event. Currently, for track and field competition, there are five wheelchair classes and five ambulatory classes with the recent addition of three jumping classes for certain field events.

SUMMARY

This chapter has described the conditions of amputations, dwarfism, and les autres as they relate to physical education and sport. Physical and motor needs were described and program and activity suggestions presented. Recognizing the medical nature of these conditions, teachers and coaches are encouraged to plan activities in consultation with allied medical professionals and the person's personal physician.

REFERENCES

Arthritis Foundation (2001). *Arthritis in children.* Atlanta, GA: The Arthritis Foundation.

Cassidy, J.T., & Petty, R.E. (Eds.) (2001). *Textbook of pediatric rheumatology.* Philadelphia: Saunders.

DiRocco, P. (1999). Muscular strength and endurance. In J. P. Winnick & F. X. Short (Eds.), *The Brockport physical fitness training guide* (pp. 39-73). Champaign, IL: Human Kinetics.

Frey, G., & Palmer, D. (1999). Achondroplasia (dwarfism). In L. Phelps (Ed.), *Health-related disorders in children and adolescents: A guidebook for understanding and educating* (pp. 29-35). Washington, DC: American Psychological Association.

Little People of America (2003). *Facts and resources.* Retrieved from www.lpaonline.org/resources_faq.html.

Lockette, K.F., & Keyes, A.M. (1994). *Conditioning with physical disabilities.* Champaign, IL: Human Kinetics.

Muscular Dystrophy Association (2001). *Facts about myasthenia gravis.* Tucson, AZ: Muscular Dystrophy Association.

National Federation of State High School Associations (2003). *Football rules book.* Indianapolis, IN: National Federation of State High School Federations

National Institute of Neurological Diseases and Strokes (2001). *Guillain-Barré Syndrome.* Bethesda, MD: National Institutes of Health (NIH).

Osgenesis Imperfecta Foundation (2003). *OI: A guide for medical professionals, individuals, and families affected by OI.* Gaithersburg, MD: Osteogenesis Imperfecta Foundation.

Pitetti, K.H., & Pedrotty, M.H. (2003). Lower-limb amputation. In J.L. Durstine & G.E. Moore (Eds.), *ACSM's Exercise management for persons with chronic diseases and disabilities* (2nd ed.), (pp. 230-235). Champaign, IL: Human Kinetics.

Short, F.X., McCubbin, J., & Frey, G. (1999). Cardiorespiratory endurance and body composition. In J.P. Winnick & F.X. Short (Eds.), *The Brockport physical fitness training guide* (pp. 13-37). Champaign, IL: Human Kinetics.

Surburg, P. (1999). Flexibility/range of motion. In J.P. Winnick & F.X. Short (Eds.), *The Brockport physical fitness test training guide* (pp. 75-119) Champaign, IL: Human Kinetics.

Tarnopolsky, M.A. (2003). Muscular dystrophy. In J.L. Durstine & G.E. Moore (Eds.), *ACSM's Exercise management for persons with chronic diseases and disabilities* (2nd ed.), (pp. 254-261). Champaign, IL: Human Kinetics.

Waubant, E., & Goodkin, D. (2000). Multiple sclerosis. In R. Evans, D. Baskin, & F. Yatsu (Eds.), *Prognosis of neurological disorders,* (2nd ed.), (pp. 291-313). New York, NY: Oxford Press.

Winnick, J.P., & Short, F.X. (1999). *The Brockport physical fitness test manual.* Champaign, IL: Human Kinetics.

WRITTEN RESOURCES

Water exercise: Pools, spas and arthritis (2000). Atlanta, GA: The Arthritis Foundation.

This brochure provides the reasons for water exercise along with a variety of exercises and activities. The brochure can be obtained by writing to the Arthritis Foundation, P.O. Box 7669, Atlanta, GA 30357 or visiting their Web site at www.arthritis.org.

Porter, P., Hall, C., & Williams, F. (1999). *A teacher's guide to Duchenne muscular dystrophy.* Tucson, AZ: Muscular Dystrophy Association.

This manual provides information on developmental issues, school behaviors and attendance, and physical education participation. It can be obtained by writing the Muscular Dystrophy Association (MDA) at 3300 East Sunrise Dr., Tucson, AZ, 85718-3208 or by contacting your local MDA Chapter.

AUDIOVISUAL RESOURCES

What is DS/USA? (Videotape, n.d.) Disabled Sports, USA, 451 Hungerford Dr., Suite 100, Rockville, MD 20850.

This video features the organizational structure of Disabled Sport, USA as well as competition footage and interviews of DS/USA athletes and staff.

Exercise interventions for infants and children with Osteogenesis Imperfecta. (Videotape, n.d.). Osteogenesis Imperfecta Foundation, 804 W. Diamond Ave., Suite 210, Gaithersburg, MD 20878, (301) 947-0083, e-mail: bonelink@oif.org.

This tape addresses issues of exercise for infants and children followed by questions and answers about exercise.

Aerobics for amputees. (Videotape, n.d.). Disabled Sport, USA, 451 Hungerford Dr., Suite 100, Rockville, MD 20850.

This video depicts vigorous exercises for ambulatory—individuals who have impaired balance or coordination—people who can exercise standing up but cannot do fancy footwork that might upset balance.

ELECTRONIC RESOURCES

Amputee Coalition of America: www.amputee-coalition.org.

This Web site provides information and education regarding limb loss and limb differences. The organization provides publications, peer support, and various programs and events (e.g., Bio-fit) with special attention to youth. The mailing address for this organization is: 900 East Hill Ave., Suite 285, Knoxville, TN 37915-2568.

CHAPTER 16

Spinal Cord Disabilities

Luke E. Kelly

Jerry and Rick are playing one-on-one basketball. Whoever reaches 15 first wins. The score is 14 all, and Jerry has the ball. Rick is on defense and knows he has to stop Jerry, or he will have to listen to him bragging the rest of the day. Rick positions himself in the center of the lane and gives Jerry an alley to his right. Rick knows Jerry has no left-hand shot and figures he can overplay his right side. Jerry starts at midcourt and drives toward Rick. Jerry makes a head fake first to the left and then to the right and then pulls up and shoots. Rick immediately yells "Travel!" as the shot swishes through the net.

"Travel? Who are you kidding?" responds Jerry. "You overcommitted and got skunked."

"Keep dreaming," says Rick. "You took four pushes on your rims without dribbling before taking that shot—that's traveling in my book."

Jerry smiles. "I didn't think you could count and play defense at the same time."

Rick takes the ball out and drives to Jerry's right. Jerry moves to block the lane. Rick does a 180 in his chair, dribbles the ball once on the floor, puts the ball on his lap, gives two quick pushes on his rims, picks up the ball, and shoots. "That's all she wrote!" he yells as the ball banks off the backboard and in.

"Nice move," says Jerry. "Another game?"

Rick and Jerry both have spinal cord injuries resulting in the loss of the use of their legs. They met at a rehabilitation center after their injuries and began playing wheelchair basketball. They now both play on the local wheelchair basketball team.

The focus of this chapter is to review the common spinal cord disabilities and the implications for physical education. After reading this chapter, teachers should be able to modify their programs or develop appropriate alternative programs to accommodate the needs of students with spinal cord disabilities. Spinal cord disabilities are conditions that result from injury to, or disease of, the vertebrae or the nerves of the spinal column. These conditions are almost always associated with some degree of paralysis caused by damage to the spinal cord. The degree of the paralysis is a function of the location of the injury on the spinal column and the number of neural fibers subsequently destroyed. Three such spinal cord disabilities will be examined in this chapter: traumatic injuries to the spine resulting in quadriplegia and paraplegia, poliomyelitis, and spina bifida. This chapter will also review several common spinal column postural deviations: scoliosis, kyphosis, lordosis, spondylolysis, and spondylolisthesis, which can adversely affect body mechanics and pre-dispose the spine to injury. Finally, this chapter will cover orthotic devices commonly associated with spinal cord disabilities, as well as physical education and sport implications.

CLASSIFICATIONS

The physical education teacher should be aware of the different systems for categorizing spinal cord disabilities. Medical classifications are based on the segment of the spinal cord that is impaired, whereas sport organizations choose to classify people by their abilities in order to match similarly able athletes for competition.

Medical

As illustrated in figure 16.1, spinal cord injuries are medically labeled or classified according to the segment of the spinal column (i.e., cervical, thoracic, lumbar, or sacral) and the number

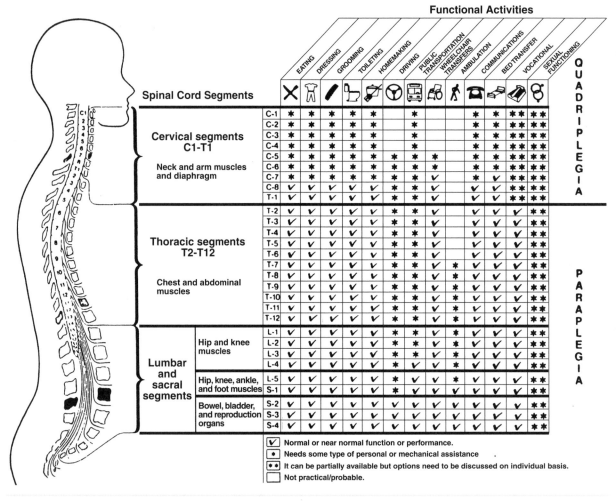

Figure 16.1 Functional activity for spinal cord injuries.

Courtesy of Healthsouth Harmarville Rehabilitation Hospital, Pittsburgh, PA 15238.

of the vertebra at or below which the injury occurred. For example, an individual classified as a C6 complete has a fracture between the sixth and seventh cervical vertebrae that completely severs the spinal cord. The location of the injury is important because it provides insight related to the functions that might be affected. The extent of the spinal cord lesion is ascertained through muscle, reflex, and sensation testing.

The actual impact of a spinal cord injury is best understood in terms of what muscles can still be used, how strong these muscles are, and what can functionally be done with the muscles in the context of self-help skills (eating, dressing, grooming), movement (wheelchair, ambulation, transfers, bed), vocational skills, and physical education skills.

Table 16.1 provides a summary of the major muscle groups innervated at several key locations

Table 16.1 Potential Functional Abilities by Select Lesion Locations

Lesion locations	Key muscles innervated	Potential movements	Associated functional abilities	Sample physical education activities
C4	Neck, diaphragm	Head control, limited respiratory endurance	Control of an electronic wheelchair and other computer electronic devices that can be controlled by a mouth-operated joystick	Riflery, bowling
C5	Partial shoulder, biceps	Abduction of the arms; flexion of the arms	Can propel a wheelchair with modified rims; can assist in transfers; can perform some functional arm movements using elbow flexion and gravity to extend the arm	Swimming
C6	Major shoulder, wrist extensors	Abduction and flexion of the arms, wrist extension and possibly a weak grasp	Can roll over in bed; might be able to transfer from wheelchair to bed; improved ability to propel wheelchair independently; partial independence in eating, grooming, and dressing using special assistive devices	Billiards, putting
C7	Triceps, finger extensions, finger flexions	Stabilization and extension of the arm at the elbow, improved grasp and release but still weak	Independent in wheelchair locomotion, bed, sitting up, and in many cases, transferring from bed to wheelchair; increased independence in eating, grooming, and dressing	Archery, crossbow, table tennis
T1	All upper-extremity muscles	All upper body lacks trunk stability and respiratory endurance	Independent in wheelchair and bed transfers, eating, grooming, dressing, and toileting; can ambulate with assistance using long leg braces, pelvic band, and crutches	Any activities from a wheelchair
T6	Upper-trunk muscles	Trunk stability, improved respiratory endurance	Can lift heavier objects because of improved stability; can independently put their own braces on; can ambulate with low spinal attachment, pelvic band, long leg braces, and crutches, using a "swing" gait but still depends on wheelchair as primary means of locomotion	Track and field, bowling, weight lifting
T12	Abdominal muscles and thoracic back muscles	Increased trunk stability, all muscles needed for respiratory endurance	Can independently ambulate with long leg braces including stairs and curbs; uses a wheelchair only for convenience	Competitive swimming, marathon racing
L4	Lower back, hip flexors quadriceps	Total trunk stability, ability to flex the hip and lift the leg	Can walk independently with short leg braces and bilateral canes or crutches	Some standing activities
S1	Hamstring and peroneal muscles	Bend knee, lift the foot up	Can walk independently without crutches; might require ankle braces or orthotic shoes	Normal physical education

along the spinal column, with implications for the movements, abilities, and physical education activities that might be possible with lesions at these locations. The functional abilities remaining are cumulative as one progresses down the spinal column. For example, an individual with a lesion at or below Tl would have all the muscles and abilities shown at and above that level.

Sport

Sport organizations that sponsor athletic events for individuals with spinal cord disabilities use different classification systems to equate athletes for competition. The most widely used system is the one used by Wheelchair Sports, USA (formerly the National Wheelchair Athletic Association [NWAA]). This system classifies athletes by functional ability into one of several classes based on the sporting event, the degree of muscular functioning, and actual performance during competition. Muscular functioning includes the evaluation of such actions as arm function, hand function, trunk function, trunk stability, and pelvic stability in relation to their importance in performing a given sporting event. This classification system provides an efficient way of equating competition among a diverse group of athletes with varying types of spinal cord disabilities. The functional classification system is illustrated in table 16.2. It is important to note that, although functional abilities are the key criteria in functional classification systems, there is a relation between these sport classifications and the level of spinal cord damage. The approximate spinal cord lesion level associated with the National Wheelchair Basketball Association (NWBA) and several of the functional sport classifications are shown in figure 16.2 (p. 283).

Table 16.2 Functional Classifications

Sport or class	Description
Archery	
AR1	Defined as tetraplegic archers in a wheelchair. The archer with upper cervical lesions, with triceps not functional against resistance (i.e., test grades 0-3) and the archer with lower cervical lesions, with good normal triceps power (i.e., test grades 4-5), wrist extensors and flexors, but having no finger flexors or extensors of functional value (i.e., below grade 3 on the muscle test scale), might use a release, compound or recurved bow, strapping, and body support. All AR1 archers are allowed to use a compound or recurved bow, a release or finger, or any combination of the above. The equipment will be standard FITA equipment rules with the exception of the addition of the release and compound bow. The sighting aids must be according to current FITA shooting rules, (A) outdoor target archery, article 504, archer's equipment, (a) (v). Archers who use mechanical release may receive assistance in putting arrow in their bows.
AR2	An open class for wheelchair archers. The archers use equipment according to FITA rules. For AR2 division, there must be no more than 15-cm slackness in the back upholstery of the wheelchair to be measured from the front of the main vertical support of the chair back. No strapping to the chair is allowed in the AR2 classification. The height of body support from the top of the chair to the armpit shall be no less than 11 cm.
AR3	A standing division for disabled archers will be permitted at some USA-sanctioned wheelchair archery events.
Field events	
F1-51	Events: Club, discus *Functional:* No grip with nonthrowing arm. (Use resin or adhesive substance for grip.) Discus—little control of the discus because finger movements are absent. Throws with a flat trajectory. Club—might throw forward or backward over the head. Use either thumb and index finger, or index and middle finger, or middle and ring finger grip. (Club—when throwing backward, the athlete is using his or her strong elbow flexors.) *Neurological Level C6 anatomical level:* Functional elbow flexors and wrist dorsiflexors. Might have elbow extensors (up to power 3) but usually not wrist palmar flexors. Might have shoulder weakness. No sitting balance. *Old level* 1A complete (*Note:* This system applies to the spinal injured athlete.) Athletes whose disability is a result of polio or other causes might show different movement and function than described here. However, the total function of the athlete in this specific event shall be similar to that of the spinal cord injury description.

Sport or class	Description
	Field events
F2-52	Events: Shot, discus, and javelin *Functional:* Difficulty gripping with nonthrowing arm. Shot—unable to form a fist, thus usually no finger contact with the shot at the release point. Unable to spread fingers apart. Discus—no functional finger flexors (i.e., unable to form a fist). Difficulty placing fingers over the edge of the discus, but might do so with the aid of contractures or spasticity. Javelin—usually grip the javelin between the index and middle fingers but might use the gap between the thumb and index finger or between the middle and ring fingers. These athletes might have slight function between the digits of the hand. *Neurological level C7 anatomical capability:* Functional elbow flexors and extensors, wrist dorsiflexors, and palmar flexors. Good shoulder muscle function. Might have some finger flexion and extension but not functional. *Old level 1b* complete: no sitting balance. Also 1A incomplete with the ability to lift trunk off the back of a chair and to perform backward and forward movement. Might also be able to rotate the trunk. (*Note:* This system applies to the spinal-injured athlete.) Athletes whose disability is a result of polio or other causes might show different movement and function than described here. However, the total function of the athlete in this specific event shall be similar to that of the spinal cord injury description.
F3-53	Events: Shot, discus, and javelin. *Functional:* Nearly normal grip with nonthrowing arm. Shot—usually a good fist can be made. Can spread the fingers apart but not with normal power. Use some spreading of the fingers, and can "grasp" the shot put when throwing. Discus—good finger function to hold discus; might be able to import spin on the discus. Able to spread and close the fingers but not with normal power. Javelin—usually grip javelin between the thumb and index finger. Have ability to hold javelin because of presence of hand muscles that spread and close the fingers. *Neurological level C8 anatomical capability:* Full power at elbow and wrist joints. Full or almost full power of finger flexion and extension. Functional but not normal intrinsic muscles of the hand (demonstrable wasting). *Old class:* 1C complete (no sitting balance). Also 1B incomplete with trunk movements.
F4-54	Events: Shot, discus, and javelin *Functional:* No sitting balance. Usually holds onto part of the chair while throwing. Complete class 2 and upper-class 3 athletes have normal upper limbs. They can hold the throwing implement normally. They have no functional trunk movements. Incomplete 1C athletes who have trunk movements with hand function like F3. *Neurological level T1-T7 anatomical capability as above. Old class 1C* incomplete, 2 complete, upper 3 complete.
F5-55	Events: Shot, discus, and javelin. *Functional:* Three trunk movements might be seen in this class: (1) off the back of a chair (in an upward direction); (2) movement in the backward and forward plane; (3) some trunk rotation. They have fair to good sitting balance. They cannot have functional hip flexors (i.e., ability to lift the thigh upward in the sitting position). They might have stiffness of the spine that improves balance but reduces the ability to rotate the spine. Shot and javelin—tend to use forward and backward movements, whereas the discus predominantly uses rotary movements. *Neurological level T8-L1 anatomical capability:* Normal upper limb function. Have abdominal muscles and spinal extensors (upper or more commonly upper and lower). Might have nonfunctional hip flexors (grade 1). Have no adductor function. *Old class:* lower 3, upper 4

(continued)

Table 16.2 *(continued)*

Sport or class	Description
Field events	
F6-56	Events: Shot, discus and javelin.
	Functional:
	Good balance and movements in the backward and forward plane. Have good trunk rotation. Can lift the thighs (i.e., off the chair); hip flexion. Can press the knees together (hip adduction). Might be able to straighten the knees (knee extension). Might have some ability to bend the knees (knee flexion). *Neurological level L2-L5 anatomical capability.*
	Old class lower 4, upper 5
F7-57	Events: Shot, discus, and javelin
	Functional:
	Very good sitting balance and movements in the backward and forward plane. Usually very good balance and movements toward one side (side-to-side movements) because of presence of one functional hip abductor (on the side that movement is toward). Usually can bend one hip backward (i.e., push the thigh into the chair). Usually can bend one ankle downward (i.e., push the foot onto the foot plate). The side that is strong is important when considering how much it will help functional performance.
	Neurological level S1-S2 anatomical capability.
	Old class: lower 56
F8-58	Events: Shot, discus, and javelin
	Normal sitting balance and trunk movements in all planes. Usually able to stand and possibly walk with braces or by locking knees straight. Unable to recover balance in standing position when balance is challenged and will fall when attempting throws with full effort in standing position.
	U.S. class only. (*Note:* Any athlete who wishes to be considered for international competition in F8 must (a) not have more than 70 points in the lower limbs and (b) compete from a standing position at a regional or national competition.
F9-42	*Standing:* Internationally, this class would compete in the 42, 43, 44 class with other ambulatory classes. *Justification:* Internationally there is no longer a wheelchair standing class.
Track	
T1	*Functional:*
	Might use elbow flexors to start (back of wrist behind pushing rim). Hands stay in contact or close to the pushing rim, with the power coming from elbow flexion. The old technique is to use the palms of the hands and to push down on the top of the wheel in a forward direction.
	Neurological level C6 anatomical capability:
	Functional elbow flexors and wrist dorsiflexors. No functional elbow extensors or wrist T1 palmar flexors. Might have shoulder weakness.
	Old class: 1A complete
T2	*Functional:*
	Usually uses elbow flexors to start but might use elbow extensors. Power from pushing comes from elbow extension, wrist dorsiflexion, and upper chest muscles (Matson technique). Additional power might be gained by using the elbow flexors when the hands are in contact with the back of the wheel. The head may be forced backward (by the use of neck muscles), producing slight upper trunk movements.
-T2A	*Neurological level C7 anatomical cabability:*
	Functional pectoral muscles, elbow flexors and extensors, wrist dorsiflexors, radial wrist movements, some palmar flexors. No finger flexors or extensors.
	Old class: 1B complete
-T2B	*Neurological level C8 anatomical capability:*
	Functional pectoral muscles, elbow flexors and extensors, wrist dorsiflexors and palmar flexors, radial and ulnar wrist movements, finger flexors and extensors. Do not have the ability to perform finger abduction and adduction (spread fingers and bring them together).
	Old class: 1C complete

Sport or class	Description
Track	
T3	*Functional:* Normal or nearly normal upper limb function. No active trunk movements. When pushing, the trunk is usually lying on the legs. The trunk might rise with the pushing action. Usually use a hand flick technique for power (or friction technique). Might use the shoulder to steer around curves. Interrupt pushing movements to steer and have difficulty resuming the pushing position. When braking quickly, the trunk stays close to pushing position. (*Note:* scoliosis (curvature of the spine) usually interferes with abdominal and back muscle function). *Neurological level T1-T7 anatomical capability:* Have normal or nearly normal upper limb function. No abdominal function. Might have weak upper spinal extension. Old class: incomplete 1C 2, upper 3
T4	*Functional:* Backward movement of the trunk. Usually rotation movements of the trunk. Might use trunk movements to steer around curves. Usually do not have to interrupt pushing stroke rate around curves. When stopping quickly, the trunk moves toward an upright position. Use abdominals for power particularly when starting but also when pushing. *Neurological level T8-S2 anatomical capability:* Back extension, which usually includes both upper and lower extensors. Usually trunk rotation (i.e., abdominal muscles). *Old class:* lower 3 4–5-6
Swimming	
S1-S10	Freestyle, backstroke, butterfly
S1	Very severe quadriplegic with poor head and trunk control (e.g., CP1)
S2	Quadriplegic, complete below C5/6; severe muscular dystrophy; amputation of 4 limbs
S3	Quadriplegic complete below C6; a lower quadriplegic with an additional handicap; severe muscular dystrophy
S4	Quadriplegic complete below C7; some incomplete C5; polio with nonfunctional hands for swimming; muscular dystrophy comparable with C7
S5	Complete quadriplegic below C8; incomplete C7 or C6 with ability to keep legs horizontal and functional hands for swimming
S6	Complete paraplegia below T1-T8; incomplete C8 with ability to keep legs horizontal
S7	Complete paraplegia below T9-L1; double above-the-knee amputee shorter than one-half
S8	Paraplegia L2-L3 with no leg propulsion but ability to keep legs straight; double above-the-knee amputee; double below-the-knee amputee, not longer than one-third
S9	Paraplegia L4-L5; polio with one nonfunctional leg; single above-the-knee amputee; double below-the-knee amputee with stumps longer than one-third
S10	Polio or cauda equina lesion with minimal affection of lower limbs; single below-the knee-amputee; double forefoot amputation
SB1-SB10	Breaststroke
SB1	Quadriplegic complete below C6; a lower quadriplegic with an additional handicap; severe muscular dystrophy
SB2	Quadriplegic complete below C7; muscular dystrophy comparable with C7 complete quadriplegia with no finger extension

(continued)

Table 16.2   (continued)

Sport or class	Description
	Swimming
SB3	Complete quadriplegic below C8; complete paraplegic T1-T5; incomplete C7
SB4	Complete paraplegia T6-T10; incomplete C8, or comparable polio
SB5	Complete paraplegia below T10-L1; incomplete T5, double above-the-knee amputee shorter than one-fourth
SB6	Paraplegia and polio L2-L3 with no leg propulsion, double above-the-knee amputation longer than one-fourth
SB7	Paraplegia and polio L4 poor leg propulsion, below-the-knee amputation shorter than one-half
SB8	Paraplegia L5; polio with one nonfunctional leg; double below-the-knee amputee longer than one-half; single above-the-knee amputee.
SB9	Single below-the-knee amputee less than three-quarters
SB10	Single below-the-knee amputation longer than three-quarters
SM1-SM10	Individual medley—medley classes are calculated by (3 × S class) + (1 × SB class) divided by 4.

Note: Wheelchair Sports, USA also has functional classifications for table tennis and weightlifting.

SPINAL CORD INJURIES

Damage to the spinal cord can occur as a result of infectious diseases or from a variety of genetic and environmental causes. This section describes the common causes of spinal cord disabilities and the implications for planning and delivering physical education.

Traumatic Quadriplegia and Paraplegia

Traumatic quadriplegia and paraplegia refer to spinal cord injuries that result in the loss of movement and sensation. Quadriplegia is used to describe the more severe form, in which all four limbs are affected. Paraplegia refers to the condition in which primarily the lower limbs are affected.

The amount of paralysis or loss of sensation associated with quadriplegia and paraplegia is related to the location of the injury (how high on the spine) and the amount of neural damage (the degree of the lesion). Figure 16.1 shows a side view of the spinal column, accompanied by a description of the functional abilities associated with various levels of injury. The functional abilities indicated for each of the levels should be viewed cautiously because the neural damage to the spinal cord at the site of the injury might be complete or partial. If the cord is severed completely, the individual will have no motor control or sensation in the parts of the body innervated below that point. This loss will be permanent because the spinal cord cannot regenerate itself. In many cases the damage to the spinal cord is only partial, resulting in retention of some sensation and motor control below the site of the injury. In a case involving partial lesion, the individual might experience a gradual return of some muscle control and sensation over several months following the injury. This is a result not of regeneration of damaged nerves, rather it is due to the alleviation of pressure on nerves at the injury site caused by bruising or swelling. Although damage to the spinal cord currently results in a permanent loss of function, a wealth of research is being conducted looking for ways to reverse this process. Promising research results have been found in animals using innovative drug therapies, reactivating dormant nerve cells, and using embryotic transplant therapy. For additional information on these and other advances, consult the electronic resources at the end of this chapter.

Incidence

The National Spinal Cord Injury Association (2003) estimates that about 7,800 people suffer spinal cord

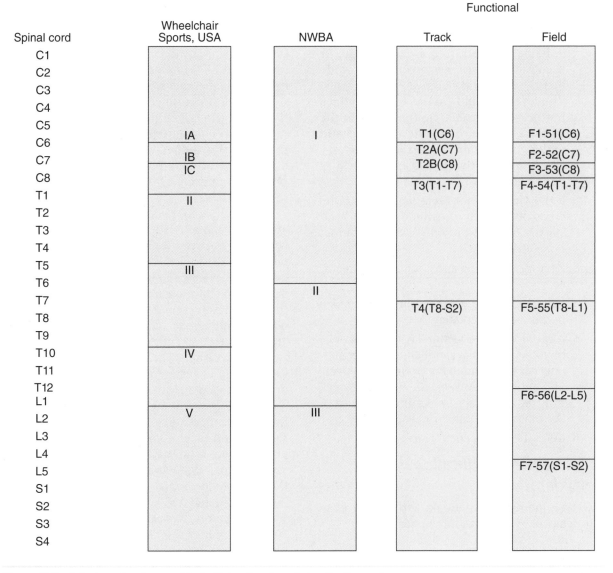

Figure 16.2 Spinal cord levels associated with functional sport classification systems.

Reprinted, by permission, from Wheelchair Sports, USA.

injuries each year in the United States. Among the major causes are automobile accidents (44 percent), acts of violence (24 percent), falls (22 percent), athletic injuries (8 percent), and other accidents (2 percent). Unfortunately, a large percentage of these injuries happen to students of high school age, with the incidence being greater among males (82 percent) than females (18 percent). It should be noted that, when spinal cord injury is suspected, proper handling of the patient immediately after the injury can play a major role in minimizing additional damage to the spinal cord.

The American Medical Association (1990) recommends the following procedures whenever a neck injury is suspected:

A neck injury should be suspected if a head injury has occurred. *Never* move a victim with a suspected neck injury without trained medical assistance unless the victim is in imminent danger of death (from fire, explosion, or a collapsing building, for example). WARNING: Any movement of the head (forward, backward, or side-to-side) can result in paralysis or death. (pp.191-192)

Immediate Treatment If the Victim Must Be Moved

Do not wait and hope someone else will know what to do in this situation. Do the following:

1. Immobilize the neck with a rolled towel or newspaper about four inches wide

wrapped around the neck and tied loosely in place. (Do not allow the tie to interfere with the victim's breathing.) If the victim is being rescued from an automobile or from water, place a reasonably short, wide board behind the victim's head and back. The board should extend to the victim's buttocks. If possible, tie the board to the victim's body around the forehead and under the armpits. Move the victim very slowly and gently. Do *not* let the victim's body bend or twist.

2. If the victim is not breathing or is having great difficulty in breathing, tilt the head *slightly* back to provide and maintain an open airway.

3. Restore breathing and circulation if necessary.

4. Summon paramedics or trained ambulance personnel immediately.

5. After moving the victim, lay folded towels, blankets, clothing, sandbags, or other suitable objects around his or her head, neck, and shoulders to keep the head and neck from moving. Place bricks or stones next to the blankets for additional support.

6. Keep the victim comfortably warm.

Treatment and Educational Considerations

The treatment of individuals with spinal cord injuries usually involves three phases:

Hospitalization

Rehabilitation

Return to the home environment

Although the three phases are presented as separate, there is considerable overlap between the treatments provided within each phase. During the hospital phase, the acute medical aspects of the injury are addressed, and therapy is initiated. Depending on the severity of the injury, the hospital stay can last up to several months. Many people with spinal cord injuries are then transferred from the hospital to a rehabilitation center. As indicated by its name, the rehabilitation phase centers on adjustment to the injury and mastery of basic living skills (e.g., toileting, dressing, transfers, and wheelchair use) with the functional abilities still available. Near the end of the rehabilitation phase, a transition is begun to move the individual back into the home environment. In the case of a

student, the transition involves working with parents and school personnel to make sure that they have the appropriate skills and understanding of the individual's condition and needs and that they know what environmental modifications will be required to accommodate those needs.

The abilities outlined in table 16.1 (p. 277) are those that can potentially be achieved by people with spinal cord injuries. Unfortunately, to achieve these abilities, individuals must accept their conditions, not be hindered by any secondary health problems, and be highly motivated to work in rehabilitation.

One of the major secondary problems associated with spinal cord injuries is psychological acceptance of the limitations imposed by the injury and the loss of former abilities. Counseling is usually a major component of the treatment plan during rehabilitation. It should be recognized that the rate of adjustment and the degree to which different individuals learn to cope with their disabilities vary tremendously.

People with spinal cord injuries are susceptible to a number of secondary health conditions. One of their most common health problems is pressure sores or decubitus ulcers. These are caused by the lack of innervation and reduced blood flow to the skin and most commonly occur at pressure points where a bony prominence is close to the skin (buttocks, pelvis, and ankles). Because of the poor blood circulation, these sores can easily become infected and are extremely slow to heal. The prevention of pressure sores involves regular inspection of the skin, the use of additional padding in troubled areas, and regular pressure releases (changes in position that alleviate the pressure). Individually designed seat cushions can be made and are used by many people to help better distribute pressure and avoid pressure sores. Keeping the skin dry is also important because the skin is more susceptible to sores when it is wet from urine or perspiration.

A problem closely related to pressure sores is bruising of the skin. Because no sensation is felt in the limbs that are not innervated, it is not uncommon for them to be unconsciously bruised or irritated from hitting or rubbing against other surfaces. Injuries of this nature are quite common in wheelchair activities such as basketball if appropriate precautions are not taken. Because these bruises are not felt, they can go unnoticed and eventually can become infected.

A third health problem commonly encountered in individuals with spinal cord injuries is urinary tract infections. Urination is controlled by some form of catheterization on an established schedule. Urinary infections occur when urine is retained in the bladder and backs up into the kidneys. Urinary tract infections can be very severe and usually keep the patient bedridden for a prolonged period of time, which is counterproductive for attitude, rehabilitation, and skill development. Bowel movements must also be carefully monitored to prevent constipation and incontinence. Bowel movements are usually controlled by a combination of diet and mild laxatives. In cases where bowel movements cannot be controlled by diet, a tube is surgically inserted into the intestine. The tube exits through a small opening made in the side and is connected to a bag that collects the fecal excretions.

Two other closely associated problems that frequently accompany spinal cord injuries are spasticity and contractures. Spasticity is an increase in muscle tone in muscles that are no longer innervated because of the injury. This increased muscle tone can nullify the use of other, still innervated muscles. The term "spasm" is frequently used to describe sudden spasticity in a muscle group that can be of sufficient force to launch an individual out of a wheelchair. The best treatment for spastic muscles is to stretch them regularly, particularly before and after rigorous activity. Contractures can frequently occur in the joints of the lower limbs if they are not regularly, passively moved through the full range of motion. A high degree of spasticity in various muscle groups can also limit the range of motion and contribute to contractures.

The last problem commonly associated with spinal cord injuries is a tendency toward obesity. The loss of function in the large-muscle groups in the lower limbs severely reduces the caloric burning capacity of people with spinal cord injuries. Unfortunately, a corresponding loss in appetite does not also occur. Many individuals with spinal cord injuries tend to resume their habitual caloric intake or even to increase it because of their sedentary condition. Weight and diet should be carefully monitored to prevent obesity and the secondary health hazards associated with it. Once weight is gained, it is extremely difficult to lose.

A major key to success in rehabilitation and in accepting a disability is motivation. Many individuals with spinal cord disabilities initially have great difficulty accepting the loss of previous abilities and, subsequently, are reluctant to work hard during the tedious and often painful therapy. Recreational and sport activities are commonly used in both counseling and therapy to provide reasons for working hard and as distractions. A physical educator should be sensitive to the motivational needs of a student returning to a program with a spinal cord disability. Although sport can be a motivator for many, it can also highlight the loss of previous skills and abilities.

The physical education teacher should anticipate needs in the areas of body image, upper-body strength, range of motion, endurance, and wheelchair tolerance. These needs, together with the student's functional abilities, should be analyzed to determine what lifetime sports skills and wheelchair sports are most viable for future participation. These activities then become the annual instructional goals for the physical education program.

Although an individual with a spinal cord injury is still learning to deal with the injury, the physical educator can assist by anticipating the person's needs and planning ahead (see the Student Placement application example). This might involve reminding the student to perform pressure releases at regular intervals (lifting the weight off the seat of the chair, by doing an arm press on the arm supports of the chair, or just shifting the sitting position) or bringing extra towels to class to absorb extra moisture in the chair. Because spasticity and spasms are common, stretching at the beginning of class and periodically during the class is recommended. Finally, pads should be provided to prevent bruising in active wheelchair activities. As the student becomes accustomed to the condition, most of these precautions will become automatic habits. A student who has an external bag should be reminded to empty and clean it before physical education class. In contact activities, care should be taken to protect the bag from contact. For swimming, the bag should be removed and the opening in the side covered with a watertight bandage.

Poliomyelitis

Poliomyelitis, commonly called polio, is a form of paralysis caused by a viral infection that affects the motor cells in the spinal cord. The severity and degree of paralysis vary with each individual and depend on the number and location of the motor cells affected. The paralysis might be temporary, occurring only during the acute phase of the illness (in which case the motor cells are not destroyed), or permanent if the motor cells are destroyed by the virus. Bowel and bladder control, as well as sensation in the involved limbs, are not affected in this condition.

Student Placement

Setting: Individualized education program committee meeting

Student: Fran is 16 years old and returning to school after suffering a complete T6 spinal cord lesion as a result of a motorcycle accident. Prior to the accident, Fran was an excellent athlete. During rehab Fran was cooperative and worked hard. She has expressed concerns about returning to school, particularly physical education class.

Issue: What is the best way to transition Fran back into physical education? What would be the most appropriate physical education placement?

Application: On the basis of the above information and a meeting with Fran, her parents, and the rehab staff, the following is decided:

- Fran will receive an adapted physical education program, which will include an individually designed strength-training and endurance program.

- The program will be initiated in a weight-training unit in an integrated setting with support services as needed.

- Prior to inclusion in the integrated setting, the physical education staff will work with Fran on learning how to safely perform the exercises in her routine.

- Special arrangements will be worked out with Fran to address any concerns she has related to changing clothes for physical education.

Incidence

The occurrence of polio is rare in school-age children today because of the widespread use of the Salk vaccine. The Centers for Disease Control (1995) has reported that there were no new cases of polio reported in the United States from 1985-1994. This is in comparison to over 20,000 reported cases in the United States in 1952. It is projected that polio could be eradicated worldwide by 2005. Although new cases of polio are uncommon, many individuals who have previously had polio have experienced a recurrence of many of the symptoms of polio later in life. This reoccurrence of symptoms, referred to as postpolio syndrome, affects about 25 percent of former polio victims, usually 35 to 40 years after the original onset of the disease. This condition is caused by the overuse of the remaining muscle fibers over time resulting in muscle pain, joint pain, increased fatigue, and loss of strength.

Treatment and Educational Considerations

During the acute, or active, phase of the illness, the child is confined to bed. The illness is accompanied by a high fever and pain and paralysis in the affected muscles. After the acute phase, muscle testing is conducted to determine which muscles were affected and to what degree. Rehabilitation is then begun to develop functional abilities with the muscles that remain.

Depending on the severity of the paralysis, a child might require instruction in walking with crutches or long leg braces or using a wheelchair. When the lower limbs have been severely affected, it is not uncommon for bone deformities to occur as the child develops. These deformities can involve the hips, knees, ankles, or feet and frequently require surgery to correct.

Specific activity implications are difficult to provide for children with polio because their range of abilities can be so great. Physical educators need to accurately evaluate the abilities and limitations imposed by the condition for each student and then make appropriate placement and instructional decisions.

Many children with only one involved limb or mild involvement of two limbs will already have learned to compensate for the condition and can participate in an integrated physical education setting. Others with more extensive or severe involvement might require a more restrictive setting for the provision of adapted physical education services. Care should be taken not to totally remove these children from inclusive physical education. Whatever the degree of involvement, these children have typical play interests and the desire to be with their classmates.

Regardless of the physical education placement, the emphasis should be on optimal development of the muscles the student does have. Priority should be given to lifetime sports skills and activities that can be carried over and pursued for recreation and fitness when the school years are past. Swimming is an excellent example of an activity that promotes lifetime fitness, provides recreation, and prepares one for other activities such as sailing and canoeing.

Spina Bifida

Spina bifida is a congenital birth defect in which the neural tube fails to close completely during the first four weeks of fetal development. Subsequently, the posterior arch of one or more vertebrae fails to develop properly, leaving an opening in the spinal column. There are three classifications of spina bifida, based on which structures, if any, protrude through the opening in the spine.

Myelomeningocele is the most severe and, unfortunately, the most common form of spina bifida. In this condition the covering of the spinal cord (meninges), cerebrospinal fluid, and part of the spinal cord protrude through the opening and form a visible sac on the child's back (see figure 16.3a). Some degree of neurological damage and subsequent loss of motor function are always associated with this form.

Spina bifida meningocele is similar to the myelomeningocele form, except that only the spinal cord covering and cerebrospinal fluid protrude into the sac (see figure 16.3b). This form rarely has any neurological damage associated with it.

Occulta is the mildest and least common form of spina bifida. In this condition, the defect is present in the posterior arch of the vertebra, but nothing protrudes through the opening (see figure 16.3c). No neurological damage is associated with this type of spina bifida.

Once detected soon after birth and surgically corrected, the meningocele and occulta forms of spina bifida have no adverse ramifications. The greatest threat in these conditions is from infection prior to surgery.

Incidence

Because some degree of neurological damage is always associated with the myelomeningocele type of spina bifida, it will be the form discussed in the remainder of this section. About 1 child out of every 1,000 live births has spina bifida (Spina Bifida Association of America, 2003), and 80

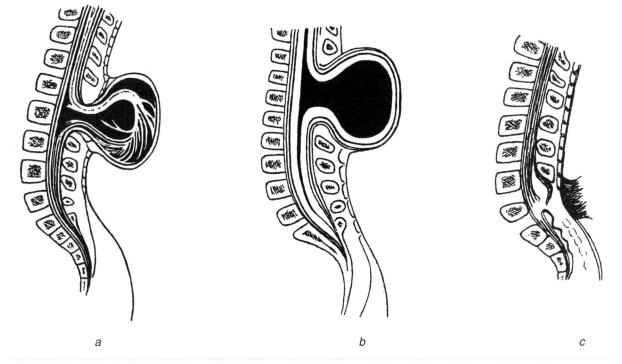

a   *b*   *c*

Figure 16.3 Diagram of the three types of spina bifida: (a) myelomeningocele, (b) meningocele, and (c) occulta.

Reprinted from *Yearbook of Physical Medicine and Rehabilitation*, G.G. Deaver, D. Buck, and J. McCarthy, Spina bifida, pg. 10, Copyright 1952, with permission from Elsevier.

percent of these children have the myelomeningocele form. The degree of neurological damage associated with spina bifida myelomeningocele depends on the location of the deformity and the amount of damage done to the spinal cord. Fortunately, spina bifida occurs most commonly in the lumbar vertebrae, sparing motor function in the upper limbs and limiting the disability primarily to the lower limbs. Bowel and bladder control are almost always lost. The muscle functions and abilities presented in table 16.1 for spinal cord lesions in the lumbar region can also be used to ascertain what functional abilities a child with spina bifida will have.

In addition to the neurological disabilities associated with damage to the spinal cord, myelomeningocele is almost always accompanied by three other conditions: hydrocephalus, Chiari II malformation, and tethering of the spinal cord. **Hydrocephalus** is a condition in which the circulation of the cerebrospinal fluid is obstructed in one of the ventricles or cavities of the brain. If the obstruction is not removed or circumvented, the ventricle begins to enlarge, putting pressure on the brain and enlarging the head. If not treated, this condition can lead to brain damage and mental retardation, and ultimately to death. Today, hydrocephalus is suspected early in children with spina bifida and is usually treated surgically by insertion of a shunt during the first few weeks after birth (see figure 16.4, a-c). The shunt, a plastic tube equipped with a pressure valve, is inserted into a ventricle and drains off the excess cerebrospinal fluid. The fluid is usually drained into either the heart (ventriculoatrial) or the abdomen (ventriculoperitoneal) to be reabsorbed by the body. Additional information regarding shunts can be found in the electronic resources section the end of the chapter.

Chiari II malformation also called Arnold Chiari malformation (ACM) refers to a condition in which the cerebellum and lower brain stem are stretched and pulled through the base of the skull and into the top of the spinal column. This condition is always present in children with myelomeningocele. In mild cases the condition does not cause any problems and is left untreated. In more severe cases, where the functions controlled by the brain stem and cerebellum are compromised, surgery is performed to decompress the brain stem by widening the opening at the base of the skull and at the top of the spinal column.

The spinal cord should float in the spinal canal allowing it to move up and down as the child grows. **Tethering of the spinal cord** refers to anchoring of

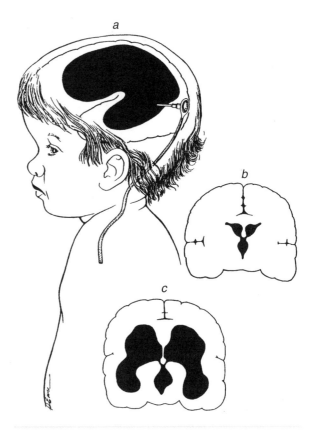

Figure 16.4   Illustration of a shunt being used to relieve hydrocephalus: (a) the shunt in place, (b) normal ventricles, and (c) enlarged ventricles.

the cord within the spinal canal at the site where the spina bifida occurred and was surgically closed. All children with myelomeningocele have tethered cords. The issue is whether the tethering results in stretching of the cord and loss of function caused by reduced circulation. Common symptoms include loss of muscular strength and tone, reductions in gait quality, and further loss of bowel and bladder functions. Tethering usually does not present problems until the adolescent growth spurt. When tethering problems are diagnosed, the problem can be treated by surgically untethering the cord. It is estimated that approximately 60 percent of all individuals with myelomeningocele experience tethering symptoms that could benefit from surgical treatment.

Treatment and Educational Considerations

As mentioned earlier, all forms of spina bifida are diagnosed and surgically treated soon after birth. The major treatment beyond the immediate medical procedures involves physical and occupational therapy for the child and counseling and training for the parents. The therapy has two focuses: using assistive devices to position children so that they parallel the developmental positions (e.g., sitting, crawling, standing) through which a normal child progresses and maintaining full range of motion and stimulating circulation in the lower limbs. In conjunction with their therapy, children with spina bifida are fitted with braces and encouraged to ambulate. Even if functional walking skills are not developed, it is very important for the child with spina bifida to do weight-bearing activities to stimulate bone growth and circulation in the lower limbs. Parents are counseled to provide the child with as normal and as many appropriate stimuli as possible. Many parents, unfortunately, frequently overprotect and confine their children with spina bifida, which results in further delays in growth and development.

Although still in the experimental stage, several innovative surgical treatments are being developed that involve surgically closing the opening in the fetus's spinal cord between the 25th to 30th weeks of the pregnancy. Although it is still too early to evaluate the long-term impact of these new procedures, the results look promising.

There are several important similarities and differences in the treatments of spina bifida and of the spinal cord injuries discussed earlier in this chapter. The similarities concern the muscle and sensation loss and the common problems related to these deficits:

Bone deformities

Bruising

Obesity

Postural deviations

Pressure sores

Urinary tract infections

The differences are related to the onset of the conditions. Different circumstances result in different emotional and developmental ramifications.

Generally, children with spina bifida have fewer emotional problems dealing with their condition than do children with acquired spinal cord disabilities, probably because the condition has been present since birth and they have not suffered the loss of any former abilities. However, this is not to imply that they do not become frustrated when other children can perform skills and play activities that they cannot because of their dependence on a wheelchair or crutches.

A major ramification of the early onset of spina bifida is its effect on growth and development. The lack of innervation and subsequent use and stimulation of the affected limbs retard their physical growth. The result is a greater incidence of bone deformities and contractures in the lower limbs and a greater need for orthotics (braces) to help minimize these deformities and assist in providing functional support. A concurrent problem is related to sensory deprivation during the early years of development because of restricted mobility. This deprivation is frequently compounded by overprotective parents and medical problems that confine the child to bed for long periods.

Children with spina bifida are vulnerable to infections from pressure sores and bruises. Pressure sores are most common in those who are confined to wheelchairs. Bruising and skin irritation are particular concerns for children with spina bifida who use crutches and long leg braces. These children have a tendency to fall frequently in physical activities and to be susceptible to skin irritations from their braces if the braces are not properly put on each time. About 7 out of 10 children with spina bifida have also been found to have an allergic reaction to latex. Latex can be found in rubber balls and other materials used in physical education such as balloons. Physical educators must diligently check all equipment and materials used in physical education to ensure they do not contain latex.

Bowel and bladder control present significant social problems for the child with spina bifida during the early elementary school years. Bowel movements are controlled by diet and medication, which are designed to prevent constipation. Urination is commonly controlled today by a regular schedule of catheterization, performed during the day with assistance by the school nurse or an aide. This dependence on others for help with personal functions and the inevitable occasional accident in class can have negative social implications for children with spina bifida and their classmates.

Finally, children with spina bifida have a tendency toward obesity. Several causes contribute to this tendency. The loss of the caloric expenditure typically made by the large-muscle groups in the lower limbs limits the number of calories that can be burned. Caloric expenditure is frequently further limited by the sedentary environment of these children and their limited mobility during the early years. Control of caloric intake is essential to avoid obesity. Unfortunately, food is frequently highly gratifying to these children and is overprovided by indulging parents and caregivers. Obesity should be avoided at all costs because it further limits the children's mobility and predisposes them to other health problems.

Children with spina bifida will most likely be placed initially in some combination of adapted and regular physical education settings during the early elementary years and will be fully integrated into regular physical education settings by the end of the elementary years. It is important not to remove these children unnecessarily from inclusive physical education settings. They have the same play and social needs as the other students in their classes. On the other hand, the primary goal of physical education, to develop physical and motor skills, should not be sacrificed purely for social objectives. If the student's physical and motor needs cannot be met in an inclusive setting, the student should receive appropriate support or supplemental adapted physical education to meet these needs in a more restricted setting.

Although there has been little systematic and experimentally controlled research on the learning attributes of children with spina bifida, there is a growing body of literature that demonstrates that many children with spina bifida display a range of learning problems involving attention, memory, and organization. Although each child's individual needs should be assessed and individually addressed, physical educators should be aware of potential problems in these areas and how to modify their instruction accordingly to accommodate these needs.

In summary, children with spina bifida need to pursue the same physical education goals targeted for other students. As they pursue these goals, their objectives might be different. Modifications might be needed to accommodate their modes of locomotion (crutches or wheelchair) and to emphasize their upper-body development. Emphasis should be placed on physical fitness and the development of lifetime sports skills.

SPINAL COLUMN DEVIATIONS

Mild postural deviations are quite common and can often be remediated through proper instruction and practice in physical education. It is estimated that 70 percent of all children have mild postural deviations and that 5 percent have serious ones. The prevalence of serious postural deviations is, unfortunately, much greater among students with disabilities.

Poor posture can result from any one or a combination of factors, such as ignorance, environmental conditions, genetics, physical or growth abnormalities, or psychological conditions. In many cases children are unaware that they have poor posture because they do not know what correct posture is and how their posture differs. In other cases, postural deviations can be traced to simple environmental factors, such as poorly fitting shoes. In students with disabilities, poor posture can be caused by factors affecting balance (e.g., visual impairments), neuromuscular conditions (e.g., spina bifida and cerebral palsy), or congenital defects (e.g., bone deformities and amputations). Finally, poor posture can occur as a result of attitude or self-concept. Students who have a poor body image or who lack confidence in their abilities to move tend to display defensive postures that are characterized by poor body alignment.

Physical educators should play an important role in the identification and remediation of postural deviations in all students. The physical educator is often the one educator in the school with the opportunity and background to identify and address postural problems. Unfortunately, postural screening and subsequent remediation are overlooked in many physical education programs. This is ironic because the development of kinesthetic awareness and proper body mechanics is fundamental to teaching physical education and is clearly within the domain of physical education as defined in IDEA.

Several excellent general posture screening tests are available that can be used easily by physical educators and involve minimal preparation and equipment to administer. Two examples, included in the resources list at the end of this chapter, are the Posture Grid (Adams & McCubbin, 1991), and the New York Posture Rating Test (figure 16.5; New York State Education Department, 1966). Posture screening should be an annual procedure in all physical education programs. Particular attention should be paid to children with disabilities because of their generally higher incidence of postural deviation. The appropriate school personnel, as well as the parents or guardians of all children identified as having present and potential postural problems, should be informed of and requested to pursue further evaluation of all these students. The instructor can remediate most mild postural deviations within the regular physical education program by educating the children about proper body mechanics and prescribing exercises that can be performed both in and out of class. Sample exercises are described on pages 297-298.

Viewed from the back, the spinal column should be straight with no lateral (sideways) curves. Any lateral curvature in the back is abnormal and is referred to as scoliosis. Viewed from the side, the spinal column has two mild curves. The first natural curve occurs in the thoracic region, where the vertebrae are concave forward (curving slightly in a posterior or outward direction). An extreme curvature in this region is abnormal and is known as kyphosis. The second natural curve occurs in the lumbar section, where there is mild forward convexity (inward curvature) of the spine. An extreme curvature in this region is also abnormal and is called lordosis. An exaggerated lumbar curve in lower elementary-age children is natural but should disappear by the age of eight.

Scoliosis

Lateral deviations in the spinal column are generally classified according to whether the deviation is structural or nonstructural. Structural deviations are generally related to orthopedic impairments and are permanent or fixed changes in the alignment of the vertebrae that cannot be altered through simple physical manipulation, positioning, or exercise. Nonstructural, or functional, deviations are those in which the vertebrae can be realigned through positioning or removal of the primary cause—such as ignorance or muscle weaknesses—and remedied with practice and exercise.

Structural scoliosis is also frequently classified according to the cause of the condition. Although scoliosis has many possible causes, the two most common are labeled idiopathic and neuromuscular. Idiopathic means that the cause is unknown. Neuromuscular means that the scoliosis is the result of nerve or muscle problems.

Structural idiopathic scoliosis occurs in about 2 percent of all school-age children. The onset of scoliosis usually occurs during the early adolescent years, when children are undergoing a rapid growth spurt. This form of scoliosis is characterized by an S-shaped curve, usually composed of a major curve and one or two minor curves. The major curve is the one causing the deformity. The minor curves, sometimes called secondary or compensatory curves, usually occur above or below the major curve and are the result of the body's

attempt to adjust for the major curve. Although both genders appear to be equally affected by this condition, five times as many females have the progressive form that becomes more severe if not treated. The cause of this progressive form of scoliosis is unknown, but there is some evidence that suggests a possible genetic link in females.

A second type of structural scoliosis, more commonly found in children with severe disabilities, is caused by neuromuscular problems. This form of scoliosis is usually characterized by a C-shaped curve. In severe cases, this form of scoliosis can lead to balance difficulties, pressure on internal organs, and seating problems (pressure sores) for students in wheelchairs.

Nonstructural scoliosis can be the result of several causes and can be characterized by either an S- or a C-curve. The primary causes can be broadly classified as either skeletal or muscular. An example of scoliosis with a skeletal cause would be a curve that has resulted from one leg being shorter than the other. An example of scoliosis with a muscular cause would be a curve that has resulted because the muscles on one side of the back have become stronger than the muscles on the other side and have pulled the spinal column out of line. Fortunately, nonstructural scoliosis can usually be effectively treated by identification and correction of the cause—that is, inserting a lift in the child's shoe to equalize the length of the legs, or strengthening and stretching the appropriate muscle groups in the back (see the Correcting Postural Deviations application example).

Assessment of Scoliosis

Early identification is extremely important for both structural and nonstructural scoliosis so that help can begin and the severity of the curve can be reduced. Scoliosis screening should be conducted annually for all children, particularly from the 3rd through the 10th grade, when the condition is most likely to occur. If a child is suspected of having scoliosis, the parents or guardians, as well as other appropriate school personnel, should be notified and further evaluation conducted. Students suspected of having scoliosis should be monitored frequently, approximately every three months, to ascertain if the condition is progressing. A scoliosis assessment, which can be performed in less than a minute, involves observing the student shirtless. The assessments should be done individually and by an assessor of the same gender as the children being assessed because children

APPLICATION EXAMPLE

Correcting Postural Deviations

Situation: During the annual posture screening evaluation of her fourth grade students, the physical education teacher notices that one of her students has a mild lateral curvature to the right when viewed from behind. When the teacher asks the student to hang from a pull-up bar, the curve disappears.

Student: This 10-year-old boy is very coordinated and active in many sports. His favorite sport is baseball, and he was the star pitcher last year. The physical educator deduces that this student has a nonstructural postural deviation probably caused by his baseball pitching, which overdeveloped and tightened the back muscles on the right side.

Application: On the basis of the information presented here, the physical educator takes the following actions:

- Develops an exercise routine designed to stretch the muscles on the right side of the upper back and strengthen the muscles on the left side of the upper back.

- Contacts the parents and informs them that their son has a mild, nonstructural postural deviation of his back. She tells them that at this time the deviation can be corrected by a routine of exercises. She asks for their assistance in encouraging their son to regularly perform the exercises and in monitoring the remediation of the deviation. She also asks them to identify a reward their son can earn for doing his exercise routine.

- Meets with the student and explains the problem and how it can be corrected by a regular exercise routine. The teacher demonstrates the exercises and has the student perform them a few times to ensure they are done correctly.

- Develops a progress chart she and the student can use to monitor the degree of his curvature and the student's exercise compliance. She gives the student a copy of this chart each month to share with his parents.

---

of these ages are usually self-conscious about the changes occurring in their bodies and about being seen undressed.

To perform a scoliosis assessment, check the symmetry of the child's back while the child is standing and then when the child is bent forward. First, with the child standing erect, observe from a posterior view for any differences between the two sides of the back, including the following points (see figure 16.5, rows A-D):

1. Does the spinal column appear straight or curved?

2. Are the shoulders at the same height, or does one appear higher than the other?

3. Are the hips at the same horizontal distance from the floor, or does one appear higher than the other?

4. Is the space between the arms and trunk equal on both sides of the body?

5. Do the shoulder blades protrude evenly, or does one appear to protrude more than the other?

Then ask the child to perform the Adam's position, bent forward at the waist to about 90 degrees (figure 16.6, p. 295). Examine the back from both a posterior and an anterior view for any noticeable differences in symmetry, such as curvature of the spine or one side of the back being higher or lower than the other, particularly in the thoracic and lumbar regions.

Care and Remediation of Scoliosis

The treatment of scoliosis depends on the type and degree of curvature. As mentioned earlier, nonstructural scoliosis can frequently be corrected when the cause is identified and the condition remediated through a program of specific exercises and body awareness. With structural scoliosis, the treatment varies according to the degree of curvature. Children with mild curvatures (less than 20 degrees) are usually given exercise programs to keep the spine flexible and are monitored on a regular basis to make sure the curves are not becoming more severe.

Children with more severe curves (20 to 40 degrees) are usually treated with braces or orthot-

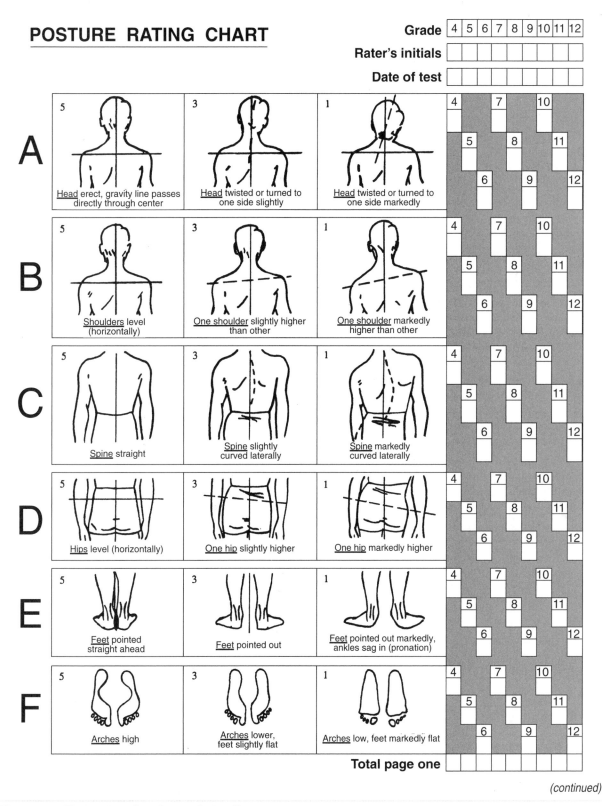

Figure 16.5 The New York State Posture Rating Chart.

293

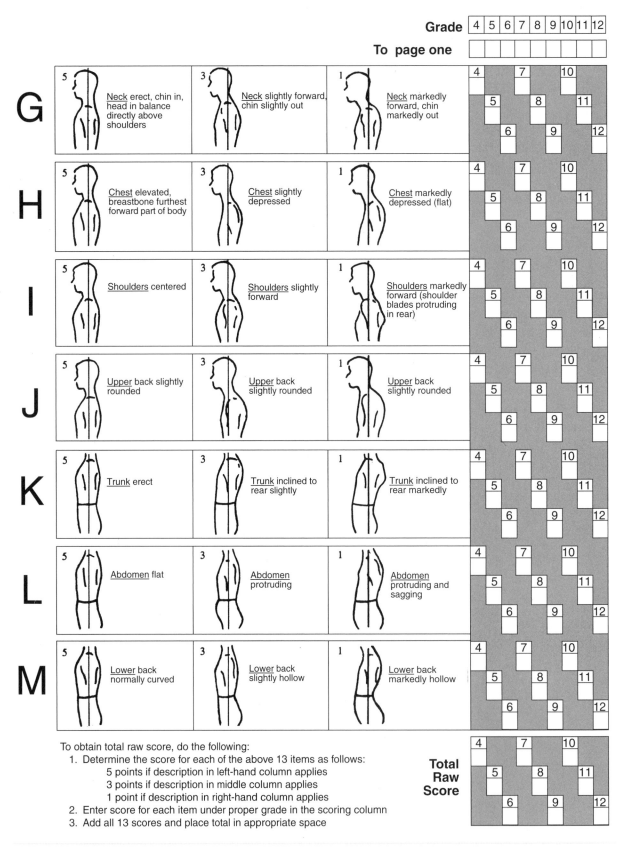

Grade 4 5 6 7 8 9 10 11 12

To page one

G — **Neck** erect, chin in, head in balance directly above shoulders (5) | **Neck** slightly forward, chin slightly out (3) | **Neck** markedly forward, chin markedly out (1)

H — **Chest** elevated, breastbone furthest forward part of body (5) | **Chest** slightly depressed (3) | **Chest** markedly depressed (flat) (1)

I — **Shoulders** centered (5) | **Shoulders** slightly forward (3) | **Shoulders** markedly forward (shoulder blades protruding in rear) (1)

J — **Upper** back slightly rounded (5) | **Upper** back slightly rounded (3) | **Upper** back slightly rounded (1)

K — **Trunk** erect (5) | **Trunk** inclined to rear slightly (3) | **Trunk** inclined to rear markedly (1)

L — **Abdomen** flat (5) | **Abdomen** protruding (3) | **Abdomen** protruding and sagging (1)

M — **Lower** back normally curved (5) | **Lower** back slightly hollow (3) | **Lower** back markedly hollow (1)

To obtain total raw score, do the following:
1. Determine the score for each of the above 13 items as follows:
   5 points if description in left-hand column applies
   3 points if description in middle column applies
   1 point if description in right-hand column applies
2. Enter score for each item under proper grade in the scoring column
3. Add all 13 scores and place total in appropriate space

Total Raw Score

Figure 16.5 *(continued)*

Reprinted, by permission, from New York State Education Department, 1999, *New York State physical fitness test for boys and girls 4-12*. (New York: New York State Education Department).

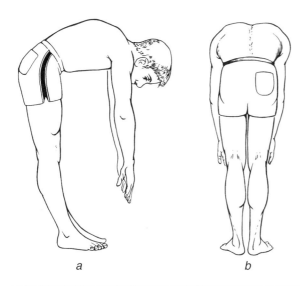

Figure 16.6 Illustration of the Adam's position showing normal spinal symmetry: (a) side view, (b) back view.

ics, which force the spine into better alignment or prevent it from deviating further. It is important to understand that the purpose of the bracing is not to correct the condition but to keep it from becoming worse. The Milwaukee and Charleston Twisting braces shown in figure 16.7 are the two most effective and commonly used braces for the treatment of scoliosis. To see the latest changes to the Milwaukee brace, consult the electronic resources referenced at the end of the chapter. Several more cosmetic braces, developed in recent years, are made of molded orthoplast and are custom fitted to the individual. These braces are also referred to as "low profile" braces, TLSO braces (Thoracic Lumber Sacral Orthosis), or underarm braces, and have been found to be effective in treating mild and moderate curves. One of the major advantages of the orthoplast braces is that they are less conspicuous and tend to be worn more consistently. These braces must be worn continuously until the child reaches skeletal maturity—in many cases, for four to five years. The brace can be removed for short periods for activities such as swimming and bathing. The treatment of scoliosis in individuals who are wheelchair-bound might also involve modifying the chair to improve alignment and to equalize seating pressures. For the latest information on braces used to treat scoliosis, check the electronic resources listed for this chapter at the end of the book.

In extremely severe cases of scoliosis, in which the curve is greater than 40 degrees or does not respond to bracing, surgery is employed. The surgical treatment usually involves fusing together the vertebrae in the affected region of the spine by means of bone grafts and the implantation of a metal rod. Following surgery, a brace is typically worn for about a year until the fusion has solidified.

Kyphosis and Lordosis

Abnormal concavity forward (backward curve) in the thoracic region (kyphosis) and abnormal convexity forward (forward curve) in the lumbar region (lordosis) are usually nonstructural and the result of poor posture (figure 16.5, rows G-M). These deformities are routinely remediated by

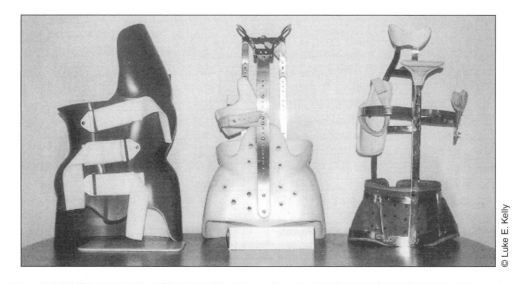

© Luke E. Kelly

Figure 16.7 The Milwaukee and Charleston Twisting braces are commonly used in the treatment of scoliosis.

exercise programs designed to tighten specific muscle groups and stretch opposing muscle groups and through education designed to make students aware of their present posture, proper body mechanics, and the desired posture.

The physical educator can assess kyphosis and lordosis by observing children under the conditions described previously for scoliosis screening but from the side view. Look for exaggerated curves in the thoracic and lumbar regions of the spinal column. Kyphosis is usually characterized by a rounded appearance of the upper back. Lordosis is characterized by a hollow back appearance and a protruding abdomen.

Structural kyphosis, sometimes referred to as Scheuermann's disease or juvenile kyphosis, is similar in appearance during the early stages to the nonstructural form described earlier, but it is the result of a deformity in the shape of the vertebrae in the thoracic region. Although the cause of this vertebral deformity is unknown, it can be diagnosed by X rays. This form of kyphosis is frequently accompanied by a compensatory lordotic curve. The prevalence of this deformity is not known, but it appears to affect both genders equally during adolescence.

Early detection and treatment of structural kyphosis through bracing can result in effective remediation of the condition. The treatment typically involves wearing a brace continuously for one to two years until the vertebrae reshape themselves. A variety of braces and orthotic jackets have been developed for the treatment of this condition. The Milwaukee brace used for the treatment of scoliosis is considered one of the more effective braces for treating this form of kyphosis.

Spondylolysis and Spondylolisthesis

Spondylolysis refers to a congenital malformation of the neural arches of the fourth, or more commonly, the fifth lumbar vertebra. Individuals with spondylolysis might or might not experience any back pain, but they are predisposed to acquiring spondylolisthesis. Spondylolisthesis is similar to spondylolysis, except that, in this condition, the fifth lumbar vertebra has slid forward. The displacement occurs because of the lack of the neural arch structure and the ligaments that normally hold this area in place. Spondylolisthesis can be congenital or can occur as a result of trauma to the back. It is usually associated with severe back pain and pain in the legs.

Treatment in mild cases involves training and awareness of proper posture. Individuals with spondylolisthesis frequently have an exaggerated lordotic curve in the back. In more severe cases, surgery is performed to realign the vertebrae and fuse that section of the spine.

Medical consultation should be pursued before any students with spondylolysis or spondylolisthesis participate in physical education. Children with mild cases might be able to participate in a regular physical education program with emphasis on proper posture, additional stretching, and avoidance of activities that involve severe stretching or trauma to the back. In more severe cases, an adapted physical education program might be required to provide more comprehensive posture training and exercises and to foster the development of physical and motor skills that will not aggravate the condition.

Working With Individuals With Spinal Column Deviations

As discussed earlier, physical educators can play a major role in screening for postural deviations in the spinal column. Children identified as having mild, nonstructural postural problems should receive special instruction and exercises to remediate their problems. Following are several general guidelines that should be considered whenever a physical educator is designing, implementing, or monitoring an exercise program to correct postural deviations.

- Establish and follow policies and procedures for working with students suspected of having structural or serious postural deviations of the spinal column.

- In an exercise program to remediate a postural deviation, the general objective is to strengthen the muscles used to pull the spinal column back into correct alignment and to stretch or lengthen the muscles that are pulling the spinal column out of alignment. The stretching program should be performed at least twice a day, and muscle-strengthening exercises should be performed at least every other day. A number of different exercise and stretching routines should be developed to add variety and keep the exercise routine interesting. Setting the exercise routines to music and establishing reward systems are also recommended, especially for students who are not highly motivated to exercise.

- All exercise and activity programs should begin and end with stretching exercises, with the greatest emphasis on static stretching. Stretches should each be performed five times and held for a count of 15 seconds.

- The exercise program should be initiated with mild, low-intensity exercises that can be easily performed by the children. The intensity of the exercises should be gradually increased as the children's strength and endurance increase.

- In most cases, individual exercise programs should be initiated and taught in adapted physical education. After the student has learned the exercise routine, he or she can perform the routine in the regular physical education class, monitored by the regular physical education teacher. First, explain to the student the nature of the postural deviation being addressed, the reasons that good posture is desirable, and the ways in which the exercises will help. The exercises should then be taught and monitored until the child clearly understands how to perform them correctly. The importance of making the student aware of the difference between the present posture and the desired posture cannot be overemphasized. Many children with mild postural deviations are simply unaware of the problem and thus do not even try to correct their postures. Mirrors and videotapes are useful for giving students feedback on posture. When working with students with visual impairments, the teacher will need to provide specific tactile and kinesthetic feedback to teach them the feeling of the correct postures. Cratty (1971) has described a tactile posture board, composed of a series of movable wooden pegs projecting through a vertical board, that can be placed along a student's spine to provide tactual feedback related to both postural deviations and desired postures.

- Children should follow their exercise programs at home on the days they do not have physical education. Some form of monitoring system, such as a log or progress chart, should be used. Periodically the children should be evaluated and given feedback and reinforcement to motivate them to continue working on their exercise programs.

- Exercises that make the body symmetrical

are recommended. The use of asymmetric exercises, especially for children being treated for scoliosis, should be used only following medical consultation.

- When selecting exercises to remediate one curve (i.e., the major curve), take care to ensure that the exercise does not foster the development of another curve (i.e., the minor curve).

- The exercise program should be made as varied and interesting as possible to maintain the student's motivation and involvement. Alternating between routine exercises and activities like swimming and rowing will usually result in greater compliance with the program. Motivation is an even greater concern with students with mental disabilities, who might not comprehend why they need to exercise or why better posture is desirable; they will require more frequent feedback and reinforcement. Showing students random Polaroid snapshots is a good technique for keeping their attention on their postures and rewarding them when they are displaying the desired postures.

- Students wearing braces such as the Milwaukee brace can exercise and participate in physical education, although activities that cause trauma to the spine (e.g., jumping and gymnastics) might be contraindicated. As a general rule, the brace will be self-limiting.

Recommended Exercises

Using the guidelines just presented and drawing on an understanding of the muscles involved in a spinal column deviation, a physical educator should be able to select appropriate exercises and activities. The following lists include sample exercises for the upper and lower back that can be used in the remediation of the three major spinal column deviations discussed in this chapter. These exercise lists provide examples and are far from complete. Several resources that provide additional exercises and more detailed descriptions of their performance are listed for this chapter at the end of the book.

Sample Upper-Back Exercises

The following sample exercises can be used to remediate nonstructural deviations in the upper spine.

- Symmetrical swimming strokes such as the backstroke and the breaststroke. If a pool is not available, the arm patterns of these strokes can be performed on a bench covered with a mat. Hand weights or pulley weights can be used to control the resistance.

- Rowing using either a rowboat or a rowing machine. The rowing action can also be performed with hand weights or pulley weights.

- Various arm and shoulder lifts from a prone position on a mat. Small hand weights can be used to increase resistance.

- Hanging from a bar. This is a good stretching exercise.

- Lateral (sideways) trunk bending from either a standing or a kneeling position. Forward bending should be avoided.

Sample Lower-Back Exercises

The following sample exercises can be used to remediate nonstructural deviations in the lower back.

- Any form of correctly performed sit-ups commensurate with the student's ability. Emphasis should be placed on keeping the lower back flat and performing the sit-ups in a slow, continuous action, as opposed to performing a large number of repetitions. Raising of the hips and sudden jerky movements should not be allowed.

- Pelvic tilt. This can be done from a supine position on a mat or standing against a wall.

- Alternating or combined knee exchanges (bringing the knee to the chest) from a supine position on a mat.

- Doing a bicycling action with the legs from a supine position on a mat.

- Leg lifts. Any variation of leg lifts is appropriate as long as the lower back is kept flat and pressed against the floor.

New techniques and treatments for spinal column postural deviations are constantly being developed. To find the latest information, look at the electronic resources at the end of the chapter.

IMPLICATIONS FOR PHYSICAL EDUCATION

Assessment is the key to successfully addressing the physical education needs of students with spinal cord disabilities. Physical educators must work as part of a team to obtain the assessment data they need to provide appropriate instruction. By consulting with each other, the physical educator and the physical or occupational therapist can share essential information about goals and objectives for each student. The physical therapist can provide pertinent information about the muscles that are still innervated and those that have been lost, the existing muscle strength and prognosis for further development, the range of motion at the various joints, and the presence or absence of sensation in the limbs. The physical or occupational therapist can also provide useful information about adapted appliances (e.g., a device to hold a racket when a grip is not possible) as well as practical guidance on putting on and removing braces, adjusting wheelchairs, positioning and using restraints in wheelchairs, lifting and handling the student, and making transfers to and from the wheelchair.

Within the domain of physical education, the physical educator must be able to assess the physical fitness and motor skills of students with spinal cord disabilities. There is currently only one health-related criterion-referenced physical fitness test available, the Brockport Physical Fitness Test (BPFT) (Winnick & Short, 1999a), which is designed to accommodate individuals with spinal cord disabilities and provides appropriate standards for the evaluation of physical fitness for this population. The BPFT recommends that individuals with spinal cord injuries be evaluated in the areas of aerobic functioning, body composition, and musculoskeletal function. Criterion-referenced test items are provided for each area, with modifications for different levels of functioning based on the level of the spinal cord injury. For example, the following test items would be recommended for a youngster who is a paraplegic and uses a wheelchair: for aerobic functioning, the 15-minute target aerobic movement test; for body composition, the sum of the triceps and subscapular skinfold test; and for musculoskeletal function, the seated push-up, dominant grip strength, and modified Apley test.

In general, individuals with spinal cord disabilities have placed significantly below students without disabilities at the same age level on physical fitness measures and in motor skill development. Winnick and Short (1985), for example, have reported that 52 to 72 percent of individuals with spinal cord disabilities in their Project UNIQUE study had skinfold measures greater than the median value for same-age subjects who were not impaired and that only about 19 percent of the girls and 36 percent of the boys with spinal cord disabilities scored above the nonimpaired median on grip strength. Winnick and Short (1984) have also reported that youngsters with paraplegic spinal neuromuscular conditions have generally lower fitness levels than normal youngsters of the same age and gender and that these youngsters do not demonstrate significant improvement with age or show significant gender differences as do those found among youngsters without disabilities. These results should not be misinterpreted to mean that people with spinal cord disabilities cannot develop better levels of physical fitness. Research has shown, on the contrary, that with proper instruction and opportunity to practice, these individuals can make significant improvements in physical fitness. The key is appropriate instruction and practice designed to address individual needs.

Fitness programs for individuals with spinal cord disabilities should focus on the development of all components of physical fitness. Although flexibility in all joints should be a goal, particular emphasis should be placed on preventing or reducing contractures in joints in which muscles are no longer innervated. These situations require a regular routine of stretching that moves the joints through the full range of motion.

Strength training should focus on restoring or maximizing the strength in the unaffected muscles. Care must be taken not to create muscle imbalances by overstrengthening muscle groups when the antagonist muscles are affected. Most common progressive resistance exercises are suitable for individuals with spinal cord disabilities with little or no modification. Posture and correct body mechanics should be stressed during all strength-training activities.

One of the most challenging fitness areas for individuals who have spinal cord disabilities is cardiorespiratory endurance. Work in this area is frequently complicated by the loss of the large-muscle groups of the legs, which makes cardiorespiratory training more difficult. Research has shown that individuals with paraplegia typically have about only half the cardiac output compared to individuals without spinal cord injuries; and individuals with quadriplegia tend to have about only a third of the cardiac output of individuals with paraplegia (ACSM, 2003). In these cases, the principles of intensity, frequency, and duration must be applied to less traditional aerobic activities that use the smaller muscle groups of the arms and shoulders. A number of wheelchair ergometers and hand-driven bicycle ergometers have been designed specifically to address the cardiorespiratory needs of individuals with spinal cord disabilities. Although it is more difficult to attain the benefits of cardiorespiratory training using the smaller muscle groups of the arms and shoulders, it is not impossible. There are several highly conditioned wheelchair marathoners who clearly demonstrate that high levels of aerobic fitness can be attained.

Obesity, unfortunately, is very common in individuals with spinal cord disabilities, largely because the loss of the large-muscle groups of the lower limbs diminishes their capacity to burn calories. Weight control is a function of balancing caloric intake with caloric expenditure. Because, in many cases, caloric expenditure is limited to a large degree by the extent of muscle damage and the subsequent activities that can be undertaken, the obvious solution is to control food intake.

When working on physical fitness with individuals with spinal cord injuries, safety must be a major concern. Individuals with spinal cord injuries, particularly individuals with injuries above T6, are subject to a number of unique problems, such as hypotension, problems of thermoregulation, and limits on their maximal exercise heart rates. **Hypotension** (low blood pressure) is caused by a disruption of the sympathetic nervous system. During aerobic exercise, the body depends on the large muscles in the legs to contract and assist in pumping blood back to the heart. When the legs are not involved, blood can pool in the legs, reducing the amount of blood returned to the heart and, subsequently, the heart's stroke volume. Some precautions that can be taken to reduce hypotension include exercising in a reclined position and including appropriate warm-up and cool-down periods as part of the workout so the body can gradually adapt to the increased workload.

Thermoregulation refers to the body's ability to regulate its internal temperature in response to the outside temperature. The higher the injury on the spine, the greater the problem individuals experience with thermal regulation. When thermal regulation is an issue, care should be taken to have individuals avoid exercising in extremely cold or hot environments. Physical educators should also keep cool compresses available to help individuals cool down after aerobic workouts.

Individuals with spinal cord injuries above T6 are also subject to autonomic dysreflexia and limitations in their maximal exercise heart rates. **Autonomic dysreflexia** refers to a rapid increase in heart rate and blood pressure to dangerous levels, which can be triggered by several factors, including bowel or bladder distension, restrictive clothing, or skin irritation. In reaction to these events, a reflex is triggered to constrict blood vessels and increase blood pressure. Another set of reflexes should also be triggered that monitors and subsequently relaxes these blood vessels Normally, these reflexes would monitor the HR and BP and respond to these changes at the spinal cord level—without conscious thought on the part of the individual. In individuals with T6 and higher lesions, the second set of reflexes is not triggered, possibly resulting in dangerously high blood pressure levels. Care should be taken to ensure that individuals empty their bowels and bladders before exercise and that their heart rates and blood pressures are monitored during exercise. If not monitored and treated in a timely fashion, this can be a life-threatening condition. Disruption to the normal integration of the parasympathetic and the sympathetic nervous systems also limits the maximum heart rate in individuals with injuries above T6 to approximately 120 beats per minute, which limits the aerobic training effects that can be achieved.

In recent years, several excellent resources have been published to assist physical educators in planning and implementing safe fitness programs for individuals with spinal cord injuries (American College of Sports Medicine, 2003; Goldberg, 1995; Lockette & Keyes, 1994; Miller, 1995; Rimmer, 1994; Winnick & Short, 1999b).

In addition to physical fitness and motor skill areas, physical educators should concentrate on posture and body mechanics. Individuals with spinal cord disabilities frequently have poor body mechanics as a result of muscle imbalances and contractures. Exercises and activities that contribute to body awareness and alignment should thus be stressed.

In terms of sports skills, the most valuable activities are those with the greatest carryover potential for lifetime participation. The selection of activities should provide a balance between warm- and cold-weather sports as well as indoor and outdoor sports. Preference should be given to sports that promote physical fitness and for which there are organized opportunities for participation in the community. Just about any sport (e.g., softball, golf, tennis, swimming, skiing) can be adapted or modified so that individuals with spinal cord disabilities can participate. Figure 16.8 shows a batter playing wheelchair softball on a wheelchair softball field in Chicago.

INCLUSION

The goal of assessment is to obtain the most accurate and complete data possible so that the

© Steven Kavanagh/Eclipse Images

Figure 16.8 Wheelchair softball.

most appropriate placement and instruction can be provided (Kelly & Melograno, 2004). Physical educators must be willing to devote both the time and effort required to obtain this assessment data if they wish to help their students reach their maximum potential in physical education. Because of the uniqueness of each spinal cord disability, physical educators need to use their skills in task analysis to develop their own authentic assessment tools and scoring rubrics to evaluate and teach functional motor skills. Working cooperatively with a team is the key to maximizing staff efficiency and the benefits for the students. Additional information on assessment and development of physical fitness and motor development is presented in other chapters in this text.

Once goals and objectives have been established for a student with a spinal cord disability, the next challenge is how to provide the instruction to achieve these goals in as inclusive a physical education setting as possible. Some physical education content, such as physical fitness, lends itself to inclusion because the content must be individualized for all of the students. Because all students are at different levels of fitness in terms of their flexibility, strength, and endurance, it is common to develop individual routines based on the students' assessed needs and then to use a circuit approach to have students work on their programs. In an individualized setting like this, it is easy to accommodate the unique needs of individuals with spinal cord disabilities by defining fitness routines to meet their unique needs around the same stations as the other students. Other physical education content, such as working on sports skills (e.g., the volleyball serve), can initially appear more difficult to modify because skills like this are traditionally taught to the class as a whole, and then activities and games are used in which everyone is expected to perform the same skill. For example, how do you include a student with a spinal cord injury who uses a wheelchair in a volleyball game if the student cannot hit the ball hard enough when serving to get the ball over the net and cannot move quickly enough in the wheelchair to defend part of the court? What are some possible modifications? The weight of the ball could be adjusted. The student could be allowed to serve closer to the net. The student could be given a smaller zone to defend on the court after the ball is served. More students could be assigned to each side to reduce the amount of space needing to be defended.

Although the physical educator is responsible for creating an inclusive setting in which the needs of all students are addressed, it is also important that students with spinal cord disabilities be taught how to advocate for themselves. This form of self-advocacy involves students being able to analyze new games and activities and then offer suggestions on how the activities could be modified so that they can successfully participate. This is a critical skill for all students with disabilities because the physical educator will not always be there to orchestrate the modifications. A common transition step from teacher-directed accommodations to those that are student directed is to have the class help to develop modifications and accommodations. This process also sensitizes the other students to the value of making activities appropriate for all participants. The golden rules to making accommodations are that the activity must still serve its original purpose and the individuals with disabilities must be working on the same skills or similar skills modified to meet their unique needs. Assigning students with spinal cord impairments to roles such as scorekeeper because they are in wheelchairs is not appropriate inclusion because they are not developing the skills they need to live and maintain an active healthy lifestyle. In the long term, inclusive physical education settings are beneficial for everyone. Inclusion requires that instruction be based on assessment and be individually designed. It also requires successful participation of all students in the planned drills, games, and activities, which should result in positive learning outcomes for all students.

ORTHOTIC DEVICES

Because of the neuromuscular limitations imposed by spinal cord disabilities, many individuals with these disabilities use orthotics to enhance their functional abilities. Orthotic devices are a variety of splints and braces designed to provide support, improve positioning, correct or prevent deformities, and reduce or alleviate pain. The use of orthotic devices is not limited to individuals with spinal cord disabilities. For example, the Milwaukee and Charleston braces are commonly used to treat scoliosis, which can occur in any adolescent. Orthotic devices are prescribed by physicians and fitted by occupational therapists, who also instruct users in wearing and caring for the devices. Examples of the more common orthotics are shown in figure 16.9. They are used both by individuals who are ambulatory to provide better stability and by individuals in wheelchairs to prevent deformities. These devices are commonly referred to by abbreviations that describe the joints they cover: AFO—ankle-foot orthotics, KAFO—knee-ankle-foot orthotics, and HKAFO—hip-knee-ankle-foot orthotics. Additional information on orthotics can be found in the electronic resources at the end of the chapter.

Many of the newer plastic orthotics can be worn inside regular shoes and under clothing. Under normal circumstances, orthotics should be worn in all physical education activities with the exception of swimming. In vigorous activities, physical educators should periodically check that the straps are secure and that no abrasion or skin irritation is occurring where the orthotics or straps contact the skin. Orthotics can also be used to improve positioning to maximize sensory input. Figure 16.10 shows a series of assistive devices often used with children with spina bifida. The purpose of these orthotics is to allow these children with spina bifida to view and interact with the environment from the normal developmental vertical postures that they cannot attain and maintain on their own. The last device is a parapodium, or standing table, which allows individuals who otherwise could not stand to attain a standing position from which they can work and view the world. The parapodium frees the individual from the burden or inability to balance and bear weight and also affords complete use of the arms and hands. The parapodium can be used effectively in physical education to teach skills such as table tennis. In recent years, several companies have devised ingenious modifications of the parapodium so that the table can be easily adjusted to many vertical and horizontal positions.

A secondary category of orthotic devices includes canes and walkers used as assistive devices for ambulation. The Lofstrand or Canadian crutches are most commonly used by individuals with spina bifida and spinal cord disabilities who ambulate with leg braces and crutches. Physical educators should be aware that a person using only one cane or crutch employs it on the strong side, thus immobilizing the better arm. This should be considered, and appropriate modifications (i.e., to maintain balance) should be made for skills in which use of the better arm is desired. For additional information on canes and crutches, consult the electronic resources at the end of the chapter.

ADAPTED SPORT ACTIVITIES

Today, many organizations sponsor athletic programs and sporting events for individuals with spinal cord disabilities. These organizations have evolved from the need to provide athletic and recreational opportunities for individuals with spinal cord disabilities who want to participate in sport.

The NWAA, now known as Wheelchair Sports, USA, was formed in 1956 and is one of the most notable organizations sponsoring athletic events for people with neuromuscular disabilities result-

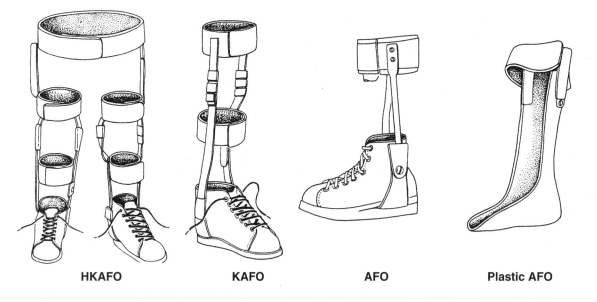

HKAFO   **KAFO**   **AFO**   **Plastic AFO**

Figure 16.9 Common orthotic devices worn by individuals with spinal cord disabilities.

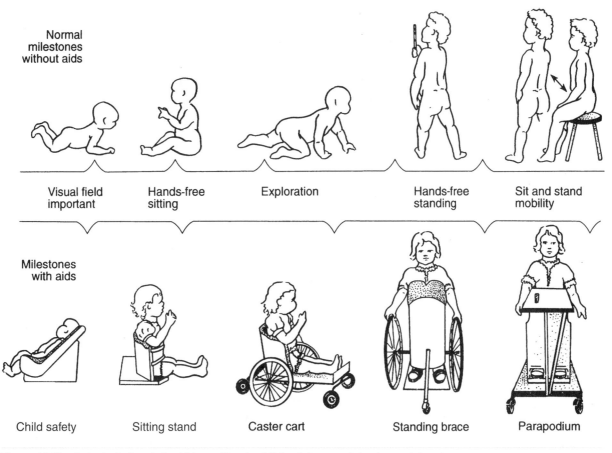

Normal
milestones
without aids

| Visual field important | Hands-free sitting | Exploration | Hands-free standing | Sit and stand mobility |

Milestones
with aids

| Child safety | Sitting stand | Caster cart | Standing brace | Parapodium |

Figure 16.10 Orthotic devices help children with spina bifida attain normal developmental postures.

ing from spinal cord injuries, spina bifida, or polio. Wheelchair Sports, USA, sponsors competitive events in pistol shooting, riflery, swimming, table tennis, weightlifting, archery, fencing, wheelchair slalom, and track and field. Competitors are classified into divisions by age and functional ability (table 16.2). There are two age divisions: adult, for individuals age 16 and older, and junior, for youngsters 8 to 15 years old. As discussed earlier in this chapter, there is growing interest in replacing the system with a functional classification system (figure 16.2), which is now used for international competitions.

Disabled Sports, USA, plays a major role in organizing and sponsoring both competitive and noncompetitive winter sports events for individuals with disabilities. Disabled Sports, USA, was formally called National Handicapped Sports (until 1994) and the National Handicapped Sport and Recreation Association (until 1976). Disabled Sports, USA, is a leader in the development and dissemination of recreation and fitness and training materials related to sport and recreation for individuals with disabilities. One example is Disabled

Sports USA's Aerobics Tapes, which is a series of aerobic dance videotapes designed especially to help individuals with paraplegia, quadriplegia, amputations, and cerebral palsy develop endurance, strength, and flexibility (for more information consult the audiovisual resources for this chapter). Disabled Sports, USA, also serves as the official governing body for sport competitions for individuals with amputations.

Several special organizations sponsor athletic competitions in a specific sport. Although many of these organizations employ the Wheelchair Sports, USA, classification system, the National Wheelchair Basketball Association (NWBA) has its own system. The NWBA was formed in 1949 and sponsors competition for men, women, and youth. In the NWBA classification system, each player is classified as a I, II, or III, depending on the location of the spinal injury and the degree of motor loss. Each class has a corresponding point value of one, two, or three. A team can comprise players in any combination of classes as long as the total point value for the five players does not exceed 12 and there are not more than three class

III players playing together at the same time. The classifications are made according to the following criteria (National Wheelchair Basketball Association, 2003):

> Class I: Complete motor loss at T7 or above or comparable disability in which there is total loss of muscle function originating at or above T7.
>
> Class II: Complete motor loss originating at T8 and descending through and including L2 in which there might be motor power of hips and thighs. Also included in this class are individuals with amputations with bilateral hip disarticulation.
>
> Class III: All other physical disabilities as related to lower-extremity paralysis or paresis originating at or below L3. All lower-extremity amputees are included in this class except those with bilateral hip disarticulation (see class II).

The NWBA classification system provides an excellent model for equating team sports competition in physical education classes that include integrated students with spinal cord disabilities. A similar classification system based on students' skill levels could also be designed and used in physical education classes.

Over the past decade, wheelchair sports have evolved from primarily recreational activities into highly sophisticated and competitive events. Many of the initial advances in wheelchair sports were the direct result of technical advances in wheelchair design and research related to the postural and body mechanics of wheelchair propulsion. In recent years, attention has shifted to defining and improving training and conditioning programs for wheelchair athletes (Ferrara & Davis, 1990; Gayle & Muir, 1992; Wells & Hooker, 1990).

Specialized, organized sports programs serve as an extension of the physical education curriculum. Such programs provide students with spinal cord disabilities with equal opportunities to gain the benefits and experiences all athletes derive from sport; they are also a good source of motivation. These activities give participants an opportunity to meet and interact socially with others who have similar characteristics, interests, and needs. Finally, these sport experiences expose students with spinal cord disabilities to positive role models who demonstrate the difference between having a disability and being handicapped. To maximize the probability that students with disabilities will both attempt and succeed in sports, physical educators must ensure that the physical education curriculum provides instruction in the fundamental sports skills and the appropriate transition from skill development to skill application in actual sport situations.

SUMMARY

Individuals with spinal cord disabilities need to pursue the same physical education goals as other students. This chapter includes the information that teachers and other professionals need to successfully meet the needs of these students. Physical educators must have a thorough understanding of the nature of the disabilities and the functional abilities that can be attained. They can then build on this knowledge base to determine the most appropriate placement and instructional programming for each student. Particular emphasis in the program should be placed on body awareness and proper body mechanics to minimize the negative impact of spinal column deviations. In addition, special attention should be given to physical fitness. Many individuals with spinal cord disabilities are predisposed for obesity and have imposed constraints on how they can train because of the nature of their disability. Finally, all programs for individuals with spinal cord disabilities should be designed so that they leave the program with functional lifetime sports skills that can be used to maintain their health and fitness. Adapted sports, using functional ability classification systems, provide excellent opportunities for individuals with spinal cord disabilities to apply and practice the skills learned in physical education.

REFERENCES

Adams, R.C., & McCubbin, J.A. (1991). *Games, sports, and exercises for the physically disabled* (4th ed.). Philadelphia: Lea & Febiger.

American College of Sports Medicine. (2003). *ACSM's exercise management of persons with chronic diseases and disabilities* (2nd ed.). Champaign, IL: Human Kinetics.

American Medical Association (AMA). (1990). *Handbook of first aid & emergency care.* New York: Random House.

Centers for Disease Control (CDC). (1995). Progress toward global poliomyelitis eradication, 1985-1994. *Morbidity and Mortality Weekly Report,* 44(14), 273-275, 281.

Cratty, B.J. (1971). *Movement and spatial awareness in blind children and youth.* Springfield, IL: Charles C Thomas.

Ferrara, M.S., & Davis, R.W. (1990). Injuries to wheelchair athletes. *Paraplegia, 28,* 335-341.

Gayle, G.W., & Muir, J.L. (1992). Role of sportsmedicine and the spinal cord injured: A multidisciplinary relationship. *Palaestra,* 8(3), 51-56.

Goldberg, B. (Ed.). (1995). *Sports and exercise for children with chronic health conditions.* Champaign, IL: Human Kinetics.

Kelly, L.E., & Melograno, V. (2004). *Developing the physical education curriculum: An achievement-based approach.* Champaign, IL: Human Kinetics.

Lockette, K., & Keyes, A.M. (1994). *Conditioning with physical disabilities.* Champaign, IL: Human Kinetics.

National Spinal Cord Injury Association (NSCIA). (2003). *Causes of spinal cord injury.* Retrieved October 5, 2003, from the Internet: www.spinalcord.org.

National Wheelchair Basketball Association (NWBA). (2003). *National wheelchair basketball association official rules and case book 2001-2002.* Retrieved October 5, 2003, from the Internet: http://nwba.org/rules.html.

New York State Education Department (1966). *New York State physical fitness test for boys and girls grades 4-12.* Albany, NY: Author.

Miller, P.D. (Ed.). (1995). *Fitness programming and physical disability.* Champaign, IL: Human Kinetics.

Rimmer, J. (1994). *Fitness and rehabilitation programs for special populations.* Madison, WI: WCB Brown & Benchmark.

Spina Bifida Association of America (SBAA). (2003). *Facts about spina bifida.* Retrieved October 5, 2003, from the Internet: www.sbaa.org/html/sbaa_facts.html.

Wells, C.L., & Hooker, S.P. (1990). The spinal injured athlete. *Adapted Physical Activity Quarterly, 7,* 265-285.

Winnick, J.P., & Short, F.X. (1999a). *The Brockport physical fitness test manual.* Champaign, IL: Human Kinetics.

Winnick, J.P., & Short, F.X. (Eds.). (1999b). *The Brockport physical fitness training guide.* Champaign, IL: Human Kinetics.

Winnick, J.P., & Short, F.X. (1985). *Physical fitness testing of the disabled.* Champaign, IL: Human Kinetics.

Winnick, J.P., & Short, F.X. (1984). The physical fitness of youngsters with spinal neuromuscular conditions. *Adapted Physical Activity Quarterly, 1,* 37-51.

WRITTEN RESOURCES

American College of Sports Medicine. (1997). *ACSM's exercise management of persons with chronic diseases and disabilities.* Champaign, IL: Human Kinetics.

This book provides guidelines for exercise testing and programming for individuals with spinal cord injuries, polio, and postpolio syndrome. Excellent recommendations are provided regarding safety and precautions that should be taken to reduce risks during exercise.

New York Posture Rating Test (1966). In *New York State physical fitness test for boys and girls grades 4-12.* Albany, NY: New York State Education Department.

This is any easy-to-use and comprehensive screening test for upper and lower back postural deviations.

Posture Grid (1991). In R.C. Adams, and J.A. McCubbin, *Games, sports and exercises for the physically disabled* (4th ed.), (pp.155-162). Philadelphia: Lea & Febiger.

This document describes how to make your own posture grid, which can then be used to evaluate postural deviations of the head, spine, legs, and feet.

AUDIOVISUAL RESOURCES

Aerobics for quadriplegia; Aerobics for Cerebral Palsy; Aerobics for paraplegia; Aerobics for amputees. (Videotapes, 1995). Disabled Sports USA, 451 Hungerford Drive, Suite 100, Rockville, MD 20850.

These four videotapes provide aerobic routines for individuals with varying physical disabilities that progress from easy to demanding workouts. The instructors on the tapes provide guidelines to ensure the exercises are performed correctly and safely; the exercises are demonstrated by youngsters and adults in wheelchairs.

National Scoliosis Foundation. Phone: (800) 673-6922; E-mail: NSF@scoliosis.org or mail: 5 Cabot Place, Stoughton, MA 02072.

This is an excellent source for videotapes on the history, nature, and treatment of scoliosis. Tapes range in length from 8 to 60 minutes and in cost from $5 to $50.

Strength and flexibility for individuals with all types of physical disabilities. (Videotape, 1995). Disabled Sports USA, 451 Hungerford Drive, Suite 100, Rockville, MD 20850.

This tape provides a strength and flexibility routine using rubber tubes for resistance. Each exercise is presented by the instructor and then modeled by an individual with a disability.

ELECTRONIC RESOURCES

Association for Spina Bifida and Hydrocephalus: www.asbah.demon.co.uk/.

This site contains the latest information on the treatment of spina bifida and shunts used to treat hydrocephalus.

National Spinal Cord Injury Association: www.spinalcord.org.

This site provides extensive coverage of the current treatment and latest research developments related to spinal cord injuries.

Scoliosis Research Society: www.srs.org.

This site contains extensive reference lists and reviews

Other Health-Impaired Students

Francis M. Kozub

Jesse is a six-year-old boy recently diagnosed with viral induced asthma. This means when Jesse gets a cold he is susceptible to asthma attacks. On most days this condition does not affect Jesse's ability to participate in physical education, but during periods of illness Jesse needs to use an inhaler frequently to keep breathing normally. The medication contained in these treatments has side effects that affect motor performance and attention. Further, Jesse's teacher has expressed concern over being responsible for helping him with the inhaler if an attack occurs during physical education time. What activity modifications must a physical educator consider for children like Jesse? What type of related services might such children need to benefit from educational programs? Should Jesse and children like him be excluded from regular physical education because they might not be able to play at the level of their peers on some days?

The purpose of this chapter is to provide information to program planners about the varied conditions known in IDEA as "other health impaired" (OHI; see sidebar). Although OHI is considered a low-incidence disability, much debate has centered on the use of this category by school district personnel. Some children are inappropriately categorized as OHI in response to parent requests for services that might or might not be required under IDEA (Grice, 2002). For this reason, it is important to understand what types of learner needs result in a child receiving educational services under the category of OHI.

The key concept of the definition for OHI, based on IDEA, is the adverse effect of a condition on educational performance in both academic and nonacademic skills (Grice, 2002). In this chapter we will present information on the conditions of seizure disorders, asthma, cancer, cardiac disorder, anemia, and acquired immunodeficiency syndrome (AIDS) and human immunodeficiency virus (HIV). Also provided are physical education implications for each condition and a checklist for inclusion of children with OHI.

DIABETES MELLITUS

Diabetes mellitus is a condition affecting the body's ability to process, store, and use glucose.

Two types of diabetes exist: type 1 (formerly called insulin-dependent) and type 2 (formerly called non–insulin dependent), which typically occurs later in life and thus does not affect most school-age children. Each year about 13,000 children are diagnosed with the more serious type 1 diabetes (Juvenile Diabetes Foundation International, 2003). Given the prevalence and chronic nature of type 1 diabetes, the focus of this chapter is on children with this disease and physical activity.

In the human body adequate blood glucose levels must be maintained. In this process, the pancreas secretes insulin needed to break down glucose and allow for storage in the liver (Hornsby & Albright, 2003). Without insulin (hyperglycemia), glucose is not broken down into glycogen and stored in the liver, resulting in damage to other parts of the body, such as the kidneys, eyes, heart, and blood vessels. Alternatively, when too much insulin is present in the blood stream because of improper management of injections, food intake, or exercise (which can facilitate the body's production of insulin in persons with type 1 diabetes), a serious condition known as hypoglycemia or low blood sugar can result (Hornsby & Albright, 2003). If left untreated, hypoglycemia (low blood sugar) can result in sudden coma.

Warning Signs

Low blood sugar (hypoglycemia) or lack of insulin (hyperglycemia) both mark situations that require attention by program leaders. Although low blood sugar is easily treated from a first aid standpoint, like low insulin, the consequences for improper medical care are severe. See the sidebar (on page 309) for symptoms and treatment of hypoglycemia and hyperglycemia. Children with diabetes vary in the nature of signals indicating low blood sugar. Further, many children and adults with diabetes vary in their willingness to monitor their blood sugar or ignore early warning signs that might help avoid either low or high blood sugar, resulting in both short- and long-term medical problems.

Key Factors

Many factors affect blood glucose in children with diabetes, including diet, exercise, and insulin injection levels. Stress, hormonal changes, periods of growth, medications, illness, and general fatigue are some major issues that make diabetes difficult to manage in children (Juvenile Diabetes Research Foundation International, 2003). Many

Symptoms and Treatment of Insulin Shock and Diabetic Coma

Insulin shock results from excessive insulin in the blood stream. Diabetic coma results from too much glucose and not enough insulin.

Insulin Shock (Hypoglycemia)

Symptoms

Rapidly occurring symptoms such as fast pulse, dizziness, weakness, irritability, and eventual loss of consciousness occur with insulin shock.

Treatment

If conscious, provide person with some fast acting sugar such as honey, juice, or soft drink (nondiet).

Diabetic Coma (Hyperglycemia)

Symptoms

Slower-acting symptoms occur, developing more gradually in diabetic coma than with insulin shock. Thirst and frequent urination over a period of days coupled with nausea and other signs of distress such as irregular breathing and abdominal pain are seen.

Treatment

Take the person to an emergency room immediately. This is a serious medical situation, and you might not have adequate knowledge on how much or what type of insulin to inject. A person who is suffering from diabetic coma needs prompt medical care.

Note: The symptoms for these two different diabetic conditions are similar, and it is helpful to talk with the affected person (if possible) before deciding whether to treat as hypoglycemia or hyperglycemia. However, keep in mind that insulin shock can occur quickly and if a person loses consciousness, medical attention must be sought immediately.

The American National Red Cross, 2001.

---

of these factors are difficult to identify and are not directly controllable by physical educators; thus cooperation by educational team members is necessary. On this team, parents are the first line of defense, followed by teachers and other school or facility support staff. Without a collaborative effort, younger children in particular run the risk of repeated issues with low and high blood sugar resulting in further complications later in life. To avoid low blood sugar, periodic monitoring of glucose levels is encouraged. This involves drawing a small sample of blood from a pinprick that is then placed on a strip and either compared to a chart or placed in a monitor. Both methods provide estimates of blood sugar that can be used to adjust food or insulin intake.

Physical Education and Students With Diabetes

Exercise and diet are two related factors important in children with diabetes. When individuals with diabetes are about to exercise, proper attention to food intake, insulin levels, and exercise amount is critical. Further, balancing these factors also requires attention to the type of physical activity anticipated. In individuals with diabetes, insulin and blood sugar levels vary depending on the nature of physical activity, making it difficult some-times to estimate nutritional needs. For example, Colberg (2000) highlights research showing that very intense exercise such as lifting weights can actually cause blood sugar to rise because of increases in counterregulatory hormones. These and other factors such as stress, temperature, or growth spurts make it important that blood sugar levels are monitored regularly; children are encouraged to learn through experience to manage their diabetes by learning to calculate energy expenditure. In physical activity settings, coordinating nutrition and each individual's response to exercise, insulin, and curricular offerings is important (Hornsby & Albright, 2003).

Physical educators must be aware of issues related to circulation in children with diabetes. Circulatory system problems are cause for concern specifically in foot health and general skin care. In this regard it is not recommended for individuals with diabetes to participate in physical activity barefooted for any period of time (Conti & Chaytor, 1995). In most physical activity situations this is not an issue, but with the rise of beach volleyball, martial arts, and other activities in which footwear is optional, program leaders need to encourage proper foot care in individuals with diabetes. Socks, water slippers, and other types of footwear are available for individuals with diabetes to use during physical activity to avoid risk of cuts, blisters, and other foot injuries.

With proper attention to diet and insulin, children with diabetes can take part in intense physical activity, such as fitness testing. Further, children with type 1 diabetes can be tested using the same physical fitness formats as children without this condition unless they have had the condition for more than 15 years or have suspected coronary artery disease or other diabetic complications (Hornsby & Albright, 2003). Again, when bouts of extreme physical activity are anticipated, prior planning and pre-exercise monitoring of blood glucose is important, along with provisions for first aid when symptoms arise (see the Symptoms and Treatment sidebar). The highest risk factor with intense physical activity is hypoglycemia (low blood sugar) provided that the individual has taken the correct dose of insulin (Hornsby & Albright, 2003).

The nature of food intake is an important consideration for active individuals with diabetes. It is important to coordinate carbohydrate intake with the activity. A short physical education class with a brief warm-up followed by 10 minutes of vigorous activity might require a child to eat a rapidly absorbed carbohydrate, such as a piece of fruit. If a child plays for a longer time or an entire game, such as in a youth soccer league, intermittent food intake might be required in which the child consumes carbohydrates every 30 minutes or between periods of a game (Birrer & Sedaghat, 2003). For strenuous activities of higher intensity, blood glucose must be monitored during the activity. For longer duration activities, such as an all-day wrestling tournament, more complicated fruit and protein consumption is required, along with faster- and slower-acting insulin doses (changes in a child's insulin might require a doctor's prescription) (see application example).

SEIZURE DISORDERS

Seizures result when abnormal electrical activity occurs in the brain, causing involuntary movements, varied sensations, perception, behavior, or altered level of consciousness. Although seizures are common, occurring in 1 of 10 people (Colson Bloomquist, 2003), the focus of this section is the condition known as epilepsy, in which seizures

APPLICATION EXAMPLE

Monitoring Blood Glucose

Setting: Varsity Football

Student: Jeffrey is a ninth grader with type 1 diabetes playing varsity football for his school. His size and physical maturity is at a level comparable to the senior level athletes in this football program, which prompted his coaches to allow Jeffrey to try out for the varsity squad. During the first two weeks of practice, Jeffrey was able to earn a starting position on the defense.

Issue: Coaches have had problems with Jeffrey's experiencing hypoglycemia during practices. Some of this is because Jeffrey has neglected to test his blood sugar before practice. Coaches are concerned that allowing Jeffrey to start and stay in the game for long periods might lead to safety issues.

Application: The physical educator proceeds in the following way:

- Teammates are informed of Jeffrey's diabetes so they can help monitor on the field during huddles if Jeffrey appears confused or dizzy.

- Another strategy is incorporated to avoid problems in the second half by having an assistant coach assigned to take Jeffrey aside during halftime and ensure that blood sugar is checked and that Jeffrey eats a light snack.

- Even with these precautions, Jeffrey still has problems early in the season gauging food intake and insulin. As a freshman athlete starting on defense and playing intermittently on offense as a fullback, it is not always possible to anticipate how many plays Jeffrey will be on the field during the game.

- Further, some plays last longer and require more energy as Jeffrey begins to run the ball and become more prominent in the offense. Through monitoring and contacting Jeffrey's physician (through Jeffrey's parents), the problem is reduced, and Jeffrey becomes one of the top players on his team.

occur with relative frequency. Epilepsy is less common in young people, affecting less than 1 percent of children. Uncontrolled prolonged seizures can have serious long-term consequences or even cause death. Thus, proper attention to help reduce seizures as well as monitor the frequency and duration of episodes is important.

Types

Types of seizure disorders depend on the system used for categorization. Common in educational settings and supported by the Epilepsy Foundation of America (2003) are classifications of seizures into groups as either generalized or partial seizures. Generalized seizures can be tonic clonic (grand mal) and result in a loss of consciousness and jerking movements; other generalized seizures (akinetic, atonic, myoclonic) produce a sudden change in muscle tone, sometimes causing a child to fall (Weinstein, 2002). Seizures can also be categorized as "partial" and result from disturbance in a single portion of the brain, thus affecting one area of control or mental activity. Whether a person remains aware or conscious further differentiates partial seizures from those that are complex partial. Children are less frequently affected by partial seizures than adults are. More common in children are generalized tonic- clonic seizures, with the noticeable loss of consciousness followed by thrashing movements, foaming at the mouth, and loss of bladder control.

The onset of seizure activity can be predicted to some extent. Grand mal seizures are the most common and often preceded by an aura (or warning) that precludes many seizures. Also, a trigger—flashing lights, intense pain, psychological stress, or even fatigue—can stimulate the occurrence of a seizure in many people.

Medications are a common treatment for seizures, along with care to avoid triggers that may spur on an episode. However, seizure episodes can occur despite consistent efforts to avoid them. First aid is an important aspect of helping children to manage seizures. The sidebar presents basic first aid information for educators when children have seizures. Care must be taken to maintain the dignity of the learner when urination or other embarrassing situations occur during the seizure. Having the class go to some other area (and sit) away from the child who is having a seizure might help prevent further injury and preserve the dignity of the learner. However, as is the case for most forms of diversity that exist in a learning setting,

First Aid for Tonic–Clonic (Grand Mal) Seizures in Physical Education

1. In many situations children who have experienced repeated seizures have an aura or warning sign that a seizure is about to happen. In this case help the child to the floor and make sure to cushion his or her head.

2. If a child has glasses, remove them. If a child has some type of mouth guard or prosthetic dental work, remove (if possible) so the child's airway remains open. Turning the head to the side allows saliva to drain and keeps the airway open.

3. Do not attempt to restrain or put any object in a child's mouth. Make sure the child is safe from bumping into objects during the seizure.

4. Make sure to note the length of the seizure because a prolonged loss of consciousness is a medical emergency. For seizures lasting more than a few minutes, first time seizures, or if the seizure occurs in the water, the American Red Cross recommends calling emergency medical personnel.

5. If emergency medical personnel are not needed, be sure to let the child who has had a seizure rest if needed and then inform him or her of what happened. Be sure to discuss missed events or information with the child.

The American National Red Cross, 2001.

educating children about the nature of seizures in general might help them distinguish fact from fiction.

Physical Education and Students With Seizure Disorders

Exercise as an important consideration for seizure activity is noted in Colson Bloomquist (2003), who states that physical activity tends to normalize electrical function in the brain. Thus, seizures are less likely to occur during regular exercise than in resting states. However, it should be noted that although it is believed that exercise has a positive impact on individuals with epilepsy, children with epilepsy might tend to avoid exercise, thus making exercise something that produces stress, pain, and other potential triggers for seizures.

Although individuals with a history of epilepsy might have a lower capacity (due to inactivity) to tolerate physical activity, the ability to experience training effects comparable to peers is supported in the literature and, with proper supervision, considered appropriate (Sirven & Varrato, 1999).

Activity selection is an important consideration for children with seizures only if the condition is not under control. Lack of control refers to periods of time where seizures are occurring on a frequent basis. When children are experiencing frequent seizures and medication is not keeping episodes from occurring, activities at height, such as walking on a high balance beam or rope climbing, might be hazardous if a seizure occurs at the wrong time. However, once seizures are under control, it is common practice to let children participate in any and all age-appropriate activities. Even contact sports can be safely played under appropriate supervision, allowing the child to benefit from sport in a manner consistent with peers without epilepsy (Sirven & Varrato, 1999).

One exception to the general unrestricted physical activity recommendation for children with seizure disorders is to exercise caution in water. Even if the seizure disorder is under control, a buddy system is recommended in both the pool and locker room because of difficulties in keeping all children in site during swimming and changing clothes. These types of strategies increase safety for all kids, not just those with known seizure disorders.

ASTHMA

Asthma is both a common childhood condition and life-threatening illness. A chronic inability to breathe accompanied by wheezing, cough, and swelling in the bronchial tubes is what is commonly referred to as asthma (or, in some cases, reactive airway disease). Defining asthma is difficult because the cause of difficulties in breathing has changed somewhat over the last decade (Woodruff & Fahy, 2001). Further, as was the case in seizure disorders, different people might have different triggers for asthma attacks. Exercise, upper respiratory infections, and other factors might trigger attacks in individuals who otherwise experience no breathing difficulties at all. Asthma is on the rise worldwide, and Woodruff and Fahy (2001) estimate that 5 percent of the U.S. population has asthma. Half of these cases include children younger than 10.

Symptoms and Treatment of Asthma

Exacerbations of asthma in susceptible individuals are first observed in an inability to breathe or a persistent cough. Physical educators should be aware of children in their class who have a documented pattern of asthma and should have access to fast-acting inhalers when appropriate. Some children, however, do not use inhalers but might require medication administration via more involved nebulizers that require an electrical outlet and 20 minutes to administer. Knowledge about each child's triggers, rate of decline, and treatment is important for helping children engage in structured physical activity. Further, age and developmental level of the child might dictate a need for help by an educator with respect to using an inhaler. Inhalers typically have a dosage and a protocol, requiring the child to hold medication in the lungs for a set time. In addition to time needed for a child to return to normal breathing after the use of an inhaler, keep in mind that these medications typically have a stimulant effect, raise the heart rate, and might affect behavior.

Physical Education and Students With Asthma

Asthma as a condition affecting physical activity is most noted when exercise is the trigger. Exercise-induced asthma (EIA) or exercise-induced bronchospasm (EIB) are conditions in which physical activity triggers breathing difficulties. It is estimated that up to 90 percent of asthma sufferers have EIA, and it is very likely that physical educators have children in their programs who are affected (Mahler, 1993). Asthma, whether exercise induced or activated by other triggers, presents a challenge to physical activity programmers. Young children or developmentally immature learners might lack an understanding of time and not be able to regulate hourly dosages or even be able to remember when they last took their medicine. Further, physical educators might not always be told when inhalers were last used. For this reason, parents and educators should come up with a documentation system of communicating when inhalers are used so that the child is not overmedicated. Placing a small spiral notebook in a child's book bag or pocket is one way for teachers and parents to communicate with each other. Each time the child uses the inhaler, an entry is made recording the time of day and dosage. Some additional recommendations for dealing with children with asthma include the following:

- Be sensitive to periods when children might not be functioning at their best. Prolonged intense physical activity during asthmatic episodes is not recommended. Allow children to put off fitness tests or other activities where a reward or attention is given for achievement if the child is suffering from symptoms prior to testing.

- Children with EIA might need to avoid physical activity in conditions such as high humidity (Friedman et al., 2001).

- If fitness levels are low, gradual increases in exercise intensity might help the child with EIA tolerate higher levels of physical activity.

- Children with asthma might need to cough up mucus. Have provisions for children to spit or dispose of mucus, particularly in indoor activities.

Children with asthma can perform at high levels when symptoms are not present, as seen in figure 17.1. However, significant activity restrictions for children with EIA might be warranted in some rare situations in which adequate warm-ups, moderate intensity levels, and other preventative measures do not reduce the incidence of breathing difficulties. In these situations accurate medical information, parent input, and helping the child understand the differences between shortness of breath caused by training rather than asthma are important. It is important to talk with medical personnel and parents to help determine when a child is short of breath because of general fatigue instead of restricted airways (indicating an asthma attack). Initially, teachers must acknowledge that a child with a history of asthma is having an attack based on any signs of breathing difficulty, including coughing or wheezing. However, similar symptoms can also occur in a child who is unfit and is exercising for the first time.

CANCER

Cancer, although perceived as a single disease, involves many conditions and symptoms that can influence short- and long-term well-being. Further, cancer attacks children at a high rate and is the second leading cause of death in those under age 14 (American Cancer Society, 2002). Bone tumors affect adolescents after age 15 at a higher rate than adults; thus it is likely that educators in the public schools will be faced with this potentially disabling condition. In treatment and overall well-being, physical activity will play a vital role in helping children recover and adjust to any permanent outcomes of the disease.

© Francis M. Kozub

Figure 17.1 This boy has had asthma since he was four years old and continues to be active in such activities as basketball, baseball, and judo, even though this condition at times results in difficulty breathing and the need for restricted play.

Types

Background information about cancer focuses on two factors: the nature of the disease and the treatment. Cancer is categorized based on the tissue affected. In cancer, cells grow at an abnormal rate and replace healthy tissue. The mechanism of cell growth and division is not clearly understood in cancer, but any body cells can be attacked. Further, treatment varies in patients from surgery to remove the abnormal growths, radiation to destroy or reduce tumor mass, and chemotherapy, which involve drugs that retard growth in cancerous cells. Prolonged hospital stays and the side effects from chemotherapy might affect normal development in children. Children might experience pain, anemia, loss of hair, and other visible and unseen outcomes of the treatment, which might create a need for extra program considerations in physical education.

Physical Education and Students With Cancer

All children, including those diagnosed with cancer, can develop fitness (Schwartz, 2003). Physical activity and fitness type activities play an important role in recovery from the physical effects of the disease and treatments. However, much of the empirical evidence on exercise as a mediator for recovery is based on adults (Lee, 1995). For children, no studies have focused on the effects of exercise; however, Sternberg (1997) reports many benefits in adults following regular physical activity during the recovery phase. Considering the lack of studies in the published literature demonstrating benefits for children with cancer exercising, care must be taken to prescribe physical activity in moderation based on the guidance of a physician during treatment phases of the disease.

When appropriate, a general recommendation is to provide programs that have influence on multiple systems in the child. These include exercise at a level that affects not only fitness but psychosocial systems. Fatigue is a big factor, and regular exercise can decrease these feelings in adults (Courneya, Mackey, & Jones, 2000). Speculatively, these same results might generalize to children and have the potential to affect overall well-being. For example, a child experiencing depression because of cancer might benefit from successful physical activity experiences by being more motivated to play. A child in recovery from losing a limb because of cancer might benefit from games and exercise that enhance balance and thus open up avenues for integrated participation with peers. In all, children should be encouraged to engage in play, physical activity, and even more intense fitness training when they are physically and emotionally ready. Educators might benefit significantly from talking to a child who has cancer about physical activity participation, locker room issues, and apprehensions about play. This will allow the educator to anticipate learner needs and avoid unnecessary problems that could affect learning outcomes for other students if the learner is overdependent on the teacher or unwilling to participate in certain activities.

CARDIOVASCULAR DISORDERS

Children with a disability caused by a cardiovascular disorder can be classified as "other health impaired" if the disease affects learning. A child with disease affecting the heart, veins, or lymphatic system suffers either from a congenital defect or acquires the condition from some other illness. Depending on the nature of the cardiovascular disorder, exercise might or might not be warranted at the time of acute symptoms. However, in the long term, all children need physical education, and even children with serious conditions warranting heart replacement will benefit from exercise prescription at an appropriate level.

Rheumatic Heart Disease

A condition resulting from a streptococcal infection that then progresses to rheumatic fever and eventually (in about half of the cases) results in permanent damage to the heart is referred to as rheumatic heart disease. More often than not, mild effects on the heart occur when a child is infected with streptococcal infections. This occurs without obvious symptoms in many children (Bisno, 1991). However, in about 500,000 school-age children, the cardiac problems associated with rheumatic fever are present and result in heart murmurs, cardiomegaly (enlarged heart caused by additional stress on the muscle itself), pericarditis (swelling around the lining of the heart, which might cause chest pain), and congestive heart failure (Surburg, 2000). Symptoms of rheumatic heart disease include shortness of breath, weight gain, dizziness, edema, and palpitations.

Treatment for infections resulting from rheumatic fever include antibiotics which, based on Bisno (1991), have little impact on the later development of cardiac problems once rheumatic attack occurs. When damage to the valves of the heart occurs, treatment can include surgery to repair or replace the heart. Prevention is the best measure, and educators who find students with severe sore throats should refer children to the school nurse, given the high prevalence of streptococcal infections in school-age children. Recommendations for children with cardiovascular disorders including those related to rheumatic heart disease follow.

Physical Education and Children With Cardiovascular Disorders

Factors that need to be considered in planning physical education experiences include the nature of the disorder and the treatment, specifically the medication being used and the accompanying side effects. Program providers should consult physicians to learn how prescribed medications affect physical activity. In general, basic weight bearing and large muscle movements promote the recovery process for individuals with cardiovascular disorder. Resistance training can help develop functional levels of fitness needed for independent living (Clark & Sherman, 1998; Franklin, 2003).

Intensity, frequency, and duration of exercise need to be discussed with medical care providers to ensure that individuals with cardiovascular disorders exercise for both recovery and health-related fitness. Short, McCubbin, and Frey (1999) suggest several methods for estimating intensity that is more problematic than the other frequency and duration factors. Most notably, it is common to use heart rate to monitor exercise intensity. Predicted heart rate is estimated by taking 220 minus current age for a heart rate maximum that is then compared to the following values to note light (35 to 54 percent of maximal heart rate), moderate (55 to 69 percent of maximal heart rate), or vigorous exercise (>70 percent of maximal heart rate) (see Short, McCubbin, & Frey, 1999, for other methods for estimating intensity). These values used in conjunction with recording the day and minutes exercised provide practitioners with an easy method to quantify and communicate about exercise frequency, intensity, and duration.

The broad range of cardiovascular diseases that exist in children carry different recommendations for physical activity. Here are suggestions to help educators individualize programs for children with cardiovascular disorders:

- Before starting an exercise program, make sure children are in stable condition (Braith, 2002).
- Walking on three nonconsecutive days per week is recommended at about 70 percent of a person's maximal heart rate for patients involved in cardiac rehabilitation (Franklin, 2003; Thompson, 2001).
- Competition might be a contraindication for some children following surgery, but some children respond well to surgical procedures and experience no residual effects. Those without residual effects might be able to participate in competitive sports (Riner & Sabath, 2003).
- Weight training, previously considered a contraindication for many individuals with cardiovascular disease, might be appropriate for some as part of the rehabilitation program (Thompson, 2001).
- Warm-up and cool-down periods should be longer for individuals with chronic heart problems (Braith, 2002).
- Watch for symptoms of cardiac problems during exercise, such as excessive coughing, difficult or labored respiration, low blood pressure, bluish discoloration of the skin, and light-headedness indicating distress (Briath, 2002).
- Rest intervals are important for individuals with cardiac heart conditions.
- Intensity levels in activities can be modified without eliminating key curricular staples. For example, playing lead-up games in basketball, shortening playing areas in soccer (or playing goalie), and playing sitting versions of games (e.g., sit volleyball) might help children with cardiac problems participate in physical activity.

ANEMIA

Anemia has many causes, including poor diet and heredity. In anemia a marked reduction in red blood cells or general change in quality of hemoglobin occurs. This in turn affects the oxygen-carrying capabilities of individuals affected. The heart is then forced to increase output to compensate for the needs of cells in the body. In general, anemia affects young children, particularly girls before their initial menstrual cycle. However, this condition can be present in both males and females of all ages. The most common form of anemia is iron deficiency, which can result in shortness of breath, lack of energy, dizziness, and digestive problems. Treatments involving changes in diet and supplements are common.

Sickle Cell Anemia

The genetic condition known as sickle cell anemia is potentially classifiable as "other health impaired" if the condition affects a child's ability to learn. Sickle-shaped cells resulting from defective hemoglobin is a genetic condition that occurs most frequently in African Americans, with about 10 percent of individuals from this ethnic group carrying the abnormal gene. When both parents are carriers, the condition emerges. The incidence of this condition is high, with estimates of 1 in 400 children being affected (Surgburg, 2000). Children with sickle cell anemia at one time or another need some form of activity modification in physical education. The symptoms most likely to affect physical activity participation include fatigue, bone and joint pain, and leg ulcers.

Physical Education and Students With Anemia

Although sickle cell anemia exists at a high frequency in African American children, and anemia in general occurs in all races, visible symptoms requiring daily attention are minimal. However, sickle cell anemia has been cited in the literature as an increased risk factor for sudden death, making it imperative that educators be aware of this form of anemia and what to do to help prevent symptoms. Risks to individuals with sickle cell anemia are associated with intense exercise, hot weather, and high altitudes that can increase the severity of symptoms (Eichner, 1993). Children with anemia and specifically sickle cell require close contact between educator, parent, child, and physician to address specific symptoms.

Anemia carries specific activity recommendations based on the nature of the disease and symptoms noted in the child. In some cases, excusing a child from physical education class for anemia can make the situation worse. Poor diet coupled with inactivity leads to a pattern that, in the long run, negatively affects the ability of the heart and other body systems to meet the demands of daily life. Students who are anemic and undergoing treatment might require a modified program less intense with respect to exercise load until the condition improves. Walking instead of running or light lifting can affect fitness goals of children with anemia who are undergoing medical treatment. As the condition improves higher workloads and more intense fitness activities are possible.

Sickle cell anemia offers more long-term implications for physical activity. Specifically, joint inflammation is a major concern in sickle cell anemia, given the nature of physical education curricula. If this is an issue for a child with sickle cell anemia, a reduction in impact activities may be warranted. However, high-profile athletes with sickle cell are found on basketball courts and other activities involving impact, indicating that a general concern for all individuals with sickle cell might not be warranted. Children should be planned for individually, and monitoring the child's symptoms and motor needs is recommended. Educators must focus on the affective domain in children with sickle cell anemia to ensure that learners are not provided a reinforcement history for inactivity caused by fear of injury or death. For some adolescents in particular the need to keep up with peers might result in high-risk activity that, with proper monitoring of symptoms, is appropriate and recommended.

HEMOPHILIA

Hemophilia is a hereditary condition that affects the body's ability to stop bleeding. Deficiencies in coagulation factors mark the conditions known as hemophilia A and B. Hemophilia A is the most prevalent, affecting 1 in 5,000 to 10,000 males. Because hemophilia is linked to the X chromosome, it is not common in females. Hemophilia B is another form that results from deficiency in the protein referred to as Factor IX.

Classification of Hemophilia

Hemophilia is classified in three levels of severity. Mild hemophilia is characterized by its appearance later in adolescence or adulthood and the presence of excessive bruising, nosebleeds, and other related symptoms. Moderate hemophilia involves the same symptoms with greater severity and some occasional bleeding noted in the joints. Severe hemophilia is a serious condition that causes pain, swelling, and severe bleeding in all areas of the body. Bleeding in general is a serious condition that can be life threatening. However, in individuals with hemophilia, the lack of blood coagulants make any bleeding or bruising an issue of concern for school-age children affected. With proper care and medication, individuals with hemophilia can be physically active, and life expectancy does not have to be diminished.

Physical Education and Students With Hemophilia

Severe hemophilia type A is a serious condition that limits the nature of physical activity for children. Safety has to be in the forefront for designing a suitable physical education program for children with severe hemophilia type A. Contact sports and other high-impact activities in which a child might receive a blow from a blunt object, such as baseball or racket, can be hazardous and requires communication between educators, parents, and doctors. Training to help educators recognize when potential injury symptoms are present and a plan to care for injury-related emergencies are needed. The benefits of appropriate physical activity outweigh the hazards; however, physical educators might want to consider individual-type activities such as jogging and some forms of light resistance training. It is important to consult the child's physician for guidance on suitable exercise intensities and warning signs indicating internal bleeding and suitable first aid measures. In cases in which bleeding injuries (internal or external) require blood factor replacement, cooperation among the school nurse, child's physician, and parents should ensure that an emergency plan to administer medication in the event of an injury is in place prior to physical activity programming.

Aside from safety concerns related to injury, individuals with hemophilia type A are recommended to engage in physical activity to optimize physical conditioning (Bell, Canty, & Audet, 1995). Mild to moderate amounts of appropriate physical activity are important for children with hemophilia who might have apprehensions about moving. Fast walking is recommended by Surburg (2000) as an appropriate way to develop cardiovascular fitness in individuals with hemophilia type A. Risks related to running and jumping activities include joint bleeding, and in many children with hemophilia these types of activities are not recommended. Consulting the child's physician and medical records to determine if joint or other central nervous system problems exist that might further limit physical activity is warranted. Individual and dual recreational activities are also recommended provided that steps are taken to ensure the safety of the child with hemophilia. Archery, golf, and badminton are excellent activities that can be done in school and in the home or community environment. Perhaps the best activity is swimming, given the low impact and potential benefits in all areas of fitness (Moore & Brubaker, 2003). The key to successful participation is to avoid contact or collisions that are contraindicated because of the issues with bleeding.

ACQUIRED IMMUNODEFICIENCY SYNDROME AND HUMAN IMMUNODEFICIENCY VIRUS

On a global scale, more than 1,500 children are infected with human immunodeficiency virus (HIV) daily (UNAIDS, 2002). Although the majority of these cases occur abroad, the United States Centers for Disease Control (2003) reports that over 9,000 children are diagnosed with acquired immunodeficiency syndrome (AIDS) annually. As a result of these numbers and increased social pressure for integration, educators must be well informed and equipped to serve learners with AIDS. Most important is making educators aware that being HIV positive is not the same as having AIDS. Only some people who are infected with the virus (HIV positive) develop AIDS symptoms. From a disease control standpoint, those who are HIV positive are carriers of the virus and thus able to infect other individuals. This is perhaps the issue that most alarms individuals in educational settings. For this reason, factual information about how AIDS and HIV are spread is important in service and community education topics. Children with AIDS/HIV can integrate into schools without putting peers and teachers at risk.

Facts About AIDS and HIV

It has long been known that HIV, the virus that causes AIDS, is present in the bodily fluids of infected individuals. However, it is only through direct contact through an open wound, sexual intercourse, or sharing of needles that the disease spreads. Airborne exposure or general casual contact will not spread AIDS, and the Centers for Disease Control consistently monitors the spread of the disease to ensure that children and adults are not put at undue risk. Although the reported number of AIDS cases has declined since 1992, it is likely that children with HIV will attend public school settings. New drugs (increasing life expectancy and decreasing viral load) and a more informed public have opened the doors for children with HIV to lead normal lives. Children with AIDS have been found eligible for services under IDEA through the category of OHI when this condition affects educational progress and the need for a specialized program of study is warranted (Grice, 2002).

Physical Education and Students With AIDS or HIV

Physical education modifications for children with AIDS depend on the presence of secondary opportunistic illnesses. Once acute symptoms such as open sores, cough, or diarrhea begin to show up, children might need modifications in programs depending on the extent of the symptom. In general, these are conditions that might be present in any child, and notification of appropriate school personal about medical and hygiene issues is important. Children with AIDS should be treated in a manner consistent with all kids when bleeding, vomiting, or other biohazards are present and at risk for exposing others. In general, all schools and institutions should have a plan or universal precautions for handling biohazards whether children with AIDS or HIV are present or not. This includes wearing rubber gloves to wipe up blood, use of bleach on surfaces on which body fluids have been spilled, and a separate waste container for paper towels used to clean biohazards. Extra care in all cases in which bleeding has occurred is a precaution that addresses the issue of unreported illness and other potentially dangerous pathogens in any child.

In general, children with AIDS or HIV who are not showing symptoms require less physical education modifications than other disability categories. However, it is important to keep in mind that some children with AIDS might suffer from related conditions, such as hemophilia, developmental delays, and other environmental deprivation effects. In these cases, activity modifications might be warranted to ensure that educational benefit is possible. One additional factor that might affect the nature of school-based programming is the potential impact on learning as a result of frequent absences from school, a situation that might require a specialized program of study (Grice, 2002).

Primarily what is known about children with AIDS and exercise are generalized from adult studies. The positive effects of exercise are noted in light of many side effects of medications used to treat the disease. Specifically, many medications are now being linked to redistribution of fat and general weight gain. From a health-related fitness standpoint, children with AIDS or HIV can benefit both mentally and physically from exercise without further complications (Spence, Galantino, Mossbert, & Zimmerman, 1990; Stringer, Berezovskaya, Obrien, Beck, & Casaburi, 1998; Wagner, Rabkin, & Rabkin, 1998). Adults were found to benefit from exercise by Roubenoff et al. (1999), who found reduced trunk fat resulting from appropriate exercise interventions. Resistance training has also had positive effects on strength and the issue of lean body mass (Roubenoff et al., 1998). Individuals with HIV are prone to fatigue, and in Smith et al. (2001), supervised aerobic exercise did decrease this symptom in a group of adults with HIV. In light of the need for more study on children, an individualized approach is recommended.

INCLUSION

Inclusion for children with OHI provides a challenge to educational teams because of the need for case-by-case modifications based on unique learner needs. Table 17.1 outlines some of the areas for consideration related to medical conditions discussed in this chapter. This checklist is recommended when the disability warrants concern for physical activity involvement. Physical educators are encouraged to address each of these points at a child's IEP meeting to ensure that appropriate activities are selected, attention to medical aspects of the disability occur, the child's social needs are addressed, parents understand implications for home programming, and appropriate placement occurs.

SUMMARY

This chapter included information to help promote educational, healthful, and safe involvement in physical education experiences for several categories of youngsters referred to as OHI. What separates OHI from other disabilities are chronic or acute medical conditions that place this category more in line with disease than disability. However, like disability, the affect on a child's education is important in making OHI classification decisions for school-age children (Grice, 2002).

Table 17.1 Inclusion Checklist for Children With Other Health Impairments

	Diabetes	Seizures	Asthma	Cancer	CV*	Anemia	Hemophilia	AIDS
Exercise intensity	I	S	S	S	I	I	S	S
Social interactions	S	N	N	I	N	N	N	I
Overemphasis on medical or illness aspect of disability	I	S	S	S	S	S	S	S
Regular parental support	I	S	I	I	I	I	I	I
Appropriateness of select curricular offerings in general PE	N	S	N	S	S	I	I	S

* CV = cardiovascular disorders

Note: These are some general areas to focus on prior to inclusion that are not necessarily an issue for each child based on medical condition; rather, use as a checklist to begin gathering information critical for the IEP process and successful integration experiences.

I: important consideration that needs to be addressed for many children with this condition

S: in some cases, this issue may warrant consideration for successful inclusion

N: no more of a concern than for any other child without a disability

REFERENCES

American Cancer Society. (2002, November 11). *What are the differences between cancer in adults and children?* Author. Retrieved May 22, 2003, from www.cancer.org/docroot/home/index.asp?level=0.

American National Red Cross. (2001). *American Red Cross Standard First Aid.* Boston MA: Staywell.

Bell, B., Canty, D., & Audet, M. (1995). Hemophilia: An updated review. *Pediatric Review, 8,* 290-298.

Birrer, R.B., & Sedaghat, V. (2003). Exercise and diabetes mellitus. *The Physician and Sportsmedicine, 31*(5), 29-41.

Bisno, A.L. (1991). Group A streptococcal infections and acute rheumatic fever. *New England Journal of Medicine, 325,* 783.

Braith, R.W. (2002). Exercise for those with chronic heart failure: Matching programs to patients. *The Physician and Sportsmedicine, 30*(9), 29-38.

Clark, J.R., & Sherman, C. (1998). Congestive heart failure: Training for a better life. *The Physician and Sportsmedicine, 26*(8), 49-57.

Centers for Disease Control. (2003, March 31). Division of HIV/AIDS Prevention: Basic Statistics. Author. Retrieved May 23 from www.cdc.gov/hiv/stats.htm.

Code of Federal Regulations, 34 C.F.R.–Office of the Federal Register National Archives and Records Administration § 300.7 (2002).

Colberg, S.R. (2000). Practical management of Type 1 diabetes during exercise. *Journal of Physical Education, Recreation and Dance, 71*(2), 24-27, 35.

Colson Bloomquist, L.E. (2003). Epilepsy. In J.L. Durstine & G.E. Moore (Eds.), *American College of Sports Medicine's Exercise management for persons with chronic diseases and disabilities* (pp. 262-280). Champaign, IL: Human Kinetics.

Conti, S.F., & Chaytor, E.R. (1995). Foot care for active patients who have diabetes. *The Physician and Sportsmedicine, 23*(6), 53-68.

Courneya, K.S., Mackey, J.R., & Jones, L.W. (2000). Coping with cancer: Can exercise help? *The Physician and Sportsmedicine, 28*(5), 49-74.

Eichner, E. R. (1993). Sickle cell trait, heroic exercise, and fatal collapse. *The Physician and Sportsmedicine, 21*(4), 51-64.

Epilepsy Foundation Kansas and Western Missouri. (2003, Jan 1). Seizure Types. Author. Retrieved August 24, 2004 from www.epilepsyfoundation.org/local/kansas/seizuretypes.cfm.

Franklin, B.A. (2003). Myocardial Infarction. In J.L. Durstine & G.E. Moore (Eds.), *American College of Sports Medicine's Exercise management for persons with chronic diseases and disabilities* (pp. 24-39). Champaign, IL: Human Kinetics.

Friedman, M.S., Powell, K.E., Hutwagner, L., Graham, L.M., & Teague, W.G. (2001). Impact of changes in transportation and commuting behaviors during the 1996 summer Olympic games in Atlanta on air quality and childhood asthma. *The Journal of the American Medical Association, 285,* 897-905.

Grice, K. (2002). Eligibility under IDEA for Other Health Impaired Children. School Law Bulletin, 33(3), 7-12.

Hornsby, W.G., & Albright, A.L. (2003). Diabetes. In J.L. Durstine & G.E. Moore (Eds.), *American College of Sports Medicine's Exercise management for persons with chronic diseases and disabilities* (pp. 133-163). Champaign, IL: Human Kinetics.

Juvenile Diabetes Foundation International. (2003, February 1). Juvenile (type 1) diabetes facts. Author. Retrieved May 20, 2003, from www.jdrf.org/index.cfm?fuseaction=home.viewPage&page_id=14AF69BC-BE51-4.

Lee, F. (1995). Exercise and physical health: Cancer and immune function. *Research Quarterly for Exercise and Sport, 66,* 281-286.

Mahler, D.A. (1993). Exercise-induced asthma. *Medicine and Science in Sports and Exercise, 25,* 554-561.

Moore, G.E., & Brubaker, P.H. (2003). Bleeding and clotting disorders. In J.L. Durstine & G.E. Moore (Eds.). *American College of Sports Medicine's Exercise management for persons with chronic diseases and disabilities* (pp. 202-208). Champaign, IL: Human Kinetics.

Riner, W.F., & Sabath, R.J. (2003). Considerations regarding physical activity for children and youth. In J.L. Durstine & G.E. Moore (Eds.). *American College of Sports Medicine's Exercise management for persons with chronic diseases and disabilities* (pp. 16-22). Champaign, IL: Human Kinetics.

Roubenoff, R., McDermott, A., Wiess, L., Suri, J., Wood, M., Block, R., & Gorbach, S. (1998). Short-term progressive resistance training increases strength and lean body mass in adults infected with human immunodeficiency virus. *AIDS,* 13, 231-239.

Roubenoff, R., Weiss, L., McDermott, A., Heflin, T., Clouteir, G.J., Wood, M., & Gorbach, S. (1999). A pilot study of exercise training to reduce trunk fat in adults with HIV-associated fat redistribution. *AIDS,* 13, 1373-1375.

Schwartz, A.L. (2003). Cancer. In J.L. Durstine & G.E. Moore (Eds.), *American College of Sports Medicine's Exercise management for persons with chronic diseases and disabilities* (pp. 185-188). Champaign, IL: Human Kinetics.

Short, F.X., McCubbin, J., & Frey, G. (1999). In J.P. Winnick and F.X. Short (Eds.), *The Brockport Physical Fitness Test Training Guide* (pp. 19-29). Champaign, IL: Human Kinetics.

Sirven, J.I., & Varrato, J. (1999). Physical activity and epilepsy: What are the rules? *The Physician and Sportsmedicine,* 27(3), 63-72.

Smith, B.A., Neidig, J.L., Nickel, J.T. Mitchell, G.L., Para, M.F., & Fass, R.J. (2001). Aerobic exercise: Effects on parameters related to fatigue, dyspnea, weight, and body composition in HIV infected adults. *AIDS,* 15, 693-701.

Spence, D.W., Galantino, M., Mossbert, K.H., & Zimmerman, S.O. (1990). Progressive resistance exercise: Effect on muscle function and anthropometry of select AIDS population. *Archives of Physical Medicine and Rehabilitation,* 71, 644-648.

Sternberg, S. (1997, May 3). Exercise helps some cancer, heart patients. *Sciencenewsonline,* 151, 269, Retrieved May 23, 2003, at www.sciencenews.org/pages/sn_arc97/5_3_97/fob2.htm.

Stringer, W., Berezovskaya, M., O'Brien, W.H., Beck, K.C., & Casaburi, R. (1998). The effect of exercise training on aerobic fitness, immune indices, and quality of life in HIV+ patients. *Medicine and Science in Sport and Exercise,* 30, 11-16.

Surburg, P.R. (2000). Other health-impaired students. In J. P. Winnick (Ed.), *Adapted physical education and sport* (3rd ed.), (p. 235-249). Champaign, IL: Human Kinetics.

Thompson, P.D. (2001). Exercise rehabilitation for cardiac patients: A beneficial but underused therapy. *The Physician and Sportsmedicine,* 29(1), 69-75.

UNAIDS. (2002). *Pediatric HIV infection and AIDS: UNAIDS Point of view.* Geneva, Switzerland: Author.

Wagner, G., Rabkin, J., & Rabkin, R. (1998). Exercise as a mediator of psychological and nutritional effects of testosterone therapy in HIV+ men. *Medicine and Science in Sports and Exercise,* 30, 811-817.

Weinstein, S. (2002). Epilepsy. In M.L. Batshaw (Ed.). *Children with disabilities* (5th ed.), (pp. 493-524). Baltimore, MD: Paul H. Brookes Publishing Co.

Woodruff, P.G., & Fahy, J.V. (2001). Asthma: Prevalence, pathogenesis, and prospects for novel therapies. *The Journal of the American Medical Association,* 286, 395-398.

WRITTEN RESOURCES

Barfield, J.P., & Michael, T.J. (2002). Responses to physical activity among children and youths with exercise-induced asthma. *Palaestra,* 18(2), 26-32.

Misconceptions about exercise and children with EIA are discussed. Recommendations for educators are provided.

Batshaw, M.L. (2002). *Children with disabilities* (5th ed.). Baltimore, MD: Paul H Brookes Publishing Co.

This source has been used by teachers across the country and is an easily understood source for medical types of conditions. Information related to contraindications that can help physical educators decide on programming options is provided.

Durstine, L.J., & Moore, G.E. (2000). *ACSM's Exercise management for persons with chronic diseases and disabilities.* Champaign, IL: Human Kinetics.

This book is an excellent source of current medical implications for children with disabilities known as "other impaired." Activity recommendations and tables help determine appropriate frequencies and intensities.

Verity, L.S., & Aufsesser, P.M. (1999). Type 2 Diabetes and disabilities—A dangerous duo: What are the recommendations? *Palaestra,* 15(4), 43-48.

Basic information on type 2 diabetes is presented along with information on blood glucose monitoring. Further, detailed information on activity recommendations based on the needs of individuals with type 2 diabetes is also included.

Weiss, C.B., Jeon, J.Y., Suh, M., & Steadward, R.D. (1998). Modifying diet and exercise to reduce risk factors for diabetes mellitus and cardiovascular disease in people with spinal cord injury. *Palaestra,* 14(1), 25-27.

Although specific to spinal cord injury, this article highlights some of the important issues related to individuals with multiple needs. In many situations, disabilities do not exist in isolation, and individuals with disabilities can have other diseases that affect physical activity.

AUDIOVISUAL RESOURCES

Cancer: A personal voyage (Videotape and DVD, 1997). Films for the Humanities & Sciences, PO Box 2053, Princeton, NJ 08543.

The issues associated with cancer from the perspective of a younger male. Mortality is discussed with relation to terminal cancer and the two-year chronicle of an individual's struggle with cancer. Running time is 58 minutes.

Diagnosing and treating diabetes. (Videotape, 1998). Films for the Humanities & Sciences, PO Box 2053, Princeton, NJ 08543.

Factual information about diagnosing and treatment of diabetes are provided. These include information about the metabolic facts related to diabetes, diet, and exercise. Running time is 22 minutes.

Just like me: Talking about AIDS (Videotape, 1997). Films for the Humanities & Sciences, PO Box 2053, Princeton, NJ 08543.

The social effects of AIDS and HIV are discussed to help older adolescents understand the facts and myths of disease transmittal. Physical effects of the disease are also discussed to help educators understand the effects of opportunistic infections on individuals with AIDS. Running time is 21 minutes.

Sickle cell anemia (Videotape 2001). Films for the Humanities & Sciences, PO Box 2053, Princeton, NJ 08543.

Interviews with adults and adolescents with sickle cell anemia are included along with some recent advancement in managing this hereditary disease. Further, information about the disease and leading clinics are presented. Running time is 29 minutes.

ELECTRONIC RESOURCES

American Cancer Society: www.cancer.org/docroot/home/index.asp?level=0.

This site contains factual as well as practical information on cancer that is geared to all audiences. Educators, parents, and children can access this site and gain valuable information about treatment and other medical aspects of cancer.

American Diabetes Association: www.diabetes.org/main/type1/medical/ketoacidosis/ketoacidosis.jsp.

This site provides information about symptoms prior to diabetic coma that will help educators understand the early warning signs of this medical emergency.

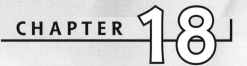

Students With Temporary Disabilities and Other Special Conditions

Christine B. Stopka

Two high school students are participating in the Special Olympics Unified Sports program. During the first half of the basketball game, the student without a disability slightly sprains his ankle. Immediate care for this injury is administered. Rest, cold, compression, and elevation (RICE) are immediately applied. During the second half of the game, one of the participants with an intellectual disability sustains a similar type of injury, and the same type of care is provided. The following week, both students were in their physical education classes. Although these injuries were mild sprains, the physical education teacher followed the appropriate protocols, as described in this chapter, to promote full participation and recovery.

As noted in chapter 4, students without a designated disability but with unique physical education needs should have an individualized physical education program (IPEP). For example, a middle school student who has Osgood-Schlatter's condition might not be able to engage in all types of physical education activities. Similarly, a person with an injured ankle might be temporarily limited in the physical education setting (figure 18.1). People with long-term disorders benefit from physical education programs modified to meet their present unique needs. Ironically, some of the information offered in this chapter to help students with temporary disorders might also apply to students with disabilities. Topics discussed under the heading Long-Term Disorders are conditions that individuals with disabilities might also exhibit. Thus, the content of this chapter is applicable to both students with and without disabilities.

ACTIVITY INJURIES AND REHABILITATIVE EXERCISES

Students might sustain activity or sports injuries in different settings. Although some injuries might originate in a physical education class, more occur during free time or recreational pursuits.

If an injury occurs in physical education class, immediate care should be provided in the RICE (rest, ice, compression, elevation) sequence: *Rest* should be given immediately to the injured part or joint. *Ice* or a cold application should be administered immediately and removed after 20 minutes. Cold may be reapplied in one to one and a half hours, depending on the extent of injury. The unavailability of commercial cold packs should not deter this critical treatment; food storage bags can be filled with ice cubes or crushed ice. An even more convenient home method is to place a bag of frozen vegetables on the injured area; frozen corn or peas conform nicely to an injured joint. *Compression* and *elevation* reduce internal bleeding and swelling. Unfortunately, in the recreational setting, these procedures are not always followed, and the injury might be exacerbated. Without the ice and compression, intraarticular pressure from the swelling might stretch structures, such as ankle ligaments, just as if a person had twisted the joint. Some type of immobilization or rest is needed for musculoskeletal injuries; rest promotes healing and reduces the risk of a prolonged recovery time.

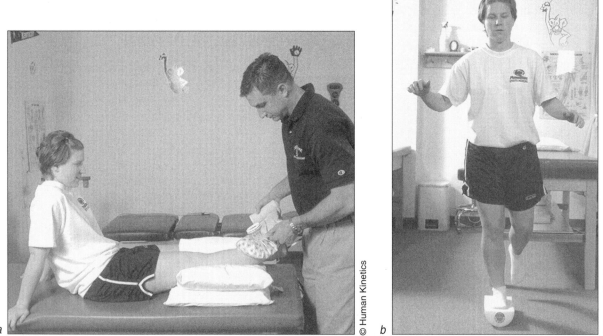

© Human Kinetics

Figure 18.1 *(a)* Initial treatment to an ankle injury. If such a cold pack is not available, then a bag of frozen peas or frozen corn works very well, easily conforming to the joint, and there's no need to refill a messy ice bag, making frozen peas or corn a perfect option for reusable, inexpensive, ice-pack treatments. *(b)* Preparing for return to participation. A tilt/balance board can also be made by slicing a softball in two and placing the flat sides on a small board and drilling it in place, thus affording everyone the opportunity to have access to such equipment, even when budgets are limited.

Unless injured students are on an athletic team, there is probably no type of rehabilitation service available to them at their school. Still, although physical educators cannot act in the capacity of athletic trainers, they might provide valuable assistance. If an injury is not being managed in an appropriate manner, the physical educator might recommend that the student see a medical professional. Many hospitals provide sports medicine services; these clinics or departments are staffed by sport physical therapists or athletic trainers.

If the injured student is progressing normally toward recovery, the physical education class might provide an opportunity for exercises or activities that ameliorate the condition. The Brockport Physical Fitness Test is health related and criterion referenced. This test may be used to assess aerobic functioning, body composition, musculoskeletal functioning, and flexibility development, following recovery from activity injuries.

Ankle

Ankle sprains are a risk for anyone who actively engages in sports or physical activity. Jumping and other movements might cause a person to roll over on an ankle and stretch the medial or lateral side of the joint. Because of the structural configuration of the bones and ligaments of this joint, 85 percent of all ankle sprains are of the inversion type (in which the ligaments on the lateral side of the ankle are stretched).

Table 18.1 provides an exercise protocol for inversion sprains after primary care and treatment have been administered. Although eversion sprains are less frequent, this injury tends to be more serious and entails a longer recovery period. Most of the exercises listed in table 18.1 could be used for an eversion sprain; the eversion exercises, being the mechanism of injury for this type of sprain, should be eliminated.

Table 18.1 Rehabilitation Protocol for a Moderate Inversion Sprain of the Ankle

Stage	Activity	Purpose
I. Control and decrease foot swelling and pain	A1. Flexion, extension, and spreading of toes 2. Exercises for noninvolved leg and upper extremities 3. Crutch walking with touch weight bearing	A1. Work on intrinsic muscles and certain muscles that go across the ankle 2. Keep rest of body in good condition 3. Involve ankle in a minimal amount of motion, but replicate a normal gait pattern as closely as possible
II. Begin restoration of strength and movements	B1. Ankle circumduction movements 2. Toe raises 3. Eversion exercises—isometric then isotonic 4. Achilles tendon stretch in sitting position with toes in, out, and straight ahead 5. Shift body weight from injured side to uninjured side	B1. Involve ankle in the four basic movements of this joint 2. Begin to develop plantar flexors 3. Reinforce side of ankle that has been stretched 4. Improve dorsiflexion and slight inversion and eversion 5. Begin to retain proprioception
III. Restore full function to ankle	C1. Ankle circumduction 2. Achilles tendon stretching in standing position 3. Eversion exercises 4. Plantar flexion, dorsiflexion, and inversion exercises	C1. Continue to improve range of motion 2. Work on dorsiflexion 3. Improve strength for protection 4. Develop main muscle groups of ankle
IV. Restore full function of ankle	D1-4. As in previous stage 5. Tiltboard exercises 6. Walk–jog 7. Jog faster, stop 8. Run and sprint 9. Jog figure eights 10. Run figure eights 11. Cutting–half-speed 12. Cutting–full speed 13. Run Z-shaped patterns 14. Backward running	D1-4. As in previous stage 5. Work on proprioception 6. Develop function and sport-specific activities

Although the primary focus of this chapter is on activity and exercise, the reader should be aware that other rehabilitative measures might have been or are currently being used. Hydrotherapy or cryotherapy is used to treat sprained ankles; taping the ankle is another mode that might be used for participation in physical education class. Sports medicine practitioners differ on the value, duration, and methods of taping or strapping. If ankle taping has been prescribed by sports medicine personnel, compliance by the student should be encouraged. The physical educator, however, should not make a practice of taping ankles because this could set a precedent for a time-consuming practice.

Knee

A variety of conditions and situations involving the knee might affect physical education performance. Table 18.2 provides basic rehabilitation programs for common knee problems. Several terms in this table are briefly described. A common condition in

adolescents and young adults, especially females, is called patellar–femoral pain syndrome (PFPS), which is usually caused by overuse accompanied by a less than optimal joint alignment. PFPS often includes a specifically painful knee condition termed chondromalacia patella, which refers to a degeneration or softening of the posterior surface of the patella or the femoral cartilage. Quad sets are isometric contractions of quadriceps femoris muscle groups. A six-second contraction of this muscle group constitutes a repetition. Straight-leg lifts involve having a student assume a supine position and flex one leg at the hip while keeping the knee in complete extension. Short arc exercises are isotonic knee-extension exercises done from 30 or 40 degrees of knee flexion to full or 0 degrees of knee extension. For chondromalacia patella, 30 to 0 degrees is appropriate, whereas for anterior cruciate ligament problems 90 to 45 degrees of motion is recommended. There is an individualized exercise program for each of these problems. A protocol that might be used in the latter stages of a rehabilitation program is the daily adjustable

Table 18.2   **Rehabilitation Exercise Programs for Common Knee Problems**

Diagnosis	Rehabilitation areas to stress	Method
Chondromalacia patella, subluxating patella, s/p surgery for chronic dislocations or chronic irritative processes	Strengthen the quads, particularly VMO, without putting additional stress on patellofemoral surface Achieve or maintain full ROM Strengthening of hamstrings, abductors, adductors, and lower-leg musculature	Quad sets, straight lifts, terminal extensions, lifts, short arcs with progressive resistance ROM and strengthening of hamstrings, abductors, and adductors can be done conventionally
Anterior cruciate deficient knees, chronic/acute; s/p casting; s/p reconstruction, intra-articular or extra-articular	Achieve full ROM Emphasis is placed on strengthening secondary stabilizers to the anterior cruciate	Active ROM exercies Hamstring strength aims to equal quad strength of the nonaffected leg, done with programs of isometrics; isotonic with concentric and eccentric contractions; isokinetics Quad strength to be elevated by use of isometrics at 90 degrees, 60 degrees, 30 degrees, and full extension; isotonic resistance done only in 90 to 45 degrees flexion
Medial collateral ligament sprains, chronic/acute, s/p reconstruction; s/p immobilization	Place special emphasis on strengthening quads and adductors General ROM Strengthen hamstrings, adductors, and lower-leg musculature	Achieve or maintain full ROM Quad sets Straight leg lifts with progressive resistance in hip flexion and adduction Isotonics for quads and hamstrings Isokinetics for quads and hamstrings

s/p = status/post

V/MO = vastus medialis obliquus muscle

ROM = range of motion

Table 18.3 **Daily Adjustable Progressive Resistance Exercise (DAPRE)**

Set	Weight	Repetitions
1	50% of working weight	10
2	75% of working weight	6
3	100% of working weight	Maximum
4	Determined by repetitions done in third set*	Maximum number determines working weight for next session

Working weight adjustments	
Repetitions during third set*	**Working weight for fourth set**
0–2	Decrease 5 to 10 lb
3–4	Decrease 0 to 5 lb
5–7	Keep the same
8–10	Increase 2.5 to 5 lb
More than 10	Increase 5 to 10 lb
Repetitions during fourth set	**Working weight for next session***
0–2	Decrease 5 to 10 lb
3–4	Keep the same
5–7	Increase 2.5 to 7.5 lb
8–10	Increase 5 to 10 lb
More than 10	Increase 10 to 15 lb

* From Knight, K. Rehabilitating chondromalacia patellae. *The Physician and Sportsmedicine,* 1, 147-148.

progressive resistance exercise (DAPRE), developed by Dr. Ken Knight (Arnheim & Prentice, 2000). This strength-development (table 18.3) program provides precise modification between sets of an exercise bout and between workouts.

Shoulder

The shoulder is composed of several major joints: sternoclavicular, acromioclavicular, scapulocostal, and glenohumeral. In many instances, activity-related strains or overuse syndromes involve the glenohumeral joint. Rotator cuff impingement syndrome, tendinitis, bursitis, and other glenohumeral problems might benefit from a general mobilizing and conditioning program for this joint (table 18.4, p. 328). This program, however, is contraindicated for students suffering from anterior glenohumeral dislocation. In its chronic form, this condition is sometimes called a "trick shoulder."

Mobilization for this condition consists primarily of adduction or internal rotation exercises. During the immobilization stage, isometric exercises are the exercises of choice; following immobilization, the exercise regimen might progress from isometric exercises, such as pulling against rubber tubing, to pulley or free-weight exercises that emphasize adduction and internal rotation. It should be noted that external rotation and abduction are movements associated with the mechanism of injury.

An important phase of many rehabilitation programs is the development of proprioception and kinesthesia. Because of this position-sense deficit, a comprehensive rehabilitation and conditioning program should include proprioceptive neuromuscular facilitation (PNF) exercises (Voss, Knott, & Iona, 1986) as well as other exercises, such as moving the arm into functional positions without the benefit of sight.

Types of Exercises

Terms commonly used to describe lower-extremity exercises are open and closed kinetic chain exercises, both of which are used in rehabilitation

Table 18.4   Shoulder Exercise Protocol for the Glenohumeral Joint

Stage	Activity	Purpose
I. During period of immobilization	A1. Isometric contractions of major muscle groups of shoulder 2. Isotonic wrist exercises of involved extremity 3. General conditioning exercises for the other three extremities	A1. Reduce muscle atrophy 2. These muscles might be kept in condition without involving shoulder muscle 3. These muscle groups should be kept in good condition
II. Mobilization of the shoulder	B1. Work on moving the shoulder through abduction and external rotation 2. Codman's exercise[a] 3. Wall-climbing exercise 4. Continue conditioning of other extremities	B1. Begin to gain appropriate range of motion 2. Begin to enhance four motions of the shoulder 3. Help to develop abduction and external rotation 4. Improve body fitness
III. Development of the shoulder	C1. Isotonic exercises that involve shoulder flexion, extension, abduction, adduction, medial rotation, and lateral rotation 2. Specific exercise involvement: bench press, pullovers, push-ups, parallel bar dips 3. PNF[b] exercises, replicate arm positions without the use of sight 4. Resistance movements that replicate sport activities	C1. Develop muscles that cause specific motions 2. Develop muscles for aggregate muscle action 3. Improve kinesthesis 4. Conform to the principle of specificity

Note: Not to be used with glenohumeral dislocations.

[a]Explained in text under the heading "Selected Exercises."

[b]PNF = proprioceptive neuromuscular facilitation

and physical fitness programs to develop strength, flexibility, and proprioception. Open kinetic chain exercises are non–weight bearing with the distal end (foot) free to move; they generally involve motion in one joint. Common examples of open kinetic chain exercises include seated, or prone, knee flexion and extensions.

Closed kinetic chain exercises are weight bearing in nature, with the distal segment in contact with a supporting surface and several joints involved in the execution of movement. A half deep-knee bend would be an example of a closed kinetic chain exercise. This type of exercise is often suggested for individuals with certain types of knee injuries, such as anterior cruciate ligament problems and patellofemoral problems. It has been suggested that closed kinetic exercises put less strain on the ligament (Fitzgerald, 1997).

A question that naturally arises is, *What is the best type of exercise?* The answer is that both open and closed kinetic chain exercises should be part of a rehabilitation and physical fitness program. If one thinks of a very basic movement, such as walking, there are both open (swing phase) and closed (stance phase) components to this motor skill.

Open and closed kinetic chain exercises might apply to the area of proprioception and kinesthesis. One could think of closed kinetic chain exercises as a means to promote proprioception. The tilt-board exercise described in the next section is a closed kinetic chain exercise. Exercises such as PNF might help kinesthesis, or the sense of the position of the joint in space, in addition to facilitating the improvement of flexibility, and are often done as open kinetic chair exercises. For more information on PNF, consult *Achieving the Ultra-Stretch* (Stopka & Follenius, 1995) and chapter 4 of *The Brockport Physical Fitness Training Guide* (Surburg in Winnick & Short, 1999). Kinesthetic and proprioceptive defects are present not only after an injury but are problems for students who have various types of physical and learning disabilities.

Selected Exercises

This section describes selected exercises for rehabilitation programs (tables 18.1 through 18.4) that might be unfamiliar. Table 18.1 refers to tiltboard exercises. The apparatus used with this exercise, which is available commercially or could easily be constructed, is basically a circle of three-quarter-inch plywood one foot in diameter (figure 18.2a). Attached to the center of the board is half of a pool ball or similar wooden ball. Standing with both feet on the board, the student attempts to balance on the board. This apparatus could be used to develop proprioceptive capabilities following an injury to the lower extremity. This exercise would be appropriate for balance and proprioceptive training of students with and without disabilities.

Terminal extension exercises are listed as strength exercises for quadriceps development in the exercise programs for common knee problems (table 18.2, p. 326). Ideally, these exercises

are done with a knee extension machine rather than a weight boot or weights wrapped around the ankle. Weights around the ankle cause a traction or pulling effect on the knee, which could stretch ligaments. Terminal extension exercises are initiated with the knee completely extended and resistance applied to the extremity (figure 18.2b). In subsequent exercise sessions, isotonic contractions are started with 5 degrees of extension. Over several sessions, the degree of extension is increased until the individual can extend against resistance through 25 degrees of motion.

In table 18.4 Codman's exercise is listed as an exercise to mobilize the shoulder. In this exercise the participant bends at the waist to achieve 90 degrees of trunk flexion and holds on to a chair or the end of a table. In this position the arm of the affected side should hang in a relaxed state. The individual initiates motion first in a flexion–extension direction, then adduction–abduction, and finally circumduction. All of these motions are pendular in nature without benefit of muscular contractions at the shoulder joint. Progressions in this exercise include wider circumduction motions and holding 2.5- and 5-pound weights as motions are performed (see figure 18.2c). As with the tilt board for proprioceptive development, Codman's exercise may be used to promote range of motion and flexibility of students with certain types of disabilities.

LONG-TERM DISORDERS AND SUGGESTED ADAPTED PHYSICAL ACTIVITIES TO IMPROVE THESE CONDITIONS

This section deals with several conditions classified as long-term disorders. The designation implies a condition or a problem that lasts longer than 30 days. This time span is, to an extent, an arbitrary designation because a third-degree ankle sprain might not be totally rehabilitated within 30 days. Several conditions—fractures, common knee and foot anomalies, adolescent hip diseases, and weight control problems—are the primary focus here, but the principles and procedures relevant to these conditions may also be applied to the integration of students with virtually any long-term disorders or conditions into regular physical education classes.

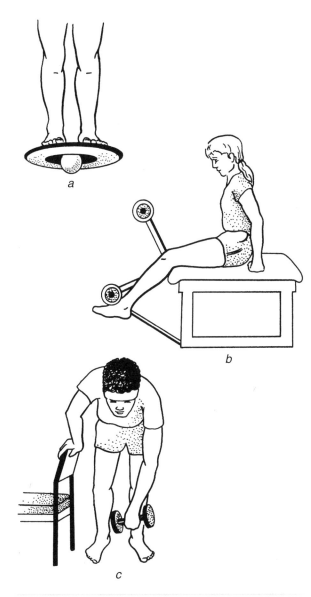

Figure 18.2 *(a)* Tiltboard exercise for common ankle problems, *(b)* daily adjustable progressive resistance exercise (DAPRE), and *(c)* shoulder exercise protocol for the glenohumeral joint.

Fractures

Bones in the upper and lower extremities are often fractured in activity-related accidents, such as when landing on an outstretched arm. Although the focus of this chapter is activity, readers should be aware that fractures might result from other situations, such as child abuse and pathologic bone-weakening conditions (e.g., cancer).

For physical educators, a student with a fracture presents two challenges: developing a program for a student immobilized in a cast and providing assistance after removal of the cast to integrate the student into the regular physical education program.

The first challenge must be dealt with from the perspective that the unaffected three fourths of the extremities have normal movement. A student with a broken arm has no problem with ambulation and can easily maintain a high level of cardiovascular fitness. Strength development of three extremities can be pursued with only minimal modification or adaptation. With a broken arm, certain lifts such as the bench press would have to be eliminated, but development of the triceps of the nonaffected arm could be accomplished through other exercises, such as elbow-extension exercises. Involvement of the affected arm should be predicated on recommendations from the physician and on good judgment. For example, any type of isometric exercise involving muscles immobilized in a cast should be approved by the physician. Exercises, isotonic or isometric, involving joints above or below the cast area should also have physician approval; this, however, does not mean that exercises are contraindicated for these joints.

Participation in physical education activities is based on the nature of the activities in the curricular unit. Although a track unit might mean little restriction for the student with a broken arm, a unit on gymnastic activities might require considerable restriction. For the person with a broken radius of the nondominant arm, a badminton unit will need very little modification. An archery unit, although less demanding as a vigorous activity, does require use of both upper extremities; however, the student could use a crossbow, which needs dexterity of one arm and could be mounted on a camera tripod. When unit activities preclude participation because of a fracture, physical fitness of the remaining three extremities might be the focus of the student's involvement in physical education class.

Once the cast is removed, the curricular focus should be on integrating the student into normal class activities. Part of this integration process might be to help develop range of motion, flexibility, strength, and muscular endurance in the affected limb. This assistance might be very important for students from low socioeconomic levels who might not have the benefit of appropriate medical services. Most students can benefit from a systemic reconditioning program. Activities and exercises described in an earlier section (Activity Injuries and Rehabilitative Exercises) might be incorporated into this program. The student's total integration into the regular physical education program depends on a group of factors: the nature of the fracture, the extent of immobilization, the duration of the reconditioning period, and the nature of activities involved in the unit.

Common Knee and Foot Conditions

A long-term condition of the knee that often presents a dilemma for the physical educator is Osgood-Schlatter's condition. Not a disease, as some books describe it, the condition involves incomplete separation of the epiphysis of the tibial tubercle from the tibia. Whether Osgood-Schlatter's condition is a result of singular or plural causes, it affects primarily adolescents during their most rapid growing periods. The treatment varies from immobilization in a cast to restriction of explosive extension movements at the knee, such as jumping and kicking (Wall, 1998). Variation in treatment depends on the severity of the condition and the philosophy of the attending physician concerning its management.

The physical educator should help the student with this condition during both its stages: the acute stage of involvement and the recovery stage. Because 60 to 75 percent of all cases are unilateral, affected students might be considered to have normal status for three fourths of their extremities. In essence, the approach discussed in the earlier section on fractures might be applied here. The comparison is applicable not only from a programmatic standpoint but also from a causality perspective, because with Osgood-Schlatter's condition there is a type of avulsion or fracture of bone from the tibial tuberosity. Involvement of the affected knee in activity must be based on a physician's recommendation. For example, certain physicians might approve isometric contractions of the quadriceps and stretching of the hamstrings in the affected extremity. Ankle exercises might also be considered appropriate for the affected limb. When all symptoms have disappeared and the physician has approved full participation, the student should begin a general mobilizing program in physical education class. Development of strength and flexibility of the affected limb should be part of the student's physical education program. Exercises such as straight-leg raises, short-arc exercises, and wall-slide arc are used to improve quadriceps strength. Stretching of the quadriceps and hamstrings should be part of the student's fitness program (Meisterling, Wall, & Meisterling, 1998). The physical educator should evaluate (and improve where needed) the student's gait pattern following the occurrence of Osgood-Schlatter's condition. Consider the application example concerning a student with Osgood-Schlatter's condition.

Knock knees, or genu valgum, refers to a valgus alignment problem in which the tibia bow outward from the midline and the knees are too close to midline (they are actually touching; see figure 18.3b; versus the normal alignment shown in 18.3a, on page 332). Genu valgum is a common postural deviation in children who are obese. Poor alignment of the knee results in a disproportionate amount of weight being borne by the medial aspect of the knee and predisposes the joint to potential strain and injury. Physical educators should carefully consider this point when selecting physical education or athletic events for students with this condition. Activities that increase the possibility of trauma to the knees (e.g., jumping from heights, running on hard or uneven surfaces, playing games or sports in which the knees could be hit laterally) should be avoided.

Bowlegs, or genu varum, refers to a varus alignment in which the tibia bows inward from the midline, resulting in the ankles touching; the knees are too separated, far apart from the midline (see figure 18.3c; versus the normal alignment shown in 18.3a). The bowing, usually bilateral, can occur in either the femur or the tibia but is most common in the tibia. This structural deformity is frequently accompanied by compensatory deformities in the feet. When the condition is suspected, the physical educator's major responsibility is to refer the child to a physician for possible treatment.

Although many foot deformities can be caused by skeletal and neuromuscular abnormalities, most are caused by compensatory postures required to offset other postural misalignments in the legs, hips, and spine. Physical educators should review the medical files and be aware of any students who have foot deformities. In most cases, the students will be able to participate in the regular physical education setting; however, the physical educator might need to monitor specific students to ensure they are wearing any needed braces or orthotics and that they are performing exercises as prescribed by their physicians.

Talipes deformities, which involves deformities of the foot and ankle, refer to a number of conditions, such as talipes equinus, a result of a plantar-flexed ankle caused by tight tendo-Achilles structures, or talipes calcaneus, the opposite condition, usually caused only iatrogenically (e.g., by the surgeon), a result of overzealous TAL (tendo-Achilles lengthening) surgery. Two others conditions are not uncommon: talipes varus, in which the foot and ankle are inverted—that is, the toes and sole of the foot are turned inward, or supinated, so the individual walks on the outside

---

APPLICATION EXAMPLE

Weight Training

Setting: Middle school physical education class

Student: 13-year-old student with Osgood-Schlatter's condition

Task: Develop a suitable strength program for a weight-training unit

Application: The physical educator might include the following modifications:

- Use the daily adjustment progressive resistance exercise for all waist-up exercises and the uninvolved leg.

- For the leg with Osgood-Schlatter's condition, work on strength exercises for the ankle and hip.

- Do flexion and extension range of motion exercises for the knee with Osgood-Schlatter's condition.

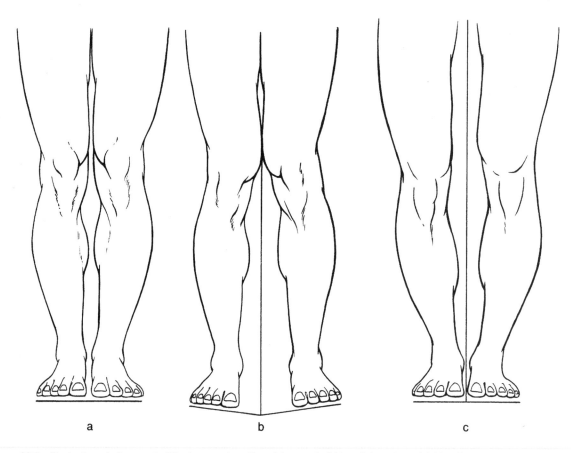

a   b   c

Figure 18.3 Illustration of alignment of the lower extremities: *(a)* normal, *(b)* knock knees, and *(c)* bowlegs.

edge of the feet—and talipes valgus, in which the foot and ankle are everted—that is, the toes and sole of the feet are turned outward, or pronated, so the individual walks on the inside edge of the feet. Mild forms of the conditions are treated with special shoes with orthotics. More severe forms might require braces, surgery, or a combination of the two.

Pronation is a foot deformity in which the individual walks on the medial (inside) edge of the feet. The condition is frequently accompanied by the toes facing laterally (outward). The use of corrective shoes (or surgery in severe cases) can help minimize the deformity and relieve any associated pain. Pes planus, or flatfoot, is usually caused by a congenital condition that results in a lowered, or flattened, longitudinal arch. Pain is a common symptom; obesity exacerbates the condition. Students might need to be referred to a physician for evaluation for surgery, orthotics, or exercises to relieve the pain and, in severe cases, correct the alignment.

Hollowfoot, or pes cavus, the opposite of flatfoot, is characterized by an extremely high longitudinal arch which, because of a finite flexor tendon length, results in a flexion of the toes, that appear clawlike in appearance—thus the nickname, "clawfoot." This condition is usually congenital and associated with an extremely high arch, which reduces the foot's ability to absorb and distribute force. Although surgery might be indicated in severe situations, the use of orthotics is often sufficient to relieve pain and prevent further deformities.

Adolescent Hip Diseases

Legg-Calve-Perthes disease (LCPD) and slipped capital femoral epiphysis (SCFE) are two common hip diseases affecting children and adolescents, mostly males. Legg-Perthes disease, or osteochondrosis of the capital epiphysis of the femur, is characterized by the degeneration of the femoral head. It occurs in children 3 to 12 years of age and runs a definitive course of pain, necrosis, and regeneration, often with some degree of residual deformity (Stopka & Todorovich, 2005). Slipped capital femoral epiphysis involves the subluxation, or slippage, of the head of the femur at the epiphyseal plate (the growth plate). It usually affects children during their periods of rapid growth, 10 to 16 years of age (Stopka & Todorovich, 2005). SCFE is similar to Osgood-Schlatter's condition, discussed above, in that they both involve an epiphysioloysis, or a degeneration of a physis, or growth plate. Rather than a degeneration of an apophysis, or a growth plate of a tubercle, as in Osgood-Schlatter's condition, SCFE involves the degeneration of the growth plate through the entire femoral head.

In both LCPD and SCFE, early diagnosis is essential to minimize the damage. But early diagnosis can be a challenge because both conditions involve pathologies of the center of the hip bone, the femoral head, in which pain is not easily perceived; indeed, this relatively internal pain is actually referred to the knee region, similar to the referred pain experienced when other internal organs are damaged. Thus, in a child or adolescent complaining of nonspecific, generalized knee pain, the hip should always be evaluated (at least radiographically) to rule out LCPD or SCFE, which should be suspected. If these conditions are left untreated until the student can no longer bear weight on the hip, the damage is so severe that, in most cases, only surgery can provide hope for a full recovery. For example, in SCFE, the hip must undergo an innominate osteotomy—that is, an actual reshaping (cutting of the hip and placement of pins for the duration of the healing). The physical educator's job is clear: When a student complains of diffuse, nonspecific knee pain, for no apparent reason, refer him or her to medical authorities. After diagnosis, the treatment will be directed at prevention of further involvement, avoidance of weight bearing through crutches, casting or bracing, and surgery, if indicated. Although these directives must be observed, safe, appropriate physical education activities are essential at this time. Specifically, all activities are indicated in which the child can participate successfully and safely in the brace. Activities that aggravate the hip are contraindicated; the hip must heal by removal of pressure on the femoral head and the acetabulum. Strength, endurance, flexibility, coordination, and balance must be maintained and trained as much as possible. To improve participation, self-confidence, and overall health, acceptance of the full treatment program of bed rest, wheelchair, or brace wear (while providing, safe, motivating activities for the student) is essential (Stopka & Todorovich, 2005).

Weight-Control Problems

Many people associate weight-control problems with the obese person going for the fourth serving at an all-you-can-eat smorgasbord. In reality, there are two types of weight control problems: overweight and underweight, and both pose serious threats to a student's health. Weight control might be the only condition a student must cope with, or it might be an accompanying condition or syndrome of a disability.

Underweight

Only recently have the terms anorexia nervosa and bulimia become familiar to the general public. School staff and faculty, including physical educators, should realize that a coordinated effort among parents, students, physicians, and school personnel is needed to deal with these problems.

Anorexia nervosa is a preoccupation with being thin that is manifested in willful self-starvation and might be accompanied by excessive physical activity. These individuals are 15 percent below what is considered normal for their weight and height, have a distorted body image, and females often develop primary or secondary amenorrhea. There is also what physicians call the "female athlete triad," which consists of eating disorders, amenorrhea, and osteoporosis. Increases in stress fractures are related to the third element in this triad (Rencken, Chestnut, & Drinkwater, 1996). During the early stages, both parents and student might be unaware that the condition is developing. As it progresses, the student becomes emaciated and hungry but denies the existence of the problem. Anorexia nervosa is not to be regarded lightly, for mortality rates range from 5 to 15 percent among diagnosed anorexics. Death is the result of circulatory collapse or cardiac arrhythmias caused by electrolyte imbalance.

Bulimia is a condition associated with anorexia nervosa; it involves obsessive eating with ritualistic purging of ingested food through means of self-induced vomiting or laxatives. This condition is not a problem exclusive to girls and female athletes but is also common in male gymnasts and wrestlers, who engage in these practices to make their weight classes (Arnheim & Prentice, 2000). These practices can lead to electrolyte imbalance, impaired liver and kidney functioning, stomach rupture, tooth decay, and esophagitis.

The goals of treatment to promote weight gain in these conditions are simple in nature but challenging in execution. Hospitalization in a medical or psychiatric unit might be needed to initiate treatment, with a brief stay of two weeks or a longer period of several months to a year. Treatment consists of behavior modification, vitamin and mineral supplements, appropriate diet, and psychotherapy for the student and family. Low self-esteem, guilt, and anxiety are often part of the student's underlying problems.

The physical educator might be one of the first to recognize these problems. Anorexic or bulimic students present a profile of being compliant high-achievers. A preoccupation with thinness, apparent weight loss, and an increasing involvement in aerobic activities might be signs that referral to an appropriate health professional is needed. Whatever the stage of the student's disorder, physical education activities must be monitored to ensure an appropriate level of exertion. A caloric deficit—more calories being used than are taken in—should not be allowed to develop through or in conjunction with physical education activities. Fitness enhancement should be a gradual process, with strength gains achieved before cardiovascular endurance is attempted. Precautions or exercise contraindications for students with cardiovascular conditions, to be discussed in a subsequent section, are applicable in this situation. Dual and individual sports, some with certain modifications, are of suitable intensity and good for promoting social interaction. A priority with the anorexic or bulimic student should be enhancement of self-esteem.

Overweight and Obesity

Obesity is defined as an excessively high amount of body fat or adipose tissue in relation to lean body mass (Winnick & Short, 1999). Body fat distribution can be estimated by skinfold measures, waist-to-hip circumference ratios, or techniques such as ultrasound, computed tomography, or magnetic resonance imaging. The body mass index (BMI) is a mathematical formula that is a common method used for determining whether someone is overweight or obese. BMI is calculated by determining body weight in kilograms and dividing the result by the square of the height in meters (i.e., weight divided by height × 2). Although this method is imperfect because it lacks precision for mesomorphic (heavily muscled) and ectomorphic individuals—producing artificially high or low scores, respectively—because of its convenience and overall validity and reliability, it remains a popular method. According to the

National Center for Chronic Disease Prevention and Health Promotion (NCCDPHP), the term "overweight" is defined by having a BMI ranging from 25 to 29.9; individuals with a BMI of 30 or more are considered "obese."

• *Incidence.* Behind smoking, obesity is the second leading preventable cause of death in the United States. Thus, a major public health concern today is the rapidly growing numbers of overweight and obese students. Furthermore, NCCDPHP reports that the percentage of children defined as overweight has more than doubled since the early 1970s. In a follow-up report, the NCCDPHP states that there are almost three times as many overweight adolescents as there were in 1980. By 1999, an estimated 61 percent of U.S. adults were either overweight or obese (an increase of 74 percent since 1991), and by 2000, nearly 40 million American adults were classified as obese. Demographic variables related to obesity are gender, age, and socioeconomic level. Although women, especially those of Hispanic and African American descent, have higher percentages of obesity, this epidemic is pervasive and clearly affects all ages, ethnicities, disabilities, and gender. Indeed, it is very important that teachers provide physical education experiences for overweight and obese students. When students with disabilities (who might have less mobility than others and are thus at higher risk for becoming obese) grow older, it is critical that they have the desire and skills to engage in an active adult lifestyle that maintains their physical fitness levels and improves their overall health and well-being while combating the ravages of a sedentary lifestyle.

• *Causes.* The causes of overweight and obesity are multifaceted. At least three factors seem to play a significant role: (1) *behavior*—eating too many calories teamed with not getting enough physical activity is a bad combination; (2) *environment*—home, work, school, and community significantly influence opportunities for an active lifestyle; and (3) *genetics*—heredity plays a large role in determining how susceptible people are to overweight and obesity. Genes also influence how the body burns calories for energy or stores fat. The behavioral and environmental factors are the two principal contributors to overweight problems and obesity, yet fortunately, provide the greatest opportunities for prevention and treatment. In addition, emotional factors seem to play a significant role; for example, some people eat as a means of compensation or to reduce feelings of anxiety; others eat excessively when content and happy. An increase in the number (hyperplastic obesity) or size (hypertrophic obesity) of the fat cells that make up adipose tissue might lead to obesity. There are two periods during which there are rapid increases in fat cell production (hyperplasia): the third trimester of pregnancy through the first year of life and during the adolescent growth spurt. Thus, the need for providing adolescents with appropriate education in nutritional choices and physical activity programs is enormous.

• *Characteristics and associated problems and health consequences.* People who are overweight are more likely to develop health problems such as heart disease, stroke, diabetes, cancer, gallbladder disease, sleep apnea, and osteoarthritis. The more overweight the person is, the more likely these health problems will occur. The NCCDPHP provides an exhaustive list of health consequences related to the above health problems for which individuals with BMIs of 25 and above are at increased risk to experience. These unfortunately common physical ailments are numerous and severe (see sidebar below). Without question, the need for high-quality strategies for weight control, including excellent teaching content and methods, motivating activities, opportunities for athletic participation, and the skills to implement a safe, active way of life through adulthood and beyond, is crucial to combat this insidious and fearsome epidemic of obesity (Must & Strauss, 1999; National Institutes of Health, 1998).

Health Consequences of Being Overweight or Obese

• High blood pressure and hypertension
• High bad cholesterol and low good cholesterol levels (high LDLs and low HDLs)
• Type II (non–insulin dependent) diabetes
• Insulin resistance (decrease in insulin sensitivity) and glucose intolerance
• Coronary heart disease and stroke
• Atherosclerosis, peripheral vascular disease, and intermittent claudication
• Congestive heart failure
• Gallstones, gout
• Diabetic retinopathy, angiopathy, nephropathy, and neuropathy
• Osteoarthritis
• Obstructive sleep apnea and respiratory problems
• Some types of cancer (e.g., endometrial, breast, prostate, colon)
• Complications of pregnancy
• Poor female reproductive health (e.g., menstrual irregularities, infertility, irregular ovulation)
• Bladder control problems (e.g., stress incontinence)
• Psychological disorders (e.g., depression, eating disorders, distorted body image, and low self-esteem)

Strategies for Losing and Controlling Weight

The physical educator is one member of a team who might help a student with a weight-control problem. Just as exercise alone cannot remediate a weight problem, the physical educator alone cannot solve this problem. A team effort is needed, with the physician overseeing medical and dietary matters, the parents providing appropriate diet and psychological support, and the physical educator selecting the exercises and activities best for the student who is overweight or obese.

There are basically three ways to lose weight: diet, exercise, and a combination of the two. Diet alone is the most common method used by adults and is often the most abused method and least effective. The criterion frequently used to judge success with this approach is how quickly the maximum number of pounds can be lost. A crash diet might even trigger a starvation reaction, which causes the basal metabolic rate to diminish, thus triggering the body to use less calories throughout the day, both at rest and during physical activity. In this way, the body counteracts certain effects of the crash diet and does not lose the desired weight. A far more effective method is to use a gradual approach, such as a reduction of 500 calories a day, which in a week equals 3,500 calories (the number of calories needed to lose a pound of fat). Under the direction of a physician, an obese student might be on a diet that reduces intake by more than 500 calories per day.

Several keywords—*pyramid, plastic, fast foods,* and *drinks*—come into play when attempting to help students in the diet phase of a weight-control program. Students should be reminded that the bottom part of the food pyramid contains the foods of choice: fruits, vegetables, and whole grains. Students should be advised to avoid eating anything wrapped in plastic, such as candy and potato chips. Lunch should include fruits and vegetables, *not* food from fast-food restaurants. Finally, students should be cautioned about what they drink. Water should be selected over diet sodas, but diet sodas are better choices than sugared sodas (Sallis, 1998). Necessary nutrients are plentiful in reduced-calorie fruit juices and fat-free milk.

Dietary and Physical Activity Considerations for Weight Loss

Although there seems to be a genetic component to some forms of obesity, in all cases, a healthy diet combined with the proper types, durations, frequencies, and intensities of physical activities can result in successful improvements in body weight and body composition for the long term. This works because: (1) participation in physical activity affects body composition and weight favorable by facilitating fat loss while preserving, or increasing, lean body mass; (2) the rate of weight loss is positively related to the frequency and duration of the physical activity session, as well as to the duration (e.g., months, years) of the physical activity program; and (3) the rate of weight loss resulting from increased physical activity is enhanced as compared to engaging in physical activity alone, or dieting alone. Thus, an effective weight-loss program must include both diet and physical activity considerations. Examples of diet and physical activity guidelines are presented in the sidebars below.

Dietary Considerations to Promote Weight Loss

- Restrict calories to 10 kilocalories per pound of body weight (e.g., 1,600 kilocalories for a 160-pound person).
- Reduce the amount of fats (daily intake should not exceed 30 percent of total calories), particularly saturated fats and trans fatty acids (daily intake should not exceed 10 percent of total calories).
- Increase dietary fiber and complex carbohydrates (starches).
- Reduce simple carbohydrates (sugars).
- Use lean meats and trim excess fat.

- Reduce or eliminate cooking oils and fats in the preparation of foods (e.g., substitute canola or olive oil; minimize saturated fats and avoid trans fat as much as possible).
- Avoid fried foods; broil or bake instead.
- Reduce sugar and fat in all recipes.
- Look for fat-free and cholesterol-free alternatives.
- Feature fruits and vegetables at snack time.
- Avoid fast-food restaurants.

Adapted from Short, McCubbin, & Frey, 1999.

Physical Activity Guidelines for Weight Loss

- Expending at least 1,000 kilocalories per week engaged in physical activities is a goal for everyone.
- For youth ages 10 to 17, a frequency of 4 to 7 days a week of physical activity is recommended, with a duration of 30 to 60 minutes of accumulated activity time per day. The intensity should be 55 to 75 percent of maximal heart rate (about 115 to 145 beats per minute, or 5 to 7 METs at a rate of perceived exertion of 12 to 13).

- For students with disabilities, the frequency and total duration are similar, yet each exercise bout might need to be more intermittent (with more breaks), as needed. The intensity might need to be adjusted, or reduced, depending on the amount of actively engaged lean body mass (actively working muscles) and initial fitness level.

Adapted from Short, McCubbin, & Frey, 1999.

Finally, it is important to select the appropriate type, or mode, of exercise. To accomplish this, the FITT (frequency, intensity, time, and type) principle is often employed. Activities that promote the acquisition of more lean body mass, such as high-resistance exercises (e.g., weight training) have a positive effect on the basal metabolic rate, by increasing it, throughout the day, because muscle mass requires more calories for maintenance than adipose tissue does.

Also of critical importance is the acquisition of cardiorespiratory endurance, which burns calories while it is being performed and for several hours after the session has ceased. The types of activities selected should engage large muscle groups and be rhythmic in nature, allowing for continuous participation. Such activities can include swimming, jogging, cycling, rowing, wheeling, dancing, hiking, cross-country skiing, in-line skating, and walking. Additional characteristics of a desirable weight-training program for students who are overweight or obese are shown in the sidebar below.

Physical Education and the Student With an Overweight Problem

A well-designed physical education program for overweight and obese students might contribute to increased caloric expenditure. There are, however, certain limitations or problems the physical educator must recognize and cope with in developing such a program. These barriers include lack of motivation, time, facilities, and equipment; anxiet-ies and previous negative experiences; and poor balance, discomfort, or pain.

The physical education teacher is in an excellent situation to offer new and appropriate activities and advice to deal with these barriers. For example, it might be helpful to provide evidence of successful control by assessing the percentage of weight lost rather than the pounds lost. The teacher can help celebrate the progress being made. Time in each physical education period might be devoted to weight-control activities. Being in a physical education class provides access to both facilities and equipment to enhance a weight-control program. An atmosphere of commitment to students' goals and positive feedback from teacher and peers can counter previous negative experiences. As noted in the next paragraph, there are many activities that a student might engage in that are suited to students with excessive weight. The physical education teacher might work on balance and proprioceptive activities and provide activities such as water aerobics that minimize weight on joints and reduce reliance on balance skills. The physical educator should ease a person into a physical activity program and provide activities that are enjoyable. This is the best antidote for anxiety. Appropriately selected activities that reduce intensity, duration, and weight-bearing situations will minimize or eliminate discomfort and pain associated with exercise.

The physical education program should be developed to provide successful experiences for the student who is overweight or obese. Activities

Characteristics of a Desirable Training Program for Youth Who Are Overweight or Obese

- The activity should emphasize the use of large muscle groups in low-impact, aerobic activities.
- Intensity should be de-emphasized and duration should be stressed.
- The frequency of activities should be daily, or nearly so, thus raising the total daily energy expenditure.
- There should be a gradual increase in frequency, time, and intensity.
- It should be recognized that participation time (daily duration) can be accumulated throughout the day, thus encouraging intermittent activities, especially for younger children and those beginning an exercise program.
- Encourage participation in active household chores.
- Activities should be well liked and pain free.
- Encouraging the participation of others such as partners, small groups, and especially the family is very helpful for program maintenance, motivation, and enjoyment.

Adapted from Short, McCubbin, & Frey, 1999.

that require lifting or excessively moving the body weight will not result in positive experiences. Gymnastic activities, distance running, rope climbing, and field events such as the long jump might need extensive modification for the students who are overweight or obese. Gradual enhancement of endurance capabilities should be part of the student's program. Fast walking, bicycle riding, and certain swimming pool activities might help to develop aerobic endurance. Students can wear pedometers to measure their distances covered throughout the day (Morgan, Pangrazi, & Beighle, 2003). Awards can be given for such progress through the President's Council on Physical Fitness and Sport, or individualized Physical Best (AAHPERD) programs, or informally through the teacher's own programs. Additionally, the reader is encouraged to consult the *Brockport Physical Fitness Test Training Guide,* which provides specific details regarding assessment guidelines for weight loss and much more. Items from The Brockport Physical Fitness Test might be used to evaluate health-related components of fitness. Preferred general standards of body fat for children and adolescents range from 10 to 20 percent for males and from 17 to 25 percent for females (Short, McCubbin, & Frey, 1999).

Furthermore, aquatic activities are well worth the extra effort needed in making them a part of your program. They are usually deemed appropriate for nearly all types of special populations as the constraints of gravity are reduced to allow those with physical limitations to experience more freedom of movement and thus an improvement in flexibility, strength, and endurance, in addition to the acquisition of aquatics skills. Indeed, students with conditions causing them to be underweight, including those lagging behind in coordination and motor skills, often find the water to be a very forgiving and positive learning environment. For example, learning locomotor skills in the water eliminates the fear of falling or "looking uncoordinated" to one's peers and is terrific for skill learning, balance, and fitness. Plus, its amusing quality invites positive social (peer) interactions (indeed, it is hard to skip or gallop in waist deep water without laughing and just having fun). In addition, for students who are obese, activities such as water calisthenics might be quite appropriate, because buoyancy might reduce stress on joints such as the knees, ankles, and feet. As the students gain in fitness, they can gradually work out in shallower water, thus eventually gaining the ability to tolerate the higher gravitational stresses of the land based environment. Also, if swimming skills are an objective, excessive buoyancy might be counterproductive, as Sherrill (2004) points out, because this force might keep parts of the body out of the water, thus impeding the execution of certain swimming strokes. So, the varying amount of buoyancy offered by the water allows it to be a very individualized, yet very effective, medium for all. It can be enjoyed by anyone of virtually any age and disability and result in an extremely therapeutic and positive experience.

Activities for Achieving Cardiorespiratory Endurance and Weight Loss

It is critical that instructors planning weight-loss programs carefully consider the factors that increase the chances that participants will want to engage in the activities and want to continue the program. Students must understand how to incorporate physical activity into their personal lifestyles (Twisk, 2001). If they are going to participate in sports or other activities, they must learn the skills to do so. For example, one cannot expect a student to participate in a lap swimming program without having learned the necessary swimming skills. Often such details are overlooked. For most children and adolescents, participation in games and sports that have a lifetime emphasis are especially desirable to make the activity both enjoyable and inviting to family and friends. Developmentally appropriate activities are also essential. Children cannot be expected to experience success on a basketball or soccer team when they have not yet mastered their basic locomotor and manipulative skills such as running, skipping, sliding, dribbling, kicking, and much more. Well-planned obstacle courses and climbing activities are excellent for younger children for motivating enjoyment and the development of motor skills. Slightly older children might benefit significantly by participating in creative dance and music games, as well as lead-up games of low-organization that encourage teamwork and allow the practice of motor skills. Once these skills are learned, older children can successfully participate in sports (basketball, soccer, etc.), as well as sport-related conditioning and training activities, if so desired. Other types of activities that downplay team competition but encourage the learning of skills on a more individual basis are walking, hiking, swimming, jogging, running, skiing cycling, skating, rowing, and hiking. Group activities such as aerobic dance, aerobic aquatics,

Suggestions to Enhance and Maintain Participation in Physical Activities

- Select activities that are developmentally appropriate.
- Ensure that students have the necessary skills to participate successfully and safely.
- Select well-liked activities and participate, or play, in pleasant surroundings.
- Emphasize that accumulated physical activity is beneficial.
- Give guidance regarding the amount of activity, intensity, and duration.
- Start easy, progress gradually; avoid doing "too much, too fast, too soon."

- Teach skills for lifetime activities and those that invite the involvement of others.
- Provide for individualized guidance, reinforcement, and personal attention.
- Empower the participants by encouraging self-assessment and self-monitoring.
- Provide feedback regarding physiological and other skill and functional improvements.
- Develop knowledge, understanding, and values regarding health-related fitness.
- Develop and implement award systems and other incentives for participation.

Adapted from Short, McCubbin, & Frey, 1999.

spinning, and other similar activities encourage socialization without having to participate with a specific team. To this end, the suggestions in the sidebar above are offered to help promote the participation students in physical activities.

Many of the typical units covered in a physical education class might need considerable modification for students who are obese. A basketball or football unit might focus on developing certain fundamental skills, such as passing, catching, kicking, and shooting. Softball might include the development of fundamental skills and might involve modification of some rules, for example, allowing for courtesy or pinch runners. Dual and individual sports with modifications such as boundary or rule changes (i.e., the ball may bounce twice in handball) are appropriate activities. Golf, archery, and bowling need no modification, whereas tennis and racquetball might be feasible only in doubles play.

All curricular experiences should be oriented toward helping obese students develop a positive attitude toward themselves and toward physical activity. Physical education experiences—whether doing a caloric analysis of energy expenditures, learning to drive a golf ball, or being permitted to wear a different type of sport clothing than the typical gym uniform—should help obese students cope with their condition and should contribute directly or indirectly to the solution of the weight-control problem. Finally, any strategy to improve self-image will help these students deal with their situation.

Likewise, any strategy that changes the other students' attitudes toward those with weight problems will facilitate integration of students who are overweight or obese into the social environment. In the final analysis, the focus of a physical education class must be on suitable physical activity. Short, McCubbin, and Frey (1999) provide helpful physical activity guidelines for weight loss in chapter 2 of *The Brockport Physical Fitness Training Guide*.

SUMMARY

This chapter has addressed conditions that students with and without disabilities might experience. Although activity injuries and long-term disorders might be found among students with and without disabilities, these conditions should not preclude participation in physical education class or physical activity outside of the school setting. Suggestions for appropriate physical activity and physical fitness experiences have been provided for students with activity injuries, long-term disorders, and weight-control problems.

REFERENCES

Arnheim, D., & Prentice, W. (2000). *Principles of athletic training* (10th ed). Boston, MA: McGraw-Hill.

Backburn, G.L., Duzer, J., Flonelers, W.D., et al. (1994). Report of the American Institute of Nutrition steering committee on healthy weight. *Journal of Nutrition,* 124, 2240-2243.

Fitzgerald, G.K. (1997). Open versus closed kinetic chain exercise: Issues in rehabilitation after anterior cruciate ligament reconstructive surgery. *Physical Therapy, 77,* 1747-1754.

Meisterling, R.C., Wall, E.J., & Meisterling, M.R. (1998). Coping with Osgood-Schlatter disease. *The Physician and Sportsmedicine, 26,* 39-40.

Morgan, C.F., Pangrazi, R.P., & Beighle, A. (2003). Using pedometers to promote physical activity in physical education. *JOPERD, 74*(7), 33-38.

Must, A., & Strauss, R.S. (1999). Risks and consequences of childhood and adolescent obesity. *International Journal of Obesity, 23*(Suppl. 2), S2-S11.

National Center for Chronic Disease Prevention and Health Promotion, Centers for Disease Control and Prevention; Atlanta, GA; *Obesity consequences,* www.cdc.gov/nccdphp/dnpa/obesity/consequences.htm, 2003; *Defining obesity,* www.cdc.gov/nccdphp/dnpa/obesity/defining.htm, 2003; *Frequently asked questions,* www.cdc.gov.nccdphd/dnpa/obesity/faq.htm, 2003; *Obesity trends,* www.cdc.gov/nccdphp/dnpa/obesity/trend/obesity_diabetes_states.htm, 2003.

National Institutes of Health. (1998). *Clinical guidelines on the identification, evaluation, and treatment of overweight and obesity in adults.* Bethesda, MD: Department of Health and Human Services, National Institutes of Health, National Heart, Lung and Blood Institute.

Parr, R.B. (1996). Exercising when you're overweight: Getting in shape and shedding pounds. *The Physician and Sportsmedicine, 24,* 81-82.

Rencken, M.L., Chestnut, C.H., & Drinkwater, B.L. (1996). Bone density at multiple skeletal sites in amenorrheic athletes. *Journal of the American Medical Association, 276,* 238-240.

Sallis, R.E. (1998). Four diet tips for teens. *The Physician and Sportsmedicine, 26,* 33.

Sherrill, C. (2004). *Adapted physical activity, recreation, and sport: Crossdisciplinary and lifespan* (6th ed). Boston, MA: McGraw-Hill.

Short, F., McCubbin, J., & Frey, G. (1999). Cardiorespiratory endurance and body composition. In J. Winnick & F. Short (Eds.), *The Brockport physical fitness training guide.* Champaign, IL: Human Kinetics.

Stopka, C. & Follenius C. (1995). *Achieving the ultra stretch.* Boston, MA: Pearson Publishing.

Stopka, C. & Todorovich, J. (2005). *Applied special physical education and exercise therapy* (3rd ed). Boston, MA: Pearson Publishing.

Surburg, P. (1999). Flexibility/range of motion. In J. Winnick & F. Short (Eds.), *The Brockport physical fitness training guide.* Champaign, IL: Human Kinetics.

Twisk, J.W. (2001). Physical activity guidelines for children and adolescents: A critical review. *Sports Medicine, 31*(8), 617-27.

Voss, D., Knott, M., & Iona, B. (1986). *Proprioceptive neuromuscular facilitation.* Philadelphia: Harper & Row.

Wall, E.J. (1998). Osgood-Schlatter disease. *The Physician and Sportsmedicine, 26,* 29-34.

Winnick, J.P., & Short, F.X. (1999). *The Brockport physical fitness test manual.* Champaign, IL: Human Kinetics.

WRITTEN RESOURCES

Surburg, P.R., & Schroder, J.W. (1997). Proprioceptive neuromuscular facilitation techniques in sports medicine: A reassessment. *Journal of Athletic Training, 32,* 34-39.

This article explains the basis of proprioceptive neuromuscular facilitation (PNF), the different types of techniques, and the use of these techniques by athletic trainers. Compares the use of PNF techniques between these dates and a previous study and provides ideas regarding practical applications.

U.S. Department of Health & Human Services. (2000). *Healthy People 2010.* Washington, DC.

Winnick, J., & Short, F. (1999). *The Brockport physical fitness training guide.* Champaign, IL: Human Kinetics.

This training manual provides information regarding the development of health-related physical fitness of children and adolescents with disabilities. An introductory chapter on health-related physical fitness concepts is included as well as three subsequent chapters on cardiorespiratory endurance and body composition, muscular strength and endurance, and flexibility and range of motion.

ELECTRONIC RESOURCES

Centers for Disease Control and Prevention (2003). *Physical Activity and Good Nutrition: Essential Elements to Prevent Chronic Diseases and Obesity,* Department of Health & Human Services, National Center of Chronic Disease Prevention and Health Promotion, Atlanta, GA. (www.cdc.gov.nccdphp/dnpa).

www.cdc.gov/nccdphp/dnpa/obesity/consequences.htm, 2003.

This Web site details the health consequences experienced by individuals who are overweight or obese. References include the latest (1998) NIH clinical guidelines for the identification, evaluation, and treatment of overweight and obesity in adults.

Developmental Considerations

This third part of the book focuses on early childhood development and services for youngsters with disabilities at the youngest ages. Chapters 19 through 22 discuss motor development (chapter 19), perceptual–motor development (chapter 20), adapted physical education services for infants and toddlers (chapter 21), and early childhood physical education (chapter 22).

The information presented in chapters 19 and 20 is intended to review and build on foundational knowledge related to motor development classes taken in a student's professional program. Chapter 21, which deals with the infant and toddler population, opens with a discussion of the role of teachers of physical education in programs for infants and toddlers. Following this, topics include assessment, goals, and objectives for programs, along with recommendations for interacting with infants, toddlers, and their families. Chapter 22 presents information related to program objectives, developmentally appropriate teaching approaches and activities, and assessment emphasizing the early childhood (ages three to five) years.

Motor Development

John C. Ozmun and David L. Gallahue

Do you remember when you were young, about four or five, and wanted to learn to tie your shoelaces? It seems a very easy task now, but back then, the first time you managed to tie your own shoes was a monumental accomplishment. First, there were the fine motor requirements of the task itself (T). Second, there were the individual differences in the rate of learning among you and your preschool playmates (I). Finally, there were environmental factors, such as the fact that your mom or dad might have dressed you in shoes with Velcro fasteners, and you had little need to learn how to tie laces (E). Motor development and the learning of new movement skills involve for all of us, with and without disabilities, a transaction among the requirements of the task at hand as well as a variety of personalized factors within the individual and the environment itself. Keep the letters T, I, E in mind as you read this chapter, focusing on how the task, individual, and environment combine to determine the sequence, rate, and extent of learning any movement skill.

For years the topic of motor development has been of considerable interest to physical educators in general and adapted physical educators in particular. Without knowledge of the process of development, teachers can only guess at appropriate educational techniques and intervention strategies to be used to maximize students' learning potential. Educators who are developmentally based in their instruction incorporate learning experiences geared to the needs of their students. They reject the all-too-frequent textbook ideal of students being at the same level of development at given chronological age markers. In fact, one of the most valuable outcomes of studying human development has been less reliance on the concept of age appropriateness and more attention to the concept of individual appropriateness.

In a very real sense, adapted physical education is developmental education. Program content and instructional strategies, by their nature, are designed to meet individual developmental needs. Unfortunately, human development is frequently studied from a compartmentalized viewpoint. That is, the cognitive, affective, and motor domains are viewed as unrelated entities. Although valid perhaps from the standpoint of basic research, such a perspective is of little value when it comes to understanding the learning process and devising appropriate intervention strategies. It is essential for teachers of students with developmental disabilities to be knowledgeable about the typical process of development so that they have a baseline for comparing the individuals with whom they are working. The totality and integrated nature of the individual must be recognized, respected, and accommodated in the educational process.

In this chapter we focus on defining motor development and describing the categories of human movement. Developmental theory is briefly examined from the viewpoints of two popular theoretical frameworks: dynamic systems theory and the phases of motor development. Applications and variations as they relate to adapted physical educators and individuals with disabilities are discussed throughout the text.

MOTOR DEVELOPMENT DEFINED

Development is a continuous process of change over time, beginning at conception and ceasing only at death. Motor development, therefore, is progressive change in movement behavior through-out the life cycle. Motor development involves continuous adaptation to changes in an individual's movement capabilities in a never-ending effort to achieve and maintain motor control and movement competence. Such a perspective does not view development as domain specific—nor does it view development as stagelike or age dependent. Instead, a lifespan perspective suggests that *some* aspects of a person's development can be conceptualized into domains, as being stagelike and age-related, whereas others cannot. Furthermore, the concept of achieving and maintaining competence encompasses all developmental change, both positive and negative.

Motor development can be studied as both a process and a product. As a process, it is viewed from the standpoint of underlying factors that influence the motor performance and movement capabilities of individuals from infancy through old age. As a product, motor development may be studied from a descriptive or normative standpoint and is typically viewed in broad time frames, phases, and stages.

Dynamic systems theory (Kamm, Thelen, & Jensen, 1990; Thelen & Smith, 1993) is popular among developmentalists as a means of better understanding the *process* of development, whereas the phases of motor development (Gallahue & Ozmun, 2002) serve as a descriptive means for better understanding and conceptualizing the *product* of development. Both concepts will be briefly discussed, but we will first have a look at the categories of human movement.

CATEGORIES OF MOVEMENT

Both the processes and products of motor development are revealed through changes in a person's movement behavior across the lifespan. All of us—infants, children, adolescents, and adults—are involved in learning how to move with control and competence in response to the daily movement challenges we face. Educators can observe developmental differences in motor behavior by observing changes in body mechanics and motor performance scores. In other words, a "window" is provided through which the individual's actual movement behavior can be observed.

Observable movement takes many forms and may be grouped into categories. One technique involves three categories—stability, locomotion, and manipulation—and combinations of the three

(Gallahue & Donnelly, 2003; Gallahue & Ozmun, 2002). **Stability** is the most basic form of movement and is present to a greater or lesser extent in all movement. A stability movement is any movement that places a premium on gaining and maintaining equilibrium in relation to the force of gravity. Gaining control of the muscles of the head, neck, and trunk represent the first stability tasks of the newborn. Sitting with support, sitting unaided, and pulling oneself to a stand are important stability tasks for most developing infants. Standing without support, balancing momentarily on one foot, and being able to bend and stretch, twist and turn, and reach and lift are all important stability tasks of childhood through old age.

Many disabling conditions are associated with deficits in stability and can result in the delay of some of the movement tasks. Central nervous system disorders such as cerebral palsy can delay the onset of independent sitting, standing, and walking in infants. Muscular strength deficits associated with conditions such as Down syndrome can inhibit children from developing key stability skills often mastered during childhood. Because of a variety of orthopedic conditions or sensory impairments, an older adult might lack the necessary state of stability to prevent falls.

The **locomotion** movement category refers to movements that involve a change in location of the body relative to a fixed point on the surface. To walk, run, jump, hop, skip, or leap is to perform a locomotor task. In our use of the term, activities such as a forward or backward roll might be considered to be both locomotive and stability movements—locomotive because the body is moving from point to point, and stability because of the premium placed on maintaining equilibrium in an unusual balancing situation.

The development of the locomotor skills used by wheelchair users might involve moving the chair forward, backward, or in a zigzag pattern. More advanced locomotor skills include moving the chair forward or backward while riding on two wheels in a "wheelie" position. Individuals with lower limb amputations might also need to modify their locomotor patterns to compensate for the use of a prosthesis.

The **manipulation** movement category refers to both gross and fine motor manipulation. The tasks of throwing, catching, kicking, and striking objects are all gross motor manipulative movements. Activities such as sewing, cutting with scissors, and typing are fine motor manipulative movements.

The development of very basic manipulative movements, such as grasping and releasing a fork or raising a spoon to the mouth with control and accuracy, is of significant importance for the individual who is severely disabled. A person with a spinal cord injury that is high enough on the spinal column to be classified as quadriplegia might strive for the development of these manipulative skills in an effort to decrease his or her level of dependence on others.

Many of our movements involve a combination of stability, locomotive, and manipulative movements. In essence, all voluntary movements involve an element of stability; this is why stability is viewed as the most basic category of movement—and why stability is absolutely essential for progressive development in the other two categories. For individuals with disabilities, certain strategies might be necessary to provide the requisite stability to carry out a variety of movement tasks. Using supportive devices such as balance bars, walkers, or peer assistance might be sufficient to compensate for the lack of stability and facilitate the performance of many movement skills.

MOTOR DEVELOPMENT AS A DYNAMIC SYSTEM

Theory should undergird all research and science. The study of motor development is no exception. Motor development theory is based on the observation of individuals without disabilities as they acquire and refine movement skills. This information provides insight into the influence of developmental disabilities on the learning of new movement skills, thereby permitting adoption of appropriate instructional strategies.

To be of practical benefit, developmental theory must be **descriptive** and **explanatory**. It is important to know about the products of development in terms of what people are typically like during particular age periods (description). It is equally important, however, to know what causes these changes (explanation). Many motor developmentalists use explanatory models in an attempt to understand more about the underlying processes that actually govern development. Dynamic systems theory is popular among many (Kamm et al., 1990; Caldwell & Clark, 1990; Thelen, 1989; Thelen & Smith, 1994).

In brief, the term "dynamic" conveys the concept that developmental change is **nonlinear** and **discontinuous,** rather than linear and continuous.

Because development is viewed as nonlinear, it is seen as a discontinuous process. That is, individual change over time is not necessarily smooth and hierarchical, and it does not necessarily involve moving toward ever higher levels of complexity and competence in the motor system. Individuals, particularly those with disabling conditions, are encumbered by impairments that tend to impede their motor development. For example, children with spastic cerebral palsy are frequently delayed in learning to walk independently. When independent walking is achieved, the gait pattern will be individualized and achieved at a point in time appropriate for each child. Although, by definition, development is a continuous process, it is also a discontinuous process. In other words, from a dynamical perspective, development is viewed as a "continuous–discontinuous" process. The dynamics of change occur over time but in a highly individual manner influenced by critical factors within the system.

The term "systems" conveys the concept that the human organism is self-organizing and composed of several subsystems. A human is self-organizing in that it is natural for humans to strive for motor control and movement competence. It is the subsystems—namely, the task, the individual, and the environment—operating separately and in concert that actually determine the rate, sequence, and extent of development. In other words, a person's development does not follow some preprogrammed universal plan that unfolds on an inflexible schedule.

Dynamic systems theory attempts to answer the "why?" questions—that is, the process questions that result in the observable product of motor development. For instance: What are those enabling factors (termed *affordances*) that allow or promote developmental change, and what are those inhibiting factors (termed *rate limiters*) that restrict or impede development? For children with cerebral palsy, rate limiters are neurological and biomechanical in nature, whereas affordances might include assisted support, handholds, encouragement, and guided instruction.

For years, developmentalists have recognized the interactive role of two primary systems—heredity and environment—on the developmental process. Interestingly, many have now taken this view one step further in recognizing that the demands of a movement task itself actually transact with the individual (i.e., hereditary or biological factors) and the environment (i.e., experience or learning factors) in the develop-

ment of stability, locomotor, and manipulative movement abilities. Such a transactional model implies that factors within various subsystems of the task, individual, and environment not only interact with one another but also have the potential for modifying and being modified by the other as a person strives to gain motor control and movement competence. These factors serve as variables on which task analyses and ecological task analysis of skills should be founded. The adapted physical educator should be prepared to manipulate these variables to stimulate optimal teaching and learning (figure 19.1).

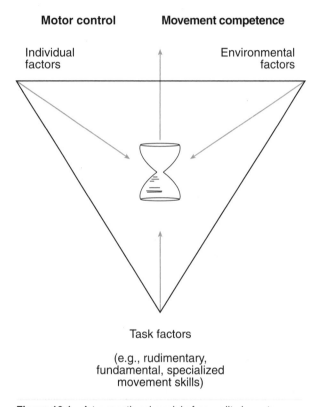

Motor control   **Movement competence**

Individual factors   Environmental factors

Task factors

(e.g., rudimentary, fundamental, specialized movement skills)

Figure 19.1 A transactional model of causality in motor development and movement skill acquisition.

Both the processes and the products of motor development should constantly remind us of the individuality of the learner. Individuals have their own timetables for the development and extent of skill acquisition. Although our "biological clocks" are rather specific when it comes to the sequence of movement skill acquisition, the rate and extent of development is individually determined and dramatically influenced by the specific performance demands of the task itself. Typical age periods of development are just that—*typical*—and nothing more. Age periods represent merely approximate time ranges during which certain behaviors might be observed for the mythical "average" individual. Overreliance on these time periods would negate the concepts of continuity, specificity, and individuality in the developmental process, and these time periods are of little practical value when working with individuals with development disabilities.

THE PHASES OF MOTOR DEVELOPMENT

If movement serves as a "window" for viewing motor development, then one way of studying

development is through examining the typical sequential progression in the acquisition of movement abilities. The phase of motor development (figure 19.2) and the developmental stages within each phase (table 19.1, p. 348) serve as a useful descriptive model for this study (Gallahue & Ozmun, 2002).

Reflexive Movement Phase

Our very first movements are reflexive. **Reflexes** are involuntary, subcortically controlled movements. Through reflex activity, the infant gains information about the immediate environment.

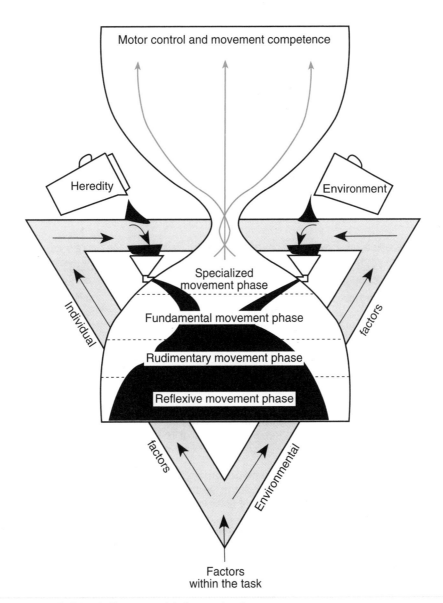

Figure 19.2 The Hourglass: Gallahue's lifespan model of motor development.

Reprinted, by permission, from D. Gallahue and J. Ozmun, 2002, *Understanding motor development: Infants, children, adolescents, adults*, 5th ed. (New York: McGraw-Hill Companies). © McGraw-Hill Companies.

Table 19.1 **The Phases and Stages of Motor Development**

Phase of motor development	Approximate periods of development	The stages of motor development
Reflexive movement phase	In utero to 4 months old 4 months to 1 year old	Information encoding stage Information decoding stage
Rudimentary movement phase	Birth to 1 year old 1 to 2 years old	Reflex inhibition stage Precontrol stage
Fundamental movement phase	2 to 3 years old 4 to 5 years old 6 to 7 years old	Initial stage Elementary stage Mature stage
Specialized movement phase	7 to 10 years old 11 to 13 years old 14 years old and up	Transition stage Application stage Lifelong utilization stage

Reprinted, by permission, from D. Gallahue and J. Ozmun, 2002, *Understanding motor development: Infants, children, adolescents, adults,* 5th ed. (New York: McGraw-Hill Companies). © McGraw-Hill Companies.

The infant's reactions to touch, light, sounds, and changes in pressure trigger involuntary movements. These movements, coupled with the increasing cortical sophistication in the early months of life, play an important role in helping a child learn more about his or her body and the outside world. Involuntary movements are typically referred to as primitive reflexes or postural reflexes.

Primitive reflexes are information gathering, nourishment seeking, and protective responses. Postural reflexes resemble later voluntary movements and are used to support the body against gravity or to permit movement. See tables 19.2 and 19.3 for a summary of common primitive and postural reflexes, respectively. The reflexive movement phase may be divided into the two overlapping stages of information encoding and decoding.

Table 19.2 **Sequence of Emergence of Selected Primitive Reflexes of the Newborn**

Reflex	Onset	Inhibition	Stimulus	Behavior
Moro	Birth	3rd month	**Supine position** Sudden loud noise causes rapid or sudden movement of infant's head.	Stimulation will result in extension of the infant's extremities, followed by a return to a flexed position against the body.
Tonic neck (asymmetrical)	Birth*	6th month	**Supine position** Neck is turned so head is facing left or right.	Extremities on side of body facing head position extend; those on side opposite flex.
Tonic neck (symmetrical)	Birth*	6th month	**Supported sitting** Flexion or extension of infant's neck	Extension or flexion of neck will result in extension of arms and flexion of legs.
Grasping	Birth	4th to 6th month	**Supine position** Stimulation of the palm of the hand or the ball of the foot	Stimulation will result in a grasping action of the fingers or toes.
Babinski	Birth	6th month	**Supine position** Stimulation by stroking the sole of the foot	Stimulation will result in extension of the toes.
Sucking	Birth	3rd month	**Supine or supported sitting** Stimulus applied directly above or below the lips	Touching area of mouth will result in a sucking action of the lips.

* Not seen in all children.

Table 19.3 Sequence of Emergence of Selected Postural Reflexes of the Newborn

Reflex	Onset	Inhibition	Stimulus	Behavior
Labyrinthine righting	2nd month	12th month	**Supported upright position** Tilting of trunk forward, rearward, or to side	Infant will attempt to keep head in an upright position by moving head in opposite direction from tilt.
Supportive reactions	4th month (arms) 9th month (legs)	12th month	**Prone or upright supported** Movement of the child's extremities toward a surface	Extension of the extremities to a position of support
Pull-up	3rd month	4th month	**Upright sitting supported by hands** Tilting of child from side to side and front and back	Infant will flex arms in an attempt to maintain equilibrium.
Stepping	2nd week	5th month	**Supported upright position** Infant is held in upright position and soles of feet are allowed to touch a surface.	Definite stepping action of only the lower extremities
Crawling	Birth	4th month	**Prone unsupported position** Stimulus is applied to sole of one foot.	Crawling action exhibited by both the upper and lower extremities
Swimming	Birth	5th month	**Prone held over water** Infant is held over or in water.	Swimming movements elicited in both the upper and lower extremities

Information Encoding Stage

The information encoding (gathering) stage of the reflexive movement phase is characterized by observable involuntary movement during the fetal period until about the fourth month of infancy. During this stage, lower brain centers are more highly developed than the motor cortex and are essentially in command of fetal and neonatal movement. These brain centers are capable of causing involuntary reactions to a variety of stimuli of varying intensity and duration. During this stage, reflexes serve as the primary means through which the infant is able to gather information, seek nourishment, and seek protection through movement.

Information Decoding Stage

The information decoding (processing) stage begins around the fourth month of postnatal life. There is a gradual inhibition of many reflexes as higher brain centers continue to develop. Lower brain centers gradually relinquish control over skeletal movements and are replaced by voluntary movement mediated by the motor area of the cerebral cortex. The decoding stage replaces sensorimotor activity with perceptual–motor behavior. That is, the infant's development of voluntary motor control involves processing sensory stimuli with stored information, not merely reacting to stimuli.

Developmental Divergence

The evaluation of an infant's reflexes is a much-used method of screening for developmental problems. One means of diagnosing possible central nervous system disorders in the infant is through observation and reflex testing. The complete absence of a reflex is usually less significant than a reflex that remains too long. Other evidence of possible neurological problems might be found in a reflex that is too strong or too weak. In addition, a reflex that elicits a stronger response on one side of the body than on the other might indicate central nervous system dysfunction. An asymmetrical tonic neck reflex, for example, that shows full arm extension on one side of the body and only weak extensor tone when the other side is stimulated might provide evidence of developmental complications. Figure 19.3 (p. 350) summarizes the reflexive behaviors that might indicate neurological dysfunction.

- Nonexistence of reflex response
- Weakness of reflex response
- Asymmetrical reflex response
- Persistence of reflex response

Figure 19.3 Infant reflexive behavior indicating possible neurological developmental delay.

Examination of reflexive behaviors in the neonate serves as a primary means of diagnosing central nervous system integrity in full-term, premature, and at-risk infants. Furthermore, such examination serves as a basis for intervention by the physical and occupational therapists and by the adapted physical education specialist working with individuals displaying pathological reflexive behavior. One such intervention investigated over the past decade is the use of a small treadmill to elicit the stepping reflex in developmentally delayed infants. Dr. Beverly Ulrich and Dr. Dale Ulrich have been able to demonstrate that when supported in an upright position with feet placed on the treadmill an infant will begin stepping reflexively once the treadmill belt begins to move (Ulrich, Ulrich, Angulo Barroso, & Yun, 2001; Ulrich, Ulrich, Collier, & Cole, 1995). The Ulrichs and their associates have demonstrated that treadmill-trained infants with Down syndrome tend to walk independently much sooner than infants with the same condition who did not train. They speculate that the treadmill training plays a role in muscular strength development as well as promoting the practicing of the movement pattern of walking.

Rudimentary Movement Phase

The first forms of voluntary movement are rudimentary. **Rudimentary movements** are maturationally determined behaviors seen in the normally developing infant from birth to about age two. Rudimentary movements are characterized by a highly predictable sequence that is resistant to change under normal conditions. The rate at which these abilities appear, however, vary from child to child and relies on biological, environmental, and task-specific factors. The rudimentary movement abilities of the infant represent the basic forms of voluntary movement required for survival. See table 19.4 for a descriptive profile of selected rudimentary stability, locomotor, and manipulative abilities.

Table 19.4 Developmental Sequence of Selected Rudimentary Movement Abilities

Movement pattern	Selected abilities	Approximate age of onset
Control of head and neck	Turns to one side	Birth
	Turns to both sides	1 week
	Held with support	1st month
	Chin off contact surface	2nd month
	Good prone control	3rd month
	Good supine control	5th month
Control of trunk	Lifts head and chest	2nd month
	Attempts supine-to-prone position	3rd month
	Success in supine-to-prone roll	6th month
	Prone-to-supine roll	8th month
Sitting	Sits with support	3rd month
	Sits with self-support	6th month
	Sits alone	8th month
	Stands with support	6th month
Standing	Supports with handholds	10th month
	Pulls to supported stand	11th month
	Stands alone	12th month
Horizontal movements	Scooting	3rd month
	Crawling	6th month
	Creeping	9th month
	Walking on all fours	11th month
Upright gait	Walks with support	6th month
	Walks with handholds	10th month
	Walks with lead	11th month
	Walks alone (hands high)	12th month
	Walks alone (hands low)	13th month
Reaching	Globular ineffective	1st to 3rd month
	Definite corralling	4th month
	Controlled	6th month
Grasping	Reflexive	Birth
	Voluntary	3rd month
	Two-hand palmar grasp	3rd month
	One-hand palmar grasp	5th month
	Pincer grasp	9th month
	Controlled grasping	14th month
	Eats without assistance	18th month
Releasing	Basic	12th to 14th month
	Controlled	18th month

Reprinted, by permission, from D. Gallahue and J. Ozmun, 2002, *Understanding motor development: Infants, children, adolescents, adults,* 5th ed. (New York: McGraw-Hill Companies). © McGraw-Hill Companies.

The rudimentary movement phase can be subdivided into two stages: reflex inhibition and precontrol. These stages represent progressively higher orders of motor control and movement competence.

Reflex Inhibition Stage

The reflex inhibition stage of the rudimentary movement phase begins at birth. Although reflexes dominate the newborn's movement repertoire, the infant's movements are increasingly influenced by the developing cortex. Development of the cortex and the lessening of certain environmental constraints cause several reflexes to gradually disappear. Primitive and postural reflexes are replaced by voluntary movement behaviors. At the reflex inhibition level, voluntary movement is poorly differentiated and integrated. That is, the neuromotor apparatus of the infant is still at a rudimentary stage of development. Movements, though purposeful, appear uncontrolled and unrefined. If, for example, the infant desires to make contact with an object, there will be global activity of the entire hand, wrist, arm, shoulder, and even trunk. In other words, the process of moving the hand into contact with the object, although voluntary, lacks control.

Precontrol Stage

Around one year of age, most developing children begin to bring greater precision and control to their movements. The process of differentiating between sensory and motor systems and integrating perceptual and motor information into a more meaningful and congruent whole takes place. The rapid development of higher cognitive processes as well as motor processes makes for rapid gains in rudimentary movement abilities during this stage. Children learn to gain and maintain their equilibrium, manipulate objects, and locomote throughout their environment. The maturational process might partially explain the rapidity and extent of development of movement control during this stage, but the growth of motor proficiency is no less amazing.

Developmental Divergence

A number of disabling conditions exist that place an infant or toddler at risk for delayed development of various rudimentary movements. Central nervous system disorders, orthopedic conditions, and mental disabilities can hinder motor development during this initial phase of voluntary movement.

Sensory impairments can also represent hurdles in the developmental process. In particular, infants and toddlers who are visually impaired often experience delays in motor development (Elisa et al., 2002; Prechtl, Cioni, Einspieler, Bos, & Ferrari, 2001). Intervention strategies, however, can help minimize such delays. By incorporating auditory cues where visual cues usually exist, infants who are visually impaired can be stimulated to interact with their environment and smooth the progress of their motor development opportunities.

Fundamental Movement Phase

The fundamental movement abilities of early childhood are an outgrowth of the rudimentary movement phase of infancy. Fundamental movements are generally viewed as basic movement skills, such as walking, running, throwing, and catching, that are building blocks for more highly developed and refined movement skills. This phase of motor development represents a time at which young children are actively involved in exploring and experimenting with the movement capabilities of their bodies. It is a time for discovering how to perform many of the basic stabilizing, locomotor, and manipulative movements, first in isolation and then in combination with one another. Children who are developing fundamental patterns of movement are learning how to respond with motor control and movement competence to a variety of stimuli. Tables 19.5, 19.6, and 19.7 (pp. 352-354) present a descriptive overview of the typical development sequence of several fundamental stability, locomotor, and manipulative movements.

Several researchers and assessment instrument developers have attempted to subdivide fundamental movements into a series of identifiable sequential stages (McClenaghan & Gallahue, 1978; Haubenstricker & Seefeldt, 1986; Roberton & Halverson, 1984; Gallahue & Ozmun, 2002). For the purposes of our model, we will view the entire fundamental movement phase as having three separate but often overlapping stages: the initial, elementary, and mature stages.

Initial Stage

The initial stage of a fundamental movement phase represents the child's first goal-oriented attempts at performing a fundamental skill. Movement itself is characterized by missing or improperly sequenced parts, markedly restricted or exaggerated use of the body, and poor

Table 19.5   **Sequence of Emergence of Selected Fundamental Stability Abilities**

Movement Pattern	Selected Abilities	Approximate age range of onset
Dynamic Balance Dynamic balance involves maintaining one's equilibrium as the center of gravity shifts.	Walks 1-inch straight line	2-4 years
	Walks 1-inch circular line	3-5 years
	Stands on low balance beam	2-3 years
	Walks on 4-inch-wide beam for a short distance	2-4 years
	Walks on same beam, alternating feet	3-5 years
	Walks on 2- or 3-inch beam	2-5 years
	Performs basic forward roll	3-7 years
	Performs mature forward roll*	6-7 years
Static Balance Static balance involves maintaining one's equilibrium while the center of gravity remains stationary.	Pulls to standing position	7-10 months
	Stands without handholds	9-11 months
	Stands alone	10-12 months
	Balances on one foot 3-5 seconds	3-5 years
	Supports body in basic three-point inverted positions	3-5 years
Axial Movements Axial movements are static postures that involve bending, stretching, twisting, turning, and the like.	Axial movement abilities begin to develop early in infancy and are progressively refined to a point where they are included in the emerging manipulative patterns of throwing, catching, kicking, striking, trapping, and other activities.	2 months to 6 years

* The child has the developmental "potential" to be at the mature stage. Actual attainment will depend on task, individual, and environmental factors.

rhythmical flow and coordination. In other words, the spatial and temporal integration of movement is poor during this stage.

Elementary Stage

The **elementary stage** involves greater control and better rhythmical coordination of fundamental movements. The temporal and spatial elements of movement are better coordinated, but patterns of movement are still generally restricted or exaggerated. Children of normal intelligence and physical functioning tend to advance to the elementary stage primarily through the process of maturation. Many individuals, adults as well as children, fail to get beyond the elementary stage in many fundamental patterns of movement.

Mature Stage

The **mature stage** within the fundamental movement phase is characterized by mechanically efficient, coordinated, and controlled performances. The majority of available data on the acquisition of fundamental movement skills suggest that most developing children can and should be at the mature stage in most fundamental skills by age five

or six years. Manipulative skills, however, which require tracking and intercepting moving objects (catching, striking, volleying), develop somewhat later because of the sophisticated visual motor requirements of these tasks.

Developmental Divergence

As children advance through their preschool and elementary years their movement requirements become increasingly more complex. As they grow older, children with disabilities might experience a widening of the gap between themselves and their peers without disabilities. This disparity might be due to a child's physical limitations, limited learning capabilities, or inadequate instruction. Children with physical limitations might benefit from an instructional focus on the outcome of a task (i.e., how far, how fast, how many) rather than the mechanics of a particular skill. A child who has limited learning capabilities might possess the ability to complete a task but might not grasp the concept of a required set of movements. By breaking a task down into meaningful parts, the student might be able to experience a certain degree of success (see the application example on page 355). Inadequate

Table 19.6 **Sequence of Emergence of Selected Fundamental Manipulative Abilities**

Movement Pattern	Selected Abilities	Approximate age range of onset
Reach, grasp, release Reaching, grasping, and releasing involve making successful contact with an object, retaining it in one's grasp, and releasing it at will.	Primitive reaching behaviors	2-4 months
	Corralling of objects	2-4 months
	Palmar grasp	3-5 months
	Pincer grasp	8-10 months
	Controlled grasp	12-14 months
	Controlled releasing	14-18 months
Throwing Throwing involves imparting force to an object in the general direction of intent.	Body faces target, feet remain stationary, ball thrown with forearm extension only	2-3 years
	Same as above but with body rotation added	3.5-5 years
	Steps forward with leg on same side as the throwing arm	4-5 years
	Boys exhibit more mature pattern than girls	5 years and over
	Mature throwing pattern*	4-6 years
Catching Catching involves receiving force from an object with the hands, moving from large to progressively smaller balls.	Chases ball; does not respond to aerial ball	18-24 months
	Responds to aerial ball with delayed arm movements	2-3 years
	Needs to be told how to position arms	2-5 years
	Fear reaction (turns head away)	3-5 years
	Basket catch using the body	3-5 years
	Catches using the hands only with a small ball	5-6 years
	Mature catching pattern*	6-7 years
Kicking Kicking involves imparting force to an object with the foot.	Pushes against ball—does not actually kick it	14-18 months
	Kicks with leg straight and little body movement (kicks at the ball)	18-36 months
	Flexes lower leg on backward lift	3-4 years
	Greater backward and forward swing with definite arm opposition	4-5 years
	Mature pattern (kicks through the ball)*	5-6 years
Striking Striking involves sudden contact with objects in an overarm, sidearm, or underhand pattern.	Faces object and swings in a vertical plane	2-3 years
	Swings in a horizontal plane and stands to the side of the object	4-5 years
	Rotates the trunk and hips and shifts body weight forward	4-6 years
	Mature horizontal pattern with stationary ball	5-7 years

*The child has the developmental "potential" to be at the mature stage. Actual attainment will depend on environmental factors.

Reprinted, by permission, from D. Gallahue and J. Ozmun, 2002, Understanding motor development: Infants, children, adolescents, adults, 5th ed. (New York: McGraw-Hill Companies). © McGraw-Hill Companies.

instruction might require the intervention of parents or other advocates to discuss achievable strategies with school administrators.

Specialized Movement Phase

The specialized phase of motor development is an outgrowth of the fundamental movement phase. Instead of continuing to be closely identified with learning to move for the sake of movement itself, movement now becomes a tool applied to specialized movement activities for daily living, recreation, and sport pursuits. This is a period when fundamental stability, locomotor, and manipula-

tive skills are progressively refined, combined, and elaborated on so that they can be used in increasingly demanding situations. The fundamental movements of hopping and jumping, for example, might now be applied to jumping rope, performing folk dances, and performing the triple jump (hop-step-jump) in track and field.

The onset and extent of skill development within the specialized movement phase depends on a variety of task, individual, and environmental factors. Task complexity; individual physical, mental, and emotional limitations; and environmental factors such as opportunity for practice, encouragement, and instruction are but a few of these

Table 19.7 **Sequence of Emergence of Selected Fundamental Locomotor Abilities**

Movement pattern	Selected abilities	Approximate age range of onset
Walking		
Walking involves placing one foot in front of the other while maintaining contact with the supporting surface.	Rudimentary upright unaided gait	9-15 months
	Walks sideways	13-16 months
	Walks backward	14-17 months
	Walks up stairs with help	18-20 months
	Walks up stairs alone–follow step	20-24 months
	Walks down stairs alone–follow step	22-25 months
Running		
Running involves a brief period of no contact with the supporting surface.	Hurried walk (maintains contact)	14-18 months
	First true run (nonsupport phase)	2-3 years
	Efficient and refined run	4-5 years
	Speed of run increases, mature run*	4-6 years
Jumping		
Jumping takes three forms: (1) jumping for distance; (2) jumping for height; and (3) jumping from a height. It involves a one- or two-foot takeoff with a landing on both feet.	Steps down from low objects	14-18 months
	Jumps down from object with one foot lead	18-24 months
	Jumps off floor with both feet	24-28 months
	Jumps for distance (about 3 feet)	4-5 years
	Jumps for height (about 1 foot)	4-5 years
	Mature jumping pattern*	5-6 years
Hopping		
Hopping involves a one-foot takeoff with a landing on the same foot.	Hops up three times on preferred foot	2-3 years
	Hops from four to six times on the same foot	3-4 years
	Hops from eight to ten times on same foot	4-5 years
	Hops distance of 50 feet in about 11 seconds	4-5 years
	Hops skillfully with rhythmical alteration, mature pattern*	5-6 years
Galloping		
The gallop combines a walk and a leap with the same foot leading throughout.	Basic but inefficient gallop	3-5 years
	Gallop skillfully, mature pattern	5-6 years
Skipping		
Skipping combines a step and a hop in rhythmic alteration.	One-footed skip	3-4 years
	Skillful skipping (about 20%)	5-6 years
	Skillful skipping for most*	5-7 years

*The child has the developmental "potential" to be at the mature stage. Actual attainment will depend on task, individual, and environmental factors.

Reprinted, by permission, from D. Gallahue and J. Ozmun, 2002, Understanding motor development: Infants, children, adolescents, adults, 5th ed. (New York: McGraw-Hill Companies). © McGraw-Hill Companies.

factors. There are three identifiable stages within the specialized movement phase.

Transitional Stage

Somewhere around seven or eight years of age, children commonly enter a transitional stage in their movement skills. They begin to combine and apply fundamental movement skills to the performance of specialized skills in sport and recreational settings. Walking on a rope bridge, jumping rope, and playing kickball are examples of common transitional skills. These skills contain the same elements as fundamental movements, but greater form, accuracy, and control of movement are required. The fundamental movement skills that were developed and refined for their own sake during the previous phase now begin to be applied to play, game, and daily living situations. Transitional skills are simply an application of fundamental movement patterns in somewhat more complex and specific forms.

Application Stage

From about age 10 to age 13, interesting changes take place in skill development. During the previous (transitional) stage, children's limited cognitive abilities, affective abilities, and experiences, coupled with a natural eagerness to be active, caused the normal focus (without adult interference) on movement to be broad and generalized to "all" activity. During the application stage, increased cognitive sophistication and a broadened experience base enable children to make many learning and participation decisions

APPLICATION EXAMPLE

Improvement of Throwing and Catching Skills

Setting: An adapted physical education class

Students: A group of students with intellectual disabilities

Task: The adapted physical education teacher is interested in improving these students' throwing and catching skills. The objective is for them to be able to use these fundamental manipulative skills more effectively in play, game, and sport activities.

Application: Assess the students' present skill levels in overhand throwing and ball catching, and use this information when engaging them in individually appropriate skill-development activities. Use the four-step approach that follows:

- *Preplan* a partner throwing and catching activity to create a situation for observing the students' present levels of developmental skills (initial, elementary, mature).

- *Assess* each student's present skill level from a location in which unobtrusive observation is possible. While they are playing catch, do a total-body configuration analysis by watching each student's entire throwing or catching pattern. After identifying students at less than the mature level, do a segmental analysis by breaking their movement pattern down and observing individual body segments.

- *Plan and implement* a series of individually appropriate movement lessons designed to bring lagging body parts in line with more advanced ones.

- Take time to *evaluate students* and revise lessons. Use ongoing observation and evaluation to determine if they have made progress in throwing and catching. Make modifications in subsequent lessons as appropriate.

based on various factors. Children begin to make conscious decisions for or against participation in certain activities. These decisions are based largely on their perceptions regarding the extent to which factors within the task, themselves, and the environment either enhance or inhibit chances for personal enjoyment and success.

Lifelong Utilization Stage

The lifelong utilization stage typically begins around age 13 and continues through adulthood. This stage represents the pinnacle of the process of motor development and is characterized by the use of one's acquired movement repertoire throughout life. The interests, competencies, and choices made during the previous (application) stage are carried over to this stage, further refined, and applied to a lifetime of daily living, recreational, and sports-related activities.

Developmental Divergence

Continuing to develop motor skills through adolescence and adulthood is an extremely important endeavor for individuals with disabilities. The enhancement of movement skills plays a

significant role in maintaining or increasing the level of independence a person with a disability possesses. Certain locomotor and manipulative skills are needed to access opportunities in the community, be they occupational or recreational in nature. The development of movement skills also increases the options for physical activity, which in turn enhances the potential for health benefits and functional daily living, particularly in the older adult.

SUMMARY

The acquisition of motor control and movement competency is an extensive process beginning with the early reflexive movements of the newborn and continuing throughout life. The process through which an individual progresses from the reflexive movement phase, through the rudimentary and fundamental movement phases, and finally to the specialized movement skill phase is influenced by factors within the task, individual, and environment.

Reflexes and rudimentary movement abilities are largely maturationally based. They appear and disappear in a fairly rigid sequence deviating only in the rate of their appearance. They do, however, form an important base on which fundamental movement abilities are developed.

Fundamental movement abilities are basic movement patterns that begin developing around the same time that a child is able to walk independently and lead to freely moving through the environment. These basic locomotor, manipulative, and stability abilities go through a definite, observable process from immaturity to maturity. A variety of stages within this phase have been identified for a number of fundamental movements; these are the initial, elementary, and mature stages. Attainment of the mature stage is significantly influenced by opportunities for practice, encouragement, and instruction in an environment that fosters learning. These same fundamental skills will be elaborated on and refined to form the specialized movement abilities so highly valued for recreational, competitive, and daily living tasks.

The specialized movement skill phase of development is in essence an elaboration of the fundamental phase. Specialized skills are more precise than fundamental skills. They often involve a combination of fundamental movement abilities and require a greater degree of exactness in performance. Specialized skills have three related stages. From the transition stage onward, children are involved in the application of fundamental movement skills and their purposeful utilization in play, games, sport, and daily living tasks. If the fundamental abilities used in a particular activity are not at the mature stage, the individual will have to resort to the use of less mature patterns of movement.

Principles of development emerge as we study the process of growth and motor development. These principles serve as an avenue for theory formulation. Dynamic systems theory and the phases of motor development serve as helpful means for conceptualizing both the process and the product of motor development.

Individuals with disabilities might experience a delay in their motor development; in some cases, development occurs that diverges somewhat from the usual course of progression. By examining the characteristics of the individual, task demands, and environmental factors, intervention strategies can be devised to increase the opportunity for successful motor performance across the lifespans of all individuals.

REFERENCES

Caldwell, G.E., & Clark, J.E. (1990). The measurement and evaluation of skill within the dynamical systems perspective. In J.E. Clark & J.H. Humphrey (Eds.), *Advances in motor development research.* New York: AMS Press.

Elisa, F., Josee, L., Oreste, F., Claudia, A., Antonella, L., Sabrina, S., & Giovanni, L. (2002). Gross motor development and reach on sound as critical tools for the development of the blind child. *Brain & Development, 24,* 269-275.

Gallahue, D.L., & Donnelly, F.C. (2003). *Developmental physical education for all children.* Champaign, IL: Human Kinetics.

Gallahue, D.L., & Ozmun, J.C. (2002). *Understanding motor development: Infants, children, adolescents, adults.* Boston: McGraw-Hill.

Haubenstricker, J.L., & Seefeldt, V.D. (1986). Acquisition of motor skills during childhood. In V.D. Seefeldt (Ed.), *Physical activity and well-being* (pp. 42-102). Reston, VA: AAHPERD.

Kamm, K., Thelen, E., & Jensen, J.L. (1990). A dynamical systems approach to motor development. *Physical Therapy, 70,* 763-774.

Magill, R. (1993). *Motor learning.* Dubuque, IA: Brown & Benchmark.

McClenaghan, B.A., & Gallahue, D.L. (1978). *Fundamental movement: A developmental and remedial approach.* Philadelphia: Saunders.

Prechtl, H., Cioni, G., Einspieler, C., Bos, A., & Ferrari, F. (2001). Role of vision on early motor development: Lessons from the blind. *Developmental Medicine and Child Neurology, 43,* 198-201.

Roberton, M.A., & Halverson, L.E. (1984). *Developing children— their changing movement: A guide for teachers.* Philadelphia: Lea & Febiger.

Thelen, E. (1989). Dynamical approaches to the development of behavior. In J.A.S. Kelso, A.J. Mandell, & M.E. Schelsinger (Eds.), *Dynamic patterns in complex systems* (pp. 348-362). Singapore: World Scientific.

Thelen, E., & Smith, L.B. (Eds.) (1993). *A dynamic systems approach to development: Applications.* Cambridge, MA: MIT Press.

Thelen, E., & Smith, L.B. (1994). *A dynamic systems approach to the development of cognition and action.* Cambridge, MA: MIT Press.

Ulrich, D.A., Ulrich, B.D., Angulo Barroso, R., & Yun, JK. (2001). Treadmill training of infants with Down syndrome: Evidence-based developmental outcomes. *Pediatrics, 108,* e84.

Ulrich, B.D., Ulrich, D.A., Collier, D.H., and Cole, E.L. (1995). Developmental shifts in the ability of infants with Down syndrome to produce treadmill steps. *Physical Therapy, 75,* 14-23.

RESOURCES

Block, M.E. (2000). A teacher's guide to including children with disabilities into general physical education (2nd ed.). Baltimore: Paul H. Brookes.

This is a very user-friendly, theoretically grounded text containing developmentally appropriate instructional strategies for teaching students with disabilities.

Gallahue, D.L., & Donnelly, F.C. (2003). *Developmental physical education for all children.* Champaign, IL: Human Kinetics.

This text contains an expanded and updated version of the *Fundamental movement pattern assessment instrument* originally developed by McClenaghan & Gallahue in 1978. Assessment guidelines for conducting both total body configuration and segmental analysis are provided for 23 fundamental movement skills. Corresponding videotapes, developed by Arlene Ignico, are also available.

Gallahue, D.L., & Ozmun, J.C. (2002). *Understanding motor development: Infants, children, adolescents, adults.* Boston: McGraw-Hill.

This source contains a wealth of information on 23 fundamental movement skills. Line drawings depict initial, elementary, and mature stages of each.

Ulrich, D.A. (2000). *Test of Gross Motor Development* (2nd ed.). Austin, TX: Pro-Ed.

This is a 12-item test of selected fundamental movement skills with norm-referenced and criterion-referenced interpretations.

Ulrich, D.A., Ulrich, B.D., Angulo Barroso, R., & Yun, JK. (2001). Treadmill training of infants with Down syndrome: Evidence-based developmental outcomes. *Pediatrics,* 108, e84.

This source describes ground-breaking research exploring the use of small treadmills to promote the motor development of infants with disabilities.

Wessel, J.A., & Zittel, L.L. (1995). SMART START: A preschool movement curriculum for children of all abilities. Austin, TX: Pro-Ed.

This source describes a comprehensive program of motor and play skills for all preschool children, including those with special developmental and learning needs.

Perceptual–Motor Development

Joseph P. Winnick and Barry W. Lavay

Margaret is a totally blind four-year-old who would like to move independently in her preschool gymnasium. Her teacher has encouraged Margaret to orient herself to play areas according to sound cues associated with each. In essence, she is encouraging Margaret to develop her auditory perceptual abilities to help compensate for her loss of sight. Do you think that Margaret's teacher should help her develop her auditory perceptual abilities? If yes, which components of auditory perception should be developed? What are some physical education activities that could help?

The ability to learn and function effectively is affected by perceptual–motor development, which permits an individual to receive, transmit, organize, integrate, and attach meaning to sensory information and formulate appropriate responses. These responses are important for the individual to move, and to learn while moving, in a variety of environments. Thus, they have direct or indirect impact in physical education and sport.

Ordinarily, perceptual–motor development occurs without the need for formal intervention. In other instances, perceptual–motor abilities need attention because they have not developed satisfactorily. For example, deficits related to perceptual–motor ability are often named as characteristics of individuals with learning disabilities. These deficits might include poor spatial orientation, poor body awareness, immature body image, clumsiness or awkwardness, coordination deficits, and poor balance. This higher incidence of perceptual–motor deficits among people with cerebral palsy or intellectual disability is well known. Perceptual–motor experiences are particularly important in cases in which sensory systems are generally affected but residual abilities might be enhanced, and in cases where perceptual–motor abilities must be developed to a greater degree to compensate for loss of sensory abilities. People with visual or auditory disabilities exemplify these situations.

In this introductory section it is important to comment on the influences of perceptual–motor programs. In the 1960s and early 1970s, such programs were strongly advocated and supported because of the belief that they led to a significant improvement in academic and intellectual abilities. Research conducted has not supported this notion (Gallahue & Ozmun, 2006; Kavale, & Mattison, 1983). On the other hand, research indicates clearly that perceptual–motor abilities, as measured by various tests, may be attained through carefully sequenced programs (Cheatum & Hammond, 2000; Winnick, 1979). For example, it is clear that balance, a perceptual–motor ability basic to movement skill, might be enhanced through systematic training. Because these perceptual–motor abilities are fundamental to many motor, academic, and functional daily living skills, the nurturing or remediation of these skills is vital and relevant to physical education and adapted physical education.

After reading this chapter it should be clear that all the movement activities experienced in physical education are perceptual–motor experiences.

When perceptual–motor abilities require nurturing or when they have developed inadequately, there might be a need to plan programs to enhance their attainment. This chapter is designed to serve as a resource for planning and program implementation.

OVERVIEW OF THE PERCEPTUAL–MOTOR PROCESS

To implement perceptual–motor programs most effectively, it is helpful to have an understanding of how the process works. A simplified four-step schematic of perceptual–motor functioning is presented in figure 20.1.

Sensory Input

The first step in the perceptual–motor process, sensory input, involves receiving energy forms from the environment and from within the body itself as sensory stimuli and processing this information for integration by the central nervous system. Tactile (touch), kinesthetic (movement), vestibular (balance), visual (sight), and auditory (hearing) sensory systems gain information that is transmitted to the central nervous system through sensory (afferent) mechanisms.

Sensory Integration

The second step in the perceptual–motor process involves sensory integration. Present and past sensory information is integrated, compared, and stored in short- or long-term memory. An important phase occurs as the individual selects and organizes an appropriate motor output based on the integration. The resultant decision becomes part of long-term memory, which is transmitted through the motor (efferent) mechanisms.

Motor–Behavioral Output and Feedback

The third major step in the perceptual–motor process is motor–behavioral output. Overt movements or behavior occur as a result of decisions from the central nervous system. As output occurs, information is also continually fed back as sensory input about the nature of the ongoing response by the human organism. This feedback

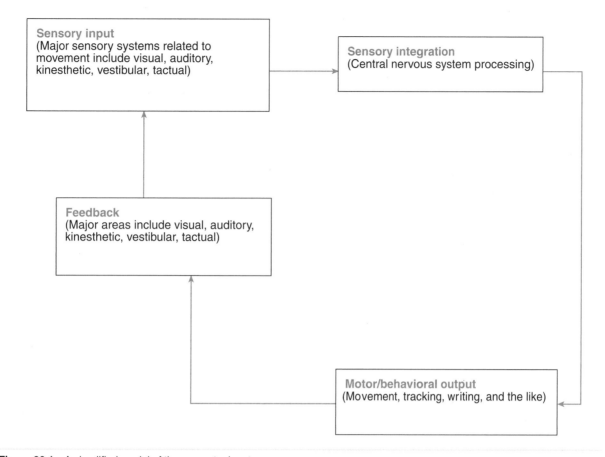

Figure 20.1 A simplified model of the perceptual motor process.

constitutes step 4 and serves as sensory information to continue the process. Similar to sensory input, feedback in movement settings is usually kinesthetic, tactile, visual, or auditory. During feedback, the adequacy or nature of the response is evaluated or judged. If it is judged inadequate, adjustments are made; if it is successful, adjustments are not required.

Terms Associated With the Process

Terms associated with the perceptual–motor process are used in many ways. The following are definitions of some terms used in this chapter.

Perception is the monitoring and interpretation of sensory data resulting from the interaction between sensory and central nervous system processes. Perception occurs in the brain and enables the individual to derive meaning from sensory data. **Perceptual–motor development** is the process of enhancing the ability to integrate sensory stimuli arising from or relating to observable movement experiences. It involves the ability to combine kinesthetic and tactual perceptions with and for the development of other perceptions, the use of movement as a vehicle to explore the environment and develop perceptual–motor abilities, and the ability to "perceive" tactually and kinesthetically. Perception occurs as sensory information is interpreted or given meaning. Because perceptual–motor includes both an individual's interpretation and response to sensory stimulation, it requires cognitive ability. On the other hand, sensorimotor activity occurs at a subcortical level and does not involve meaning, interpretation, or cortical-level functioning. Sensorimotor activity is characterized by motor responses to sensory input. The sensory integration process results in perception and other types of sensory data synthesis. Thus, perception is one aspect of sensory integration.

During the 1980s and continuing today there has developed in the physical education literature a view on perception that appears to have implication for perceptual–motor development. This view, known as the direct or **ecological approach** to perception, is based on the writings of J.J. Gibson

(1977, 1979) and emphasizes that perception is specific to each individual and that the environment is perceived directly in terms of its utility or usefulness for the perceiver. Individuals perceive the environment in terms of the actions they can exert on it—that is, the affordances provided by the environment. For example, children might perceive a chair predominantly in terms of their ability to crawl under it, whereas adults perceive it as an object to sit on (although they might also recognize its other possibilities). Advocates of this orientation feel that perceptual deficits might be defined in terms of inadequate perception of affordance. Thus, perception might become a prime candidate in the search for potential rate-limiters in children with movement problems (Burton, 1990; Davis & Burton, 1991).

An Example of a Perceptual–Motor Skill

Batting a pitched softball can be used to illustrate these basic introductory concepts of the perceptual–motor process described in figure 20.1. As the pitched ball comes toward the plate, the batter focuses on the ball and tracks it. Information about speed, direction, spin, and other flight characteristics is picked up (stimulus reception) by the visual system (sensory input) for further processing. The information is transmitted via sensory neurons to the central nervous system, where it undergoes sensory integration. Because of the various characteristics in the environment, the nature of the sensory information, and past experience, the incoming object is perceived as a softball (perception) to be struck (perceptual-motor). The batter's past experience will influence the ability to fixate and track the softball and process information about how to hit it. How to hit it involves comparative evaluations in which, for example, the arc of the ball is compared with that from previous instances when the act was performed (feedback).

The batter decides on the appropriate swing (decision about motor behavior) on the basis of earlier steps in the process. This decision becomes part of the long-term memory to be used for future reference. During the pitch, the brain is constantly kept informed about the position of the bat and the body (kinesthetic) and will use this information to enhance the overt behavior of swinging the bat. Once the nature of the motor behavior or response has been determined, messages are sent to appropriate parts of the body to initiate the response (motor output). As the batter moves and completes the task, the information is provided on which to judge whether the response is successful or inadequate (feedback). If the pitch was missed, the batter might decide that adjustments are necessary in similar future instances; this information is stored in long-term memory and serves as a basis for learning. Perceptual–motor functioning is concerned with the entire process and batting a pitched ball is thus one type of perceptual–motor skill.

If the ecological perspective on perception is applied to this example described previously, the ball will be perceived by each observer in terms of ability to hit the ball or to hit the ball to a particular place on the field given one's body size and skill rather than a focus on the ball's velocity, spin, and so on. Thus, individuals will perceive the ball in terms of their ability to hit it, and based on this perception, they will decide what to do and respond accordingly.

Perceptual–Motor Deficit

Because figure 20.1 depicts perceptual–motor processing, it is a useful reference for breakdowns in the process: breakdowns at the input, integration, output, and feedback sites. A breakdown at the input site might occur for a variety of reasons. For example, individuals with sensory impairments such as blindness or deafness might not be able to adequately take in visual or auditory information from the environment, and the result is that this information does not appropriately reach the central nervous system. Students with intellectual disabilities, learning disabilities, attentional deficit disorder, or autism might not attend to, and thus might not receive, relevant information. People with neuromuscular impairments might be inhibited by the lack of appropriate kinesthetic, vestibular, or tactual information basic to quality input.

Sensory integration might be affected by factors such as intellectual disability or neurological conditions that impair the functioning of the central nervous system. Also, sensory integration might be influenced by the quality of information received and the ability to process sensory input. For example, a student with a learning disability might have difficulty with motor planning.

Motor output can be affected by inappropriate functioning during previous steps as well as conditions influencing movement, including transmission of information. Conditions associated with cerebral palsy, muscular dystrophy, and other neurological or orthopedic impairments are examples. Breakdowns at the feedback site can result from factors that affect earlier steps and any additional factors that bear on the ability to modify or correct behavior. The child with developmental coordination disorder, for example, might lack body awareness because of faulty kinesthetic perception; this would impair the adequacy of feedback.

Related to the ecological approach, Burton (1987, 1990) has suggested that the influence of perception be examined more closely when movement problems occur. Consistent with this view, it is suggested that perceptual judgments be assessed using actual performance as a criterion to determine if the motor outcomes are due to faulty perception. The game of golf provides a good example of this concept. In golf, the club used for a particular shot is selected on the basis of distance, height desired, and so on. If, after selecting a club, the golfer makes a shot short of the target, it is possible that this inadequate performance resulted from selecting the wrong club (faulty perception of shot requirements) rather than from poor skill. For example, the golfer might have underestimated the distance, wind resistance, and so on. Although the shortness of the shot might have been caused by other reasons, the possibility for faulty perception exists and should be assessed.

Many of the factors causing perceptual–motor deficits are associated with student disabilities seen in the school environment. Because of the influence on perceptual–motor development, physical educators might need to develop programs to nurture development or remediate performance. The nature of an individualized program depends on the cause of the perceptual–motor breakdown, the student's perception and abilities, and the purpose of the program. In the case of a student who is totally blind, for example, it might be necessary to focus on heightening auditory perceptual–motor components to improve orientation to school grounds and focus on kinesthetic perception to enhance efficient movement in the environment. Table 20.1 presents an analysis of prominent perceptual–motor need and deficit areas as a function of specific impairments.

Sensorimotor Stimulation

As stated earlier, perceptual–motor deficits might be a result of sensory input and processing problems. Physical educators who have reviewed and analyzed research and literature on the value of sensory stimulation (Cheatum & Hammond, 2000; Cratty 1986a and 1986b; Seaman, DePauw, Morton, & Omoto, 2003; Sherrill, 2004) agree with the authors of this chapter that sensorimotor stimulation enhances development and learning. There is also agreement in the literature that acceptable levels of sensorimotor development generally occur without the need for special intervention by professionals. However, programs including

Table 20.1 An Analysis of Prominent Perceptual–Motor Need and Deficit Areas

Disability	Prominent need and deficit areas
Visual disability (visual impairments)	Need to focus on the development of residual visual perceptual abilities and to help the child compensate for visual perceptual–motor deficits by enhancing auditory, vestibular, tactual, and kinesthetic perception. Give particular attention to input and feedback steps in the perceptual–motor process.
Auditory (Deaf and hard of hearing)	Need to focus on the development of residual hearing and vestibular abilities (if affected) and help the child compensate by enhancing development associated with sensory systems that are intact. Give particular attention to input, integration, and feedback steps in the perceptual–motor process.
Haptic disabilities (primarily, children who are clumsy; children with orthopedic, neuromuscular, or neurological impairments)	Need to focus on the development of vestibular, kinesthetic, and tactual perception and to integrate motor experiences with visual and auditory perception. There may be a particular need to focus on input, motor response, and feedback steps.
Mental or affective disabilities (children with intellectual disabilities, emotional disturbance, and the like)	Need to focus on needs determined through assessment of perceptual motor abilities. Involvement throughout the perceptual–motor process might exist.

sensorimotor activity are sometimes recommended for individuals with disabilities, especially those exhibiting severe disabilities. This stimulation is designed to overcome sensorimotor developmental delays or deficits caused by such factors as inadequate central nervous system development or functioning, diseases, disabilities, and opportunities for development. Programs designed to nurture sensory systems have been conducted by professionals, including educators as a part of early childhood or physical education, movement therapists as a part of movement education programs, and occupational therapists as a part of sensory integration programs. Goals of programs established by professionals influence purposes and approaches in programs. The authors of this chapter recommend sensorimotor stimulation to promote adequate perceptual motor and motor development.

Programs designed for sensorimotor nurturing emphasizing movement have several identifiable commonalties. First they are closely associated with the major sensory modalities associated with movement (tactile, kinesthetic, vestibular, visual, and auditory). Second, they involve and focus on subcortical activity—that is, activity not dependent on cerebral cortex and cortical tracts. A key distinction between sensorimotor activity and perceptual–motor activity is that the former is subcortical and the latter includes cognition. Third, in program implementation, there is considerable overlap in sensorimotor and perceptual–motor activities. In fact, perceptual–motor functioning depends on sensorimotor functioning because sensory information is processed, integrated, and organized in the cerebral cortex, and this activity is key to perceptual–motor functioning. For example, if a youngster is blindfolded and is holding an orange and it feels squishy, that is sensorimotor. When the youngster gives meaning to what is felt and says it is an orange that is perceptual–motor. So when meaning is given to sensorimotor information, it is perceptual–motor.

Factors that affect sensorimotor function include muscle and postural tone, reflexes and postural reactions, and sensory input systems (Sherrill, 2004). In this regard, this chapter is delimited to an introduction of activities associated with the stimulation of sensory systems. The information presented in table 20.2 serves as a good beginning resource for physical educators called on to provide or coordinate programs designed to nurture sensory input systems. Components as well as sample activities typically associated with such programs are shown in table 20.2. The components include tactile, kinesthetic, vestibular, visual, and auditory integration. Although activities are grouped with a single component, most activities involve and stimulate two or more components as they are conducted. These components correspond closely to the perceptual–motor components to be discussed subsequently in the chapter.

Table 20.2 Typical Components and Activities Associated With Sensorimotor Development

Components	Typical activities
Tactile integration	Water activities; massage; stroking; partner activities; bare-footed activities; movement education activities; activities performed on various surfaces; handling objects of various textures; crawling through tunnels; tactually discriminating between familiar and unfamiliar objects
Kinesthetic integration	Naming body parts; moving body parts for a purpose; active movements that develop a knowledge of body parts, their position in space, and the ability to innervate them (time, space, force, flow of movement)
Vestibular integration	Rocking and cradling in arms, cribs, or chairs; simple bouncing activities on spring-type or trampoline equipment; scooter and vestibular board activities; simple swinging activities using hammocks or other simple swing-type supplies; therapy ball activities; sitting and standing postures; nonlocomotor movements
Visual integration	Activities involving object manipulation, including ball handling in which speed, distance, size, color, and mass are modified; recognition and tracking of objects; looking; sorting; fundamental visual–motor activities; finding objects
Auditory integration	Activities involving sound recognition; auditory discrimination; sound localization; auditory–figure ground fundamental motor activities; listening and responding to auditory stimuli; making sounds and talking; activities involving auditory memory

Facilitating Development

The teacher has an important role in nurturing or remediating perceptual–motor abilities. The exact role and teaching styles to be employed should vary with characteristics of the learner. Because perceptual–motor abilities appear to develop optimally between the ages of 2 and 7, indirect teaching styles such as movement exploration, guided discovery, and open-ended tasks that allow more than one response are generally appropriate. As children reach ages 6 and 7, more direct teaching styles are developmentally appropriate and thus more effective.

Burton (1987) suggested two implications for teaching to enhance perceptual skill that might have important potential for enhancing perceptual–motor development. First, he emphasized that teachers should provide purposeful movement because it is most motivating and encourages attention to the information in the environment. Movements are most purposeful when they are performed in natural settings as a means to an end rather than as the end itself. Key to the provision of purposeful movement is to select an activity involving an objective beyond the actual movement itself. For example, assume that the teacher wishes to improve the accuracy of kicking a playground ball. A purposeful movement would be to kick the ball into a goal in a soccer lead-up activity or game. This is more motivating to the student than a drill of kicking a ball for the sake of kicking a ball.

A second teaching implication is for students to become more accurately attuned to affordances in the environment (Burton, 1987). One way this is done is by encouraging students to make perceptual judgments and to assess the accuracy of their judgments. Applied to a golf example, the question posed might be, "Can I hit the ball to the green using the nine iron?" In another example, a question posed might be, "Can I pass the ball to a teammate without it being intercepted by a defensive player?" In these situations the congruency between perception and action or movement is evaluated. The accuracy of one's perception of the environment or the affordances available is evaluated. The influence of perception on motor performance might be evaluated to determine if poor performance results from faculty perception.

SENSORY SYSTEMS

Many sensory systems are associated with perceptual–motor development. In the remainder of this chapter we will discuss tactual, kinesthetic, visual, and auditory perception. Each sensory system includes a description with subsequent parts of that system and is followed by examples of physical education and sport activities. The reader must understand that during a movement response the different sensory systems work collectively and simultaneously. For example, visual motor coordination combines the use of the visual, kinesthetic, and tactual sensory systems. A multisensory approach that emphasizes the teacher using more than one sensory system is one of the more accepted instructional practices used to teach children with disabilities. Chapter 11, Specific Learning Disabilities, includes further discussion of the merits of the multisensory approach.

Tactile Perception

Tactile perception is the ability to interpret sensations from the various layers of the skin surfaces of the body. Tactile perception is externally related and responds to touch, feel, and manipulation. Through these aspects of the tactile system the individual experiences various sensations that contribute to a better understanding of the environment. For example, tactile perception enables one to distinguish wet from dry, hot from cold, soft from hard, and rough from smooth. For students with a learning disability, instruction is enhanced and made more concrete when they touch, feel, hold, and manipulate objects. The term *soft* becomes more meaningful and tangible when students feel something soft and distinguish it from something hard.

Some individuals might have a disorganized tactile system and consequently exhibit tactile dysfunction. A lack of tactile perception or the inability to localize touch might occur with children with learning problems related to a lack of body awareness (discussed in the proprioception section of this chapter). Other children (i.e., with serious emotional disturbance) might be tactile defensive and very sensitive to normal touch. For example, the feelings of clothes or a touch on the body causes a negative or painful reaction. They perceive touch as irritating and avoid contact with objects and people. They dislike tag games, tumbling, and contact sports such as football, wrestling, and soccer. Other children who have not received necessary amounts of stimulation might be tactile deprived and crave touch, seeking physical contact (Cheatum & Hammond, 2000).

Gross motor activities in physical education and sport offer many opportunities to use tactile perception. Relevant activities include those involving contact of the hands or the total body with a variety of surfaces, such as touching body parts with a wet sponge. Tactile perception combines with kinesthetic sensations as youngsters crawl through a tunnel, walk along a balance beam, jump on a mini-trampoline, climb a ladder, wrestle, or tumble. Individuals might walk barefoot on floors, lawns, beaches, balance beams, or mats or in swimming pools; they might climb ropes, cargo nets, ladders, and playground equipment. Swimming activities are particularly important because of the unique sensations that water provides.

Proprioception

Proprioception consists of those perceptual–motor abilities that respond to stimuli arising within the individual. These include sensory stimuli arising from skin, muscles, tendons, joints, and vestibular sense receptors. Such abilities emphasize movement and are discussed within the categories of kinesthetic perception and balance.

Kinesthetic Perception

It is apparent even to the casual observer that we use information gained through auditory and visual receptors to move within and learn from the environment. Just as we know a sight or sound, we also have the ability to know a movement or body position. We can know an action before executing it, and we can feel the correctness of a movement. The awareness and memory of movement and position is **kinesthetic perception** and is internally related. It develops from impulses that originate from the body's proprioceptors. Because kinesthetic perception is basic to all movement, it is associated with visual–motor and auditory–motor abilities.

Like all perceptions, kinesthetic perceptions depend on sensory input (including kinesthetic acuity) provided to the central nervous system. The central nervous system, in turn, processes this information in accordance with the perceptual–motor process. Certain conditions might cause kinesthetic perception to be impaired. For example, in the case of a person who has had an amputation, all sensory information that normally would be processed by a particular extremity could be missing. Cerebral palsy, muscular dystrophy, and other diseases or conditions affecting the motor system might result in a pattern of input or output different from that of an individual without disabilities. A student with a learning disability

and developmental coordination disorder might have difficulty selecting appropriate information from the many sources in the body. Inadequate kinesthetic perception might manifest itself in clumsiness due to lack of opportunity for participation in movement experiences. Abilities closely associated with kinesthetic perception are body awareness, laterality, and verticality.

Body Awareness

Body awareness is an elusive term that has been used in many ways by authors (among others) representing different but related disciplines. Used here, **body awareness** is a comprehensive term that allows an individual to derive meaning from his or her body and includes body schema, body image, and body concept or knowledge. **Body schema** is the most basic component and is sometimes known as the sensorimotor component because it depends on information supplied through activity of the body itself. It involves awareness of the body's movement capabilities and limitations, including the ability to create appropriate muscular tensions in movement activities, and awareness of the position in space of the body and its parts. At basic levels, body schema helps the individual know where the body ends and external space begins. Thus, an infant uses feedback from body action to become aware of the dimensions and limitations of the physical being and begins to establish separateness of the body from external surroundings. As body schema evolves, higher levels of motor development and control appear and follow a continuous process of change throughout life.

Body image refers to the feelings one has about one's body. Body image is affected by biological, intellectual, psychological, and social experiences. It includes the internal awareness of body parts and how they function. For example, people learn that they have two arms and two legs or two sides of the body and that, at times, these work in combination and at other times function independently.

Body concept, or body knowledge, is the verbalized knowledge one has about one's body. It includes the intellectual operation of naming body parts and the understanding of how the body and its parts move in space. Body concept builds on body schema and body image.

The importance of movement experiences for the stimulation and nurturing of body awareness and the importance of body awareness for movement are obvious. Virtually all gross motor activities involve body awareness at some level. Movement experiences that might serve in the developmental years to enhance body awareness include those in which parts of the body are identified, named, pointed to, and innervated (i.e., playing "Simon Says"). Imitation of movements, balance activities, rhythmic or dance activities, scooterboard activities, mimetic activities, movement and exploration, swimming games, activities conducted in front of a mirror, stunts and tumbling, and other exercises are all examples of helpful movement experiences.

Laterality and Verticality

Laterality and verticality refer to internal awareness of the body's right and left and up and down, respectively. Laterality is the internal awareness of both sides of the body and their relations as well as differences. With good laterality the child can catch a ball on the right side with the right hand, the left side with the left hand, or toward the center of the body with both hands. He or she can use the two limbs of the body to perform opposite tasks, such as using one hand to hold a paper and the other hand to write (Cheatum & Hammond, 2000).

Verticality refers to an internal awareness of up and down. Development of verticality is also believed to be enhanced through experimentation in upper and lower parts of the body. Laterality and verticality should be conceived as very much related to body awareness. Laterality and verticality are significantly included in many physical education activities, and nurturing these abilities enhances their successful development and performance. Examples include most balance, locomotor, and object-control activities.

Balance

As mentioned previously, proprioception includes sensation pertaining to vestibular sense reception. The vestibular system provides the individual with information about the body's relation to gravitational pull and thus serves as the basis for balance or equilibrium. Vestibular sense perception combines with multiple sources such as visual, auditory, kinesthetic, and tactual information to enhance in the attainment of distinctly different static (stationary) and dynamic (moving) forms of balance.

Balance is a key element in the performance of movement activities. Many activities might be used to nurture or remediate balance during the perceptual–motor developmental years. These include activities conducted on tiltboards, balance boards, and balance beams. Examples of everyday functional activities that require balance are stepping off a sidewalk curb to get on a bus or walking up a set of bleachers to attend a game. Mimetic activities, stunts and tumbling, and a variety of games might also be used to develop balance.

Visual Perceptual–Motor Development

Visual perceptual–motor abilities are important in academic, physical education, and sport settings. In the academic setting, visual perceptual abilities are used in writing, drawing, reading, spelling, and arithmetic. In physical education and sport they are important for performing such fundamental movements as running, catching, throwing, and kicking objects, playing tag, and balancing. Age-appropriate visual perceptual–motor abilities are built on visual acuity, which affects the ability to see, fixate, and track, and thus is required for the input step of the perceptual motor process. On the basis of input, the individual develops the abilities or components of visual perceptual–motor development associated with central nervous system processing and output. Components closely associated with this process that affects movement include visual figure-ground perception, spatial relations, visual constancy, and visual–motor coordination.

Figure-Ground Perception

Figure-ground perception involves the ability to distinguish the main figure or target from its background and give meaning to the forms or the combination of forms or elements that constitute the figure. It requires the ability to differentiate and integrate parts of objects to form meaningful wholes and to appropriately shift attention and ignore irrelevant stimuli. Visual figure-ground perception is called on when students are asked to pick out a specific letter of the alphabet from a field of extraneous items. Students with inadequate perception might exhibit difficulties in differentiating letters, numbers, and other geometric forms, combining parts of words to form an entire word, or sorting objects. For example, in the classroom, the child with visual figure ground difficulty might place her paper closer to her face to block out background information. In physical education, figure-ground perception is required in games that depend on tracking moving objects, observing lines and boundaries, and involving concentration on relevant stimuli. These include activities in which children move under, over, through, and around perception boxes, tires, hoops, or playground equipment, as well as activities in which they follow or avoid the lines and shapes associated with obstacle courses, geometric figures, maps, mazes, hopscotch diagrams, or footprints. In sport, figure-ground perception is clearly demonstrated in baseball—a batter must distinguish a white ball from a background in attempting to hit it. See the application example.

Spatial Relationships

The perception of spatial relationships means locating objects in space relative to oneself, or self-space (egocentric localization), and locating objects relative to one another or general space (objective localization). Egocentric localization, often referred to as perception of position in space, is demonstrated as youngsters attempt to move through hoops without touching them. Objective localization is seen as a player attempts to complete a pass to a guarded teammate.

Spatial relationship, which affects virtually all aspects of academic learning, involves knowing direction, distance, and depth. Position in space is basic to the solution of reversal or directional problems (such as the ability to distinguish *d, p,* and *q,* 36 and 63, *saw* and *was, no* and *on*). Perception of spatial relationship also encompasses temporal ordering and sequencing. Individuals demonstrating difficulty placing objects in order will have difficulty in various academic areas, including arithmetic sequencing problems (per-

forming operations in correct order). In physical education students with spatial relationship difficulties might need to be oriented to their position on the court. Some authors have contended that spatial awareness is preceded by body awareness and that the awareness of relationships in space grows out of an awareness of relationships among the parts of one's own body.

Visual Perceptual Constancy

Perceptual constancy is the ability to recognize objects despite variations in their presentation. It entails recognizing the sameness of an object although the object might in actuality vary in appearance, size, color, texture, brightness, shape, and so on. For example, a football is recognized as having the same size even when seen at a distance. It has the same color in daylight as in twilight and maintains its shape even when only its tip is visible during a spiral pass. Development of perceptual constancy involves seeing, feeling, manipulating, smelling, tasting, hearing, naming, classifying, and analyzing objects. Inadequate perceptual constancy affects the recognition of letters, numbers, shapes, and other symbols in different contexts. Physical education and sport provide a unique opportunity for the nurturing of perceptual constancy because objects are used and manipulated in many ways and are viewed from many perspectives.

Visual–Motor Coordination

Visual–motor coordination is the ability to coordinate vision with body movements. It is the aspect of visual perceptual–motor ability that

---

APPLICATION EXAMPLE

Perceptual Motor Development: Perceptual–Motor

Setting: A classroom teacher asks the physical education teacher to suggest motor activities to help develop visual figure-ground activities for a six-year-old student named Jimmy.

Student: This six-year-old boy has a learning disability involving serious difficulty with visual figure-ground differentiation and integration.

Issue: What are some possible strategies for handling this situation?

Application: The physical educator suggests the following activities:

- Have Jimmy use a scooter to follow roads in his community drawn on the gym floor.
- Involve Jimmy in partner activities in which soft, large balls and balloons are rolled, tossed, and stopped.
- Have Jimmy walk, hop, or jump on and off shapes, various spots, hula-hoops, or lines drawn on a mat or on the floor.

combines visual with tactual and kinesthetic perception; thus, it is not an exclusively visual ability. Although coordination of vision and movement might involve many different parts of the body, eye–hand and eye–foot coordination are usually most important in physical education and sport activities. Effective eye–limb coordination is also important in such pursuits as cutting, pasting, finger painting, drawing, tracing, coloring, scribbling, using the chalkboard, and manipulating clay and toys. Eye–limb coordination is particularly important in writing. It is also necessary for such functional activities of daily living (ADL) as putting on and tying shoes, putting on and buttoning clothes, eating or drinking without tipping glasses and plates, and using simple tools.

Development of Visual Perceptual–Motor Abilities

Many experiences in physical education and sport call on and might be used to stimulate visual perceptual–motor abilities. Although motor activities are not generally limited to the development of one ability, some activities are especially well suited for figure-ground development. These include rolling, throwing, catching, kicking, striking, dodging, chasing different objects in different ways; moving under, over, through, and around perception boxes, tires, hoops, geometric shapes, ropes, playground equipment, pieces of apparatus; following or avoiding lines associated with obstacle courses, geometric shapes, maps, mazes, hopscotch games, or grids; stepping on or avoiding footprints, stones, animals, or shapes painted on outdoor hardtops or floors; imitating movements as in Leapfrog, Follow the Leader, or Simon Says; and doing simple rope activities, such as moving under and over ropes and jumping rope (figure 20.2).

Spatial relationships are involved in tumbling, swimming, rope jumping, rhythms and dance, and obstacle courses. Activities particularly useful in helping an individual develop spatial abilities include moving through tunnels, tires, hoops, mazes, and perception boxes. Activities in which one must locate objects in space relative to oneself (egocentric localization) or relative to one another (objective localization) also promote perception of spatial relations.

Visual–motor coordination is clearly important in physical education and sport. Exhibiting difficulty moving around other players and objects, not tracking an object, and a student turning their head or blinking when attempting to catch a ball are all examples of potential visual problems. Games that include throwing, catching, kicking, and striking balls and other objects are among those activities requiring such coordination. Age-appropriate games are highly recommended because they enhance the purposefulness of movement and motivate the learner.

Auditory Perceptual–Motor Development

Age-appropriate auditory perceptual–motor abilities are built on auditory acuity and perception. The ability to receive and transmit auditory stimuli as sensory input is the foundation of the development of auditory figure-ground perception, sound

© Robert Freligh

Figure 20.2 Leaping over a rope is a fun activity to stimulate visual perceptual–motor abilities.

localization, discrimination, temporal auditory perception, and auditory-motor coordination.

Auditory Figure-Ground Perception

Auditory figure-ground perception is the ability to distinguish and attend to relevant auditory stimuli against a background of general auditory stimuli. It includes ignoring unimportant auditory sensations or irrelevant stimuli (such as those in a noisy gym in which different activities are conducted simultaneously) and attending to relevant stimuli—such as teacher directions. In situations in which irrelevant stimuli are present, people with inadequate figure-ground perception might have difficulty concentrating on the task at hand, responding to directions, and comprehending information received during the many listening activities of daily life. They might not attend to a honking horn, a shout, or a signaling whistle. Their problems in physical education and sport might be associated with transitions when beginning, changing, or ending activities are signaled through sound. Methods to ensure smooth transitions are touched on later in this chapter.

Auditory Discrimination

Auditory discrimination is the capacity to distinguish among different frequencies, qualities, and amplitudes of sound. It involves the ability to recognize and discriminate among variations of auditory stimuli presented in a temporal series, as well as auditory perceptual constancy. The latter is the ability to recognize an auditory stimulus as the same under varying presentations. Auditory discrimination thus involves the ability to distinguish pitch, loudness, and constancy of auditory stimuli. People with inadequate auditory discrimination might exhibit problems in games, dances, and other rhythmic activities that depend on this ability. Another potential auditory discrimination problem is the player who cannot distinguish the official's whistle from the noise of the crowd.

Sound Localization

Sound localization—the ability to determine the source or direction of sounds in the environment—is used, for example, during a basketball game to find an open player calling for the ball. Sound localization is basic to goal ball, in which blindfolded players attempt to stop a ball emitting a sound (see figure 20.3).

Temporal Auditory Perception

Temporal auditory perception involves the ability to recognize and discriminate among variations of auditory stimuli presented in time.

Figure 20.3 Sound localization is basic to goal ball, in which blindfolded players attempt to stop a ball emitting a sound.

It entails distinguishing rate, emphasis, tempo, and order of auditory stimuli. Individuals with inadequate temporal auditory perception might exhibit difficulties in rhythmic movement and dance, singing games, and other physical education activities.

Auditory–Motor Coordination

Auditory–motor coordination is the ability to coordinate auditory stimuli with body movements. This coordination is readily apparent when an individual responds to a beat in music (ear–foot coordination) or to a particular cadence when football signals are called out. Auditory–motor coordination is evident as a dancer, skater, or gymnast performs a routine to musical accompaniment.

Development of Auditory Perceptual– Motor Abilities

Physical education and sport offer many opportunities to develop auditory perception. Participants might follow verbal directions or perform activities in response to CDs, tapes, or records; the activities might be suggested by the music itself. For example, children might walk, run, skip, or gallop to a musical beat; they might imitate trains, airplanes, cars, or animals, as suggested by music. Dances and rhythmic activities with variations in the rate and beat are useful, as are games and activities in which movements are begun, changed, or stopped in response to various sounds. Triangles, drums, bells, sticks, or whistles might direct children in movement or serve as play equipment. A teacher conducting such activities should minimize distracting stimuli and vary the tempo and loudness of sound. It might be necessary to speak softly at certain times so that the participants must concentrate on listening.

SUMMARY

Perceptual–motor development is a process of enhancing the ability to integrate sensory stimuli arising from or relating to observable movement experiences. It is associated with all the sensory systems. This chapter discussed sensorimotor stimulation and perceptual–motor development, focusing on how movement activities are involved in and can be used for sensorimotor stimulation and perceptual–motor development, and how they thereby contribute to an individual's development and consequent movement experiences.

REFERENCES

Burton, A.W. (1987). Confronting the interaction between perception and movement in adapted physical education. *Adapted Physical Activity Quarterly,* 4, 257-267.

Burton, A.W. (1990). Assessing the perceptual–motor interaction in developmentally disabled and handicapped children. *Adapted Physical Activity Quarterly,* 7, 325-337.

Cheatum, B.A, & Hammond, A.A. (2000). *Physical activity for improving children's learning and behavior.* Champaign IL: Human Kinetics.

Cratty, B.J. (1986a). *Perceptual motor development in infants and children.* Englewood Cliffs, NJ: Prentice Hall.

Cratty, B.J. (1986b). *Adapted physical education in the mainstream.* Denver, CO.: Love Publishing Company.

Davis, W. E., & Burton, A.W. (1991). Ecological task analysis: Translating movement behavior theory into practice. *Adapted Physical Activity Quarterly,* 8, 154-177.

Gallahue, D.L., & Ozmun, J. C. (2006). *Understanding motor development: Infants, children, adolescents and adults* (6th ed.). Boston: McGraw Hill.

Gibson, J.J. (1977). The theory of affordance. In R. Shaw & J. Bransford (Eds.), *Perceiving, acting, and knowing: Toward an ecological psychology.* Hillsdale, NJ: Earlbaum.

Gibson, J.J. (1979). *The ecological approach to visual perception.* Boston: Houghton Mifflin.

Kavale, K.A., & Mattison, P.D. (1983). One jumped off the balance beam: A meta-analysis of perceptual motor training programs. *Journal of Learning Disabilities,* 16, 165-173.

Keogh, J., & Sudgen, D. (1985). *Movement skill development.* New York: Macmillan.

Seaman, J.A., DePauw, K.P., Morton, K.B., & Omoto, K (2003). *Making connections: From theory to practice in adapted physical education.* Scottsdale AZ: Holcomb Hathaway Publishers.

Sherrill, C. (2004). *Adapted physical activity, recreation, and sport: Crossdisciplinary and lifespan* (6th ed.). Boston: McGraw-Hill.

Winnick, J.P. (1979). Early movement experiences and development: *Habilitation and remediation.* Philadelphia: Saunders.

WRITTEN RESOURCES

Capon, J. (1994). Byron, C.A: *Front row experience.*

This is a perceptual motor series of five books covering basic movement activities; ball, rope, hoop activities; balance activities; beanbag, rhythm, stick activities; and tire and parachute activities.

Cheatum, B.A, & Hammond, A. A. (2000). *Physical activity for improving children's learning and behavior.* Champaign IL: Human Kinetics.

Provides a comprehensive easy-to-read approach to neurological development and the sensory systems. Part two of the text devotes a chapter to each of the different sensory systems.

Cowden, J.E., Sayers, L.K., & Torrey, C.C. (1998). *Pediatric adapted motor development and exercise.* Springfield, IL: Clarke C. Thomas.

Provides exercises for increasing muscle tone and strength, decreasing muscle tone and reflex integration, and sensory motor development (postural reactions and vestibular stimulation, visual–motor control, auditory discrimination, tactile stimulation, and kinesthetic and spatial awareness). Emphasis is on organizing and conducting infant and toddler movement intervention programs.

Cratty, B.J. (1986a). *Perceptual motor development in infants and children.* Englewood Cliffs, NJ: Prentice Hall.

This comprehensive book provides a theoretical overview of perceptual–motor development and practical suggestions for programs.

Cratty, B.J. (1986b). *Adapted physical education in the mainstream.* Denver, CO: Love Publishing Company.

Chapter 5 reviews and summarizes theories and models (perceptual–motor theories, recapitulation theories, cognitive approaches) related to movement abilities. Chapter 25 provides information and guidelines for in–out stimulation, including sensory stimulation.

Huettig, C., Pyfer, J., & Auxter, D. (2005). *Gross motor activities for young children with special needs.* (10th ed.), Boston: McGraw Hill.

A supplement handbook to the textbook, *Principles and Methods of Adapted Physical Education,* this source offers over 200 activities and suggested songs for professionals serving young children. Activities are designed to promote central nervous system development (equilibrium, sensory stimulation and discrimination, body image, basic locomotor skills, motor planning, object control skills, cross lateral integration, aerobic fitness, animal actions, and cooperative play and games).

Johnson-Martin, N.M., Attermeier, S.M., & Hacker, B.J. (2004). *The Carolina curriculum for infants and toddlers with special needs* (3rd ed.). Baltimore, MD: Paul H. Brookes Publishing Company.

This text includes a chapter on sensorimotor development and curriculum sequences related to visual pursuit and object permanence; auditory localization and object permanence; understanding space; visual perception; and gross motor skills including posture and locomotion, stair activity, jumping, and balance.

Johnson-Martin, N.M., Attermeir, S.M. & Hacker, B. (2004). *The Carolina curriculum for preschoolers with special needs* (2nd ed.). Baltimore, MD: Paul H. Brookes Publishing Co.

This source presents curriculum sequences encompassing object manipulation, locomotion (walking, galloping, skipping, running, and hopping), stair activities, jumping, balancing, and ball throwing and catching.

Kranowitz, C.S. (2003). The out-of-sync child has fun: Activities for kids with sensory integration dysfunction. New York: Perigee.

This book features more than 100 enjoyable activities that reinforce the different sensory systems for young children.

AUDIOVISUAL RESOURCES

Cassettes, records, CDs, and books related to sensorimotor stimulation, perceptual–motor development, and interdisciplinary teaching may be purchased from Kimbo Educational, P.O. Box 477, Long Branch, NJ 07740-0477. Phone: 800-631-2187; fax: 732-870-3340.

Another excellent source for these materials is Educational Activities, Inc., 1937 Grand Ave, Baldwin, NY 11510. Phone: 800-645-3739; fax: 516-623-9282.

ELECTRONIC RESOURCES

The Center for the Ecological Study of Perception and Action: http://ione.psy.uconn.edu/~cespaweb/info.html.

This site features a discussion on the ecological approach to perception and action in the tradition of the late James J. Gibson.

P.E. Central: www.pecentral.org.

A Web site designed for health and physical education teachers, parents, and students whose goal is to provide the latest information about developmentally appropriate physical education programs for children and youth. The site includes lesson plan ideas to promote perceptual–motor development.

CHAPTER 21

Infants and Toddlers

Cathy Houston-Wilson

Maria, an early childhood adapted physical education teacher at the United Cerebral Palsy Center for Young Children, sets up her motor room with incline mats, soft balls, scarves, and tunnels to accommodate infants and toddlers with special needs and their caregivers. She has specific objectives for each child: weight bearing for Adam, balancing and ambulating for Molly, and visual tracking for Juan. The children and their caregivers enter the motor room and immediately begin acting on the equipment that has been set out for them. Maria greets the children individually as they enter and talks with their caregivers about the progress the children are making and what objectives have been developed for the day with the equipment that has been set up. Maria and the caregivers follow the young children's lead as they begin to play with the equipment.

The purpose of this chapter is to present an overview of adapted physical education as it relates to infants and toddlers with unique needs. The following topics will be covered: the role of teachers in early childhood adapted physical education; goals and objectives of early childhood motor programs for young children with and without unique needs; and the importance of families in the development of the young child.

LEGISLATION

Infants and toddlers, caregivers, and adapted physical education? Do these groups belong together, you might ask. The answer is yes. As a result of federal legislation, particularly PL 99-457, the Education of the Handicapped Amendments of 1986, now reauthorized as PL 105-17, the Individuals with Disabilities Education Act (IDEA) Amendments of 2002, infants and toddlers with developmental delays or at risk for developmental delays are provided early intervention services to enhance their development and minimize their potential for delays. According to federal legislation (PL 105-17), infants and toddlers with disabilities are defined as individuals under three years of age who are experiencing developmental delays in one or more of the following functional areas: cognitive development (learning and thinking); physical development (growth, gross and fine motor abilities); communication development (understanding and using words); social or emotional development (relating to others); adaptive development (self-help skills, such as feeding); or who have a diagnosed physical or mental condition that has a high probability of resulting in developmental delay. Infants and toddlers with disabilities might also include, at a state's discretion, at-risk infants and toddlers.

To determine if infants and toddlers experience developmental delays or are "at risk" for developmental delays, states develop criteria to be met. Based on these criteria, decisions are made about who is eligible to receive early intervention services. Definitions of developmental delays vary depending on criteria set by individual states. For example, in New York, a developmental delay would be established if the child demonstrates any of the following:

- A 12-month delay in one functional area
- A 33 percent delay in one functional area or a 25 percent delay in each of two areas

- A score of at least two standard deviations below the mean in one functional area
- A score of at least 1.5 standard deviations below the mean in each of two functional areas *(NYS Department of Health—The Early Intervention Program: A Parent's Guide,* 1999)

Early childhood experts agree that determining eligibility for early intervention services for children who are so young is a complex process. A variety of methods for determining eligibility are thus recommended, including direct observation, play-based assessment, standardized tests or developmental inventories, clinical opinion, and, most important, reports by parents or caregivers. In addition to assessing the child, a family may choose to be involved in what is known as a family assessment. With this process, the family identifies their concerns, priorities, and resources in relation to maximizing the potential for their child's development and shares these wishes with the early intervention team. *(NYS Department of Health—The Early Intervention Program: A Parent's Guide,* 1999).

To determine if the child is experiencing a developmental delay in one or more of the functional areas listed previously, a comprehensive multidisciplinary assessment must be conducted on the child. Tests used to determine unique needs must be valid and administered by trained professionals from the multidisciplinary team. Members of the multidisciplinary team include the parents, a service coordinator, advocates, professionals from at least two disciplines (e.g., a speech and language specialist, an occupational therapist, or a teacher of adapted physical education), and any other individual with an interest in the child. The team members engage in various forms of data collection to determine the strengths and needs of the child. Once a developmental delay has been established, an Individualized Family Service Plan (IFSP) is developed by the team members. The IFSP is a written document that contains the following information:

- The child's present level of performance in the five functional areas of development
- A statement of the family's resources, priorities, and concerns relating to enhancing the development of the child
- A statement of major outcomes to be achieved and the criteria, procedures, and timelines used to determine the degree to

which progress is being made and whether modifications or revisions are necessary

- A statement of early intervention services necessary to meet the unique needs of the child and his family, including frequency, intensity, and method of delivery
- A statement of the natural environments in which early intervention services shall be provided, including a justification of the extent, if any, to which the services will not be provided in a natural environment (the child's home or daycare)
- The projected dates for initiation of services and the anticipated duration of the services
- The identification of the service coordinator from the profession most immediately relevant to the child's or family's needs who will be responsible for the implementation of the plan and coordination with other agencies and persons
- The steps to be taken to support the transition of the toddler with a disability to preschool or other appropriate services (Office of Special Education and Rehabilitative Services, 2002)

THE ROLE OF TEACHERS OF EARLY CHILDHOOD ADAPTED PHYSICAL EDUCATION

Where do teachers of early childhood adapted physical education fit into this process? Infants and toddlers with developmental delays, whether they be cognitive, physical, or emotional, might also demonstrate psychomotor delays. Psychomotor delay creates a major disadvantage to the child because movement serves as an important basis from which children initially learn. For example, if children lack the ability to maintain an upright position or ambulate across a room, they are unable to interact with their environments in a meaningful way. Teachers of early childhood adapted physical education are in a unique position to develop and implement appropriate motor programs that can stimulate and enhance the movement abilities of infants and toddlers with special needs. These teachers may serve as valuable members of the multidisciplinary team

by conducting motor assessments or observing motor behavior, thereby helping to select goals and objectives to enhance the child's development. They may provide direct teaching services or serve in a consultant role to early intervention providers and parents. As resource consultants, they can provide appropriate activities that stimulate development in areas beyond the motor domain, including cognitive, social or emotional, communication, and adaptive development.

In summary, teachers of early childhood adapted physical education conduct assessments and teach or serve as consultants to caregivers of infants and toddlers with special needs. Because the ability to conduct valid assessments is essential to determining eligibility for services, the following section provides information that can help teachers of early childhood adapted physical education to accurately test and assess the motor needs of infants and toddlers with developmental delays.

ASSESSMENT

As noted, assessment serves as the primary means of determining eligibility for and implementing early intervention services. Various assessment techniques are used to determine the status of infants and toddlers. These techniques and examples of each are provided in the following sections.

Screening

Prior to a comprehensive assessment, infants and toddlers might first be screened to determine if there is a probable delay. On completion of the screening procedure, recommendations are made regarding the need for further evaluation. One example of a motor screening test is the Milani-Comparetti Motor Development Screening Test for Infants and Young Children (1987). The Milani-Comparetti was designed to test the development of children from approximately birth to two years of age. The majority of the test items are scored within the first 16 months of a child's life; however, the test provides the most detailed information regarding children between the ages of 3 and 12 months. The test assesses primitive reflexes, righting reactions, protective reactions, equilibrium reactions, postural control, and active movement. Another popular screening test is the Denver II Developmental Screening

Test (Frankenburg et al., 1992). The Denver II assesses children from birth to six years of age in the areas of personal and social development, language, fine and gross motor ability, and adaptive behavior. The Denver II relies heavily on the input of caregivers as well as on direct observation of developmental tasks to determine performance level. Teachers of early childhood adapted physical education should have a solid background in motor development so that these screening tests and subsequent assessments can be administered with relative ease.

Standardized Assessment

After initial screening, if it is determined that a child might have a delay, a formal assessment is conducted. One way to determine the unique needs of infants and toddlers with special needs is through the use of standardized assessments. Standardized assessments are often used because they lend themselves to the determination of developmental status, are technically sound, and are relatively easy to administer by educators. Standardized assessment instruments might be norm referenced or criterion referenced or both. Norm-referenced assessments allow testers to compare the child's performance against others of similar age and characteristics, whereas criterion-referenced tests compare the child's performance against pre-established criteria. Tests that are both norm and criterion referenced help not only with identification of unique needs but also with program planning and implementation.

One example of a motor assessment instrument that is both norm and criterion referenced is the *Peabody Developmental Motor Scales–2nd Edition* (PDMS–2) (Folio & Fewell, 2000). This test provides in-depth assessment and training of gross and fine motor skills for children from birth through age five. The test is broken down into six subtests that measure reflexes, stationary positions, locomotion, object manipulation, grasping and visual–motor integration. The test yields fine motor and gross motor quotient scores as well as a total motor quotient score. The total motor quotient is the best estimate of the child's overall motor abilities. The PDMS–2 also provides a motor activity program with units of instruction organized developmentally by skill area to aid in the development and implementation of appropriate goals and objectives to meet the unique needs of the child.

Another example of a standardized test that is both norm and criterion referenced is the Brig-ance Inventory of Early Development (Brigance, 1999). The Brigance is unique in that it contains both a screening test and formal assessment. Once the child has been screened and a delay is suspected, the child is further evaluated with the formal assessment. The Brigance is designed for children from birth to seven years. Areas assessed include motor skills, self-help skills, speech and language, general knowledge and comprehension, and early academic skills. The Brigance tends to be one of the most widely used comprehensive assessments because it targets all areas of functional development, generating a valid picture of the child's current level of performance.

Curriculum-Based Assessment

Curriculum-based assessment has also become a popular means in which to generate data relative to a child's present level of performance. Curriculum-based assessment takes place in natural environments and is based on a predetermined set of curriculum objectives. The Carolina Curriculum for Infants and Toddlers with Special Needs (Johnson-Martin, Jens, Attermeier, & Hacker, 1991) and the Hawaii Early Learning Profile (HELP) Strands (Parks, 1992), are both examples of curriculum-based assessment. The Carolina Curriculum was developed for infants and toddlers from birth to 24 months, whereas the HELP Strands was developed for infants and toddlers from birth to 36 months. Both tests assess the child in five functional areas of development: cognitive skills, communication and language, social–emotional adaptation, fine motor skills, and gross motor skills. Each area assessed is embedded in a naturally occurring activity. Based on the assessment data, a profile of the child is developed. Because these assessments are linked to a curriculum, there is a smooth transition from the assessment phase to the intervention phase. Both the Carolina Curriculum and the HELP Strands provide activities to develop skills assessed.

Transdisciplinary Play-Based Assessment

The final form of assessment presented in this chapter is transdisciplinary play-based assessment (Linder, 1993), which differs from traditional forms of assessment in several ways. Traditional forms of assessment typically involve experts in various domains determining the strengths and needs of the child for a particular domain. For example, a teacher of adapted physical education might provide data related to motor abilities, whereas a speech and language teacher might provide information regarding communication. These experts then come together and report their findings and generate a comprehensive picture of the youngster's current level of performance. Transdisciplinary play-based assessment, also known as arena assessment, calls for a play facilitator to interact with the child, her parents, and a peer. The interactions are based on a set of criteria observed unobtrusively in both structured and unstructured play environments by representatives from various disciplines knowledgeable about all areas of development (Linder, 1993). During the interactions, observations of cognitive, social–emotional, communication and language, and sensorimotor development are assessed. Based on the observations, developmental level, learning style, interaction patterns, and other relevant behaviors are analyzed and recorded onto observation sheets, which are later transferred to summary sheets during postobservation sessions (Linder, 1993). The role of the parents in transdisciplinary play-based assessment cannot be overemphasized. Parents are involved in the process from start to finish by completing a developmental checklist, directly interacting with the child during the assessment, and developing the IFSP. This form of assessment has many benefits; most notably it helps to provide an accurate picture of the youngster's present level of performance, because data are collected in natural environments with caregivers directly involved in the assessment process. Youngsters are typically more at ease and perform more as they normally would with this type of assessment. In addition, by using a play facilitator, the child is exposed to only one professional individually assessing the child rather than the traditional three to five members of an assessment team. Teachers of early childhood adapted physical education can easily serve as play facilitators, because their primary means of developing motor abilities is through the use of play.

Because well-prepared teachers of adapted physical education should be able and willing to provide assessment services, they might serve as valuable members of the multidisciplinary team responsible for direct screening and assessment of motor behaviors for infants and toddlers with disabilities. In addition to their abilities to provide screening and assessment data, teachers of early childhood adapted physical education can help infants and toddlers achieve their motor objectives by providing developmentally appropriate activities and environments. The next section identifies goals and objectives of early childhood motor programs for infants and toddlers. For additional information on assessments see chapter 4.

GOALS AND OBJECTIVES IN MOTOR PROGRAMS FOR INFANTS AND TODDLERS

Infants and toddlers learn by experiencing their environments in several ways: through their senses (seeing, hearing, tasting, smelling, and feeling), through reciprocal adult–child interactions, and through movement actions and reactions (Bredekamp & Copple, 1997). For example, when an infant cries, a natural reaction on the part of the parent or caregiver is to interact with the child to determine his or her needs. Similarly, if a child swats at a mobile (i.e., movement action), the natural reaction is for the mobile to move. These constant interactions among the child, the environment, and those within the environment serve as the basis for cognitive, affective, and psychomotor development of infants and toddlers.

Within these early years, adult–child interactions need to be warm and positive so that infants and toddlers can develop a sense of trust in the world and feelings of self-competence (Bredekamp & Copple, 1997). As trust is established, infants and toddlers become receptive to new experiences. Teachers of early childhood adapted physical education are in a unique position to provide safe and secure motor environments in which infants, toddlers, and their caregivers can discover and explore the world around them. Thus, a primary goal of motor programs for infants and toddlers is to develop a sense of trust in both their caregivers and their environments.

A second goal of motor programs for infants and toddlers is to aid in the development of independence. Whereas infants might not be ready to function independently of their caregivers, they should be provided opportunities to engage in isolated activities independently from time to time. Toddlers, however, will need guidance and support as they begin to release their total dependence on their parents or caregivers and learn to function more independently. This need for independence helps shape positive psychosocial behaviors later in life. Play is seen as crucial to the development of the child's independence because it allows children to function within their own boundaries, not the boundaries established by others. As youngsters attempt new skills, they need to feel successful so that they will continue to attempt either the same skill, leading to more refined movement, or try out new skills. Self-initiated repetition is one way to foster this independence (Bredekamp & Copple, 1997). Teachers of early childhood adapted physical education are responsible for developing environments that allow for ample opportunities to practice already learned skills as well as new skills. For example, if a toddler finds rolling a ball stimulating, a variety of balls with various shapes and sizes should be available to the child. It is important to keep in mind that, in terms of play, toddlers are egocentric and should not be expected to share. Enough equipment that is the same or similar in nature should be available to the children (figure 21.1).

A third goal of motor programs for infants and toddlers relates to providing opportunities for active movement. Typically developing infants and toddlers will naturally progress from reflexive movement to rudimentary movement, which includes three categories: stability, locomotion, and manipulation. Stability—the ability to maintain control of the head, neck, and trunk—serves as the basis for locomotion and manipulation. The enhanced motor ability that comes with rudi-

mentary movement such as crawling, creeping, and walking allows infants and toddlers to move freely within their environments. Once there, the ability to reach, grasp, and release allows infants and toddlers to make meaningful contact with objects within the environment. Together, these movement interactions help to shape the overall development of infants and toddlers and lead to more refined movement forms, known as fundamental movement. The need for active movement cannot be overstated. Recently, the National Association for Sport and Physical Education (2002) developed a position statement that notes "all children birth to age five should engage in daily physical activity that promotes health-related fitness and movement skills" (p. 2). Guidelines regarding active movement for these young children are identified for infants, toddlers, and preschoolers.

Infant Guidelines

1. Infants should interact with parents or caregivers in daily physical activities dedicated to promoting the exploration of their environment.

2. Infants should be placed in safe settings that promote physical activity and do not restrict movement for prolonged periods of time.

3. Infants' physical activity should promote the development of movement skills.

Figure 21.1 Plenty of toys similar in nature should be readily available.

4. Infants should have an environment that meets or exceeds recommended safety standards for performing large muscle activities.

5. Individuals responsible for the well-being of infants should be aware of the importance of physical activity and promote the child's movement skills.

Toddler Guidelines

1. Toddlers should accumulate at least 30 minutes daily of structured physical activity.

2. Toddlers should engage in at least 60 minutes and up to several hours per of daily unstructured physical activity and should not be sedentary for more than 60 minutes at a time except when sleeping.

3. Toddlers should develop movement skills that are building blocks for more complex movement tasks.

4. Toddlers should have indoor and outdoor areas that meet or exceed recommended safety standards for performing large muscle activities.

5. Individuals responsible for the well-being of toddlers should be aware of the importance of physical activity and promote the child's movement skills.

Providing activities and objects within the environment that elicit active movement is a key role of teachers of early childhood adapted physical education.

In summary, motor programs for typically developing infants and toddlers should seek to provide a safe nurturing environment in which trust and independence can flourish. It should also provide opportunities for motor activities that allow infants and toddlers to use their newly found motor skills, such as crawling, walking, grasping, and releasing, so that they may have meaningful contacts with persons and objects within their environments and remain active most times of the day. These combined goals realized through a series of objectives help to shape motor development in infants and toddlers as well as their cognitive and social development.

Infants and toddlers with unique needs, however, might have motor delays that inhibit their abilities to move freely and interact with their environments. Whereas the goals and objectives previously discussed are applicable to all infants and toddlers, the following section identifies unique motor needs that teachers of early childhood adapted physical education might encounter, as well as strategies to promote the development of children with unique needs.

GOALS AND OBJECTIVES IN MOTOR PROGRAMS FOR INFANTS AND TODDLERS WITH UNIQUE NEEDS

Although typically developing infants and toddlers move from the stage of reflexive movement to rudimentary movement in a smooth, integrated fashion, infants and toddlers with special needs might demonstrate unique motor problems that benefit through intervention.

Cowden, Sayers, and Torrey (1998) identify several areas of emphasis in which motor programs for infants and toddlers with unique needs are developed. The first deals primarily with increasing muscle tone and strength. Infants and toddlers lacking in muscle tone are said to be **hypotonic.** Disabilities associated with hypotonicity include Down syndrome, muscular dystrophy, or metabolic disorders (Cowden, Sayers, & Torrey, 1998). Infants with low muscle tone often demonstrate delays in primitive reflex integration, especially with the tonic neck group of reflexes (Cowden, Sayers, & Torrey, 1998). Teachers of early childhood adapted physical education should provide physical assistance as needed to move the child through various strength-enhancing activities. Strength-control activities should occur in four positions: prone, supine, side lying, and upright. In the prone position, the child is developing greater control of the head and trunk. These prerequisite skills aid in the development of locomotor movements, such as crawling and creeping. A typical prone position stimulus that elicits head control involves squeaking or rattling a favorite toy above the child's head (see figure 21.2). The child will attempt to reach for the toy and in so doing will lift his or her head from the floor. Control of the trunk can be realized by encouraging and assisting, if necessary, the child to roll from stomach to back. Again, a favorite toy just out of reach will motivate the child to roll over. After the child has accomplished the task, it is important to allow him or her to interact with the toy. Once head and trunk control have been established, crawling and creeping positions should be maintained.

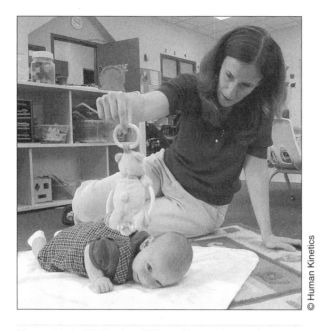

Figure 21.2 Eliciting head lifting with a toy fosters the infant's control of the head.

Activities in the supine and side-lying positions also stimulate muscle strength. However, it is important to note that for children with extremely high or low muscle tone, supine positions should be avoided and activities should be done in the side-lying position for greater control. A typical supine or side-lying activity involves offering the child a toy just slightly out of reach. The child will then reach for the toy (extend arms), obtain it, and bring the toy into midline (flex arms). These types of activities can be repeated in several different ways by using a variety of equipment to stimulate the child's interest. Finally, activities that enhance strength can be attained in upright positions. For example, in a sitting position, children can interact with caregivers and their environments. Any activity that maintains the child's interest, such as Peek-a-Boo, done over and over again often stimulates a child and fosters an upright position. As the child gains additional strength, standing and finally walking will be achieved.

The second area of motor emphasis for infants and toddlers with special needs is to decrease muscle tone and enhance reflex integration. Increased muscle tone, also known as hypertonicity, results from delayed reflex integration. Infants and toddlers with spastic cerebral palsy exhibit hypertonicity. The lack of reflex integration interferes with typical movement skills, thus creating substantial motor delays. Activities that involve relaxation techniques, massage, therapy

exercise balls, and appropriate positioning help to minimize and alleviate hypertonicity. Figure 21.3 illustrates a young child being placed in a prone position on a therapy ball with legs slightly separated and toes pointed outward. The child is gently rocked forward and backward. This position on the therapy ball helps to normalize muscle tone by relaxing the muscles.

Figure 21.3 Child on therapy ball.

Stimulation and development of the sensory motor system are also areas of emphasis for infants and toddlers with unique needs. Cowden, Sayers, and Torrey (1998), and chapter 20 of this book identify five components of the sensory system and provide activities to enhance each. These components include vestibular integration, visual–motor control, auditory discrimination, tactile stimulation, and kinesthetic and spatial awareness. Vestibular integration activities are needed so that youngsters can "right" themselves, that is, maintain an upright position. Infants and toddlers who lack the ability to right themselves can easily be injured and demonstrate delayed locomotion and balance abilities. Therapy balls are useful in helping to enhance postural reactions. With the child lying over the ball, the ball is rolled forward so that the child extends arms in a protective fashion. Activities that use incline mats, balance boards, and scooters, as well as a variety of other movement activities, are all appropriate for enhancing postural reactions because they stimulate opportunities for movement in a variety of positions and situations. The ability to track objects, discriminate between shapes and sizes, and distinguish objects from a background is all under the guise of visual–motor control (figure 21.4). Activities that can enhance children's visual–motor control should be incorporated into the repertoire of early childhood motor programs. Simple tasks such as tracking a rolling ball, matching shapes, and walking on overlapping geometric shapes are all appropriate for enhancing visual–motor control.

© Human Kinetics

Figure 21.4 Tracking a slow moving scarf is one way to enhance visual–motor control.

Auditory discrimination (i.e., the ability to distinguish sounds) can be enhanced by having children search for sounds in a room, move their bodies to the rhythm of music, and follow simple directions. Some children might be hypersensitive to touch or lack reactions to touch. In these instances, carefully sequenced tactile stimulation activities can be incorporated into the program.

Allowing the child to interact with a variety of textured equipment such as scooters, mats, balance boards, and ropes will prove helpful in the child's ability to distinguish hard and soft objects. Physically stroking a child with various textures in a manner that is tolerated by the child is also helpful. Finally, kinesthetic and spatial awareness can be enhanced by providing activities that allow the child to move through space, such as obstacle courses with tunnels, mats, and scooters.

The ability to manipulate objects might also be a needed area of emphasis for infants and toddlers with unique needs. The ability to reach, grasp, hold, and release is crucial for acquiring self-help skills, such as eating, and for making meaningful contacts within the environment, such as swinging on a swing.

In summary, areas of emphasis associated with infants and toddlers with unique needs might include increasing muscle tone and strength, decreasing muscle tone and enhancing reflex integration, stimulating the sensory motor system, and enhancing manipulative abilities. The following section describes developmentally appropriate interactions parents, caregivers, and teachers of early childhood adapted physical education should embrace in implementing programs.

DEVELOPMENTALLY APPROPRIATE INTERACTIONS WITH INFANTS AND TODDLERS

Traditional formats for teaching physical education obviously do not apply to teaching infants and toddlers. Teachers of early childhood adapted physical education are primarily responsible for setting up an environment that is intriguing to youngsters and their parents or caregivers. Direct teaching is not recommended with such young children; rather, indirect approaches to attain goals such as discovery and exploration are embedded within the learning environment. Infants and toddlers should be free to explore and engage in self-initiated repetition as much as desired. Teachers and caregivers should use indirect teaching strategies such as following the child's lead in activities that are initiated by the child rather than the teacher or caregiver. The adult watches and interacts at the child's level by describing what the child is doing rather than telling the child what he should be doing (McCall

& Craft, 2000). For example, if a young child is interacting with blocks, the caregiver can label the blocks by their colors or shapes with statements such as, "Shannon is stacking the red block." Adults also play a role in providing choices for young children. A child should be able to choose to play in any of several suitable environments; for example, a motor room might contain push toys, stacking toys, balls, and tunnels. Any of these activities would be suitable, as each has specific embedded values. Tunnels and balls allow children to enhance their gross motor abilities, whereas push toys and stacking toys enhance fine motor abilities. Activity participation will have naturally occurring consequences; that is, if a child climbs to the top of the slide, the natural consequence would be to slide down. These activities contribute to an understanding of the environment and sensorimotor development. Refer to the application example, which describes a developmentally appropriate motor environment.

As noted, typically parents or caregivers will accompany the young child in the motor environment; thus, teachers of early childhood adapted physical education need to respect and embrace the role of parents in their programming. The following section provides tips for interacting with parents or caregivers to effectively enhance the development of the child.

INTERACTING WITH FAMILIES

Teachers of early childhood adapted physical education for infants and toddlers should understand that their programs should be based on a **family-centered** philosophy and that goals and objectives are developed not in isolation of the family but rather in conjunction with the family. One of the basic underlying assumptions of the development of the IFSP is that infants and toddlers depend on their families for survival (McGonigel, 1991); thus, the role of families in early intervention cannot be minimized. Bennett, Lingerfelt, and Nelson (1990) developed family-centered principles that teachers of early childhood adapted physical education may adopt as effective methods for interacting with families. The first principle deals with basing intervention efforts on the needs and aspirations identified by the family. Fiorini, Stanton, and Reid (1996) identify several questions one might ask regarding motor development, such as, "What types of activities would you like your child to be doing now that she is not doing at the present time?" "What worries you most about your child's motor ability?" "What are you most excited about in terms of your child's motor ability?" This process enables parents to set the goals and objectives they feel are important to their child's development. The role of the early childhood adapted physical educator is to help prioritize the goals.

The second family-centered principle is based on expanding and developing the family's repertoire of skills and competencies. Teachers of early childhood adapted physical education can consult with and demonstrate appropriate motor interactions that parents or caregivers can model. As parents or caregivers engage their child in developmentally appropriate activities and see gains in motor development, confidence in their abilities to do so is strengthened.

Finally, the most important family-centered principle is communication. Teachers of early

---

APPLICATION EXAMPLE

Developing an Appropriate Motor Environment

Setting: Motor room at a daycare facility

Students: Toddlers with and without unique needs

Task: Setting up a developmentally appropriate motor environment that promotes the movement of the young children

Application: The environment contains the following areas:

- Push toys for fine motor development

- Stack toys for fine motor development
- Balls for gross motor development
- Tunnels for gross motor development

The teacher allows the children to interact within the environment and follows their lead as they move from one piece of equipment to another. Children with special needs might need to be brought to various areas if they are unable to ambulate independently. Choosing an area should be encouraged.

childhood adapted physical education need to maintain constant open communication with parents or caregivers. The development of the young child is based on the combined efforts of parents and supportive professionals whose major role is to guide the family in the development of their child not to direct the development of the child. With a strong collaborative partnership, infants and toddlers with special needs and their families can benefit from early intervention services, and the child's development can be significantly enhanced.

SUMMARY

This chapter has provided an overview of the role of teachers of early childhood adapted physical education as it relates to infants and toddlers with unique needs. As noted, teachers of early childhood adapted physical education might be involved in early intervention services for infants and toddlers with unique needs by serving as members of the multidisciplinary team convened to determine unique needs, conduct valid assessments of the child's motor abilities, develop appropriate motor goals and objectives for the IFSP, and implement motor programs. In some instances, teachers of early childhood adapted physical education might serve as consultants to caregivers or parents on providing appropriate motor programs.

Although all infants and toddlers can benefit from developmentally appropriate motor programs, infants and toddlers with unique needs will have specific goals and objectives embedded in their activities. Goals might include increasing muscle tone and strength, decreasing muscle tone and enhancing reflex integration, stimulating the sensory motor system, or enhancing manipulative abilities. A variety of suggested activities were presented to assist teachers of early childhood adapted physical education realize these goals; however, the reader is encouraged to seek out recommended resources outlined in the resources for this chapter to further develop motor programs for infants and toddlers with unique needs.

Finally, this chapter has highlighted the importance of family in the lives of infants and toddlers. It is suggested that teachers of early childhood adapted physical education embrace three family-centered principles when working with infants and toddlers with unique needs. These family-centered principles include basing intervention efforts on the needs and aspirations identified by the family, expanding and developing the family's repertoire of skills and competencies, and maintaining open communication.

Teachers of early childhood adapted physical education are in a unique position to help minimize further delays of infants and toddlers with unique needs by creating movement environments that allow children to discover, explore, and interact with their environments. These interactions enhance motor development and improve cognitive and social development.

REFERENCES

Bennett, T., Lingerfelt, B.V., & Nelson, D.E. (1990). *Developing individualized family support plans: A training manual.* Cambridge, MA: Brookline Books.

Bredekamp, S., & Copple, C. (1997). *Developmentally appropriate practice in early childhood programs—Revised.* Washington, DC: National Association for the Education of Young Children.

Brigance, A. (1999). *Brigance diagnostic inventory of early development.* Billerica, MA: Curriculum Associates.

Cowden, J.E., Sayers, L.K., & Torrey, C.C. (1998). *Pediatric adapted motor development and exercise: An innovative, multisystem approach for professionals and families.* Springfield, IL: Charles C Thomas.

Fiorini, J., Stanton, K., & Reid, G. (1996). Understanding parents and families of children with disabilities: Considerations for adapted physical activity. *Palaestra,* 12(2), 16-23.

Folio, M.R., & Fewell, R. (2000). *Peabody developmental motor scales* (2nd ed.). Austin, TX: Pro-Ed.

Frankenburg, W.K., Dodds, J., Archer, P., Bresnick, B., Maschka, P., Edelman, N., & Shapiro, H. (1992). *Denver II training manual* (2nd ed.). Denver, CO: Denver Developmental Materials.

Johnson-Martin, N., Jens, K.G., Attermeier, S.M., & Hacker, B.J. (1991). *The Carolina curriculum for infants and toddlers with special needs.* Baltimore, MD: Paul H. Brookes.

Linder, T. (1993). *Transdisciplinary play-based assessment.* Baltimore, MD: Paul H. Brookes.

McCall, R., & Craft, D.H. (2000). *Moving with a purpose: Developing programs for preschoolers of all abilities.* Champaign, IL: Human Kinetics.

McGonigel, M.J. (1991). Philosophy and conceptual framework. In M.J. McGonigel, R.K. Kaufman, & B.H. Johnson (Eds.), *Guidelines and recommendations for the Individualized Family Service Plan.* Bethesda, MD: Association for the Care of Children's Health.

Milani-Comparetti Motor Development Screening Test manual. (1987). Available from Meyer Children's Rehabilitation Institute, University of Nebraska Medical Center, 444 South 44th Street, Omaha, Nebraska 68131-3795.

National Association for Sport and Physical Education (2002). *Active Start: A statement of physical activity guidelines for children birth to five year.* Reston, VA: Author.

New York State Department of Health—The Early Intervention Program: A parent's guide. (1999). New York, NY: Author.

Office of Special Education and Rehabilitative Services (OSE/RS), 34 CFR 306 (2002).

Parks, S. (Ed.). (1992). *HELP strands: Curriculum-based developmental assessment birth to three years.* Palo Alto, CA: VORT.

WRITTEN RESOURCES

Blanche, E.I., Botticelli, T.M., & Hallway, M.K. (1995). *Combining neuro-development treatment and sensory integration principles: An approach to pediatric therapy.* Tucson, AZ: Therapy Skill Builders.

Explains both NDT and SI principles and offers suggestions for combining these two forms of treatment to enhance the motor development of infants and toddlers with special needs. Provides activities and worksheets to assist teachers in programming.

Bly, L. (1994). *Motor skills acquisition in the first year: An illustrated guide to normal development.* Tucson, AZ: Therapy Skill Builders.

Illustrations of infant development during the first years are depicted. Allows teachers to note normal development and deviations in development. Suggests activities to enhance development.

Bricker, D., Pretti-Frontczak, K., & McComas, N. (1998). *An activity-based approach to early intervention.* Baltimore, MD: Paul H. Brookes.

Details how and why the activity-based approach can benefit any child ages birth to five.

Johnson, L.J., LaMontagne, M.J., Elgas, P.M., & Bauer, A.M. (1998). *Early childhood education: Blending theory, blending practice.* Baltimore, MD: Paul H. Brookes.

Combines best practices in early childhood education and early childhood special education to create environments in which all children can achieve.

Jordan, J.B., Gallagher, J.J., Hutinger, P.L., & Karnes, M.B. (1990). *Early childhood special education: Birth to three.* Reston, VA: Council for Exceptional Children—Early Childhood Division.

Provides readers with updated information on early intervention policies and procedures.

ELECTRONIC RESOURCES

National Association for the Education of Young Children: www.naeyc.org

This is the primary site for resources and best practices for the education of young children aged 0 to nine years.

Early Childhood Adapted Physical Education

Lauriece L. Zittel

Mr. Sanchez and Ms. Brooks are elementary physical education specialists at North Ridge Elementary School. Recently, their district instituted an inclusive early childhood program for preschoolers. Young children ages three to five with disabilities or developmental delays from the community who have been identified as needing special education services are enrolled in this program. The district combined this special education program with an already existing preschool program housed in the elementary school. Federal legislation (IDEA) requires that all preschool-age children with diagnosed disabilities or developmental delays receive special education programming. Additionally, those children experiencing motor delays are entitled to receive adapted physical education services at the discretion of individual states. The teachers decided that rather than just providing instruction to the children with developmental delays, they would design a preschool physical education program for all of the young children in this new program. The teachers are aware that the majority of children in the preschool program have communication delays in addition to their disability diagnosis or general developmental delay. They are anxious to collaborate with the classroom teachers and speech therapist to develop a movement program to enhance motor and communication skills. The challenge, as they recognize it, will be to design a preschool program that builds a skill foundation for the children as they prepare to enter their elementary physical education program.

The early childhood physical education instructors in this vignette are not alone. It is not uncommon to find preschool classrooms for children with developmental delays in an elementary school building. Many physical educators have had experience teaching children with disabilities in kindergarten through the third grade, but teaching a preschool-age population might be new to them. The purpose of this chapter is to present readers with information about accurately assessing the abilities of young children, the developmental differences between preschool-age children and those entering elementary school, and planning for instruction and developmentally appropriate teaching practices.

IDENTIFYING YOUNG CHILDREN WITH DEVELOPMENTAL DELAYS

Federal legislation, now known as PL 105-17 the Individuals with Disabilities Education Act Amendments, was passed to enhance opportunities for young children with special needs. According to the act, children aged three through nine who are experiencing developmental delays are to be provided early educational opportunities and might qualify for these services if they are:

> (1) . . . experiencing developmental delays, as defined by the State and as measured by appropriate diagnostic instruments and procedures, in one or more of the following areas: physical development, social or emotional development, or adaptive development; and (2) Who, by reason thereof, need special education and related services. (Federal Register, 1999, p. 12421)

In the preschool and early childhood years (ages three through nine), a noncategorical approach is used to classify students as eligible to receive special education services. This noncategorical approach in the early childhood years allows for programming based on the functional areas of development of each child rather than disability-specific programming. Federal legislation also requires that instruction be provided to these youngsters in the least restrictive and most natural learning environment. Thus, inclusive programs designed to accommodate children with and without unique needs should be the norm rather than the exception. Teachers of physical education are thus faced with the challenge of determining movement delays and structuring movement programs to meet the needs of young children with varying levels of abilities.

Accurately assessing the abilities of these youngsters' abilities will enhance the planning and implementation of early childhood adapted physical education programs. Children with diagnosed developmental delays, as well as disabilities, present individual challenges for instructors. In the next section we will present appropriate assessment procedures that can assist teachers of early childhood adapted physical education in determining the functional abilities of the young children in their classrooms. Identifying a gross motor developmental delay is an essential component in determining a child's eligibility to receive an individualized adapted physical education program. Planning and implementing developmentally appropriate physical education instruction for children with gross motor delays depends on the accuracy of the assessment results.

ASSESSMENT OF PERFORMANCE

Making accurate decisions about children's individualized program needs requires an understanding of their current ability. Professional guidelines and federal legislation recommend that assessment information come from several measures and sources. Additionally, with children at risk for developmental delay, each child should be observed in variety of settings. A complete picture of a young child's present level of performance (in all areas of learning) can be drawn from a group of individuals most familiar with the child's routines and behaviors. A multidisciplinary team should collect screening information while observing the child in structured settings as well as unstructured play environments. Members of the multidisciplinary team should include classroom teachers, adapted or regular physical educators, therapists, parents or guardians, and others who see the child regularly. These individuals will develop the child's individualized educational program (IEP) and participate as part of the IEP planning committee.

The assessment process may be completed using a formal, standardized procedure or an informal, play-based procedure (Linder, 1993), the difference lying primarily in the level of intrusiveness. Before selecting an instrument to assess young children, the purpose of testing should be clear (Zittel, 1994). Will the results be used to document a developmental delay, or is information needed for planning and teaching? Norm-referenced, standardized tests are administered to determine a child's gross motor developmental level and provide comparison information of same-age children without delays. Criterion-referenced instruments typically provide more information about delays in skill areas (e.g., locomotor, object control) to assist with teaching program planning.

Standardized Formal Testing

Selecting standardized test instruments that are both norm- and criterion-referenced will assist adapted physical education specialists in making program eligibility decisions as well as provide instructional information. Instruments that incorporate flexible testing procedures (i.e., equipment selection and testing environments) will be more sensitive to the testing characteristics of young children with disabilities and thus have a more positive impact on the accuracy of test results. Good examples of standardized, norm- and criterion-referenced tools used to assess the gross-motor skill of young children include the *Brigance: Diagnostic Inventory of Early Development-Revised* (Brigance, 1991), the *Peabody Developmental Motor Scales-2* (PMDS) (Folio & Fewell, 2000), and the *Test of Gross Motor Development-2* (TGMD) (Ulrich, 2000). Each of these assessment instruments is designed to assist early childhood physical education specialists in determining a child's gross-motor developmental level as well as provide information for instructional programming. Additionally, each of these tools will assist specialists in developing goals and objectives for the child's IEP. The testing procedures outlined for the *Brigance,* the *PMDS-2,* and the *TGMD-2* provide test administrators with flexibility in the way the test environment is structured, what equipment is selected, and how instructions are provided. For example, the *Peabody* test manual suggests that a station-testing format be used for evaluating several young children at a time. And the materials used to administer the *PMDS-2* are those commonly found in preschool or primary programs and familiar to most children.

Federal guidelines encourage early childhood teachers to use data from multiple observations and measures for gathering information to make decisions about performance ability. Informa-tion collected in standardized settings should be combined with observations made in natural play environments.

Informal Testing

The authenticity of data collected in natural settings provides instructors with useful information about the child's preferences and abilities. The ability to write accurate instructional objectives and structure an effective teaching environment is maximized when teachers observe and record behaviors of children during typical games and activities and watch them interact with age-appropriate equipment. Criterion-referenced skill checklists are used in curriculum-based assessment and yield information about the child's abilities in the context of a predetermined set of curriculum objectives (McLean, Wolery, Bailey, 2004).

In the area of early childhood adapted physical education two curriculum-based tools are recommended here to assist teachers of physical education in securing performance assessment data. *SMART START: A Preschool Movement Curriculum* (Wessel & Zittel, 1995) and *I CAN Primary Skills K–3 (Revised)* (Wessel & Zittel, 1998) are programs that include skill checklists for teachers to use to collect information for individualizing movement programs. In both programs the authors have organized the skill checklists into a LOOP model. The *SMART START* preschool checklists include Locomotor (e.g., jumping, hopping), Orientation (e.g., body awareness, imitative expressive movements), Object Control (e.g., throwing, kicking) and Play Skills (e.g., parachute play, tricycle riding). The *I CAN K-3* skill checklists also include the fundamental skill areas (locomotor, orientation, and object control) but instead of play skills, Personal–social participation (e.g., problem solving, self-control) skills are assessed. Participation checklists were added to the I CAN K-3 curriculum because of a need expressed by teachers. The LOOP organization in both of these early childhood programs allows instructors to assess children according to skill areas relevant for both the preschool and elementary years. Additionally, the model gives instructors the freedom to select skill objectives from different areas for different units of instruction. For example, a preschool adapted physical educator might choose to assess three locomotor skills (vertical jumping, hop, gallop) and two play skills (parachute play, tricycle riding) to organize one six-week unit of instruction.

The *Carolina Curriculum for Preschoolers with Special Needs* (Johnson-Martin, Attermeier, & Hacker, 1990) and the *Assessment, Evaluation, and Programming System for Infants and Children* (AEPS) (Bricker & Pretti-Frontczak, 1996) are multidomain, curriculum-based programs designed for preschool-age children with disabilities or those who are at risk of developmental delays. The *Carolina* assesses children in five learning domains and provides a curriculum sequence in each area. The gross-motor domain assesses skills in locomotion, stair climbing, jumping, balance, balls, and outdoor equipment. The *AEPS* includes a functional skill assessment across six learning domains and a curriculum to provide programming and teaching suggestions for instructors. The gross-motor domain includes two skill strands. Strand A is balance and mobility in standing and walking and focuses on stair climbing. Strand B is called play skills and includes five goals in these areas: jumps forward; runs avoiding obstacles; bounces, catches, kicks, and throws; skips; and rides and steers a two-wheel bicycle.

Teacher-made checklists and rubrics can also be useful methods for assessing motor and play skill performance. Standards of performance can be written to address the unique movement abilities of children, and progress on those standards can be used to evaluate improvement on instructional objectives. These methods give teachers the freedom to collect performance information on skills or behaviors that might not be found in published checklists. Additionally, task-analyzing skills for children with severe disabilities will give early childhood teachers the opportunity to assess functional abilities by individualizing the critical elements in a checklist. For example, a teacher might be assessing the galloping abilities of preschool-age children while they pretend that yardsticks are their horses. One child in the class with cerebral palsy uses a gait trainer and, with the horse attached, is working on stepping. In this example, the teacher might use the *SMART START* galloping checklist for some of the children in the class and create his or her own stepping checklist to evaluate the ability of the child with cerebral palsy.

Portfolio assessment is a means of gathering information about a child in order to monitor progress on teaching objectives or to inform teaching practice (Lynch & Struewing, 2001). In collaboration with the classroom teacher, information from the movement environment can be added to a child's portfolio, or the adapted physical educator can begin a portfolio system for a child on his or her own. Because the purpose of a portfolio is to enhance teaching, a collaborative effort is recommended. Ideally, movement skills will be practiced not only in the physical education class but at home and during movement times that the classroom teacher arranges. All who work with a child should add samples of a child's activity or practice on certain IEP objectives. Written comments from teachers, parents, or teaching assistants, videotapes, photos, and drawings related to movement skills and practice are examples of items to include in a movement portfolio. At the end of each evaluation period, the adapted physical educator should organize all of the material and provide an overview and reflection about the child's year. For children who will remain in a preschool program for multiple years, the portfolio can be used to document progress and then shared with the elementary specialists during the transition to kindergarten.

Performance data gathered formally or informally, should provide a direct link to designing and evaluating an individualized intervention plan. The activities a teacher uses should be designed to address each child's gross-motor strengths and challenges. Teachers of early childhood adapted physical education should become familiar with appropriate curriculum designs and instructional strategies that are both age and individually appropriate.

OBJECTIVES OF EARLY CHILDHOOD PROGRAMS

The development of early childhood physical education programs should be aligned with best practices in early childhood and early childhood special education. Young children experiencing delays in their motor development should receive opportunities and instruction designed to parallel what their same-age peers receive but modified to address individual challenges. Preschool movement programs should provide children with the opportunity to explore and act on objects in their physical environment. The preschool years give instructors the opportunity to guide children through games and activities in order to build a skill foundation. It follows then that the early elementary years (kindergarten–third grade) allow the teacher to integrate the knowledge and skill that children have acquired and begin a focus on refining fundamental skills required for more advanced games and activities. The importance of seeing the developmental connection in the early childhood years is critical for physical education curriculum development. Moving toward mastery of the basic fundamental movements and skills and beginning to integrate those skills into games and activities are processes.

Activity environments designed to provide instruction for young children with developmental delays and those with disabilities should be individualized according to assessment information. Arbitrarily selecting games and activities because they "seem fun" and the children "appear to enjoy them" is not necessarily in line with good practice. Specifically, learning environments should parallel the strengths and challenges identified during the assessment process and written on the IEP as instructional objectives. Instruction is based on a good understanding of each child's present level of performance. An activity setting should be carefully planned to build on what children already know and promote the acquisition of new skills. Figure 22.1 shows a young child attempting the

Figure 22.1 A young child attempting the objective of jumping. The platform she is jumping from is wide and sturdy to allow her to engage in the targeted skill with confidence.

objective of jumping. The platform from which she is jumping is wide and sturdy to allow her to confidently engage in the targeted skill.

Developmental theorists support instruction that encourages children to explore and manipulate their environment in order to construct meaning (Piaget, 1952; Vygotsky, 1978). Individualizing instruction for each child in the class is the challenge faced by teachers providing early childhood adapted physical education in an integrated setting. An understanding of the child's developmental abilities (physically, socially, and cognitively) and the effect that a certain disability might play on this development must be considered.

Developmental Differences Between Preschoolers and Primary-Age Children

The cognitive and social developmental status of a four-year-old differs from that of a six-year-old. As children develop cognitively and socially, they incorporate their movement strategies in different ways. Teachers providing adapted physical education services must understand age-related developmental differences in order to construct appropriate learning environments for children who exhibit delays in one or more areas of learning.

Developmentally appropriate movement environments designed for preschool-age children (three to five years of age) differs from those planned for kindergarten and elementary school children (six to eight years of age). A "watered down" kindergarten curriculum presented to children in preschool is not appropriate. Games, activities, and equipment meaningful to a four-year-old might be of little interest to a seven-year-old, and vice versa. For example, preschool-age children love to experiment with speed, direction change, and space. Figure 22.2 (p. 390) shows a young girl maneuvering around obstacles placed on the activity floor. With a little creativity and imagination, teachers of early childhood physical education can create stimulating and motivating learning environments. A refrigerator box that has holes cut for climbing and hiding might lure a preschooler to explore and move for a long period of time. Preschool-age children are intrigued by new spaces and the opportunity to explore these seemingly simple environments. On the other hand, a seven-year-old might find these activities simplistic and boring. He or she would be much more interested and challenged by moving under

Figure 22.2 A young girl experimenting with speed and space. The objects on the floor become "challenges" as she moves around, between, and over the obstacles.

and through a parachute lifted by classmates. A child in first or second grade (six to seven years) might be challenged by activities that encourage a higher level of problem solving. They have more of an ability to reason and logically integrate thoughts than younger children do. For a three- or four-year-old, a parachute activity that includes anything more than moving the parachute up and down is often frightening and unpredictable. The National Association for the Education of Young Children (NAEYC) (Bredekamp & Copple, 1997) provides guidelines for developmentally appropriate practice in early childhood and discusses the differences between preschool- and primary-age children in their physical, social, cognitive, and language development. Teachers providing adapted physical education should keep in mind that the cognitive and social development of young children cannot be ignored when developing goals and objectives in the pychomotor domain. The interplay between each of these functional areas of learning and an individual child's development within each area must be considered when planning movement environments and instruction.

Developmental Considerations for Young Children With Disabilities

The effect of a disability on the communication, social, cognitive, or physical development of a child must be recognized prior to planning instruction. Knowing how a child's disability affects motor learning and performance is essential for the development of an appropriate physical education program. Young children with orthopedic impairments, for example, might begin independently exploring their physical environments by using a walker, wheelchair, or crutches but might also require accommodations in order to benefit from age-appropriate activities. Instructors should be aware of physical barriers that exist in the activity setting and design the environment in a way that encourages interactions with peers and equipment. Assistive devices that allow children with orthopedic impairments to initiate tasks that are both physically and intellectually challenging should be made available to these youngsters to promote independence. Young children with delays in social interaction, for example children with autism, will require modifications in the manner in which games and activities are introduced and delivered. Small- or large-group activities might be difficult for children with autism, and practicing motor skills might need to be completed in social environments that offer solitary or parallel play options. For young children with autism, interaction with others might not be the best instructional approach or least restrictive environment for learning new skills. On the other hand, children with intellectual disabilities often benefit from an environment that is consistent, predictable, and repetitive. As shown in figure 22.3, a predictable environment is set up in such a way that the young child knows where to throw the ball.

The cardboard box cut out into to the shape of a triangle also demonstrates ways in which cogni-

Figure 22.3 Consistent and predictable environments promote learning among children with disabilities.

tive concepts, such as shapes, can be embedded within the learning activity. Physical educators need to be aware of the characteristics of young children with disabilities and plan activities and environments accordingly.

Facilitating Communication in a Movement Lesson

Interacting with others requires some level of communication. Some young children with disabilities use speech and language to communicate, whereas others who are nonverbal might use alternative methods and strategies. Although speech or language impairment is considered the most prevalent disability category among preschool-age children, children with many different diagnoses might have communication needs (U.S. Department of Education, 2002). The movement setting, typically a motivating setting for young children, can be an ideal environment to enhance communication skills. Collaboration with classroom teachers and speech therapists will assist the early childhood physical educator in determining what communication goals and objectives can be integrated within an early childhood physical education setting. Further, collaboration might be necessary to determine which communication strategies work best for individual children according to their IEP goals and objectives.

Young children with disabilities or developmental delays who are verbal might use speech and language to communicate with peers and teachers. The movement setting is a natural place to incorporate concepts such as under, over, more, through, and around. To reinforce the meaning of movement concepts and model the use of speech, a physical educator should talk with children as they participate in each movement lesson. For example, as children are pretending to be in the jungle climbing over rocks (bolsters under mats) and jumping over cutout ants and snakes (taped to the floor) you might hear a teacher say, "I like the way everyone is jumping *over* the creatures in the jungle. Everyone find a creature and say OVER as we jump. Ready?" Prompting children to use the words to identify the concept (in this example "over") as they practice the skill (in this example "horizontal jump") reinforces the meaning of commonly taught concepts in early childhood and encourages children to use speech. Similarly, identifying shapes, colors, or equipment can become a natural part of an early childhood movement setting. The end of a class session or particular activity is an appropriate time to talk about what happened during that lesson. Asking children to reflect on the lesson or activity encourages them to speak, which can be a confidence booster. Talking about the snakes in the jungle or asking children to name the color of the scarf they used for a catching activity is a good strategy for prompting children to talk.

Children with speech and language delays or those who are nonverbal as a result of a particular disability or multiple disabilities might use augmentative and alternative systems to communicate (DiCarlo, Banajee, & Stricklin, 2000). Sign language and picture systems are nonverbal options used by teachers to communicate with young children. Sign language has become very popular as a method of communicating with very young children of all abilities. However, children with communication delays and those who are hard of hearing might benefit in particular. Physical educators not proficient in sign language should consult with classroom teachers, interpreters, or speech therapists to learn the signs used by young children in the classroom.

Picture systems can also be used in a movement setting to increase communication between the child and teacher. Young children with autism often have very sophisticated picture systems in place to assist with identifying activities, equipment, activity directions, and transitions. Picture systems can increase the probability that children with communication delays have the opportunity to be engaged in movement activities to the maximum extent possible. Having a child understand *what to do* and *when to do it* often decreases the time needed to manage unwanted behaviors. Pictures posted in the activity area or taped to pieces of equipment is a great communication strategy for all children. A sequence of pictures posted to a board or paper might be a functional method for communicating an activity or skill sequence to a child who is nonverbal.

Voice output devices are another method used by students to communicate with children who are nonverbal. A voice output system makes use of pictures and symbols along with prerecorded words and phrases (DiCarlo et al., 2000). Programming movement concepts, names of equipment or activities, and general statements provide a child with functional communication during physical education. For young children using a voice output system, a movement setting might reinforce practice with a new voice output device.

Stories and songs are also great methods for integrating movement and communication skills. Reading stories such as *The Balancing Girl* (Rabe,

1981) after a balancing lesson or *We're Going on a Bear Hunt* (Rosen, 1989) during a lesson emphasizing concepts such as under, over, and through might prompt a dialog. Asking children to communicate about the story as they are acting out parts of it or to tell the story using key words related to movements they used might promote verbal and nonverbal communication. Collaboration with classroom teachers to develop a reading list or vocabulary list for use in the classroom and movement setting is a functional strategy to address communication skills during movement lessons.

PLANNING FOR INSTRUCTION

Curriculum, including assessment and instruction, should be designed according to what is known about how children learn (Bredekamp & Rosegrant, 1992). What is age appropriate must be balanced with what is individually appropriate when designing physical education instruction for young children with disabilities or developmental delays. The three Cs of curriculum design— content, construction, and contact (Wessel & Zittel, 1995, 1998)—can serve as a guide for teachers of adapted physical education working toward attaining this balance for preschool- and primary-age children. First, the skills selected as instructional content must be considered. The instructional focus of a preschool physical education program might include community-based, neighborhood activities such as tricycle riding or pulling a wagon, whereas it might be appropriate to teach primary age children how to use a jump rope. The selection of appropriate content depends on how well the teacher has examined assessment information and understands the developmental differences between children of the same or similar chronological age. Second, construction of a teaching environment must be carefully planned. How the teacher of adapted physical education constructs the physical environment and how activities are introduced will differ for preschool- and primary-age children. Given the developmental premise that a three-year-old differs from a seven-year-old, the manner in which children of different ages interact in a physical environment will vary. Physical environments should be designed to promote interactions for the purpose of skill development. The organization of the physical environment, as well as how and when activities are introduced, must be considered. Finally, a critical consideration in planning for instruction

is the thought given to strategies that maximize the contact a young child has with equipment and peers versus their contact time with adults (teachers). Young children, regardless of developmental level, must be given the opportunity to explore their physical environment in order to develop impressions about their world. Young children with disabilities or developmental delays might require additional prompting during exploration so they are not denied opportunities to interact with equipment and peers. Instructors working with young children have the primary responsibility of promoting interactions within the movement environment as an alternative to providing direct instruction. Table 22.1 lists strategies physical educators can use to promote effective teacher and environmental interactions.

Organization of the curriculum might vary in different preschool and primary grade programs. Teachers of early childhood adapted physical education might choose to set up an instructional unit to focus on a certain fundamental skill area at a certain time of the year or to introduce skills in a particular sequence. For example, a specialist might design a unit that targets locomotor skills at the beginning of the school year. All games and activities during that unit will include the ongoing assessment and teaching of skills such as hopping, jumping, and galloping. Other instructors might choose to organize instructional material around themes (Clements, 1995). Often, the theme approach is used in collaboration with classroom teachers and the instructional concepts they are teaching. For example, a physical education *Day at the Zoo* or *Day at the Circus* provides children with the opportunity to practice different fundamental and motor fitness skills while interacting within a familiar theme. The curricular vehicle used to organize instruction (units or themes) often depends on the instructor's style of teaching and comfort level with this younger age group. The number of skill objectives taught and the time needed to learn each objective depends on the severity of the child's delay. However, what should never be compromised in any early childhood program is developmentally appropriate instruction for this young age group.

DEVELOPMENTALLY APPROPRIATE TEACHING APPROACHES

The following sections will deal with developmentally appropriate teaching approaches that should

Table 22.1   **Key Indicators in Assisting Teachers to Be Effective Facilitators**

Teacher interaction	Effective implementation
Teacher as observer	• Pursue student involvement. • Collect data on the needs and interests of the children. • Monitor activity environment to ensure success.
Teacher as facilitator	• Allow for choice making (assist when necessary). • Maximize opportunities to practice skills with child-directed repetition. • Maintain physical proximity and provide support as needed. • Model activity behavior, challenge present performance level, guide or redirect to alternative activity, if necessary. • Encourage development of positive social skills (helping, sharing, negotiating).
Environmental interaction	**Effective implementation**
Equipment	• Use familiar and meaningful objects mixed with novel challenging objects. • Arrange according to spatial and safety constraints to allow for active activity involvement. • Provide enough material for multiple trials without waiting.
Peers	• Create a motivating environment in which children can model appropriate skill performance, demonstrate alternative play activities, and encourage task persistence.

Adapted, by permission, from J.A. Wessel and L.L. Zittel, 1995, *SMART START: Preschool movement curriculum designed for children of all abilities* (Austin, TX: PRO-ED).

be used by teachers for planning and delivering adapted physical education programs for preschool- and primary-age children.

Preschool-Age Children

Preschool classrooms typically include 12 to 18 children, with one teacher and an assistant. Classrooms for young children with severe developmental delays and disabilities often have fewer children. One challenge in providing instruction for this age group is that many preschool programs have multiage classrooms, meaning that three-, four-, and five-year-olds are taught in the same class. As has been stated earlier in this chapter, planning instruction requires teachers to consider the developmental status of each child in the class, regardless of chronological age or how a disability might affect his or her development. Although ages and abilities might differ for children in the same class, the approach to intervention should remain similar for this age group. Developmentally appropriate practice in preschool physical education emphasizes the role of teachers as one of guide or facilitator. Teachers structure the environment with objectives in mind, for example throwing and kicking, and guide students toward these movement objectives. Environments are adapted to allow for several choices to meet the objectives and for maximum active participation (Avery, Boos,

Chepko, Gabbard, & Sanders, 1994). This style of teaching, known as child directed, differs from the teacher-directed style of instruction in which the instructor focuses on one task at a time and students move as a group from one activity to the next on the teacher's signal. It would be developmentally inappropriate to expect preschool children to respond to a teacher-directed format.

One example of a child-directed approach to early childhood education is known as Activity-Based Intervention (ABI) (Bricker & Cripe, 1992). ABI is designed to embed each child's IEP goals and objectives within activities that are naturally motivating to young children. Strategies can be used by teachers to design activity areas that are motivating for children and that encourage skill practice within the environment (see application example). Young children with disabilities or developmental delays benefit from structured movement environments that incorporate the following principles:

- Child-directed versus teacher-directed learning
- Opportunity for choice
- Self-initiated exploration
- Experience with novel and familiar equipment
- Exposure to peer models

APPLICATION EXAMPLE
Child-Directed, Teacher-Facilitated Lesson

Setting: The early childhood teacher has selected the following content objectives: body space awareness (under, over, through) and jump down.

Issue: What environmental construction would be appropriate to ensure child-directed learning?

Application: The goal in this setting is to minimize teacher interaction and maximize each child's interaction with peers and equipment. The teaching/learning environment should contain multiple opportunities to practice the lesson objectives. Children will choose equipment, and teachers will facilitate learning by providing verbal prompts, demonstrations, physical assistance, or redirection as necessary. The following equipment will prompt child-directed activity:

- Tunnels, cardboard boxes, and archways with scarves attached will prompt movement through and under.
- Bolsters covered with mats will prompt climbing over.
- Various platforms or steps with pictures of letters, numbers, smiley faces, or bugs will prompt stepping up and jumping down.

The following scenario highlights how each of these principles of best practice can be seen within one preschool physical education activity setting.

A structured movement environment should allow children to direct the process through which they manipulate the physical environment. **Child-directed learning** *is not* synonymous with

Emma and her classmates are on their way to physical education class, where they will soon discover that today is a wheel toy adventure. As they enter the activity area, they see tricycles, ride toys, wagons, and scooters scattered throughout the area. They also notice that jump ropes have been laid down to create pathways, cardboard trees have been spaced throughout the activity area, and arches held up with orange cones have been scattered around as obstacles to move under and through. As Mr. Sanchez welcomes the children into the activity environment, he announces, "Let's take a ride through the park today."

As the children scurry into the activity area to select their mode of transportation, Mr. Sanchez takes notice of Emma. He knows that Emma has autism, and on reviewing her IEP he is aware of that she has a gross motor IEP objective focused on pulling an object around obstacles, a social skill objective focused on initiating social interactions, and a communication objective focused on making verbal requests. He notices that Emma gets on a ride toy and begins to maneuver through the "park." As Emma crosses the room, she slows down to take notice of a teddy bear sitting in a wagon. Emma knows that she has been given a ride in a wagon before and decides that she will give the teddy bear a ride. Mr. Sanchez sees that Emma has directed her attention toward the wagon. Knowing that pulling an object is one of her objectives, he begins to interact with Emma, telling her how nice it is that she is giving the teddy bear a ride. Emma continues to pull her wagon through the pathways and around the cardboard trees. Mr. Sanchez is able to promote communication (another of Sara's IEP objectives) by suggesting that Emma ask Misha if she would like to go for ride. Once Misha is in the wagon, Mr. Sanchez suggests that Emma ask Misha where she would like to go. In this manner, Mr. Sanchez is facilitating work on Emma's IEP objective focused on initiating social interactions. Misha's request will encourage Emma to move through her physical environment encountering different inanimate obstacles in the park as well as other children moving with wheel toys.

free play. Teachers of preschool adapted physical education are responsible for designing environments to motivate children to initiate practice on skills outlined in their individualized plans. Interaction with equipment and practice on certain IEP objectives will be far more probable, and children will persist with the task much longer, if they initiate the interaction themselves. The teacher then becomes a facilitator within the movement environment. He or she follows the child's lead and promotes challenges based on the choices the child has made. The intensity with which children practice a skill or explore a new task depends on how interested they are in the task itself. The fact that Emma recognized the teddy bear sitting in the wagon and related that to her own previous experience was enough to interest her in the task and encourage further exploration. Mr. Sanchez was able to accommodate the interests and abilities of different children in his class by using multiple pieces of equipment and structuring his activity environment around one theme. The opportunity to view peer models and initiate social interactions was built into the structure of the activity. This activity design now gives Mr. Sanchez the opportunity to facilitate the children's viewing of peer models. For example, he may now prompt Erik to follow Emma while riding his tricycle.

Primary-Age Children

Primary grade classes, including kindergarten through third grade, typically vary in size in accordance with school policies. A newer approach in primary education is to incorporate multiage class groupings. In this structure, kindergarten and first-grade students may be educated in the same classroom. Designing developmentally appropriate instruction for this age group can only follow if a good assessment of individual abilities has been completed. As children grow and mature physically, discrepancies in movement abilities among children in the same age range might become more evident. However, young children with disabilities or developmental delays between six and eight years of age will have an interest in participating in the same physical activities as their same-age, typically developing counterparts. Planning instructional content for this age group should focus on fundamental movement skills (locomotion, object control, perceptual motor) and build on the rudimentary skills learned in preschool. For some children, this means refining skills and for others it will be a time to begin to integrate fundamental skills into organized games and activities.

Integrating fitness concepts within the curriculum will also become important. Regardless of the curricular focus, it is critical that children learn to move and enjoy movement at this age in order to increase the possibility that they will continue to be physically active as they mature.

Designing instructional settings for primary-age students of differing abilities should combine movement exploration and guided-discovery techniques with specific skill practice. With an exploration style of teaching, the teacher selects the instructional materials to be used and designates the area to be explored (Pangrazzi, 1998). Rather than having the environment already set up with embedded goals and objectives, students choose a piece of equipment and figure out ways to interact with the equipment. Teachers might offer directives such as, "Get a hoop and see how many ways you can make it spin." This style of teaching takes advantage of children's desire to move and explore. It emphasizes self-discovery, which is a necessary and important part of learning, and allows children to note variations in movement forms and equipment usage. However, when using this teaching style, the instructor should avoid praising students for their creative movements too early because this might lead to imitative or noncreative behavior (Pangrazzi, 1998).

Guided discovery is used when there is a predetermined choice or result that the teacher wants students to discover (Pangrazzi, 1998). With this approach to teaching, students are presented with many methods to perform a task and then are asked to choose the method that seems to be most efficient or that works best. Students with disabilities might often find that their movement choice might differ from what typically developing peers choose as the appropriate movement form. This discovery reinforces the idea that just because a movement form is different does not mean it is incorrect.

Children should also have the opportunity to use fundamental skills in low-organization type games. Equipment and instruction should be modified, if necessary, to accommodate the physical, sensory, behavioral, or cognitive abilities of each child in the class. The activity environment should be organized to accommodate the varying learning styles (visual, kinesthetic) of children in the class (Coker, 1996). General principles guiding the design of developmentally appropriate adapted physical education lessons for primary grade students include:

- different teaching styles used to individualize instruction for the variety of learning styles (visual, auditory) present in one classroom,

- varied equipment (e.g., different size rackets) available to incorporate student choice,

- rule flexibility in tasks to be completed to encourage creativity and problem solving,

- varied classroom designs (activity stations, small group, large group), and

- the opportunity for peer observation and interaction.

The following scenario provides an example of how the principles can be used to accommodate children in one first-grade classroom.

Louis is selected as the line leader by his classmates as they prepare to leave for physical education. Ms. Brooks greets the children outside of their classroom and walks with them to the gym. As they walk together, Ms. Brooks explains to the children they will continue working on striking activities today. Once inside the gym, the children see a familiar sight. Ms. Brooks has set up five activity stations, each with a different task to complete. Ms. Brooks asks the children, "What type of implements do we use for striking?"

The children's responses to Ms. Brooks' question are varied. As they look around the gym they are reminded of some answers. "We strike with bats," says Claire. "We can use Styrofoam rackets," yells Mia. "I like the hockey sticks," exclaims Jose. Ms. Brooks explains that everyone will have an opportunity to use all of the implements today as they spend time in each activity station. She informs the children they will select an implement out of the station bin and begin practice at one station until they hear the sound of the drum. At that time they will put their implements back into the bin and follow the floor arrows to the next station, select their new implement, and begin the task. Ms. Brooks has asked Louis to begin at the racket and balloon station. As Ms. Brooks designates other stations for children in the class, Louis turns to Sammy and whispers, "That's my favorite!" Ms. Brooks is familiar with Louis' IEP and has written his gross motor objectives. Striking is a focus for Louis in addition to working on increasing his static and dynamic balance. He will be working on both today. Louis has spina bifida and uses braces on his legs. He ambulates slowly but is proud of the fact that over the summer months, before first grade began, he stopped using his walker for most activities. The activities that Louis will participate in today are functional for him. He will work on striking, just like the rest of his classmates, but this activity will also address his balance goals as he swings different implements and moves among stations.

Ms. Brooks has constructed enough activity stations to accommodate this class of 28 children and given them the opportunity to explore different movements with different striking implements. The equipment used to accomplish the skill objective in a few of the stations has been changed (e.g., some stations have rackets whereas others might have bats), but for the most part the students are familiar with the activity structure and have been practicing their striking for several classes now. This activity environment allows Ms. Brooks to individualize instruction, provide specific skill feedback to children at different times, and modify equipment and tasks to accommodate the learning abilities of all the children in the class. Ms. Brooks knows that in her next period first-grade class she will see Micah. He has a severe mental disability, and Ms. Brooks will use a "location station" approach for him. This means that she will use the same environmental structure to practice striking, but when the drum sounds Micah will remain in the same balloon-striking station, and his cross-age peer model will assist him in selecting another implement to strike the balloon. The rest of the class will rotate stations. All of this has been planned by Ms. Brooks because she is familiar with the children she teaches and their ability level. So, for now, she admires Louis' stability as she watches him swing the racket to hit the suspended balloon to his classmate Bryce. As Bryce tracks the balloon and gets ready to hit it back, he exclaims, "Here it comes, Louis!"

ACTIVITIES

Developmentally appropriate activities for preschool- and primary-age students are those selected, designed, sequenced, and modified to maximize learning and active participation. Fundamental motor skills and patterns form the basis for higher-level movement sequences and skills and should thus be emphasized in early childhood motor programs. Activities that develop and promote body awareness, perceptual motor skills, communication, and other academic abilities should also be incorporated into the program. Using the strategies presented in this chapter, physical educators can select games and activities to meet IEP goals and objectives that are both age and developmentally appropriate and presented in a way that fosters child-directed interactions. The *SMART START* (1995) and the *I CAN Primary Skills K-3* (1998), both created by Wessel and Zittel, provide many games and activities that can be used in early childhood physical education programs and that can be easily adapted to youngsters with unique needs.

SUMMARY

The increase in early childhood motor programs has brought new challenges to physical educators. Children as young as three years old might, at the discretion of states, be included in adapted physical education programs designed to meet their unique needs. Although some physical educators might have experience in working with older students with developmental delays or disabilities, the opportunity to work with young children presents new and exciting challenges. This chapter has provided information to assist teachers of early childhood adapted physical education by suggesting strategies and tools necessary for the development of appropriate goals, objectives, and activities for young children with unique physical education needs. Specifically, information related to assessment, program planning, and program implementation has been highlighted. With an understanding of what constitutes developmentally appropriate intervention, teachers of adapted physical education should be able to positively influence the movement abilities of young children. Intervention that is planned and delivered in settings that challenge and reinforce motor learning in a positive manner provide young children with opportunities to experience success and enjoy movement.

REFERENCES

Avery, M., Boos, S., Chepko, S., Gabbard, C., & Sanders, S. (1994). *Developmentally appropriate practice in movement programs for young children ages 3-5.* Reston, VA: Council on Physical Education for Children.

Bredekamp, S., & Copple, C. (1997). *Developmentally appropriate practice in early childhood programs (revised).* Washington, DC: National Association for the Education of Young Children.

Bredekamp, S., & Rosegrant, T. (Eds.). (1992). *Reaching potentials: Appropriate curriculum and assessment for young children* (Vol. 1). Washington, DC: National Association for the Education of Young Children.

Bricker, D., & Pretti-Frontczak, K. (1996). *AEPS measurement for three to six years.* Baltimore, MD: Paul H. Brooks.

Bricker, D., & Woods Cripe, J.J. (1992). *An activity-based approach to early intervention.* Baltimore, MD: Paul H. Brooks.

Brigance, A. (1991). *Brigance diagnostic inventory of early development.* Billerica, MA: Curriculum Associates, Inc.

Clements, R. (1995). *My neighborhood movement challenges.* Oxon Hill, MD: AAHPERD Publications.

Coker, C. A. (1996). Accommodating students' learning styles in physical education. *Journal of Physical Education, Recreation and Dance,* (67), 66-68.

DiCarlo, C., Banajee, M., & Stricklin, S. (2000). Embedding augmentative communication within early childhood classrooms. *Young Exceptional Children,* 3(3), 18-26.

Federal Register (1999, March 12). *Assistance to states for the education of children with disabilities and the early intervention program for infants and toddlers with disabilities.* 34 CFR Parts 300-303. Vol. 64, No. 48. Washington D.C. Department of Education.

Folio, M.R., & Fewell, R. (2000). *Peabody developmental motor scales-2.* Austin, TX: Pro-Ed.

Johnson-Martin, N., Attermeier, M.A., Hacker, B.J. (1990). *The Carolina curriculum for preschoolers with special needs.* Baltimore, MD: Paul H. Brooks.

Linder, T. (1993). *Transdisciplinary play-based assessment.* Baltimore, MD: Paul H. Brooks.

Lynch, E., & Struewing, N. (2001). Children in context: Portfolio assessment in the inclusive early childhood classroom. *Young Exceptional Children,* 5(1), 2-10.

McLean, M., Wolery, M., & Bailey, D. (2004). *Assessing infants, toddlers and preschoolers with special needs.* Upper Saddle River, New Jersey: Pearson Merrill Prentice Hall.

Pangrazzi, R.P. (1998). *Dynamic physical education for elementary school children.* Needham Heights, MA: Allyn and Bacon.

Piaget, J. (1952). *The origins of intelligence in children.* New York: International Universities Press.

Rabe, B. (1981). *The balancing girl.* New York: Penguin Books.

Rosen, M. (1989). *We're going on a bear hunt.* New York: Simon & Schuster Children's Publishing.

Ulrich, D.A. (2000). *Test of motor development* (2nd ed.). Austin, TX: Pro-Ed.

U.S. Department of Education. (2002). *Twenty-fourth annual report to congress on the implementation of the Individuals with Disabilities Education Act.* www.ed.gov.

Vygotsky, L. (1978). *Mind in society: The development of higher psychological processes.* Cambridge, MA: Harvard University Press.

Wessel, J.A., & Zittel, L.L. (1998). *I CAN primary skills: K-3.* Austin, TX: Pro-Ed.

Wessel, J.A., & Zittel, L.L. (1995). *Smart Start: Preschool movement curriculum designed for children of all abilities.* Austin, TX: Pro-Ed.

Zittel, L.L. (1994). Gross motor assessment of preschool children with special needs: Instrument selection considerations. *Adapted Physical Activity Quarterly,* 11, 245-260.

WRITTEN RESOURCES

Clements, R.L. (1995). *My neighborhood movement challenges.* Oxon Hill, MD: AAHPERD Publications.

This source contains a comprehensive overview of movement narratives and provides sample narratives for commonly used themes to teach movement skills and concepts.

Landy, J., & Burridge, K. (2000). *Motor skills and movement station lesson plans for young children.* West Nyack, NY: The Center for Applied Research in Education.

The program is a motor skills program for teachers, professionals, and parents teaching fundamental motor skills to children who have coordination difficulties.

Linder, T. (1999). *Storybook activities for young children: Read, play, and learn.* Baltimore, Maryland: Paul H. Brookes Publishing.

This play-based, storybook-oriented curriculum allows teachers to incorporate skills in all domains of learning while providing a motivating experience for the young learner.

McCall, R., & Craft, D. (2000). *Moving with a purpose: Developing programs for preschoolers of all abilities.* Champaign, IL: Human Kinetics.

This resource is designed to provide information to teachers responsible for structuring movement programs for preschool-age children. Games and activities are presented. A section is also devoted to children with special needs.

Winders, P. (1997). *Gross motor skills in children with Down syndrome.* Bethesda, MD: Woodbine House.

This resource addresses the physical development of children with Down syndrome and provides guidelines for promoting gross motor development. Activities and strategies are provided.

AUDIOVISUAL RESOURCES

Pica, R., & Gardzina, R. (1990). *More music for moving and learning.* Champaign, IL: Human Kinetics.

This is a set of six audiocassettes with 62 songs that focus on typical early childhood themes. A great package for both the preschool and primary years.

ELECTRONIC RESOURCES

National Association for the Education of Young Children: www.naeyc.org.

This Web site serves as the primary site for resources and "best practices" for the education of young children.

Activities for Individuals With Unique Needs

Part IV includes separate chapters on physical fitness (chapter 23); rhythms and dance (chapter 24); aquatics (chapter 25); team sports (chapter 26); individual, dual, and adventure sports (chapter 27); winter sports (chapter 28); and the enhancement of wheelchair sport performance (chapter 29). Although the content of each chapter is influenced by the nature of the activities discussed, there are several common threads. To the extent relevant and appropriate, the chapters identify skills, lead-up activities, modifications, and variations associated with activity areas. In many instances, these include modifications and variations used in established organized sport programs. In fact, some chapters provide information on organized sport programs. Chapters provide information helpful for the enhancement of education in a variety of settings, including inclusive settings.

The importance of the use of wheelchairs in physical education and sport is recognized by including an entire chapter (chapter 29) on ways to enhance performance when using wheelchairs. Although this section is last in the book, it is of great importance because it applies much information presented earlier to the content associated with physical education and sport. This chapter focuses on how the content of the program is adapted or modified to meet unique needs. It is this part of the book that will serve as a great resource to service providers on the job because it provides answers on how they might modify an activity for a youngster with unique needs to be active, physically educated, and working toward self-actualization.

Health-Related Physical Fitness and Physical Activity

Francis X. Short

Two teachers, Mr. Barnett, a social studies teacher, and Ms. Novak, a physical education teacher, were in the teachers' lounge.

"What are you working on?" Mr. Barnett asked.

"I'm just planning some fitness activities for my third-period class."

"Isn't that the class with the students in wheelchairs? How are they doing? Are the athletes in the class treating them okay?"

"Well," said Ms. Novak with a smile, "some of my students who use wheelchairs *are* athletes, but what I do in my class is more health related than sport related."

"Health related? Is that really necessary? I mean, I haven't heard of too many junior high school students dying of heart attacks lately."

"Well, that's right, but good fitness and physical activity habits should be established early, and besides, health-related fitness, especially for kids with disabilities, is not just about reducing the risk of disease. Having good health-related fitness also means having the independence to perform important day-to-day skills, like pushing a wheelchair uphill or even getting dressed. In fact, fitness might actually be more important to students with disabilities than it is for the general student body."

"By the way," continued Ms. Novak, *"your* 'general student body' looks like it could stand some health-related fitness."

"Hey . . ." said Mr. Barnett while sucking in his stomach.

The relations among physical fitness, physical activity, and health are explored in this chapter. We pay particular attention to how physical activity can be used to promote health-related physical fitness. Although some examples of modifications for students with disabilities are provided, the chapter is written primarily from a "noncategorical" perspective; that is, most of the information is generic and not specific to any one category of disability. Disability-specific fitness information can be found in other chapters of this book.

DEFINITIONS

Physical activity is defined as any bodily movement produced by skeletal muscle resulting in a substantial increase in resting energy expenditure (Bouchard & Shephard, 1994). Bouchard and Shephard (1994), citing seven categories of physical activity (exercise, sport, training, play, dance, work, and domestic chores), suggested that patterns of physical activity could be described by manipulating the variables of frequency (how often), intensity (how hard), and duration (how long).

Health has been defined as "a human condition with physical, social, and psychological dimensions, each characterized on a continuum with positive and negative poles. Positive health is associated with a capacity to enjoy life and to withstand challenges; it is not merely the absence of disease. Negative health is associated with morbidity and, in the extreme, with premature mortality" (Bouchard & Shephard, 1994, p. 84). Winnick and Short (1999) suggested that in broad terms health can be categorized and include physiological or functional aspects. **Physiological health** relates to the organic well-being of the individual. Indices of physiological health include traits or capacities associated with well-being, absence of a disease or a condition, or low risk of developing a disease or condition. **Functional health** relates to the physical capability of the individual. Indices of functional health include the ability to perform important tasks independently and the ability to independently sustain the performance of those tasks (see figure 23.1).

Caspersen, Powell, and Christenson (1985) defined **physical fitness** as a "set of attributes that people have or achieve that relates to the ability to perform physical activity" (p. 129). The components of physical fitness can be categorized into two groups: one related to health and the other to skills that are necessary for athletic ability. **Heath-related physical fitness** "refers to those components of fitness that are affected by habitual physical activity and relate to health status. It is defined as a state characterized by (a) an ability to perform and sustain daily activities and (b) demonstration of traits or capacities that are associated with a low risk of premature

Figure 23.1 Musculoskeletal functioning (strength, endurance, and flexibility) can contribute to functional health.

development of diseases and conditions related to movement" (modified from Pate, 1988). Most experts agree that the components of health-related fitness include aerobic functioning, body composition, muscular endurance, muscular strength, and flexibility (the latter three are sometimes referred to as musculoskeletal functioning). The components of skill-related physical fitness (also known as performance-related fitness) generally include agility, balance, coordination, speed, power, and reaction time. In this chapter primary attention is given to development of health-related aspects of physical fitness, but teachers and coaches are reminded that developing the skill-related components is also necessary to foster certain types of physical activity (e.g., sport performance).

As these definitions suggest, relations exist among health-related physical fitness, physical activity, and health. These relations are depicted in figure 23.2. In essence, each of these areas can influence, and be influenced by, each of the others. Increases in physical activity and in physical fitness can both contribute to posi-

tive health status. Increases in physical activity usually result in improved physical fitness, whereas improved physical fitness will likely affect the potential types (exercise, sport, etc.) and patterns (frequency, intensity, duration) of physical activity available to the individual. Finally, reductions in health status (i.e., negative health) typically reduce participation in physical activity and restrict progress in physical fitness. The relations among physical fitness, physical activity, and health are explored further in the following sections.

PHYSICAL FITNESS AND HEALTH

Physical fitness has long been viewed as an important vehicle for improved sport performance. From the ancient Greeks to the modern athlete, sportspersons have trained their fitness to improve their athletic performance. Often, the relation between fitness development and improved sport performance is obvious, and

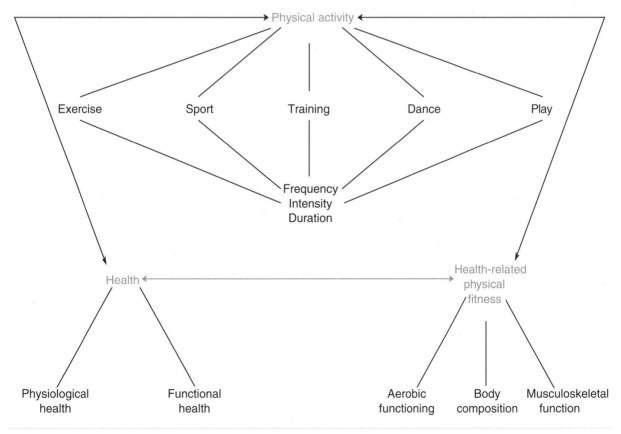

Figure 23.2   Relations among physical activity, health, and health-related fitness.

Adapted, by permission, from F.X. Short, J. McCubbin, and G. Frey, 1999, Cardiorespiratory endurance and body composition. In *The Brockport physical fitness training guide,* edited by J.P. Winnick and F.X. Short (Champaign, IL: Human Kinetics), 24.

sometimes it is dramatic. The relation between physical fitness and health, however, is usually less obvious. Many nonathletes have attempted to get into shape because of the common belief that being fit is "good for you," without really knowing *how* it is "good for you."

Since the 1980s, researchers have been working to improve their understanding of the relations between physical fitness and health. We now know, for instance, that acceptable levels of aerobic capacity are associated with a reduced risk (in adults) of hypertension, coronary heart disease, obesity, diabetes, some forms of cancer, and other health problems. For these reasons, measures of aerobic capacity are thought to be linked to indices of physiological health, as previously defined. A similar relation exists between body composition and physiological health. Obesity has been associated with an increased risk of diabetes, coronary heart disease, high blood pressure, arthritis, and several forms of cancer. Obesity has also been linked to higher rates of all-cause mortality and to increased risk factors for heart disease in children.

Researchers have had a more difficult time establishing relations between muscular strength or muscular endurance and physiological health (although relations between strength and low back pain and osteoporosis are suspected). Still, there is a logical relation between muscular strength and endurance and functional health. Clearly, minimal levels of strength and endurance are necessary to perform many activities of daily living and to participate in leisure activities. Similarly, a logical relation exists between flexibility and functional health—that is, having sufficient range of motion in the joints to perform important daily activities. There is also some evidence that hamstring flexibility is linked to low back pain in some people.

Over the years, several studies have compared the physical fitness performance of youth with disabilities to that of youth without disabilities. With few exceptions, research using subjects with intellectual disabilities, cerebral palsy, spinal cord injuries, and visual impairments has found that the fitness performance of youngsters with disabilities is below that of their peers without disabilities. To the extent that the fitness of youngsters with disabilities falls below acceptable levels, it is probable that students with disabilities are at greater risk for the health concerns mentioned previously than are students without disabilities.

PHYSICAL ACTIVITY AND HEALTH-RELATED PHYSICAL FITNESS

People with or without disabilities generally can improve their health-related physical fitness through physical activity. In fact, despite the fact that many children and youth with disabilities have levels of fitness below those of youngsters without disabilities, the fitness of children and youth with disabilities ordinarily responds very favorably to increases in physical activity. This section of the chapter focuses on improving the health-related physical fitness of students with disabilities through physical activity. The first two subsections deal with the importance of personalizing physical fitness and how physical activity can be measured and arranged into patterns to achieve fitness objectives. The third subsection addresses physical activity recommendations for promoting each of the components of health-related fitness, and the final subsection discusses a few general considerations for fitness development.

Personalizing Physical Fitness

When programming for students with disabilities, the physical educator must first ask, "Physical fitness for what purpose?" Objectives vary widely from student to student. Fitness objectives for a student with a disability can be influenced by several factors, including present level of physical fitness, functional motor abilities, physical maturity, age, nature of the disability (and how the disability affects activity selection), student interests or activity preferences, and availability of equipment and facilities. In an adapted physical education program, objectives can range from fitness for the execution of rudimentary movements (e.g., sitting, reaching, creeping) to fitness for the execution of specialized movements (sports skills, recreational activities, vocational tasks) to fitness for the pursuit of a healthier lifestyle (better daily functioning and reduced risk of acquiring diseases or conditions).

With the help of the student, as appropriate, teachers should design personalized fitness programs. In personalizing physical fitness, certain elements of the fitness program are emphasized for each student. For instance, for each student the teacher might ask the following questions:

- What are the highest priority fitness needs for this student (including any health-related concerns) and what would be the objectives of the program (or personalized "profile")?

- Which components of health-related or skill-related physical fitness should be targeted for development given the identified needs and objectives? Which areas of the body will be trained?

- Which tests will be used to measure physical fitness for this student, and what standards will be adopted for evaluative purposes?

The Brockport Physical Fitness Test, for instance, provides opportunities for teachers to personalize the test according to the needs and abilities of the student. Test users have the option of adopting a set of tests and standards identified for students with a particular disability or modifying the recommended test battery and standards based on the unique fitness needs of the student.

Patterns of Physical Activity

Once the objectives of the personalized program have been established and baseline testing has been conducted, the teacher must arrange "patterns" of physical activity for the student in such a way that fitness is improved and objectives attained. As shown in figure 23.2, patterns of physical activity can be arranged by manipulating the variables of frequency, intensity, and duration of various types of activity (e.g., games, sports, exercise, and dance).

Monitoring appropriate levels of frequency and duration is fairly straightforward. Frequency generally is expressed in terms of the number of times a day or days in a week that activity is performed (e.g., three to five days per week; twice a day for five to seven days per week). Duration is simply monitored by timing the length of the activity period (6 to 10 seconds, 20 to 40 minutes) or counting the number of repetitions of an exercise. Duration of activity also can be measured by the number of steps one might take as counted by a pedometer.

Tracking intensity, particularly in a field setting, however, is somewhat less objective and sometimes a bit more difficult. Different indices of intensity are used with different components of fitness. For instance, for muscular strength and endurance, intensity could be estimated from the degree of exertion or the amount of resistance (e.g., a certain percentage of the maximum weight that can be lifted one time). In the case of flexibility, intensity could be a function of perceived discomfort or length of a stretch (e.g., touching toes rather than ankles). The intensity of activity selected to improve either aerobic functioning or body composition might be measured by heart rate, ratings of perceived exertion (RPE), or estimated metabolic equivalents (METs) (see table 23.1). Heart rate monitors are becoming increasingly popular in public schools and provide an easily determined, objective measure of intensity. Pulse rate taken manually by either teachers or students provides an inexpensive alternative to the heart rate monitor. Maximal heart rate is usually estimated from the simple formula 220 − age (e.g., the estimated maximal heart rate for a 10-year-old is 210).

RPE provides a subjective, but nevertheless valid, measure of intensity in which participants

Table 23.1 Estimating Activity Intensity by Three Methods

Intensity	Method		
	% maximal heart rate	RPE	METs
Very light	<35	<10	<2
Light	35-54	10-11	2-4
Moderate	55-69	12-13	5-7
Vigorous	70-89	14-16	8-10
Very vigorous	>90	17-19	>10
Maximal	100	20	12

Adapted from U.S. Department of Health and Human Services. *Physical Activity and Health: A Report of the Surgeon General.* Atlanta: U.S. Department of Health and Human Services, Centers for Disease Control and Prevention, National Center for Chronic Disease Prevention and Health Promotion.

gauge effort by sensations, such as perceived changes in heart rate, breathlessness, sweating, muscle fatigue, and lactate accumulation. Participants then translate these sensations to a numerical scale, such as one suggested by Borg (1998) and shown in figure 23.3. Borg's RPE scale has good utility for adapted physical education programs and has been used successfully in research projects employing subjects with intellectual disabilities, asthma, spinal cord injuries, and cerebral palsy.

6	No exertion at all
7	Extremely light
8	
9	Very light
10	
11	Light
12	
13	Somewhat hard
14	
15	Hard (heavy)
16	
17	Very hard
18	
19	Extremely hard
20	Maximal exertion

Borg RPE scale
© Gunnar Borg, 1970, 1985, 1994, 1998

Figure 23.3 Borg's ratings of perceived exertion scale.

Reprinted, by permission, from G.A. Borg, 1998, *Borg's perceived exertion and pain scales* (Champaign, IL: Human Kinetics), 47.

MET values represent multiples of resting energy expenditure. For instance, when an individual participates in an activity that is four METs, the body is using four times more oxygen than it does at rest. Estimated MET values, often published in charts in exercise physiology and fitness books, reflect an "average" person's energy expenditure for a particular activity (e.g., running a 10-minute mile = 10.2 METs, playing basketball = 8.3 METs). In adapted physical education programs, the use of METs to estimate intensity has the most relevance for youngsters without physical disabilities (e.g., mental retardation, learning disabilities, visual impairments) and the least relevance for those students who have physical disabilities (cerebral palsy, spinal cord injuries, and amputations)

because the theoretical "average" person does not have a physical disability.

Physical Activity Recommendations for Health-Related Physical Fitness

Recommendations for developing health-related fitness follow under the headings aerobic functioning, body composition, muscular strength and endurance, and flexibility and range of motion. Adjustments to those recommendations for youngsters with disabilities, as well as some suggested activities, are also included.

Aerobic Functioning

Aerobic functioning refers to that component of physical fitness that permits one to sustain large-muscle, dynamic, moderate-to-high intensity activity for prolonged periods of time. Aerobic functioning can be estimated by measuring aerobic capacity (an index of physiological health) and/or aerobic behavior (an index of functional health). Aerobic capacity refers to the highest rate of oxygen that can be consumed by exercising and ordinarily is the preferred measure of aerobic functioning. Field tests of aerobic capacity include a 1-mile run and the 20-meter multistage shuttle run (i.e., the PACER). Estimating aerobic capacity in a field setting, however, is not always possible for students with disabilities because the estimates are based on equations developed for people without disabilities. Aerobic behavior provides an alternative measure of aerobic functioning and refers to the ability to sustain physical activity of a specific intensity for a particular duration. Field tests of aerobic behavior include measuring the length of time one can exercise in a target heart rate zone (e.g., the Target Aerobic Movement Test). Aerobic behavior can be measured in any youngster who can sufficiently elevate the heart rate through physical activity.

Frequency, intensity, and duration guidelines for improving the aerobic functioning of school-age youngsters are summarized in table 23.2. In essence, children are encouraged to be active on all, or most, days of the week for at least 30 to 60 minutes each day. The intensity of activity ranges from "deemphasized" for younger children to moderate (and sometimes vigorous) for older children. Adolescents may reduce their frequencies and durations somewhat in exchange for higher levels of intensity (moderate to vigorous).

Table 23.2   **Guidelines for Developing Aerobic Functioning**

Group	Frequency	Intensity	Duration
Adolescents (13-17)	3-5 days per week	55-90% HR max (~115-180 beats/min) 12-16 RPE 5-10 METs	20-60 min per day (accumulated: >10 min per bout)
Older children (10-12)	4-7 days per week	55-70% HR max* (~115-145 beats/min) 12-13 RPE* 5-7 METs*	30-60+ min per day (accumulated, intermittent)
Younger children (6-9)	4-7 days per week	Deemphasized; participation is encouraged	30-60+ min per day (accumulated, intermittent)
Adjustments for youngsters with disabilities	No change unless disability can be exacerbated by regular activity	Reduce as a function of fitness level; adjust THRZ for individuals using arms-only activity and for individuals with SCI quadriplegia	Accumulate more intermittent activity or reduce total time if necessary

* These values represent moderate physical activity; ideally, this level will be exceeded to vigorous levels at times.

Reprinted, by permission, from F.X. Short, J. McCubbin, and G. Frey, 1999, Cardiorespiratory endurance and body composition. In *The Brockport physical fitness training guide,* edited by J.P. Winnick and F.X. Short (Champaign, IL: Human Kinetics), 24.

Higher levels of intensity are usually necessary to improve aerobic capacity.

Many youngsters with disabilities can meet these guidelines without modification. Some adjustments, however, are appropriate in certain situations. Ordinarily, frequency will not have to be adjusted; as with students without disabilities, students with disabilities should be encouraged to participate regularly in aerobic activity. Greater periods of recovery from physical activity, however, might be necessary for youngsters with neuromuscular diseases, arthritis, or other disabilities requiring greater periods of rest. Similarly, youngsters with disabilities should strive to attain the same duration guidelines as their peers without disabilities. When students with disabilities cannot maintain continuous activity for the recommended length of time, the first alternative would be to accumulate more intermittent activity (i.e., shorter bouts of activity more often to achieve the recommendations) before electing to reduce the duration guidelines.

Adjustments to intensity will likely be necessary when youngsters have a history of inactivity. For these students, activity might be more appropriately conducted at lighter intensities, particularly if the frequency and duration guidelines can be achieved. Intensity should be gradually increased over time. If intensity is being measured via heart rate, it will be necessary to adjust the target heart rate zone (THRZ) for students who use their arms

to propel wheelchairs, for those who engage in other "arms-only" forms of activity, or for those with spinal cord injuries (SCI). Subtracting 10 beats per minute from the THRZ values given in table 23.2 constitutes a reasonable adjustment in intensity for arms-only activity.

A range of activities can be used to meet the aerobic functioning guidelines in table 23.2. Teachers should select age-appropriate developmental activities for children (ages 6 to 12). Included in this group might be jump rope activities, relay races, obstacle courses, climbing activities (e.g., jungle gyms or monkey bars), active lead-up games, active games of low organization, and rhythmic activities including creative dance and "moving to music."

Adolescents (ages 13 to 18) generally are ready for more sport-related activities and should be exposed to activities that have a lifetime emphasis. Appropriate activities might include fast walking, jogging or running, swimming, skiing, racket sports, basketball, soccer, skating, cycling, rowing, hiking, parcourse (fitness trail) activities, and aerobic dance or aerobic aquatics.

Many youngsters with disabilities can participate in most of the activities listed in the previous paragraphs, although some modifications might be necessary. As with all good teaching in physical education, teachers should "start with the student" and select, modify, or design appropriate activities rather than start with an activity and hope that it is somehow appropriate for the student. Youngsters in wheelchairs or those who are blind often require alternative activities (or activity modification) to meet the aerobic functioning guidelines. Some ideas for youngsters using wheelchairs might include slalom courses, free wheeling (e.g., "jogging" in a wheelchair), speed bag work (i.e., rhythmically striking an overhead punching bag), arm ergometry, seated aerobics, and active wheelchair sports (e.g., sled hockey, basketball, track, rugby, and team handball). Students with visual impairments might participate in activities such as calisthenics, rowing, stationary or tandem cycling, wrestling or judo, step aerobics, aerobic dance, swimming, or track.

Body Composition

Body composition shows the percentage of one's body weight that is fat versus the percentage that is muscle, bone, connective tissue, and fluids, or indicates the appropriateness of one's body weight to height. Skinfold measures can be used in field settings to estimate percent of body fat, whereas body mass index (a weight to height ratio) is often used to assess the appropriateness of one's weight. This section of the chapter will focus on weight-loss strategies associated with physical fitness. When people fall outside the appropriate range of body composition, most do so because they are too fat (or are too heavy for their heights). Readers should remember, however, that some youngsters might be outside the healthy range because they are too lean (or too light for their heights). Excessive leanness is also a health-related concern. When physical educators believe that a student's excessive leanness might be a result of an inadequate diet, an eating disorder, or the possible existence of a medical condition, the school's medical staff should be consulted.

Strategies for improving body composition (i.e., for weight loss) are similar to those associated with aerobic functioning. In most cases, weight-loss recommendations can be achieved by following the guidelines for improved aerobic functioning (see table 23.2, p. 407). In fact, there would be little reason to ever adjust those recommendations for achieving weight-loss in children. In the case of adolescents (and adults), however, there may be circumstances in which weight loss might be a more important goal than improved aerobic functioning. In such cases, the aerobic functioning guidelines could be adjusted slightly to meet weight-loss recommendations for adoles-

cents (and adults). These weight-loss recommendations would be to participate in moderate-level activity, four to seven days per week, for 30 to 60 or more minutes per day. When compared to the aerobic functioning guidelines for adolescents, the recommendations for weight loss generally are less intense but more frequent and, at least potentially, for longer durations. Another weight-loss recommendation is to attain a minimal energy expenditure of at least 1,000 kilocalories (kcals) per week. If MET estimates are available, kilocalories can be calculated from the following equation:

$$\text{kcals/min} = \text{METs} \times 3.5 \times \text{body weight (kg)} / 200$$

As mentioned earlier in the chapter, published MET estimates might not be particularly appropriate for youngsters with physical disabilities. This is because of differences in mechanical efficiency that might exist between participants without disabilities and those with physical disabilities. Estimating kilocalorie expenditure for students with physical disabilities, however, is still possible. Let us say that Eddie is a 14-year-old, 150-pound (68-kilogram) boy with spastic paraplegia. He uses forearm crutches to walk and run. He enjoys playing floor hockey, and his dad devised a way to attach the blade of a floor hockey stick to the end of one of his crutches so that he could play in his regular physical education class. Because there are no MET estimates for youngsters with cerebral palsy playing floor hockey with forearm crutches (and a modified stick), energy cost will have to be estimated in a different way. Eddie's teacher, for instance, could determine Eddie's average heart rate during the game. (This most easily could be done with a monitor but could also be done by taking manual pulse rates periodically.) If Eddie averaged 155 beats per minute over the course of the game, he would have been working at about 75 percent of his maximal heart rate (220 − 14 = 206; 155 / 206 = 0.75). By consulting table 23.1, the teacher can see that Eddie is at the low end of "vigorous" activity. The low end of vigorous intensity roughly corresponds to 8 METs (the range for vigorous intensity is 8 to 10 METs). If 8 METs are used to estimate the energy cost of Eddie's activity, his energy expenditure in kilocalories per minute would be:

$$\text{kcals/min} = 8 \times 3.5 \times 68 / 200 = 9.5$$

To expend 1,000 kilocalories for the week, Eddie will need to participate in floor hockey (or some other 8-MET activity) for 105 minutes (1,000 / 9.5

= 105). If he plays twice a week, he could meet the 1,000 kilocalories goal if he played for 53 minutes each time (105 / 2 = 52.5), or he could play three times per week for 35 minutes each time to reach 1,000 kilocalories. Less intense activities will require greater frequencies and/or durations to meet the goal.

Muscular Strength and Endurance

Muscular strength is the ability of the muscles to produce a maximal level of force over a short period of time. We can measure strength by using dynamometers (e.g., grip strength) or by recording the maximum amount of weight that can be lifted in a single repetition. Muscular endurance refers to the ability to sustain submaximal levels of force over an extended period of time. Curl-ups and flexed arm hang are examples of field-based tests of muscular endurance. Exercise is traditionally the type of physical activity selected to improve muscular strength and muscular endurance. Recommendations generally call for an activity pattern characterized by performing 8 to 10 different dynamic (i.e., isotonic or isokinetic) exercises at least twice a week with at least one day of rest between each exercise. It is also recommended that 1 set of 8 to 12 repetitions maximum be performed when strength is the primary goal, and 12 to 15 repetitions maximum when endurance is being tar-

geted. (The intensity of the activity is a function of the amount of resistance that can be overcome within the range of maximum repetitions.)

Exercise tends to be the preferred mode of activity for strength and endurance because muscle groups can be more easily isolated and intensity more easily monitored. For gains in strength and endurance to be made, muscles must be overloaded; that is, they must work at a greater level than normal. To achieve overload, resistance of some kind (e.g., gravity, one's body weight, free weights, exercise machines, elastic bands, medicine balls, weighted cuffs) usually is necessary (figure 23.4). When resistance is used, a very light load (or possibly no load at all) is recommended initially, followed by a progressive increase in resistance as exercise skill is mastered and as muscles develop. The level of resistance generally should never require a maximum exertion to attain a single repetition (i.e., one repetition maximum) in prepubescent children.

The exercise recommendations discussed in this section are appropriate for a wide range of individuals, including many youngsters with disabilities. Some youngsters with disabilities might need to work at lighter intensities (lower resistance) but might still be able to meet the frequency and repetition guidelines given earlier. Others might benefit from a reduction in the number of separate

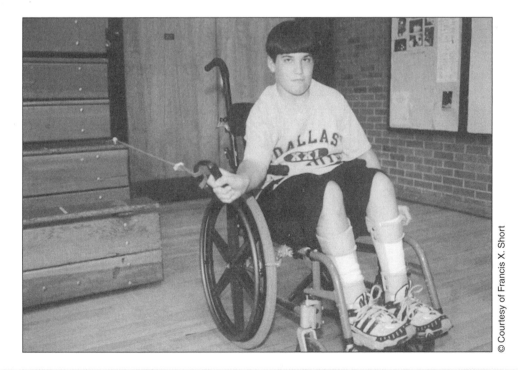

© Courtesy of Francis X. Short

Figure 23.4 Elastic exercise bands help to overload this student's muscles, which increases his muscular strength and endurance.

exercises recommended per day (down from 8 to 10) or from a pattern that increases the frequency of exercise but reduces the intensity and duration. Programs for youngsters with medical conditions should be developed with medical consultation.

Although exercise may be the preferred type of activity for enhancing strength and endurance, other types of activities certainly can contribute. In fact, children will likely benefit from a wide range of developmentally appropriate activities. Activities that require children to move their own weights or the weight of an object against gravity might be most appropriate. Examples include climbing on monkey bars, jungle gyms, ropes, or cargo nets; crawling through obstacle courses; pushing a wheelchair up a ramp; propelling scooterboards with legs or arms or by pulling on a rope; and emphasizing fundamental movements that require power such as throwing, kicking, jumping, leaping, and hopping.

Flexibility and Range of Motion

Flexibility is conceptualized as the extent of movement possible in multiple joints while performing a functional movement. The backsaver sit-and-reach and the shoulder stretch are measures of flexibility. Range of motion is defined as the extent of movement possible in a single joint. An objective measure of range of motion can be obtained through goniometry; the target stretch test provides a subjective alternative (see appendix C). As with muscular strength and endurance, exercise is usually the preferred activity mode for improving flexibility and range of motion. Again, properly selected exercises can be used to isolate muscles or muscle groups, and intensity can be monitored or controlled. When exercises are used by teachers to improve flexibility and range of motion (ROM), general recommendations call for performing exercise sessions at least three days per week. Each exercise should be conducted for a period of 10 to 30 seconds and repeated three to five times per session. The intensity of a flexibility exercise is judged by a feeling of mild discomfort; that is, muscles should be stretched to a point at which a slight pulling or "burning" sensation is felt and held there for 10 to 30 seconds.

Although some stretching activities are generally recommended at the start of a physical activity program for warm-up, specific flexibility and ROM training will be more successful when conducted toward the end of the activity session. Muscular and collagenous tissues are more likely to be warm toward the end of the session and be more receptive to stretching (Surburg, 1999). There are several stretching techniques to use to improve flexibility and ROM, including passive stretching, active-assisted stretching, active stretching, and proprioceptive neuromuscular facilitation (PNF).

In passive stretching the person is not actively involved in the exercise. The muscle is stretched by some outside force (e.g., a weight, sandbag, gravity, machine, therapist). Passive stretching is usually used in rehabilitative settings when individuals are weak, when muscles are paralyzed, or when exercise protocols require sustained stretches. Nevertheless, passive stretching can be used in educational settings as well. Physical educators who wish to employ passive stretching techniques should consult qualified professionals.

Active-assisted stretching combines the efforts of the individual and a partner assistant (e.g., teacher, therapist, aide). The individual stretches the muscle as far as she can, and then the partner assists the movement through the full (or functional) range of motion.

Active stretching is characterized by the participant moving the joint through its full (or functional) range of motion without outside assistance. Active stretching exercises have been categorized as static (slow stretches to a point of mild discomfort and holding for a time generally ranging from 6 seconds to 45 seconds) and ballistic (a "momentum exercise" in which "bouncing" or twisting movements are used to elongate a muscle for a brief time) (Surburg, 1999). Although ballistic stretching might replicate certain sport-related movements, it generally is not a recommended technique for improving flexibility and ROM. The preferred method is static stretching.

Proprioceptive neuromuscular facilitation is an exercise system designed to improve strength, coordination, and kinesthesia, as well as flexibility (Surburg, 1999). Surburg (1999) has described five PNF techniques used specifically to increase flexibility and ROM:

- Rhythmic stabilization—the participant performs rhythmical, alternating, isometric contractions of agonists and antagonists.
- Contract-relax—a partner or teacher passively stretches the muscle to elongation; the participant contracts the muscle against resistance provided by the partner or teacher until the body part has returned to its original resting position; the muscle is relaxed for five seconds prior to the next repetition (five to six repetitions).

- Hold–relax—a partner or teacher passively stretches the muscle to elongation; the participant then performs a six-second isometric contraction in that position followed by a five-second rest.

- Hold–relax–contract—this stretch is the same as hold–relax except that following the isometric contraction of the target muscle (i.e., the muscle to be stretched) the participant contracts the opposite muscle group isotonically and without resistance.

- Contract–relax–contract—this stretch is similar to contract–relax but adds an isotonic contraction of the antagonist following the isotonic contraction of the target muscle (the agonist).

Most youngsters with disabilities will benefit from one or more of the stretching techniques just described. The general recommendations for frequency, intensity, and duration described at the beginning of this section also may be appropriate when youngsters have unique flexibility and ROM needs; however, some modification in these recommendations might be necessary. Although intensity (stretches to a point of mild discomfort) ordinarily would remain the same, flexibility and ROM training for youngsters with unique needs likely should consist of greater frequency (exercise sessions conducted two to three times daily) and duration (individual stretches lasting 10 minutes or more). For longer stretches (more than five minutes) it would be appropriate to limit the number of exercise repetitions to one (recommendations generally call for three to five repetitions per exercise for shorter stretches).

General Considerations

When developing programs of physical fitness, the physical educator should be aware of students' initial levels of fitness and select activities accordingly. See the application example below. In all cases the procedure should be to start

---

APPLICATION EXAMPLE

Physical Fitness

Setting: A 15-year-old girl with a thoracic spinal cord injury is in an inclusive physical education class. One of the class goals is to improve the students' physical fitness. Present level of performance (i.e., baseline data) was established using the Brockport Physical Fitness Test. Improvements in aerobic functioning and body composition (i.e., weight loss) were identified as the primary fitness objectives.

Issue: What strategies should be used to help the student achieve these goals?

Application: The teacher might recommend or pursue the following strategies:

- Use Activitygram (or some other self-report instrument to monitor activity levels).

- Encourage the student to achieve the CDC/ACSM recommendation to engage in at least moderate-level activity—with a minimum heart rate of 103 beats per minute (220 – 15 = 205 × 0.55 = 112.75 – 10 for arm activity = 102.75)—for at least 30 minutes per day on most, preferably all, days of the week.

- If the student has difficulty achieving these guidelines, reduce criteria for intensity (i.e., heart rate) but maintain frequency and duration (i.e., days and minutes).

- If the student is able to achieve the CDC/ACSM recommendation on a regular basis, modify the activity pattern so that some of the activity is done within a target heart rate zone of 134 to 164 (i.e., 70 to 85 percent of predicted maximum heart rate with a 10-beat adjustment for arm-only activity) for at least 20 minutes a day for three days of the week (such a pattern more likely will contribute to improved aerobic functioning).

- Recommend enjoyable aerobic-based activities for use in and outside of class, such as wheelchair slaloms, free wheeling, speed bag work, swimming, arm ergometry, seated aerobics and dance, scooterboard activities, and wheelchair sports.

- Consult with parents on the nature of the program; encourage their support at home and possibly include a dietary component with their help.

slowly and progress gradually. Students should be taught to warm up prior to a workout and cool down afterward. The physical educator should motivate students to pursue higher levels of fitness by keeping records, charting progress, and presenting awards. Selecting enjoyable activities will also help to maintain interest in physical fitness; for instance, charting a class's cumulative running distances on a map for a "cross country run" will be more interesting and motivating than simply telling them to "run three laps." The physical educator should also be a good role model for students; this includes staying fit and participating in class activities whenever possible. Finally, the physical educator should view physical fitness as an ongoing part of the physical education program and not just one unit of instruction. Although different units will be taught throughout the year, activities within a unit (exercises, games, and drills) should be arranged to enhance, or at least maintain, physical fitness.

PHYSICAL ACTIVITY AND HEALTH

Although it certainly is true that physical activity can enhance physical fitness, which, in turn, can positively influence one's health, the idea that regular participation in physical activity, in and of itself, can enhance an individual's health status is now firmly established. Regular physical activity can reduce the risk of premature mortality and the risk of acquiring coronary heart disease, hypertension, colon cancer, and diabetes mellitus; it also appears to reduce depression and anxiety, improve mood, and enhance ability to perform daily tasks (U.S. Department of Health and Human Services, 1996). Physical activity is one of the 10 leading health indicators in the Healthy People 2010 goals for the nation. "The health benefits of moderate and vigorous physical activity are not limited to adults. Physical activity among children and adolescents is important because of the related health benefits (cardiorespiratory function, blood pressure control, and weight management) and because a physically active lifestyle adopted early in life may continue into adulthood" (U.S. Department of Health and Human Services, 2000, p. 22-23).

As a result of the relation between physical activity and health, the Centers for Disease Control and Prevention (CDC) and the American College of Sports Medicine (ACSM) published joint recommendations that all Americans accumulate at least 30 minutes of moderate-level physical activity on most, preferably all, days of the week (Pate et al., 1995). Perhaps the most significant aspect of this recommendation is the notion that moderate-level activity is of sufficient intensity to act as a buffer against certain diseases and conditions. In contrast, physical activity recommendations for improving physical fitness generally require more vigorous levels of intensity. Furthermore, the CDC/ACSM recommendation suggests that *any* moderate-level activity can enhance health status. Traditional activity recommendations for the development of physical fitness, on the other hand, have focused on specificity of training and have been dominated by one form of activity, namely exercise.

The Council for Physical Education for Children (COPEC, n.d.) has suggested that the CDC/ACSM recommendation be modified for children. In defense of a modified recommendation, COPEC cites some significant differences when comparing children to adults, including a relatively short attention span, a tendency toward concrete rather than abstract thought, normal activity patterns that are more intermittent than continuous, a weaker relation between physical activity and physical fitness, and the possibility that participation in more intense activities will be perceived as too difficult, thus leading to withdrawal from physical activity. The COPEC guidelines include the following:

- Elementary school children should accumulate *at least 30 to 60 minutes* of age-appropriate and developmentally appropriate physical activity on all, or most, days of the week.
- An accumulation of *more than 60 minutes, and up to several hours per day,* of age-appropriate and developmentally appropriate activities is *encouraged* for elementary school children.
- Some of the children's activity each day should be in periods lasting 10 to 15 minutes or more that includes moderate to vigorous activity.

Although there is relatively little data on the physical activity habits of people with disabilities, it is generally believed that individuals with disabilities are less active than those without disabilities (U.S. Department of Health and Human Services, 2000). It has been suggested that people with disabilities are less active because (1) there is a lack of knowledge regarding the importance of physical activity and health, (2) there is limited access to transportation to and from physical activity-related facilities, (3) many facilities are inaccessible to people with disabilities, and (4) there is a perception that exercise is inappropriate for people with disabilities (Rimmer, Braddock, and Pitetti, 1996). It is important that children and adolescents with disabilities be encouraged to meet either the CDC/ACSM or COPEC recommendations for physical activity. Those who participate in structured physical fitness development programs will have a "head start" because many of the recommendations for fitness development are more rigorous than either the CDC/ACSM or COPEC recommendations, especially with regard to intensity. Nevertheless, those implementing adapted physical education programs might find the CDC/ACSM and COPEC guidelines more appropriate for certain students than traditional "exercise prescriptions" for fitness for several reasons. First, it might be difficult or impossible to measure fitness in some students with disabilities (but increases in physical activity will likely lead to increases in physical fitness even if fitness cannot be validly assessed). Second, because the CDC/ACSM and COPEC recommendations tend to be less intense, they might be more attainable by some youngsters with disabilities. Finally, a wider range of possible activities is available to meet the CDC/ACSM or COPEC guidelines than is usually recommended for fitness development.

As mentioned in chapter 4, the computer program Activitygram can be used to track the physical activity behaviors of students with and without disabilities. Another important resource for teachers interested in increasing the activity levels of their students is the President's Council on Physical Fitness and Sports (PCPFS). In addition to a variety of physical fitness awards, the PCPFS sponsors the Presidential Active Lifestyle Award (PALA). Students who accumulate 60 minutes of activity per day (or 11,000 pedometer steps), five days per week, for six weeks, qualify for PALA (which can be earned multiple times by a single student) (PCPFS, n.d.). The PCPFS supports modifications for students with disabilities in all of its award programs.

SUMMARY

Physical fitness is critical to the person with a disability. In addition to improved performance, health, and appearance, high levels of fitness can foster independence, particularly among individuals with physical disabilities. The goals of a fitness program for individuals with unique needs depend on the type and severity of the disability and current levels of physical fitness. Increasing fitness for developing physiological or functional health and for improving skill or performance are all reasonable goals in adapted physical education. Fitness programs should be "personalized" to meet the goals of each student. Teachers must understand that, with few exceptions, students with disabilities will exhibit a favorable physiological response to increases in physical activity. Increasing physical activity likely will result in improvements in both health status and physical fitness. In many cases, the recommendations for frequency and duration of activity for improving fitness do not differ significantly from those made for the student without disabilities. The mode, or type of activity, and intensity, however, frequently must be modified to provide the student with an appropriate workout. At the very least, students with and without disabilities should pursue the CDC/ACSM guidelines (or the COPEC adjustments) for physical activity: at least 30 minutes of moderate-intensity activity on most, preferably all, days of the week.

REFERENCES

Borg, G.A. (1998). *Borg's perceived exertion to heart rate and pain scales.* Champaign, IL: Human Kinetics.

Bouchard, C., & Shephard, R.J. (1994). Physical activity, fitness, and health: The model and key concepts. In C. Bouchard, R.J. Shephard, & T. Stephens (Eds.), *Physical activity, fitness and health: International proceedings and consensus statement.* Champaign, IL: Human Kinetics.

Caspersen, C.J., Powell, K.E., & Christenson, G.M. (1985). Physical activity, exercise, and physical fitness: Definitions and distinctions for health-related research. *Public Health Reports,* 100, 126-131.

Pate, R.R. (1988). The evolving definitions of fitness. *Quest,* 40, 174-178.

Pate, R.R., Pratt, M., Blair, S.N., Haskell, W.L., Macera, C.A., Bouchard, C., et. al. (1995). Physical activity and public health: A recommendation from the Centers for Disease Control and Prevention and the American College of Sports Medicine. *Journal of American Medical Association,* 273, 402-407.

President's Council on Physical Fitness and Sports (n.d.). *Presidential active lifestyle award.* Retrieved December 20, 2003 from www.fitness.gov.

Rimmer, J.H., Braddock, D., & Pitetti, K.H. (1996). Research on physical activity and disability: An emerging national priority. *Medicine, Science, Sports, and Exercise,* 28(8), 1366-1372.

Surburg, P. (1999). Flexibility/range of motion. In J.P. Winnick & F.X. Short (Eds.), *The Brockport Physical Fitness Training Guide,* Champaign, IL: Human Kinetics.

U.S. Department of Health and Human Services (1996). *Physical activity and health: A report of the Surgeon General.* Atlanta: Author.

U.S. Department of Health and Human Services (2000). *Healthy People 2010.* Washington, DC: Author.

Winnick, J.P., & Short, F.X. (1999). *The Brockport physical fitness test manual.* Champaign, IL: Human Kinetics.

WRITTEN RESOURCES

American College of Sports Medicine. (2003). *Exercise management for persons with chronic diseases and disabilities.* Champaign, IL: Human Kinetics.

How to effectively manage exercise for someone with chronic disease or disability. This source includes 49 chapters categorized by disabilities, diseases, or conditions written by persons with research or clinical experience in exercise programming. Prominent in the book are suggestions for exercise testing and exercise programming.

Goldberg, B. (Ed.). (1995). *Sports and exercise for children with chronic health conditions.* Champaign, IL: Human Kinetics.

This source presents information on general issues related to sports, exercise, and chronic health conditions and provides specific information on these topics in chapters organized according to 20 disabilities and conditions.

Lockette, K.F., & Keyes, A.M. (1994). *Conditioning with physical disabilities.* Champaign, IL: Human Kinetics.

This book covers general principles of physical conditioning, including strength, aerobic, and flexibility training, and applies these principles to a number of physical disabilities, including cerebral palsy, stroke, head injury, spinal cord injury, spina bifida, poliomyelitis, amputations, visual impairments, and multiple sclerosis. Separate chapters for upper-extremity, abdominal and trunk, and lower-extremity exercises are included.

Miller, P. (Ed.). (1995). *Fitness programming and physical disability.* Champaign, IL: Human Kinetics.

An excellent book providing information on principles of conditioning for the development of health-related physical fitness; guidelines for developing resistance-training programs; modifications for using stretch bands or tubing as the mode of exercise; ways of maintaining and developing flexibility; exercises for the neck, shoulder, elbow, wrist, trunk, hip, knee, and ankle; and other topics.

Winnick, J.P., & Short, F.X. (Eds.). (1999). *The Brockport physical fitness training guide.* Champaign, IL: Human Kinetics.

This guide is designed to be used in conjunction with the Brockport Physical Fitness Test. Provides principles for fitness development in the areas of cardiorespiratory endurance, body composition, muscular strength and endurance, and flexibility and range of motion. CDC/ACSM physical activity guidelines are incorporated. Focuses on youngsters with intellectual disabilities, visual impairments, cerebral palsy, spinal cord injury, and amputations.

AUDIOVISUAL RESOURCES

Fitness for everyone. (Videotape series, 1995). Disabled Sports, USA, 451 Hungerford Drive, Suite 100, Rockville, MD 20850.

Developed by the National Handicapped Sports and Recreation Association; series includes an aerobics videos for those with quadriplegia, cerebral palsy, paraplegia, and amputations; another video in the series demonstrates strength and flexibility training for people with a variety of disabilities.

ELECTRONIC RESOURCES

Fitness Challenge Software. (1999). American Fitness Alliance, Youth Fitness Resource Center, P.O. Box 5076, Champaign, IL 61825-5076.

Supports the Brockport Physical Fitness Test. Prints goals, results, and fitness plans for individual students; separate reports can be generated for instructors or parents. Also includes the technical manual for the BPFT, which provides validity and reliability information for test items.

Fitnessgram 6.0 Software. (1999). American Fitness Alliance, Youth Fitness Resource Center, P.O. Box 5076, Champaign, IL 61825-5076.

Provides a sophisticated computerized system for administering Fitnessgram. Has both teacher and student components. The student component allows students to enter their own scores and track their progress. It also provides a system for monitoring their levels of physical activity through Activitygram, a subcomponent of the software.

Rhythmic Movement and Dance

Boni B. Boswell

Shawn dreaded his fifth-grade creative educational dance (CED) class. His success in physical education was close to zero, and he believed it would sink lower in dance. His extreme muscle tightness made throwing and kicking look like slashing and punching. Playing the usual ball games using his wheelchair wasn't considered cool. He figured dance would just be another round of trying to copy the movements of people with perfect bodies.

But Shawn felt encouraged when the teacher explained that CED focused on discovering different ways of moving by changing things, such as speed and energy level. The class tried different ways of reaching into space, while changing levels and speeds. Several classes later, Shawn's perception of dance and his ability to dance began to change. Students in the class were asked to travel on a straight path, stop, and slowly show strong movements that changed levels. The teacher described the movements as deliberate, tense, forceful and characterized these actions as "pressing" movements. Students then changed the speed (tempo) of their strong movements to fast. These quick movements were described as sharp, bold, piercing and identified as punching, thrashing actions.

The teacher asked students to create a sequence of movements that included traveling through space, pausing, and performing actions described as pressing and punching. As Shawn created his sequence, he noticed that his body demonstrated these qualities easily. He was surprised that he felt good about sharing his sequence with the class, and he was shocked that the teacher used his movements as a model for other students. As students created sequences based on Shawn's movements, he began to think that dance might be his favorite class.

What if someone told you that a joyous and meaningful part of your physical education curriculum was missing? When rhythmic activities and dance are omitted from a physical education program, this is indeed the case. Rhythmic and dance activities offer opportunities not only to improve motor skills but also to have fun and gain valuable learning experiences in problem solving and creative expression. In this chapter we present a practical approach that teachers with little or no dance background can use to present rhythmic movement and dance in physical education programs for students with a wide range of ability levels.

TEACHING DANCE: WHAT IS IT?

Typically, dance in physical education includes three movement forms: rhythmic movement, creative educational dance (CED), and structured dances (e.g., folk, social). This chapter presents an overview of the content of these forms, suggestions for ways to include students with disabilities, and sample lessons. Although in most cases these dance forms are taught separately, there are important links between the forms. These links include movement principles that relate to balance, transfer of weight, and alignment as well as to such movement concepts as time, space, and force. The degree of emphasis of these principles and concepts differs among movement forms, but each content can lead into the others, supporting and strengthening student development in the other two forms. Through overlapping activities from these movement forms, teachers can provide a richer base for achieving student objectives than could be achieved through using one of these movement forms exclusively.

TEACHING DANCE: WHAT IS IT NOT?

It is important to note differences as well as commonalities between dance therapy and educational dance used with students with unique differences. First, the overall purpose of each is strikingly different. Whereas dance therapy is a psychotherapeutic use of movement focused on the emotional as well as physical integration of individuals, educational dance is designed to meet the educational and aesthetic needs of students

with and without disabilities. Dance therapy is a treatment used primarily with clients with mental illness or emotional or behavioral problems. Dance therapists earn a degree that qualifies them as therapists. Clearly, teachers of educational dance classes are not therapists—they are instructors—and the participants are not clients—they are students. On the other hand, in regard to commonalities, anyone with or without a disability who dances can experience therapeutic effects. For example, any student who moves rhythmically can release tension, both physically and psychologically, and thus derive therapeutic benefit. So, while educational dance in inclusive settings and dance therapy have different goals they both offer potential therapeutic effects.

SELECTION OF AGE-APPROPRIATE CONTENT

Each of these three movement forms contains age-appropriate content, but each form can be extended or simplified to accommodate a range of age and ability levels. For example, CED content is considered most applicable to kindergarten through fifth grade, but by extending CED content to focus on progressively more complex forms for creative expression, teachers can easily adapt the content for sixth- through eighth-grade students. Structured or pattern dance content might be considered most age appropriate for upper elementary and middle school students, but many folk dances are easily modified for kindergarten students. Although some social dances, such as the salsa and tango, might be considered best suited for high school students, other social dances are age appropriate for middle school students. Selection of age-appropriate content is guided primarily by practical information about the developmental needs as well as social behaviors and interests of students. For an overview of the general order of dance forms suggested for K through 12 in regard to traditional age-appropriate dance content, Kassing and Jay (2003) present the sequence shown in figure 24.1.

RHYTHMIC MOVEMENTS

"Of all the ingredients in . . . dance, rhythm is the most persuasive and most powerful element . . ." (Humphrey, 1980, p. 104). The primary purpose of a rhythmic movement program is to provide

Preschool – kindergarten	Lower elementary	Upper elementary	Middle school	High school
Creative movement and dance				
		Modern dance		
			Jazz Dance	
		Ballet		
Tap dance				
Folk dance				
		Square dance		
		Contra dance		
			Social dance	
			Aerobic dance	

Figure 24.1   Sample curriculum overview of dance in K-12 education.

Reprinted, by permission, from G. Kassing and D. Jay, 2003, Dance teaching methods and curriculum design (Champaign, IL: Human Kinetics), 200.

opportunities for students to become competent in moving to various rhythmic patterns. In their simplest form, rhythmic movements can be described as a balance of contracting and expanding movements that are connected and repeated, such as inhaling and exhaling. When two movements are connected and repeatedly performed, a rhythm is created. Try the following exercise. Lift, then lower one arm. Perform these two movements as if they were parts of the same movement. In other words, connect the movements. Repeat the connected movements several times without stopping. Notice the resulting rhythmic pattern? You can continue to perform rhythmic arm movements in sync with an internal rhythm, such as your breathing, or you can match the movements to an external rhythm, such as a drumbeat.

Rhythm and Movement

As an integral part of movement, rhythm can be said to characterize the quality of movement. Although all children possess a sense of rhythm, they do not all possess the same degree of rhythmic sense. For several reasons, such as lack of appropriate rhythmic experience, poor concentration, and physical differences, some children might appear to lack a sense of rhythm. When students experience difficulty in moving rhythmically or "in time," their movements often appear choppy or awkward. In truth, a sense of rhythm can be developed and refined through carefully selecting appropriate rhythmic activities that offer fun as well as challenging opportunities and result in feelings of accomplishment. When individuals develop a refined sense of rhythm, the quality of their movements reflects this change.

Content of Rhythmic Movement Programs

The essential content of a rhythmic program includes four elements: pulse, tempo, accent, and patterns. Pulse is defined as the underlying beat of the rhythm. The pulse repeats continuously, with each beat taking an equal amount of time, unless the tempo of the pulse is slowed down or speeded up. Students need opportunities to explore internal rhythms—in other words, to explore movements at their own speed—before being challenged to demonstrate movements in sync with external beats. Tempo can be defined simply as the speed of the rhythm. Pulse and tempo are the simplest of these four rhythmic elements for students to master. An accent can be described as the emphasis or stress placed on certain beats. Students need opportunities to listen to different rhythms for the sole purpose of identifying which beats are accented. Students should know that accents reflect the basic structure of the rhythm. To understand the basic structure of rhythm, students should know that beats are grouped together in measures. Measures are composed of series of beats in twos, threes, or fours. In most of the popular music in the United States, the first beat in each measure is accented. As each measure or series of beats is repeated, the first beat in each measure continues to be accented, and there continues to be the same number of beats in each measure. When students are able to hear or feel the accented beats, they can count the number of beats in each measure. In music, measures are considered fundamental units. The meter of a musical piece reflects the number of beats in each measure and what kind of note equals one beat. For example, music with a meter of 3 / 4 has three beats in each measure, and a quarter note receives one beat. Music in a 4 / 4 meter has four beats in each measure, with a quarter note receiving one beat. Understanding this aspect of rhythm is especially important in structured dance because the steps in these dances (folk, social, and square dance) reflect the basic structure of the rhythmic accompaniment.

The term **rhythmic patterns** connotes variety in rhythm and presents a level of complexity not found in pulse, tempo, and accent. Simply stated, rhythmic patterns are recurring groups of beats or movements in which each group includes different tempos. For example, if a rhythmic pattern is composed of a group of four steady beats, a combination of two or more different tempos would be included within the four beats. Translating this into movement, this four count rhythmic pattern can include two walking steps (counts 1 and 2) and four running steps (counts 3 and 4). Locomotor patterns such as galloping, sliding, rolling, or skipping can be used in this example by replacing the walking steps (counts 1 and 2) with the new locomotor pattern followed by the four running steps (counts 3 and 4). After the teacher guides practice combining movements of different tempos to match a group of set beats, students should be encouraged to create their own rhythmic patterns using other movements. Most students need to feel a rhythmic pattern while stationary by clapping or tapping the pattern before moving through space using rhythmic patterns.

Teaching Style

Guided discovery offers a natural avenue for presentation of rhythmic activities. The teacher guides students by asking questions and presenting tasks that require students to engage in self-discovery. The rhythmic movement lesson presented in this chapter also includes opportunities for problem solving. Students are asked to solve movement problems that relate to the rhythmic material explored. Through the process of solving these problems, students generate a broad range of "solutions" or responses. Depending on the developmental level of the students, the solutions could range from a brief sequence of simple movements that reflect the students' breathing rhythms to a movement sequence focusing on the changing accents combined with changes in direction, pathway, and levels.

Speaking Rhythmically

A significant part of presenting rhythmic activities is the skill of beginning the class in unison and in rhythm with the beat of the activity. The beginning signal given by the teacher or student leader is traditionally a verbal cue presented in a fashion described as "speaking rhythmically." The instructor speaks loudly, clearly, and in rhythm with the beat of the activity. An example of speaking rhythmically would be counting an introductory set of eight beats and ending the set of counts with verbalizing, ". . . *five–six–ready, and . . .*" Instructions given during the activity for changing the task must be announced before the change is to take place. For example, the instructor would say, ". . . *five–six–ready, change.*" For students with auditory difficulties, verbal cueing must be accompanied by visual cues. In these classes, simple hand responses, such as beating in time with the tempo of the activity, can be easily added.

Developmental Progression of Activities

Perhaps all teachers would agree that rhythmic activities should be presented in a developmental manner, but often teachers present rhythmic challenges that are too complex for many of their students. Although assessment of rhythmic development can determine which activities are appropriate, it is usually beyond the scope of physical education programs. The following guidelines can help teachers sequence rhythmic activities for a range of developmental levels.

- Focus on internal rhythmic awareness before focusing on external rhythms.
- Provide opportunities for listening to the pulse before moving to the pulse.
- Begin with nonlocomotor movements before using locomotor movements.
- Begin with nonlocomotor movements using various hand movements before using other body parts.
- Gradually increase the number of and difficulty of the concepts introduced. For example, use *moving forward,* before incorporating other directions.
- Begin with students moving individually, then moving with partners, and then moving with a small group.

Suggestions for Individuals With Differences

The following suggestions apply to any group of students who need to increase awareness of internal rhythms and develop awareness of external rhythmic patterns. This might include not only students with severe disabilities but also students who appear to lack a sense of rhythm. As mentioned previously, lack of appropriate rhythmic experiences, poor concentration, and physical differences can hinder rhythmic ability. Initially, these students might demonstrate difficulty moving to an external rhythm. Teachers can begin working with rhythms that originate from the students themselves by encouraging students to explore nonlocomotor and locomotor movements at their own speed before introducing activities that require moving in sync with external beats.

One teaching strategy for students who need to develop beginning rhythmic awareness is to match these students with peers or cross-age tutors. Matching students (with or without disabilities) with partners requires careful consideration of many variables, including level of maturity of the students, student preferences, body weights, and level of rhythmic ability. In regard to students using wheelchairs, teachers might ask selected peers to attend an introductory class so that partners can be introduced to each other and the strengths of each student can be emphasized. Relevant information about wheelchairs and assistive devices can be highlighted. For students who remain in their wheelchairs during the rhythmic activities, peers can sit in chairs facing their partners or sit side by side. When appropriate, instruction can be presented to partners of students with severe disabilities about providing physical support, such as physically helping to guide a partner's hands through movements. To actively engage and foster responses of students with severe cognitive and physical disabilities in rhythmic movements, the following steps are suggested: (1) focus attention—secure eye contact, (2) provide opportunities for passive movements, (3) provide opportunities for mirroring movements of a partner, and (4) provide opportunities for creating original movement responses.

Clarifying the objectives for a class is a crucial step in developing a rhythmic program. These might be based on national curriculum guides, state or locally developed guidelines, or knowledge of typical development. The objectives of the Beginning Rhythmic Movement sample lesson were based on typical rhythmic development. The activities included in the sample lesson were adapted from a program designed for middle school students with severe differences (Boswell & Vidret, 1993). Even though the original discussion (Boswell & Vidret, 1993) focused on students with severe cognitive and physical disabilities, the activities lend themselves to a wide range of adaptations.

The following sample of a beginning lesson was designed for students who need opportunities to move to their own internal rhythms and to increase awareness of external rhythms. The content of this sample lesson is primarily rhythmic movement, but it includes group activities leading to readiness in structured dances.

Sample Lesson: Beginning Rhythmic Movement

Student Objectives:

1. Show awareness of internal rhythms by demonstrating movements that reflect breathing patterns.
2. Demonstrate matching a partner's rhythmic pattern with movements.
3. Move in sync with simple external rhythm by demonstrating tapping movements while stationary.

Warm-Up Activity: Modified Structured Dance—"Seven Jumps"

Instructions: The class listens to the music "Seven Jumps" for two or three minutes (perhaps while the teacher checks roll). The teacher stops the music and explains that the music alternates between the melody heard for 32 counts and a series of single, long notes of 4 to 8 counts. The teacher replays the music and provides a physical signal, such as lifting his or her arms, when the series of long notes is heard. Each time the melody stops and the long single notes are heard, a long note is added. Thus, one long note is heard after the first melody change, then two long notes after the second melody change, proceeding in an "add-on" pattern until seven long notes are heard.

The following is a modification of the traditional steps

(continued)

(continued)

of the simple folk dance "Seven Jumps." In circular formation, students travel when they hear the melody, then stop and reach in any direction, changing body parts, when they hear the long notes. Students can use any locomotor pattern that is appropriate. Stepping "on the beat" is not emphasized. With each "long" note, students reach out into space; thus, during the last section of long notes, students reach seven times in different directions.

Communicate the Goal of the Class to Students.

The goal of the class is to increase awareness of rhythms, beginning with breathing. Explain that everyone has a comfortable rhythm of breathing, and the rhythms of one person's breathing might differ from that of others.

Sequence of Activities

1. Explore internal rhythm of breathing. Ask students to focus on their natural rhythm of breathing. Stress that it doesn't matter if exhales and inhales last two or eight counts—the point is to be aware of the rhythm. If any students need additional structure to focus on their breathing, ask them to count to five as they exhale and to five again as they inhale.

   a. Ask students to add movements that reflect the rhythm of their breathing. Describe and demonstrate. While inhaling, add lifting both arms forward and high. While exhaling, add lowering arms down and backward. Students match arm movements to their breathing pattern, using their own pace.

   b. Students add lateral rocking with breathing. Describe and demonstrate. Begin with palms of both hands touching the floor or a chair at the sides of the body. With inhales, lean trunk to one side and lift opposite arm over head, then reverse the movement when exhaling. Students are encouraged to move at their own pace.

   c. Students "mirror" a partner's rhythm. One in each pair of students is designated as the "mirror" and copies his or her partner. Facing each other, the mirror students match their

partner's breathing and movement pattern. Partners take turns mirroring each other's breathing as movements are added.

   d. Present a movement problem. Ask students to create a rhythmic sequence of four breaths with at least two different arm movements, repeated twice.

   e. After independent practice creating a sequence including various movements, partners can volunteer to perform their sequences for the class.

   f. The teacher provides feedback and encourages students to observe variations in tapping rhythms.

2. Explore tapping to a simple external rhythm.

   a. Provide an external rhythm with any instrument, such as a drum.

   b. Explain that tapping movements are short, gentle movements performed quickly. Demonstrate tapping using different body parts. Students explore tapping fingers or hands on knees, shoulders, feet, or floor.

   c. Provide a steady, moderate-tempo drum beat. Ask students to match their tapping movements to the beat.

   d. Provide a steady beat using a different instrument, such as a tambourine. Ask students to travel through space to the tambourine beat and tap in place to the drum beat.

   e. The teacher divides the class in half. One half performs their sequence while the other half observes, and then groups switch roles.

   f. The teacher provides feedback and encourages students to observe variations in tapping rhythms.

Closure Activity

Ask students to demonstrate the movements they liked best as they take deep breaths and review the purpose of the lesson.

CREATIVE EDUCATIONAL DANCE

Creative educational dance (CED) can be defined as a movement form that focuses on refining natural movements as students explore the elements of movement (i.e., space, time, force, and the body). In this discussion, an integral part of CED is creating dances through problem solving. The simplest dance created through this process is defined as a movement sequence that includes a clear beginning and ending and a middle section that demonstrates a creative use of the elements of movement. As students learn and master the content, they begin to create dances that communicate ideas or themes. One of the joys of CED for students comes from giving form to their natural movements so that they can communicate ideas as they perform their dances for their peers. There are many avenues through which one can approach the process of creating dances. In this chapter we will focus on creating dances through the process of solving movement problems.

Several terms have been used to describe programs that focus on exploration of space, time, and force. Related terms include *movement education, creative movement,* and *creative dance.* Kassing and Jay (2003) summarize the history of these related dance forms, highlighting the influence of Margaret H'Doubler and Rudolf Laban. Although these terms might stress different aspects of exploration of the elements and emphasize different outcomes, Kassing and Jay underscore that "regardless of what titles they are given," these approaches "provide age-appropriate movement and dance experiences that support learning in other dance forms, other art forms, and in physical education" (2003, p. 215).

Teaching Style

Similar to the content of rhythmic movement, CED content lends itself to the use of guided discovery and divergent teaching styles. The teacher poses questions that encourage students to analyze and explore the body and movement concepts. For example, the teacher might ask, "Can you jump higher if you use a different body shape?" The terms *exploration* and *improvisation* are used frequently in relation to CED. The heart of each CED lesson is exploration of the basic elements of movement. In this context, exploration is defined as "a systematic investigation, examination, search for making specific discoveries and learning about something." (Smith-Autard, 2000, p. 80) The process of exploration of CED content is filled with improvisation, which is defined as spontaneously responding to a stimulus, or "invention without preparation" (Smith-Autard, 2000). In CED lessons, exploration is replete with questions and "movement problems" (also termed assignments) that require students to consider possible "spontaneous responses" and then select one of the responses to include in the dance. Specifically, in implementing exploration, teachers present questions that guide students in using "improv" as a strategy for exploring. For example, teachers ask students, "What body parts can make an angular shape like the letter S? Now, how can you create a different angular S shape with a different body part? Select one of these shapes

and explore making that shape at different levels." Clearly, there are different levels of improvisation. Teachers can pose highly specified questions that offer few options, or they can ask questions that are completely free and open ended.

Figure 24.2 (p. 422) presents students engaged in an improvisation activity. To begin, one student is asked to perform a nonlocomotor rhythmic movement accompanied by a sound. Dancers are asked to individually add their rhythmic movements and sounds to the rhythmic movement of the first dancer, thus creating a Rhythm Machine. Dancers reverse the process of adding movements so that each dancer individually breaks away from the Rhythm Machine, leaving the initial dancer to end the dance.

When teachers present problem-solving activities that have many possible solutions, they provide opportunities for divergent thinking. Movement problems are posed to the class that require students to create a dance that adheres to boundaries related to aspects of space, time, and force, but there are many possible solutions. Through the process of solving movement problems, students can create a diverse collection of dances, ranging in scope from the flickering movements of a candle to the powerful movements of a hurricane.

Content

The heart of CED is exploring the elements of movement: space, time, force, and the body. Space, time, and force are concepts that allow us to think about and to analyze movement. These concepts, as well as the body, are considered four of the basic elements of movement and, as such, provide the rich content of CED. These basic concepts are defined in physical education and as well as dance texts, but terminology varies from text to text. For example, the term "force" might be replaced by other terms, such as "effort," "energy," or "weight." The following brief descriptions of the elements are similar to definitions found in physical education texts, such as *Children Moving: A Reflective Approach to Teaching Physical Education* (Graham, Holt/Hale, Parker, 2001), and in texts on creative dance, such as *First Steps in Teaching Creative Dance to Children* (Joyce, 1994).

Space can be defined as the medium in which our bodies move and create designs. Space includes terms that relate to specific areas in space. Typically, space is described as self or general space and includes a description of level and focus. The area closest to the body is called "self space" or kinesphere. The area beyond the

Figure 24.2   *The Rhythm Machine* performed by an inclusive dance troupe at East Carolina University, Greenville, NC.

body's reach is termed general space. Levels in space are described as high, middle, or low. The focus of the body in space can be near or far away or can be directed to a certain level in space. Space designs related to the body include shape, size, direction, and pathway. Body shapes can be small or large in size. Identification of the direction of a movement is based on where the body is facing, whether forward, backward, diagonally, or sideward. One of the first ways to explore direction is to ask the students to lead with different parts of their bodies. For example, leading with the back, students would travel backward, and when leading with one side of the body, students travel sideward. *Pathway* describes a different aspect of space. The pathway the body follows can be described as the floor pattern, such as straight, curved, or any combination. Thus, you can move backward (direction) while traveling on a curved pathway (floor pattern).

Force describes the energy level of movements. Other related terms include *quality* and *flow*. Force can be powerful, described as strong or gentle. *Quality* refers to how the energy moves the body, often described as swinging, smooth (sustained), sharp (sudden), or shaking. *Flow* describes whether the energy is bound (controlled, tensed) or free (uncontrolled, free flowing).

Time includes the terms beat, tempo, accent, and pattern. *Beat* refers to the underlying pulse of the rhythm. *Tempo* describes whether the beat is fast or slow. Stressed beats (or emphasized movement) are *accents*. *Patterns* refer to the combinations of rhythms—they are created by changing tempos, placements of accents, or including uneven rhythms. Uneven rhythmic patterns simply include both quick and slow movements or beats, such as the rhythm of galloping (quick, quick, slow).

Suggested CED Themes

In concert with Graham, Holt/Hale, and Parker (2001), each of the basic elements can be considered a "movement theme" that serves as a basis for lesson development. A suggested progression of movement themes for planning a series of lessons is shown in table 24.1. In this progression, space and body are combined. It is suggested that teachers begin with level A themes Body and Space and progress from left to right, incorporating movement themes from level A Time and Force. Teachers can build on these by adding themes from level B, and then level C.

Although using various images can motivate students to explore the elements of movement, many images support stereotypic movements and actually distract students from exploring movement. Animal images, such as bunnies and dogs, are especially difficult to use because students "fall into" stereotypic movements and thereby miss exploration of movement.

Lesson Format

The CED content is organized into lessons that include objectives, warm-up, and closure phases. In addition, the CED lesson format includes four sequential phases that provide a framework for students to explore, create, perform, and respond. The following format can be used with a broad range of ability levels.

1. *Exploration.* This is the heart of the lesson. Teacher guides the students in exploring selected elements.

2. *The teacher presents movement problem or assignment.* Problems are based on the material covered in exploration. The problem is similar to an assignment, specifying the parameters or boundaries that students can follow to create dances.

3. *Students create dances.* Individually, with a partner, or in a small group, students create dances by following the boundaries or instructions specified in the problem.

Table 24.1 CED Progression of Movement Themes

Body and space themes	Time themes	Force themes
A. Exploring motion and stillness	**A. Exploring internal rhythms and external rhythms**	**A. Exploring movement qualities**
• Travel short distances and stop (stillness) on cue. • Change ways of travel (galloping/jumping) and stop (stillness) on cue. • Create a traveling sequence with 2 points of stillness without teacher cue. • Travel and rise to high level, showing stillness and holding a high body shape. • Travel and rise to high level and sink to low level and stop with low body shape. • Create traveling sequences with 2 rising and sinking movements and 2 points of stillness. Begin with body lifted and end with body close to floor. • Travel using any locomotor pattern with a partner, stopping and one rises and one sinks; reverse roles.	• Stationary—sit and focus on internal beats (heartbeats and breathing); lifting and lowering arms in rhythm with breathing. • Tap fingers to internal rhythm on different body parts. • Draw circles with different body parts to internal rhythm. • Stationary—use internal, natural rhythm; sway side to side 4 to 6 times, turn, then stop. Repeat, using natural, internal rhythm. • Stationary—Navajo Greeting Game: hands patting knees and floor with verse.* • Listen to steady drum beat and sway side to side. • Travel using internal rhythm, stopping on teacher cue and swaying side to side in rhythm to drum, repeat. • Create sequence, traveling to internal rhythm, stopping on teacher's cue and tapping and swaying to external, even drum beat.	• Stationary—explore qualities of shaking, tapping, swinging, bending, twisting, reaching. • Body isolations—use different body parts to perform qualities. • Travel and stop and perform different qualities (with teacher cues). • Create sequence of traveling and stopping independently and performing qualities; add level changes.

(continued)

Table 24.1 *(continued)*

Body and space themes	Time themes	Force themes
B. Exploring spatial relationships	**B. Exploring changing tempo**	**B. Exploring strong/light**
• Stationary—different body parts reach toward spatial areas: front, back, side, high, low.	• Stationary—sit and tap quickly on floor, then slowly clap hands.	• Stationary—strong-punch, pushing, stamping
• Stationary—body parts perform different qualities of force (shaking, swinging) in different locations.	• Stationary—echo teacher's clapping: 4 slow claps, then 2 quick claps; repeat.	• Stationary—light tapping, brush, patting, rocking
• Travel through space, stopping and reaching with various body parts into different spatial areas.	• Travel, changing from slow to fast.	• Travel using strong then light force.
• Create a traveling sequence including body parts reaching into different spatial areas and 2 stationary points with body parts performing selected qualities of force; begin and end with body shape that includes reaching away from body into space.	• Create a traveling sequence, changing tempo and adding stillness.	• Create sequence of traveling, stopping, and using strong and light force.
	• Select 2 body shapes, then do changes quickly from one shape to another; then do slowly; repeat several times.	
• Travel with partner—any locomotor pattern, stop, reach out into space with any body part; repeat and replace reaching with shaking different body parts.	• Create a sequence—traveling quickly and slowly with 2 points of stillness in which the body pauses then quickly changes shape.	

C. Exploring body shapes	C. Exploring accents and patterns	C. Exploring flow
• Stationary—shake entire body, then freeze to hold "shaking" shape.	• Stationary—sitting and listening to a steady 4/4 rhythm, accents on first beat of the 4 counts by clapping; repeat, adding voice on accented beat.	• Stationary—energy flowing, swinging, free movements with different body parts, then whole body.
• Stationary—whole body control: reach body wide and hold shape, reaching, expanding into large shapes.	• Stationary—clap 3 beats, accenting first beat by clapping at high level.	• Stationary—energy bound, tight, frozen, body parts then whole body.
• Large shapes changing into small shapes	• Stationary—sit or stand and perform a punching movement on the accented beats of 4/4 rhythm.	• Traveling—with free flowing energy.
• Travel with large shapes, then with large shapes changing into small shapes.	• Traveling—travel and accent the first beat of each 4 counts, with voices of students counting "1."	• Create a sequence combining traveling and stationary movements using free and bound flow.
• Isolate body parts—exploring shapes focusing on back (cat back, long back, and so on) shoulders, heads, and other parts.	• African rhythm game—students repeat a rhythm using stomp, clap, pat and hold (rest) for a beat.	
• Balance using different body parts as base of support and holding shapes.		
• Create a shape dance sequence. Begin with large whole-body shapes, then isolate a body part and focus on changing shape of that body part; add traveling and definite ending shape.		

4. *Perform/Respond.* Students share their dances with peers. Responses after each performance focus on how the content of the dances "solved" the movement problem.

The following sample CED lesson was designed for a range of ability levels and would be appropriate for most typically developing primary school students. Although the content of this lesson is primarily CED, it includes valuable opportunities for rhythmic development.

Sample Lesson: CED

Student Objectives

1. Demonstrate traveling and stopping with auditory and visual cues.
2. Demonstrate stopping and showing a shape with a round back and a shape with an arched back.
3. Travel for three beats and hold on fourth beat; repeat to music.

Warm-Up Activity

Directions: Students travel through space, carefully avoiding colliding with others, as the teacher beats a drum beat at a moderate tempo. When the beats stop, students stop and extend any body part out into space for four counts. (Another percussion instrument such as a bell or maracas can be played to provide an auditory cue for reaching into space, or teachers can verbalize the sequence.) The teacher repeats the sequence—travel, stop, reach several times—changing the tempo of the drumbeat. If developmentally appropriate, other non-locomotor movements can be added, such as an elbow tapping a knee, or a hand tapping the sole of a foot for four counts. Teachers can guide students to use different body parts for tapping or twisting for four counts. By varying the tempo of the sequence (travel, stop, reach, tap, and twist), teachers can add complexity as needed. (For children with hearing losses, simple visual cues can easily be added. Depending on the developmental level of the students, teachers might add different kinds of visual cues, such as a color code in which certain colors are matched with specified movements.)

Communicate the Goals of the Class to Students

1. Demonstrate body control while traveling, stopping, and shaping with round and arched backs.
2. Create a dance that includes shapes with rounded and arched backs.

- *Exploration.* Students melt to the floor in four counts and explore shapes with rounded backs on count five. Teachers use age-appropriate feedback to encourage students to repeat melting and shaping with rounded backs. Primary grade students might begin exploration by focusing on the concept of size of the

shape. For example, teachers ask the students to keep their rounded back shapes while they change the size of their shapes. As suggested in table 24.1, under "exploring body shapes," students' small rounded shapes can grow into large ones while maintaining rounded backs and vice versa. Teachers can add traveling while changing the size of their shapes, or they can ask students to travel through space and then stop on a certain cue before shaping with rounded backs. After students demonstrate traveling and shaping with rounded backs, teachers may guide students in exploring shapes with arched backs. Slowly stretching into a shape with an arched back and then slowly curving into a rounded back shape provides opportunities for students to refine upper body control while increasing awareness of their abdominal muscles. To add complexity, teachers can ask students to explore changing level as well as shape and size: "Can you lift and expand your arched back shape to a high level and then change to a small rounded back shape as you melt toward the floor?"

- *Teacher presents movement problem (assignment).* Create a shape dance that includes traveling and shaping with rounded and arched backs and which begins and ends with definite shapes. Teachers add complexity to the problem to match the abilities of the students by including size, level, and tempo changes.

- *Students create dances.* Students create dances independently (or with a partner). Teachers circulate through the class and provide feedback and encouragement. As students complete the assignment, ask them to repeat their dances and think of possible titles for their dances.

- *Perform/Respond.* Half the class shares their dances while the other half observes quietly. Then the groups switch roles so that all students perform their dances. Teachers encourage all students to watch for the rounded and arched shapes and to focus on how other students solved the movement problem.

- *Closure.* Students form a circle and breathe deeply as they stretch high, melt low, reach into the circle, then reach out of the circle, turn, and stretch. Cue words for the sequence include *reach up, down, in, out, turn,* and *stretch.* Repeat the sequence several times and verbally review the purpose of the lesson.

Extending the Content

When students create dances that demonstrate their understanding of the basic content (space, time, force, and the body), teachers can offer greater challenges by extending the content into exploration of the qualitative aspects of movement. In this discussion, examination of qualitative aspects of movements is limited to the introduction of the eight basic effort actions, as presented in table 24.2. The eight effort actions correspond to eight different qualities of movement. They are described as basic effort actions "because they form the base from which more subtle qualities are drawn" (Preston-Dunlop, 1990, p. 60). Although performing even simple movements such as reaching for a glass of water might contain a blend of basic effort actions, the overall quality or dynamics of reaching for the glass can be described in terms of space, time, and force—thus, they can be identified as one of the basic effort actions. For example, the movement of reaching slowly, lightly, and directly toward the glass can be described as the effort action called "gliding." In contrast, if the movement of reaching is performed quickly, with strong force, and directly, the movement can be described as the effort action "thrusting" or "punching." As presented in table 24.2, in addition to gliding and thrusting, the eight basic effort actions include slashing, floating, wringing, pressing, flicking, and dabbing.

Lessons devoted to exploration of the eight basic effort actions provide opportunities for students to refine their movements in terms of force, space, and time and improve their abilities to use movement in creative expression. As students master the effort actions, teachers can provide meaningful opportunities to concentrate on refining creative expression. Presenting words that clarify the moods or feelings associated with effort actions can help students understand the various expressions characterized by each effort. For example, words such as "quietness," "balance," and "peaceful" can be used when exploring the effort actions floating or gliding. Using words such as "sparkling," "sharp," "glittering," and "excited" with the effort actions flicking and dabbing helps students become more aware of the connection of movement qualities and expression.

Understanding the effort actions begins with focusing on each of the elements of movement and then progresses to focusing on how these elements of movement combine to form the basic effort actions. First, imagine that each element exists on a continuum, a range between two ends of a spectrum of movement expression. Clarification of each element in relation to this continuum is the first step in understanding and experiencing the eight basic effort actions.

Space: Movements ranging from indirect to direct express the continuum of *space*.

Indirect*_____SPACE_____*Direct

When people enter a classroom to find a seat, they might travel on a straight path directly to a seat or wander around the room before finding a seat. If the person looks straight ahead and moves through the room on a straight path with a definite idea of where to go, the spatial focus of that person is *direct*. If another person scans the room and wanders through space, weaving freely between seats before finally spiraling into a seat, his or her spatial focus is indirect. Students need to explore moving both indirectly and directly, when stationary in self space as well as when traveling through general space.

Time: Movements varying from slow to sudden or abrupt express the *time* continuum.

Slow*_____TIME_____*Sudden

To simplify this discussion, we will consider time only in respect to tempo. Slow movements extend into time, whereas sudden movements are performed quickly. Cows often demonstrate both slow and sudden movements simultaneously. Typically, cows grazing in a green field travel slowly from one grassy spot to another. But at the same

Table 24.2   **Eight Basic Effort Actions**

Basic effort action	Space	Time	Force
Float	Indirect	Sustained	Light
Wring	Indirect	Sustained	Strong
Press	Direct	Sustained	Strong
Glide	Direct	Sustained	Light
Dab	Direct	Sudden	Light
Flick	Indirect	Sudden	Light
Slash	Indirect	Sudden	Strong
Punch	Direct	Sudden	Strong

time the cows' bodies are moving slowly, the cows' tails are moving suddenly and repeatedly to swish away flies and mosquitoes.

> Force: Movements described as light and resisting gravity ranging to movements that are strong and powerful express the continuum of *force*.

Light_____FORCE_____Strong

Force can be described as an amount of energy. Force relates to gravity in that it is influenced by the degree of energy needed to overcome the pull of gravity on the weight of the body or an object. For example, if you need to move a piano, you will need to use your weight (with gravity) and push with a strong force. However, if you are moving a delicate crystal vase, you need to withhold your full body weight and use light force.

So, what happens when aspects of space, time, and force of a movement are clarified? The result is that you can identify the effort action that describes the quality of that movement. Simply stated, when a movement is described in respect to time (fast or slow), space (direct or indirect), and force (light or strong), one of the basic effort actions is identified. Exploration of the effort actions builds on the basic CED content. In other words, students explore effort actions while exploring the body and aspects of the other elements, such as direction, size, level, and shape. For example, pressing (direct-slow-strong) can be explored at a low level using the whole body or at a high level using an isolated body part. Teachers can gradually increase the complexity of the movement problem from lesson to lesson, thus allowing students time to learn and master the concepts while continuing to present new and challenging content.

Exploring the eight basic effort actions in pairs of opposites is suggested for beginning students (Preston-Dunlop, 1990). Working with opposite effort actions within one lesson allows teachers to focus primarily on one effort and to use the opposite one to balance the experience. For example, exploring effort actions characterized by strong force and fast tempo interspersed with light, slow actions provides opportunities to experience the contrast of the two actions and provides recovery or rest time for the body. Using opposite effort actions, teachers would pair the effort actions as follows: wringing with dabbing, slashing with gliding, punching with floating, and pressing with flicking.

One quick and easy way to begin exploring opposite effort actions is to ask students to work with partners using a structured activity, such as "Together and Apart." In this activity, partners begin several feet apart from each other, then travel "together" (toward each other), then travel "apart" (back to their beginning point). Students begin by focusing on only one element of movement, such as time, then broaden their focus to include force followed by space. For example, to explore floating and punching using "Together and Apart," students can begin by focusing on the time continuum. Students travel together (toward a partner) in slow motion, pause, and then rush quickly apart. Teachers add the concept of force to the exploration of time. In other words, students travel slowly with light or gentle force, pause, then separate and travel apart quickly with strong force. After experiencing the contrast between slow, light movements and quick, strong movements, students add a layer related to space. Teachers guide students to explore traveling indirectly, slowly, with light force "together" and directly while traveling quickly and forcefully "apart." By providing a wide range of possible movements that can be used to explore the effort actions, teachers can more easily include students with disabilities. In other words, traveling can be rolling, scooting, or any form of moving through space. To bring the basic effort actions to life and give meaning to the exploration, teachers and students can match the movements to selected traveling or descriptive words. Selection of words used to motivate students to explore these effort actions is based on the developmental level and interests of the students. The application example includes potential words for exploring opposite pairs of basic effort actions and many possible movements.

CED and Individuals With Disabilities

All students should have opportunities to explore the interactions of space, time, and force, but how can students with severe physical disabilities participate? The following discussion introduces an approach based not on "normalizing" the movements of students with disabilities but on perceiving differences associated with disabilities as potential sources of artistic material. The approach requires expansion of the definition of dance to include a new aesthetic—the aesthetics of disability. Within the scope of this chapter we cannot present a detailed description of this

APPLICATION EXAMPLE

Exploring Opposite Pairs of Effort Actions

Setting: A physical educator uses words to guide and motivate students in exploring an opposite pair of basic effort actions: floating and thrusting.

Students: A middle school class including a student with hypertonia (excessive muscle tightness) who walks with a scissors gait.

Application: The physical educator presents exploration floating and thrusting by offering a variety of movement choices and using age-appropriate descriptor words.

- Students are asked to travel in slow motion for eight drum beats, pause, then, with the speed of light, on that spot, clap, stamp, or jump for four drum beats. Students can use any form of traveling as long as they use slow tempo. Using a variety of travel words, such as plodding, creeping along, lingering, or descriptive words such as sleepily, calmly, serenely, quietly, gradually or leisurely, can help students move in slow motion.

- Students are asked to perform the stationary, quick movements with any body parts, such as a knee, elbow, wrist, or shoulder and focus on force. "As you travel, breathe deeply and move gently, drifting along, then surprise me with strong, vigorous, jolting, powerful, exploding movements with any body parts. You can clap, stamp, jump, or use any movements. Your sequence is drift, pause, explode."

- Words used to characterize the use of space for floating include vaporous, roundabout, carefree, or meandering. Making sure to clearly highlight the contrast of the direct use of space of thrusting actions, teachers describe them as pointed, piercing, or jabbing movements.

---

approach, but we can offer a brief overview of the key components.

As described by Elin and Boswell (2004) the process of "Re-envisioning Dance" begins with adopting the notion that all students bring talents to class and that sometimes these talents are disguised as limitations. In other words, whether students present postural misalignments, limited mobility, lack of range of motion, or other obvious differences, they enter class bringing strengths. And, what appears to be a limitation can be perceived as an asset. This process allows us to begin to see motor differences associated with disabilities as potential sources of artistic expression. Recognition of the potential value of movements previously considered "unacceptable" is a central theme in the process.

The concept of motif is an integral component of Re-envisioning Dance. Motif is defined as a single movement, spatial design, or brief movement phrase used as the basis for creating a dance. An excellent discussion of motif and development by Blom and Chaplin (1982) clarifies motif as a device or method for building dances:

> . . . the motif is manipulated; it is performed upside down, backward, inside out. Its original sequence (order of its parts) is not sacred as in theme and variation. Fragments of the movement are used and developed separately, then put together with no specific regard for the original order. But there is a definite sense of form that comes from developing the motif. (pp. 101-102)

Re-envisioning Dance involves guiding students to explore the development of motifs as they focus on the effort actions. As highlighted in the chapter-opening scenario, the movements of students with disabilities can serve as the basis of motifs. At first, these movements might appear to be unacceptable for dance, but teachers are encouraged to "re-envision" these movements as potential sources of artistic material.

STRUCTURED DANCE

Building on the knowledge and skills gained in rhythmic activities and CED, students can discover the joy of learning structured or patterned dances. Structured dances, as the term implies, have specific sequences of steps. The terms "structured," "patterned," and "recreational" dances can be used interchangeably and include many types of dances, such as international folk dances, American Heritage dances (e.g., the Virginia Reel), contemporary line dances, and social dances (e.g., swing and salsa). The degree of structure of these types of dance, varies greatly from dance to dance. Many folk dances are characterized by a basic step and have a common figure or movement design performed by two or more persons. Common dance figures in folk dances include do-si-do for partners and turning under arches for three dancers. Structured dances also have a range of group formations, such as a circle, line, or square arrangement and diverse musical accompaniments. Use of age-appropriate music and inclusion of current steps are especially important in middle school and high school levels. When high school students have opportunities to increase their skills and confidence in social dances, they experience dance as a lifelong physical activity that provides social as well as physical benefits throughout their lives.

Learning a structured dance should be accomplished in a minimum amount of time and result in a feeling of accomplishment. Variations of locomotor and nonlocomotor movements previously experienced in rhythmic activities and CED are the basic ingredients. It is a natural progression from exploring running with a partner to learning a structured dance that uses running as the basic step. It is also a natural progression from exploring ways of traveling using a wheelchair with a partner to discovering ways of moving together to learn a structured dance. Approaching the process of teaching structured dances with a problem-solving perspective can contribute to the fun of modifying a dance and to the awareness of the importance of inclusion.

As forms of recreational dance, participation in structured dances offers lifetime health and social benefits. Moving in unison with others to music should be a fun activity that students return to with pleasure and develop as a meaningful lifetime physical activity. Also, learning international folk dances provides excellent opportunities for students to increase their understanding of other cultures. Introductory information such as country of origin and cultural significance of the dance can be covered quickly and reinforced through handouts.

Content

The basic nonlocomotor (bend, reach, twist) and locomotor (walk, run, jump, hop, leap) movement patterns form the basic materials of struc-tured dances. Combinations of these locomotor movements produce the gallop, slide, and skip. Variations and combinations of these locomotor patterns form the traditional dance steps, such as the two-step, schottische, polka, grapevine, and waltz. Most folk and line dances consist of one or two of these basic steps performed in a sequence. The sequence of steps is performed repeatedly to a simple rhythmic pattern. Many references for folk dances classify the dances according to the basic step used. One of the guidelines for selecting a structured dance for a class is to review the basic step of the dance in light of the developmental level of the students. The step should already be part of the students' movement repertoire and one that can be modified easily so that all students can participate. The movement content of the dance should match the developmental level of the students to ensure that the class can learn the dance easily and practice it quickly with a sense of enjoyment and accomplishment.

Teaching Style and Method of Presentation

Weikart (1989, 1997) provides an excellent description of her teaching style, "Say and Do." The "Say and Do" strategy involves verbalizing cue words as steps are performed. As well as capitalizing on the power of verbalizing the steps as they are performed, this procedure includes a developmental analysis of the movements included in folk dances. Dances are grouped developmentally into levels of motor difficulty.

The following list presents dances grouped according to general motor complexity. Developmental considerations include the level of difficulty of locomotor patterns, number of weight transfers, complexity of the rhythm, and directional information (knowing left and right). Other factors such as previous motor experience, cultural differences, and levels of social development must be considered when selecting dances for a particular class.

Level 1 (corresponding to K through second grade)

Seven jumps

Apat apat

Irish stew

Sneaky snake

La raspa

Troika

Level 2 (corresponding to grades three through five)

> Close encounters
>
> Alley cat
>
> Hustle
>
> Popcorn
>
> Cotton-eyed Joe
>
> Hora

Level 3 (corresponding to middle school grades to adults)

> Dirlada
>
> Jambo
>
> Mayim mayim
>
> Tarantella
>
> Korobushka
>
> Misirlou
>
> Doublebska polka
>
> Jessie polka

In respect to teaching styles appropriate for presenting structured dances, Kassing and Jay (2003) provide a description of the inclusive teaching style, which is based on allowing students to work on different variations of the content. Teaching variations of certain steps when presenting structured dances is an essential part of including all students. For example, some students might be working on refining the grapevine step while other students who use wheelchairs are working on traveling forward on a curved path with a partner. The teacher can present options to the entire class or to small groups of students.

An inclusive teaching style used in teaching structured dances can be extended to incorporate a divergent teaching style. This extension would involve the students in discovering other variations of steps through problem solving. In other words, students would work not only on different levels of the same combination but also on discovering different variations of the steps. Once the students understand the sequence of steps, the figures, and how the steps reflect the phrasing of the music, the teacher can use these as boundaries or parameters in the movement problem. To incorporate problem solving into teaching structured dances, the teacher must be willing to allow changes in the original dance that might alter the dance's essential pattern and style. The teacher must carefully consider what changes are appropriate and set acceptable boundaries for changes to the dances. Certain changes that dis-

tort any semblance of the original pattern and style of the dance might not be acceptable. But if altering certain steps and eliminating others allows all students to participate with enthusiasm and to develop a love for movement and dance, the result likely outweighs the loss of authenticity of the dance. See the section on modifications.

The method of presentation will vary according to the features of the dance and the needs of the students. The teaching process outlined in the following section is primarily the add-on method. As the term implies, after specific steps are learned, remaining steps are added. Depending on the complexity of the dance and the developmental level of the students, use of the part-whole-part method might be appropriate. Regardless of method of presentation, students need to hear the music and have opportunities to listen to the beat at the beginning of the lesson. For deaf or hard-of-hearing students, the instructor should use visual cues. Also, sitting close to a speaker on the floor might allow these students to feel vibrations of the music. Clapping in time to the music emphasizes the underlying beat and can help students identify accented beats.

1. Students listen and clap or tap to the music. Emphasize the tempo and meter.

2. Teacher (or student leader) provides a brief demonstration of the dance with the musical accompaniment and introduces verbal cues. Students with visual differences can be paired with a peer who can verbally describe the steps as performed by the instructor.

3. Introduce the basic step. This activity can serve as a warm-up. Demonstrate the step, facing the same direction as the students, and suggest a modification if needed. In circular formation or while traveling across the room, the class performs the step to music or a drum beat.

4. If a difficult step is included, this step can be "pulled out" of the entire sequence and taught separately. Modifications are explored and developed to match the students' developmental level. The step is practiced with music.

5. The remaining steps are combined, and the sequence is performed to music. Teacher cues (verbal and visual) along with additional demonstrations are provided as needed.

The following sample lesson is designed for any students who have responded successfully to changing tempos while performing nonlocomotor and locomotor movements. These students can dance with a partner or small group and follow simple sequences of movements performed to an external rhythm. Although the content is primarily structured dance, the lesson includes opportunities for rhythmic development.

Modifications for Meeting Unique Needs and Differences

Possible ways to modify dances will evolve as the teacher and students engage in problem solving.

The following questions are offered to encourage teachers to be inventive in the process. It is better to change certain aspects of the dance than to exclude any students or to abandon the dance altogether.

- If the dance consists of several sections, can a section be eliminated or a certain section shortened? Dancing only two of three sections might be preferred to help students remember the dance and leave the class with a feeling of accomplishment.

- If the dance includes movements that require considerable balance skills, such as hops or

Sample Lesson: Structured Dance

Student Objectives

1. Demonstrate the basic step, the schottische, to a steady external beat.
2. Demonstrate two of the three sections of the African Creole folk dance, Bele Kawe, with music.
3. Explore variations for the movements in the third section of Bele Kawe, the four-count turn or jump.

Warm-Up Activity: Movements to "Happiness Runs in a Circular Motion"

Directions: Students listen to the music and sway side to side in rhythm to the four simple lines of verse. The teacher asks students to watch as he or she demonstrates a basic step, the schottische, composed of three walking steps and a hop. She repeats the schottische step several times, then asks the students to perform the step (or an appropriate variation) with her without the music. To practice with music, students divide into two or three groups to form small circles. Each circle travels forward on the circular path, in the same direction, repeating the schottische step (or appropriate modification) to music.

Communicate Goals of the Lesson to Students

Perform two of the three sections of Bele Kawe with a small group to music.

Explore variations of the step that includes a turn or jump.

Sequence of Activities

1. Listen to the music for Bele Kawe and clap or tap in sync with the beat.

2. Students learn part 1. Facing the same direction as the students, the instructor demonstrates a simple version of "step, touch." Beginning with either foot, the first step is forward, and the other foot touches (no transfer of weight) close to the first; then "step, touch" is repeated moving to the back. In circular formation, the class practices the step with the instructor and then performs the step to music.

3. Students use the same procedure for learning part 2, "touch heel, step." Students touch the heel of the foot forward, then step with the same foot. They alternate feet and practice in circular formation with the teacher.

4. Students practice parts 1 and 2 to music.

5. The teacher demonstrates the three-step turn or jump and asks students to brainstorm about variations for this movement. Examples of variations include performing the basic schottische step forward (four counts) and backward (four counts) or repeating the step for two sets of eight counts.

6. Students independently explore variations for the third section and select one to perform to music.

7. The class divides into groups of six to eight, shares their variations, and selects the best fit to the music.

Closure

The class performs the schottische step to contemporary music with a moderate or slow tempo in a circular path. Teacher slows the tempo and asks the class to use walking steps as she reviews the purpose of the lesson.

jumps, how can these movements be modified? What movements can be substituted for these movements?

* Can the tempo of the music be slowed or can the movements be performed using twice as many counts? Acquiring a CD player or tape player with variable speed control allows teachers to easily slow or speed up the tempo of the music.

* If the dance includes a difficult turn, what other ways can the turn be performed? What other movements might be substituted?

SUMMARY

The guiding theme of this chapter is that rhythmic movement and dance are powerful content areas for developing problem solving, creative expression, and motor skills of students with and without disabilities. Rhythmic movement can be considered the beginning point for dance, a beginning that is strengthened through participation in CED and structured dance. Teaching structured dances enables teachers to involve the class quickly in physical activity and provide meaningful opportunities to learn a lifetime physical activity. Although the content of these movement forms can be taught separately, each content can lead into the others, thus resulting in a more powerful medium for strengthening student development. This chapter also emphasized that the basic content of CED can be extended into exploration of the basic effort actions. This expansion of content provides opportunities for students to refine their ability to communicate through movement; it also provides opportunities for teachers to re-envision movements associated with disabilities as potential sources of artistic material.

REFERENCES

Blom, L.A., and Chaplin, T.L.(1982). *The intimate act of choreography.* London: Dance Books.

Boswell, B., & Vidret, M. (1993). Rhythmic movement and music for adolescents with severe and profound disabilities. *Music Therapy Perspectives,* 11, pp. 37-41.

Elin, J., & Boswell, B. (2004). *Re-envisioning dance: Aesthetics of disability.* Dubuque, IA: Kendall Hunt Publishers.

Graham, G., Holt/Hale, S., & Parker, M. (2001). *Children moving: A reflective approach to teaching physical education.* (5th ed.). Mountain View, CA: Mayfield.

Harris, J., Pittman, A., Waller, M., & Dark, C.L. (1998). *Social dance.* (2nd ed.). San Francisco: Benjamin Cummings.

Humphrey, D. (1980). *The art of making dances.* New York: Grove Press.

Joyce, M. (1994). *First steps in teaching creative dance.* (3rd ed.). Palo Alto, CA: Mayfield.

Kassing, G., & Jay, D.M. (2003). *Dance teaching methods and curriculum design.* Champaign, IL: Human Kinetics.

National Association for Sport and Physical Education. (1995). *Moving into the future: National standards for physical education.* St. Louis, MO: Mosby.

Preston-Dunlop, V. (1990). *Modern educational dance.* (Rev. ed.). Boston: Plays Inc. Publishers.

Sherrill, C. (1998). *Adapted physical activity, recreation and sport* (5th ed.). Boston: McGraw-Hill.

Smith-Autard, J.M. (2000). *Dance composition.* (4th ed.). London: Routledge.

Weikart, P.S. (1989). *Teaching movement and dance* (3rd ed.). Ypsilanti, MI: High Scope Press.

Weikart, P.S. (1997). *Teaching folk dance: Successful steps.* Ypsilanti, MI: High Scope Press.

WRITTEN RESOURCES

Benjamin, A. (2002). *Making an entrance.* London: Routledge.

A must-read for anyone interested in new dance or inclusive theatre dance.

Bennett, J.P., & Reimer, P.C. (1995). *Rhythmic activities and dance,* Champaign, IL: Human Kinetics.

Edwards-Duke, B., Boswell, B., McGhee, S., & Decker, J. (2002). Creative educational dance and children with behavior disorders. *Journal of Dance Education,* 2, 23-31.

Elin, J., & Boswell, B. (2004). *Re-envisioning Dance: Aesthetics of disability.* Dubuque, IA: Kendall Hunt Publishers.

Gilbert, A.G. (1992). *Creative dance for all ages: A conceptual approach.* Reston, VA: American Alliance for Health, Physical Education, Recreation and Dance.

The author provides clear and simple discussions of content and lesson examples.

Hills, S. (1999). Shall we dance? *WE Magazine,* 3, 46-52.

Presents organizations for dancers with disabilities: Dancing Wheels and the Axis Dance Co.

Joyce, M. (1984). *Dance technique for children.* Palo Alto, CA: Mayfield.

This is an excellent book that clarifies how dance provides opportunities for students to learn movement principles and move effectively.

Kuppers, P. (2000). Accessible education: Aesthetics, bodies and disability. *Research in Dance Education,* 1(2), p. 119-131.

Landalf, H., & Gerke, P (1996). *Movement stories.* Lyme, NH: Smith and Kraus, Inc.

Authors present a series of movement sequences for children aged three to six years.

Lloyd, M.L, (1998). *Adventures in creative movement activities.* (2nd). Dubuque, IA: Eddie Bowers Publishing, Inc.

The author summaries fundamental concepts for educational dance and provides examples of CED lessons adaptable for many skill levels.

Mentzer, M.C., & Boswell, B. (1995). Effects of a movement poetry program on creativity of children with behavioral disorders. *Impulse,* 3, 183-199.

Preston-Dunlop, V. (1998). *Looking at dances.* Great Britain: Bath Press.

AUDIOVISUAL RESOURCES

All bodies speak: Five DanceAbility performances. (Videotape, 2000). Obtained through Insight Media, 2162 Broadway, NY, 10024.

Humorous, playful, and insightful, this program presents five works by the well-known DanceAbility Project. The project highlights prejudices that inhibit artistic diversity. Running time is 55 minutes.

Common ground: Dance and disability. (Videotape, 1990).

Obtained through Insight Media, 2162 Broadway, NY, 10024. Individuals with a variety of abilities explore movement and dance. Presents scenes of people in and out of wheelchairs practicing balances and lifts as well as creating improvisational movement sequences. Running time is 20 minutes.

Dancing from the inside out. (Videotape, 1994). Fanlight Productions, 4196 Washington Square, Boston, MA 02131.

An excellent video that profiles three dancers from the acclaimed AXIS Dance Troupe, which includes dancers with and without disabilities. By Thais Mazur and Sarah Shockley. Running time is 28 minutes.

ELECTRONIC RESOURCES

www.artslynx.org/heal/dance.htm.

This site includes resources related to dance and disabilities. An excellent source of information about dance companies such as AXIS, Bilderwerfer, Dancing Wheels, Light Motion, and Full Radius Dance. Also provides great info and links to companies including dancers who are deaf and blind. In addition, dance companies including older adults, such as the fabulous Liz Lerman Dance, and resources for dance therapy are included.

www.lunakidsdance.com.

Luna Kids Dance is an arts education organization with an emphasis on teacher education and building alliances between school-based teachers and dance artists.

CHAPTER 25

Aquatics

Monica Lepore

Jack is an eight-year-old boy needing full physical assistance to participate in his general physical education class. Jack's parents have asked the school district for a physical education assessment to determine if Jack is benefiting from his current support and placement. Jack's parents have noticed Jack exhibits more independence when placed in a flotation device in his backyard pool than he does anywhere else. Thus, they have asked that a swimming component be part of the assessment.

During the land portion of the physical education assessment, it was evident that Jack could not participate in physical activities without adult intervention. He was not able to consistently perform voluntary movements against gravity and could not raise his heart rate unless physically assisted. In contrast, during the pool assessment, Jack was able to raise his heart rate by 40 beats using a head–neck flotation device without teacher intervention. In addition, he continually moved his arms and legs for nine minutes without prompting. On the basis of this information, Jack's IEP committee decided that he should receive adapted aquatic instruction at the expense of the school district in addition to general physical education instruction.

This scenario demonstrates that adapted aquatic instruction can complement a land-based adapted physical education program. The purpose of this chapter is to assist the reader in identifying benefits of aquatic instructional programs, illustrate the best practices in adapted aquatics, and provide information for meeting the needs of students with disabilities in aquatic programs.

BENEFITS OF ADAPTED AQUATICS

Aquatics provide physical fitness and motor skill development within a physical education program for children with disabilities. In the chapter-opening scenario, Jack's parents are within their legal rights to request swimming as part of their son's IEP because aquatics is listed as a component of physical education under PL 105-17 (Individuals with Disabilities Education Act). School districts have to realize that aquatics is neither a luxury nor a therapeutic (related) service. **Adapted aquatics** means modifying the teaching environment, skills, facilities, equipment, and instructional strategies for individuals with disabilities. Adapted aquatics includes aquatic activities of all types, including instructional and competitive swimming, small-craft boating, water aerobics, and skin diving and scuba diving (AAHPERD-AAALF, 1996).

Physical educators, school administrators, parents, related service personnel, and special education teachers must be educated about the benefits of aquatics and its role in a child's education. The physical and psychosocial benefits of aquatics for children with disabilities are more pronounced and significant than for individuals without disabilities. Because of the buoyancy afforded by water, many people whose disabilities impair mobility on land can function independently in an aquatic environment without the assistance of braces, crutches, walkers, or wheelchairs. Although adapted aquatics does not focus on therapeutic water exercise, warm water facilitates muscle relaxation, joint range of motion, and improved muscle strength and endurance (Koury, 1996). Swimming strengthens muscles that enhance postural stability necessary for locomotor and object control skills. Water supports the body, enabling a person to possibly walk for the first time, thus increasing strength for ambulation on land. Adapted aquatics activities also enhance breath control and cardiorespiratory fitness. Blowing bubbles, holding one's breath, and inhalation–exhalation during swimming strokes improve respiratory function and oral motor control, aiding in speech development (Martin, 1983; see figure 25.1).

© Monica Lepore

Figure 25.1 Breath control exercises help improve oral motor control.

Benefits are not limited to the physical realm. Water activities that are carefully planned and implemented meet individual needs by providing an environment that contributes to psychosocial and cognitive development. As an individual with a physical disability learns to move through the water without assistance, self-esteem and self-awareness improve. Moreover, the freedom of movement made possible by water boosts morale and provides an incentive to maximize potential in other aspects of rehabilitation (Koury, 1996).

The motivational and therapeutic properties of water provide a stimulating learning environment. Some instructors even reinforce academic learning, successfully reinforcing cognitive concepts during water games and activities centered on math, spelling, reading, and other concepts. Participants might count laps, dive for submerged plastic letters, or read their workouts. These activities also help participants improve judgment and orientation to the surrounding environment.

GENERAL TEACHING SUGGESTIONS

Each person is unique, and individualization is the key to safe, effective, and relevant programming. Thus, it should never be assumed that all characteristics associated with disabilities are endemic to each person with that diagnosis. Generalizations serve merely to present a wide scope of information that might pertain to swimmers with any particular disability. Each swimmer should be taught sufficient safety and swimming skills to become as safe and comfortable as possible during aquatic activities. Choice and presentation of skills should be tailored to meet the needs of each individual (Lepore, Gayle, & Stevens, 1998).

Prior to instruction the teacher must gather information from written, oral, and observational sources. In addition to reading previous records and interviewing the swimmer and significant others, an aquatic assessment must be conducted to determine present level of functioning. General instructional suggestions include writing long-term goals and short-term performance objectives, task analyzing aquatic skills, determining proper lift and transfer methods, establishing communication signals, and developing holding and positioning techniques to facilitate instruction. Knowledge of typical growth and developmental patterns are helpful in understanding the difference between movements that are developmentally inappropriate and movements that have just not developed yet. For example, a bicycle kick is a typical developmentally appropriate sequence for most children, but after more experience and decreased fear, this type of kick is an inappropriate swim skill during the crawl stroke.

Teaching basic safety skills first, such as mouth closure, rolling over from front to back, changing directions, recovering from falling into the pool, vertical recovery from front and back positions, and holding onto the pool wall, helps to alleviate fear of more difficult skills. A balanced body position in the water is an important prerequisite for skills. The aquatic instructor must experiment with horizontal and vertical rotation and appropriate placement of arms, legs, and head to teach the development of proper buoyancy, balance, and water comfort in relation to the unique physical characteristics of the student. One method of teaching balance and body positions in adapted aquatics is the Halliwick method (Stanat & Lambeck, 2001).

Finally, presenting swimming cues in a concise manner, connected to something that the individual already is familiar with, strengthens learning. Because swimming takes place in such a unique setting, swimmers with disabilities need cues that refer to situations or things they already know or know how to do. An example of this is the use of the phrase "move your hands as if you are opening and closing curtains" to depict the movement of the hands during treading water or sculling.

AQUATIC ASSESSMENT

Individualized instructional planning begins with defining which skills a participant needs to learn and assessing the present level of performance in those skills. Before performing the assessment, an instructor should determine the skills to be assessed. To help prioritize, questions such as these should be asked of the participant or caregiver: What is the participant interested in learning? What are important safety skills for the participant to acquire? Where will the participant use the skills outside of class? What are same-age peers performing in aquatics? What equipment does the family have available? What are the medical, therapeutic, educational, and recreational needs of the participant? After looking at all the possible skills important to teach or test for a participant, an instructor looks at the list to determine if there are any repeat skills. Skills common to many of the questions just listed should become the priorities to assess (and then be taught, if they are lacking). Assessment items that determine the present level of performance in these skills should be developed (Block, 2000).

Swimming instructors typically use curriculum-based or ecologically based assessment checklists or a rubric to determine the extent of aquatic skills an individual possesses (figure 25.2). Curriculum-based assessment items include skills that the swimmer needs to function effectively within an integrated class. The American Red Cross Progressive Swim Levels 1-6 (American Red Cross, 2004), YMCA swim levels (YMCA of the USA, 1999), and the SwimAmerica (SwimAmerica, n.d.) skills programs are examples of curricula from which a swim instructor would draw skills for a curriculum-based assessment checklist.

An ecologically based aquatic assessment might also be considered. Ecologically based assessments include skills needed for an individual's current and future environment. Aquatic skill assessments of this nature might include components of the curriculum-based assessment but also

SKILL EVALUATION CHART

Student: _____

Scoring codes:

O = cannot perform   V = verbal cues   G = gesture cues

X = independent   PC = picture cues   P = physical cues

• More than one code might describe a step (e.g., V, PC)

Target steps or skills	Dates	Target steps or skills	Dates
I. Entries		• Arm stroke, with underwater recovery, face in, kicking (10 feet)	_____
• Ladder entry	_____	• Arm stroke with over water recovery (10 feet)	_____
• Side roll in	_____	• Arm stroke with kick (20 feet)	_____
• Jump: shallow	_____	• Front crawl with rhythmic breathing to front (20 feet)	_____
• Jump: deep	_____	• Front crawl with breathing to side (20 feet or more)	_____
• Dive: kneel	_____	**V. Breaststroke**	
• Dive: compact	_____	• Push off in streamlined position for beginning breaststroke	_____
• Dive: stride	_____	• Breaststroke arms (on deck)	_____
• Dive: front	_____	• Breaststroke arms while standing in water	_____
II. Exits		• Breaststroke arms over a noodle (30 feet)	_____
• Ladder	_____	• Breaststroke kick correctly on deck (5 times)	_____
• Pull-up (side of pool)	_____	• Breaststroke kick over a noodle (30 feet)	_____
III. Water orientation		• Breaststroke combined arms and kick (30 feet)	_____
• Washes face	_____	**VI. Back propulsion**	
• Puts chin in water	_____	• Back float (5 seconds)	_____
• Puts mouth in water	_____	• Back glide off wall with a noodle	_____
• Puts mouth and nose in water	_____	• Back glide (10 feet)	_____
• Puts face in water	_____	• Back glide with kick (20 feet)	_____
• Puts whole body in water	_____	• Back glide with finning or sculling (10 feet)	_____
• Blows bubbles	_____	• Back crawl arms (on deck)	_____
• Blows bubbles with face in water	_____	• Back crawl arms over a noodle	_____
• Blows bubbles lying on front with face in water	_____	• Back crawl arms with kick (20 feet)	_____
• Blows bubbles with full body underwater	_____	**VII. Side propulsion**	
• Bobs 5 times in shallow water	_____	• Side stroke glide	_____
• Bobs 10 times in shallow water	_____	• Side stroke legs (on deck)	_____
• Bobs 5 times in deep water	_____	• Side stroke legs over a noodle (20 feet)	_____
• Bobs 10 times in deep water	_____	• Side stroke arms (on deck)	_____
IV. Front propulsion		• Side stroke arms over noodle (20 feet)	_____
• Pushes off side with face out of water	_____	• Side stroke (30 feet)	_____
• Pushes off side with face in water	_____		
• Pushes off side with face in water and kicks	_____		
• Arm stroke while walking	_____		
• Arm stroke, with underwater recovery (5 feet)	_____		
• Arm stroke, with underwater recovery face in water (5 feet)	_____		

Figure 25.2 Aquatic activity achievement checklist.

From *Adapted Physical Education and Sport, Fourth Edition* by Joseph P. Winnick, 2005, Champaign, IL: Human Kinetics.

include individual skills not addressed in the general curriculum, such as entering and exiting the pool area, dressing, using appropriate language in a swim group, performing stretching exercises before swimming, knowing how to swim in a circle, using a flotation device, or clearing the mouth of water. These are skills that need to be learned but would not usually appear within a general swim curriculum. Ecologically based assessments are recommended to assess all areas of the aquatic experience. These assessments should be developed on the basis of individual needs.

ADAPTING SWIMMING SKILLS

Before adapting skills to meet an individual's needs, an instructor must first look at why the skill is needed and how and where the skill will be used. Some swimmers want to pass the competencies for the American Red Cross Swim Levels, some might want to improve cardiorespiratory functioning, and yet others might want to enter a swim meet. These differing purposes for performing the front crawl (freestyle) might cause an instructor to take a different approach to adapting strokes and other aquatic skills. Important considerations in adapting strokes include the following:

- What are the physical constraints of the disability?
- What is the most efficient way to propel through the water, given the constraints?
- What movements will cause or diminish pain or injury?
- What adaptations can be made to make the stroke or skill as much like the nonadapted version as possible?
- What equipment is available to facilitate the skill?
- What is the reason the swimmer wants to learn this skill (competition, relaxation)?

The instructor might need to:

- adjust the swimmer's body position by adding flotation or light weights,
- change the propulsive action of the arms or legs, or
- adapt the breathing pattern.

Adjusting the swimmer's body position is typical for people who have disabilities such as cerebral palsy, stroke, traumatic brain injury, spina bifida, obesity, limb loss, muscular dystrophy, polio, or traumatic spinal cord injury. Because of variations from the norm, in regard to muscle mass and body fat in many individuals with physical disabilities, the center of gravity and center of buoyancy might be atypical. It is important to find an efficient body position and experiment with different flotation devices and weights (e.g., scuba diving and ankle weights, inflatable arm floaties, foam swim noodles, rescue tubes, lifejackets, ski belts). A body position close to horizontal is the most streamlined and effective.

The swimmer's arm and leg actions might need adjustment also. Typical efficient propulsive action might not be feasible because of contractures, muscle atrophy, or missing limbs. Adaptations such as changing the ideal "S" curve of the front crawl arms to a modified "C" or "J" should be experimented with. Lower-body propulsive adaptations might include bending the knees more during flutter kicking, using the scissors kick while breathing in the front crawl, or using fins while doing the butterfly dolphin kick during any of the strokes.

Breathing patterns can be changed from one-side breathing to alternate-side breathing, front breathing, rolling over onto back to breathe, or using a snorkel. Swimmers can be taught explosive breathing, breathing using the mouth only, or breathing using a closed-throat technique.

Nonphysical adaptations include developmentally appropriate progressions, frequent practice of skills, detailed traditional and ecological task analysis, verbal and visual cues, repeating directions, and altering the skill objective.

ORIENTATION TO WATER

Acquisition of aquatic skills is based on the learner's readiness to receive the skill, readiness to understand the goal, opportunities to practice at a challenging but manageable level, and ability to receive feedback. Orientation to water focuses on the readiness of the learner and other psychological and physiological factors. Physiological factors are those in which anatomical and physiological variations in an individual's body affect how and what he or she learns. This includes how disability and medication affect each body system. A swimmer might not be neurologically ready to perform a skill because of brain damage, lack of central nervous system maturity, or a developmental delay. When the instructor understands the effect of a disability on learning and provides developmentally appropriate skill progressions, learning is increased (Langendorfer & Bruya, 1995).

Psychologically, each person is unique and learns at an individual rate, depending on several psychological factors. Individuals with disabilities might have psychological characteristics that hinder the acquisition of aquatic skills. Some psychological factors, such as anxiety and cognitive readiness, should be examined before developing instructional strategies.

Most anxiety during swim instruction stems from fear and discomfort and inhibits mental adjustment to the aquatic environment. Although mental adjustment takes time for new or frightened swimmers, it might be even more difficult for individuals with disabilities. Poor breath control as a consequence of oral muscle dysfunction, asthma, or high- or low-muscle tone limits the ability to develop rhythmic breathing and breath holding. These and other issues, such as not being able to grasp and hold the pool gutter, make it likely that some individuals with disabilities are at high risk of having their openness to learning affected by fear and anxiety. Factors that might cause anxiousness in a swimmer include fear of drowning, past frightening water experiences, submerging unexpectedly and choking on water, fear reinforced by warnings (e.g., "Don't go near that water or you'll drown"), capsizing in a boat, being knocked down by a wave, or feelings of insecurity caused by poor physical ability or unfamiliar surroundings (Lepore, Gayle, & Stevens, 1998).

Fear stimulates physiological responses, such as heightened muscle tone, increased involuntary muscle movements, and inability to float. Fear and insecurity prevent success in swimming. Helping participants get past fear and anxiety to practice aquatic skills that will make them safer in the water is an initial step in teaching swimming. When participants are free of fear, they are free to learn. The following tips, taken from the *YMCA of the USA Parent/Child and Preschool Aquatic Program Manual* (1999a), will promote comfort and reduce fear. These suggestions can be used for all ages of participants:

- Allow more reluctant participants extra time for water acclimation activities.
- Use patience without pampering.
- Gently guide; don't force.
- Explain everything in a calm, quiet, matter-of-fact voice.

- Teach in shallow water (e.g., on pool steps, water tables, or water docks) or on a gradually sloping ramp.
- Emphasize noncompetitive activities.
- Provide a mask or goggles if water in the eyes is an issue.
- Provide redirection of crying or anxious behaviors by using a colorful piece of equipment or a discussion of the swimmer's favorite food.
- Use the swimmers' names frequently; smile and praise small steps in the progression of water adjustment.
- Assess an individual's readiness for swim lessons. Use an assessment such as the Aquatic Readiness Assessment tool by Langendorfer & Bruya (1995). Areas to assess with this tool are water entry, breath control, buoyancy and body position, arm actions, leg actions, and combined movements.

Fear is diminished when the aquatic instructor and swimmer easily communicate. In addition to communication skills, a thorough understanding of proper participant positioning, guiding, and supporting is essential. Proper methods of transferring, touching, and supporting participants in the locker room, on the pool deck, and in the pool will also develop relationships based on trust. Knowing how to use and work all the adapted equipment, wheelchairs, and flotation devices provides an atmosphere of efficiency and safety that makes everyone feel comfortable. Likewise, holding someone with a firm and balanced grip, as close as safety and comfort allow, communicates care and establishes trust and rapport (Lepore, Gayle, & Stevens, 1998). In addition, an environment in which the instructor exhibits a consistent personality, provides discipline methods that are flexible but consistent, uses caring verbal assurances, and provides balanced and controlled physical handling promotes trust, security, and mental adjustment.

The aquatic instructor should use fun activities instead of drills to promote a more comfortable atmosphere. Games, music, and props help a fearful student become more ready to accept the aquatic setting. Activities such as a flower hunt with plastic flowers inserted into the gutters at various intervals help acclimate the fearful student in a nonthreatening manner. Other activities include square dance and social dance; physical education games, such as cooperative musical chairs using hoops; land games; and activities such as basketball and sponge tossing to inflatable tubes. These activities build on what a person is familiar with, and the aquatic instructor can progress from there.

FACILITY AND EQUIPMENT CONSIDERATIONS

For participants and instructors alike, facilities and equipment must be accessible and safe and lend themselves to successful and satisfying experiences. Familiarity with the *Americans with Disability Act (ADA) Accessibility Guidelines* (Architectural and Transportation Barriers Compliance Board, 2004), state and local health codes for aquatic facilities, and resources for equipment and supplies that promote aquatic participation (see this chapter's references and resources section) help provide quality swimming experiences.

Facilities

Facility characteristics should be discussed with the participant before the first session. This discussion should center on information about the locker room, pool deck, and pool itself. Locker rooms can cause frustration for individuals with disabilities. Factors such as shower handles and locker shelves too high for people with dwarfism, inadequate lighting for individuals with visual impairment, and combination-only lockers that impede independence for those with arthritis, do not motivate individuals to use a facility. Other factors inhibiting independence include benches cemented into the floor in front of lockers; shower area ledges or lips that limit access for participants in wheelchairs; and lack of Braille signs on lockers, entrances, and exits. Since the Architectural and Transportation Barriers Compliance Board published their final ruling on accessibility and recreation facilities, it is easier to know exactly what meets the standards (Architectural and Transportation Barriers Compliance Board, 2004).

Facility design must enable participants to make transitions between the locker area, pool deck, and water. Newly designed, newly constructed, or significantly altered pools must have at least one primary means of access (lift or sloped entry) and a secondary means of access provided if the pool has over 300 linear feet of pool wall or if access is limited to one place (e.g., a lazy river pool at a water park; Brown, 2003). A lift (figure 25.3a) or sloped entry (figure 25.3b) must be one of the primary means of access; secondary means can be a lift, sloped entry, transfer wall (see figure 25.3c), transfer system (see figure 25.3d), or pool stairs that meet the ADA code (Scott, 2003b). A sloped entry (sometimes called a "wet ramp") connects the deck directly to the water through a gradual slope entry ramp. It has handrails and a flat landing area at the bottom.

Another primary means for access could be a lift (which is generally categorized as equipment and thus covered in the next section). Secondary access to the pool may be provided via one of the means just mentioned or by a transfer wall, transfer system, or pool stairs (not the ladders built into the walls of the pool). A transfer wall (sometimes called a dry ramp because it is outside the pool on the deck) is constructed so that the deck of the pool slopes down below the pool edge so that it is flush with the wheelchair seat. This method of access is the least used because of its limitations for exiting the pool and the extensive strength and stability requirements to use it. Another means of access is a transfer system (discussed in the equipment section). Gradually sloping steps are a helpful adaptation for many pool participants. Gradual pool steps are either built into the pool or are portable and placed into the pool as needed. These steps must meet the ADA accessibility guidelines for depth, height, and width.

Facilities already in existence can use any or all of the access means mentioned earlier to make reasonable accommodations to remove existing architectural and service barriers. New guidelines will set a high standard for reasonable accommodations (Architectural and Transportation Barriers Compliance Board, 2004), so facility managers of already existing pools would be prudent to develop a long-term barrier removal plan to bring their pool up to code.

In addition to the structure and architecture of a pool, pool temperature and chemical composition of the pool must be compatible to the groups it serves. In general, children with disabilities perform better with pool water temperature between 86 and 90 degrees. Air temperature should be about four degrees higher. Participants should be made aware of the type of water purification used because some people have chemical sensitivity to chlorine.

a

© Aquatic Access, Inc.

b

© Monica Lepore

c

© Monica Lepore

d

© Monica Lepore

Figure 25.3 *(a)* Water powered lift from Aquatic Access is a primary means of access according to the ADA guidelines. *(b)* Gradual slope entry, also known as a wet ramp, is a primary means of access. *(c)* A dry ramp provides access to a transfer ledge. *(d)* A transfer system can be a secondary means of access.

Equipment

Proper equipment and supplies are even more important for classes serving individuals with disabilities than for the general population. Adapted equipment is often necessary for entry and exit, safety, maintaining a proper body position in the water, arm or leg propulsion, fitness purposes, and motivating swimmers.

Safe entrances and exits are crucial to accessible swim instruction. In addition to the method of entry afforded by the facility design, lifts, and portable ramps, stairs, and transfer systems are important items for entrance and exit when equipment is not built into the facility. Lifts often provide primary access to pools for individuals with severe orthopedic disabilities. A lift is a pneumatic, water-powered, mechanical, or fully automated electrical assistive device that permits a user to transfer from wheelchair to a seat or sling and move from deck to pool using little strength. According to the newest guidelines (ATBCB, 2004), the lift should be arranged for independent operation by the swimmer and should have a hard plastic seat rather than a sling seat. Independent usage is best facilitated when hand controls are located at the front edge of the seat, are operational with one hand, do not require tight grasping, and require five pounds or less of force to operate.

Portable ramps and gradual steps have been used for many years to offer access to pools when the facility design does not provide any other means of access. These items take up extra room on the deck when they are removed and do not provide the most independent access (because users need to rely on the aquatic staff to place them into the water when needed). Portable equipment also breaks more frequently as a result of wear and tear from its removal and storage.

For individuals who have good upper-body function but cannot negotiate stairs or ladders because of lower-body involvement, a transfer system often allows more independent pool access. A transfer system is a platform 19 by 24 inches wide and 16 by 19 inches above deck (see figure 25.3d). This platform is connected to a series of "steps" (14 to 17 inches deep by 24 inches wide) that one uses to transfer onto and then gradually lower oneself into the water from the chair, to the platform, to each step. The process is reversed for exiting.

Another useful piece of equipment is an aquatic chair with push rims (especially if the pool has a gradual sloped ramp as its primary means of access). It is recommended that an aquatic facility provide an aquatic wheelchair that can be used on the sloped entrance because an individual's personal wheelchair is not appropriate for submersion.

Safety equipment—absolutely mandatory to an adapted aquatics program—includes typical rescue equipment as well as such items as a floor covering to decrease slipping, closed-cell foam mats for use during seizures, and transfer mats to cover pool gutters.

Equipment used to maintain body position is the most prominent equipment typically seen in an adapted aquatic program. Support equipment useful in an adapted swim program might include personal flotation devices (PFDs), foam noodles, sectional rafts, and flotation collars. A large variety of flotation devices, including PFDs, water wings, pull buoys, dumbbell floats, and sectional rafts, give an extra "hand" when working with individuals who are dependent on others to stay above the water. Flotation devices can ensure safety (if they are Coast Guard approved PFDs) and might also reduce or even eliminate fear. Because flotation devices help to support, stabilize, and facilitate movement, they open a new world to individuals with mobility impairments, allowing freedom of movement not possible on land.

Although flotation devices are useful, they might pose certain concerns. For example, they might impair independence if swimmers rely on them too long after they should have progressed to independent, unaided swimming. Also, devices typically tested on individuals without disabilities often fall short of their goal when used with swimmers who have atypical body postures, uneven muscle development or tone, or poor head control. Thus, if students use flotation devices for support, proper supervision must be provided, even if the PFDs are Coast Guard approved. Generally speaking, each person with a disability has such unique needs that it is very difficult to make blanket statements or recommendations regarding safety and buoyancy. It is important to know each swimmer and his or her abilities and to assess horizontal balance through experimentation under supervision with buoyancy and floating in various positions. Buoyancy can be used to resist or assist movement or to support the swimmer (Koury, 1996).

Propulsion equipment affords an individual with a disability the ability to move in ways he or she might not be able to on land. Propulsion is affected by variances in streamlined position, difficulty with horizontal and lateral body positions, inadequate strength, poor range of motion, atypical buoyancy, and other factors, including poor coordination and disproportionate body shape contributing to drag (USA Swimming, n.d.). The first step to efficient propulsion is to put the body in the most streamlined and balanced position possible, using other support as necessary. If the participant is still having difficulty with propulsion, try other devices such as hand paddles and fins to increase surface area and press against the water for propulsive efficiency. Remember that in official competition none of these devices are allowed. Those who have part or all of their arms missing might be able to use a swimming hand prosthesis or Plexiglas paddles attached to the residual stump. For ideas and possible uses of these devices, see Paciorek and Jones (2001) and Summerford (1993).

An increased interest in water fitness has resulted in a greater diversity of fitness supplies. Underwater treadmills, aquacycles, water workout stations, and aqua-exercise steps provide cardiovascular conditioning, muscle toning, and strength training. Water fitness participants also use supportive and resistive equipment and supplies in the water that are handheld, pushed, or pulled, including finger and hand paddles, balance bar floats, upright flotation vests and wraps, aquashoes, webbed gloves, waterproof ankle and wrist weights, workout fins, buoyancy cuffs, water-ski belts, aquacollars, and water jogging belts.

Motivational equipment provides swimmers of all ages the "push" necessary to attempt and complete tasks that might be otherwise overwhelming or boring. The developmental levels, interests, and attention spans of adapted aquatic participants require a different approach to aquatic instruction and recreation. Attractive, brightly colored equipment; nontoxic and sturdy supplies; toys; flotation devices; and balls help enhance instructional strategies that focus on fun. Other devices include swim belts, bubbles, and foam squares, many of which come with modules to increase or decrease flotation. Water logs—also known as water noodles or woggles—are hefty, flexible buoyant logs that encourage water exploration and kicking in a fun way.

MEETING UNIQUE NEEDS OF PARTICIPANTS

To meet the needs of a variety of individuals in providing safe, effective, and relevant aquatic opportunities, it is necessary to know certain unique attributes or characteristics of learners. However, it is important not to assume that these attributes or characteristics apply to every individual in an identified category. Suggestions for teaching people with intellectual disabilities, visual impairments, or deafness are quite similar to the land-based teaching tips; thus, the reader is referred to chapters 8 through 13 and asked to generalize the information in those chapters to an aquatic setting.

Individuals With Cerebral Palsy

Individuals with cerebral palsy (CP) exhibit a variety of skills because of type and severity of CP and the different body parts affected. See the tips in the sidebar on page 445 for teaching swimming to individuals with CP.

Individuals With Orthopedic Disabilities

Although individuals with orthopedic disabilities reflect a range of characteristics, there are simi-larities that can be considered within the aquatic environment. Balance, buoyancy, body position, and range of motion might be affected. Individuals with arthrogryposis, amputations, dwarfism, spina bifida, spinal cord injuries, osteogenesis imperfecta, traumatic brain injury, stroke, spinal cord injury, orthopedic disabilities, multiple sclerosis, muscular dystrophy, or myasthenia gravis might benefit from the teaching tips in the sidebar on page 446.

Individuals Who Are Seizure Prone

Individuals with seizure disorders need aquatic instructors who have a plan of action in case of a seizure incident. Current practice suggests that steps be taken to ensure that the person having the seizure has an open airway and is protected from physical injury caused by contact with other people, objects, or water ingestion or aspiration. When in doubt, always activate the emergency medical system (EMS). The following section describes how to manage a seizure effectively.

The first-aid objectives for assisting an individual having a seizure in the pool are to keep the individual's face above the water, to maintain an open airway, and to prevent injury by providing support with a minimal amount of restraint. One position that meets these objectives is to stand low in the water behind the individual's head and place him or her in a supine position. Then support the individual under the armpits, shoulders, and head. Remember to provide only the support needed to keep the participant's face out of the water, as unnecessary restraint might cause injury to the participant or rescuer. Remove the person from the water when it is safe to do so. If the individual is kept away from the pool edge, equipment, and other people, the natural qualities of the water provide buoyancy and support during a seizure, but do not allow him or her to remain in the pool if the seizure lasts for more than several minutes, continues in rapid succession, or if injury or hypothermia are imminent. The Epilepsy Foundation Web site offers the following suggestions:

> If a seizure occurs in water, the person should be supported in the water with the head tilted so his face and head stay above the surface. He or she should be removed

Suggestions for Teaching Swimming to Individuals With Cerebral Palsy

Many stroke adaptations are based on limited range of motion; try having the individual use an underwater versus out-of-water recovery of the arms, especially for the front crawl.

- Maintain water temperature between 86 to 90 degrees Fahrenheit and air temperature 4 degrees higher than the water temperature.
- Guard against sudden submersion of the face; people with CP often have a weak cough and cannot clear water from their throat effectively.
- Consider hand paddles for participants with wrist flexion contractures.
- Develop strokes executed in the back lying position thus eliminating the need for head control with rhythmic breathing.
- While in a prone position, have the participant wear a ski belt or rescue tube across the chest and under the armpits (with closing clip on back) to elevate chest and face area.

For individuals with primitive reflex retention, the following suggestions apply:

- Keep in mind that sudden noises, movements, or splashing may cause sudden reflex activity, possibly causing the participant to lose a safe position. Maintain a position at or near the participant's head to prevent sudden submersion.
- For individuals with primitive reflex retention, consider allowing participants to wear a flotation collar to hold their heads above water.
- Neck hyperextension or turning of the head to the side may affect arm and leg control in persons with reflex retention. Encourage a full body roll for breathing or the use of a snorkel.
- Avoid quick movements and sudden hands-on and hands-off movements. Slow movements and a steady touch are best with persons who have high muscle tone.
- Be aware of sudden spastic movements during transfers in and out of the pool. Have adequate personnel during transfers and use a mat under the transfer area.
- Encourage participants to flex their heads slightly while on their backs. When their heads are in extension and they are lying on their backs, the mouths tend to open and their arms tend to extend.
- Keep the participant stable, as unstable positions in the water or a feeling of falling causes the body to stiffen, the arms and legs to involuntarily extend and flex, and the mouth to open.
- Use positions that inhibit reflexes, such as a neutral or slightly tucked chin position and the head in midline of the shoulders. Hips and knees should be slightly flexed.
- Use symmetrical activities as much as possible (both sides of the body doing the same thing at the same time) such as breaststroke, elementary backstroke or inverted breaststroke, finning, or sculling.
- Use caution with the scissors kick and the flutter kick as these tend to promote the crossed extension reflex, causing scissoring of the legs. If scissoring occurs, place a comfortable piece of cushioning between the knees during swimming.

from the water as quickly as possible with the head in this position. Once on dry land, he should be examined and, if he is not breathing, artificial respiration should be begun at once. Anyone who has a seizure in water should be taken to an emergency room for a careful medical checkup, even if he or she appears to be fully recovered afterwards. Heart or lung damage from ingestion of water is a possible hazard in such cases. (Epilepsy Foundation, 2003)

If the participant requires removal from the pool during a seizure, several rescuers or aides can lift the participant from the water. One type of lift requires several instructors/lifeguards standing on one side of the individual, rolling the individual toward their chests, and laying the individual on a mat or towels on the side of the pool. The participant's medical or participation form should indicate the exact protocols for care in the event of a seizure. Refer to the tips in the sidebar (on page 446) for working with a person who is seizure prone.

Suggestions for Teaching Swimming to Individuals With Orthopedic Disabilities

- Use in-water tables or in-water benches or docks for rest areas or for people with short stature who cannot rest on the bottom of the pool due to pool depth.
- Look for ways to streamline the body, such as changing head position or attaching flotation devices or weights to lower or raise body position. Achieve a balanced body position by experimenting within proper safety limits.
- Check skin for abrasions before and after swimming if the person has decreased sensation.
- Encourage use of aquashoes to decrease lesions caused by transferring and scraping feet when swimming.
- Be aware that muscle spasms and strange sensations may sometimes interrupt the aquatic session.
- Become knowledgeable about proper assistance in taking off and putting on braces and other orthotic devices.

- Alter stroke mechanics as necessary due to uneven muscle strength and abnormal centers of gravity and buoyancy. Change strokes as little as possible from normal efficiency. If necessary, use smaller range of motion or sculling arm movements with participants.
- If upper-body impairment causes difficulty in lifting the head to breathe, a participant should use a mask and snorkel or roll over onto the back to breathe. Initially, teach the back crawl or elementary backstroke.
- Ensure that all excretion collection bags are emptied before swimming.
- Allow the individual to wear a neoprene vest or wet suit to keep warm in cooler pools.
- Provide assistance for balance problems while on deck.

Suggestions for Teaching Swimming to Individuals Who Are Seizure Prone

- Obtain medical clearance and a list of any contraindicated activities.
- Fill out an appropriate incident report following a seizure.
- Maintain supervision during aquatic activities.
- Factors provoking onset of seizure include playing games of holding breath for "as long as you can" as well as hyperventilation before underwater swimming; excessive drinking of pool water,

which can lead to hyperhydration or hyponatremia; hyperthermia; and excessive looking into the sun.
- Discuss scuba diving with participants and their physicians before attempting deep dives.
- Be aware that some seizure medications increase photosensitivity. When outdoors it may be important to swim in the early evening. Use sunscreen or wear T-shirts.

SWIMMING AS A COMPETITIVE SPORT

As with other sports, integration of athletes with disabilities into general competition has been a goal of disability sport advocates for over a decade. In the United States, USA Swimming has done an exemplary job of advocating for vertical integration—the inclusion of people with disabilities into general aquatic meets and teams. USA Swimming is the national governing body for all United States swimming competition and has a national adapted swimming committee. This committee acts as consultants to the USA Swimming Disability Championships and as advocates for swimmers with disabilities; the committee has written several resources for coaches, local swim committees, officials, meet directors, parents, and swimmers with disabilities (USA Swimming, n.d.). The *USA Swimming Rules and Regulations* manual (2003) has guidelines for officiating swimmers with a disability.

USA Swimming's goal is for swimmers with disabilities to train with their local swim clubs and participate in swim meets combining swimmers with and without disabilities during events. In addition to integrated swim meets, the USA Swimming Disability Championships are held once a year in the spring. This multidisability swim championship is conducted for elite disabled swimmers who have met qualifying times for their events. USA Swimming Rules and Regulations apply during these meets; however, disability sport classifications are used so that swimmers can compete against others of similar functioning. Swimmers with disabilities often have atypical stroke mechanics or atypical power because of missing limbs, neurological issues, cognitive delays, or paralysis that do not afford them to compete equally with one another—or even with swimmers who have the same disability. Swimmers are classified into categories according to their functional ability rather than just separated by gender and swim stroke.

USA Swimming encourages the integration of swimmers with disabilities into meets by providing reasonable accommodations to barriers that might otherwise preclude them. According to USA Swimming (n.d.), local swim committees are encouraged to develop special administrative procedures and circumstances that encourage swimmers with disabilities to participate, such as the following:

- Including a statement welcoming swimmers with disabilities to provide notice of needed accommodations.
- Development of standards for seeding a swimmer that do not interfere with the timeline and flow of the meet but would not place undue spotlight on the athlete with a disability. (For example, swimmers who have cerebral palsy might be placed in a 100-meter event but swim 50 meters if their 50-meter time is similar to the 100-meter times of peers without disabilities.)
- Waiving qualifying time standards.

Additional guidelines for officiating swimmers with disabilities meets might include some of the following accommodations from the 2003 *USA Swimming Rules and Regulations* manual:

- Allowing the swimmer to start in the water
- Allowing the swimmer's assistant on the deck or in the water to assist the start
- Use of a visual starting system (e.g., a strobe light or hand signals) for deaf and hard-of-hearing participants
- Leniency in the time it takes to get into their starting positions
- Modified starting positions on blocks, deck, or gutter (see figure 25.4)
- "Tappers" for swimmers with vision impairment (assistants who hold a pole with a soft tip to tap the swimmer at turns and finishes)
- Physical touch to signal a relay swimmer when their teammate has touched the wall
- Not judging a part of the body that is absent or not used as part of a legal–illegal stroke technique

Although within the United States, most competitive training takes place within USA Swimming

© Brian Butcher

Figure 25.4 Competitive swimming for athletes with disabilities.

clubs, the YMCA and other organizations conduct integrated club teams as well. For those who would prefer training with only swimmers who have disabilities, segregated disability sports organizations such as Special Olympics (for athletes with intellectual disabilities) and USA Deaf Sports Federation (who participate in Deaflympics) provide segregated competitive opportunities for individuals within disability-specific meets (although Special Olympics include some "unified" swimming events that provide reverse inclusion of athletes without disabilities). Deaf or hard-of-hearing swimmers may participate in the Deaflympics through USA Deaf Sports Federation; people with dwarfism may participate as members of the Dwarf Athletic Association of America in their regional and national games; athletes with cognitive disabilities may swim in Special Olympics International; and swimmers who are blind or visually impaired may participate in United States Association for Blind Athletes competitions. These competitions are limited in number and are usually far from a swimmer's home pool.

Although swimming is the primary means of aquatic competition in the disability sports world, competitive diving (Special Olympics) and water polo (USA Deaf Sports Federation) are other options, though they generally need to be pursued in inclusive team settings.

OTHER AQUATIC ACTIVITIES

Activities such as water skiing, scuba diving, and boating can serve as avenues for increasing independence and normalization. Individuals with disabilities of all ages enjoy water sports as much as their counterparts without disabilities. Water sports provide outlets for individuals with disabilities to participate in aquatic recreational opportunities with their peers, families, and community members. With legal mandates for accessibility, more chances exist for participation in instructional, recreational, and competitive water sports. The Architectural and Transportation Barriers Compliance Board rulings on accessibility and recreation facilities include boat docks and fishing piers (Architectural and Transportation Barriers Compliance Board, 2004).

Water Skiing

Prerequisites to water skiing include consultation with a swimmer's physician, acquisition of basic swim skills, and knowledge of using a personal floatation device (PFD). All skiers should practice using a PFD for support and buoyancy in a controlled environment before using a PFD in open water. The driver of the boat, the observer, and the skier should agree beforehand on communication techniques (e.g., hand or head movement signals) to make the activity safe for all.

To make skiing easier for the beginner and for those with disabilities, equipment modifications must be made, especially for those with lower-extremity involvement. A ski bra is one piece of equipment that keeps the skis together for those with leg weakness or paralysis. A kneeboard, ski biscuit (inflatable inner tube with a cover), or specially designed sit-ski can accommodate the skier who cannot stand up. One popular water sit-ski is the KAN SKI available through Access to Recreation at www.accesstr.org. These feature high seatbacks, aluminum seat tube or "cage," and quick-release tow rope attachments and foot bindings on a wide- or regular-width ski. Outriggers are also available for the novice or skier with severe balance impairment. Similar equipment is used in snow skiing (see chapter 28).

Scuba Diving

Traditionally, scuba diving was not a sport open to individuals with disabilities, but scuba and snorkeling have become part of a core of adventure-based activities offered to individuals with numerous disabilities. Before beginning training, the instructor and diver need to discuss water access and entry techniques from the pool, beach, or boat (Petrofsky, 1995; Robinson & Fox, 1987) and medical issues that affect breathing, mobility, and vision. Once in the water, however, no architectural barriers prevent interaction with nature, and mobility is enhanced by a minimal amount of gravity. Some modifications to equipment might include pressure gauges that have Braille numbers or that emit auditory signals, divers tethered together, hand paddles or swim mitts, diving boots, low-volume masks, octopus regulators, jacket-type buoyancy compensators, flexible vented fins, Velcro on wet suits, and diver propulsion vehicles for those who cannot propel themselves (Paciorek & Jones, 2001; Jankowski, 1995).

Handicapped Scuba Association International has programs to train individuals with disabilities to scuba dive and also trains scuba instructors to meet the needs of individuals with disabilities. Founded in 1981 by Jim Gatacre, HSAI uses a multilevel credential that classifies divers according to physical performance standards regardless of type of disability. Level A consists of diving students who can care for themselves and others; level B are students who need partial support; and level C are students who need full support. Another organization that is international in scope is the International Association for Handicapped Divers (IAHD), founded in 1993. Based in The Netherlands, the IAHD is very similar to HSAI in that it has three levels of divers and conducts instructor-training programs. The IAHD publishes the *IAHD Newsletter* for its members and conducts seminars, symposiums, and dive conventions.

Although all agree that certified divers should possess requisite knowledge and skills for a safe and successful experience, controversy surrounds the diving community in regard to medical clearance and certification. Scuba diving has been generally accepted for most individuals with orthopedic, sight, and hearing disabilities. However, secondary disabilities such as limited breathing capacity, osteoporosis, poor circulation, temperature regulation disorders, psychological conditions, and medical conditions such as seizure disorders, insulin-dependent diabetes, and asthma present a real concern for physicians and dive instructors (Lin, 1987; Petrofsky, 1995). Presently, the only sound advice for the prospective diver with a disability is to consult a physician experienced in hyperbaric medicine, use caution when diving, and be conservative.

Boating

Boating activities are enjoyed by all but are especially good for people with lower-body involvement because paddling, rowing, and sailing emphasize upper-body strength. Adaptations to equipment are the primary concern, along with embarking and disembarking and seating and balance. People with cognitive disabilities have similar needs for instructional modifications in boating as they do in swimming: simplify, demonstrate, and repeat. People with vision impairments should have land-based training and a chance to practice their skills in shallow water or in a pool first. This land practice is important because it is very difficult to have a person who needs to use tactile modeling (putting hands on the person demonstrating to feel their movements) if they are out in a boat and cannot move around because of safety concerns or capsizing. Two-person tandem kayaks are ideal for paddlers who have visual impairment to use with a sighted partner.

Paddlers with mobility disabilities often need modifications to the access points of paddle sports. Hard-surface runways on beachfronts—including accessible routes to accessible boat launch ramps, slips, and boarding piers—are needed for those who use wheelchairs, crutches, or canes and those who have balance problems. When these are not available, a beach wheelchair could be made available. Once a person with a mobility disability reaches the boat, it is recommended that a mat or cushion be placed over the gunwale, the boat steadied, and a plan of action for embarking established. Entry and exit procedures can be modified in several ways. For example, a modification might be as simple as the instructor standing or swimming in the water stabilizing a boat, or two assistants helping to lift a boater onto a transfer mat from the dock to the bottom of a boat. If the river or lake bed is firm enough, it might be possible to push a water wheelchair into shallow water for water entries, with assistants, if necessary, to help lift and transfer.

Commercial equipment for seating is available, such as sling-back seats, rubber materials to prevent slipping on the seat, and materials to protect individuals with sensitive skin. Several models of canoes and kayaks lend themselves to various needs. Instructors should analyze the movements, stability, cognitive ability, and strength of the participant to determine what type of canoe or kayak would be best. Open-decked or sit-on-top kayaks are advisable for warm water and for individuals who have difficulty in transferring. These vessels are easy to enter and exit but have a high center of gravity and don't lend themselves to seating adaptations (Adaptive Adventures, n.d.). People who need adaptive seating systems or have poor balance would work best in an inflatable kayak (called a "duckie"). Sea kayaks are also helpful for those who need seating systems because they have deep wells and come in many shapes.

Propulsion in paddle sports can be adapted by using mitts or tubing to secure a paddler's hands to the paddle shaft. Further modifications of equipment to enhance propulsion techniques include printing the words "right" and "left" on the opposite paddle blades on a double-blade paddle or on the inside of the boat to help a paddler with an intellectual impairment, painting the inside of the boat with nonslip paint, using suction-cup bathmats on the bottom or seats of the boat, keeping a variety of paddle lengths available, and having participants use rubber or leather palm gloves for a better grip.

In the United States, the primary organization for paddle sports is the American Canoe Association (ACA). The ACA sponsors the Adaptive

Paddling Committee, which dedicates itself to promoting canoeing, kayaking, and rafting as lifetime recreational activities for individuals with physical disabilities. In addition, their mission includes full integration of paddlers with varying abilities in all aspects of paddle sports. The members of the ACA Adaptive Paddling Committee publishes articles, consults with current paddling clubs to promote inclusion of paddlers with disabilities, publishes *Adaptive Paddling* newsletter and works with designers to develop adaptive equipment. Adaptive paddling workshops are conducted nationally and designed to provide already certified paddling instructors with the information needed to integrate paddlers with disabilities into their programs (American Canoe Association, 2003). On completion of the four-day workshop, including classroom instruction, hands-on learning, and a pool and open-water session, the adaptive paddling endorsement is achieved by already certified paddling instructors. Because of new accessibility regulations for marinas, advancements in technology, and creative designs of adapted seating and paddles, more people with disabilities can now experience boating.

In addition to canoeing and kayaking, sailing opportunities have expanded rapidly through new programs and adapted boats for individuals with disabilities. Worldwide, the International Foundation for Disabled Sailing (IFDS) provides positive contributions to the sport (IFDS, 2002). The IFDS promotes disabled sailing through compilation and publication of events throughout the world on their Web site and reports of recent events and articles pertinent to the sport bimonthly in their bulletin. The IFDS publishes *World Disabled Sailor* once per year and contains information related to current and future trends in adapted sailing. The organization also conducts the World Disabled Sailing championship, which is a qualifier for Paralympic competition. Just as in Paralympic swimming, Paralympic sailing is conducted by classifying sailors according to a functional classification system prior to races based on stability, hand function, maneuverability, visibility, and hearing (International Paralympic Committee, n.d.). Sailors who have physical disabilities have been able to compete in the Paralympics since its demonstration in 1996 and full medal status in 2000. Sailors with intellectual disabilities may participate in international competition through Special Olympics, which has included sailing in their world games since 1995. Individual and Special Olympian teams as well as "Unified" teams exist at the local, national, and international levels. Athletes are placed in divisions according to age, gender, and ability.

Nationally, the United States Sailing Association promotes sailing at all levels. One of the first adapted sailing programs in the United States, the Lake Merritt Adapted Boating Program of the Office of Parks and Recreation in Oakland, California, began in 1981. Glo Webel, boating programs coordinator, pioneered the development of sailing facilities for individuals with disabilities. Another pioneer and innovator in sailing is Harry Horgan, founder of Shake-A-Leg of Newport, Rhode Island. His boat design, with its adapted seating, proved to be successful, and participants consider it to be the benchmark of modified sailing vessels. In addition, the National Ocean Access Project, now associated with Disabled Sports USA, has continued to improve accessibility of sailing vessels by modifying traditional designs, such as with the Kaufman "drop-in seat" and by otherwise customizing boats for sailors with disabilities. Competitive sailing opportunities continue to grow nationally, and elite sailors with disabilities strive to participate on the U.S. Disabled Sailing Team.

People with disabilities also pursue rowing for recreation or competition. At the international level, adaptive rowing is a subcommittee of the Rowing for All Commission within the world rowing organization, Fédération Internationale des Sociétés d'Aviron (FISA). The goals of this subcommittee include elaboration of an international adaptive rowing calendar, collection and distribution of information on adaptive rowing, development of a classification and ranking system for racing, and application to the International Paralympic Committee for adaptive rowing as a Paralympic sport in the 2008 games. The first World Championships within the international governing body FISA were held in 2002. At present, four classes have developed (with the first three being used in world competitions thus far):

> Class LTA4+: Four athletes in a shell who can row using legs, trunk, and arms; plus a coxswain (sliding seat boat)
>
> Class TA2X: Two athletes in a fixed-seat shell who can use their trunk and arms to row
>
> Class TA1X: One athlete in a fixed-seat shell who can use only arms for rowing
>
> Class A: One athlete in a single fixed-seat scull with pontoons. (FISA, 2002)

The U.S. Rowing Association is the national governing body for rowing in the United States and is a member of FISA. Its adaptive rowing committee is active in recruiting members for the national team and is committed to the goal of rowing in the Paralympics in 2008 (U.S. Rowing, n.d.). One of the most active programs is the Philadelphia Rowing Program for the Disabled, held in the prestigious "boat house row section" of the Schuylkill River.

Safety and risk management are concerns for everyone in boating, but some individuals with disabilities need to take extra precautions. Those who are interested can become certified as instructors through the American Canoe Association or the Level I Coaching Program, available through U.S. Rowing. Webre and Zeller (1990) suggest that safety planning of any boating class should include swim skill assessment of participants, considerations for accessibility to the boating site, review of medical information, and considerations involved with any medical condition. In addition, assessing what the participant can do on land and determining what medical information needs to be shared with others in the group in relation to an emergency action plan are crucial. Other safety issues include stumbling over unseen items on the boat or dock for blind boaters, failure to hear a shouted warning for deaf or hard-of-hearing individuals, bowel and bladder management issues for those who are incontinent, change of weather conditions related to those with temperature-regulation disorders, and problems with rough seas as a result of lack of balance or reduced ability to grip for holding on.

The amount of responsibility a paddler, sailor, or rower should have depends on functional ability. It is important to test balance, stability, and buoyancy of the boat with the person in it, in shallow, calm water, and to test equipment before undertaking a river or lake trip. Other elements of safety include planning for embarkation and disembarkation, instructor-to-student ratio, and—as with all water sports—an emergency action plan. To determine which boat, method, and paddle are most appropriate, consider the participant's balance, grip strength and endurance, coordination, and upper-extremity range of motion. Consider, too, how much sight and hearing the person possesses, the ability to make decisions, and knowledge of cause and effect.

Water orientation should include instruction in safety, personal rescue, and proper PFD use. After the water orientation, boat orientation may begin on land, move into a pool and then calm outdoor water, and finally progress to moving and open water. Boat orientation should take into account terminology that is understandable to the partici-

pant, exploration of the boat by blind participants, entry and exit procedures, and propulsion and steering techniques. Participants and instructors must work together to modify equipment through trial and error, based on knowledge of available commercial equipment.

INCLUSION IN AQUATIC ACTIVITIES

Including an individual with a disability in an aquatic activity with peers without disabilities requires the teacher to review the results of the individual skill assessment and to look at the goals of the program, class, or activity in which the student will be placed. Clearly, the aquatic setting is unlike the gym and sport field settings. Even if a student is included in a general physical education environment on land, several questions must be answered by the IEP team before the student begins an aquatic program within an inclusive setting. Typical questions might include the following: How many of the participant's targeted goals and objectives match those that are possible within the general aquatic program? Can the participant follow rules and guidelines within the general aquatic program so as not to compromise the safety of all? Is there an age-appropriate class available? Does the placement provide an emotionally and physically safe environment? Is the ultimate goal of the placement to be able to participate in aquatic activities in an integrated setting? Does the placement meet other goals in addition to instructional goals (e.g., recreational or therapeutic goals)? Refer to the aquatics application example (p. 452) for a practical situation describing the inclusion of a student with disabilities.

A critical factor in the successful inclusion of individuals with disabilities into the general aquatic program is the instructor. Instructors should work with their swimmers and caregivers to provide the most appropriate placement and curriculum for teaching aquatic skills. Studies show that aquatic instructors have more positive attitudes toward including students with mild disabilities and that in order to feel more successful in all inclusion programs, aquatic instructors have expressed perceived needs in the areas of adapted aquatics training, equipment, and class management (Conatser, Block, & Lepore, 2000). Currently, there are two formal adapted aquatics national training programs in the United States: the AAHPERD-AAALF Aquatic Council Teacher of

APPLICATION EXAMPLE

Diving

Setting: A child with multiple physical disabilities has been included in the general sixth-grade aquatics class during her physical education period. The class is learning how to dive, but the child does not have the prerequisite skills to participate.

Student: This 12-year-old girl has no cognitive disabilities but has spastic cerebral palsy and uses an electric wheelchair. She has head control and can close her mouth in response to splashing water. She can also hold onto the pool gutter and use her arms to do a modified elementary backstroke.

Application: The adapted aquatic instructor suggests the following modifications:

- An aide or additional aquatic instructor trained in adapted aquatics must be available.

- While the rest of the class is practicing kneeling or standing dives, the student practices sitting on the pool edge with maximal support while wearing a lifejacket. With an aide in the water, the assistant on the pool deck helps the student fall into the pool and recover on her back.

- During diving practice, she can work on surface dives in the deep end with an aide to assist her to plunge under the water and then to help her recover onto her back.

- Have the student work on her IEP aquatic goals in the shallow end.

- Encourage her to work on diving tasks (e.g., streamlined body position and pike or tuck position) but not the dive itself.

Adapted Aquatic Credential and the YMCA Swim Lessons for Individuals with Disabilities Instructor Certification.

Another critical factor to successful aquatic inclusion programs is the match of the participants' prerequisite skills with the programs or classes they are put into. Participants should have a minimal level of basic skill competencies and possess several prerequisite skills for safe and successful experiences in an integrated class. Participant prerequisites might include such factors as social, cognitive, and aquatic readiness skills vital to inclusive group integrity and learning. Medical and health conditions are also issues. Lepore, Gayle, and Stevens (1998) contend that some medical and health conditions, such as the following, might warrant a more segregated setting.

- Open sores, such as decubitus ulcers
- Uncontrolled seizures leading to emergency removal from the pool and causing clearing of the pool for each seizure incident
- Tracheotomy tubes or ventilator dependency that might require shallow water, qualified health care professionals, heavily grounded electrical cords, and calm water with no splashing

- Neuromuscular conditions that require a water temperature not available in the general aquatic facility
- Neurological conditions that require gradual change from water to air temperature because of inadequate thermoregulation systems
- High susceptibility to infection, needing more sterile environments
- Allergies to chlorine, requiring pools with alternative chemicals
- Behavior disorders, such as uncontrolled aggression, compromising the safety of others
- Hemophilia, possibly requiring calm water, limited bumping into other participants and equipment, and modified pool temperatures because of arthritic conditions
- Detached retinas, requiring the need to avoid projectiles and any bumping of the head and face

Aquatic skill prerequisites are necessary for success in aquatic classes. Regardless if the tasks are as simple as holding the pool gutter, closing the mouth when someone splashes, or not drinking pool water, these skills might be necessary for success and safety in the general class. Support services often need to be provided to assist with skill prerequisites.

Unlike land-based physical activities, some individuals with a disability cannot safely participate in aquatic groups with same-age peers without disabilities because of lack of ability. For example, if an entire instructional unit is taking place in a diving well, and the individual is overly fearful, the caregiver and individual must communicate with the instructor about what is needed, desired, and feasible.

Ways that inclusion can be enhanced include modifications to equipment, rules, instruction, and the environment. Many suggestions and recommendations have been integrated into the information in this chapter. Here are other strategies to try:

- Provide an alternative swimming activity to one that might be inappropriate (e.g., participants can complete a cannonball jump instead of a dive).

- Use an instructor aide to provide physical support within an inclusive aquatic class. (AAALF Teachers of Adapted Aquatics can provide training and give credentials for Teaching Assistants of Adapted Aquatics.)

- Provide a temporary segregated program in a small group or one on one when the skills in the inclusion group do not match the goals or abilities of the swimmer.

- Have the swimmer work with a teacher of adapted aquatics in another area of the pool.

- Use peers trained as water safety aides or teaching assistants of adapted aquatic who can provide assistance (e.g., repeating directions or providing positive reinforcement).

SUMMARY

Aquatics can be an important part of a physical education program for individuals with disabilities. This chapter summarized the benefits of adapted aquatics, the importance of assessment to the success of the adapted aquatics program, issues related to facilities and equipment, and general teaching tips for adapted aquatics. Physical educators should be familiar with the many possibilities afforded by water to advocate for aquatic experiences within the physical education program for individuals with disabilities. After-school recre-

ational and competitive opportunities also exist in other aquatic pursuits, including swim team, boating, water skiing, and scuba.

REFERENCES

Adaptive Adventures. (n.d.) *Adaptive canoeing, kayaking and rafting: A level paddling field.* www.adaptiveadventures.org.

American Alliance for Health, Physical Education, Recreation and Dance–American Association for Active Lifestyles and Fitness. (1996). *Adapted aquatics: Position paper.* Reston, VA: Author.

American Canoe Association. (2003). *What is the adaptive paddling committee?* www.acanet.org.

American Red Cross. (2004). *Water safety instructor's manual.* Boston: StayWell.

Architectural and Transportation Barriers Compliance Board (ATBCB). (2004). Americans with Disabilities Act Accessibility Guidelines for Buildings and Facilities; Final Rule, *Federal Register,* 36 CFR Parts 1190 and 1191, July 23. 2004.

Block, M.E. (2000). *A teacher's guide to including students with disabilities in regular physical education* (2nd ed.). Baltimore, MD: Paul H. Brookes.

Brown, A. (2003). Access points: Ground rules. *Aquatics International,* 15(2), 14-16.

Conatser, P., Block, M.E., & Lepore, M. (2000). Aquatic instructors' attitudes toward teaching students with disabilities. *Adapted Physical Activity Quarterly,* 17, 197-207.

Epilepsy Foundation. (2003). *First aid in special circumstances.* www.epilepsyfoundation.org/answerplace/Medical/treatment/firstaid/seizurespecial.cfm.

Fédération Internationale des Sociétés d'Aviron (FISA). (2002). *A new breed of rowers—Adaptive rowers at Seville, June 9, 2002,* www.worldrowing.com.

International Foundation for Disabled Sailing. (2002). IFDS Bulletin, December 19, 2002.

International Paralympic Committee. (n.d.). *Sailing.* www.paralympic.org.

Jankowski, L.W. (1995). *Teaching persons with disabilities scuba diving.* Montreal, Canada: Quebec Underwater Association.

Koury, J.M. (1996). *Aquatic therapy programming.* Champaign, IL: Human Kinetics.

Langendorfer, S.J., & Bruya, L. (1995). *Aquatic readiness.* Champaign, IL: Human Kinetics.

Lepore, M., Gayle, G.W., & Stevens, S.F. (1998). *Adapted aquatics programming: A professional guide.* Champaign, IL: Human Kinetics.

Lin, L.Y. (1987). Scuba divers with disabilities challenge medical protocols and ethics. *The Physician and Sportsmedicine* 15(6), 224-228, 233, 235.

Martin, K. (1983). Therapeutic pool activities for young children in a community facility. *Physical and Occupational Therapy in Pediatrics,* 3, 59-74.

Paciorek, M.J., & Jones, J.A. (2001). *Disability sport and recreation resources* (3rd ed.). Traverse City, MI: Cooper Publishing Group.

Petrofsky, J.S. (1995). Diving with spinal cord injury. Part I. *Palaestra,* 10(4), 36-41.

Robinson, J., & Fox, A.D. (1987). *Diving with disabilities.* Champaign, IL: Human Kinetics.

Scott, J.P. (2003a). Access points: Act now! *Aquatics International,* 15(4), 20,22-23.

Scott, J.P. (2003b). Access points: The fine print. *Aquatics International,* 15(3), 16-18.

Stanat, F., & Lambeck, J. (2001). The Halliwick method. *AKWA,* 15(1), 39-41.

Summerford, C.F. (1993). Apparatus used in teaching swimming to quadriplegic amputees. *Palaestra,* Spring, 54-57.

SwimAmerica. (n.d.) *Organizational documents provided by SwimAmerica,* 2101 N. Andrews Ave., Suite 107, Fort Lauderdale, FL 33311.

USA Swimming. (n.d.). *Including swimmers with a disability.* Colorado Springs, CO: Author.

USA Swimming. (2003). *Rules and regulations.* Colorado Springs, CO: Author.

Webre, A., & Zeller, J. (1990). *Canoeing and kayaking for persons with physical disabilities.* Newington, VA: American Canoe Association.

YMCA of the USA. (1999a). *The parent/child and preschool aquatic program manual.* Champaign, IL: Human Kinetics

YMCA of the USA. (1999b). *The youth and adult aquatics program manual.* Champaign, IL: Human Kinetics.

WRITTEN RESOURCES

USA Swimming. (n.d.). *Including swimmers with a disability.* Colorado Springs, CO: Author.

USA Swimming has published a series of five brochures including a guide for coaches, officials, swimmers and parents, meet directors, and local swimming committees. These are an excellent resource, published after 2001, that covers in-depth issues related to inclusion of swimmers with a variety of disabilities into general swim competitions and teams.

AUDIOVISUAL RESOURCES

Adapted aquatics teacher training. (Videotape, 1997). Available from the Department of Physical Education and Athletics, SUNY, Stony Brook, NY.

Running time is approximately 60 minutes.

Aquatics for children with disabilities. (Videotape, 1997). Available from Courage Center of Minnesota, Golden Valley, MN.

This video includes training about swimming for children with disabilities. Running time is approximately 30 minutes.

The Halliwick Method. (Powerpoint and videoclips.)

This video presents critical factors to consider when handling individuals with disabilities in the water using the Halliwick method, www.halliwick.net. Approximately 28 slides.

ELECTRONIC RESOURCES

Aquatic Access: www.aquatic-access.com.

This site includes information related to aquatic lifts and ADA pool access.

National Center on Accessibility: www.indiana.edu/~nca.

This site contains information on all types of accessible recreation and on the swimming pool access project. The site includes an extensive bibliography on accessibility and pools.

U.S. Paralympics: www.usparalympics.org.

This organization creates selection procedures for athletes (including swimmers) with disabilities to be on elite and national teams. Information on providing uniforms and funding is also included.

USA Swimming: www.usaswimming.org.

Information on adapted competitive swimming and brochures previously mentioned are included on this Web site.

USRowing Association: www.usrowing.org.

This site presents information about rowing programs, including the Adaptive Rowing committee.

OTHER RESOURCES

Access to Recreation.

Adapted products designed to put people with disabilities into recreation and physical activities, including pool lifts and ramps, bath and shower chairs, pool floats, beach access chairs and adapted water skis. Web site: www.accesstr.com; phone: 800-634-4351; mailing address: Access to Recreation, 8 Sandra Court, Newbury Park, CA 91320.

Team Sports

David L. Porretta

Joe, a 15-year-old, has just moved into a new school district and is to receive regular physical education with his chronological-age peers. Joe is functioning academically at grade level, is socially well adjusted, and has a mobility impairment that requires him to use a wheelchair. Joe's physical education teacher, Mr. Bailey, was consulted about whether Joe could safely and effectively participate in regular physical education. Mr. Bailey, believing that students with disabilities should be included with peers without disabilities whenever possible, agreed to the arrangement, knowing that the way in which the high school secondary curriculum was now structured, some accommodations would need to be made, especially because there were many team sports units. Although unsure about how these accommodations would be made, Mr. Bailey would do his best—he was committed to teaching *all* students.

In this chapter, variations and modifications of selected team sports are presented to promote involvement in them and to promote the inclusion of students with disabilities into team sports. These variations and modifications are designed to help physical education teachers such as Mr. Bailey provide the best possible physical education programs for students with disabilities.

GETTING INVOLVED

Team sports are a popular way for individuals with disabilities to become involved in physical activity. In elite or inclusive settings, individuals with disabilities have excelled and continue to excel in amateur as well as professional team sports, and many interscholastic and recreational sport programs encourage participation of individuals with disabilities on an integrated basis.

Fully integrated sport is especially encouraged for people with auditory impairments. In fact, as early as the late 19th century people with auditory impairments were excelling in sport with nonimpaired individuals. For example, William Ellsworth "Dummy" Hoy, was a Major League baseball player from 1886 to 1902 and was noted as the first person with profound deafness to become a superstar in the game. He is regarded as the first person to use hand signals typically used by umpires and coaches. Hoy was inducted into the Cincinnati Reds Hall of Fame in 2003. Kenny Walker (professional football) and Curtis Pride (professional baseball) are other examples of Deaf individuals who have excelled in sport. Both got signals from managers or coaches and team players while on the field. In other sports, including floor hockey, basketball, and volleyball, which are played in a relatively small area, very few modifications might need to be made. In volleyball, an official pulling the net might signal the beginning or ending of play. On the other hand, sports played out-of-doors on a large field might require more modification. For instance, in football and soccer, flags and hand gestures can supplement whistles as signals. For Deaf players, a bass drum on the sideline might signal the snap of the ball instead of the quarterback's verbal cadence (National Federation of State High School Associations, 2003). There are teams composed entirely of Deaf players who compete against individuals without disabilities.

Many organizations now provide sport programs for athletes with disabilities. The USA Deaf Sports Federation (USADSF) and its international counterpart, The International Committee on Sports for the Deaf (CISS—Comité International des Sports des Sourds) offer competition solely for those with hearing impairments. CISS is a member of the International Olympic Committee (IOC). USADSF team events include baseball, basketball, ice hockey, soccer, softball, team handball, and volleyball, in which athletes are classified according to gender and degree of hearing loss. These sports are regularly featured at the Deaflympics (formerly the World Games for the Deaf) and follow international sports federation rules with some minor adjustments. The Deaflympics occur every two years, alternating between the summer and winter games. Because few modifications are needed for people with hearing impairments to participate in team sports, the focus in the remainder of this chapter is on individuals with other types of disabilities.

Other sport organizations, such as the National Beep Baseball Association (NBBA), Special Olympics, and the National Disability Sports Alliance (NDSA) have been formed to meet the needs of individuals with disabilities for segregated sport competition. However, Special Olympics promotes team sports competition for individuals with intellectual disabilities in totally inclusive settings. This program is known as Unified Sports. Beep baseball, goal ball, quad rugby, and wheelchair softball are relatively new team sports designed for players with disabilities.

Only the significant modifications of each sport are presented in this chapter. Information regarding a more detailed description of the rules and regulations for each sport can be obtained from each sponsoring sport organization.

BASKETBALL

Basketball is a popular activity in both physical education and sport programs. It incorporates the skills of running, jumping, shooting, passing, and dribbling. Varying or modifying skills, rules, or equipment can allow individuals with disabilities to effectively participate in the game. Generally, most ambulatory individuals can participate in basketball with few or no modifications. However, those with severe mental disabilities or mobility problems might need greater modifications—for example, wheelchair basketball for people in wheelchairs.

Game Skills

Important basketball game skills include shooting, passing, and dribbling. Selected modifications are provided for each skill.

• *Shooting and passing.* Bounce passing is advised for partially sighted players because the sound of the bounce lets them know from which direction the ball is coming. Bounce passing also provides more time for players with unilateral upper-limb involvement to catch the ball. One-hand shots and passes should be encouraged for players who have upper-limb impairments. Players in wheelchairs find the one-hand pass useful for long passes; when shooting at the basket, however, they often prefer the two-hand set shot (especially for longer shots) because both arms can put more force behind the ball. For people with ambulation difficulties, a net placed directly beneath the basket during shooting practice facilitates return of the ball. Players with upper-limb involvement might find it helpful to trap or cradle the ball against the upper body when trying to catch a pass.

• *Dribbling.* For players with poor eye–hand coordination or poor vision, dribbling can be performed with a larger ball. For those having poor body coordination, it might be necessary to permit periodic bouncing when running or walking, although they can dribble the ball continually when standing still. Players in wheelchairs will need to dribble to the left or the right of the chair and carry the ball in the lap when wheeling.

Lead-Up Games and Activities

Lead-up games and activities are important prerequisites to learning the game of basketball. Selected lead-up games and activities are provided.

• *Horse.* Two or more players might play this shooting game, competing against each other from varying distances from the goal. To begin the game, a player takes a shot from anywhere on the court. If the shot is made, the next player must duplicate the shot (type of shot, distance, etc.). Failure to make the shot earns that player the letter H. If, however, the second player makes the shot, an additional shot may be attempted from anywhere on the court for the opponent to match. Players attempt shots that they feel the opponent might have difficulty making. The first person to acquire all of the letters H-O-R-S-E loses.

• *Circle shot.* This activity involves shooting a playground ball in any manner to a large basket about 1.1 meters (45 inches) high from six different spots on the floor, ranging from about .64 meter (2 feet) to 1.5 meters (5 feet) away surrounding the basket. Two shots are attempted from each spot

for a total of 12 shots. The player's score is the number of successful shots made.

• *Other activities.* Other basketball lead-up activities might include bouncing a beachball over a specified distance and shooting or dropping a playground ball into a large barrel or container.

Sport Variations and Modifications

Basketball is an official sport of the Dwarf Athletic Association of America (DAAA). The only modification to the game is that players use a slightly smaller ball (the size used in international play by women) for better dribbling and shooting control.

In Special Olympics competition, the game follows rules developed by the Fédération Internationale de Basketball Amateur (FIBA) for all multinational and international competition (Special Olympics, 2000). Both full-court (5 on 5) and half-court basketball (3 on 3) are offered by Special Olympics. The only significant modifications are as follow:

• A smaller basketball 72.4 centimeters (28 1/2 inches) in circumference and .51 kilograms (18 ounces) to .57 kilograms (20 ounces) in weight might be used for women's and junior division play.

• A shorter basket 2.4-meter (8 feet) might be used for junior division play.

• Players might take two steps beyond what is allowable. (However, if the player scores or escapes the defense, a violation is called).

The National Wheelchair Basketball Association (2001) has also modified the game for wheelchair users. Examples of some major rule modifications include the following:

• The wheelchair is considered part of the player.

• Players must stay firmly seated in the chair at all times.

• An offensive player shall not remain for 4 seconds in the key.

• Dribbling consists of simultaneously wheeling the chair and dribbling the ball (a player cannot take more two consecutive pushes without bouncing the ball).

• Taking more than two consecutive pushes results in a traveling violation.

- No player of the team with a thrown-in into the front court shall enter the free-throw lane until the throw-in starts.
- Personal fouls are charged to players who block, push, charge, or impede the progress with either the body or wheelchair.

Skill Event Variations and Modifications

Special Olympics offers individual skills competition in shooting, dribbling, and passing for individuals with lower ability levels, not for athletes who can already play the game. Scores for all three events are added together to obtain a final score. The shooting competition is called spot shot and measures the athlete's skill in shooting a basketball. Six spots are marked on the basketball floor—three spots to the left of the basket and three spots to the right of the basket. The athlete attempts two shots from each of the six spots. The first six shots are taken from the right of the basket, and the second six shots are taken from the left of the basket. Points are awarded for every field goal made. The farther the spot is from the basket, the higher the point value. For any shot that hits the backboard or rim and does not go into the basket, one point is scored. The athlete's score is the sum of all 12 shots.

The 10-meter event requires the athlete to dribble with one hand as fast as possible for a distance of 10 meters (32 feet 9 inches). If control of the ball is lost, the athlete can recover the ball. If, however, the ball goes outside of the designated 1.5-meter (4 feet 9 inch) lane, the ball may be retrieved, or a backup ball placed outside of the lane 5 meters (16 feet 4 inches) at the start of the event might be picked up. Points are awarded depending on how long it takes to dribble the entire 10 meters (32 feet 9 inches). A 1-second penalty is added for each illegal (e.g., two-handed) dribble. Two trials for this event are allowed. The athlete's score is the better of the two trials.

In the target pass event, the athlete must stand within a 3-meter (9 feet 8 inches) square and pass the ball in the air to a 1-meter (3 feet 3 inches) square target 1 meter (3 feet 3 inches) from the floor from a distance of 2.4 meters (7 feet 8 inches). Five attempts are allowed. The athlete receives 3 points for hitting the inside of the target, 2 points for hitting the lines of the target; 1 point for hitting the wall but no part of the target, and 1 point for catching the ball on the return from the wall. The final score is the sum of all five passes.

Other Variations and Modifications

Game rules might be simplified by reducing the types of fouls players are allowed to commit. A playground ball might be used, and the basket can be lowered or enlarged. The game area might be restricted to half-court for players with mobility impairments, such as those using lower-limb prostheses. Shorter play periods and frequent substitutions might be incorporated into the game for players with cardiac or asthmatic conditions. Those with insufficient arm strength can use lighter-weight balls.

FLOOR HOCKEY

The game of floor hockey is gaining popularity in physical education and sport programs across the country. Game skills include stickhandling, shooting, passing, checking, and goalkeeping. With appropriate variations and modifications, most individuals with disabilities can play the game.

Game Skills

Important floor hockey game skills include stickhandling, shooting, passing, checking, and goalkeeping. Selected modifications are provided for each skill.

- *Stickhandling.* The key to successful stickhandling is being able to keep the head up. Keeping the head up allows the player to attend to the field of play and opponents rather than the puck. To promote better stickhandling, the stick blade can be enlarged for players with motor control problems or visual impairments. The size and length of the stick are important factors for some individuals. Lighter sticks should be available for smaller players and those with muscle weaknesses, and shorter sticks for those in wheelchairs. Players with crutches might use the crutch as a stick to strike the puck, as long as sufficient balance can be maintained. Those with crutches or leg braces can hit the puck more successfully from the stationary position. Players with unilateral upper-limb deficiencies or amputations can control the stick with the nonimpaired limb because sticks are light in weight. However, for those with poor grip or poor arm or shoulder strength, the stick can be secured to the limb with a Velcro strap. Players in wheelchairs might need to stress passing or shooting rather than trying to dribble past opponents. When moving the chair, they usually place the stick in their laps.

• *Shooting and passing.* Shooting and passing in floor hockey requires quickness, accuracy, and the ability to shoot the puck when moving. Making a pass is a difficult skill and requires good timing and eye–hand coordination. In the initial stages of learning this skill, the player should make passes from a stationary position to a player who is also in a stationary position. More advanced stages of passing might include passing the puck from a stationary position to a moving player. When passing or shooting on goal, players with visual impairments can push the puck with the stick rather than using a backswing before striking the puck. They will find playing with a larger, brightly colored puck very helpful. It is also helpful if a coach or a sighted teammate calls to them when the puck is passed in their direction.

• *Checking.* Checking requires the player to gain control of the opponent's puck. Here, the player positions the stick under the opponent's stick and attempts to lift the opponent's stick away from the puck. Once the opponent's stick is raised, the puck can be controlled. Players should first practice checking in a stationary position and in a slow manner and then gradually increase in the speed of movement. The highest level of checking is when both players are moving.

• *Goalkeeping.* Goalies try to keep the puck from going into the goal and thus need to make quick movements. They might stop the puck in several different ways, with either the stick or feet or by blocking it with the body or catching it. Once the puck is controlled, it may be put back into play by using the stick or actually throwing it into the playing area. Goalies need a larger stick and wear a facemask, pads, and gloves. Players with asthma or poor cardiorespiratory endurance levels can be successful at the goalie position because little running is needed.

Lead-Up Games and Activities

Lead-up games and activities are important prerequisites to learning the game of floor hockey. Selected lead-up games and activities are provided.

• *Stop the puck.* Three players face the net at a distance of 5 meters (16 feet 4 inches). One player is positioned in front of the net, and the other two players position themselves 3 meters (9 feet 8 inches) to the left and right of middle player. Each of the three players has two pucks. On command, players in rapid succession shoot their pucks at the goal, attempting to score. The goalie makes as many saves as possible.

• *Puck dribble race.* The player starts the race from behind a starting line. On command, the player dribbles the puck as quickly as possible in a forward direction for a distance of 10 meters (32 feet 8 inches).

• *Other activities.* Additional activities include pushing a puck to the goal as fast as possible using a shuffleboard stick, kicking the puck with the feet as fast as possible to the goal, dribbling the puck as quickly as possible around a circle of cones, or shooting a sock stuffed in the shape of a ball (sockball) with a poly hockey stick into a large box turned on its side.

Sport Variations and Modifications

As played under Special Olympics rules (Special Olympics, 2003), floor hockey is similar to ice hockey. The game can be played on any safe, level, properly marked surface with minimum dimensions of 12 meters × 24 meters (40 feet × 80 feet) and maximum dimensions of 15 meters × 30 meters (49 feet × 98.5 feet). The backs of the goals are set 1.2 meters (4 feet) from the endlines to allow play behind them. Additional official floor dimensions (e.g., center circle, goal line, faceoff circles) can be found in the *Winter Sports Rule Book* (2003). Six players compose a team (one goalkeeper, two defenders, and three forwards). Players use wooden or fiberglass sticks that resemble broom handles, except for the goalie, who uses a regulation ice hockey stick. The goalie must wear a mask, helmet, and protective gloves; pads may be used if desired. All other players must wear helmets with protective cages and shinguards; pads, gloves and mouthguards can also be worn. All players wear a shirt with distinctive team markings. The puck is a circular felt disc (about 20 centimeters [8 inches] in diameter and 2.5 centimeters [1 inch] thick) with a 10-centimeter (4-inch) hole in the center. The end of the stick is placed in the hole to control the puck. Faceoffs, offsides, and minor and major violations are part of the game. Games consist of three 9-minute periods of running time, with 1 minute of rest between periods.

There are three line shifts per period. A line shift refers to all on-ice players from one team being replaced by substitute players at the same time. For penalties, "frozen" puck situations, time-outs, and line changes, the clock is stopped.

Skill Event Variations and Modifications

Special Olympics offers individual skills competition for floor hockey in shooting (two events), passing, stickhandling, and defense for individuals with lower ability levels, not for athletes who can already play the game. A final score is determined by adding the scores of all five events. Shooting competition has two events: Shoot Around the Goal and Shoot for Accuracy. In the shoot-around-the-goal event, the athlete takes one shot from five different locations around the goal with each location being 6 meters (19 feet 7 inches) from the goal. The athlete has a 10-second time limit to shoot all the pucks. One puck will be at each location before the athlete starts shooting. Each puck that goes into the goal is worth 5 points. The score is the total of the 5 shots. In the shoot-for-accuracy event, the athlete takes five shots from directly in front of the goal from a distance of 5 meters (16 feet 4 inches). The goal is divided into the following point sections: 5 points for a shot entering the goal in either of the upper two corners, 3 points for a shot entering the goal in either of the lower two corners, 2 points for a shot entering the goal in the upper-middle sections, 1 point for a shot entering the goal in the lower middle section, and 0 points for a shot not entering the goal.

The passing event requires that the athlete make five passes from behind a passing line located 8 meters (26 feet) from two cones placed 1 meter (39 inches) apart. The athlete is awarded 5 points each time the puck passes between the two cones; 3 points are awarded whenever the puck hits a cone and also crosses the line. The total score is the sum of scores for the five passes made.

In the stickhandling event, the athlete stickhandles the puck in a figure-eight fashion past six cones 3 meters (9 feet 8 inches) apart for a distance of 21 meters (68 feet 8 inches) and then shoots the puck at the goal. The time elapsed from the beginning of the event to the shot on goal is subtracted from 25. One point is also subtracted for each cone missed, and 5 points are added to the score if the goal is made.

In the defensive event, the athlete gets two attempts to steal the puck from two opponents who try to keep it away from the athlete within a 12-meter (39 feet 4 inches) square area. Fifteen seconds on each attempt is given. Each steal is worth 10 points. If the puck is not stolen, the athlete might score up to 20 points for pressing opponents, stick checking the opponent with the puck, or staying between opponents.

Other Variations and Modifications

To accommodate players with differing abilities, the game might be played on a smaller playing surface and with larger or smaller goals. To make the game less strenuous, a Wiffle ball, sockball, foam ball, or a large reinforced beanbag might be used. If players have impaired mobility, increasing the number of players on each team might be helpful. Body contact can be eliminated for players with bone or soft tissue conditions, such as juvenile rheumatoid arthritis or osteogenesis imperfecta. Penalties might be imposed on players who deliberately bump into opponents in wheelchairs.

FOOTBALL

Football utilizes the skills of passing, catching, kicking, blocking, and tackling. Most individuals can participate effectively in football or some variation of it. People with mild impairments who are in good physical condition can play the regulation game of tackle football. A small number of players possessing partial sight can and do participate on high school and collegiate teams. In fact, individuals who are legally blind can be successful place kickers. However, people with total blindness are unable to play the regulation game. Those with unilateral amputations either below the knee or above or below the elbow will be able to participate in regulation football as long as their prostheses do not pose a safety risk. Flag or touch football is more commonly offered in physical education and recreation sport programs. Most individuals with intellectual disabilities, except those with severe or profound impairments, can be safely integrated with other players. Individuals with significant physical impairments might prefer modified or less integrated participation.

Game Skills

Important football game skills include passing, catching, and kicking. Selected modifications are provided for each skill.

• *Passing.* Players possessing partial sight are able to pass the ball as long as distances are short and receivers wear bright-colored clothing. For players with poor grip strength or pronounced contracture of the hand or wrist or for those on crutches, a softer and smaller ball might be used to promote holding and gripping. People in wheelchairs will be able to effectively pass the ball if they have sufficient arm and shoulder strength. Wheelchair users will find it almost impossible to perform an underhand lateral pass while facing the line of scrimmage, so this type of pass must be performed facing the receiver.

• *Catching.* Players with partial or no available sight and those who are wheelchair users should be facing the passer when attempting to catch the ball. Instead of trying to catch with the hands, they should be encouraged to cradle the ball with both hands or to trap the ball in the midsection. The ball should be passed from short distances without great speed; a foam ball should be used for safety purposes. Players who have unilateral arm deformities should catch the ball by stopping it with the palm of the nonimpaired hand and trapping it against the body. Wheelchair users will be able to catch effectively if the ball is thrown accurately (using a chair limits a person's catching range).

• *Kicking.* Players with partial or no available sight might be encouraged to practice punting without shoes so they can feel the ball contacting the foot. In learning this punt, players should be instructed to point the toes (plantarflex the foot) while kicking. A player with unilateral arm amputation can punt the ball by having it rest in the palm of the nonimpaired hand. A punting play might begin with the player already holding the ball instead of with a snap from center.

Lead-Up Games and Activities

Lead-up games and activities are important prerequisites to learning the game of football. Selected lead-up games and activities are recommended here.

• *Kickoff football.* The game is played on a playground 27.4-meter (30 yards) by 54.8-meter (60 yards) by two teams of six to eight players each. The object of the game is to return the kickoff as far as possible before being touched. The football is kicked off from the center of the field. The player with the ball returns it as far up the field as possible without being touched (two-handed) by opposing team members. The team returning the ball might use a series of lateral passes to advance it; forward passes are not permitted. Play stops when the ball carrier is touched. The other team then kicks off from the middle of the field. The winner is the team advancing farthest up the field.

• *Football-throw activity.* A player attempts to pass a football from a distance of 9.1 meters (30 feet) through a hole of a large rubber tire suspended 1.2 meters (4 feet) from the ground on a rope. Ten attempts are given; the player's score is the number of successful passes out of 10.

• *Other activities.* Other lead-up activities include placekicking or punting the ball for distance; centering the ball to a target for accuracy; performing relays in which players hand the ball off to each other; and guessing the number of throws or kicks it will take to cover a predetermined distance.

Sport Variations and Modifications

Wheelchair football has steadily gained in popularity since it began in 1948. For over 20 years the Santa Barbara (CA) Parks and Recreation Department–Adapted Programs has been sponsoring wheelchair football tournaments. Because of its growing popularity, the Universal Wheelchair Football Association (UWFA) was formed in 1997 to promote the game. Wheelchair football is played on any hard, flat surface. The boundaries for a standard basketball court work well. The degree of physical contact is determined by how hard one blocks or tackles others. Some players, through mutual consent, like to play more aggressively. Most contact occurs wheelchair to wheelchair. With few exceptions, the game is similar to touch football. Team size varies, but six per side is preferred to avoid too much on-the-field confusion. A standard foam football is used, and players can participate in manual chairs, motorized chairs, or scooters. Protective equipment is optional but could include a bike helmet, gloves, seatbelt, and eyewear. Players are classified into one of three classification levels according to their ability to catch the ball and ability to tag (tackle) a player. For example a level 1 player (with fully functional arms and hands) must catch and hold on to the ball, whereas a level 3 player (with minimal or no arm movement) can be considered "catching" the ball when the ball hits him or her anywhere above the waist from the front or the side of the body or in the back of the head or headrest. Individuals without disabilities are encouraged to play the game (using wheelchairs). Of course, they would be classified as level 1 players. Each team should have players of similar ability on the field at the same time. Major rule modifications are as follows:

- Throwing the ball down the field simulates a kickoff or punt.
- The game can be played with a delayed rush. However, the defense must count off three seconds before beginning the rush.
- One blitz is allowed per series of downs.
- A first down is from the foul line on the basketball court to half-court or any equivalent distance identified (a first down could be two parking spaces).
- Contact behind the opponent's rear axle is considered clipping; grabbing an opponent's chair is considered holding.
- When playing indoors, the walls behind the end zones are considered in the field of play for kickoffs and punts. Balls hitting the walls are considered in play until the player takes possession of the ball and is tackled (or downs the ball).

Skill Event Variations and Modifications

Various skill events are possible. A catching event might require a player to run a specified pattern (e.g., down and out) and catch the ball. Five attempts are given, with the total number of catches constituting the player's score.

In a field goal kicking event, players attempt to placekick a football over a rope suspended 2.4 meters (8 feet) from the ground between two poles 15.2 meters (50 feet) apart. Kicks might be attempted from 4.6 meters (5 yards), 9.1 meters (10 yards), 13.7 meters (15 yards), 18.3 meters (20 yards), or 22.9 meters (25 yards) from the rope. Ten kicks are given; players might kick from any or all of the five distances. Points are awarded according to the distance kicked, as follows: 1 point for a 4.6-meter kick, 2 points for a 9.1-meter kick, 3 points for a 13.7-meter kick, 4 points for an 18.3-meter kick, and 5 points for a 22.9-meter kick. The total number of points after 10 successful kicks is the player's score.

Other Variations and Modifications

Simplified game situations that include only the performance of specific game skills can be used. For example, the game might be played allowing only passing plays. The field can be shortened and narrowed, and the number of players on each team can be reduced. In addition, first-down yardage can be reduced to less than 9.1 meters (10 yards). Individuals of low skill might play the game with a kickball or volleyball. Individuals with arm or leg deformities or visual impairments can play most line positions.

SOCCER

Soccer is included in many physical education and sport programs. Skills in soccer include running, dribbling, kicking, trapping, heading, and catching (goalie only) the ball. Because of its large playing area and continuous play, soccer requires stamina. However, the game can be varied or modified so that individuals with disabilities can participate in any setting. For those with very minimal impairments (e.g., mild learning disability), no modifications in the game are necessary. When regular sport competition is not possible, NDSA and Special Olympics provide competition only between players with disabilities.

Game Skills

Important soccer skills are kicking, trapping, heading, and goalkeeping. Selected modifications are provided for each skill.

- *Kicking.* Whether for dribbling, passing, or shooting, kicking is of paramount importance in the game of soccer. People with upper-limb amputations can learn to kick the ball effectively, but they might have difficulty with longer kicks because the arms are normally abducted and extended to maintain balance. Individuals with unilateral lower-limb amputations might use a prosthesis for support when passing or shooting the ball. Players might be unable to kick the ball effectively with a prosthetic device and thus might wish to play in a wheelchair. Wheelchair users will be able to dribble the ball by using the footrests of the chair to contact the ball and push it forward. They are also allowed to throw the ball because they do not have use of the lower limbs.

- *Trapping.* Most players can effectively learn to trap the ball. Foam balls are good to use with players who are hesitant to have the ball hit the body. Individuals in wheelchairs might have some difficulty trapping because the sitting position impedes the reception of the ball on the chest and abdomen. However, some players learn to trap the ball in their laps.

- *Heading.* Most players can learn to head the ball successfully, although heading should not be encouraged for players with conditions such as brain injury or atlantoaxial instability. Players with mental or visual impairments might find using a balloon or beachball helpful for learning to head because these balls are soft and give players time to make body adjustments before ball contact. Players with upper-limb amputations can be very effective in heading the ball. Players in wheelchairs will be able to head the ball effectively as long as it comes directly to them. However, the distance the ball can be headed will be limited because the chair's backrest and the sitting position limit the player's ability to exert force on the ball.

- *Goalkeeping.* Goalkeeping requires that the goalie be able to catch (or at least trap the ball with the hands) and kick the ball. It also requires that the goalie be able to react quickly to the ball. Because playing this position requires little cardiorespiratory endurance, many players with limited endurance can successfully play goalie. Those in wheelchairs can catch effectively as long as upper-limb involvement is minimal. Most players with one arm find it difficult to catch in the goalie position. In this case, they should be encouraged to slap, trap, or strike the ball. For some players with limited mobility, reducing the size of the goal can help.

Lead-Up Games and Activities

Lead-up games and activities are important prerequisites to learning the game of soccer. Selected lead-up games and activities are provided.

- *Line soccer.* The game might be played on a playground with two teams, preferably of 8 to 10 players each. Players on each team stand beside each other about 2 feet (.64 meter) apart. Both teams face each other from a distance of about 8 meters (26 feet 2 inches). Players on each team try to kick a soccer ball below shoulder level past their opponents. After each score, players

on both teams rotate one position to the right. A team scores 1 point each time the ball passes the opponents' line, and 1 point is scored against a team that uses their hands to stop the ball.

- *Accuracy kick.* This activity involves kicking a playground ball into a goal area 1.5 meters (5 feet) wide from a distance of 3 meters (9 feet 8 inches). A player is allowed three kicks from either a standing or sitting position. The player receives 3 points each time a ball is kicked into the goal, 2 points each time the ball hits a flag stick (placed at either side of the goal) but does not pass through the goal, and 1 point each time the ball is kicked in the direction of the goal but does not reach the goal. Following three kicks, players' scores are compared.

- *Other activities.* Additional activities include heading a beachball into a large goal area from a short distance, dribbling a soccer ball in a circular manner around stationary players as fast as possible, throwing the ball in-bounds for distance, keeping a balloon in the air by kicking it, punting a soccer ball for distance, and playing scooter soccer.

Sport Variations and Modifications

Modifications in the sport of soccer have been introduced by several sport organizations. Disabled Sports, USA (DS/USA) sponsored soccer competition for players with amputations. Players missing part or all of one leg participate on forearm crutches; the crutch is treated as an extension of the arm.

Sport modifications have also been introduced by the NDSA. That organization has developed rules for competition in both indoor wheelchair soccer and seven-a-side soccer (NDSA, 2003). In indoor wheelchair soccer players are assigned to one of two divisions (Division A or Open Division). Generally, Open Division players have higher skill levels than Division A players. Players are assigned to one of five classes. These classes generally follow the NDSA 8-level functional classification system presented in chapter 14; in this system, assignment to one of the higher classification levels (e.g., class VII) is a result of greater function than assignment to one of the lower classification levels (e.g, class II). Consideration for class assignment is given to the player's ability and function related to catching, throwing, and manipulating the ball in addition to his or her degree of sitting balance and wheelchair operation. Class 1 players have less function than class 5 players. For example, class 1 players use a motorized wheelchair because they are not able to propel a manual wheelchair, whereas class 5 players have near normal function of the upper extremities and good to normal trunk control and thus use manual wheelchairs. Each team must field at least one player who uses a motorized chair and no more than two players from class 5. Teams are composed of at least four but not more than six on-court players (one of which is the goalie). The following are modifications to be applied to indoor wheelchair soccer:

- The game is played on a gym floor with boundaries not less than 15.2 meters (50 feet) wide and 28.6 meters (94 feet) long, or not more than 15.2 meters (50 feet) wide and 30.5 meters (100 feet) long.
- A rubber playground ball 25.4 centimeters (10 inches) in circumference is used.
- The goal measures 1.7 meters (5 feet 6 inches) high, 1.5 meters (5 feet) wide, and .9 meter to 1.5 meters (3 to 5 feet) deep.
- Penalty boxes are located at midcourt on the opposite side of team benches.
- Penalty shots and power plays are used.
- Goalies might leave the goal area with the ball or to gain possessions of the ball.
- The ball is considered "tied-up" when a team is unable to move the ball for two seconds.
- The wheelchair, a limb, or any part of the body can be used to move the ball.
- Dribbling the ball with one or both hands simultaneously is permitted.
- Players are not permitted to rise from the wheelchair to gain an advantage.
- A maximum of three seconds is permitted for a player to hold or maintain possession of the ball before attempting a pass, dribble, or shot.
- Unnecessary roughness, holding, hooking, or ramming into another wheelchair results in penalties.

Players who can ambulate (NDSA Classes V-VIII) are eligible to play 7-a-side soccer. Rules generally follow Fédération Internationale de Football Association (FIFA) standards (NDSA, 2002). Along with the seven-player limit, some modifications are as follows:

- One class 5 or class 6 player must be a member of the team, and one of these players must be on the field at all times.
- Players are not allowed to use crutches.
- No offside rule is applied.
- An underhand throw-in is permitted.
- Teams might consist of male and female players.
- The field dimensions are 75 meters (82 yards) by 55 meters (60 yards); standard junior-size goals are 5.2 meters (19 feet) by 2.1 meters (7 feet).

In Special Olympics, the sport is played as either 11-a-side or 5-a-side soccer, and rules follow Fédération Internationale de Football Association (FIFA) standards (Special Olympics, 2000). There are no major modifications for 11-a-side soccer. However, the standard length of the game (two 45-minute periods) can be shortened to account for ability levels and the physical condition of players. The following modifications, among others, are applied for 5-a-side soccer:

- The field dimensions must be a maximum of 50 meters (164 feet) by 35 meters (114 feet 9 inches) and a minimum of 40 meters (131 feet) by 30 meters (98 feet 4 inches). The smaller field is recommended for lower-ability teams.
- The goal should be about 4 meters (13 feet) by 2 meters (6 feet 6 inches).
- A ball over the sideline results in a kick-in by a player from the opposing team to the player who last touched it.
- There are two 25-minute periods.

The game of soccer is also modified for individuals in power wheelchairs. The game known as power soccer originated in Canada and is played on an indoor court (regulation basketball court) with a 45.7- to 60-centimeter (18- to 24-inch) physioball. Teams are composed of four players each, either male or female. The strategy is similar to rugby. Bumpers on footrests (to maneuver the ball and protect the chair and player) and anti-tip bars on chairs are mandatory because of safety and ball control issues. To score, the ball must travel through a goal at the end of the court designated by two cones 7.6 meters (25 feet) apart.

Skill Event Variations and Modifications

Special Olympics offers individual skills competition in dribbling, shooting, running, and kicking for athletes with lower ability levels. Athletes perform each of the three events twice, and all scores are then added for a total score. In the dribbling event, the player dribbles the ball 15 meters (49 feet 2), while staying in a 5-meter (16 feet 4 inches) lane, into a 5-meter (16 feet 4 inches) finish zone, which is marked with cones. The clock stops when both the player and the ball are stopped inside the finish zone. If players overdribble the finish zone, they must dribble it back into the zone to finish. If the ball runs over the sideline, the referee places another ball in the center of the lane opposite the point at which the ball went out. The elapsed time it takes to do this is converted into points by a point system. The maximum number of points that can be obtained is 60, and the minimum is 10 (less a deduction of 5 points each time the ball runs over the sideline or a player touches the ball with his or her hands).

In the shooting event, the player runs forward a distance of 2 meters (6 feet 6 inches) and then kicks a stationary ball into a 4-meter (13 feet 1 inch) wide by 2-meter (6 feet 6 inches) deep goal from a distance of 6 meters (19 feet 7 inches). Once the kick is made, the player returns to the starting line. A total of 5 kicks are allowed, and each successful kick is worth 10 points.

In the run-and-kick event, the player stands 4 meters (13 feet 1 inch) from four balls (one to the left, one to the right, one in front, and one in back). The player begins by running to any ball and kicking it 2 meters (6 feet 6 inches) through a target gate, which is 2 meters (6 feet 6 inches) wide and formed by cones. Play continues until all four balls have been kicked. From when the player starts to when the last ball is kicked, total time is recorded in seconds. The time is then converted into points. The maximum number of points is 50; the minimum number is 5. In addition, a bonus of 5 points is added for each ball kicked successfully through the target.

Other Variations and Modifications

For a simplified game, fewer than 11 players can participate, and field dimensions can be reduced. For players with low stamina, a partially deflated ball (which does not travel as fast as a fully inflated ball) can be used, and frequent rest periods, substitutions, or time-outs can be incorporated into the game. A soft foam soccer ball can be used; in some cases, a cage ball can replace a soccer ball. Players with upper limb deficiencies might be allowed to kick the ball in-bounds on a throw-in. Additional players might be situated along the sidelines to take throw-ins for their teams. Penalty kicks can be employed for penalties occurring outside of goal areas. To avoid mass conversion on the ball, players can be required to play in specific zone areas.

SOFTBALL

Softball uses the skills of throwing, catching, fielding, hitting, and running. With certain modifications, the game can be played in an integrated setting by most individuals with disabilities, although players with visual or mobility impairments might find competing in a segregated setting more appropriate. The National Wheelchair Softball Association (NWSA) sponsors competition for athletes in wheelchairs, NBBA sponsors competition for players with blindness, Special Olympics sponsors competition for players with intellectual disabilities, and the DAAA sponsors competition for players with dwarfism. The DAAA follows American Softball Association rules with no modifications.

Game Skills

Game skills important to softball are throwing, catching, fielding, and batting. Selected modifications are offered for each skill.

* *Throwing.* People with visual impairments throw with better accuracy if the person receiving the ball communicates verbally with the thrower. For players with small hands or hand deformities, the use of a smaller or foam ball is recommended. Individuals with cerebral palsy, because of control problems, might find using a slightly heavier ball advantageous. Individuals with lower limb disability will be able to throw the ball quite well. However, they will have difficulty throwing for distance because body rotation might be limited. A player with one upper limb will be able to throw the ball without much difficulty.

* *Catching and fielding.* Players with visual impairments will more easily learn to catch if a

large, brightly colored ball is initially rolled or bounced. A beep baseball, described in this section under the heading "sport variations," will be most helpful. Individuals using wheelchairs and those with crutches or with braces might wish to use a large glove. Players with one upper limb will be able to catch with one hand as long as eye–hand coordination is well developed. A glove is helpful to most players with one arm who have a remaining segment of the affected limb, provided they have mastered the technique of catching the ball and then freeing it from the glove for a throw. (After the catch, the player removes the glove with the ball by placing it under the armpit of the limb segment; the hand is then quickly drawn from the glove to grasp the ball for the throw). Jim Abbott, a former Major League pitcher, used this technique.

An oversize glove can facilitate fielding for players with poor eye–hand coordination. Fielders should face the direction from which the ball is being hit, and players with visual impairments should be encouraged to listen for a ground ball moving along the ground. Players with assistive devices or in wheelchairs can be paired with sighted players without disabilities for assistance in fielding. Although a fielder in a wheelchair should be able to intercept a ball independently, the assisting player can retrieve it from the ground after interception and hand it to the player with a disability for the throw.

- *Batting.* Players with one upper limb will be able to bat as long as the nonimpaired limb possesses enough strength to hold and swing the bat. To promote hitting, the player might use a lighter bat, grasping it not too close to the handle. Players in wheelchairs or on crutches must rely more on arm and shoulder strength for batting because they will be unable to shift their body weight from the back leg to the front leg to provide power for the swing. Plastic bats with large barrels will be helpful for people with poor arm and grip strength or poor eye–hand coordination. In this case, a large Wiffle ball should be used.

Lead-Up Games and Activities

Lead-up games and activities are important prerequisites to learning the game of softball. Selected lead-up games and activities are provided.

- *Home run softball.* The game is played on a softball field with a pitcher and catcher, a batter, and one fielder. The object of the game is for the batter to hit a pitched softball into fair territory, then run to first base and return home before the fielder or pitcher can get the ball to the catcher. The batter is out when three strikes are made, a fly ball is caught, or the ball reaches the catcher before the batter returns home.

- *Lead-up team softball.* The game is played in any open area, with six players constituting the team. Players position themselves in any manner about 3.6 meters (12 feet) from each other. To begin play, the first player throws the ball to the second player. Each player attempts to catch the softball and throw it (in any manner) accurately to the next one. The sixth player, on catching the ball, attempts to throw it to a 1-meter square (3 feet by 3 feet) target from a distance of 4 meters (13 feet). Following that throw, players rotate positions until each player has had an opportunity to throw the ball to the target.

- *Other activities.* Additional activities include throwing beanbags in an underarm manner through a hoop suspended from the floor, hitting balls for distance from a batting tee, punching a volleyball pitched in an underarm manner, keeping a balloon in the air by hitting it with a plastic stick, and batting a ball suspended from the ceiling or a tetherball pole.

Sport Variations and Modifications

Beep baseball, designed for athletes with visual impairments, is sanctioned by the NBBA. The object of the game is for the batter to hit a regulation 16-inch audio softball equipped with a special sound-emitting device and to reach base before an opposing player fields the ball. (The ball is manufactured by Qwest Communications International, Inc., and distributed by the Denver Beep Ball Group in Colorado. To obtain a beep ball, visit the National Beep Baseball Association Web site.) The Telecom Pioneers (formerly the Telephone Pioneers of America), a volunteer organization, have been largely responsible for the success of Beep baseball (figure 26.1). Teams are composed of six players. Each team might have two additional teammates on the roster; they play blindfolded only when no other player with visual impairment is available to play. All players, even those with visual impairment, must wear blindfolds. In addition to the two teammates who might be on the roster, two sighted players function as the pitcher and catcher, while on offense. The pitcher throws the ball (from a distance of 6.1 meters [20 feet]) in an underarm motion to the batter in an attempt to "give up" hits. The pitcher must give two verbal cues to the batter before the pitch. These are; "ready" and "pitch" (or "ball"). The catcher assists batters by positioning them in the batter's box, and he or she also retrieves pitched balls. On defense, both sighted players (spotters) stand in the field and assist their six teammates in fielding the ball by calling out the number of the defensive player closest to the ball. The spotters cannot field balls themselves. If a hit ball presents a chance of injury to a player,

the spotter might yell a warning. Also, a spotter might knock down an unusually hard hit ball headed directly toward a player; however, a run will be awarded to the offensive team. To assist players and spotters, position markers can be spray painted on the field to identify defensive positions. A batter gets four strikes before being called out. A batter might allow one ball to go by without penalty. Any additional pitched balls that are not swung at shall be called strikes. Bunting is not allowed. Each side has three outs per inning; there are six innings to an official game unless more are needed to break a tie.

Figure 26.1 Beep baseball competition.

On hitting the ball beyond the foul line (see figure 26.2), the batter runs to one of two bases (one located down the third base line and one located down the first base line) that are at least 122 centimeters (48 inches) high. Bases are padded cylinders that contain battery-powered, remotely controlled buzzers that emit a steady buzz when activated; the umpire predetermines which buzzer is to be activated by giving a hand signal to the base operator before the ball is hit. The bases are located off the foul line to prevent a defensive player from colliding with a base runner. To score a run, the batter must touch the appropriate base before an opposing player cleanly fields the ball. However, if the opposing player fields the ball before the batter reaches base, the batter is out.

The game of softball has been modified for players in wheelchairs by the NWSA (see figure 26.3). The game is played under official rules for 40.6-centimeter (16-inch) slow-pitch softball as approved by the Amateur Softball Association of America with the following major modifications:

- Manual wheelchairs with foot platforms must be used.

- The field is a smooth, level surface of blacktop or similar material.

- Bases are 15.2 meters (50 feet) in length from each other; home plate to second base is a length of 21.5 meters (70 feet 8 inches).

- The pitching stripe is located 8.5 meters (28 feet) from home plate.

- Second base is composed of a 1.2-meter (4-feet) diameter circle; first and third bases are composed of 1.2-meter (4-feet) semi-circles.

- Teams are balanced by a point system.

- Neither a hitter nor fielder (when playing the ball) can have any lower extremity in contact with the ground.

- Fielders cannot play the ball with any lower extremity in contact with the ground.

- Teams must have a player with quadriplegia on the team and in active play.

- Each team is composed of 10 players.

The game of softball is also modified for Special Olympics play (Special Olympics, 2000). Official events include slow-pitch team competition and tee-ball competition. Both events follow Fédération Internationale de Softball (FIS) and national governing body (NGB) rules for slow-pitch softball. The following are some modifications used for the slow-pitch game:

- The distance from home plate to the pitching rubber can be modified to a distance of 12.2 meters (40 feet).

- A 30.5-centimeter (12-inch) restricted flight softball must be used.

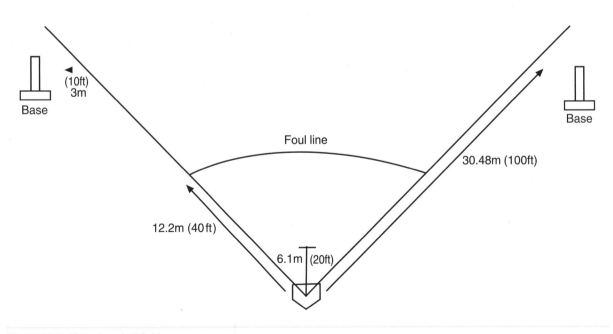

Figure 26.2 Beep baseball field.

Figure 26.3   Player participating in a wheelchair softball game.

* Ten players play defense at any one time.
* An extra player may be used. If one is used he or she must play the entire game. The extra player might be substituted for at any time.
* If an extra player is used, all 11 players must bat, and any 10 are allowed to play defense.
* If the batter has two strikes and fouls off the third pitch, the batter is out.
* The catcher must wear a facemask and batter's helmet.

Skill Event Variations and Modifications

Special Olympics offers individual skill competition designed for athletes with lower abilities (not for athletes who can already play the game) in four events: base race, throwing, fielding, and hitting. The scores for each of the four events are added together to obtain the athlete's final score. In the base-running event, the player must start at home plate, run the bases, positioned 19.8 meters (65 feet) apart, and return home as fast as possible. The time needed to run the bases is subtracted from 60 to determine the point score. A 5-second penalty is given for each base missed or touched in improper order. The better of two trials is counted.

In the throwing event, the object is to throw a softball as far and as accurately as possible. Two attempts are given, and the player's score is the distance of the longest throw (measured from the restraining line to the point where the ball first touches the ground). The score reflects the throwing distance in meters minus the error distance (the number of meters the ball landed to the left or right) of a perpendicular throwing line marked from the restraining line. Similar events sponsored by the NDSA include a soft shot and a club throw for distance. NDSA junior events also include a softball throw. Distance-throwing events such as the shot and club throws are also offered in competition sponsored by Wheelchair Sports, USA (WS/USA).

The fielding event requires the player to stand between two cones 3 meters (10 feet) apart and catch a total of 10 ground balls (five attempts per trial for a total of two trials) thrown by an official from 19.8 meters (65 feet) away. The throw from the official must hit the ground before traveling 6.1 meters (20 feet). The athlete can move aggressively to the thrown ball. Five points are received for catching the ball in the glove or trapping it against the body but off the ground; 2 points are scored for a ball that is blocked; no points are scored for a missed ball.

The hitting event requires the player to bat for distance by hitting a softball off a batting tee.

Three attempts are allowed, and the longest hit is the player's score. The distance is measured in meters from the tee to the point at which the ball first touches the ground. If the score falls between meters, the score is rounded down to the lower meter.

Other Variations and Modifications

To accommodate players' varying ability levels, the number of strikes a batter is allowed can be increased. In some cases, fewer than four bases can be used, and distances between bases can be shortened. Half-innings might end when three outs have been made, six runs have been scored, or 10 batters have come to bat. In addition, lighter-weight and large-barreled bats might be used. For players with poor eye–hand coordination, such as those with cerebral palsy or traumatic brain injury, the ball might be hit from a batting tee. A larger ball or restricted-flight softball, which travels a limited distance when hit, might be used. For players with more severe impairments, the ball might be rolled down a groove or tubelike channel when they are at bat. A walled or fenced area is recommended for players with mobility impairments so that distances to be covered can be shortened. In addition, a greater number of players on defense might be allowed, especially if players have mobility problems. The game can also be modified so that it is played in a gym with a Wiffle ball and bat.

VOLLEYBALL

Volleyball is a popular game included in most programs. Game skills include serving, passing, striking, and spiking the ball. Most individuals with disabilities can be integrated into the game. However, for players with severe intellectual disabilities, or those with significant visual or mobility impairments, the game might require modifications.

Game Skills

Important volleyball game skills consist of serving and striking. Selected modifications are provided for each skill.

- *Serving.* Players with disabilities can learn to serve quite effectively. It is helpful to begin with an underhand serve. The nondominant hand is beneath the ball, and the dominant hand (fisted) strikes the ball in an underhand motion. Very young players or those with insufficient arm and shoulder strength can move closer to the net. As players develop coordination, they can progress to the overhand serve. Players with one functional arm can serve overhand effectively by tossing the ball into the air with the nonimpaired arm and then hitting it with the same arm. Wheelchair users will be able to perform both the underhand and overhand serves, though for the underhand serve, it is important to be in a chair without armrests.

- *Striking.* Players with visual impairments can competently hit the ball with two hands if the ball is first allowed to bounce. This gives the player more time to visually track the ball. Because of limited mobility, players on crutches will need to learn to return the ball with one hand. However, players in wheelchairs can use both hands to return the ball within their immediate area. As these players become more adept in predicting the flight of the ball, they are able to make a greater percentage of returns.

Lead-Up Games and Activities

Lead-up games and activities are important prerequisites to learning the game of volleyball. Selected lead-up games and activities are provided.

- *Keep It Up.* This game is played by teams that form circles about 4.6 meters (15 feet) to 6.1 meters (20 feet) in diameter. Any number of teams of six to eight members each may play. To begin the game, a team member tosses the volleyball into the air within the circle. Teammates, using both hands, attempt to keep hitting the ball into the air (it must not hit the ground). A player may not strike the ball twice in succession. The team that keeps the ball in the air the longest scores 1 point; the team with the most points wins the game.

- *Serving activity.* A player hits a total of 10 volleyballs, either underhand or overhand, over a net and into the opposite court. Point values are assigned to various areas within the opposite court, with areas farther away from the net having higher values. The player's score is the point total for all 10 serves.

- *Other activities.* Additional activities might include setting a beachball or large balloon to oneself as many times as possible in succession, serving in the direction of a wall and catching the ball as it returns, or spiking the ball over a net about 30.8 centimeters (1 foot) higher than the player.

Sport Variations and Modifications

Disabled Sports, USA (DS/USA), DAAA, and Special Olympics offer team sport competition in volleyball. Volleyball competition is governed internationally by International Sports for the Disabled (ISOD) and the International Paralympic Committee (IPC). Players, especially for DS/USA competition, are classified according to functional ability. For example, players with amputations are classified according to the site and degree of amputation. Two modifications of the sport under DAAA auspices consist of a slightly lowered net and court dimensions used by ISOD for seated competition. It is interesting to note that sitting volleyball was first introduced in The Netherlands as early as the mid 1950s (figure 26.4). In 1980, it became an official Paralympic sport. Table 26.1 illustrates the basic differences between sitting and standing volleyball.

Special Olympics volleyball competition is based on Federation Internationale Volleyball (FIVB) and the rules of each individual country's national governing board (NGB). Some modifications of the game (Special Olympics, 2000) include the following:

- Hitting the ball with any part of the body on or above the waist
- Moving the serving area closer to the net but no closer than 4.5 meters (14 feet 9 inches)
- Using a lightweight ball no heavier than 226.4 grams (8 ounces)

Skill Event Variations and Modifications

Special Olympics competition includes three skill events: overhead passing (volleying), serving, and passing (forearm). These events are designed for athletes with lower ability levels, not for those who can already play the game. Scores obtained in each of the three events are added together to obtain a final score. For the overhead passing event, the player stands 2 meters (6 feet 7 inches) from the net and 4.5 meters (14 feet 9 inches) from the sideline on a regulation-size court. A tosser provides the player with 10 two-handed underhand tossed balls from the backcourt 4 meters (13 feet) from the baseline and 4.5 meters (14 feet 9 inches) from the sideline in the left back position. The player sets the tossed ball to a target (a player standing 2 meters [6 feet 7 inches] from the net and 2 meters [6 feet 7 inches] from the front left sideline position). If any toss is not high enough for the player to set, it is repeated. The peak of the arc of each set should be above net height. The height of each set is measured. One point is awarded for setting the ball 1 meter (3 feet 3 inches) above the

Figure 26.4 Participation in sitting volleyball.

Table 26.1 **Basic Rule Differences Between Sitting and Standing Volleyball**

Game characteristics	Sitting	Standing
Court dimensions	10 m (32 ft, 8 in.) × 6 m (19 ft, 7 in.)	18 m (59 ft) × 9 m (29 ft, 5 in.)
Attack lines	2 m (6 ft, 5 in.) from the middle of the centerline	3 m (9 ft, 8 in.) from the middle of the centerline
Net size	6.5 m (21 ft, 7 in.) × .8 m (2 ft, 6 in.)	9.5 m (31 ft, 2 in.) × 1 m (3 ft, 3 in.)
Net height	1.15 m (3 ft, 8 in.) (men) 1.05 m (3 ft, 4 in.) (women)	2.43 m (7 ft, 9 in.) (men) 2.24 m (7 ft, 3 in.) (women)
Equipment	Not allowed to sit on thick materials	NA
Play	Positions of players are determined by the position of their buttocks.	Positions of players are determined by the position of their feet contacting the ground.
	Players are not allowed to lift their buttocks from the court when carrying out any type of attack hit.	NA
	When serving, the server must be in the service zone and buttocks must not touch the court.	When serving, the server's feet must be in the service zone and must not touch the court.
	Only front-row players are allowed to block the opponent's service.	It is a fault to block the opponent's service.

athlete's head, 3 points for setting the ball above net height, and 0 points for illegal contact (a ball that goes lower than head height or goes over the net outside the court). The final score is the sum of all points awarded for each of 10 attempts.

Serving competition requires the athlete to serve a ball into the opponent's side of the court. That court is divided into three areas of equal size, and a point value is assigned to each area. One point is awarded for a serve landing in the area of the opponent's court closest to the net, 3 points are awarded for a serve landing in the middle third area, and 5 points for a serve landing in the area closest to the opponent's end line. For serves that land on a line, the athlete receives the higher point value. The final score is the total number of points made in 10 serves.

In the forearm passing event, the athlete stands on a regulation court at the right back position 3 meters (9 feet 10 inches) from the right sideline and 1 meter (3 feet 3 inches) from the baseline. A tosser standing on the same side of the net in front center court 2 meters (6 feet 7 inches) from the net makes a two-hand overhead toss. The athlete returns the toss with a forearm pass to a target (person standing on the same side of and 2 meters (6 feet 7 inches) from the net and 4 meters (13 feet 1 1/2 inches) from the side away from the tosser. Varying point values are marked on the frontcourt. This is repeated with the athlete at the left back

position. To receive the maximum number of points, the peak of the arc of the pass must be at least net height. A ball landing on a line is assigned the higher point value. One point is received if the ball passes below net height. The final score is determined by adding together the five attempts from both the left and right sides.

Other Variations and Modifications

Volleyball is easily modified for most players with disabilities. Most often, court dimensions are reduced, the net lowered, and the serving line brought closer to the net to accommodate varying abilities of players, especially for players in wheelchairs. Balls might be permitted one bounce before players attempt to return them over the net, or an unlimited number of hits by the same team might be allowed before the ball is returned. Players with arm or hand deficiencies can be allowed to carry on a hit or return. To serve, players might throw the ball over the net rather than hitting it, and they might catch the ball before returning it. Players might have greater success by using a large, colored beachball or a foam ball. Players who have mobility problems, such as those using crutches or walkers, might play the game from a seated position, or the number of players on each team might be increased.

GOAL BALL

Goal ball, a sport invented almost 60 years ago in Europe was created primarily for sport and rehabilitation for post–World War II blind veterans. The game was first introduced to world competition at the 1976 Paralympics in Toronto, Canada. Goal ball requires players to use auditory tracking, agility, coordination, and team-mindedness skills. The game is played in a silent arena in which blindfolded players attempt to score goals by rolling a ball across an opponent's goal line. Game skills are throwing, shot blocking, and ball control. Goal ball follows rules established by the International Blind Sports Association (IBSA).

Males and females compete separately. To remove any advantages for players possessing partial sight, all players are blindfolded, even those who are totally blind. Instead of actually blindfolding players, eyeshades in the form of blacked-out swim or ski goggles are generally used. A hard rubber ball 76 centimeters (30 inches) in circumference and weighing about 1.25 kilograms (2.75 pounds) is used. Each ball contains bells that allow players to track it during play. Information on purchasing goal balls can be obtained from the USABA, 33 North Institute, Colorado Springs, CO 80903.

Because of the nature of the game, many players wear protective padding covering the knees, elbows, and hips, similar to the padding worn in volleyball or ice hockey. Coaches are not permitted to communicate with their players outside of halftime or during official time-outs. Spectators must also remain silent so that players can hear the ball. However, the rules permit communication between players in the form of talking, finger snapping, or tapping on the floor.

The game consists of two 10-minute periods; halftime lasts 3 minutes. Running time is not used; rather, the clock is stopped at various points in the game (e.g., a scored goal). Three 45-second team time-outs are allowed during regulation play. Whistles are used to communicate clock times to players. Each team is allowed a total of six players. Three players are on the court at any one time, and each team is allowed three substitutions per game.

Players must remain within their respective play zones. Boundaries are marked with tape about 5 centimeters (2 inches) wide. Various textured tape is used so that players can distinguish boundaries and zones (figure 26.5). Play begins with a throw by a designated team. During the game, the ball

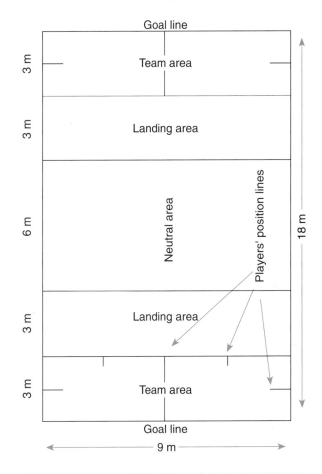

Figure 26.5 Goal ball arena (according to IBSA rules all measurements are to be within a half meter of these).

must touch the floor at least once in the neutral area. If not, the throw counts but cannot result in a score. The ball might be passed twice before each throw on goal.

All three players may play defense. Defensive players might assume a kneeling, crouching, or lying position to contact the ball, but they cannot assume a lying position on the playing surface until an opponent has thrown the ball. Defenders might move laterally within their team area. However, they cannot rush forward into the throwing area to intercept the ball except to follow a deflection. A player must throw the ball within 10 seconds after defensive control has been gained.

Should a personal or team penalty be assessed to a team, the offending team must defend a penalty throw. In such a case the player committing the penalty (personal penalty) is the only player to defend against the penalty throw. In the case of a team penalty, the player who made the last throw before the penalty was awarded will defend the throw. If a team penalty is awarded before a throw has been taken, the player to defend the throw will be at the coach's discretion. Should the game end in a tie, two additional 3-minute periods are played. The team scoring the first overtime goal is the winner.

The USABA encourages and promotes goal ball development camps across the country and provides technical assistance and professional support to members in regions throughout the country who are interested in offering these camps. The camps are designed to assist new players in learning the game.

Game Skills

Important goal ball skills are throwing, blocking, and ball control. Selected modifications are offered for each skill.

- *Throwing.* Most players can accomplish throwing easily. The ball is thrown in an underhand manner so that it rolls along the ground. Individuals with poor upper body strength or poor motor control might need to use a lighter ball. Players with one arm can effectively throw the ball, whereas players with orthopedic impairments who use scooters might need to push the ball with both hands along the ground rather than throwing it in an underhand motion. In other cases, players on scooters can "throw" the ball by striking it with a sidearm motion when it is located at their side.

- *Blocking and ball control.* Blocking and ball control are essential skills because defensive players must stop the ball from entering the goal area. Once the ball is blocked, it is brought under control with the hands so that a throw can be made. It might be helpful to have players with intellectual disabilities see the ball when learning the skill of blocking so that they can more effectively coordinate body movement with the sound of the ball. Players with amputations can wear prosthetic devices to assist in blocking, as long as the ball does not damage the device or vice versa.

Lead-Up Games and Activities

Lead-up games and activities are important prerequisites to learning the game of goal ball. Selected lead-up games and activities are provided.

- *Heads-Up.* This game involves one-on-one competition with players positioning themselves in their half of the arena. A player is given possession of the ball with the object of scoring a goal. The ball must be continuously rolled as the offen-

sive player moves about; the player cannot carry the ball. The defensive player can take control of the ball from the offensive player by deflecting or trapping a shot on goal. The first player to score three goals wins the game.

- *Speedy.* This game involves two teams of three players each who play within an enclosed area. Players on each team assume a crouching or kneeling position and form a triangle with a distance of 3.7 meters (12 feet) between players. Players position themselves on small area rugs and face the middle of the triangle. On command, a designated player rolls a goal ball as quickly as possible to the player on the immediate right, who controls the ball and rolls it to the next player on the right, and so on. In the event a player to whom it was rolled does not control the ball, that player must retrieve the ball and return to the area rug before rolling to the next player. Each time the ball returns to the player who started the game, a point is scored. The team scoring the most points in 1 minute wins the game. Teams compete one at a time so that players can hear the ball.

- *Other activities.* Other activities include throwing for accuracy to the goal and passing the ball as quickly as possible between two players for a set amount of time.

Sport Variations and Modifications

Goal ball has quickly gained popularity in the United States and is an official competitive sport of the USABA. People with other types of disabilities as well as people without impairments can participate in the game as long as blindfolds are worn.

Other Variations and Modifications

The game might be modified by increasing or decreasing the size of the play arena and the number of players on a side. People with mobility problems might play on scooterboards; a lighter ball might be used for players with poor upper-arm and shoulder strength.

QUAD RUGBY

Quad rugby (internationally known as wheelchair rugby), originally called murderball, was developed in the latter part of the 1970s by wheelchair athletes from Manitoba, Canada. In 1981 the game was introduced in the United States and quickly gained popularity. The United States Quad Rugby Association (USQRA) was formed in 1988 to promote and regulate the game at both the national and international level. The USQRA is the national governing body for quad rugby in Wheelchair Sports, USA (WS/USA) competition. To further advance the sport, the USQRA sponsors a number of instructional clinics each year around the country. Today, quad rugby is the fastest growing wheelchair sport in the world. Stoke Mandeville in England was the site of the first international competition in 1990. In 1996, the game was played at the Paralympics as an exhibition sport. The International Wheelchair Rugby Federation (IWRF) holds a world championship every four years and in 2000 the sport attained full medal status at the Paralympics.

Quad rugby is designed for players who have quadriplegia that would prevent them from participating in other sports, such as wheelchair basketball. Individuals who exhibit upper and lower extremity limitations caused by spinal cord injuries, cerebral palsy, spina bifida, and other les autres conditions are eligible to compete. Generally, quad rugby is a combination of American football, ice hockey, and wheelchair basketball. Teams are composed of four on-court players. To equalize competition, players are classified according to functional ability by a point system. Players are provided a classification number from one of seven classifications ranging from .5 (most impaired) to 3.5 (least impaired). The player classified as .5 has function comparable to C5 quadriplegia, whereas a player classified as 3.5 has function comparable to a C7 to C8 incomplete quadriplegic. The combined classification points cannot exceed eight for the four on-court players. Because of the classification process males and females can compete on the same team. A complete copy of quad rugby rules and regulations can be obtained from USQRA, 5861 White Cypress Dr., Lake Worth, FL 33467.

The game of quad rugby is played on a regulation basketball court. Cones placed at the end of each line identify the goal lines at each end of the court. In front of each goal line is a key area 8 meters (26 feet 2 inches) × 1.75 meters (5 feet 7 inches). The object of the game is to carry the ball (regulation volleyball) over the opponent's goal line. Players try to gain possession of the ball by forcing a bad pass or a violation. The team with the greatest number of goals at the end of the game wins. At no time can all four defensive play-

ers be in the restricted area. Full chair contact is allowed, and because of the nature of the game any form of hand protection might be used; however, whatever is used cannot be harmful to other players (e.g., hard or rough material). The game is composed of four 8-minute periods. Should the game end in a tie, 3-minute overtime periods are played. The team scoring the first overtime goal is the winner.

The ball-handler can make an unlimited number of pushes, but the ball must be either passed or bounced within 10 seconds or else a turnover is assessed. A player has 15 seconds to advance the ball into the opponent's half of the court; although only three defensive players can be in the key area at any one time, all four offensive players are allowed in the key area, but only for 10 seconds. Players committing personal fouls must serve time in a penalty box, which gives the opposing team a power play.

Game Skills

Important quad rugby game skills consist of wheelchair mobility, throwing, and catching. A brief description of each skill is provided.

- *Wheelchair mobility.* Chair mobility is essential in the game of quad rugby. Mobility skills consist of maneuvering the chair with the ball, picking, and sprinting. To maneuver effectively, the player must place the ball securely in the lap. Maneuverability consists of being able to move forward and backward as fast as possible as well as being able to turn the chair quickly to the left or right. Players also must be able to bounce and pass the ball while the chair is in motion. Players set picks to gain an offensive advantage. This is where an offensive player maneuvers to the side or behind a defensive player guarding an offensive teammate. This creates an offensive advantage in that the offensive player (not the one creating the pick) can move or drive around the pick. Players having the ability to quickly start from a stopped position have an advantage over other players especially when sprinting down the court. Sprinting up and down the court places the offensive player in a better position to score and places the defensive player in an advantageous position to defend against a score.

- *Throwing and catching.* Throwing (accuracy and distance) and catching are essential skills in the game of quad rugby. The nature of the game requires that the ball be advanced, and throwing (passing) the ball is the quickest way to do it. Depending on ability level, a one-hand or two-hand throw can be thrown. Those with more severe upper limb impairments might need to throw two-handed. The skill of catching needs to be mastered while the chair is either moving or stationary. Of course the ability to catch while the chair is in motion is an advantage. For players who do not have full control of the hands, catching (trapping) the ball can be done with closed fists, wrists, or forearms.

Lead-Up Games and Activities

Lead-up games and activities are important prerequisites to learning the game of quad rugby. Selected lead-up games and activities are provided.

- *Mobility relay.* Relay teams are composed of three or more players. Three cones are placed at 4-meter (13 feet 1 inch) intervals from a starting line. The distance from the starting line to the third cone is 12 meters (39 feet 4 inches). The object of the relay is to wheel forward as fast as possible in a figure-eight fashion around each of the three cones. Rounding the third cone, the player returns to the starting line by wheeling backward. The first team to successfully complete the relay wins.

- *Accuracy pass activity.* A passing line is marked on a court floor 5 meters (16 feet 4 inches) from a wheelchair situated on the court. The start line is situated 3 meters (9 feet 8 inches) behind the passing line. The total distance between the start line and the wheelchair is 8 meters (26 feet 2 inches). On command, the player begins moving forward and passes the ball to the wheelchair (facing the player) before crossing the passing line. The player gets a total of five throws. The final score is the number of times the player hits the wheelchair in the air. Should the player go over the passing line before the ball is thrown, a fault is called and the pass does not count.

- *Other activities.* A battery of quad rugby skill tests (consisting of sprinting, passing [distance and accuracy], picking, and maneuvering) have been validated (Yilla & Sherrill, 1998). Each of these skills can be used as part of practice for the competitive sport or can be used as lead-up activities in physical education classes.

INCLUSION

During physical education, and at times in athletics, players with disabilities can be included in regular or adapted sports of basketball, floor hockey, volleyball, football, soccer, and softball. The games of goal ball and quad rugby are designed for individuals with certain defined disabilities. However, individuals with disabilities as well as participants without disabilities might play them. As long as certain techniques are applied, most players with disabilities can be successfully and safely integrated into the sports identified. Many variations and modifications have already been presented. In addition, other techniques have also been successfully implemented, as shown in the application example below. One technique is to match abilities and positions; teachers and coaches should attempt to assign positions on the basis of ability levels of players. In football, players with mild intellectual disability possessing good

---

APPLICATION EXAMPLE

Transition

Setting: Interscholastic freshman football

Students: Players with mild intellectual disabilities or specific learning disabilities

Application: To accommodate the learning needs of these players, the coach could, among other strategies,

- require players to play only on "special team" (e.g., kickoff, punt return) so that they will not need to know multiple play assignments;

- use task analysis for the learning of new, more complex skills and assignments;

- allow players to wear a wristband to remind them of their play assignments;

- have teammates remind them of their play assignments in the huddle; and

- teach new plays and new skills at the beginning of practice and then review the new plays and new skills toward the end of practice as well.

catching skills could play end positions, whereas others with good speed could play the backfield. Players with upper-arm impairments can be the place-kickers in football. In specific instances, a physical disability can be used to advantage. For example, Tom Dempsey, whose partial amputation of the kicking foot allowed for a broader surface with which to kick the ball, was a very successful place-kicker in the National Football League.

Teaching to players' abilities can also enhance integration. When teaching or coaching players with intellectual disabilities, emphasize concrete demonstrations over verbal instructions. Verbal instructions, when used, should be short, simple, and direct as when coaching first and third base in softball. In football and basketball, a few simple plays that have been overlearned can promote success. In sports such as football or basketball, the player holding the ball can shout or call out to help a partially sighted player with ball location.

Modification of equipment can also foster integration. For players with visual impairments, the teacher or coach can place audible goal locators in goal areas for sports such as basketball, soccer, or floor hockey. Goals, when used, can be brightly painted or covered with colored tape. For example, the crossbar and goal posts in soccer could be brightly painted. In games played on an indoor court, such as floor hockey or basketball, mats might be placed along the sidelines to differentiate the playing surface from the out-of-bounds area.

Special Olympics now promotes competition with individuals without disabilities provided Special Olympics athletes have demonstrated the ability to participate in team sports. This ability includes not only the attainment of certain skills but also teamwork and team strategy. Special Olympics provides detailed information covering the philosophy of Unified Sports, research and evaluation results, and field implementation and sports rules for basketball, bowling, soccer, softball, and volleyball (Special Olympics, 2000, 2003).

SUMMARY

This chapter described a number of popular team sports included in physical education and sport programs. Team sports included in competition sponsored by sport organizations such as USADSF, DAAA, NBBA, DS/USA, NWBA, NWSA, Special Olympics, USABA, and NDSA, as well as team sports pertaining to various international sport organizations (e.g., IBSA, IWRF, UWFA), were also discussed. Game skills and variations and modifications specific to each sport were identified. Also presented were lead-up games and activities, as well as rules and strategies, corresponding to those found in programs for individuals without disabilities. Finally, suggestions for integrating individuals with disabilities into team sports were offered in addition to the many modifications and variations presented earlier to promote inclusion.

REFERENCES

National Disability Sports Alliance (2003). *NDSA indoor wheelchair soccer rule book.* Kingston, RI: Author.

National Disability Sports Alliance (2002). *Sports rules manual* (6th ed.). Kingston, RI: Author.

National Federation of State High School Associations (2003). *Football rules book.* Indianapolis, IN: Author.

National Wheelchair Basketball Association (2001). *Official rules and casebook 2001-2002.* Charlotte, NC: Author.

Special Olympics. (2000). *Official Special Olympics summer sports rules 2000-2003 (revised edition).* Washington, DC: Author.

Special Olympics. (2003). *Official Special Olympics winter sports rules 2003-2006 (revised edition).* Washington, DC: Author.

Yilla, A.B., & Sherrill, C. (1998). Validating the Beck battery of quad rugby skill tests. *Adapted Physical Activity Quarterly, 15,* 55-67.

WRITTEN RESOURCES

Spirit: The magazine of Special Olympics. Special Olympics International, 1325 G Street NW, Suite 500, Washington, DC 20005.

This is a quarterly publication focusing on such topics as sports, athletes, families, volunteers, world games, celebrities, and fundraising.

Bernotas, B. (1995). *Nothing to prove: The Jim Abbott story.* New York: Kodansha America, Inc.

This is the biography of Jim Abbott, who was born without a right hand. He overcame his disability and became a Little League and high school standout, a college All-American, an Olympian, and a Major League pitching star.

AUDIOVISUAL RESOURCES

Kiss my wheels. (Videotape, 2003). Fanlight Productions, 4196 Washington Street, Suite 2, Boston, MA 02131, phone (800) 937-4113.

This 56-minute video highlights a nationally ranked junior wheelchair basketball team through a regular season, culminating in tournament competition.

Goal Ball: An introductional videotape (Videotape, n.d.). Winnipeg, Manitoba, Canada: Communication Systems Distribution Group, University of Manitoba.

This tape examines the sport of goal ball.

ELECTRONIC RESOURCES

International Committee on Sports for the Deaf (CISS): www.ciss.org/enews.

This electronic newsletter ("e-news") is published monthly and covers topics such as international events and activities, sports articles, and IOC news.

World Organization Volleyball for Disabled (WOVD): www.wovd.com.

This site provides information on volleyball for individuals with physical disabilities. Sections such as history, constitution, competition schedules, statistics, refereeing, and rules (in English and Spanish) are included.

CHAPTER

Individual, Dual, and Adventure Sports and Activities

E. Michael Loovis

Kevin approached the physical education instructor at a local college and inquired about signing up for the beginning tennis course. The instructor told Kevin he was welcome, and Kevin appeared at the first class. After the normal introductory lecture, students were paired up for some basic drills. Initially, only one student would pair up with Kevin. Apparently, everyone thought Kevin was incapable of doing well in tennis. It soon became obvious that Kevin was quite capable, and other students soon wished to be paired with him. Kevin picked up the forehand and backhand strokes quickly. He did have some difficulty with the serve, but even in this area he was ahead of most of the class. Kevin completed his competency testing before anyone else in the class and was patiently waiting for the class tournament to begin. When it did, Kevin quickly dispatched all opponents. Although he needed to play while seated in a wheelchair, Kevin had clearly become the best tennis player in the class.

In this chapter we examine individual, dual, and adventure activities and sports in which individuals with unique needs can participate successfully. Participation is analyzed from two perspectives: within the context of sanctioned events sponsored by sport organizations and as part of physical education programs in the schools. In terms of organized competition, discussion is limited to the rules, procedural modifications, and adaptations that are in use and that are the only approved vehicle for participation. The remainder of the chapter is a compendium of modifications or adjustments for several activities and sports, including the use of lead-up games and activities for individuals with disabilities.

TENNIS

Because of the nature of the game and the availability of variations and modifications, tennis, or a form of it, can be played by all individuals except those with the most severe disabilities. The game can be played as a singles or doubles activity, so the skill requirements (both psychomotor and cognitive) can be modified in many ways to encourage participation. Regardless of the variations or modifications, the game's basic objective remains the same: to return the ball legally across the net and prevent the opponent from doing the same.

Sport Skills

Typically, people can play tennis quite adequately using only the forehand and backhand strokes and the serve. For the ground strokes, good footwork (for ambulatory players) or effective wheelchair mobility along with good racket preparation—moving the racket into the backswing well in advance of the ball's arrival—is fundamental to execution. Under normal circumstances, movement into position to return the ball and racket preparation are performed simultaneously.

Lead-Up Activities

Adams and McCubbin (1991) describe an elementary noncourt lead-up game, Target Tennis, that is appropriate for individuals in wheelchairs as well as ambulatory students and which can be played indoors with limited space. Players position themselves behind the end-zone line, which is 10 feet (3 meters) from a target screen. The screen has five openings, each 10 inches (25.4 centimeters) in diameter, which are the targets. The player

tosses a tennis ball into the air and, with an overhand swing, attempts to bounce the ball midway between the end-zone line and the target so that the ball goes through one of the five openings. A bonus serve is permitted for every point scored. No points are awarded if the ball bounces twice.

Special Olympics (2003) provides four developmental events that can serve as lead-up activities: target stroke, target bounce, racket bounce, and return shot. In target stroke, the athlete is given 10 attempts to drop-hit the ball within the boundaries of the opponent's singles court; one point is awarded for each successful hit. In target bounce the athlete bounces a tennis ball on the playing surface using one hand; the score is the highest number of consecutive bounces in two trials. In racket bounce, the athlete bounces the ball off the racket face as many times consecutively as possible; the score is the most consecutive bounces in two trials. In return shot, the athlete attempts to return a ball that has bounced once over the net and into the opponent's singles court. One point is awarded for each successful hit, and the greatest number of successful consecutive attempts in two rounds is counted.

Sport Variations and Modifications

In 1980 the National Foundation of Wheelchair Tennis (NFWT) was founded to develop and sponsor competition. In 1981 the Wheelchair Tennis Players Association (WTPA) was formed under the aegis of the NFWT, with the purpose of administering the rules and regulations of the sport. A Wheelchair Tennis Committee within the United States Tennis Association (USTA) was approved in 1996. In 1998, the WPTA merged with the USTA's Wheelchair Tennis Committee, making the USTA the governing body for wheelchair tennis. The rules for wheelchair tennis are the same as for regular tennis, except that the ball is allowed to bounce twice before being returned (Parks, 1997). The first bounce must land in-bounds; the second bounce can land either in-bounds or out-of-bounds.

The USTA (2003) sanctions the following singles and doubles divisions: men's and women's open; men's A, B, and C; women's A and B and women's E (novice), and boy's and girl's junior. There is also a senior doubles event. The "Quad" division (open, A, and B) was established for individuals with limited power, mobility, and strength in at least three limbs as a result of accidents, spinal cord injuries, or other conditions. Also included in this division are individuals with quadriplegia with the ability to walk, individuals who use power wheelchairs, and individuals with three amputations.

Special Olympics (2003) offers the following events: singles, doubles, Unified Sports doubles, and an individual skills contest. The latter consists of the racket bounce, "Ups" (hitting the ball into the air from the racket), forehand volley, backhand volley, forehand ground stroke, backhand ground stroke, serve into deuce court, serve into advantage (ad) court, and alternating ground strokes with movement. A player's final score is the cumulative score of all nine events.

Other Variations and Modifications

If mobility is a problem, the court size can be reduced to accommodate individuals with disabilities. This can be accomplished by having players without disabilities defending their entire regulation court while individuals with disabilities defend half of their court. It could also be accomplished by permitting players to strike the ball on the second bounce. Variations in the scoring system can promote participation. An example is scoring by counting the number of consecutive hits, which, in effect, structures the game as cooperative rather than competitive. If the player with a disability has extremely limited mobility, the court could be divided into designated scoring areas, with those closest to that player receiving higher point values. Racket control might be a concern for some students because the standard tennis racket might be too heavy. There are several solutions to this problem, including shortening the grip on the racket, using a junior-size racket, or substituting a racquetball racket. In the case of an individual with an amputation, the racket can be strapped to the stump (if one remains) to allow for effective leverage and racket use.

If mobility or racket preparation is a problem, reducing the court size, at least initially, assists in learning proper racket positioning and stroking (because footwork is minimal). If still unsuccessful, the player can be placed in the appropriate stroking position with the shoulder of the nonswinging arm perpendicular to the net. This way, all that is necessary is to move into and swing at the ball.

To serve, the player routinely tosses the ball into the air with the hand opposite the one holding the racket. In preparation for striking the ball at the optimal height, the racket is moved in an arc from a position in front of the body down to the floor and up to a position behind the back. At this point, the racket arm is fully extended to strike the ball as it descends from the apex of the toss. For individuals who lack either the coordination or strength to perform the serve as described, an appropriate variation is to bring the racket straight up in front of the face to a position in which the hand holding the racket is about even with the forehead or slightly higher. Although serving in this manner reduces speed and produces an arc that is considerably higher than normal, it does allow individuals to serve who might otherwise not learn to serve correctly. To accomplish the toss, an individual with a single-arm amputation might grip the ball in the racket hand by extending the thumb and first finger beyond the racket handle when gripped normally and hold the ball against the racket. The ball is then tossed in the air and stroked in the usual way. A player with a double-arm amputation and the racket strapped to a stump uses a different approach. The ball lies on the racket's strings, and, with a quick upward movement, the ball is thrust into the air to be struck either in the air or after it bounces. In the case of "Quad" tennis, another individual might drop the ball for a player who is unable to serve in the conventional manner (Parks, 1997).

TABLE TENNIS

As is true of tennis, all individuals but the severely disabled can play table tennis or a version of it. Table tennis can be played in singles or doubles competition and, although the requisite skills are less adjustable than in tennis, the mechanical modifications that are available make this sport quite suitable for individuals with disabilities. Regardless of the variations and modifications, the basic objective of the game remains the same: to return the ball legally onto the opponent's side of the table in such a way as to prevent the opponent from making a legal return.

Sport Skills

As in tennis, the basic strokes are the forehand and backhand. Unlike tennis, the service is not a separate stroke. A serving player puts the ball in play with either a forehand or backhand stroke. The ball is required to strike the table on the server's side initially before striking the table on the receiver's side. In addition, servers must strike the ball outside the boundary at their end of the court.

Lead-Up Activities

Appropriate for use in physical education programs is an adapted table tennis game created at the Children's Rehabilitation Center at the University of Virginia Hospital. Two or four people can play this game, which is called "surface table tennis." The game involves hitting a regulation table tennis ball so that it moves on the surface of the table and passes through a modified net. The net is constructed from two pieces of string strung parallel and attached a half-inch apart at the top of official standards, and two or three pieces of string strung parallel and attached three-quarters of an inch apart at the bottom of the standards with a two-inch opening in the middle (Adams & McCubbin, 1991). At the start of play, the ball is placed on the table. A player strikes it so that it rolls through the opening in the net into the opponent's court. Points are awarded to the player who last made a legal hit through the net. Points are lost when a player hits the ball over the net either on a bounce or in the air, when the ball fails to pass through the net, or when a player hits the ball twice in succession.

Another lead-up game, Corner Ping-Pong, was developed at the University of Connecticut (Dunn & Fait, 1997). It is played in a corner in an area 6 feet (2 meters) high and 6 feet wide on each side of the corner. One player stands on either side of the centerline. The server drops the ball and strokes it against the floor to the forward wall. The ball must rebound to the adjacent wall and then bounce onto the floor of the opponent's area. If the server fails to deliver a good serve, one point goes to the opponent. The ball may bounce only once on the floor before the opponent returns it. The ball must be stroked against the forward wall within the opponent's section of the playing area so that it rebounds to the adjacent wall and onto the floor in the server's area. Failure to return the ball is a point for the server. Scoring is similar to that for table tennis. Each player gets five consecutive serves. A ball that is stroked out of bounds is scored as a point for the other player. The winning score is 21 points, and the winner must win by 2.

Special Olympics provides three developmental events that can serve as lead-up activities. They are Target Serve, Racket Bounce, and Return Shot (Special Olympics, 2003). In Target Serve, the athlete serves five balls from the right side and five balls from the left side of the table; a point is awarded for each ball that lands in the correct service area. In Racket Bounce, the athlete bounces the ball off the racket face as many times consecutively as possible in 30 seconds; the score is the most consecutive bounces in two trials. Return Shot involves attempting to return a tossed ball to the feeder's side of the table; one point is awarded if the ball is successfully returned; five points are earned if the ball lands in one of the service boxes. The athlete attempts to return five balls, with a maximum of 25 points possible.

Sport Variations and Modifications

Table tennis is included as a sport in competitions offered by Wheelchair Sports, USA (WS/USA); the National Disability Sports Alliance (NDSA), formerly the United States Cerebral Palsy Athletic Association; Disabled Sports, USA (DS/USA); the Dwarf Athletic Association of America (DAAA); the United States of America Deaf Sports Federation (USADSF) through its affiliate, the U.S. Deaf Table Tennis Association, Inc.; and the Special Olympics. For the most part, competition is based on the rules established by the International Table Tennis Federation and International Paralympic Committee (IPC) (1999-2003). Some modifications are permitted. For example, DAAA (1998) permits the use of a riser or an elevated platform. In WS/USA and USCPAA competitions, the following rules apply (WS/USA, 2002):

- Competitors' feet and footrests may not touch the floor.
- Service shall be called a let if the ball leaves the table by either of the receiver's sides, if on bouncing on the receiver's side the ball returns in the direction of the net, or if the ball comes to rest on the receiver's side of the playing surface.
- The playing surface shall not be used as a support with the free hand while playing the ball; a player may use the playing surface to restore balance after a shot has been played as long as the table does not move.
- Strapping is permitted only below the knee.
- The playing area may be reduced, but it should not be less than eight meters long and seven meters wide.
- There are no exceptions to the playing rules for players who stand.

Special Olympics (2003) sanctions the following events: singles, doubles, mixed doubles, wheelchair competition, individual skills competition, Unified Sports doubles, and Unified Sports mixed doubles. In wheelchair competition, players who are serving may project the ball upward in any manner; they are not required to deliver the ball from the palm of the free hand. The individual skills competition is comprised of five events, including hand bounce, racket bounce, forehand volley, backhand volley, and serve. Scores from all five events are added together for a final score.

Other Variations and Modifications

Several assistive devices are available for individuals with severe disabilities (e.g., muscular dystrophy and other disorders that weaken or affect the shoulder). A ball-bearing feeder provides assistance for shoulder and elbow motion by using gravity to gain a mechanical advantage and makes up for a loss of power resulting from weakened muscles. The bi-handle paddle, which consists of a single paddle with handles on each side, was designed to encourage greater range of motion for participants in adapted table tennis. Its greatest asset is increased joint movement resulting from the bilateral nature of hand and finger positioning. A strap-on paddle has been designed for players with little or no functional finger flexion or grasp. The paddle is attached to the back of the hand with Velcro straps. The major disadvantage is that it precludes use of a forehand stroking action. A table tennis cuff is useful for individuals with limited finger movement and grip strength. The cuff consists of a clip that attaches to a metal clamp on the paddle's handle and a Velcro strap that holds the cuff securely to the hand (Adams & McCubbin, 1991). Another device, the space ball net, can replace the paddle for play-

ers who are blind (Dunn & Fait, 1997). This device, held in two hands, consists of a lightweight metal frame that supports a nylon lattice or webbing. The net is large enough and provides an adequate rebounding surface to make participation feasible for individuals who are blind. Additionally, a special table has been designed for players who are visually impaired or blind. The table is all white and, when combined with a special orange ball containing metal beads, accommodates players who have visually impairments.

ANGLING

The American Casting Association (ACA) is the governing body for tournament fly and bait casting in the United States. It sets the rules by which eligible casters can earn awards in registered tournaments. None of the contemporary sports organizations for people with disabilities sponsors competition in angling, and the activity is rarely seen in physical education programs. It is most likely used as a recreational sport.

Lead-Up Activities

Angling requires the mastery of casting and other fishing skills. In terms of lead-up activities, at least two casting games deserve mention. The game of "skish" involves accuracy in target casting at various distances. Each participant casts 20 times at each target. One point is awarded for each direct hit (plug landing inside target or similar goal). Three targets can be used simultaneously to speed up the game, with players changing position after

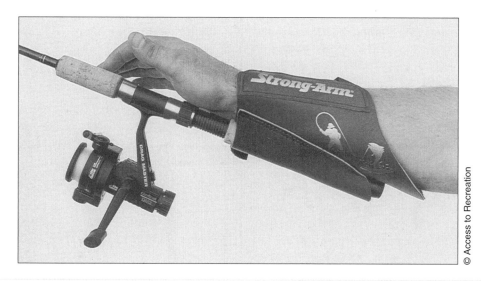

© Access to Recreation

Figure 27.1 Strong-arm rod holder.

each has cast 20 times at a target. The player with the greatest number of hits at the end of 60 casts is the winner. The second game, speed casting, is a variation of skish. Each player casts for 5 minutes at each target. The player with the high score at the end of 15 minutes is the winner (Adams, Daniel, McCubbin, & Rullman, 1982).

Variations and Modifications

Major assistive devices for use in angling have become popular in recent years. For example, the Strong-Arm rod holder (see figure 27.1) is a six-ounce sleeve into which the rod fits, enabling individuals with quadriplegia to cast. Other devices include the Ampo Fisher I, Van's EZ cast, Batick Bracket, Handi-Gear and the Freehand Recreation Belt. There are also several lines of electronic fishing reels (Adams & McCubbin, 1991).

ARCHERY

Under normal circumstances, shooting the long-bow is a six-step procedure. The steps, in order of occurrence, are assuming the correct stance, nocking the arrow, drawing the bowstring, aiming at the target, releasing the bowstring, and following through until the arrow makes contact with the target. One or more of these steps might be problematic and thus require some modification in the archer's technique.

Sport Variations and Modifications

Target archery is an athletic event sponsored by NDSA, WS/USA, and DS/USA. These groups observe the rules established by the Federa-tion of International Target Archery, with certain modifications. The following are adjustments that might be employed to encourage participation by individuals in wheelchairs, including athletes from NDSA and les autres athletes (WS/USA, 2002):

- An adjustable arrowrest and arrowplate and any movable pressure button or pressure point on the bow may be used, provided they are not electric or electronic and do not offer any additional aid in aiming; a draw check indicator, audible or visible, other than electric or electronic may be used.
- Archers with quadriplegia (Class AR 1) may use strapping and body support.
- Only archers with quadriplegia may have the bow bandaged or strapped into the hand. Archers with bow arm disability may use an elbow or wrist splint; they may also have someone load their arrows into the bow for them.
- Archers with quadriplegia may use compound bows; they may use a mechanical release aid with recurve and compound bows.
- Archers (only in junior divisions at WSUSA events) with functional use of only one side of their bodies can use a bowstand that holds the bow vertical to the target.

Other Variations and Modifications

Several assistive devices are available to aid the archer who has a disability. These include the bow sling, commercially available from most sports shops, which helps stabilize the wrist and hand for good bow control; the below-elbow amputee adapter device (see figure 27.2), which is held by

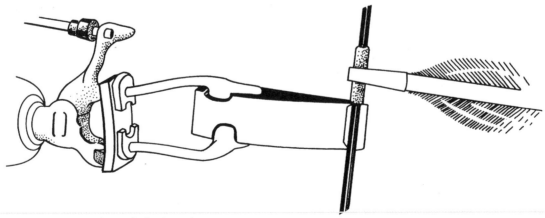

Figure 27.2 Amputee adapter device for archery.

the terminal end of the prosthesis and requires a slight rotation of the prosthesis to release the string and the arrow; the wheelchair bowstringer, which consists of an in-ground post with two appropriately spaced bolts around which the archer with a disability places the bow in order to produce enough leverage to string it independently; and the elbow brace, which is used to maintain extension in the bow arm when the archer has normal strength in the shoulder but minimal strength in the arm, possibly because of contractures (Adams & McCubbin, 1991). Additionally, the vertical bow set can accommodate individuals with bilateral upper-extremity involvement (Wiseman, 1982).

Other program adjustments include the use of a crossbow with the aid of the tripod assistive device for bilateral upper-extremity amputees. Various telescopic sights are also commercially available for the partially sighted archer.

Although the United States Association for Blind Athletes (USABA) does not sponsor competition in archery, several modifications can promote participation by individuals with visual impairments (Hattenback, 1979). These include:

- using foot blocks to ensure proper orientation with the target,
- placing an audible goal locator behind the target to aid in directional cueing,
- using a brightly colored target for partially sighted individuals, and
- placing balloons on the target as a means of auditory feedback.

BADMINTON

Special Olympics (2003) sponsors competition in badminton, but it is classified as a "recognized sport" only, which means it can be included in Special Olympics training and competitive programs but probably has not generated enough interest to be included in their regular sport offerings. Badminton was added as a new medal sport by DAAA in 1998. Competition is based on the rules of the International Badminton Federation (IBF). The game is, however, ideally suited for individuals with disabilities and is played routinely in physical education class.

Sport Skills

Badminton can be played quite adequately using only the forehand and backhand strokes and the underhand service. Beyond these strokes, devel-opment of the clear, smash, drop shot, and drive will depend on the participant's ability.

Lead-Up Activities

There are at least two lead-up games that deserve mention. Loop badminton (Dunn & Fait, 1997) is played with a standard shuttlecock, table-tennis paddles, and a 24-inch (61-centimeter) loop placed on top of a standard 46 inches (1.2 meters) in height. The object of the game is to hit the shuttlecock through the loop, which is positioned in the center of a rectangular court 10 feet (3 meters) long and 5 feet (1.5 meters) wide. Scoring is done as in the standard game of badminton. Loop badminton is well adapted for individuals with restricted movement who wish to participate in an active game that requires extreme accuracy. A second modified game is balloon badminton (Adams & McCubbin, 1991), a game in which a balloon is substituted for the shuttlecock, and table-tennis paddles are used instead of badminton rackets. People with visual impairments can play this game if a bell is placed inside the balloon to aid in directional cueing.

The three lead-up activities Special Olympics provides for badminton are target serve, return volley, and return serve (Special Olympics, 2003). In target serve, the participant has 10 chances to hit the shuttlecock within the boundaries of the opponent's singles court; one point is awarded for each successful hit. In return volley, the athlete has 10 chances to return the shuttlecock feed from the opponent's midcourt area to the opponent's single court; one point is awarded for each successful hit. Return serve involves attempting to return a serve to anywhere in the opponent's court; one point is awarded for each successful return up to a maximum of 10 points.

Sport Variations and Modifications

Special Olympics sanctions the following events: singles, doubles, mixed doubles and Unified Sports doubles, mixed doubles, and individual skills contests. The latter is unique to Special Olympics and includes six events: hand feeding, racket feeding, the "Ups" contest, forehand stroke, backhand stroke, and serve. A final score is determined by adding the scores of all six events. In Special Olympics competition, the following rules apply to wheelchair athletes (Special Olympics, 2003):

- Athletes may serve an overhand serve from either the right or left serving areas.

- The serving area is shortened to half the distance.

DAAA (1998) permits the following rules modifications:

- Sidearm serving is allowed.
- No overhead serves are permitted.

Other Variations and Modifications

Some standard modifications are routinely used. These include reducing the court size, strapping the racket to the stump of the individual with a double-arm amputation, and using Velcro on the butt end of the racket and on the top edge of the cork or rubber base of the shuttlecock to aid in shuttlecock retrieval (Weber, 1991). Several assistive devices are used to promote participation in badminton. The extension-handle racket involves splicing a length of wood to the shaft of a standard badminton racket. This is helpful for a wheelchair player or a player with limited movement. Another device is the "amputee serving tray" (see figure 27.3). Attached to the terminal end of the prosthesis, the tray permits easier service and promotes active use of the prosthesis. See also the application example below.

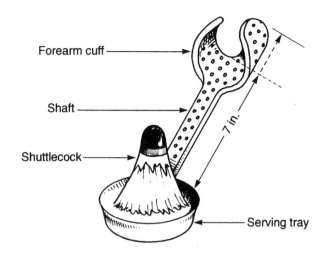

Figure 27.3 Amputee serving tray.

Adapted, by permission, from R.C. Adams and J.A. McCubbin, 1991, *Games, sports, and exercise for the physically handicapped*, 4tth ed. (Philadelphia, PA: Lippincott, Williams, and Wilkins), 218.

BOWLING

Both the ambulatory and people who use wheelchairs can participate in bowling with a high degree of success. Usually, the ambulatory bowler demonstrates a procedure that incorporates the following actions: approach (which may be modified if lower-extremity involvement exists); delivery, including the swinging of the ball; and release. A bowler who uses a wheelchair will eliminate the approach and either perform the swing and release independently or use a piece of adapted equipment to assist this part of the procedure. Two organizations that have significantly influenced the lives of bowlers with disabilities are the American Blind Bowlers Association (ABBA) and the American Wheelchair Bowling Association (AWBA).

Lead-Up Activities

Special Olympics (2003) sponsors two developmental events that qualify as lead-up activities: target bowl and frame bowl.

- *Target bowl.* In this activity participants roll two two-pound bowling balls in the direction

---

APPLICATION EXAMPLE

Individual, Dual, and Adventure Sports and Activities

Setting: Middle school physical education class

Student: Seventh-grade student with muscular dystrophy who uses a wheelchair and is able to push himself

Unit: Badminton

Task: Serving the shuttlecock

Applications: The physical educator might make reasonable accommodations in the following ways:

- Modify regular equipment to make it lighter or more manageable.
- Permit serving into a larger court area.
- Lower the net.
- Shorten distance of serve.

of two regulation bowling pins positioned on a standard bowling lane modified to equal half its normal length. Participants bowl five frames using the standard scoring systems of the American Bowling Congress (ABC).

- *Frame bowl.* In this activity the bowler rolls two frames (two rolls per frame) using plastic playground balls 30 centimeters (12 inches) in diameter. The object is to knock down the greatest number of plastic bowling pins from a traditional 10-pin triangular formation. The lead pin is set 5 meters (5 1/2 yards) from a restraining line. Bowlers either sit or stand and may use either one or both hands to roll the ball; the ball must be released behind the restraining line. Pins that are knocked down are cleared between the first and second rolls; pins are reset for each new frame. A bowler's score equals the number of pins knocked down in two frames. Five bonus points are awarded when all pins are knocked down on the first roll of a frame; two bonus points are awarded when all remaining pins are knocked down on the second roll of the frame.

Sport Variations and Modifications

Bowling is a sanctioned event in the competitions of USCPAA and Special Olympics. Both follow the rules of the ABC. The NDSA (2001) has developed the following procedures and rules for its competition:

- There are four divisions, two chute and two nonchute (chute bowling is explained soon).
- Nonchute divisions include class 3 through 8 bowlers who do not use specialized equipment; the retractable ball handle is permitted in these divisions.
- Chute divisions are for class 1 through 6 bowlers using specialized equipment. There are two divisions: closed chute, for class 1 and 2 bowlers, who need assistance with equipment (wheelchair, chute, or ball), and open chute, for classes 3 through 6 bowlers, who do not require assistance with their equipment.
- All bowlers must be able to bowl each ball independently within a 60-second period.

Special Olympics (2003) sponsors competition in bowling and follows the rules established by the ABC and the Women's International Bowling Congress. Modified rules for use in Special Olympics are as follows:

- Ramps and other assistive devices are permitted for singles competition only.
- Bowlers using ramps shall compete in separate divisions; there are two classifications of ramp bowling: unassisted and assisted.
- Bowlers are permitted to bowl up to three consecutive frames.

Other Variations and Modifications

Ambulatory bowlers use several types of assistive devices. The handle-grip bowling ball, which snaps back instantly on release, is ideal for bowlers with upper-extremity disabilities and for individuals with spastic cerebral palsy, especially those who have digital control difficulties. The ABC has approved the handle-grip ball for competitive play. Individuals with upper-extremity amputations who use a hook can use an attachable sleeve made of neoprene to hold and deliver a bowling ball. The sleeve can be made to compress by use of a spring and to expand for release with the identical action used to open the conventional hook. Stick bowling, which is similar to the use of a shuffleboard cue, was designed for individuals with upper-extremity involvement, primarily grip problems. The AWBA permits stick bowling in its national competitions, provided the bowlers apply their own power and direction to the ball.

Bowlers who are wheelchair users have several assistive devices that facilitate participation. Although not approved by the AWBA for national competition, ramp or chute bowling has become extremely popular with bowlers who are severely disabled. The counterpart of stick bowling for individuals who are wheelchair-users is the adapter-pusher device, originally designed for wheelchair bowlers lacking sufficient upper-arm strength to lift the ball. The handlebar-extension accessory, used in conjunction with the adapter-pusher device, assists ambulatory bowlers who do not have enough strength to lift the ball. Also available is the bowling ball holder ring (third arm), a device that attaches to the wheelchair arm and holds a ball while the bowler wheels down the approach lane.

Although USABA does not sponsor competition in bowling, the International Blind Sports

Federation (IBSF) sponsors nine pin bowling (or "skittles"). There are several modifications that can enhance participation in the sport for people with visual impairments. These modifications include:

- the use of a bowling rail for guidance, which is the standard method employed by most bowlers in the ABBA National Blind Bowling Championship Tournament,
- the use of an auditory goal locator placed above or behind the pins, and
- a scoring board system that tactually indicates the pins that remain standing after the ball is rolled.

FENCING

Sir Ludwig Guttmann introduced fencing as a competitive event for people with disabilities in 1953 as part of the Stoke Mandeville Games in Stoke Mandeville, England. Fencing was included in the Paralympic Games in Rome in 1960. The objective in fencing is to score by touching the opponent's target while avoiding being touched. If fencing is included in physical education, several possible variations and modifications make achievement of the sport's primary objective feasible for individuals with disabilities.

Sport Variations and Modifications

Competition in fencing for individuals who are wheelchair-users is normally conducted according to the rules of the International Wheelchair Fencing Committee (IWFC) of the International Stoke Mandeville Wheelchair Sports Federation. In competition, the following classes are recognized for all weapons: C, B, and A, which represent the old classification 1A and 1B, class 2, class 3, and class 4, respectively. This continuum represents competitors with no sitting balance and a severely affected fencing arm to competitors with good sitting balance and support legs and a functional fencing arm, respectively. When appropriate, fencers in these classes with significant loss of grip or control of the sword hand may bind the sword to the hand with a bandage or similar device (IWFC, 2001). Participants eligible to compete in wheelchair fencing include individuals with cerebral palsy, spinal cord injuries, amputations, and les autres. Among the modified rules written to ensure equal opportunity for all participants in wheelchair fencing, the following are important to note:

- A fencing frame must be used; the fencer with the shortest arms determines the length of the playing area.
- Fencers cannot purposely lose their balance, leave their chairs, rise from their seats, or use their legs to score a hit or to avoid being hit; the first offense is a warning, with subsequent offenses penalized by awarding one hit for each occurrence; accidental loss of balance is not penalized.
- The legs and trunk below the waist are not valid target areas in épée; the target area for foil and saber is exactly the same as in competition between individuals without disabilities (i.e., torso excluding arms, legs, and head and waist up including arms and head, respectively).

Other Variations and Modifications

Fencing is ordinarily conducted on a court measuring 6 by 40 feet (1.8 by 12.2 meters); however, to accommodate wheelchair participants, the dimensions of the standard court may be changed to 8 by 20 feet (2.5 by 6 meters)—or a circular court 15 to 20 feet (4.5 to 6 meters) in diameter may be used (Adams et al., 1982). Fencers who are blind will require a smaller, narrower court, which may conceivably be equipped with a guide rail (Dunn & Fait, 1997).

Basically, the only piece of adaptive equipment is the lightweight sword, which permits independent participation, especially for individuals with upper-extremity disabilities. In cases where no modification is necessary, the épée is recommended for ease of handling rather than the foil or saber (Orr & Sheffield, 1981).

HORSEBACK RIDING

The North American Riding for the Handicapped Association (NARHA), founded in 1969, is the primary advisory group to riders with disabilities in the United States and Canada. NARHA does not sponsor competition; however, it advises therapeutic, recreational, and competitive riding programs. NARHA also certifies riding instructors, accredits therapeutic riding facilities, and provides guidelines for operating safe programs.

Sport Skills

The Cheff Center in Augusta, Michigan, and the EQUEST program in Dallas, Texas, are two of the largest instructor training programs for therapeutic riding in the United States. Horseback riding involves, among other skills, mounting, maintaining correct positioning on the mount, and dismounting. At the Cheff Center, students with disabilities receive a six-phase lesson. The phases include mounting, warm-up, riding instruction, exercises, games, and dismounting (McCowan, 1972). Special consideration should be given to the selection and training of horses used for therapeutic riding programs (Spink, 1993). Horses should be suitably sized—that is, small, because children are less likely to be fearful of smaller animals. Smaller horses also permit helpers to be in a better position for assisting unbalanced riders; the shoulder of the helper should be level with the middle of the rider's back.

Lead-Up Activities

Several possibilities exist for using games in the context of horseback riding instruction. The origin of some of these games is pole bending, which is common in Western riding. It is used to teach horses how to bend and teach riders how to compensate during the bending movement. One game that encourages stretching of the arms involves placing quoits over the poles; this activity is conducted in relay fashion, with two- or three-member teams competing. Another game consists of throwing balls into buckets placed on a wall or pole. This activity has similar benefits to quoits. The traditional game Red Light, Green Light can be played as a way of reinforcing certain maneuvers, such as halts, which are taught to riders.

Sport Variations and Modifications

Special Olympics and NDSA each has its own equestrian competition or show. Les autres athletes participating in equine competition follow NDSA rules.

Special Olympics (2003) offers the following events: dressage, English equitation; stock seat equitation; Western riding; working trails; Gymkhana events including pole bending, barrel racing, figure 8 stake race, and team relays; drill teams of two or four, prix caprilli, showmanship at halter/ bridle classes, and Unified Sports team and drill relays. There are eight divisions to which riders are assigned based on a rider profile completed by the coach for each rider prior to any competition. The divisions are C-S, C-I, B-SP, B-S, B-IP, B-I, AP, and A. Distinctions among divisions range from Division C-S, which requires a leader (horse handler) and one or two sidewalkers to act as spotters, to Division A, in which a rider is expected to compete with no modifications to national governing body rules. Special Olympics (2003) has designated the following rules for riding:

- Riders who must wear other footwear as the result of a physical disability must submit a physician's statement with their entry; English tack-style riders must use either Peacock safety stirrups, S-shaped stirrups, or Devonshire boots; Western tack-style riders must use tapaderos or other approved safety stirrups.
- All riders must wear protective SEI-ASTM or BHS-approved helmets with full chin harness.
- Riders may use adaptive equipment without penalty but must in no way be attached to the horse or saddle.
- An athlete with Down syndrome who has been determined to have atlanto-axial instability is prohibited from competing in equestrian competition.

The USCPAA offers competition in the following dressage tests according to the rules established by the International Paralympic Equestrian Committee (IPEC): dressage including grades 1 to 3 (walk only, walk and trot, and walk, trot and, canter); grade 4 in derby and freestyle to music and pairs competition. For further details about the individual dressage test, consult the IPEC Web site. The IPEC (2002) has the following rules:

- No equipment is permitted that would in any way affix a rider to a horse or saddle, with the exception of Velcro to keep the rider attached to the saddle and elastic rubber bands to keep feet in the stirrups.
- Readers or callers (called "commanders") are permitted for riders with intellectual impairments, visual impairments, or head injury in all events including freestyle; commanders may use radio communication if supervised by a steward.
- For dressage tests, riders with visual impairments may either have callers or use beepers for purposes of location.

Other Variations and Modifications

Mounting is the single most important phase of a riding program for individuals with disabilities. Because for some people with disabilities the typical method of mounting is impossible (i.e., placing the left foot in the stirrup, holding onto the cantle, and springing into the saddle), some alternatives are based on the rider's abilities. Several basic types of mounting procedures are used by riders with disabilities; these range from totally assisted mounts, either from the top of a ramp or at ground level, to normal mounting from the ground (McCowan, 1972).

Once mounted, individuals with disabilities have available to them many pieces of special equipment that can make riding an enjoyable and profitable learning experience. One commonly used item is an **adapted rein bar,** which permits riders with a disability in one arm to apply sufficient leverage on the reins with the unaffected arm to successfully guide the horse; use of this bar is faded as soon as the rider learns to apply pressure with his or her knees. Another adaptation is the **Humes rein,** consisting of large oval handholds fitted on the rein; this allows individuals with involvement of the hands to direct the horse with wrist and arm movement. Body harnesses are used extensively in programs for riders with disabilities. They consist of web belts about four inches wide with a leather handhold in the back, which a leader can hold onto to help maintain a rider's balance. Most riders who have disabilities also use the **Peacock stirrup** (figure 27.4a), which is shaped like a regular stirrup except that only one side is iron and the other side has a rubber belt attached top and bottom.

This flexible portion of the stirrup releases quickly in case of a fall, reducing the chance of catching a foot. The **Devonshire boot** (figure 27.4b) is used frequently if a rider has tight heel cords or weak ankles. Designed much like the front portion of a boot, it prevents the foot from running through the stirrup, and consequently it promotes keeping the toes up and heels down, which can be invaluable if heel-cord stretching is desirable.

GYMNASTICS

Gymnastics has enjoyed considerable popularity in recent decades because of its visibility in the Olympic Games. As a result, individuals with disabling conditions have begun to participate in gymnastic programs when opportunities are available. For example, people with orthopedic involvements have participated in gymnastics programs for individuals without disabilities (Winnick & Short, 1985).

Sport Skills

Beyond possessing the physical attributes necessary to participate in gymnastics (e.g., strength, agility, endurance, flexibility, coordination, and balance), participants must learn to compete either in one or more single events or in all events, called the "all-around." Under normal conditions, men compete in the following events: pommel horse, rings, horizontal bar, parallel bars, and floor exercise. Women compete in balance beam, uneven parallel bars, vaulting, and floor exercise. In both men's and women's competitions, participation in all events qualifies athletes for a chance to win the all-around title.

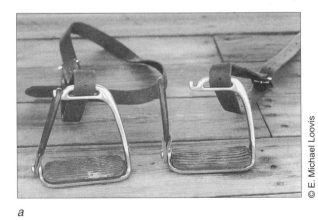

a   *b*

Figure 27.4   *(a)* Peacock stirrup. *(b)* Devonshire boot.

Lead-Up Activities

The closest thing to lead-up activities related to gymnastics can be found in the Special Olympics sports skills program and in select developmental events offered as part of the Special Olympics Games. In its sports skills program manual, *Gymnastics* (Special Olympics, n.d.), general conditioning exercises with emphasis on flexibility and strength are recommended. Doubles tumbling and balance stunts are also suggested. As an introductory experience, educational gymnastics, which uses a creative, problem-solving approach, can be used to teach basic movement concepts. This could eventually allow participants to compete in more advanced forms of gymnastic competition.

Sport Variations and Modifications

Gymnastics is offered in the Special Olympics Games. Events for men include vaulting, parallel bars, pommel horse, horizontal bar, rings, and floor exercise. Women's events include vaulting, uneven parallel bars, balance beam, and floor exercise. Both men and women can compete in the all-around competition. Mixed gender events include vaulting, wide beam, floor exercise, and tumbling with an all-around competition. Only women compete in rhythmic gymnastics in the following events: ribbon, ball, rope, hoop, and an all-around competition consisting of the four events. Exceptions are levels A and B, which are coeducational and which are performed while sitting. There are also Unified Sports events as well as group routines performed by groups of 4 to 8 athletes. Each of the individual competitions (i.e., mixed gender, men's, and women's) has a unified sports event for each of the events that make up the specific category. No significant rule modifications are required, and each participant's performance is judged according to the rules established for that event by the International Gymnastics Federation (FIG) and the national governing body (Special Olympics, 2003).

Special Olympics (2003) rules to ensure equitable competition include the following:

- Gymnasts with visual impairments have the option of performing the vault with no run; a one-step, a two-step, a multiple bounce on the board (with hands starting on the horse); or a two- or three-bounce takeoff; audible cues may be used in all routines.
- In floor exercise, the coach may signal gymnasts with hearing impairments to begin the routine.
- Gymnasts using canes or walkers may have a coach walk onto the floor and remove (and replace) walkers and other aids as needed without any deduction of points.
- Gymnasts with visual impairments may use audible cues during floor exercise; music may be played at any close point off the mat, or the coach may carry the music source around the perimeter of the mat.
- Gymnasts in levels A and B perform their rhythmic gymnastics routines while seated either in a wheelchair or a sturdy chair; gymnasts who are blind can have audible cues during competition; Deaf athletes can have a visual cue to start with music without penalty.

Other Variations and Modifications

Few modifications are used in gymnastics competition. If gymnastics is used in physical education programs, all of the modifications observed by the sports organizations in the conduct of their competitions would be valid.

WRESTLING

The sport of wrestling requires considerable strength, balance, flexibility, and coordination. If individuals with a disability possess these characteristics, and if they can combine knowledge of techniques with an ability to demonstrate them in competitive situations, then there is no reason that individuals with disabilities cannot experience success in wrestling.

Sport Skills

Wrestling consists of several fundamentals and techniques that are essential for success. These include takedowns, escapes and reversals, breakdowns and controls, and pin holds. When learned and performed well, these maneuvers assist in accomplishing the basic objective in wrestling, which is to dominate opponents by controlling them and holding both shoulders to the mat simultaneously for one second.

Lead-Up Activities

The development of lead-up activities for wrestling has apparently not been an area of creative activity. If lead-up activities are desirable, then one can conceivably use certain traditional elementary physical education self-testing activities that have some relation to wrestling. Two such activities are listed here:

- *Hand wrestling.* Standing, two people face each other and grasp right hands; each person raises one foot off the ground. On a signal, each attempts to cause the other to touch either the free foot or hand to the ground.

- *Indian leg wrestle.* Two people lie side by side but facing in opposite directions. Hips are adjacent to the partner's waist. Inside arms are hooked. Each person raises the inside leg to a count of three; on the third count, they bend knees, hook them, and attempt to force the partner into a backward roll.

Sport Variations and Modifications

Both USABA and USADSF sponsor wrestling competitions. The USABA competition takes place in one division known as the Open Division and is contested according to international freestyle rules as interpreted by the International Blind Sports Federation (IBSF). International competition is held at the following weight categories for men: up to 119.5, 127.86, 138.88, 152.11, 167.54, 187.39, 213.8, and 275.57, and for women: up to 101, 112, 123, 136.5, 149.5, and 163 pounds. The following modification has been instituted to render conditions more suitable for athletes with visual impairments:

> Opponents begin the match in the neutral standing positions with gentle overlapping of each wrestler's hand over the hand of the opponent that is directly opposite; right to left and left to right hands. When contact is broken the match is interrupted and restarted in the neutral position at mat center. (IBSF, 1997)

Both **Greco-Roman wrestling** (which prohibits holds below the waist and use of the legs in attempting to take opponents to the mat) and freestyle wrestling are sanctioned events in competitions governed by USADSF. These events are conducted according to the rules established by the International Federation of Wrestling.

Competition in judo is also sanctioned by USABA. Judo is contested according to the rules of the International Judo Federation as interpreted by the IBSF. In the Paralympic Games, World Championships, and Regional Championships, competition for all weight classifications shall be combined for classes B1, B2, and B3. There are individual men's and women's competitions and men's and women's team competitions.

Other Variations and Modifications

Wrestling is not for everyone. For people with disabilities who want to attempt this sport, several modifications can be used. For those with lower-extremity difficulties that prevent ambulation, all maneuvers should be taught from the mat with emphasis on arm technique. Bilateral upper-extremity involvement will probably restrict participation in all but leg wrestling maneuvers. After removal of prostheses, single-arm amputees can participate with emphasis placed on leg maneuvers.

TRACK AND FIELD

Because all major sports organizations for individuals with disabilities offer competitive opportunities in track and field, this section will focus on rule modifications enacted to make participation maximally available. For each organization the track portion is discussed first, followed by the field events. No attempt is made to examine sport skills, variations and modifications, or lead-up activities, except as related to Special Olympics.

Wheelchair Sports, USA

Track and field competitions are governed by the rules of The Athletic Congress (TAC). The WS/USA sponsors a classed division in track and field events. Classes include T1, T2 (including T2a and T2b for juniors competition only), T3, T4, F1, F2, F3, F4, F5, F6, F7, and F8 (standing and sitting). Classes T1 and T2 compete in 100-, 200-, 400-, 800-, 1,500-, 5,000-meter races, and a 4 × 100-meter circular relay and a 4 × 400-meter relay. Classes T3 and T4 also compete in a 10,000-meter race and a 4 × 100-meter circular relay. T3 and T4 also contest 10-, 15-, and 20-kilometer races as well as half- and full marathons. In field events all classes compete in the discus, shot put, and javelin, except class F1, which does not put the shot and which substitutes the club throw for the javelin event. Class F2 can choose between the club throw and javelin. Additionally, all classes compete in the pentathlon, which consists of five individual events. F1 competes in a 100-meter race, club throw, a 400-meter race, discus, and an 800-meter race. Classes F2 and F3 compete in shot put, javelin, discus, and 100- and 800-meter races. Classes F4 through F8 substitute 200- and 1,500-meter distances. There is also a junior division that contests mostly similar events but also includes races at shorter distances such as 60 meters as well as medley relays (all male, all female, and mixed).

The WS/USA (2002) has designated the following rules:

- Wheelchairs shall have at least two large wheels and one small wheel with only one round handrim for each large wheel; no mechanical gears or levers shall be allowed in any sanctioned WS/USA competition; only hand-operated mechanical steering devices are permitted.

- Batons are not exchanged in relay races; the takeover shall be a touch on any part of the body of the outgoing competitor within the takeover zone.

- Athletes must ensure that no part of their lower limbs can fall to the ground or track during an event; if used, strapping must be of a nonelastic material.

- Approved hold-down devices can be used to stabilize competitors' chairs in field events; classes F1 to F6 must have at least one part of the upper leg or buttock in contact with the cushion or seat until the implement is released; F7 and F8 competitors are permitted lifting as long as one foot is in contact with the ground inside the throwing circle.

- Competitors cannot use any device (e.g., taping two or more fingers together) to assist in making throws; gloves are not allowed; F1 through F3 may use strapping on the non-throwing hand or to anchor it to the chair.

United States Association of Blind Athletes

IAAF rules are employed in track and field competitions. Within the United States Association of Blind Athletes (USABA) structure, there are three visual classifications: B1, B2, and B3. The following events are provided for males and females across all three classes: 100-, 200-, 400-, 800-, 1,500-, 5,000- and 10,000-meter races. Men and women in all classes also run a marathon. There are two relays for men and women: a 4 × 100 meter and a 4 × 400 meter with combined visual classes. Both men and women in all three classes compete in long jump, high jump, triple jump, discus, javelin, and shot put. Men in all three classes throw the hammer. There are pentathlons contested by all classes and both genders. Both men and women compete in the long jump, discus, and 100-meter events. Men throw the javelin while women put the shot. Men run a 1,500-meter event, and women run a 800-meter race. Two divisions of youth events, junior and intermediate, are also contested. The IBSF (1997) has determined that the following rule modifications are necessary to provide more suitable competition for athletes with visual impairments:

- Class B1 sprinters may run the 100-meter with the help of not more than two callers, one of whom must remain behind the finish line; the second caller, if one is used, has no restriction on position taken but may not cross the finish line ahead of the athlete.

- Guides are allowed for B1 and B2 in 200-meter through marathon events. When guides are used in events between 200 and 800 meters, there is an allowance of two lanes per competitor.

- Competitors may also decide what form guidance will take. They may choose an elbow lead, a tether, or run free; at no time will the guide push or pull the competitor, nor will the guide ever precede the athlete; the runner may receive verbal instructions from the guide.

- Acoustic signals (a caller) are permitted for B1 and B2 athletes in field events.

- Class B1 high jumpers may touch the bar as an orientation prior to jumping; B2 jumpers are permitted to place a visual aid on the bar.

- Class B1 and B2 shot put, discus, and javelin throwers may enter the throwing circle or runway (run-up track) only with the assistance of a helper, who must leave the area prior to the first attempt.

United States of America Deaf Sports Federation

Track competition for men includes races at standard distances from 100-meter through 25-kilometer road racing. It also includes 110- and 400-meter hurdles, 3,000-meter steeplechase, and 20-kilometer walk. Along with the standard field events, the United States of America Deaf Sports Federation (USADSF) provides competition in pole vaulting and hammer throw. Women's competition in track and field parallels that described for women in USABA with one exception: 100-meter hurdle.

Special Olympics

Special Olympics offers a greater number and diversity of track and field events than any other sport organization for people with disabilities. Included in the list of possible events that can be offered at a sanctioned competition are 100-, 200-, 400-, 800-, 1,500-, 3,000-, 5,000-, and 10,000-meter races. There are walking races of 400 and 800 meters; women compete in 100-meter hurdles whereas men compete in 110-meter hurdles. Additionally, there are 4×100- and 4×400-meter relays. In field competition the following events are contested: long jump, high jump, shot put, and pentathlon. Each of these events is mirrored with unified sports events with the exception of the hurdle events. There are also track and field events for athletes in wheelchairs. Long-distance events combining racing and walking have expanded to include 1,500-, 3,000-, 5,000-, and 10,000-meter competitions. There is also a 15,000-m walking event, a half-marathon, and a full marathon. Unified sports competitions include 1,500-, 3,000-, 5,000-, 10,000-, and 15,000-meter walking and running events. A 15,000-meter walking event is contested along with a half- and full marathon. IAAF rules are employed in competitions sanctioned by Special Olympics (2003). Modifications to those rules include the following:

- In running events a rope or sighted guide can be used to assist athletes who are visually impaired; a tap start can be used only with an athlete who is deafblind.
- In race walking events, athletes are not required to maintain a straight support leg while competing.
- In the softball throw, athletes can use any type of throw.

- Athletes with Down syndrome who have recognized atlanto–axial instability may not participate in either the high jump or the pentathlon.

Special Olympics (2003) gets nearer than other organizations to describing lead-up activities. It does this through the provision of 18 developmental events including 25- and 50-meter dashes or walks, a 100-meter walk, the 10-, 25-, and 50-meter assisted walk, softball throw, 10- and 25-meter wheelchair races, a 30-meter wheelchair slalom, a 4×25-meter wheelchair shuttle relay, 30- and 50-meter motorized wheelchair slaloms, a 25-meter motorized wheelchair obstacle race, a tennis ball throw for distance, and the standing long jump.

United States Cerebral Palsy Athletic Association

Competition sanctioned by the NDSA is governed by rules established by TAC. Events are contested via an eight-class system and consist of races as short as 60-meter (weave) for class 1 athletes in electric wheelchairs up to 3,000 meters and cross country running for class 5 through 8. There are 4×100-meter and 4×400-meter open relays for classes 2 through 8, including wheelchair and ambulant events. The following events constitute the field portion: shot put, discus, javelin, club throw, and long jump. Additional events include the precision throw, soft shot, distance kick, high toss, and medicine ball thrust. There is also a pentathlon for classes 3 through 8. Modifications of rules (NDSA, 2001) used to ensure equitable competition include the following:

- Class 5 athletes who use canes or crutches must use their assistive devices in a manner such that they make contact with the surface of the track a minimum of one time approximately every 10 meters.
- Athletes in wheelchair relays must make personal contact with their team member to complete a successful changeover. This contact can be on any part of the outgoing teammate; either the incoming or outgoing competitor may initiate the tag within the change zone.

The NDSA (2001) incorporates the following additional modifications in its field events:

- An attendant or approved holding device may secure the chair in place; however, neither an attendant nor the apparatus may be inside the throwing area.

- The soft shot (5-inch [13-centimeter]-diameter cloth weighing a maximum of 6 ounces [170 grams]), precision throw, high toss, and soft discus (Spongedisc) are used for class 1 only.
- Distance kick and medicine ball thrust are offered for class II athletes who cannot engage in routine throwing events. In the distance kick a 13-inch (33-centimeter) playground ball is placed on a foul line; the competitors initiate a backswing and then kick the ball forward while remaining seated in their chairs. Distance of the kick is the criterion. In the medicine ball thrust, a 6-pound (2.7-kilogram) medicine ball is used. Competitors may not kick the ball; rather, the foot must remain in contact with the ball throughout the entire movement until release.

Dwarf Athletic Association of America

The Dwarf Athletic Association of America (DAAA) sanctions the following track events: 20-meter run for children under 7 years of age (futures); 20-meter run for juniors, 7 to 9 years; 40-meter run for juniors, 7 to 9 and 10 to 12 years; and a 60-meter run for juniors, 10 to 12 and 13 to 15 years, and athletes over 40 years of age (master). There is also a 100-meter open race and a 4 × 100-meter relay. The rules of TAC and wheelchair competition are typically adhered to.

Field events contested in DAAA competition include shot put, discus, and javelin in open and shot put and discus in master's classes. Juniors (13 to 15) may participate in shot put and discus. Other juniors and futures events include softball throw, flippy flyer (soft discus), and tennis ball throw for futures (DAAA, 1998).

GOLF

Golf has been an event in the Special Olympics since 1995. It is also an activity that can be effectively included in physical education programs for individuals with disabilities. The sport of professional golf achieved infamous recognition in 1998, when Casey Martin, a golfer with a chronic and debilitating circulatory disorder in his leg, sued the Professional Golf Association (PGA) under the provisions of the Americans with Disabilities Act to traverse the course using a cart. He won the right to use a cart in PGA events.

Sport Skills

Golf, as it is typically played, requires a person to grasp the club and address the ball using an appropriate stance. Being able to swing the golf club backward, then forward through a large arc including a follow-through are also requisite tasks.

Lead-Up Activities

An appropriate lead-up activity is miniature golf. This popular version of golf is quite suited to individuals with disabilities. For many people with disabilities, this might represent the extent to which the golf experience is explored. Holes should range from 8 to 14 feet (2.4 to 4.3 meters) from tee mat to hole with a width of 3 feet (1 meter), which accommodates reaching a ball lying in the center of the course from a wheelchair.

Sport Variations and Modifications

Special Olympics (2003) has created rules based on the *Rules of Golf* as written by the Royal and Ancient Golf Club of St. Andrews and the United States Golf Association. Official events include an individual skills contest (level 1), an alternate shot team play competition (level 2), an individual stroke play competition of 9 holes (level 3), an individual stroke play competition of 18 holes (level 4), and a Unified Sports team play (level 5). Individual skills contests are designed to train athletes to compete in basic golf skills. Competition is held in short putting, long putting, chipping, pitch shot, iron shot, and wood shot. The alternate shot team play competition involves pairing one Special Olympics athlete with one golfer without mental retardation who serves as a coach and mentor. The format is a 9-hole tournament played as a modified four-person scramble. Level 3 enables athletes to play in regulation 9-hole golf competition, whereas level 4 is designed to play in 18-hole competitions. Level 5 or Unified Sports team play is designed to provide the Special Olympics athlete an opportunity to play in a team format with a partner without intellectual disabilities but with similar ability.

Other Variations and Modifications

Because of limitations experienced by individuals with disabilities, the essential sport skills are often problematic. Dunn and Fait (1997) have detailed many practical considerations necessary for successful participation by golfers who are disabled. These include using powered carts for those who lack stamina to walk the golf course but who can physically play the game; having a player whose right arm is missing or incapacitated play left-handed, or vice versa; providing a chair for players who cannot balance on one crutch or who are unable to stand (Longo, 1989) (those using a chair or sitting in a wheelchair should have the chair turned so they are facing the ball); and eliminating the preliminary movement of the club (waggle) for blind golfers because this could produce an initial malalignment of the club with the ball. Additionally, information about distance to the hole can be gained by tapping on the cup or by asking others how far they are positioned from the cup; some wheelchair players also use extra long clubs to clear the footplates. The Putter Finger is an assistive device that consists of a molded rubber suction cup designed to fit on the grip end of any putter. It is used to retrieve the ball from the hole (Adams & McCubbin, 1991). J. H. Huber (personal communication, January 1971) developed another adaptation that enables golfers who are blind to practice independently. Three pieces of material, all of which produce a different sound when struck, are hung 15 to 20 feet in front of golfers as they practice indoors. Golfers are instructed about the positions of the different pieces of material and the sound made by each. Because feedback about the direction of the ball's line of flight is available, they can determine whether the ball went straight, hooked, or sliced. The golf chirper (Cowart, 1989) is used to develop independent putting skills; it serves as a cup locator and audio feedback device. The amputee golf grip developed by Synergetic Muscle-Powered Prosthetic Systems fits any standard prosthetic wrist. It permits full rotation during backswing, squared clubface at impact, and complete follow-through.

POWER LIFTING

Power lifting has developed over the years as an extremely popular sport for people with disabilities. In this chapter power lifting as a sport is distinguished from routine weight training.

Sport Skills

As administered by the International Stoke Mandeville Wheelchair Sports Federation (ISMWSF), the sport includes two lifts: the bench press and the power-lifting press. In IPC competition, the sport is restricted to the bench press. Participants are classified by weight; however, braces and other devices are not counted in the total weight. Wheelchair Sports, USA makes adjustments to recorded weight according to the site of an amputation.

Sport Variations and Modifications

DAAA, WS/USA, NDSA, and USABA offer competitive power-lifting programs. Special Olympics likewise offers power-lifting but only as a demonstration event. The IBSF (1997) sanctions three events: bench press, squat, and deadlift. Special Olympics (2003) offers bench press, deadlift, and squat. It also offers two combination events: bench press and deadlift and bench press, deadlift, and squat. Special Olympics offers Unified Sports competition that parallels the previously mentioned events. WS/USA provides competition in power-lift press and bench press. Each organization has specific rules that accommodate its athletes. Some of the more significant modifications are the following:

- A safety device engineered to protect lifters against the "clasp knife reflex" (exaggerated stretch reflex) is mandatory in all sanctioned events (NSDA, 2001).
- Strapping the legs to the bench is permissible either just above the knees or at the ankles as long as it is done with the strap provided by the organizing committee; for above-the-knee amputees, strapping is permitted between the hip and the remainder of the amputated limb (WS/USA, 2002).
- A lifter who has a physical disability may be strapped to the bench between the ankles and the hips with a strapping not to exceed 10 centimeters in length (Special Olympics, 2003).
- An athlete with Down syndrome with a recognized atlanto–axial instability may not compete in the squat lift (Special Olympics, 2003).
- Athletes may bench press with legs straight or with knees bent and feet flat on the bench (DAAA, 1998).

CYCLING

Cycling, whether bicycle or tricycle, is a useful skill from the standpoint of a lifelong leisure pursuit. It can also be a strenuous sport pursued for its competitiveness. To compete, participants must develop a high level of fitness and learn effective race strategy.

Sport Skills

Under most circumstances cycling requires the ability to maintain balance on a cycle and to execute a reciprocal movement of the legs to turn the pedals. Technological advances have enabled individuals to cycle who would never have thought previously about cycling as a leisure pursuit or as a competitive event.

Sport Variations and Modifications

The USADSF sponsors three events: the 1,000-meter sprint, a road race, and a time-trial race on the road. The USCPAA sponsors events in four divisions including Divisions 1 and 2 for tricycles and Divisions 3 and 4 for bicycles. The tricycle events include a 3K to 10K time trial and a 10K to 40K road race for classes 2, 5, and 6. The bicycle events include a 10K to 20K time trial and a 35K to 75K road race for classes 5 to 8. Classes 5 to 8 also compete in a velodrome or cycling track event, a flying 200, a pursuit 3K–4K, and a kilo. Hand-propelled tricycles are not permitted in NDSA competitions (NDSA, 2001). The IBSF (1997) offers four event categories: road races, track races, individual pursuit, and sprints. Within each category are races for men, women, and mixed tandems. Road races are 100 to 135 kilometers for men, 50 to 70 kilometers for women, and 60 to 85 kilometers for mixed teams. Track races are 1,000 meters for men and mixed teams and 500 meters for women. Individual pursuit events are 4 kilometers for men and 3 kilometers for women and mixed teams. Sprint competitions are contested over a distance of 1,000 meters for men, women, and mixed teams. With few exceptions the rules for IBSF cycling are the same as those for the United States Cycling Federation. The primary exception is that the pilot (front rider) in tandem riding events must be sighted, with a group 1 permit; the stoker (back rider) can be from any vision class and must have a group 2 permit.

Special Olympics offers the following events: 500-meter time trial; 1-, 5-, and 10-kilometer time trials; 5-, 10-, 15-, 25-, and 40-kilometer road races; 500-meter, 25- and 40-kilometer tandem time trials. Unified Sports cycling events parallel the competitions mentioned earlier with the exception of the 500-meter time trial. All events are governed by the rules established by the International Federation of Amateur Cycling (Special Olympics, 2003).

Other Variations and Modifications

Riding a bicycle can be difficult. Individuals with impaired balance or coordination might require some adaptation. Three- and four-wheeled bicycles with or without hand cranks can facilitate cycling for individuals with a disability. If riding a two-wheeled bicycle is the desirable approach, then training wheels suitable for full-size adult

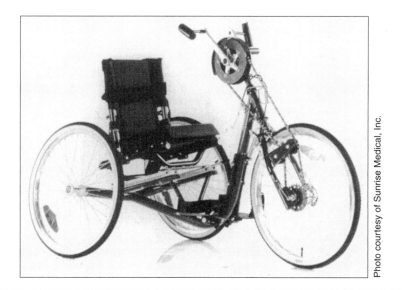

Photo courtesy of Sunrise Medical, Inc.

Figure 27.5 Quickie Kidz bike.

bikes can be constructed. Additionally, tandem cycling can be used in cases in which total control of the bicycle is beyond the ability of the person with a disability (e.g., the visually impaired). The Quickie Kidz Bike (figure 27.5) is a made-to-order, hand-cranked bicycle–wheelchair available in single speed or three- to five-speed models. It is available from Sunrise Medical, Inc.

BOCCE

Bocce, the Italian version of bowling, is generally played on a sand or soil alley 75 feet (30 meters) long and 8 feet (2.4 meters) wide. The playing area is normally enclosed at the ends and sides by boards 18 inches (46 centimeters) and 12 inches (30 centimeters) high, respectively.

Bocce made its initial appearance in the Paralympics at the 1992 Barcelona Games. Bocce is the only Paralympic sport in which men and women compete together in all events.

Sport Skills

The game requires that players roll or throw wooden balls in the direction of a smaller wooden ball or "jack." The object is to have the ball come to rest closer to the "jack" than any of the opponent's balls. To do this, players try to roll balls in order to protect their own well-placed shots, while knocking aside their opponent's balls.

Lead-Up Activities

The Empire Games for the Physically Challenged pioneered a game called crazy bocce, which con-

sists of throwing two sets of four wooden balls alternately into various size rings for specified point totals. Three smaller rings sit inside one large ring, which is 13 feet (4 meters) in circumference. Points are awarded only if the ball remains inside the large ring. If the ball lands inside the large ring (but not in any of the smaller rings), 1 point is awarded. If the ball lands inside the small blue or red ring, 2 points are earned. Landing inside the small yellow ring nets 3 points. The game is usually played with the large ring in a small wading pool (see figure 27.6). The large ring can also be attached to swimming pool sides, using a suction cup attachment. The game can also be played in the snow, on the beach, on the lawn, and on carpet. Crazy bocce is enjoyed by young and old alike.

Sport Variations and Modifications

Both individual and team bocce are sanctioned events in the national competition of NDSA, DAAA, and SO. A minor adjustment to established rules permits the use of ramps or chutes by DAAA athletes. In the Paralympic Games, athletes eligible for individual competition are classified as BC1, BC2, BC3, and BC4 according to the Cerebral Palsy International Sports and Recreation Association (CP-ISRA) and the International Boccia Commission. There are also pairs events for BC3 and 4 as well as team competition for BC1 and 2. Special Olympics (2003) offers the following events: singles, doubles, and team competitions and Unified Sports doubles and team competitions. Major modifications to the rules in either NSDA (2001) or DAAA (1998) sanctioned events include the following:

© Empire State for the Physically Challenged

Figure 27.6   Playing crazy bocce.

- The court is laid out on a tile or wood gym floor or other hard surface and measures 12.5 by 6 meters (41 feet by 19 feet 8 inches); stools, chairs, or other sitting devices are permitted in the thrower's box during matches.

- An assistant is allowed to adjust ramps or chutes and player's chair position within the throwing box; however, all direction for adjustments must be initiated by the player; assistive devices should not contain any mechanical device that aids in propulsion, such as a spring-loaded device.

- BC1 players who have difficulty holding or placing the balls can receive assistance from one aide; however, they must throw, kick, strike, push, or roll the ball independently; players may use more than one assistive device during a match only after the referee has indicated it is their turn to throw.

- All balls must be thrown, rolled, pushed, struck, or kicked into the court; use of a head pointer, chin lever, or pull lever is acceptable.

Other Variations and Modifications

There are several ways to modify bocce for participation by people with disabilities. A major concern is a lack of sufficient strength to propel the ball toward the jack. In such cases, substitution of a lighter object, such as a Nerf ball or balloon, or reduction of the legal court size would facilitate participation. Another area of concern is upper-extremity involvement, which could prohibit rolling or throwing the ball. This concern can be overcome if the individual is permitted to kick the ball into the target area or perhaps, as in regular bowling, to use a bowling cue or stick.

ADVENTURE ACTIVITIES

Another programmatic area that has gained considerable momentum over the past 25 to 30 years is the adventure curriculum. Perhaps the best-known program is Project Adventure, started by R. Lentz in 1971. Project Adventure uses a sequence of activities that encourage the development of individual and group trust, cooperation, confidence, courage, independence, and competence. These themes or goals are achieved through trust activities, cooperative games, initiative problems, rope course elements, and high ropes courses. Over the years it became clear that these experiences would benefit individuals with disabilities just as they benefit those without disabilities. In 1992, with the encouragement of Project Adventure, M.D. Havens published *Bridges to Accessibility.* The major theme of this text is the provision of integrated adventure experiences for individuals with disabilities that are accessible rather than adapted.

Individuals with disabilities engage in adventure activities such as canoeing (Wachtel, 1987), whitewater rafting (Roswal & Daugherty, 1991), kayaking (Kegel & Peterson, 1989), and backpacking (Huber, 1991). Still others participate in activities considered by many to be high-risk, nontraditional experiences, at least for individuals with disabilities. These include rock climbing (Roos, 1991), mountain biking, mountain trekking, and mountaineering (see figure 27.7).

Hal O'Leary who is the Recreation Program Director at the National Sports Center for the Disabled (NSCD) in Winter Park, Colorado, indicated

Figure 27.7   Mountaineering descent by wheelchair.

© NICAN INC. (Australia)

that whitewater rafting for individuals with disabilities is not much different than it is for individuals without disabilities (personal communication, October 1998). In the case of wheelchair users, the chair is placed on the floor of the raft, which is contrary to where one is normally positioned. Also, air mattresses or inflatable seats can be fitted in the boat to provide support and comfort. For individuals with severe disabilities the NSCD uses "beanbag" chairs to position individuals to participate comfortably in the rafting experience.

Huber (1991) reported on the successful through-hike of the Appalachian Trail by Bill Irwin. Irwin lost his sight to an eye disease at the age of 28. He made the hike from Springer Mountain, Georgia, to Mount Katahdin, Maine, in a little over eight months accompanied by only his guide dog.

Rock climbing (Roos, 1991) is becoming a favorite sport of individuals with disabilities. Mark Wellman was the first paraplegic to climb the sheer 3,000-foot granite face of El Capitan in Yosemite National Park. Eric Weihenmayer was the first person with blindness to climb El Capitan; he likewise was the first to climb the 20,320-foot summit of Denali in Alaska. More recently, mountaineering has become the talk of the world of sport for individuals with disabilities with the successful climb of Mount Everest in 1998 by Tom Whittaker, who has a below-the-knee amputation. The equally successful 1998 All Abilities Trek accompanied Whittaker's summit. A group of five people with disabilities and seven trekkers without disabilities attempted to reach the Mount Everest base camp located at 17,000 feet. These "Kripples in the Kumboo," as they called themselves, became the first group of people with disabilities to reach base camp; it took 41 days. More recently, Eric Weihenmayer succeeded in his quest to climb Mount Everest.

Many of these activities are conducted in a one-day format. Also available is the adventure or wilderness trip that might last for days or weeks. Several organizations provide separate wilderness experiences for individuals with disabilities, whereas others offer integrated experiences for people of all abilities. The more prominent organizations providing these experiences include the following:

> SPLORE—Special Populations Learning Outdoor Recreation and Education, 880 East 3375 South, Salt Lake City, UT 84106; 801-484-4128.

> C.W. HOG—Cooperative Wilderness Handicapped Outdoor Group, Idaho State University, Student Union, Box 8128, Pocatello, ID 83209; 208-282-3912.

> Wilderness Inquiry II—808 14th Avenue SE, Minneapolis, MN 55414; 612-676-9400.

> B.O.E.C.—The Breckenridge Outdoor Education Center, P.O. Box 697, Breckenridge, CO 80424; 970-453-6422.

> Bradford Woods—5040 State Road 67 North, Martinsville, IN 46151; 765-342-2915.

INCLUSION

The variations and modifications highlighted in this chapter reflect what is considered good practice in physical education as well as in sanctioned sports programs (e.g., limiting the play areas is an adaptation technique used in several sports such as tennis, badminton, and bocce). Individual, dual, and adventure sports and activities provide a unique opportunity for encouraging inclusion of people with disabilities with their peers without disabilities. From elementary school through high school, variations and modifications can be used to alter a sport in subtle ways (e.g., maintaining physical contact while wrestling). As a result of this approach, students with disabilities can participate or compete in inclusive physical education and sport programs and not only derive the benefits of instruction in activities that are themselves normalizing but also receive that instruction in the least restrictive environment. Because of the reduced temporal and spatial demands of most of the individual, dual, and cooperative sports and activities, there is every reason to believe that success in activities such as those highlighted in this chapter will be readily attainable within accessible programs in inclusive settings.

As it relates to inclusion in adventure activities, the Cooperative Wilderness Handicapped Outdoor Group (C.W. HOG) at Idaho State University uses the "Common Adventure" principle. All participants engage in planning, decision making, expense, and execution of the experience, regardless of their ability level.

SUMMARY

This chapter presented individual and dual sports currently available as parts of the competitive offerings of the major sport organizations serving athletes who have disabilities. In each case, the particular skills needed in the regular, unmodified version of the game or sport were detailed. Additionally, lead-up activities were suggested as well as variations and modifications for use in competitive sport or for use in physical education programs. It is worth noting that the rules governing sport for individuals with disabilities continue to undergo subtle modifications. National governing bodies and international federations have changed rules in ways that permit fewer and fewer modifications. Space limitations prevented discussion of other activities such as riflery and air pistol, shuffleboard, darts, and billiards; information on these activities can be found in Adams and McCubbin (1991). Also highlighted were accessible adventure activities, including brief mention of the Common Adventure principle. It is likely that wilderness experiences for individuals with disabilities will be a burgeoning area of interest in the early decades of the 21st century.

REFERENCES

Adams, R.C., Daniel, A.N., McCubbin, J.A., & Rullman, L. (1982). *Games, sports, and exercise for the physically handicapped* (3rd ed.). Philadelphia: Lea & Febiger.

Adams, R.C., & McCubbin, J.A. (1991). *Games, sports, and exercise for the physically handicapped* (4th ed.). Philadelphia: Lea & Febiger.

Cowart, J. (1989). Golf chirper for the blind. *Palaestra, 5*(3), 34-35.

Dunn, J.M., & Fait, H. (1997). *Special physical education: Adapted, individualized, developmental* (7th ed.). Dubuque, IA: Brown.

Dwarf Athletic Association of America. (1998). *Athletic handbook.* Lewisville, TX: Author.

Hattenback, R.T. (1979). Integrating persons with handicapping conditions in archery activities.In J.P. Winnick and J. Hurwitz (Eds.), *The preparation of regular physical educators for mainstreaming* (pp. 50-54). Brockport: State University of New York, College at Brockport. (ERIC Document Reproduction Service No. ED 222 028).

Havens, M.D. (1992). *Bridges to accessibility: A primer for including persons with disabilities in adventure curricula.* Hamilton, MA: Project Adventure.

Huber, J.H. (1991). An historic accomplishment: The first blind person to hike the Appalachian trail. *Palaestra, 7*(4), 18-23.

International Blind Sports Federation. (1997). *IBSA technical rulebook.* Madrid, Spain: Author.

International Paralympic Committee. (1999-2003). *IPC handbook.* Bonn, Germany: Author.

International Paralympic Equestrian Committee. (2002). *Rule book for dressage* (6th ed.). Bonn, Germany: International Paralympic Committee.

International Wheelchair Fencing Committee. (2001). *Official rules for fencing.* Bucks, UK: International Stoke Mandeville Wheelchair Sports Federation.

Kegel, B., & Peterson, J. (1989). Summer splash: A water sports symposium for the physically challenged. *Palaestra, 6*(1), 17-19.

Longo, P. (1989). Chair golf. *Sports 'N Spokes, 15*(2), 35-38.

McCowan, L.L. (1972). *It is ability that counts: A training manual on therapeutic riding for the handicapped.* Olivet, MI: Olivet College Press.

National Disability Sports Alliance. (2001). *NDSA sports rules manual* (6th ed.). Newport, RI: Author.

Orr, R.E., & Sheffield, J. (1981). Adapted épée fencing. *Journal of Physical Education, Recreation and Dance, 52*(6), 42, 71.

Parks, B.A. (1997). *Tennis in a wheelchair.* White Plains, NY: United States Tennis Association.

Roos, M. (1991). Pass the adrenaline, please. *Palaestra, 8*(1), 44-46.

Roswal, G.M., & Daugherty, N. (1991). Whitewater rafting: An outdoor adventure activity for individuals with mental retardation. *Palaestra, 7*(4), 24-25.

Special Olympics. (2003). *Official Special Olympics Summer Sports Rules, 2003-2006.* Washington, DC: Author.

Spink, J. (1993). *Developmental riding therapy: A team approach to assessment and treatment.* Tucson, AZ: Therapy Skill Builders.

United States Tennis Association. (2003). *USA tennis wheelchair.* White Plains, NY: Author.

Wachtel, L.J. (1987). Thoughts on a wilderness canoe trip. *Palaestra, 3*(4), 33-40.

Weber, R.C. (1991). Using Velcro to assist badminton players who are disabled or elderly. *Palaestra, 7*(3), 10-11.

Wheelchair Sports, USA. (1996). *Official rulebook of Wheelchair Sports, USA.* Colorado Springs: Author.

Wheelchair Sports, USA. (2002). *WSUSA Sanctioned Athletic Rules.* http://www.wusa.org.

Winnick, J.P., & Short, F.X. (1985). *Physical fitness testing of the disabled.* Champaign, IL: Human Kinetics.

Wiseman, D.C. (1982). *A practical approach to adapted physical education.* Reading, MA: Addison-Wesley.

WRITTEN RESOURCES

Grosse, S. (Ed.) (1991). Sport instruction for individuals with disabilities: The best of practical pointers. Reston, VA: AAHPERD.

This book contains previously published *Pointers* as well as new articles on increasing opportunities for those with disabilities to participate in instructional sport programs. Adaptations are presented for students with crutches and with unilateral and bilateral upper-arm amputations in badminton, golf, archery, bowling, tennis, and table tennis.

Paciorek, M.J., & Jones, J.A. (2001). *Disability sport and recreation resources* (3rd ed.). Traverse City, MI: Cooper Publishing Group.

Perhaps the most comprehensive resource currently available, this manual uses a cross-categorical approach in discussing sports and recreation for people with disabilities. Information is provided on sport-governing bodies for individuals both with and without disabilities. An overview of each sport, along with adapted equipment suppliers and manufacturers, accompanies each description.

Parks, B.A. (1997). *Tennis in a wheelchair.* White Plains, NY: United States Tennis Association.

The best nuts and bolts manual on playing tennis in a wheelchair provides information not only on the history and rules and regulations of the game but also on drills, specialty shots, wheelchair mobility, and singles and doubles strategy.

Special Olympics. (2003). *Official Special Olympics summer sports rules, 2003-2006,* (Revised Edition). Washington, DC: Author.

This manual contains information that organizers will need to conduct equitable competitions including how to conduct official sporting events, how to place athletes in appropriate ability groups, and how coaches should prepare athletes for competition.

AUDIOVISUAL RESOURCES

Beyond the barriers. (Videotape, 1998). Aquarius Health Care Videos. 5 Powerhouse Lane, P.O. Box 1159, Sherborn, MA 01770.

This video features Mark Wellman, the first paraplegic to climb El Capitan in Yosemite National Park and other individuals with disabilities engaging in such activities as sailing, body-boarding, scuba diving, and hang gliding. This video demonstrates the breadth of activities in which individuals with disabilities can engage and provides an inspirational message for individuals of all ability levels.

Making of a champion: Track and field (Videotape, no date). Special Olympics International. 1325 G Street, N.W., Suite 500, Washington, DC 20005.

This video can be used as a training aid for athletes. It provides instruction on various techniques used to prepare athletes for competition.

Summer sports officials/coaches training video. (Videotape, no date). United States Association of Blind Athletes. 33 N. Institute Street, Colorado Springs, CO 80903.

This video provides information about fundamentals, basic rules, and their modifications from companion sports for athletes without disabilities. Special equipment and adaptations are addressed. Sports include track and field, gymnastics, power lifting, and wrestling.

ELECTRONIC RESOURCES

EQUEST: www.equest.org.

This is the home of the nationally recognized and accredited equine-assisted therapy and rehabilitation program for children and adults with mental, emotional, and learning disabilities located in Dallas, Texas.

National Sports Center for the Disabled: www.nscd.org.

This is the home of the innovative, nonprofit organization in Winter Park, Colorado, that serves the year-round recreational needs of children and adults with disabilities.

Success Oriented Achievement Realized: www.soarnc.org.

This is the home of SOAR, which sponsors success-oriented, high-adventure programs, such as wilderness backpacking, rock climbing, whitewater rafting and canoeing, mountaineering, and wildlife studies for students with disabilities or ADHD school-aged youth at six locations in North and Central America.

Winter Sport Activities

Luke E. Kelly

"It's 7:00 A.M., going to be partly sunny, high around 15 degrees, with winds out of the west today," blares the DJ on the radio as Andrew and Emily drive into the sunrise toward the mountains.

"It's going to be a great day for skiing," Emily says.

"Yeah," Andrew agrees, "I hope they have the black diamond run open. I want to get some big air off that run of moguls near the top."

"Come on!" says Emily. "You can't get big air! The way you ski, you'll be lucky if you don't get taken out by a tree. I know—let's make a little wager on who can get down black diamond the fastest."

Andrew grins. "Sorry, but no way—you're not getting another free lunch off me."

As they approach the lodge, Andrew says, "You want me to drop you off here, and I'll go park?"

"That would be great," says Emily. "Get my chair set up, and I'll take our skis and get in line for the lift tickets." Andrew gets Emily's wheelchair out of the trunk and sets it up. While Emily transfers from the car seat to her wheelchair, Andrew gets the skis off the roof.

"You sure you can carry your skis and mine?" asks Andrew.

"No problem," says Emily. "Just don't get lost parking the car and make me pay for the lift tickets."

The reason Andrew did not want to bet Emily on a race down the black diamond run is that she is a world-class sit-skier. Emily "broke her back" in a skiing accident when she was 13 and lost the use of both legs. After the injury, she took up sit-skiing because she loved to ski and wanted an activity she could do outdoors with her friends. She lives in Colorado, so skiing was the natural choice.

In this chapter the reader is introduced to winter sport activities that can be included in physical education and sport programs for individuals with disabilities. It is not within the scope of the chapter to cover in detail how each winter sport skill should be taught. Instead, general guidelines are provided, along with a brief description of each winter sport activity and suggested adaptations for participants with different disabilities.

VALUE OF WINTER SPORTS

A major goal of physical education for both students with and without disabilities is to provide the knowledge, skills, and experiences they need to live healthy and productive lives. At the completion of their school physical education programs, students should have the basic physical fitness and motor skills required to achieve this goal. It would be logical to assume that the emphasis on sport skills in the school curriculum would reflect the students' needs in terms of carryover value and the likelihood of continuing participation after the school years. However, one area, that of winter sport skills, is frequently underrepresented in the physical education and sport curriculum. This is a serious omission for all students and especially students with disabilities. In many parts of the country, the winter season is the longest season during the school year. Winter sport activities provide opportunities for individuals with disabilities to:

- maintain or improve physical fitness levels,
- participate in community recreation activities, and
- pursue athletic competition.

Failure to provide youngsters with disabilities with winter sport skills limits their recreational options during the winter months, which, in turn, might affect their fitness and isolate them from many social activities and settings.

Given proper instruction and practice, individuals with disabilities can pursue and successfully participate in many winter sports, including alpine skiing (downhill), snowboarding, cross-country skiing (Nordic), ice skating, ice picking, sledding, curling, and hockey. Instructional programs for individuals with disabilities should be guided by equal attention to safety, motivation (fun), and skill development. Safety concerns should encompass the areas of physical and motoric readiness, appropriate clothing and equipment, and instructor qualifications (Leonard & Pitzer, 1988).

ALPINE SKIING

Alpine (downhill) skiing is a winter sport in which most individuals with disabilities can participate with little or no modification. Skiing frees many individuals with disabilities from the limitations that hinder their mobility (figure 28.1) on land and allows them to move with great agility and at great speeds. For many individuals with physical, mental, and sensory impairments, skiing offers a unique opportunity to challenge their environment.

Figure 28.1 A double-leg amputee using a mono-ski and outriggers.

The key to learning to ski is controlling one's weight distribution and directing where the weight is applied on the surface (edges) of the skis. The goal of any introductory ski program is to provide students with the basic skills needed to enjoy and safely participate in the sport. The basic skills of downhill skiing can be grouped into six categories:

- Independence in putting on and taking off one's equipment
- Independence in using rope and chairlifts
- Falling and standing
- Walking (sidestepping, herringbone)
- Stopping (wedge, parallel)
- Turning (wedge, parallel)

Instruction

Ski instruction should be preceded by a conditioning program and the development of basic skills such as falling and standing. When actual ski instruction begins, the skill sequence must be matched to the needs and abilities of the learners to ensure safety and maximize enjoyment. Although independent recovery (standing back up on one's skis) is a required skill for independent skiing, it might not be appropriate to concentrate on this skill during early learning. For many individuals with disabilities, learning to stand up on skis after falling is very strenuous and often frustrating. Students who are made to master this skill first are likely not to experience much success or fun and will soon become disenchanted with the idea of learning to ski. Initial instruction should focus on actual skiing skills, such as a wedge stop, and the instructor should provide assistance to compensate for the lack of other skills, such as the ability to independently recover from falls. This form of instruction provides students with confidence and some of the thrills of moving on skis (figure 28.2). As skill and enjoyment increase, students become more motivated to work on mastering the other essential skills, such as independent recovery.

Assistive Devices

Assistive devices have been developed to offset some of the limitations imposed by disabilities and to compensate for the general low fitness and poor motor coordination common to many individuals with disabilities. The most commonly used device is the ski-bra (figure 28.3, p. 506), which is mounted to the tip of the skis and serves two primary functions. First, it stabilizes the skis while allowing them to move independently. Second, it assists the skier in positioning the skis in a wedge position, which improves balance and makes for easier stopping and turning. The ski-bra can be used as a temporary learning device for any skier

© Mary E. Messenger

Figure 28.2 An individual learning to sit-ski while being tethered to the instructor.

© David Burton, Kludge Children's Rehabilitation Center, University of Virginia.

Figure 28.3 Photograph of a ski-bra. Note how the ski-bra can be easily attached to any skis.

(e.g., intellectually disabled, visually impaired, orthopedically impaired) during the early stages of learning to assist with balance and control of the skis. The ski-bra may also be used as a permanent assistive device for individuals with lower-extremity orthopedic impairments who lack sufficient strength or control of their lower limbs.

Canting wedges are another common modification used to assist skiers with disabilities. Small, thin wedges are placed between the sole of the ski boot and the ski. The wedges adjust the lateral tilt of the boot and subsequently affect the distribution of the weight over the edges of the skis. Canting wedges are commonly used to assist skiers who have trouble turning to one side or the other.

Outriggers (see figure 28.4) are common assistive devices used by skiers with amputations and other orthopedic impairments who require additional support primarily in the area of balance. The outriggers are made from a Lofstrand crutch with a short ski attached to the bottom. The ski on the end of the crutch can be placed

in a vertical (up) position and used as a crutch or positioned in a horizontal position for use as an outrigger. Three-track and four-track skiing are common terms used to describe the use of outriggers. Three-track skiing refers to individuals who use only one ski and two outriggers—for example, single-leg amputees. Four-track skiing refers to those who use two skis and two outriggers.

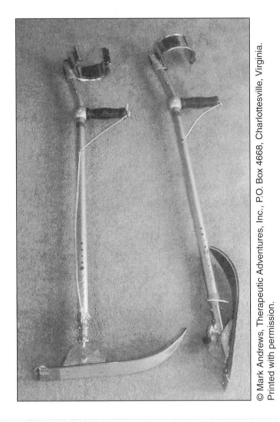

© Mark Andrews, Therapeutic Adventures, Inc., P.O. Box 4668, Charlottesville, Virginia. Printed with permission.

Figure 28.4 Outriggers. The left outrigger is in the down position for skiing, and the right outrigger is in the up position and can be used as a crutch.

Sit-skiing is really more like sledding than skiing, but it is included here because it is performed on ski slopes and is the method used by skiers with paraplegia and quadriplegia to ski. Sit-skiing involves the use of a special sled (see figure 28.5). The person with paraplegia is strapped into the sled, which contains appropriate padding and support to hold the skier in an upright sitting position. The top of the sled is covered by a water-repellent nylon skirt to keep the skier dry. The bottom of the sled is smooth, with a metal runner or edge running along each side. Skiers control the sled by shifting their weight (over the edge) in the direction they want to go. A single kayak-type pole or two short poles can be used by the skier to assist in balancing and controlling the sled. Special mittens are available to allow individuals with limited grip strength to hold on to the poles. For the protection of both the sit-skier and other skiers on the slope, the beginner sit-skier should always be tethered to an experienced ski instructor. Modified sit-skis are also available and can be used by individuals with paraplegia for cross-country skiing. Consult the electronic resources at the end of this chapter to find the latest advances in sit-skiing equipment.

Figure 28.5 Sit-skiing sleds. View of an athlete with a spinal cord injury in a stationary sit-ski.

Ski instructors use various forms of physical assistance to help and guide skiers with different disabilities. Instructors must be able to provide sufficient physical assistance during early learning to ensure safety and success. Providing physical assistance to a moving beginner skier requires skills that must be learned and perfected. As the skills of a skier with a disability increase, the instructor must also know how to gradually fade out the physical assistance to verbal cues and eventually to independence.

In addition to the more universal assistive devices described previously, many other devices have been created to address the needs of skiers with disabilities. Special prosthetic limbs, for example, have been developed to allow single- and double-leg (mono-ski) amputees to ski. Many of these devices are homemade by ski instructors trying to help specific individuals. Watch a national ski competition for individuals with disabilities for an idea of the range of devices that can be created to assist skiers with various disabilities.

SNOWBOARDING

The latest winter sport to evolve for athletes with disabilities is **snowboarding**. Snowboarding is comparable to skateboarding on snow but using a slightly longer and wider board. The snowboarder's feet are attached perpendicular to the length of the board by special bindings that require special boots. Snowboarding can be done at any facility that offers alpine skiing. The necessary snowboarding equipment costs between $250 and $600. Most beginners use slightly longer, wider, and heavier boards. The average board should be about mouth level when stood end to end and as wide as the feet (in boots) are long. Most ski resorts that offer adapted ski instruction also offer snowboard instruction for individuals with disabilities.

An adapted snowboard instructor should be consulted when selecting and adapting snowboard equipment. With modified equipment, most individuals with disabilities can learn and participate in snowboarding. The United States of America Snowboard Association (USASA) is the governing body for snowboarding competition. The USASA has a division for adaptive snowboarders at their regional and national competitions and offer events in alpine, freestyle, and boarderCross (USASA, 2002). Special Olympics initiated snowboarding as an official event in the 2001 World Winter games in Anchorage, Alaska. Athletes compete in three divisions (novice, intermediate, and advanced) in three events: super giant slalom (super G), giant slalom, and slalom. In 1998, the U.S. Deaf Skiers Association was renamed the U.S. Deaf Skiers and Snowboard Association (USDSSA). The USDSSA offers regional competitions in snowboarding that culminate in competing at the Winter Deaflympics. The instructional recommendations provided for alpine skiing also apply to teaching snowboarding. Many of the assistive devices used in teaching downhill skiing, such as outriggers and tethers, are also used when teaching snowboarding.

CROSS-COUNTRY SKIING

Cross-country skiing has become a very popular winter sport in recent years, partly because it is an excellent physical fitness and recreational activity. Because both the arms and the legs are used in cross-country skiing, this activity develops total-body fitness. Two other advantages of the sport are that it costs nothing after the initial equipment is purchased and that it can be done almost anywhere (e.g., golf courses, parks, open fields). The major disadvantage of cross-country skiing for many individuals with disabilities, when compared to downhill skiing, is that the skier must create the momentum to move. This difference precludes participation of many individuals with more severe orthopedic impairments who lack either the strength or the control to generate the momentum needed to cross-country ski. However, because the activity is performed on snow and does not require that the feet actually be lifted off the ground, many individuals with cerebral palsy who have difficulty walking (shuffle gait) can successfully cross-country ski.

A complete cross-country skiing outfit (skis, poles, gaiters [short waterproof leggings that cover the ankle and low leg and keep them dry], and shoes) is relatively inexpensive. For beginners, waxless (fish-scale or step pattern) skis are recommended over wax skis. Waxless skis require no maintenance or preparation prior to use, and they provide more than sufficient resistance and glide for learning and enjoying cross-country skiing.

Initial instruction should take place in a relatively flat area with prepared tracks. Most beginning cross-country skiers tend to simply walk wearing their skis, using their poles for balance. This, unfortunately, is incorrect and very fatiguing. The key in learning to cross-country ski is getting the feel of pushing back on one ski while the weight is transferred to the front foot and the front ski is slid forward. Instructors should focus on demonstrating this pattern and contrasting it with walking. A very effective technique is to physically assist the beginning skier through this pattern so that the learner can feel what it is like (a method that works particularly well with skiers with intellectual disabilities or visual impairments). Cross-country skiers with visual impairments must be accompanied by sighted partners who usually ski parallel to them and inform them of upcoming conditions (turns, dips, changes in

grades). The forward push-and-glide technique is the preferred pattern for most skiers with disabilities, as opposed to the more strenuous and skill-demanding skating technique used by world-class Nordic skiers.

COMPETITIVE SKIING FOR INDIVIDUALS WITH DISABILITIES

Skiing for individuals with disabilities is sponsored by several sport associations that conduct local, state, and national skiing competitions. Three of the largest and most prominent sponsors of ski competitions are Special Olympics, which sponsors competitions for individuals with intellectual disabilities; Disabled Sports, USA (DS/USA), which sponsors national skiing competitions for individuals with disabilities; and the United States Association for Blind Athletes (USABA), which sponsors an annual national competition for skiers with visual impairments.

Special Olympics sponsors local, state, and national ski competitions (Special Olympics, 2003). Competition is offered in both alpine and Nordic events. The alpine events include downhill, giant slalom, and slalom races. The Nordic events include the 500-meter, 1-kilometer, 3-kilometer, 5-kilometer, 7.5-kilometer, and 10-kilometer races, as well as a 4 × 1-kilometer unified relay race and a 4 × 1-kilometer relay race. Athletes are classified for competition into one of three classes—novice, intermediate, or advanced—on the basis of preliminary time trials in each event. There are no age or gender divisions. Special Olympics also offers developmental (noncompetitive) alpine and Nordic events. The developmental alpine events include a 10-meter walk, glide event, and super glide. The Nordic developmental events include 10-, 50-, and 100-meter cross-country skiing race and glide events. Special Olympics also offers 100-meter, 200-meter, 400-meter, 800-meter, 1,600-meter, 5-kilometer, and 10-kilometer races as well as a 4 × 100 and 4 × 400-meter relay race.

DS/USA sponsors the National Ski Championships each year. The nationals are preceded by a series of regional meets in which athletes must qualify for the nationals. The national meets involve competition in three categories: alpine (downhill, slalom, giant slalom), Nordic (5-kilometer, 10-kilometer, 15-kilometer, 20-kilometer,

30-kilometer, biathlon, and relays), and sit-skiing (as listed for alpine and Nordic). Athletes are classified according to the site and severity of their disabilities and the type of adapted equipment used in skiing (DS/USA, 2001). Skiers with orthopedic impairments are divided into 12 classes, described briefly in the next section.

Classification of Skiers With Orthopedic Disabilities

The following is a list of classifications for individuals with orthopedic disabilities:

Standing Classes

Class L1—Disability of both legs, above the knees, skiing with outriggers and using two skis or skiing on one ski using a prosthesis

Class L2—Disability of one leg, skiing with outriggers or poles and on one ski

Class L3/1—Disability in both legs below the knees; amputations, severe cerebral palsy, severe neurological impairments, skiing on two skis with poles

Class L3/2—Disability of both legs below the knees, partial paraplegia, mild CP or nerve disorder, skiing on two skis with poles

Class L4—Disability of one leg, skiing on two skis with poles

Class L5—Disability of both arms or hands, skiing on two skis with no poles

Class L6—Disability of one arm or hand, skiing on two skis with one pole

Class L9/1—Disability of a combination of arm and leg, partial quadriplegia, above-the-knee amputations, severe CP or neurological impairment, using equipment of choice

Class L9/2—Disability of a combination of arm and leg, partial quadriplegia, below-the-knee amputation, mild CP or neurological impairment, using equipment of choice

Mono-Ski Classes

Class L10—Athletes with disabilities in the lower limbs, no functional sitting balance or significant impairment of the upper limbs (e.g., tetra, para classes 1, 2, and upper 3 and standing L classes with impairment of the lower limbs together with a significant functional impairment in the upper limbs or trunk)

Class L11—Athletes with disabilities in the lower limbs and a fair sitting balance (e.g., para classes lower 3 and 4; standing L classes with impairment of the lower limbs together with a significant functional impairment of the trunk or hips). Athletes who have functions in the lower limbs are not allowed to use them outside of the equipment at any time during the race.

Class L12/1—Athletes with disabilities in the lower limbs (paraplegia only with good sitting balance)

Class L12/2—Athletes with disabilities in the lower limbs, amputations, and standing L classes L1, L2, L3/1, L3/2, L4, L9/1, L9/2 with good sitting balance

Classification of Skiers With Vision Disabilities

Skiers with visual impairments are divided into three classes on the basis of visual acuity with maximum correction. These classifications are used by both USABA and DS/USA for their ski competitions. The following are the three most common classification for individuals with visual disabilities:

Class B1—Totally blind, can distinguish between light and dark but cannot discern all shapes

Class B2—Partially sighted. Best correctable vision up to 20:600 or visual field of 5 degrees

Class B3—Partially sighted. Best correctable vision from 20:600 to 20:200 or field of vision from 5 degrees to –20 degrees.

For its national ski competition, the USABA offers giant slalom and downhill alpine events as well as 5-kilometer, 10-kilometer, and 25-kilometer Nordic events (USABA, 2003). Separate competitions are offered for each gender within each classification; there are no age divisions. Sighted guides are used in all of the events to verbally assist the skiers who are visually impaired. USABA sponsors several Nordic skiing training camps each year to promote skiing for individuals with visual impairments.

In addition to the DS/USA classifications just described, there are three age divisions: ages 0 through 16 (juniors), ages 17 through 39, and age 40 and over (seniors). Separate competitions are offered for each gender in each age division except when there are not enough participants of one gender to compose a heat. The same classifications apply for both alpine and cross-country skiing. The only difference between the men's and women's events is that females are limited to the 5-kilometer and 10-kilometer cross-country events.

Sit-Skiing Classifications

Sit-skiing competition is conducted only in the United States; thus athletes competing in this category are not classified according to the international classification system. Sit-skiers are classified into one of two groups. Group 1 is composed of athletes with disabilities in the lower limbs, with injury between T5 and T10 inclusive. (Athletes with higher injuries, above T5, typically are not able to sit-ski.) Group 2 is for athletes with all other disabilities resulting from injury below T10 and conditions such as spina bifida, amputation, cerebral palsy, polio, and muscular dystrophy.

ICE SKATING

Ice skating is another inexpensive winter sport easily accessible in many regions of the country. Most individuals with disabilities who can stand and walk independently can learn to ice skate successfully. For those who cannot, a modified form of ice skating, ice picking, is available. Although skating is common in many areas on frozen lakes and ponds or water-covered tennis courts, the preferred environment for teaching ice skating is an indoor ice rink. An indoor rink offers a more moderate temperature and a better quality ice surface, free from the cracks and bumps commonly found in natural ice. Ice rinks frequently can be used by physical education programs during off times, such as daytime hours on weekdays.

Properly fitting skates are essential for learning and ultimately enjoying ice skating. Ice skates should be fitted by a professional experienced in working with and fitting individuals with disabilities. Either figure or hockey skates can be used. The important consideration is that the skates provide good ankle and arch support so that the skater's weight is centered over the ankles, and

the blades of the skates are perpendicular to the ice when the skater is standing.

As discussed earlier, instruction should be guided by safety and success. The greatest obstacle in learning to ice skate is the fear of falling. Although falling while first learning to skate is inevitable, steps can and should be taken to minimize the frequency and severity of the falls and, consequently, the apprehension. At the same time, the early stages of learning must be associated with success, which gives learners confidence that they will be able to learn to skate. It is recommended that padding be used around the major joints most likely to hit the ice during a fall. Knee and elbow pads reduce the physical trauma of taking a fall and also provide psychological security that alleviates the fear of falling. When teaching individuals with disabilities to ice skate, football pants with knee, hip, and sacral pads along with elbow pads have been found to be very beneficial during the early stages of learning. See the Overcoming Fear application example.

The locomotor skill of ice skating is very similar to walking. The weight, the center of gravity, is basically transferred in front of the base of support and from side to side as the legs are lifted and swung forward to catch the weight. The back skate is usually rotated outward about 30 degrees to provide resistance to sliding backward as the weight transfers to the forward skate. Because success during the early lessons is essential, one-on-one instruction from an experienced instructor is highly recommended.

The primary aid used in teaching ice skating is physical assistance. Some individuals with orthopedic and neuromuscular impairments might benefit from the use of polyproplylene orthoses to stabilize their ankles. Ankle-foot orthoses are custom made and can be worn inside the skates. The most universal skating aid is the Hein-A-Ken skate aid, which is simply a walker modified to be used on ice (Adams & McCubbin, 1991). This device does not interfere with the skating action of the legs and provides the beginning skater with a stable means of support independent from the instructor. The skate aid can be used for temporary assistance during the early stages of learning for students who need a little additional support or confidence; it can also be a more permanent assistive device for skaters with more severe orthopedic impairments. It is beneficial to add some foam padding to the top support bar in the front of the skate aid to

APPLICATION EXAMPLE

Overcoming Fear

Setting: A physical education class is starting an ice hockey skills unit. Most of the students can skate forward well and are working on speed, changing direction, and skating backward.

Student: John is an 11-year-old with mild intellectual disabilities who recently moved to Michigan from Florida. He has slightly below-average coordination for his age but is generally willing to try new skills. John has recently become a big MSU hockey fan.

Issue: John had a negative experience with ice skating the first time he tried it and now is extremely fearful and unwilling to put skates on.

Application: Based on the information available and a meeting with John's parents, the physical educator decides on the following strategies:

• Meet individually with John to discuss his fears of ice skating and to explain how these fears will be addressed.

• Contact the local university and borrow some official Michigan State hockey pads and a helmet of appropriate size.

• John will start using a padded Hein-A-Ken skate aid to give him confidence. He will then transition to using a hockey stick as a balance aid.

• An aide was prepared by the physical educator and assigned to work with John during the initial lessons to ensure he was successful and to prevent any new negative experiences.

---

further reduce the chance of injury from falls. If skate aids are not available, chairs can be used in a similar fashion.

Ice picking is a modified form of ice skating in which the participant sits on a **sledge** (a small sled with blades on the bottom) and uses small poles (picks) to propel the sledge on the ice. Ice picking can be performed by almost anyone and is particularly appropriate for individuals who have only upper-limb control (e.g., individuals with paraplegia or spina bifida). Ice picking is an excellent activity for developing upper-body strength and endurance. All skating activities and events (speed skating and skate dancing) can be modified and performed in sledges. Because individuals with and without disabilities can use the equipment, ice picking offers a unique way to equalize participation and competition in integrated settings.

Special Olympics sponsors ice skating competitions in two categories: figure skating and speed skating (Special Olympics, 2003). The figure-skating events include singles, pairs, and ice dancing; the speed-skating events include the 100-, 200,- 300-, 500-, 800-, 1,000- and 1,500-meter races; 4 × 20 lap relay, and Unified Sports 4 × 20 lap relay. For each event, athletes are divided into three classifications—novice, intermediate, and advanced—on the basis of preliminary performance and time trials. Developmental (noncompetitive) ice-skating events are also offered. These include the skills competition and the 100-meter oval, 25 meter straight-away, and 50-meter half-lap race.

SLEDDING AND TOBOGGANING

In snowy regions of the country, sledding and tobogganing are two common recreational activities universally enjoyed by children and adults. Many individuals with disabilities, however, avoid these activities because they lack the simple skills and confidence needed to successfully take part in them. The needed skills and confidence can easily be addressed in a physical education program. Given proper attention to safety and clothing, almost all children with disabilities can participate in sledding and tobogganing. Sleds and toboggans can be purchased or rented at minimal cost. Straps and padding can be added to commercial sleds and toboggans to accommodate the specific needs occasioned by individuals with different disabilities. Even individuals with the most severe disabilities can experience the thrill of sledding or tobogganing when paired with an aide who can control and steer the sled.

HOCKEY

Ice hockey is a popular winter sport in the northern areas of the United States and is the national sport of Canada. The game is played by two teams who attempt to hit a puck into the opposing team's goal using their hockey sticks. Hockey is a continuous, highly active, and exciting sport. Because of these features, many modifications and adaptations have been made to hockey to accommodate players with disabilities. Some common modifications are as follows:

- Use soft plastic balls, plastic pucks, or doughnut-shaped pucks instead of the traditional ice hockey pucks.
- Use shorter and lighter sticks made of plastic, which are more durable, easier to handle, and less harmful to other players.
- Use a less slippery surface, such as a gym floor or tennis court.
- Change the size of the goals.
- Change the boundaries, number of players per team, or the length of the playing periods to accommodate players' abilities.

Modifications can easily be made to enable sticks to be held by players with physical impairments or used from wheelchairs by using tape and Velcro. A wide range of abilities can be accommodated in a game if the teams are balanced and the players' abilities are matched to the various positions.

Special Olympics sponsors local, state, and national competition in floor hockey. A stick similar to a broomstick with a vinyl coating on the end is used in conjunction with a doughnut-shaped puck. The goalkeeper uses a regular hockey goalie stick. The goals are 1.8 meters wide and 1.2 meters high. The playing area is 30 meters × 15 meters or the size of a typical basketball court. Special Olympics offers team competition, Unified Sports team competition, and 10-meter puck dribble event.

Sledge hockey is a modified form of ice hockey played on sledges. The only difference from the regulation game of ice hockey is that the game is played from a sledge and the puck is struck with a modified stick called a pick. The pick is about 30 inches in length. On one end it has metal points that grip the ice and allow the athlete to propel the sledge. The other end, called the butt, is rubber coated. The butt end of the pick is held while the sledge is being propelled. When the athlete wants to hit the puck, the hand is slid down the shaft of the pick to cover the spiked

© Empics

Figure 28.6   Sledge hockey checking.

end, and then the butt end of the pick is used to strike the puck.

Sledge hockey is an excellent recreational and fitness activity. Using sledges is also an ideal way of allowing students with and without orthopedic disabilities to participate in the same activity. The United States won the gold metal in sledge hockey in the 2002 Paralympics in Salt Lake Games. Figure 28.6 shows a picture from a sledge hockey game. For more information on sledge hockey, consult the electronic resources for this chapter.

Logical modifications should be made to the regulation game of hockey to accommodate beginners, such as reducing the playing area, increasing the number of players on each team, increasing the size of the goal, playing without goalkeepers, or changing the size or type of puck (e.g., substituting a playground ball). The goal of all modifications should be to maximize participation and success in the basic sledge and hockey skills while gradually progressing toward the regulation game.

CURLING

Curling is a popular recreational activity and sport in Europe and Canada. The playing area is an ice court 46 yards long and 14 feet wide (or 42 by 4.3 meters), with a 6-foot (1.8-meter) circular target, called a "house," marked on the ice at each end. The game is played by two teams of four players, with pieces of equipment called stones (a kettle-shaped weight 36 inches [.9 meters] in circumference and weighing about 40 pounds [18 kilograms], with a gooseneck handle on top). A game is composed of 10 or 12 rounds called heads; a round consists of each player delivering (sliding) two stones. Players on each team alternate delivering stones until all have been delivered. After each stone is delivered, teammates can use brooms to sweep frost and moisture from the ice in front of the coming stone to keep it straight and allow it to slide farther. At the end of a round, a team scores a point for each stone they have closer to the center of the target than the other team. The team with the most points at the end of 10 or 12 rounds is the winner. If the score is tied, an additional round is played to break the tie.

Curling can easily be modified to accommodate individuals with just about any disability. The distance between the houses and the weight of stones

can be reduced to facilitate reaching the targets. The size of the targets can also easily be increased to maximize success. Audible goal locators can be placed on the houses to assist players with visual impairments. The sweeping component of the game might be difficult to modify to include players who are nonambulatory or have visual impairments. In these cases, mixed teams could be formed of players with different disabilities or combining players with and without disabilities so that each team has a few members who could do the sweeping. Finally, assistive devices like those used in bowling (ramps and guide rails) could be used to help players with more severe disabilities deliver the stones. For the latest information on curling, check the electronic resources for this chapter.

INCLUSION

Although competition is available for most winter sports, most students learn winter sports so that they can participate in them as recreational activities. As such, winter sports lend themselves to inclusion, and many modifications can be made to allow even the most severely disabled to participate. The goal of all modifications should be to capitalize on the abilities of the students and maximize their participation. For winter activities such as skiing, snowboarding, cross-country skiing, ice skating, and sledding, modifications can often easily be made to the equipment to increase stability and control and to the terrain to slow the activity down to ensure success and allow inclusion of all students in the same activity. In many cases the specialized equipment used by the students with disabilities draws the interest and respect of students without disabilities. Seeing a student with a spinal cord injury ski down a ski slope on a mono-ski and then get on the chair lift commands the admiration of any skier who is having trouble staying up on two skis. In fact, it is not uncommon for students without disabilities to want to try and ski using a mono-ski. Simple modifications can also be made to team events such as floor hockey, sledge hockey, and curling to promote inclusion. These typically involve modifying how the equipment is held to increase control, reducing the distances and boundaries to minimize the limitations imposed by reduced mobility and defining safe areas if the students must be protected from physical contact or require a little more time to react during the game. Again, the goal should be to build on the students' strengths and maximize participation. Given the physical fitness and social benefits associated with participation in winter sport activities, every effort should be made to make sure all students with disabilities have functional competency in these activities so that they can participate in them throughout their adulthood.

SUMMARY

Winter sports, in general, are excellent all-around activities. They develop motor skill, strength, and physical fitness, and at the same time provide participants with functional recreational skills they can use for the rest of their lives. For many individuals with disabilities, winter sports performed on snow and ice allow them to move with agility and speed not possible under their own power on land. Thus, winter sports should be an essential component in the physical education and sport programs of all students, and especially for students with disabilities. For this reason, activities have been discussed in this chapter with particular focus on ways to modify them for people with unique needs.

REFERENCES

Adams, R.C., & McCubbin, J.A. (1991). *Games, sports, and exercises for the physically disabled* (4th ed.). Philadelphia: Lea & Febiger.

Disabled Sports USA. (2001, June). *DS/USA Alpine competition rules.* Rockville, MD: Author. Retrieved October 20, 2003, from the Internet: www.dsusa.org/winter-guide02.html.

Leonard, E., & Pitzer, N.L. (1988). Special problems of handicapped skiers: An Overview. *Physician and Sportmedicine,* 16(3), 77-82.

Special Olympics. (2003). *Official Special Olympics winter sports rules.* Washington, DC: Special Olympics, Inc. www.specialolympics.org/Special+Olympics+Public+Web site/English/Coach/Sports_Rules/Winter+Sports.htm

United States of America Snowboard Association (2002). *USASA rule book Winter 2002/2003.* Author. Retrieved October 20, 2003 from the Internet: www.usasa.org/rulebook.html.

United States Association for Blind Athletes. (2003). *Alpine and Nordic skiing.* Colorado Springs, CO: Author. Retrieved October 20, 2003 from the Internet: www.usaba.org/index.html.

WRITTEN RESOURCES

O'Leary, H. (1994). *Bold tracks: Teaching adaptive skiing.* Boulder, CO: Johnson Books.

This book is a must for anyone who is going to be teaching skiing to individuals with disabilities.

Special Olympics. (1997). *The Special Olympics alpine skiing sports skills program guide.* Washington, DC: Special Olympics, Inc.

This manual provides a how-to approach for teaching the basic skills involved in alpine skiing, including teaching suggestions, sample drills, and activities.

Special Olympics. (1995). *The Special Olympics floor hockey sports skills program guide.* Washington, DC: Special Olympics, Inc.

This manual provides a how-to approach for teaching the basic skills involved in floor hockey. Teaching suggestions, sample drills, and activities are provided for each skill.

AUDIOVISUAL RESOURCES

Mono-ski II. (Videotape, 2003). This tape is available from Tom Cannalonga, 504 Brett Place, South Plainfield, NJ 07080; phone: 908-313-5590.

This is an inspirational video that shows mono-skiing on a variety of terrains as well as chair lifts and a few wipeouts.

No simple road. (Videotape). Available from The Children's Hospital of Denver, Sports Program Office B385, 1056 East 19th, Denver, CO 90218; phone: 303-861-6590.

This is an inspirational videotape showing children with various disabilities skiing.

Adaptive ski teaching methods. (Videotape). Available from DS/USA National Headquarters, 451 Hungerford Drive, Suite 100, Rockville, MD 20850; phone: 301-217-0960.

This is an instructional video that provides basic techniques for working with three-track, four-track and sit-skiers.

Advanced three-track and four-track methods. (Videotape). Available from DS/USA National Headquarters, 451 Hungerford Drive, Suite 100, Rockville, MD 20850; phone: 301-217-0960.

This instructional video demonstrates how to teach advanced three- and four-track skiing techniques.

ELECTRONIC RESOURCES

Abledata Database of Assistive Technology for Winter Sports: www.abledata.com/winter.htm.

This Web site provides information and links to the latest assistive devices that can be used to assist individuals with disabilities participate in winter sports.

British Sledge Hockey Association: http://info.lut.ac.uk/research/paad/wheelpower/sledge.htm.

This site provides information on sledge hockey rules, classifications, and competitions.

Sit-skiing: www.sitski.com.

This site provides information and pictures of the latest advances in sit-skiing equipment.

United States of America Snowboard Association (USASA): www.usasa.org/.

USASA is the national governing body for all snowboarding competition. This site contains the official rules and events as well as information on regional and national competitions.

United States Deaf Ski and Snowboard Association (USDSSA): www.usdssa.org.

This is the official site of the USDSSA, which governs ski and snowboard competitions for Deaf people. The site contains information on the organization and its history as well as information on upcoming events.

World Curling Foundation: www.worldsport.com/sports/curling/home.html.

This site provides information on curling history, rules, and strategies.

CHAPTER 29

Enhancing Wheelchair Sport Performance

Abu B. Yilla

She felt good, poised, and confident—it was *her* day. She leaned back slightly to get a feel for how her fifth wheel was: It felt good, not too high, and not too low: the balance felt perfect. She could sense the crowd's growing anticipation. It was unusual to have a crowd at a quad rugby game, but this was the world championship final, and they were in her native country. She touched the ball on her lap. Although she couldn't actually feel the ball (quadriplegia had seen to that), she knew from practice when she cut hard right, or left, exactly how to keep the ball with her. She scanned the court around her: Three blockers looked set, and it looked as if they were overplaying the right, where she had scored five times before. With the score tied at 20 she knew she had to be perfect. "Well, let's give them what they want," she thought. She went right, and they came with her. When at the last second she cut hard left, her blockers knew what she was going to do. As they sealed the center of the lane, her hard left cut brushed the back wheel of a teammate. It was perfect—there was the space. The clock was counting down as she drove for the key, but she hadn't noticed that last defender . . .

At the 2000 Summer Paralympic Games in Sydney, Australia, a sport that attracted standing-room-only crowds was quad rugby. For a sport that had only reached viability with the advent of the lightweight wheelchair, it was a crowning moment. Athletes who compete at quad rugby combine themselves, their chairs, and their skills into performance systems to achieve levels of excellence unheard of in the days of medically driven attitudes and regulations. The combination of body and wheelchair into a performance "system" has opened up elite disability sport to a new dimension far from what early pioneers had envisioned. There is now a functional perspective in wheelchair sports that places disability second to the demands of the specific sport. This transition has been spearheaded by the athletes themselves, who have been instrumental in developing many of the latest innovations in equipment and technique.

It was once possible for an athlete with a disability to compete at a World Championship level in several sports, but this is no longer the case. Sport for athletes with disabilities now parallels the world of athletes without disabilities; to reach the highest levels, athletes must find the sport (and often the event or position) for which they are best suited. Suitability for specific sports is most commonly determined by interest, disability type, body size and shape, and the psychological makeup of the athlete. To maximize wheelchair sport performance, event selection should be based on a system approach that considers both the athlete and the wheelchair. Keeping all of these changes and advances in mind, in this chapter we cover the process of selecting an appropriate sport and an appropriate chair; we also discuss training and performance considerations.

THE ATHLETE AND THE WHEELCHAIR: A SYSTEM APPROACH

Conceptually, the athlete and the wheelchair combined can be viewed as a performance system. This reflects the functional model of disability sport now prevalent in both the design of wheelchairs and the functional classification systems employed in elite disability sport competition. Much of the early research available in wheelchair sports examined *either* the athlete *or* the wheelchair. Many of these studies also examined wheelchair users outside of their preferred environment—that is, outside of their competitive wheelchairs. These approaches employed instruments such as ergometers that had scientific but not ecological validity. In appreciating the functional development in wheelchair sports, it is necessary to understand the importance of a system approach. A system approach incorporates the combination of athlete and wheelchair into a performance *system* defined by the needs of the specific sport. In this chapter we will examine performance enhancements for the wheelchair athlete, provide a brief description of the equipment, and then examine the combination of the athlete and the wheelchair into a performance system (see figure 29.1).

Figure 29.1 Basketball performance system.

The Athlete

Success in wheelchair sports requires that an athlete be suited to meet the performance considerations of that sport. For example, success in basketball requires height for the forward and center positions and speed and agility in the guard positions. In general, athletes with predominantly fast-twitch muscle fibers should focus on sprint events, and those with slow-twitch fibers should focus on endurance events. Those with the psychological profile that includes subsuming the self into a team mold should, of course, focus on team events; those with an individual orientation should focus on an appropriate individual sport. In the past, wheelchair athletes have not always been able to match their personal goals to the appropriate athletic challenge. After identifying the appropriate event, the athlete needs to focus on meeting the demands of that sport by identifying a training regime.

Training

Wheelchair users respond to physical training in a similar, though not identical, manner to each other and to the population of athletes without disabilities (Shephard, 1990; Wells & Hooker, 1990). In addition to developing a foundation of health-related fitness (see chapter 23) when identifying the training requirements in a given sport, athletes should develop levels of fitness associated with performance for their specific sport. The athlete should also consider factors such as individual orientation to specific sports and body anthropometry. Performance-related fitness includes components such as movement, coordination, agility, power, speed, and balance (Gallahue & Ozmun, 2002). These components are applicable to wheelchair performance and should be developed in a sport-specific manner. Ultimately, the trained athlete will demonstrate improved performance in the sport under examination (Curtis, 1981a). Note that because agility and balance require an optimal combination of the athlete and the wheelchair, they are addressed in a subsequent section.

Training regimens for athletes with disabilities parallel those for athletes without disabilities and, in many cases, appear identical. When modifications are necessary, it is usually because of the smaller active muscle mass and the lack of alternate modes of training available. Runners can train their legs through running, jumping, stair climbing, cycling, and weight training. Athletes who use wheelchairs are usually limited to weight training, pushing their chairs, or arm cranking (if they have access to this specialized equipment). This limitation makes repetitive overuse injuries a concern, although reported injury rates for athletes with disabilities are less than those reported for athletes in American football and soccer (but more than running and basketball) (Ferrara & Peterson, 2000).

Underpinning most athletic performances is the development of a sound cardiovascular "base." However, training the cardiovascular system presents unique problems to the wheelchair athlete. Cardiovascular endurance is produced by stressing the heart and respiratory system through the use of major muscle groups, which expend large amounts of energy over prolonged periods of time. For athletes without disabilities, running, cycling, and swimming use the large muscles of the trunk and lower limbs and are excellent modes of exercise. The wheelchair athlete, however, is limited to using the relatively small muscles of the arm and, in some cases, the muscles of the trunk. This smaller working muscle mass places lower demands on the heart and lungs and makes cardiovascular endurance training more difficult. However, training rollers, arm-crank ergometers, and upper-body exercise systems (modalities used in cardiovascular endurance programs of elite wheelchair athletes) can be employed in this respect. The intensity of this training can best be gauged by using rate of perceived exertion scales (Borg, 1998) because these allow the trainer to account for the unique variability of the individual independent of standard measures. There is some merit in using standardized exercise tests, and Van der Woude, Bouten, Veeger, and Gwinn (2002) identified that elite, trained athletes can be evaluated using standardized aerobic and anaerobic exercise tests provided classification and current training status were taken into account.

Although a cardiovascular base is essential, power more directly relates to the performance demands made in the anaerobic sports exemplified on the court (tennis, basketball, and quad rugby). Because of the small muscle mass involved in wheelchair propulsion and the asymmetry of the propulsion movements, systematic strength and flexibility training is critical. Stretching, both before and after exercise, might be more important for athletes with disabilities than for athletes without disabilities. Weight training will develop strength and, indirectly, power and is a major component in the regime of the elite athlete. It should be noted that the wheelchair athlete propels the wheelchair using a relatively small range of motion at the shoulder and elbow, and this action is asymmetrical in that the forces of extension (during propulsion) are far greater than the muscular forces used in recovery. This asymmetry can lead to muscle imbalance around the shoulder joint, which in turn might cause serious overuse injury and postural problems (Curtis, 1981b). Thus, an important component of the weight-training program for wheelchair users should be development of the posterior (back) muscles. A simple rule of thumb is to pair the muscles in the training program (i.e., biceps and triceps) and to include free-weight exercises that require the athlete to be face down (prone) on the work bench. Exercises for the latissimus dorsi and the trapezius muscles of the back are examples of the muscles that should be targeted in a weight program if such exercises are not contraindicated. Attention to appropriate stretching practices also improves weight-training regimes (Curtis, 1981b), and when there is a strength imbalance in the muscles caused by disability, stretching can reduce problems such as contractures. In the next section we examine other disability-specific sports medical concerns.

Medical Concerns

Wheelchair athletes face several disability-specific sports medicine problems, of which the most important are associated with thermal regulation. Damage to the spinal cord presents problems at both high and low ambient temperatures because impairment of sensory nerves means that athletes are often unable to feel heat, cold, or pain. Thus, in cold weather, they receive no sensory warning that body extremities (usually the feet) are becoming frozen. Coupled with reduced blood flow to the inactive feet, frostbite becomes an ever-present danger against which the athlete must guard.

At high ambient temperatures, the problem is damage to the nerves that initiate and control sweat production. This problem is particularly severe in athletes with quadriplegia, many of whom have little or no body sweat production, and thus no way of reducing their core temperature. The provision of shade, adequate drinking fluids, and wet towels for surface-temperature reduction can help alleviate this problem.

A particularly pernicious medical problem that has surfaced in wheelchair sport is the life-threatening but deliberate precipitation of **autonomic dysreflexia** by athletes with quadriplegia, a process referred to as "boosting." Autonomic dysreflexia is a medical condition characterized by hypertension, piloerection, headaches, and bradycardia and associated with very high levels of catecholamine. Autonomic dysreflexia is unique to individuals with spinal cord injury above the major splanchnic outflow at the sixth thoracic vertebrae.

Athletes with quadriplegia believe that "boosting" increases their athletic performance, and

experimental evidence (Burnham et al., 1993; Schmid et al., 2001) supports this view. National and international sports groups are aware of both the use of "boosting" and its dangers, and the practice is banned in Paralympic competition (Schmid et al., 2001).

The Wheelchair

Developments in wheelchair design that match the chair to the demands of the sport have led to a multiplicity of choices for the athlete wishing to enhance performance (LaMere & Labanowich, 1984 a, b, c). It is no longer feasible at the elite level to expect a general wheelchair to perform to the competitive demands of a sport. Just as the athlete without a disability wears different shoes for different sports, the elite wheelchair athlete uses different wheelchairs for different sports. Still, some commonalties in wheelchair design generalize across the spectrum of competitive wheelchairs.

The Wheelchair Frame

The wheelchair frame performs one major function. It holds the other components—the seat, the mainwheels, and front wheel(s)—in their proper relative positions (see figure 29.2). Perhaps the most important design consideration in building a wheelchair frame is to make it as light and as rigid as possible. It needs to be lightweight so that the athlete has to propel as little weight as possible during athletic performance. It needs to be rigid so that the energy that the athlete applies to the wheelchair is used to drive the chair rather than to bend and deform the frame. Frame flexing absorbs energy directly, and because the wheel alignment of the wheelchair changes as the frame flexes, additional energy is lost when the mainwheels do not point straight ahead in the direction of travel. In addition, the frame must be matched to the body size and shape of the athlete and will vary depending on the performance considerations of the sport.

Wheels

The rear wheels of racing wheelchairs are larger in diameter and narrower in cross section than those used in other sport chairs because of the differing demands of the activity. Wheels for court chairs must withstand rotational torque and, in many cases, contact with other wheelchairs. Thus, some athletes in contact sports such as basketball and quad rugby forgo lightness for additional robustness in the mainwheel and have

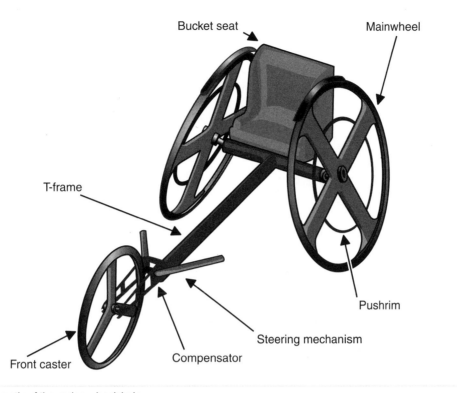

Bucket seat   Mainwheel

T-frame

Front caster   Compensator   Steering mechanism   Pushrim

Figure 29.2   Schematic of the racing wheelchair.

Image Courtesy: Per4Max Medical.

stronger, cross-spoked wheels that can withstand these extra forces.

For racing, unless the athlete is very small, the mainwheels are usually high-quality racing bicycle wheels in the European 700-centimeter or North American 27-inch size. For road racing, the narrowest possible tires (19 millimeters or less) are used, whereas for track racing there appears to be some benefit to using wider 23- to 28-millimeter tires. Because additional weight in the wheels of a wheelchair slows the athlete down twice as much as additional weight in the frame of the chair, racing wheels should be as light, strong, and rigid as possible. Although athletes have experimented with both disk and three-spoke airfoil wheels, no demonstrated performance gains have been seen over traditionally spoked wheels, probably because of their greater weight and poorer performance in cross-wind conditions (although three and four-spoked airfoil wheels are being used increasingly in tennis and, to a lesser extent, basketball). The trend for front wheel(s) has been to use as large a wheel as the rules allow, and 18- and 20-inch (.46- and .51-meter) diameter front wheels are common.

For court chairs such as those used in the basketball game pictured in figure 29.1, the size of

mainwheels ranges from 24 inches to the maximum permissible 26 inches, depending on the position played (Yilla, La Bar, & Dangelmaier, 1998). The preferred front wheel now tends to be the skateboard-type available at regular hobby shops.

Number of Wheels

A wheelchair remains stable as long as the center of gravity of the athlete plus the chair remains inside the wheelchair's base of support. The base of support is the area of ground marked by the points at which the wheels contact the surface. In four-wheeled designs, the base of support is rectangular with the base a little narrower at the front than at the rear, whereas in three-wheeled designs, the base of support is triangular. This means that as the weight of the athlete moves forward (as he or she leans forward to cut down air resistance) the center of gravity gets nearer to the edge of the base of support of the three-wheeled chair, and the chair becomes less stable. This lack of stability can be a problem for less experienced athletes or for some court sports, but for those who can handle them, three-wheeled chairs are faster. Three-wheel designs are faster because there is less resistance to passage over the ground for three rather than four wheels (Higgs, 1992a), and three-wheeled designs also have considerably less wind resistance than four-wheelers under most wind conditions (Higgs, 1992b).

Note that a performance consideration in many court sports is the necessity to extend laterally forward to the right or the left—and this might require the extra stability inherent in a four-wheeled design. Thus, caution should be exercised in selecting a three-wheeled chair for basketball or quad rugby, sports in which stability is at a premium. For tennis and racing, elite athletes almost exclusively now use a three-wheeled configuration. An additional wheel for front to rear stability can be attached to the back of the chair and is now popular in tennis, basketball, and quad rugby (see figure 29.3).

Figure 29.3 Tennis chair with "fifth" wheel—although in this case it is the fourth.

Mainwheel Alignment

To allow the wheelchair to roll with the least resistance, it is critical that the mainwheels point straight ahead. If the mainwheels point slightly outward (toe-out) or slightly inward (toe-in), they significantly slow down the wheelchair. O'Reagan and colleagues (1981) showed that, for some tires, toe-in or toe-out of as little as three degrees increased rolling resistance tenfold. Because the front wheels are essentially castors to allow turning, they are not subject to the same toe-in–toe-

out problems as mainwheels. They do, however, significantly increase rolling resistance when their bearings become worn.

Camber Angle

Sports chairs are cambered to allow for superior turning and ease of pushing. Camber is the state in which the wheels are fixed to the frame of the chair at an angle so that the top of the wheel is close to the frame and the bottom is further away. With the wheels cambered, the hands fall naturally to the pushrim. The mainwheels of a racing wheelchair are cambered to allow for maximum application of force to the pushrim. With court chairs, the camber significantly enhances maneuverability. The majority of athletes use camber angles between 6 and 12 degrees, with 8 to 10 degrees being most popular.

Seat Height

When all other factors are equal, the most effective seat height depends on the athlete's trunk and arm length and on the pushrim size selected. Higgs (1983) reported that in athletes at the 1980 Paralympic games, superior performances in racing events were recorded by those with lower seats. Experimental work by Traut (1989) showed greater propulsion efficiency when a "relatively low" seat position was used. Experimental work by Meijs and colleagues (1989) and by Van de Woude, Veeger, and Rozendal (1990) showed a relation between the elbow angle (when the athlete was sitting upright in a general sport wheelchair with hands placed on the top center of the pushrim) and propulsion efficiency. Their results showed that efficiency was greatest when the elbow angle was 80 degrees and that the energy cost of sitting too high in the chair was greater than the penalty paid for sitting too low. However, performance considerations (height in basketball or the post position in quad rugby) offset some propulsion considerations.

Additional sport-specific considerations for wheelchairs follow. Note there is a fundamental difference in the configuration of the racing wheelchair relative to court chairs.

Specific Considerations for Racing Wheelchairs

As can be seen by the racers in figure 29.4, the structure of the racing wheelchair has changed fundamentally since Bob Hall first pushed in the Boston marathon. In fact, Goosey and Campbell

(1998) concluded that wheelchair design (combined with disability) might be more important factors in pushing efficiency than propulsion techniques. Considerations for racing wheelchairs involve the weight distribution of the athlete in the wheelchair, which can be modified by the anterior–posterior seat position, the size of the pushrims, and use of accessories. Detailed explanations of these considerations follow.

Anterior–Posterior Seat Position

Little is known about the optimal anterior–posterior position of the wheelchair seat, although this position affects both the chair's stability and the effectiveness of application of force to the pushrim. If the athlete is too far toward the rear of the wheelchair, the chair might become unstable (particularly when going uphill), and the athlete could "flip" out the back. A rear seat position makes it difficult for the athlete to apply force to the front of the pushrim where the most effective application of driving force can be made. Although there is little research evidence on optimal anterior–posterior seating and positioning for elite athletes, Boninger and colleagues (2000) identified that adjustable axle positions significantly facilitate identifying the optimal seating position for maximizing propulsion.

Pushrims

The pushrims are the point at which the athlete's energy is transmitted to the wheelchair—thus, they are critical to producing optimal perfor-

mance. The three most important aspects of the pushrim are its diameter, its width, and the material with which it is covered.

- *Pushrim Diameter.* The pushrim acts like the gearing for the wheelchair. If a small-diameter pushrim is used, the athlete has selected a "high" gear that produces poor acceleration but a high top speed. Conversely, if a large-diameter pushrim is used, the benefit is greater acceleration at the cost of a lower top speed. In general, stronger athletes are able to effectively push smaller diameter pushrims, and thus the optimal pushrim diameter depends on the size of the athlete, the relative importance of acceleration and top speed in the race being run, and the strength of the athlete. Most pushrims are between 14 and 16 inches (0.35 and 0.41 meter) in diameter, and athletes usually experiment to determine what works best for them. Paralympic competition rules require that there be only one pushrim on each mainwheel.

- *Pushrim Width.* If the pushrim is made of relatively wide tubing, it is easier to grasp, which makes starts and uphill climbing easier. On the other hand, it is possible that narrower tubing would encourage higher wheeling speeds because the athlete is more likely to "strike" the pushrim rather than hold it and push. In the absence of research studies, athletes determine their optimal pushrim width through trial and error.

- *Pushrim Material.* The pushrim covering is of great importance because it is this material that the

Figure 29.4 Racing performance system.

hand strikes during propulsion. If it is too smooth or slick, the hand will slip when power is applied. For this reason, a number of materials have been used for pushrim covers. Many racers also apply adhesives to increase pushrim traction. Although the frictional grip of the pushrim is important, it is only half of the hand-wheelchair interface, and the hand covering used by the athlete is of equal or greater importance. Most athletes wear gloves that have been sculptured to their exact requirements by the application of hundreds of layers of adhesive tape. This glove and tape combination provides protective cushioning and high, instant grip between the hand and the pushrim. Again, athletes are encouraged to experiment with different materials to find the combination that best meets their needs.

Accessories

Racing wheelchair accessories are almost as numerous as the wheelchair athletes who use them, but almost all racing wheelchairs incorporate at least a steering device, a compensator, and a computer. With downhill racing speeds reaching more than 40 mph (64 kph), the need for a steering mechanism to help the athlete negotiate corners is obvious, and the usual steering device is a small handle attached directly to the front wheel mounting. This lever can be moved left or right to steer the wheelchair, although steering only occurs when the lever is held in place. Once released, the front wheel returns (under spring action) to a neutral, straight-ahead position. This process is called "active steering" because turning occurs only when steering input is applied by the racer. In addition to this active steering mechanism, the wheelchair also incorporates a compensator.

The purpose of the compensator is to permit small, long-term adjustments to the direction in which the chair moves, and it is most important in road racing. Most road races are held on public roads designed with a high crown along the midline, with the road falling away for drainage toward the curb. A chair propelled along the crown would go straight, but a chair wheeled near the curb for safety would be moving forward on a sideways sloping surface. The front of the chair would be constantly "falling away" from the crest of the crown, and the chair would tend to steer into the curb. A compensator applies a small offset to the front wheel to allow the chair to move straight ahead without the athlete needing to make constant small corrective steering adjustments. The rigidity provided by a compensator system (as opposed to rotating casters) also stabilizes the wheelchair in the event of surface irregularities.

Bicycle computers are now relatively inexpensive and are almost universally found on racing wheelchairs. These computers provide necessary information on distance traveled, cadence, and top and average speeds. This feedback is essential for developing and maintaining accurate training and racing logs that enhance performance.

Specific Considerations for Court Chairs

Because of similarities in configuration, it is easy to assume that a wheelchair that is appropriate for everyday use is also sufficient for sport. Whereas a general wheelchair might be sufficient for recreational physical activity, when examining enhancing wheelchair sport performance, a first step is to realize the importance of using sport-specific equipment. The following paragraphs contain general guidelines for selecting a wheelchair for court sports such as basketball, rugby, and tennis. Yilla (1997) provided a more detailed explanation on selecting a wheelchair specifically for basketball, and much of this information transfers to the selection of other court chairs.

When selecting a wheelchair, athletes should seek advice from someone who has experience in court sports and understands their function level at the position they play. This will help give the athlete insight into the functional demands of the sport. If this chair is the athlete's first court chair, it should be purchased from a reputable manufacturer.

There are now a bewildering number of options in performance wheelchairs and in their designs; many are experimental. It is advisable to avoid experimental designs until the athlete is comfortable with the performance demands of the sport. The athlete's first, sport-specific performance chair should be adjustable both for height and for point of balance (see figure 29.5a and b) so that it can be modified. However, because of weight and performance considerations, the athlete should avoid wheelchairs with too many adjustments. Adjustable mechanisms tend to add weight to the chair because of the need to provide a securing method that is flexible and that can be locked for rigidity. The solution is almost always heavier than the simple weld, nut, or other locking mechanism that it replaces. Performance is negatively affected because adjustment mechanisms cannot provide the same rigidity as a weld, leading to a misapplication of drive forces. Adjustments also require a level of expertise for the frame alignment to remain "true."

A = Neutral

B = Less stable (more mobile)

C = More stable (less mobile)

A = Neutral

D = Seat down

E = Seat up

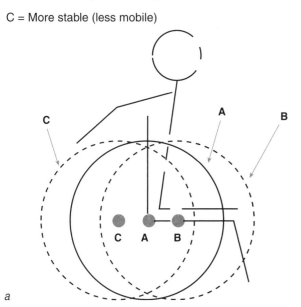

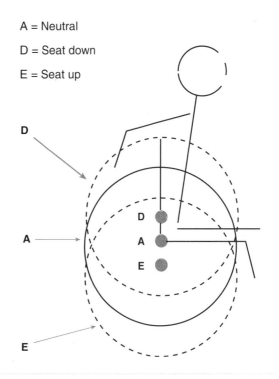

Figure 29.5 *(a)* Horizontal and *(b)* vertical mainwheel adjustments.

Wheelchairs Without Wheels

Functionality is the focus of performance wheelchairs, and these chairs can diverge from the traditional concept of the wheelchair to the point that these "wheelchairs" no longer have wheels! In particular, throwing chairs for field events, mono-skis for snow skiing, and mono-skis for water skiing are all "wheelchairs" without wheels (figures 29.6 and 29.7).

Wheelchairs without wheels are designed to provide a rigid, stable base from which the athlete can perform optimally. Throwing chairs are firmly anchored to the ground during the throw; there is no need for wheels and, as seen in figure 29.6, they are no longer part of the throwing chair design. The heavy metal frame is designed to give stability to the athlete and provide anchor points so that the chair can be tied down to prevent it from moving during throws. The seat is built as high above the ground as the rules allow, and because cushioning on the seat would absorb some of the power of the throw, the seat is usually hard. Sit-skis and mono-skis (figure 29.7) provide a similar sport-specific approach, and in meeting the functional demands of the activity, the wheels have become superfluous. Similarly, as was seen at the Winter Paralympics Games in 2002, sleds used to compete at ice hockey are an exciting addition to this category of "wheelchairs" (see figure 29.8).

© Sports 'N Spokes/Paralyzed Veterans of America

Figure 29.6 A throwing chair for field events.

Figure 29.7   Mono-ski for water skiing.

Figure 29.8   Canada versus Sweden in the 2002 Winter Paralympic Games.

THE SYSTEM APPROACH: COMBINING THE ATHLETE AND THE WHEELCHAIR

Although the process of combining the athlete and the wheelchair into a sport "system" varies depending on the sport, some general principles apply when fitting the wheelchair itself. Additionally, other performance considerations are broken down into the division between racing wheelchairs and court chairs.

Fitting the Wheelchair to the Athlete

Proper fitting of the wheelchair to the athlete is critical for high levels of athletic performance. Most manufacturers provide retail experts experienced in measuring athletes for performance wheelchairs.

In fitting the frame, the two most critical dimensions are the width and the relative positions of the seat and wheels. If the frame is too narrow for the athlete, there will be insufficient clearance between the wheels and the athlete, resulting in the wheel rubbing the athlete's body (which slows the chair and produces frictional injury to the athlete). If the frame is too wide, the pushrim is difficult to reach and even more difficult to push effectively.

The relative positioning of the seat and the mainwheels depends on the material in the wheelchair, the sport to be played, the athlete's weight, and the athlete's fitness level. Thus, an adjustment on the wheelchair for this relative position is essential no matter how experienced the athlete. Because different manufacturers present this adjustment option in different ways, this should be an important factor when selecting the chair. Refer to the application example below for considerations to keep in mind when helping athletes find the chair that is best for them.

System Considerations for Racing Wheelchairs

Several system considerations apply to racing wheelchairs. The following section identifies **propulsion techniques** and how to overcome negative

---

APPLICATION EXAMPLE

Enhancing Wheelchair Sports Performance

Setting: A community-based junior wheelchair sports program

Student: A 16-year-old junior wheelchair basketball player needs recommendations to refine his individualized transition program to incorporate adult wheelchair sports. The player is tall and has played the center and forward positions and wishes to purchase his own wheelchair.

Issue: What considerations should be taken into account in making recommendations to this athlete?

Application: Considerations for this athlete center around equipment, physical fitness, and individual skills.

- Equipment considerations:

   Athlete's height, the desire to play a certain position, athlete's classification level.

   Adjustability for height and point of balance. (Because the player has a desire to be a center/forward, the adjustability should

include being able to maximize the seat height to about 21 inches.)

   System considerations such as strapping and mobility in the wheelchair.

   A reputable manufacturer.

- Individual physical fitness:

   A strength-training program that targets the upper-body muscles in paired groups (i.e., biceps and triceps).

   A cardiovascular conditioning program that utilizes an arm crank ergometer or, preferably, a training roller.

- Individual skills targeted:

   Wheelchair mobility skills both with and without the basketball.

   Shooting skills both stationary and moving.

   Passing skills both stationary and moving.

   Studying the sophisticated strategies involved in the adult game.

forces as important considerations in developing an athlete's wheelchair racing system.

Propulsion Techniques in Track and Road Racing

Coupled with the evolution of the racing wheelchair has been the development of ever-more efficient propulsion techniques (Higgs, 1985). A six-phase technique (see figure 29.9) is most frequently used, although not all athletes use each phase with the same degree of effectiveness. A subsequent analysis by O'Connor, Robertson, and Cooper (1998) indicates a need for coaches to become more knowledgeable concerning appropriate wheelchair propulsion techniques. More comprehensive analyses of the effects of propulsion techniques in wheelchair racing can be found in the works of Goosey and Campbell, 1998; Goosey, Campbell, and Fowler, 2000; and Vanlandewijck, Theisen, and Daly, 2001.

The Basic Stroke

The **propulsion cycle** starts with the hands drawn up as far above and behind the pushrim as possible given the seating position and flexibility of the athlete. The hands are then accelerated as rapidly and forcefully as possible (acceleration phase) (see points A on figure 29.9) until they strike the pushrim. The moment of contact is the impact energy transfer phase (point B on figure 29.9), during which the kinetic energy stored in the fast-moving hand is transferred to the slower moving pushrim. With the hand in contact with the pushrim there is a force application, or push, phase (points C on figure 29.9), and this continues until the hands reach almost to the bottom of the pushrim. During the force application phase, most of the propulsion comes from the muscles acting around the elbow and shoulder. As the hands reach the bottom of the pushrim, the powerful muscles of the forearm are used to pronate the hand, which allows the thumb to be used to give a last, powerful "flick" to the pushrim. This last flicking action is reversed by a few athletes who use supination in the rotational energy transfer phase (points D on figure 29.9) to flick the pushrim with the fingers rather than the thumb, and research indicates this type of "backhand" techniques might be more efficient in endurance races (Chow, Millikan, Carlton, Morse, & Chae, 2001). Immediately following the rotational energy transfer, the hands leave the pushrim during the castoff phase (point E on figure 29.9). Here it is important that the hand be moving faster than the pushrim as it pulls away because a slower hand will act as a brake to the wheelchair. Often athletes use the

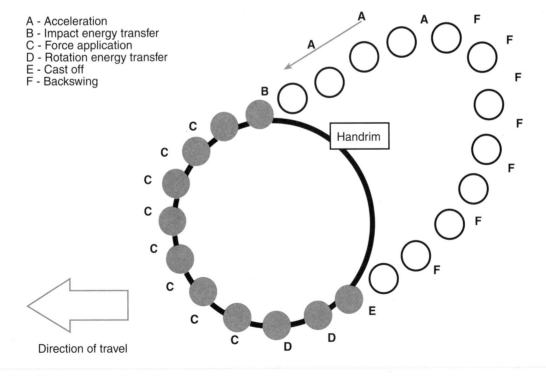

A - Acceleration
B - Impact energy transfer
C - Force application
D - Rotation energy transfer
E - Cast off
F - Backswing

Direction of travel

Figure 29.9   Six-phase propulsion cycle.

pronation or supination of the rotational energy transfer phase to accelerate the hands and arms and thus allow them to be carried up and back under ballistic motion. This upward and backward motion is called the backswing phase (points F on figure 29.9) and is used to get the hands far enough away from the pushrim to allow them to accelerate forward to strike the pushrim at high speed at the start of the next stroke. Goosey, Campbell, and Fowler (2000) reported that there was no single identifiable stroke frequency to recommend as best for wheelchair racing but that the athlete's own freely chosen frequency was the most economical in lab conditions.

This basic propulsion stroke is modified by the terrain over which the athlete is wheeling, by the tactics of the race, and by the athlete's level of disability. On uphill parts of a course, the athlete shortens the backswing and acceleration phases to minimize the time during which force is not applied to the pushrim and during which the chair could roll backward. Tactically, the athlete is either wheeling at constant speed or is making an attack and needs to accelerate. The basic stroke described previously is used at steady speed, whereas during bursts of acceleration the major change in stroke takes place during the backswing. At steady speeds the backswing is a relatively relaxed ballistic movement in which the velocity at castoff is used to raise the hand to its highest and most rearward position. This relaxed backswing is efficient and allows a brief moment of rest during each stroke. During acceleration, however, the major change in stroke dynamics is to increase the number of strokes from about 80 per minute to more than 120 per minute. This is achieved by a rapid reduction in the time taken for a more restricted backswing.

The Start

In short races, the start is critical, and a good start can provide the margin of victory. Critical aspects of the start are the upper-body action and modifications to the first few strokes. Newton's third law, the law of action and reaction, confirms that if the upper body is thrown forward at the starting gun there will be a reaction of the lower part of the body (plus the front of the wheelchair) rising up to meet it. Then, as the upper body pushes down on the pushrim and rocks back up, the legs and the wheelchair will return to the ground, and only then will the chair start to move forward. This is clearly inefficient, and for this reason it is critical that athletes start with their bodies as far forward as possible and, at the gun, the arms drive the wheelchair forward while the athlete tries to prevent the chair from rising. In this way maximum energy is transferred to the forward motion of the wheelchair.

The stroke is also modified during the start. Because the wheelchair is stationary, the hands grip the pushrim (rather than striking it), and for the first few strokes the arc of pushing is very restricted with as rapid as possible a recovery. The key is to get three or four short, hard strokes before making the transition to a striking rather than a pushing stroke.

Retarding Forces and Overcoming Them

Whereas the athlete provides the energy to drive the wheelchair forward, the twin retarding forces of rolling resistance and aerodynamic drag act to slow it down. When propulsive forces are greater than resistance, the wheelchair accelerates, and when the retarding forces are greater, the chair is slowed. Obviously, reductions in rolling resistance and aerodynamic drag translate directly into higher wheeling speeds and improved athletic performance.

Rolling Resistance

On a hard, smooth, surface the majority of rolling resistance of a wheelchair wheel occurs at the point where the tire is in contact with the ground. The energy loss in the reformation of the tire when contacting the ground is known as **hysteresis,** the major determinant of rolling resistance. The thicker and less flexible the wall of the tire, the greater the hysteresis energy loss. If the tire wall can be prevented from flexing, energy losses are reduced, and this is exactly what happens when the air pressure in the tire is increased. Thus, the road-racing athlete should inflate tires to the highest safe pressure for best performance (Higgs, 1993).

On the track, hysteresis energy losses still occur in the tires when they are compressed and allowed to rebound, but the tires also cut into the surface of the track and produce surface deformation energy losses. Thus, on a track the best athletic performance occurs at the tire pressure that minimizes the combined energy losses from both hysteresis and surface deformation. Experiments have been conducted (Higgs, 1993) that indicate that moderate tire pressures of about 90 pounds per square inch give the best results on synthetic athletic tracks.

Rolling resistance of racing wheelchairs is also affected by the mainwheel's camber angle, although the relation is complex. Wheels that are not parallel and pointing straight ahead dramatically increase the rolling resistance of a wheelchair. Athletes should do everything in their power to check and adjust alignment before every important race.

Aerodynamic Drag

The problems of aerodynamic drag of racing wheelchairs and athletes are unique in the field of sport because of the relatively low speeds at which events take place. Coutts and Schutz (1988) calculated that races on the track take place at average speeds between three and seven meters per second (6.65 and 15.75 mph). Although race times of wheelchairs have dramatically improved since 1988, wheelchair times are still considerably slower than the speeds found in cycling. These slower speeds create unusual aerodynamic conditions.

Aerodynamic drag is caused by two separate but interrelated forces called surface drag and form drag. **Surface drag** is caused by the adhesion of air molecules to the surface of an object passing through it, and it is very powerful at low speeds. To reduce surface drag there is a need to reduce the exposed surfaces of the chair and athlete. **Form drag,** on the other hand, is caused by the difference in air pressure between the front and the back of an object, which in turn is created by the swirls and eddy currents formed as the wheelchair and athlete pass through the air. Form drag is mostly reduced by ensuring that all of the exposed components of the wheelchair are streamlined and that the chair and athlete have the lowest possible frontal area (frontal area is what we see in silhouette when we look head-on at an approaching athlete).

Drafting

Because aerodynamic drag represents about 40 percent of the force acting to slow down a wheelchair racer, methods of cheating the wind pay considerable dividends. The single most effective way in which drag can be reduced is through the process of drafting. Drafting occurs when a wheelchair follows closely behind another wheelchair that acts as a wind deflector. The second wheelchair might experience aerodynamic drag forces less than half of those that would occur under nondrafting conditions. In still air or in a headwind, the wheelchair that follows gains greatest benefit when it follows directly behind the lead chair and as closely as possible. If a choice must be made between dropping back farther but remaining directly behind the lead chair, or staying closer and moving out to one side, the evidence (Pugh, 1971) is overwhelming that it is better to stay directly behind. At the end of long races, the energy saved through drafting can affect race outcome, and modern race tactics confirm this. Frequently teams work together, taking turns leading and drafting to improve overall performance.

System Considerations for Court Wheelchairs

This section does not include information on propulsion in the court sports. Although there is less research in propulsion techniques for court sports—presumably because of the wide variability in the propulsion techniques as compared to racing—Vanlandewijck, Theisen, and Daly (2001) conducted a review of propulsion biomechanics that included not only wheelchair racing but also basketball and rugby; for those interested in increasing wheelchair sport performance, this review is recommended reading.

Two fundamental properties affect the system considerations for court wheelchairs (Yilla, La Bar, and Dangelmaier, 1998): the horizontal (anterior–posterior) positioning and the vertical positioning of the chair (see figure 29.5, a and b). Appropriate adjustments of these aid in the development of the balance (vertical adjustment) and agility (horizontal adjustment) components of performance-related fitness.

Horizontal Positioning

Horizontal positioning of the mainwheels affects the mobility of the chair. The further forward the mainwheel from a hypothesized neutral position (position A in figure 29.5a), the more maneuverable the chair (position B in figure 29.5a). A backward tilt to the seat rail can also be incorporated; this shifts the center of gravity of the system to the rear and further promotes mobility. Unfortunately, the further forward the mainwheel relative to the center of gravity, the more likely it is that the chair will raise and tilt up. Thus, the forward placement of the mainwheel is restricted by the athlete's ability to force the front end of the chair down. This ability is a function of abdominal and lower-body strength and thereby a function of the athlete's disability level. Thus, disability level has been a limiting factor in how far forward the mainwheels could be placed, with more restricted athletes positioning their chairs in the more stable position (position C in figure 29.5a). This problem has been somewhat mitigated by changes in the rules of basketball, quad rugby, and tennis that allow for a "fifth" wheel (see figure 29.3). This fifth wheel can be placed on the rear of the chair, provided it stays within the area contained by the mainwheel. This wheel offsets the tendency of the chair to tilt up if the mainwheel is set forward of the neutral position (position B in figure 29.5a), thus affording more restricted athletes the capacity to move their rear wheels forward and thereby improve their mobility. In basketball, less restricted athletes are now using the fifth wheel to aid in the tilting of the chair to gain more height, particularly when rebounding or shooting in the restricted zone.

Vertical Positioning

Vertical positioning of the mainwheel affects the height at which the athlete sits and the "system's" center of gravity. This fundamentally affects the chair's handling properties. Again, using a hypothetical neutral position (position A in figure 29.5 b), the lower down the athlete sits relative to this neutral position (position D in figure 29.5b), the more maneuverable is the wheelchair. So, all other things being equal, the wheelchair athlete should sit as low as possible. However, performance considerations place a premium on height for certain positions, such as center in basketball and the post position in quad rugby. When playing these positions, it is advantageous to position the mainwheel to maximize sitting height (position E in figure 29.5b). However, because the center of gravity is higher, this position makes the chair less maneuverable; this can be offset somewhat by using larger main wheels, but this, in turn, reduces start speeds, which are vital in court sports.

Thus, when enhancing wheelchair sport performance on the court, the athlete should identify the functional aspects of the game as well as his or her roles within the competition—which will in part depend on his or her level of disability. The athlete should then select the wheelchair setup that will improve functionality most for the roles identified. Again, note that the positioning of the mainwheel fundamentally affects the performance characteristics of the chair. After the athlete has identified the appropriate wheelchair setup, consideration needs to be given to combining the athlete and the wheelchair into a performance system. This is accomplished through **strapping** and, when applicable, the use of orthotic or prosthetic devices.

Strapping

The relaxation of regulations that used to prohibit or limit the securing of the athlete to the wheelchair has radically altered performances seen in basketball, rugby, and tennis. The use of strapping helps an athlete establish a base from which to perform and results in greater "volumes of action" by allowing more leaning and stretching than could occur without being secured to the wheelchair. A striking representation of this is the practice of "tilting" or "standing" the chair now common in basketball. In basketball, the player has to remain firmly seated to the chair or else a technical foul is assessed. With the advent of strapping, innovative players found a way to lean or "stand" the chair on one side without the buttocks leaving the seat (Vernon et al., 2003), considerably raising the height of the chair on the side that is elevated. Although the maneuver was initially controversial, it is now accepted practice and seen as a means of making the game more dynamic. In fact, the Great Britain Wheelchair Basketball Association has considerably relaxed strapping regulations for the prospective 2004–2005 season because of the increased dynamism this practice has brought to the sport.

Level of loss of function can be used as a general indicator of the point at which the athlete should strap to the wheelchair. A USA class III athlete (international 4.5 to 3.5) who has good leg function may simply use a strap across the thighs to be secure to the wheelchair. A USA class II (international 3.0 to 2.0) may choose to strap at the waist and other points of the lower body. A USA class I (international 1.5 and 1.0) may, additionally, use straps across the abdomen and secured to the back of the chair to compensate for the lack of stomach function. These are general guidelines, and the choice of strapping strategies is ultimately based on personal preference. Similarly, the use of orthotics and prosthetics depends on what the individual has identified as required to achieve maximum performance. Novice participants are encouraged to experiment with several strategies to identify the performance system that works best for them.

Finally, combined to the wheelchair in a performance system, the athlete should address the skill development essential for success in the chosen sport.

Skill Development

The skill aspects of the sport are critical to the elite athlete's program. Common to skill tests in court sports is speed (which depends on power, which depends on strength) and maneuverability with the target object, be it a basketball, volleyball (as used in quad rugby), or tennis racket. Other sport-specific skills can be obtained from the research literature. Skill tests have been developed for wheelchair basketball, quad rugby, and tennis (Brasile, 1986; Brasile & Hedrick, 1996; Yilla & Sherrill, 1998; Moore & Snow, 1994).

Instructional materials that focus on the skills and strategies involved in many wheelchair sports are also available (Hedrick, Byrnes, & Shaver, 1989; Moore & Snow, 1994). Again, the system approach should be incorporated, with athletes practicing their skills in their competitive system that includes sport-specific wheelchair, strapping, bracing, and applicable prosthesis.

As pioneer Sir Ludwig Guttmann stated (admittedly with gender bias), "It is no exaggeration to say that the paraplegic *[sic]* and his chair have become one, in the same way as a first-class horseman and his mount" (Weisman & Godfrey, 1976). This is the essence of the system approach to enhancing wheelchair sport performance.

FACILITIES

In the past, advocates of wheelchair sport have experienced resistance in the use of facilities because of the perception that wheelchairs can damage the playing surfaces in the arena involved. In particular, as basketball arenas install high-tech, expensive, playing surfaces, there is a natural resistance to allowing equipment that would appear to expose these surfaces to damage. Relevant disability sport organizations already have in place rules relating to the configuration of wheelchairs intended to minimize any possible damage to facilities. The National Wheelchair Basketball Association, the United States Quad Rugby Association, and Wheelchair Sports USA all have rules requiring that players have appropriate protections and padding on wheelchairs for the safety of other athletes and the competitive facilities. Experienced athletes are used to complying with the rules, but novice athletes might not be as familiar with them; it is the responsibility of program organizers to ensure that relevant standards are strictly enforced.

Unfortunately, logical arguments regarding rules have little effect in discussions regarding wheelchair use in certain facilities, as it is the perception, not the reality, that is the primary obstacle. The author recommends advocacy by example. Many programs are using the very best facilities to provide wheelchair sport competition, and it is these examples that should be used to persuade those who are less informed about the low risk in allowing wheelchairs to use facilities. For example, the Dallas Wheelchair Mavericks regularly provide exhibitions at the American Airlines Center during NBA Mavericks competition. Because of the strict adherence by the Wheelchair Mavericks to the NWBA standards regarding wheelchair configuration over the years, the NBA Mavericks no longer have issues regarding wheelchairs using their facilities. Similar examples can and should be used when discussions arise regarding the use of facilities for wheelchair sport competition, be it on the court (basketball or tennis) or on the track.

THE FUTURE

Technological advances and improved training techniques have dramatically changed the look of wheelchair sport. Opportunities are seemingly endless. Professionalism is now part of a number of wheelchair sports, including racing, tennis, and, in Europe, even basketball. Elite athletes now travel the world competing in their chosen sport, and there is no reason to believe this trend will not become even more prevalent.

New sports are always being adapted to meet the needs of individuals with disabilities, and, with each new sport, comes the need for specialized equipment, designed to meet that sport's unique demands. The popularity of quad rugby at the 2000 Summer Paralympic Games in Sydney and sledge hockey at the 2002 Winter Paralympic Games in Utah were both indicators that wheelchair sports are a dynamic means of physical activity for individuals with mobility disabilities. The demands of each sport and the needs of athletes involved in them must be systematically assessed, and suitable equipment must then be designed and developed. The combining of the athlete and the wheelchair into a sport-specific, functional, performance system is the trend in elite wheelchair athletics, with even greater equipment and technique specialization anticipated as the wave of the future.

SUMMARY

This chapter has dealt with information for enhancing performance in wheelchair sport. We have discussed the appropriate selection of a sport by the athlete and the athlete's individual training regime and addressed sport medicine issues faced by athletes with disabilities. Basic types of sport wheelchairs were identified (racing and court), as were specific performance considerations that influence the selection of a chair that best suits the chosen activity. The chapter concluded with an examination of how the athlete and chair combine to create a performance system. Racing performance considerations (stroke analysis, starting techniques, overcoming rolling resistance, and drafting) were discussed separately from court performance considerations (adjusting the chair and individual skill development). Finally, simple strategies for safe and preferred facility use were identified.

REFERENCES

Boninger, M.L., Baldwin, M., Cooper, R.A., Koontz, A., & Chan, L. (2000). Manual wheelchair pushrim biomechanics and axle position. *Archives of Physical Medicine and Rehabilitation, 81*(5), 608-613.

Borg, G. (1998). *Borg's perceived exertion and pain scales.* Champaign, IL: Human Kinetics.

Brasile, F. (1986). Do you measure up? *Sports 'N Spokes, 12*(4), 42-47.

Brasile, F., & Hedrick, B.N. (1996). The relationship of skills of elite wheelchair basketball competitors to the International Functional Classification System. *Therapeutic Recreation Journal, 30*(2), 114-127.

Burnham, R., Wheeler, G., Bhambhani, Y., Cumming, D., Maclean, I., Sloley, B.D., Belanger, M., Eriksson, P., & Steadward, R. (1993). Performance enhancement in elite quadriplegic wheelchair racers through self-induced autonomic dysreflexia. *Vista '93 Conference,* May 14-20, Jasper, AB.

Chow, J.W., Millikan, T.A., Carlton, L.G., Morse, M.I. & Chae, W.S. (2001). Biomechanical comparison of two racing wheelchair propulsion techniques. *Medicine and Science in Sports and Exercise, 33*(3), 476-484.

Coutts, K.D., & Schutz, R.W. (1988). Analysis of wheelchair track performance. *Medicine and Science in Sport and Exercise,* 20, 188-194.

Curtis, K.A. (1981a). Wheelchair sportsmedicine: Part 3— Stretching routines. *Sports 'N Spokes, 7*(3), 16-18.

Curtis, K.A. (1981b). Wheelchair sportsmedicine: Part 2—Training. *Sports 'N Spokes, 7*(2), 16-19.

Ferrara, M.S., & Peterson, C.L. (2000). Injuries to athletes with disabilities: Identifying injury patterns. *Sports Medicine, 30*(2), 137-143.

Gallahue, D.L., & Ozmun, J.C. (2002). *Understanding motor development* (5th ed.). Dubuque, IA: McGraw/Hill.

Goosey, V.L., & Campbell, I.G. (1998). Pushing economy and propulsion techniques of wheelchair racers at three speeds. *Adapted Physical Activity Quarterly, 15*(1), 36-50.

Goosey, V.L., Campbell, I.G. & Fowler, N.E. (2000). Effect of push frequency on the economy of wheelchair racers. *Medicine and Science in Sports and Exercise, 32*(1), 174-181.

Hedrick, B., Byrnes, D., & Shaver, L. (1989). *Wheelchair basketball.* Washington DC: Paralyzed Veterans of America.

Hedrick, B., Wang, Y.T., Moeinzadeh, M., & Adrian, M. (1990). Aerodynamic positioning and performance in wheelchair racing. *Adapted Physical Activity Quarterly, 7*(1), 41-51.

Higgs, C. (1983). An analysis of racing wheelchairs used at the 1980 Olympic Games for the Disabled. *Research Quarterly for Exercise and Sport, 54*(3), 229-233.

Higgs, C. (1985). Propulsion of racing wheelchairs. In M. Ellis & D. Tripps (Eds.), *Proceedings of the 1984 Olympic scientific congress,* Eugene, Oregon. Champaign, IL: Human Kinetics.

Higgs, C. (1992a). Racing wheelchairs: A comparison of three- and four-wheeled designs. *Palaestra,* (80), 28-36.

Higgs, C. (1992b). Wheeling the wind: The effect of wind velocity and direction on the aerodynamic drag of wheelchairs. *Adapted Physical Activity Quarterly, 9*(1), 74-87.

Higgs, C. (1993). *The rolling resistance of racing wheelchairs: The effect of rolling surface, rear-wheel camber and tire pressure.* Final report, Applied Sport Science Program, Fitness and Amateur Sport, Government of Canada.

LaMere, T.J., & Labanowich, S. (1984a). The history of sport wheelchairs—Part I: The development of the basketball wheelchair. *Sports 'N Spokes, 9*(6), 6-8; 10-11.

LaMere, T.J., & Labanowich, S. (1984b). The history of sport wheelchairs—Part II: The racing wheelchair 1956-1975. *Sports 'N Spokes, 10*(1), 12-15.

LaMere, T.J., & Labanowich, S. (1984c). The history of sport wheelchairs—Part III: The racing wheelchair 1976-1983. *Sports 'N Spokes, 10*(2), 12-16.

Meijs, P.J.M., Van Oers, C.A.J.M., Van de Woude, L.H.V., & Veeger, H.E.J. (1989). The effect of seat height on the physiological response and propulsion technique in wheelchair ambulation. *Journal of Rehabilitation Science,* 2, 104-107.

Moore, B., & Snow, R. (1994). *Wheelchair tennis: Myth to reality.* Dubuque, IA: Kendall Hunt.

O'Connor, T.J., Robertson, R.N., & Cooper, R.A. (1998). Three-dimensional kinematic analysis and physiological assessment of racing wheelchair propulsion. *Adapted Physical Activity Quarterly, 15*(1), 1-14.

O'Reagan, J.R., Thacker, J.G., Kauzlarich, J.J., Mochel, E., Carmine, D., & Bryant, M. (1981). Wheelchair dynamics. In *Wheelchair Mobility 1976-1981.* Rehabilitation Engineering Center, University of Virginia, 33-41.

Pugh, L.G.C.E. (1971). The influence of wind resistance in running and walking and the mechanical efficiency of work against horizontal and vertical forces. *Journal of Physiology (London),* 213, 795-808.

Schmid, A., Schmidt-Trucksaess, A., Huonker, M., Koenig, D., Eisenbarth, I., Sauerwein, H., et al. (2001) Catecholamines: Response of high performance wheelchair athletes at rest and during exercise with autonomic dysreflexia. *International Journal of Sports Medicine,* 22, 2-7.

Shephard, R.J. (1990). *Fitness in special populations.* Champaign, IL: Human Kinetics.

Traut, L. (1989).Gestaltung ergonoisch relevanter Konstruktionsparameter am Antriebssysteem des Greifreifenrollstuhls—Teil 1. *Orthopedaedie Technik,* 7, 394-398.

Van de Woude, L.H.V., Veeger, H.E.J., & Rozendal, R.H. (1990). Seat height in hand rim wheelchair propulsion: A follow up study. *Journal of Rehabilitation Science,* 3, 79-83.

Van de Woude, L.H.V., Bouten, C., Veeger, H.E.J., & Gwinn, T. (2002). Aerobic work capacity in elite wheelchair athletes: A cross-sectional analysis. *American Journal of Physical Medicine and Rehabilitation, 81*(4), 261-271.

Vanlandewijck, Y., Theisen, D., & Daly, D. (2001), Wheelchair propulsion biomechanics: Implications for wheelchair sports. *Sports Medicine,* 31(5), 339-367.

Vernon, T., Tunstall, H., Mullineaux, D.R., Bishop, D.C., Horton, J. & Brooksbank, S.L. (2003). A biomechanical analysis of the tilt technique in wheelchair basketball (Abstract). *Journal of Sports Sciences,* 21(4), 253.

Weisman, M., & Godfrey, J. (1976). *So get on with it: A celebration of wheelchair sports.* Toronto, Canada: Doubleday.

Wells, C.L., & Hooker, S.P. (1990). The spinal injured athlete. *Adapted Physical Activity Quarterly,* 7, 265-285.

Yilla, A.B. (1997). Express yourself. *Sports 'N Spokes,* 23: 59-63.

Yilla, A.B., & Sherrill, C. (1998). Validating the Beck battery of quad rugby skill tests. *Adapted Physical Activity Quarterly,* 15(2), 155-167.

Yilla, A.B.; La Bar, R.H.; & Dangelmaier, B.S. (1998). Setting up a wheelchair for basketball. *Sports 'N Spokes* 24(2), 63-65.

RESOURCES

Davis R.W. (2002). *Inclusion through sports: A guide to enhancing sport experiences.* Champaign, Il: Human Kinetics.

This book identifies methodologies for integrating several disability sports, including wheelchair basketball and tennis, into the physical education curriculum. Descriptions of the skills to be taught and modification strategies are included.

Training Resources

Marty Morse is an expert trainer associated with the notable University of Illinois–Champaign-Urbana Wheelchair Sports Program. Morse has many publications and is considered a leader in the field of training elite wheelchair athletes. He publishes regularly in both *Sports 'N Spokes* and scientific journals. His work should be accessed for the most recent trends in enhancing wheelchair sports performance.

The History of the Sport Wheelchair

LaMere, T.J., & Labanowich, S. (1984a). The history of sport wheelchairs—Parts I–III.

These articles can be found in *Sports 'N Spokes* articles 1989–1990. A brief history of the development of wheelchairs until 1984 is described, covering most of the landmark developments. The reader is left with a vivid impression of the relentless drive of the athletes to improve their equipment.

Wheelchair Selection and Configuration

Cooper, R.A. (1998). *Wheelchair selection and configuration.* New York: Demos.

This book provides an in-depth, though somewhat technical, insight into all aspects of wheelchair design. Although brief in the area of sport-specific wheelchair design, this source belongs on the shelf of any professional with an interest in physical activity for wheelchair users. Dr. Cooper is a leader in the area of wheelchair configuration and design, and his works provide a thorough explication of this field.

AUDIOVISUAL RESOURCES

You feel the need for speed. (Videotape, 1992). K.C. Racing, 291 Comfort Drive, Henderson, NV 89014.

This instructional video, available in both North American and European VHS formats, covers all the basics of wheelchair racing, including adjustment and operation of a new chair, propulsion techniques, maintenance, and many tricks of the trade. The narrator and producer of the video is Kenny Carnes, one of the top racers in the United States.

Wheelchair basketball. (Text and Videotape, 1989). Paralyzed Veterans of America 801 Eighteenth Street, N. W. Washington D.C. 20006.

The authors (Hedrick, Byrnes, and Shaver) have all achieved considerable success as coaches in international wheelchair basketball competition. Their level of expertise is reflected in this comprehensive instructional text on wheelchair basketball and the accompanying series of videotapes.

ELECTRONIC RESOURCES

www.communityzero.com/iwbfamzone

This is the Web site of the international and North American wheelchair basketball community. The site has a wealth of information and links to other sites. Subscription is free (as of press time) and includes an electronic newsletter with information on wheelchair basketball around the world.

www.nwba.org/

The official Web site of the U.S. National Wheelchair Basketball Association.

www.cwba.ca

The official Web site of the Canadian Wheelchair Basketball Association.

www.quadrugby.com/

The official Web site of the United States Quad Rugby Association. The site includes the rules of rugby and updates on recent tournaments.

www.itfwheelchairtennis.com/111596

This is the wheelchair site of the international tennis federation, including schedule and results from the world of wheelchair tennis. The site includes many photos of well-known tennis stars interacting with wheelchair tennis athletes and beginners.

www.wsusa.org/wsusa/

The official Web site of the official governing body for wheelchair racing in the United States.

http://groups.yahoo.com/group/WHEELCHAIRacing/

The official Yahoo Site for "The WHEELCHAIRacing group"; their stated goal is to "try to help wheelchair athletes and coaches sharing racing and training tips and advices." The site provides the opportunity to join chat rooms and receive newsletters about wheelchair racing.

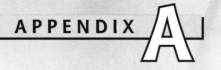

Definitions Associated With the Individuals With Disabilities Education Act (IDEA)

Several definitions are associated with infants, toddlers, and children with disabilities. To a great extent, the definitions used in this book are based on those from IDEA. Those definitions are summarized here.

INFANT OR TODDLER WITH A DISABILITY

The term "infant or toddler with a disability" means an individual under 3 years of age who needs early intervention services because the individual:

- is experiencing developmental delays, as measured by appropriate diagnostic instruments and procedures in one or more of the areas of cognitive development, physical development, communication development, social or emotional development, and adaptive development; or

- has a diagnosed physical or mental condition that has a high probability of resulting in developmental delay; and

- may also include, at a State's discretion, at-risk infants and toddlers. (Office of Special Education and Rehabilitative Services [OSE/RS] 34 CFR 300 [2002])

The term "at-risk infant or toddler" means an individual under two years of age who would be at risk of experiencing a substantial developmental delay if early intervention services were not provided to the individual.

CHILDREN WITH DISABILITIES

The term "children with disabilities" means those children having mental retardation; hearing impairments including deafness, speech, or language impairments; visual impairments including blindness; serious emotional disturbance; orthopedic impairments; autism; traumatic brain injury; other health impairments; specific learning disabilities; deaf-blindness; or multiple disabilities—and who, because of these disabilities and differences, need special education and related services.

The term "children with disabilities," for children aged three through nine may, at a State's discretion, include children:

1. who are experiencing developmental delays, as defined by the state and as measured by appropriate diagnostic instruments and procedures, in one or more of the following areas: physical development, cognitive development, communication development, social or emotional development, or adaptive development; and

2. who, for that reason, need special education and related services. (Office of Special

Education and Rehabilitative Services [OSE/RS] 34 CFR 300 [2002])

The terms used in this definition are defined as follows:

1. "Autism" means a developmental disability significantly affecting verbal and nonverbal communication and social interaction, generally evident before age three, that adversely affects a child's educational performance. Other characteristics often associated with autism are engagement in repetitive activities and stereotyped movements, resistance to environmental change or change in daily routines, and unusual responses to sensory experiences. The term does not apply if a child's educational performance is adversely affected primarily because the child has a serious emotional disturbance.

2. "Deaf-blindness" means concomitant hearing and visual impairments, the combination of which causes such severe communication and other developmental and educational needs that they cannot be accommodated in special education programs solely for children with deafness or children with blindness.

3. "Deafness" means a hearing impairment that is so severe that the child is impaired in processing linguistic information through hearing, with or without amplification, that adversely affects his or her educational performance.

4. "Hearing impairment" means harm to hearing, whether permanent or fluctuating, that adversely affects a child's educational performance but that is not included under the definition of deafness.

5. "Mental retardation" means significantly subaverage general intellectual functioning existing concurrently with deficits in adaptive behavior and manifested during the developmental period that adversely affects a child's educational performance.

6. "Multiple disabilities" means concomitant impairments (such as intellectual disability teamed with blindness, or deafness with an orthopedic impairment), the combination of which causes such severe educational problems that they cannot be accommodated in special education programs solely for one of the impairments. The term does not include deaf-blindness.

7. "Orthopedic impairment" means a severe orthopedic impairment that adversely affects a child's educational performance. The term includes impairments caused by congenital anomaly (e.g., clubfoot or absence of some member), impairments caused by disease (e.g., poliomyelitis or bone tuberculosis), and impairments from other causes (e.g., cerebral palsy, amputations, or fractures or burns that cause contractures).

8. "Other health impairment" means having limited strength, vitality, or alertness as a result of chronic or acute health problems, such as a heart condition, attention deficit disorder, attention deficit hyperactivity disorder, rheumatic fever, nephritis, asthma, sickle cell anemia, hemophilia, epilepsy, lead poisoning, leukemia, or diabetes that adversely affects a child's educational performance.

9. "Serious emotional disturbance" is defined as follows:

    a. a condition exhibiting one or more of the following characteristics over a long period of time and to a marked degree that adversely affects a child's educational performance.

        1. An inability to learn that cannot be explained by intellectual, sensory, or health factors.

        2. An inability to build or maintain satisfactory interpersonal relationships with peers and teachers.

        3. Inappropriate types of behavior or feelings under normal circumstances.

        4. A general pervasive mood of unhappiness or depression.

        5. A tendency to develop physical symptoms or fears associated with personal or school problems.

    b. The term includes schizophrenia. The term does not necessarily apply to children who are socially maladjusted, unless it is determined that they have a serious emotional disturbance.

10. "Specific learning disability" means a disorder in one or more of the basic psychological processes involved in understanding or in using language, spoken or written, that may manifest itself in an imperfect ability

to listen, think, speak, read, write, spell, or to do mathematical calculations. The term includes such conditions as perceptual disabilities, brain injury, minimal brain dysfunction, dyslexia, and developmental aphasia. The term does not apply to children who have learning problems that are primarily the result of visual, hearing, or motor disabilities, intellectual disability, emotional disturbance, or environmental, cultural, or economic disadvantage.

11. "Speech or language impairment" means a communication disorder such as stuttering, impaired articulation, or a voice impairment that adversely affects a child's educational performance.

12. "Traumatic brain injury" means an acquired injury to the brain caused by an external physical force, resulting in total or partial functional disability or psychosocial impairment (or both) that adversely affects a child's educational performance. The term applies to open or closed head injuries resulting in impairments in one or more areas, including cognition; language; memory; attention; reasoning; abstract thinking; judgment; problem solving; sensory, perceptual, and motor abilities; psychosocial behavior; physical functions; information processing; and speech. The term does not apply to brain injuries that are congenital or degenerative or to brain injuries induced by birth trauma.

13. "Visual impairment including blindness" means an impairment in vision that, even with correction, adversely affects a child's educational performance. The term includes both partial sight and blindness.

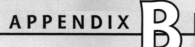

Adapted Physical Education and Sport Addresses

Multisport Organizations

Disabled Sports, USA
451 Hungerford Dr., Suite 100
Rockville, MD 20805
301-217-0960 (phone)
301-217-0968 (fax)
E-mail: information@dsusa.org
Web site: www.dsusa.org

Dwarf Athletic Association of America
418 Willow Way
Lewisville, TX 75077
972-317-8299 (phone)
972-966-0184 (fax)
E-mail: daaa@flash.net
Web site: www.daaa.org

National Disability Sports Alliance
NDSA National Center
25 West Independence Way
Kingston, RI 02881
401-792-7130 (phone)
401-792-7132 (fax)
E-mail: infor@ndsaonline.org
Web site: www.ndsaonline.org

Special Olympics
1325 G Street, NW, Suite 500
Washington, DC 20005-3104
202-628-3630 (phone)
202-824-0200 (fax)
E-mail: info@specialolympics.org
Web site: www.specialolympics.org

United States Association for Blind Athletes
33 North Institute Street
Colorado Springs, CO 80903
719-630-0422 (phone)
719-630-0616 (fax)
E-mail: mlucas@usaba.org
Web site: www.usaba.org

USA Deaf Sports Federation
102 North Krohn Place
Sioux Falls, SD 57103-1800
605-367-5761 TTY
605-367-5760 (phone)
605-367-5958 (fax)
866-273-3323 TTY (toll free)
800-642-6410 (toll free phone)
E-mail: homeoffice@usadsf.org
Web site: www.usadsf.org

U.S. Paralympics
25 N. Tejon—LL #110
Colorado Springs, CO 80903
719-471-8772 (phone)
719-471-0196 (fax)
Web site: www.usparalympics.org

The United States Olympic Committee
Disabled Sports Services Dept.
One Olympic Plaza
Colorado Springs, CO 80909-5760
Web site: www.usoc.org

Wheelchair Sports, USA
3595 E. Fountain Blvd., Ste L-1
Colorado Springs, CO 80910
719-574-1150 (phone)
719-574-9840 (fax)
E-mail: wsusa@aol.com
Web site: www.wsusa.org

Unisport Organizations

Aquatics

Aqua Sports Association for the Physically
    Challenged
9052-A Birch St.
Spring Valley, CA 91977
619-589-0537 (phone)
619-589-7013 (fax)

USA Swimming Adapted Swimming
1 Olympic Plaza
Colorado Springs, CO 80909
Phone: 719-866-4578
Web site: www.usa-swimming.org

U.S. Wheelchair Swimming, Inc.
c/o Wheelchair Sports, USA
3595 E. Fountain Blvd., Ste L-1
Colorado Springs, CO 80910
719-574-1150 (phone)
719-574-9840 (fax)

Archery

Wheelchair Archery, USA
c/o Wheelchair Sports, USA
3595 E. Fountain Blvd., Ste L-1
Colorado Springs, CO 80910
719-574-1150 (phone)
719-574-9840 (fax)

Athletics

Wheelchair Athletics of the USA
2351 Parkwood Rd.
Snellville, GA 30278
770-972-0763 (phone)
770-985-4885 (fax)

Basketball

National Wheelchair Basketball Association
Charlotte Institute of Rehabilitation
c/o Adaptive Sports/Adventures
1100 Blythe Blvd.
Charlotte, NC 28203
704-355-1064 (phone)
704-466-4999 (fax)
E-mail: nwba@carolinas.com
Web site: http://www.nwba.org

Bowling

American Blind Bowling Association
411 Sheriff
Mercer, PA 16137
412-662-5748 (phone)

American Wheelchair Bowling Association
2912 Country Woods Lane
Palm Harbor, FL 34683-6417
727-734-0023 (phone)
E-mail: bowlawba@aol.com
Web site: www.awba.org

Cycling

United States Handcycling Federation
721 N. Taft Hill Rd
Fort Collins, CO 80521
303-670-8290 (phone)
E-mail: info@ushf.org
Web site: www.ushf.org

Equestrian

North American Riding for the Handicapped
    Association
P.O. Box 33150
Denver, CO 80233
303-452-1212 (Phone)
800-369-RIDE (toll-free)
303-252-4610 (fax)
E-mail: narha@narha.org
Web site: www.narha.org

American Competition Opportunity for Riders
    with Disabilities (ACORD) Inc.
5303 Felter Road
San Jose, CA 95132
408-261-2015 (phone)
Web site: http://members.aol.com/acordcomp

Flying

Freedom's Wings
1832 Lake Ave.
Scotch Plains, NJ 07076
727-944-5756 (phone)
E-mail: president@freedomswings.org
Web site: www.freedomswings.org

International Wheelchair Aviators
P. O. Box 1126
Big Bear Lake, CA 92315
909-585-9663 (phone)
909-585-7156 (fax)
E-mail: IWAviators@aol.com
Web site: www.wheelchairaviators.org

Football

Universal Wheelchair Football Association
UC Raymond Walters College
Disability Services Office
9555 Plainfield Rd.
Cincinnati, OH 45236-1096
513-792-8625 (phone)
513-745-8300 (TTY)
513-792-8624 (fax)
E-mail: john.kraimer@uc.edu
Web site: http://dept.kent.edu/stuorg/AUWorld/
UWF.html

Golf

Association of Disabled American Golfers
P O Box 280649
Lakewood, CO 80228-0649
303-922-5228 (phone)
303-969-0447 (fax)
E-mail: adag@usga.org
Web site: www.golfcolorado.com/adag

National Amputee Golf Association
11 Walnut Hill Rd
Amherst, NH 03031-1713
800-633-6242 (toll free)
E-mail: info@nagagolf.org
Web site: www.nagagolf.org

Hockey

United States Sled Hockey Association
USSHA President
Mr. Jeff McKenney
198 Calvary Drive
Franklin, TN 37064
615-945-1089 (work phone)
615-595-7497 (work fax)
E-mail: jeff.ussha@tsha.org
Web site: www.sledhockey.org

US Electric Wheelchair Hockey Association
US EWHA Powerhockey
7216 39th Ave. No.
Minneapolis, MN 55427
763-535-4736 (phone)
E-mail: info@powerhockey.com
Web site: www.usewa.org

Quad Rugby

United States Quad Rugby
5861 White Cypress Dr
Lake Worth, FL 33467-6230
561-964-1712 (phone)
561-642-4444 (fax)
E-mail: jbishop@quadrugby.com
Web site: www.quadrugby.com

Road Racing

Achilles Track Club
42 West 38th Street Suite 400
New York, NY 10018
212-354-0300 (phone)
212-354-3978 (fax)
E-mail: achillesTC@aol.com
Web site: www.achillestrackclub.org

Crank Chair Racing Association
3294 Lake Redding Dr.
Redding CA 96003-3311
530-244-3577 (phone)

Sailing

Access to Sailing
6475 East Pacific Coast Hwy
Long Beach, CA 90803
562-881-0576 (phone)
E-mail: info@accesstosailing.org
Web site: www.access2sailing.org

Scuba Diving

Handicapped Scuba Association International
1104 El Prado
San Clemente, CA 92672-4637
949-498-4540 (phone)
949-498-6128 (fax)
E-mail: hsa@hsascuba.com
Web site: www.hsascuba.com

Shooting

National Rifle Association Disabled Services
Department
11250 Waples Mill Road
Fairfax, VA 22030
703-267-1450 (phone)
703-267-3941 (fax)
E-mail: competitions@nrahq.org
Web site: www.nrahq.org/compete/disabled.asp

National Wheelchair Shooting Federation
102 Park Ave
Rockledge, PA 19111
215-379-2359 (phone)
215-663-9662 (fax)

Skating

The Skating Association for the Blind & Handicapped (SABAH)
1200 East and West Road
West Seneca, NY 14224
716-675-7222 (phone)
E-mail: sabah@aabahinc.org
Web site: www.sabahinc.org/overview

Skiing

Ski for Light, Inc.
1455 West Lake Street
Minneapolis, MN 55408
612-827-3232 (phone)
E-mail: info@sfl.org
Web site: www.sfl.org

Adaptive Sports Center
PO Box 1639
Crested Butte, CO 81224
866-349-2296 (phone)
Web site: www.adaptivesports.org

Soccer

American Amputee Soccer Association
E-mail: rgh@ampsoccer.org
Web site: www.ampsoccer.org

Bay Area Outreach and Recreation Program
  (BORP)
830 Bancroft Way Ste 205
Berkeley, CA 94710
510-849-4663 (phone)
510-849-4616 (fax)
E-mail: info@borp.org
Web site: www.borp.org

International Paralympic Committee (7-sided
  soccer)
IPC Headquarters
Adenauerallee 212-214
53113 Bonn
Germany
+49 (228) 2097-200 (phone)
+49 (228) 2097-209 (fax)
E-mail: info@paralympic.org
Web site: www.paralympic.org/ipc/handbook/
  section4/chapter13/content.htm

Softball

National Beep Baseball Association
c/o Jeanna Weigand (Secretary)
5568 Boulder Crest Street
Columbus, OH 43235
614-442-1444
E-mail: info@nbba.org
Web site: www.nbba.org

Tennis

International Wheelchair Tennis Federation
Bank Lane, Roehampton
London, SW15 5XZ, Great Britain
011-44-208-878-6464 (phone)
011-44-208-392-4744 (fax)
E-mail: wheelchairtennis@itftennis.com
Web site: www.itfwheelchairtennis.com

National Foundation of Wheelchair Tennis
940 Calle Amanecer, Suite B
San Clemente, CA 92673
714-361-3663 (phone)
714-361-6603 (fax)
E-mail: NFWT@aol.com

United States Tennis Association (USTA)
Web site: www.usta.com/
(click on community tennis for wheelchair
  tennis and special populations)

Water Skiing

USA Water Ski
c/o Water Skiers with Disabilities Association
1251 Holy Cow Road
Polk City, FL 33868
863-324-4341 (phone)
863-325-8259 (fax)
E-mail: usawaterski@usawaterski.org
Web site: www.usawaterski.org/pages/divisions/
  WSDA/main.htm

Weightlifting

United States Wheelchair Weightlifting Federation
39 Michael Pl
Levittown, PA 19057
215-945-1964 (phone)

International Organizations

Cerebral Palsy—International Sports and Rec-
  reation Association
PO Box 16
6666 ZG Heteren
The Netherlands
E-mail: cpisra_nl@hotmail.com
Web site: www.cpisra.org

International Blind Sport Federation (IBSA)
Jose Ortega y Gasset, 18
Madrid, Spain 28006
Web site: www.ibsa.es

International Committee of Sports for the Deaf
  (C.I.S.S.)
7310 Grove Road, Suite #106
Frederick, Maryland 21704, USA
E-mail: info@ciss.org
Web site: www.ciss.org

International Stoke Mandeville Wheelchair Sports Federation (ISMWSF)
Head Office
Olympic village, Guttmann Road Aylesbury, Bucks HP21 9PP
United Kingdom
Web site: www.wsw.org.uk

International Tennis Federation
Wheelchair Tennis Department
Bank Lane
Roehampton
London SW15 5XZ
Great Britain
+44 208 878 6464 (phone)
+44 208 392 4714 (fax)
E-mail: wheelchairtennis@itftennis.com
Website: www.itfwheelchairtennis.com

Online Resources

National Center on Physical Activity and Disability (NCPAD)
NCPAD provides information and resources to enable people with disabilities to become as physically active as possible.
Web site: www.ncpad.org

PE Central
This site provides up to date information on developmentally appropriate programs for school aged children. PE Central offers resources and lesson ideas for regular and adapted physical education classes
Web site: www.pecentral.org

PE Links 4 U
Provides seven different sections related to physical education that offer links, resources, and suggestions for your program.
Web site: www.pelinks4u.org

Project Inspire
This site provides disability fact sheets for several disability types along with teaching suggestions for each. Project Inspire also offers ideas for games and activities for your classes.
Web site: http://venus.twu.edu/~f_huettig/

Brockport Physical Fitness Test

This appendix contains a brief description of the test items included in the Brockport Physical Fitness Test. Readers are reminded that a video describing the test can be found on the DVD provided in the sleeve of the book. Although all 27 test items are presented here, a test battery for a particular individual generally includes 4 to 6 items. Test-selection guidelines are included in the test manual. For a full description of the test, please see Winnick and Short, *The Brockport Physical Fitness Test,* Human Kinetics, 1999.

AEROBIC FUNCTIONING

- PACER Test (20 meters and modified 16 meters)—At the sound of a tape-recorded beep, youngsters run from one line to another, either 20 meters or 16 meters away. They must arrive at the second line prior to the next beep (initially a nine-second interval). The time between beeps gradually decreases over the length of the test, so students find it increasingly difficult to keep up with the pace the longer the test goes on. The test score is the number of laps completed on pace (scoring stops when two consecutive beeps are missed; one trial is given).

- Target Aerobic Movement Test—Youngsters engage in any type of activity to elevate their heart rates into a target heart rate zone (70 to 85 percent of predicted maximum heart rate). They then attempt to maintain the elevated heart rates for 15 continuous minutes (one trial).

- One-Mile Run–Walk—Youngsters have one trial to complete a one-mile distance as quickly as they can.

BODY COMPOSITION

- Skinfold Measures—Skinfold calipers are used to determine the youngster's skinfold thickness to estimate body fat percentage. Measures are taken at one of the following site options: triceps (only), triceps plus calf, or triceps plus subscapular. Three measures are taken at each site, and the middle score serves as the criterion.

- Body Mass Index—Height and weight measures are used in a ratio to determine if individuals are overweight or underweight for their height.

MUSCULOSKELETAL FUNCTIONING

Muscular Strength and Endurance

- Trunk Lift—From a prone position with hands under thighs, participants attempt to lift their chins up to 12 inches from the mat by arching the back. Allow two trials and count the better score.

- Dominant Grip Strength—Youngsters squeeze a grip dynamometer as hard as possible with their preferred hand. Three trials are given; the middle score is the criterion.

- Bench Press—From a supine position on a bench, youngsters are given one attempt to repeatedly lift a 35-pound barbell from the chest to a straight-arm position above the chest. Boys are limited to 50 repetitions and girls to 30 repetitions.

545

- Push-Up—Initially, participants lie prone on a mat with hands placed under the shoulders (palms flat on the mat), elbows at 90 degrees, legs straight, and toes tucked. The participant then pushes up so that the arms (and back) are straight and the body weight is supported completely by the hands and toes. Youngsters attempt to complete as many push-ups as possible in one trial by performing one push-up every three seconds.

- Isometric Push-Up—Participants are given one trial to hold the up position for the push-up for up to 40 seconds.

- Seated Push-Up—Participants who are wheelchair users (paraplegic) attempt to lift their buttocks and posterior thighs off the seats of their wheelchairs by pushing up from the armrests or tires of the chairs with their hands and arms. An alternative is to lift the buttocks off a mat using seated push-up blocks. One trial is provided; the push-up is held up to 20 seconds.

- Dumbbell Press—From a seated position, youngsters are given one attempt to repeatedly lift a 15-pound dumbbell from shoulder height to a straight-arm position directly above the shoulder. Boys and girls are limited to 50 repetitions.

- Reverse Curl—Participants (with a spinal cord injury and quadriplegia) are given one attempt to lift a one-pound weight one time from lap level to shoulder level with a tenodesis grasp and elbow flexion.

- 40-Meter Push–Walk—Youngsters with certain mobility problems are given one attempt to cover at least 40 meters in 60 seconds while maintaining a low heart rate (i.e., 10-second heart rate is generally below 19 beats).

- Wheelchair Ramp Test—Youngsters in wheelchairs are given one try to negotiate a standard ANSI ramp (12 inches of run for every inch of rise) up to a maximum of 30 feet.

- Curl-Up—Youngsters lie in a supine position with knees bent and feet flat on the mat; arms are straight at the side with palms down and fingers at the edge of a 4.5-inch-wide cardboard strip. Youngsters lift their upper backs off the mat until the fingers slide to the far edge of the strip and then return to the starting position. Youngsters perform as many curl-ups as possible (up to 75) by doing one curl-up every three seconds (1 trial).

- Curl-Up (modified)—Identical to the curl-up except there is no cardboard strip. Instead, youngsters place their hands on the top of their thighs and slide them to the kneecaps during the curl-up.

- Flexed Arm Hang—Participants grasp (palms forward) an overhead bar (feet off the floor) with elbows bent and chin above the bar and attempt to hold that position for as long as possible (one trial).

- Extended Arm Hang—Participants grasp (palms forward) an overhead bar (feet off the floor) with elbows straight and attempt to hold that position for up to 40 seconds (one trial).

- Pull-Up—Participants grasp (palms forward) an overhead bar (feet off the floor) with elbows straight. They then get one attempt to repeatedly lift the body with the arms until the chin is above the bar.

- Pull-Up (modified)—Using a special apparatus, students lie in a supine position and grasp a bar an arm's length above their chests. Keeping heels on the ground and their backs straight, participants pull their bodies toward the bar until the chin passes an elastic band placed seven to eight inches below the bar. Participants attempt to perform as many modified pull-ups as they can in one trial.

Flexibility

- Back-Saver Sit-and-Reach—The youngster places one foot against a sit-and-reach box with a straight leg while the other leg is bent at the knee with the foot flat on the floor. With one hand placed on top of the other, the youngster attempts to reach as far across the top of the box as possible while maintaining the straight leg. One trial is given for each leg.

- Shoulder Stretch—Participants attempt to touch the fingertips of their two hands behind their backs. The right hand reaches over the right shoulder between the scapulae while the left hand is brought up the back from the waist by bending the elbow. The test is repeated with the opposite arms; do one trial each.

- Apley Test (modified)—Youngsters attempt to touch with one hand one of three landmarks given here in descending order of difficulty: superior angle of the opposite scapula, top of the head, and the mouth. The test is repeated with the opposite hand; do one trial each.

- Thomas Test (modified)—Youngsters lie supine on a table and pull one knee to their chests while the tester evaluates the length of the opposite hip flexors by observing the extent of "lift" present in the opposite leg. The test is repeated with the other leg; do one trial each.

• Target Stretch Test—Participants demonstrate in one attempt their maximum movement extent for a variety of single-joint actions (e.g., wrist extension, shoulder abduction, elbow extension, forearm supination), and testers estimate the extent of movement from pictorial criteria.

THE BROCKPORT PHYSICAL FITNESS TEST KIT

The *Brockport Physical Fitness Test Kit* provides a complete package for fitness testing for youths with physical and mental disabilities. The kit includes the following:

• A comprehensive test manual that explains development of the test and testing procedures

• A training guide to assist you in improving your students' fitness

• *Fitness Challenge,* the companion software that makes test use much easier

• A video that clearly demonstrates how to use the test with this population (DVD included at the back of the textbook)

• Curl-up strips

• Skin caliper

• PACER audio CD or cassette

All materials are available from Human Kinetics Publishers at www.HumanKinetics.com.

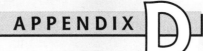
Rating Scale for Adapted Physical Education

Name of school: _____

Address: _____

Level: _____ Number of students enrolled in adapted PE: _____

Principal: _____

Director of physical education: _____

Reviewed by: _____ Date: _____

INTRODUCTION

The purpose of the rating scale is to assist school personnel in improving adapted physical education services.

When properly guided and developed, physical education becomes a purposeful and vital part of a student's school education. Physical education aids in the realization of those objectives concerned with the development of favorable self-image, creative expression, motor skills, physical fitness, and knowledge and understanding of human movement. To become a fully functioning individual, a person needs many opportunities to participate in well-conceived, well-taught learning experiences in physical education. To achieve this objective, the essentials of a quality program of physical education need to be identified.

The rating scale is designed for self-appraisal use.

USE AND INTERPRETATION OF THE SCORES

The rating scale is composed of a series of ratings for the major areas that should concern school personnel relative to the adapted physical education. There are six sections to the rating scale: curriculum, required instruction, attendance, personnel, facilities, and administrative procedures.

The individual(s) making the assessment should consider the criteria statement in terms of the degree of achievement that exists for the program. The rating score is on a scale from 0 to 4 (0 meaning inadequate achievement and 4 meaning fully achieved with excellent results). Each section can be rated by the total section score, or a program overall rating can be obtained by totaling all sections of the rating scale.

A careful analysis should be made of each statement, section, and overall rating to determine the

From *Adapted Physical Education and Sport, Fourth Edition* by Joseph P. Winnick, 2005, Champaign, IL: Human Kinetics.

areas in need of improvement. The interpretation of the score for each statement is:

0—Inadequate: extremely limited

1—Poor: exists but needs a great deal of improvement

2—Fair: adequate but needs some improvement

3—Good: well done and only needs periodic review

4—Excellent: has achieved outstanding results.

Rating Scale for Adapted Physical Education

	Inadequate (0)	Poor (1)	Fair (2)	Good (3)	Excellent (4)
Section I—Curriculum					
1. The goals and objectives of the school district plan for physical education encompass adapted physical education.					
2. Provision is explicitly made for adapted physical education in the school district physical education plan.					
3. There exists a definition of adapted physical education that is in accord with state, federal, and professional laws, regulations, and practices.					
4. Adapted physical education may include students with disabilities as well as students without disabilities.					
5. There exist a variety of activities to meet unique student needs.					
6. Instruction in adapted physical education is based on a curriculum guide that encompasses adapted physical education content.					
7. Instruction for all students is distributed among the following areas in accord with students' needs and abilities:					
a. Basic movement experiences					
b. Adventure and risk challenge activities					
c. Rhythms and dance					
d. Games and sports					
e. Gymnastics					
f. Outdoor education					
g. Motor movement skills					
h. Physical fitness					
i. Aquatics					
8. Appropriate literature and other resource materials regarding adapted physical education are made available to professional staff.					

(continued)

	Inadequate (0)	Poor (1)	Fair (2)	Good (3)	Excellent (4)
9. Students with disabilities are provided equivalent opportunities in intramural, extramural, or extra-class activities.					
10. There is an annual evaluation of the instructional program in adapted physical education.					
11. Guidelines pertaining to adapted physical education are evaluated at least every five years.					
12. There is a procedure for reporting student status and progress.					
13. The progress of students is continually measured.					
14. Cumulative records pertaining to the physical education of each student are maintained.					
Section II—Required Instruction					
1. All students not receiving regular physical education have an adapted physical education program.					
2. No student is excused from physical activity or excused from adapted physical education because of participation in extra-class programs unless by the school's committee on adapted physical education or similar committee or unless approved in a student's individualized education program (student with a disability).					
3. Instruction in adapted physical education is conducted with a time allotment that is in accord with state regulations and in a frequency and duration that is comparable to chronological-aged peers in the school district.					
4. Class periods are scheduled in time lengths that are appropriate to student needs and achievement of instructional objectives.					
5. Time allotment for physical education meets state requirements.					
6. Physical education instruction is made available to every student with a disability.					
Section III—Attendance					
1. Physical education is required of all students, ages 3 to 21, and adapted physical education is provided for students who exhibit unique physical education needs.					
2. Credit provided for adapted physical education is in accord with regular physical education credit.					
Section IV—Personnel					
1. Instruction in adapted physical education for students aged 3 to 21 is provided by a certified physical education teacher.					

(continued)

From *Adapted Physical Education and Sport, Fourth Edition* by Joseph P. Winnick, 2005, Champaign, IL: Human Kinetics.

Rating Scale for Adapted Physical Education *(continued)*

	Inadequate (0)	Poor (1)	Fair (2)	Good (3)	Excellent (4)
2. Physical education for infants and toddlers is provided by an adapted physical educator.					
3. Physical educators teaching adapted physical education who have not completed at least 12 semester hours of formal higher education in adapted physical education have access to appropriate resource personnel.					
4. Extra-class activities are provided under the supervision of personnel meeting state requirements and approved by the board of education.					
5. Physical educators teaching adapted physical education for more than 50 percent of their teaching load have completed at least 12 semester hours of formal study in adapted physical education, have a concentration in adapted physical education from an accredited college or university, or have a state credential or endorsement in adapted physical education.					
6. Supervision and coordination of all phases of adapted physical education (instruction, intramurals, extra-class programs, interscholastic athletics) is provided by a director certified in physical education and administrative and supervisory services.					
7. Aides are provided for instructional classes in physical education.					
8. The qualifications of aides are in accord with appropriate state or local regulations.					
9. A physician delegated by a district submits to appropriate committees or personnel areas of the program in which a student might participate when medical reasons are given to limit participation.					
10. Teachers of adapted physical education are involved in individualized education programming and placement decisions.					
11. Teachers of students requiring adapted physical education are involved in assessment, setting objectives and goals, and determining unique needs of students receiving adapted physical education.					
Section V—Facilities					
1. Students receiving adapted physical education have equal access to facilities required to provide equal opportunity for programmatic benefits.					
2. Indoor facilities for adapted physical education:					
a. Have adequate clear activity space					
b. Provide a safe environment for activity					
c. Have appropriate flooring and satisfactory finish					

From *Adapted Physical Education and Sport, Fourth Edition* by Joseph P. Winnick, 2005, Champaign, IL: Human Kinetics.

	Inadequate (0)	Poor (1)	Fair (2)	Good (3)	Excellent (4)
d. Have adequate lighting					
e. Have adequate acoustical treatment					
f. Have protective padding on walls					
g. Have sufficient ceiling clearance					
h. Have adequate ventilation					
3. Equipment and supplies required for reasonable accommodations are provided.					
4. For students receiving adapted physical education, the dressing, showering, and drying areas include:					
a. Adequate space for peak load periods					
b. Floors constructed to facilitate ambulation and maintenance of safe and clean conditions					
c. Lockers of proper type and sufficient quantity					
d. Sufficient number of shower heads					
e. Adequate ventilation					
f. Adequate lighting					
g. Adequate heating					
h. Adequate benches, mirrors, and toilets					
i. All facilities are clean, sanitary, and in operable condition.					
5. The outdoor adapted physical education facilities are designed for effective instruction and safety. They are:					
a. Readily accessible					
b. Free from safety hazards (glass, holes, stones)					
c. Properly fenced or enclosed for safety and efficient usage					
d. Properly surfaced, graded and drained					
e. Laid out and marked for a variety of activities					
f. Properly equipped (playground structures, backstops, physical fitness equipment, etc.)					
6. Qualified supervision of areas and facilities is provided during use.					
Section VI—Administrative Procedures					
1. Class sizes for adapted physical education are equitable with those specified for special education classroom teaching.					
2. Teacher load for teachers teaching adapted physical education is equitable with that of special education teachers.					

(continued)

Rating Scale for Adapted Physical Education *(continued)*

	Inadequate (0)	Poor (1)	Fair (2)	Good (3)	Excellent (4)
3. Teachers of adapted physical education receive support staff on the same student–teacher ratio as special education teachers.					
4. Appropriate committees use certified physical educators to assess physical education status for IEP development when unique physical education needs are suspected.					
5. Students with disabilities are integrated into regular physical education classes to the maximum extent appropriate.					
6. Students with disabilities are provided reasonable accommodations in physical education classes.					
7. Provisions are made for physical educators and appropriate committees, for all students with disabilities suspected of having unique needs in physical education.					
8. The physical education teacher is involved with individualized program development of all students who participate in physical education outside of regular or integrated classes.					
9. Physical education is included in the IEP of every student with a disability.					
10. Students are referred to appropriate planning committees and receive adapted physical education on the basis of objective criteria.					
11. The physical education abilities of all students not participating in regular physical education are assessed by a physical educator.					
12. Staff members implementing adapted physical education are provided in-service education on at least an annual basis.					
13. School districts provide placement settings that permit individualized attention in the most appropriate environment.					
14. The annual budget request for adapted physical education is prepared on the basis of an inventory of needs of the program including needs specified in individualized education programs.					
15. The adapted physical education budget includes state and federal monies earmarked for instruction of students with disabilities if such students are receiving an adapted physical education program.					
16. Up-to-date reference materials are provided for teachers providing adapted physical education.					
17. The school library contains materials on adapted physical education that are sufficient and appropriate.					
18. Budgets for instructional, intramural, extramural, and athletic programs for students with disabilities are equitable to those for students without disabilities and reflect at least a double weighting in favor of the students with disabilities.					
19. The school district plan includes provisions for regular extra-class programs for qualified students with disabilities.					

From *Adapted Physical Education and Sport, Fourth Edition* by Joseph P. Winnick, 2005, Champaign, IL: Human Kinetics.

Author Index

Subject Index

Note: The italicized *f* and *t* following page numbers refer to figures and tables, respectively.

About the Authors

Boni B. Boswell received a doctorate in kinesiology at Texas Woman's University. She currently is an associate professor at East Carolina University where she teaches adapted physical education and dance in the department of exercise and sport science. She is coauthor of *Re-envisioning Dance* as well as author of many articles concerning dance and individuals in inclusive settings.

Douglas H. Collier received his bachelor's and master's degrees from McGill University and his doctorate from Indiana University. He is a professor of physical education and sport at the State University of New York, College at Brockport, where he teaches undergraduate courses in the teacher preparation program with an emphasis on elementary and early childhood education and graduate courses in adapted physical education. His research and writing focuses on instructional strategies effective for learners with severe disabilities, the autism spectrum disorder, and positive, proactive approaches to behavior management.

David L. Gallahue is dean of the School of HPER at Indiana University, Bloomington. He holds degrees from Indiana University (BS), Purdue University (MS), and Temple University (EdD). Dr. Gallahue is active in the study of motor development, sport, and fitness education of children. He is author of several textbooks, many journal articles, and several edited book chapters. Dr. Gallahue is a past president of the National Association for Sport and Physical Education (NASPE) and former chair of the Motor Development Academy and the Council of Physical Education for Children (COPEC). He is a recognized leader in children's motor development and developmental physical activity.

Cathy Houston-Wilson received her doctoral degree from Oregon State University in Movement Studies in Disability. She is an associate professor at SUNY College at Brockport in the department of physical education and sport, where she serves as coordinator of the Teacher Certification Concentration. She teaches classes in adapted physical education and early childhood physical education.

Her research and writing focus on inclusion, early childhood physical education, and fitness education for individuals with disabilities.

Luke E. Kelly is a professor of kinesiology at the University of Virginia, where he directs the masters and doctoral programs in adapted physical education. He received his doctorate from Texas Woman's University and his bachelors and masters degrees from the State University of New York, College at Brockport. Dr. Kelly works extensively with public schools on developing functional physical education curricula based on the Achievement-Based Curriculum model so that they accommodate the needs of all students. Dr. Kelly is a fellow in the American Academy of Kinesiology and Physical Education, a past president of the National Consortium for Physical Education and Recreation for Individuals with Disabilities, and the former director of the Adapted Physical Education National Standards Project.

Patricia L. Krebs is the president and CEO of Special Olympics Maryland, Inc. (SOMD), which serves more than 10,000 athletes. Prior to this appointment, she served as Director of Education for Special Olympics, Inc. She earned her doctorate from the University of Maryland in 1979 and previously directed the undergraduate and graduate adapted physical education preparation programs at Adelphi University. In 1997 she was named one of Maryland's Top 100 Women and in 1999 led SOMD to receive the Maryland Association of Nonprofit Organizations Standards of Excellence Award, one of only 50 nonprofits (out of 16,000 nonprofits statewide) to achieve and maintain this standing.

Francis M. Kozub is an assistant professor in the department of kinesiology at Indiana University. Dr. Kozub received his PhD at Ohio State University in 1997. Both his master's and baccalaureate degrees were earned at State University of New York at Brockport in 1996 and 1995 respectively. Dr. Kozub taught and coached in the public schools of New York as a general and adapted physical educator from 1986 until 1994. Currently, Dr. Kozub studies physical activity and motivation in individuals with disabilities.

Barry W. Lavay obtained his PhD in special physical education from the University of New Mexico in 1984. He is a professor in the department of kinesiology and physical education (KPE) at California State University, Long Beach (CSULB), where he coordinates the State Adapted Physical Education Teaching Credential Program and directs the after-school and summer physical activity programs for children with disabilities. He is the 2001 CSULB Outstanding Professor Award recipient. His scholarly activity is in the area of behavior management, and he has authored or coauthored several textbook chapters, manuals, and juried articles. He is the coauthor of two textbooks: *Positive Behavior Management Strategies for Physical Educators* and *Physical Activity for Individuals with Mental Retardation: Infancy through Adulthood.* Dr. Lavay has been an active member with the American Alliance of Health, Physical Education, Recreation and Dance, where he is a fellow member. He received the 2001 AAHPERD Adapted Physical Activity Council Professional Recognition Award.

Monica Lepore, originally from New York City, resides in Wilmington, Delaware, and teaches adapted physical education professional preparation at West Chester University of Pennsylvania. Dr. Lepore holds an EdD from New York University, a MS in adapted physical education from University of Wisconsin–Lacrosse, and a BS in physical education from the College of Mt. St. Vincent–Manhattan College. She was chairperson of the Adapted Aquatics Committee and Credential for AAALF Aquatic Council from 2000-2004, and is lead author of *Adapted Aquatics Programming: A Professional Guide.* She is past assistant director and current aquatic director of Camp Abilities, a developmental sports camp for children who are blind or visually impaired. Monica has received the International Swimming Hall of Fame Adapted Aquatics Award and recently has been named to Who's Who in Aquatic Leadership.

Lauren J. Lieberman is an associate professor of physical education at SUNY Brockport. She currently teaches undergraduate and graduate classes in adapted physical education. She has taught physical education and aquatics at the Perkins School for the Blind in Watertown,

Massachusetts, in the Deafblind Program. She received her PhD from Oregon State University in the movement studies in disabilities program. In addition to teaching, she runs Camp Abilities, a developmental sports camp for children with visual impairments and deafblindness in various places around the country. She also conducts research and consults in the area of individuals with visual impairments, deafness, and deafblindness and physical activity.

E. Michael Loovis received his PhD from Ohio State University in 1975. He is currently a professor at Cleveland State University, where he teaches adapted physical education and related courses at both the graduate and undergraduate levels. On an interdisciplinary basis he teaches courses in child development and organization behavior and change in the college of education's master's and doctoral programs, respectively. His research interests include the development of fundamental motor skills and patterns in typically developing children using hierarchical linear modeling.

John C. Ozmun is chairperson of the department of physical education at Indiana State University. He holds degrees from Taylor University (BS) and Indiana University (MS, PED). He is the coauthor with David L. Gallahue of *Understanding Motor Development: Infants, Children, Adolescents, Adults*—one of the most widely used motor development textbooks nationally and internationally. His research focus is in the area of muscular strength characteristics of young children with and without disabilities.

Michael J. Paciorek received his PhD from Peabody College of Vanderbilt University. He is a professor and physical education program coordinator at Eastern Michigan University, where he teaches classes in adapted physical education and sport and motor development. Dr. Paciorek is the coauthor of the popular text *Disability Sport and Recreation Resources.* He has served on the board of directors for Special Olympics Michigan for 12 years and was co-coordinator of disabled athlete participation at the United States Olympic Festival. Additionally, he was a member of the United States Disabled Sports Team that competed at the 1992 Paralympic Games in Barcelona, Spain. He received the William A. Hillman Distinguished Service Award from the National Consortium on Physical Education and Recreation for Individuals with Disabilities in 1999 and in 2000 received the Eastern Michigan University Distinguished Faculty Award for Service.

David L. Porretta, PhD, is a professor of sport and exercise education at Ohio State University and is responsible for graduate study in adapted physical education. He earned his doctoral degree from Temple University in Philadelphia. Dr. Porretta is a fellow in the American Academy of Kinesiology and Physical Education (AAKPE) and a past president of the National Consortium for Physical Education and Recreation for Individuals with Disabilities (NCPERID). He is a recipient of the Professional Recognition Award from the Adapted Physical Activity Council of AAHPERD, as well as the G. Lawrence Rarick Research Award, and the Hollis Fait Scholarly Contribution Award from NCPERID. Broadly conceived, Dr. Porretta's research focuses on psychological variables that affect the motor behavior of individuals with mental retardation and other developmental disabilities in applied physical education and sport settings.

Francis X. Short is a professor in the department of physical education and sport at the State University of New York, College at Brockport. He teaches courses in adapted physical education and motor development. He has authored and coauthored a number of publications related to the physical fitness of individuals with disabilities, including the Brockport Physical Fitness Test. In 2000 he received the Professional Recognition Award from the Adapted Physical Activity Council of AAHPERD and the G. Lawrence Rarick Research Award from NCPERID. Dr. Short holds degrees from Springfield College and Indiana University.

Christine B. Stopka earned her PhD from the University of Virginia. She is a professor of exercise therapy and adapted physical education at the University of Florida. There, she established undergraduate and graduate specializations in athletic training and special physical education, the Student Injury Care Center, the Exercise Therapy Lab, the adapted aquatics program, and community-based programs in athletic training and adapted physical activity. Her writings and research include the study of exercise therapy programs and sports medical considerations for people with disabilities, including those with

mental disabilities; peripheral vascular disease; and adapted equipment ideas to facilitate inclusive teaching.

Joseph P. Winnick, EdD, is a distinguished service professor of physical education and sport and State University of New York, College at Brockport, where he has taught adapted physical education for more than 35 years. Renowned for his research in adapted physical education, he is the coauthor of *The Brockport Physical Fitness Test Manual* and related resources, which present the best physical fitness test available for youths with disabilities. Dr. Winnick developed and implemented America's first master's degree professional preparation program in adapted physical education at Brockport in 1968 and since that time has secured funds continually from the U.S. Department of Education to support the program. He has received the Professional Recognition Award from the Adapted Physical Activity Council of AAHPERD, the G. Lawrence Rarick Research Award, and the Hollis Fait Scholarly Contribution Award. He earned his master's and doctoral degrees from Temple University.

Abu B. Yilla received his master's and doctorate degrees from the Texas Woman's University and two bachelor's degrees, one from the University of Nottingham, England, and one from the University of Texas at Arlington. He is an assistant professor at the University of Texas at Arlington. His research focus is the explication of elite disability sport, in particular, wheelchair basketball. He is a Paralympic medalist and has won 12 national championships in wheelchair basketball (eight in Great Britain and four in the United States).

Lauriece L. Zittel earned her doctorate at Oregon State University. Currently, she is an associate professor at Northern Illinois University, where she teaches graduate coursework in adapted physical activity. Dr. Zittel was the president of the National Consortium for Physical Education and Recreation for Individuals with Disabilities and a past recipient of the Mabel Lee Award. She is the coauthor of *Smart Start: A preschool Movement Curriculum* and *I CAN K-3* (second edition). Her research focuses on the environmental variables influencing the motor development of young children with developmental delays, particularly children exposed to severe poverty and violence.